Persecutory Delusions
Assessment, Theory, and Treatment

Persecutory Delusions

Assessment, Theory, and Treatment

Edited by

Daniel Freeman

Richard Bentall

Philippa Garety

OXFORD
UNIVERSITY PRESS

OXFORD
UNIVERSITY PRESS

Great Clarendon Street, Oxford OX2 6DP

Oxford University Press is a department of the University of Oxford.
It furthers the University's objective of excellence in research, scholarship,
and education by publishing worldwide in

Oxford New York

Auckland Cape Town Dar es Salaam Hong Kong Karachi
Kuala Lumpur Madrid Melbourne Mexico City Nairobi
New Delhi Shanghai Taipei Toronto

With offices in

Argentina Austria Brazil Chile Czech Republic France Greece
Guatemala Hungary Italy Japan Poland Portugal Singapore
South Korea Switzerland Thailand Turkey Ukraine Vietnam

Oxford is a registered trade mark of Oxford University Press
in the UK and in certain other countries

Published in the United States
by Oxford University Press Inc., New York

British Library Cataloguing in Publication Data

Data available

Library of Congress Cataloging in Publication Data

Persecutory delusions: assessment, theory, and treatment/edited by
Daniel Freeman, Richard Bentall, Philippa Garety.
      p. ; cm.
   Includes bibliographical references and index.
   ISBN 978–0–19–920631–5
1. Delusions. 2. Paranoia. I. Freeman, Daniel, 1971-II. Bentall,
Richard P. III. Garety, Philippa A.
[DNLM: 1. Paranoid Disorders. 2. Delusions--psychology.
3. Paranoid Behavior. 4. Paranoid Personality Disorder. WM 205 P466 2008]
RC553.D35P47 2008
616.89'7--dc22   2008012841

Typeset by Cepha Imaging Private Ltd., Bangalore, India
Printed and bound in the UK by
CPI Antony Rowe, Chippenham, Wiltshire

ISBN 978–0–19–920631–5

1 3 5 7 9 10 8 6 4 2

Preface

The central idea underlying this book is a simple one: persecutory thinking is important to understand and treat in its own right. In the past the presence of paranoid thinking has only been given significance in relation to diagnosing illness. It has been viewed as a symptom that leads to a diagnosis—an item on a checklist of whether a person is ill—and that, more or less, is the end of it. Our view is that the distress and disruption of persecutory thoughts makes it an experience that needs understanding in its own right. Paranoid thinking, not diagnosis, is the central problem for the person. And it is a common problem. The latest epidemiological research demonstrates that paranoid thinking is regularly present in 10–15% of the general population. The experience takes centre stage in the book.

Remarkably, no previous volume brings the experts on persecutory delusions together. *Persecutory Delusions* is influenced by the spirit of two previous edited books. The first of these is another Oxford University Press publication, *Understanding Other Minds* (Baron-Cohen *et al.* 1994), which presented the emerging research on autism and highlighted the wider implications of the condition. The second influential book was *Delusional Beliefs* (Oltmanns and Maher 1988), which laid the foundations for empirical research on delusions by offering novel and coherent conceptualizations. Our view is that paranoia, like autism, is a fundamental area of human relations to explore. Decisions to trust or mistrust lie at the heart of social interaction. And since the publication of *Delusional Beliefs* an empirical literature on paranoia has emerged, which we think can provide a springboard for a dramatic increase in understanding as more people become interested in the topic.

The aim was to gather the perspectives of the leading international researchers and clinicians in one volume. We also wanted to include personal accounts. We endeavoured to obtain biological, psychiatric, psychological and social accounts of paranoia and its treatment, though it is notable that an approach focusing on persecutory experiences has been much more common from a psychological perspective. Most of all we wanted a book to stimulate ourselves and other readers. We asked contributors for empirical evidence, but encouraged speculation. After reading this book we hope readers have a comprehensive knowledge of the developments in the understanding and treatment of persecutory experiences. Equally, we hope readers are inspired to continue the work on this important topic.

London, UK	D.F.
Bangor, UK	R.P.B.
London, UK	P.G.

References

Baron-Cohen, S., Tager-Flusberg, H. and Cohen, D.J. (eds) (1994) *Understanding Other Minds*. Oxford: Oxford University Press.

Oltmanns, T.F. and Maher, B.A. (eds) (1988) *Delusional Beliefs*. New York: Wiley.

Contents

Contributors

Katie Ashcroft
Consultant Clinical Psychologist,
Hampshire Early Intervention in
Psychosis Service,
Fairways House,
Mount Pleasant Industrial Estate,
Southampton SO14 0SP, UK

Ellen B. Astrachan-Fletcher
Assistant Professor,
Department of Psychiatry,
University of Illinois College
of Medicine,
1601 W. Taylor (M/C 912) PI,
Chicago, IL 60612, USA

Paul E. Bebbington
Professor of Social and Community
Psychiatry,
Department of Mental Health
Sciences,
University College London,
Charles Bell House,
67-73 Riding House Street,
London W1W 7EJ, UK

Richard P. Bentall
Professor of Clinical Psychology,
School of Psychology,
University of Bangor,
Adeilad Brigantia,
Penrallt Road,
Gwynedd LL57 2AS, UK

Samantha E. Bowe
Clinical Lead and Clinical
Psychologist,
Psychology Department,
Greater Manchester West Mental
Health NHS Foundation Trust,
Bury New Road, Prestwich,
Manchester M25 3BL, UK

Matthew R. Broome
Associate Clinical Professor of
Psychiatry,
Health Sciences Research Institute,
Room B156,
Medical School Building,
Gibbet Hill Campus,
University of Warwick,
Coventry CV4 7AL, UK

Paul Chadwick
Professor of Clinical Psychology,
Royal South Hants Hospital &
University of Southampton,
Department of Clinical Psychology,
Department of Psychiatry,
Royal South Hants Hospital,
Southampton SO14 0YG, UK

Peter K. Chadwick
Lecturer in Psychology,
Psychology Division,
Birkbeck College Faculty of
Continuing Education,
School of Social and Natural
Sciences, University of London,
26 Russell Square, Bloomsbury,
London WC1B 5DQ, UK

Max Coltheart
ARC Federation Fellow and
Scientific Director of the Macquarie
Centre for Cognitive Science,
Macquarie University,
Sydney NSW 2109, Australia

Dennis R. Combs
Assistant Professor of Psychology,
Department of Psychology,
The University of Texas at Tyler,
Tyler, TX 75799,
USA

Rhiannon Corcoran
Associate Professor,
Division of Psychiatry,
School of Community
Health Sciences,
University of Nottingham,
A floor, South Block,
Queens Medical Centre,
Derby Road,
Nottingham NG 72UH,
UK

Marta Di Forti
Department of Psychological
Medicine,
PO Box 063,
Institute of Psychiatry,
London, SE5 8AF, UK

Mari Dominguez
Department of Psychiatry
and Neuropsychology,
South Limburg Mental Health
Research and Teaching Network,
EURON, Maastricht University,
PO Box 616 (DRT 10),
6200 MD Maastricht,
The Netherlands

David Fowler
Professor of Social Psychiatry,
School of Medicine,
Health Policy and Practice,
University of East Anglia,
Norwich NR4 7TJ, UK

Daniel Freeman
Wellcome Trust Fellow,
Department of Psychology,
PO Box 77, Institute of Psychiatry,
King's College London,
Denmark Hill, London SE5 8AF, UK

Philippa Garety
Professor of Clinical Psychology,
Department of Psychology,
PO Box 77, Institute of Psychiatry,
King's College London,
Denmark Hill,
London SE5 8AF, UK

Martin Harrow
Professor and Director of
Psychology,
Department of Psychiatry,
University of Illinois College
of Medicine, 1601 W. Taylor (M/C
912) PI,
Rm. 445, Chicago,
IL 60612, USA

Cécile Henquet
Department of Psychiatry
and Neuropsychology,
South Limburg Mental Health
Research and Teaching Network,
EURON, Maastricht University,
Maastricht,
The Netherlands & Mondriaan
Zorggroep, Division Addiction Care,
South Limburg, The Netherlands

Thomas H. Jobe
Professor of Psychiatry,
Department of Psychiatry,
University of Illinois College of
Medicine,
1601 W. Taylor (M/C 912) PI,
Chicago, IL 60612, USA

Suzanne Kaiser
Research Fellow,
School of Psychological Sciences,
University of Manchester,
Oxford Road,
Manchester M13 9PL, UK

Peter Kinderman
Professor of Clinical Psychology,
Population, Community and
Behavioural Sciences,
University of Liverpool,
Whelan Building,
Quadrangle, Brownlow Hill,
Liverpool L69 3GB, UK

David Kingdon
Professor of Mental Health
Care Delivery,
University of Southampton,
Department of Psychiatry,
Royal South Hants Hospital,
Brintons Terrace, Southampton
SO14 0YG, UK

Lydia Krabbendam
Senior Lecturer, Department of
Psychiatry and Neuropsychology,
South Limburg Mental Health
Research and Teaching Network,
EURON, Maastricht University,
PO Box 616 (DRT 10),
6200 MD Maastricht,
The Netherlands

Elizabeth Kuipers
Professor of Clinical Psychology,
Institute of Psychiatry at King's
College London,
De Crespigny Park,
Denmark Hill,
London SE5 8AF, UK

Robyn Langdon
ARC Australian Research Fellow,
Macquarie Centre for Cognitive
Science,
Macquarie University,
Sydney NSW 2109,
Australia and Schizophrenia
Research Institute (SRI),
NSW, Australia

Marc Laruelle
Associate Professor of Psychiatry
and Radiology,
Columbia University College of
Physicians and Surgeons,
New York State Psychiatric Institute,
Unit 31, 1051 Riverside Drive,
New York, NY 10032, USA

Philip K. McGuire
Professor of Psychiatry and
Cognitive Neuroscience,
Institute of Psychiatry,
Box P067, De Crespigny Park,
London SE5 8AF, UK

Ryan McKay
Research Fellow,
Institute for Empirical
Research in Economics,
University of Zurich,
Bluemlisalpstrasse 10,
Zurich, CH-8006,
Switzerland

Anthony Morrison
Professor of Clinical Psychology,
School of Psychological Sciences,
University of Manchester,
Coupland I Building,
Oxford Road,
Manchester M13 9PL, UK

Michael Moutoussis
Specialist Registrar,
Tolworth Hospital,
South West London and
St George's Mental
Health NHS Trust,
Red Lion Road, Surbiton
KT6 7QU, UK

Alistair Munro
Emeritus Professor of Psychiatry,
Dalhousie University Halifax,
Nova Scotia, Canada

Karl Murphy
c/o Ben Smith, Department
of Mental Health Sciences,
University College London,
Charles Bell House,
67-73 Riding House Street,
London W1W 7EJ, UK

Robin M. Murray
Professor of Psychiatry,
Department of Psychological
Medicine, PO Box 063,
Institute of Psychiatry,
London SE5 8AF, UK

Juliana Onwumere
Research Clinical Psychologist,
PO77, Department of Psychology,
Institute of Psychiatry at King's
College London,
De Crespigny Park, Denmark Hill,
London SE5 8AF, UK

Sophie Parker
Clinical Psychologist,
Early Detection and
Intervention Team,
Greater Manchester West
Mental Health NHS
Foundation Trust,
Bury New Road,
Prestwich M25 3BL, UK

David L. Penn
Professor of Psychology,
Department of Psychology,
University of North Carolina
at Chapel Hill, Chapel Hill,
NC 27599, USA

Stephen Pilling
Director, Centre for Outcomes
Research and Effectiveness,
Sub-Department of Clinical
Health Psychology,
University College London,
1-19 Torrington Place,
London WC1E 7HB, UK

Bart P.F. Rutten
Lecturer, Department of Psychiatry
and Neuropsychology,
South Limburg Mental Health
Research and Teaching Network,
EURON, Maastricht University,
PO Box 616 (DRT 10),
6200 MD Maastricht,
The Netherlands.

Ben Smith
Clinical Research Fellow,
Department of Mental Health
Sciences,
University College London,
Charles Bell House,
67-73 Riding House Street,
London W1W 7EJ, UK

Jayne L. Taylor
School of Psychological Sciences,
Coupland 1 Building,
University of Manchester,
Oxford Road,
Manchester M19 3PL, UK

Peter Trower
Honorary Associate Professor,
School of Psychology,
University of Birmingham,
Edgbaston,
Birmingham B15 2TT, UK

Douglas Turkington
Professor of Psychosocial Psychiatry,
Newcastle University,
Richardson Road,
Newcastle-upon-Tyne
NE1 4LP, UK

Jim van Os
Head of the Department of
Psychiatry and Neuropsychology,
Department of Psychiatry and
Neuropsychology,
South Limburg Mental Health
Research and Teaching Network,
EURON, Maastricht University,
PO Box 616 (DRT 10),
6200 MD Maastricht,
The Netherlands

Craig Whittington
Senior Systematic Reviewer,
Centre for Outcomes
Research and Effectiveness,
Sub-Department of Clinical
Health Psychology,
University College London,
1–19 Torrington Place,
London WC1E 7HB, UK

Part 1

A personal account

Chapter 1

Delusional thinking from the inside: paranoia and personal growth

Peter K. Chadwick

In defence of the single case

Some fifty years ago the case study was seen as the very foundational content of psychiatry and, to a lesser extent, clinical psychology. Of course it still is, and rightly so, in psychoanalysis but in recent years clinical psychologists and psychiatrists have tended to regard the single case as merely the lowest rung of the ladder of evidence quality in science and instead (with only a few exceptions) have aimed for generalizations gleaned from analyses of large samples of people to inform clinical practice. The personal story is regarded therefore, in these days of evidence-based medicine and the scientist-practitioner model, as being too specific, uncontrolled and as lacking needed generalizability. However, some would perceive it more positively. Parker (1994) argues, for example, that it does help to target gaps in existing research and can facilitate the refinement of ideas and theories as one sees them deployed in the service of interpreting and explaining an actual case. I also have put forward the view (Chadwick 2001a, p. ii) that it is particularly at the single case level that one does more clearly apprehend how biological, cognitive, motivational, social and spiritual factors interact to produce the experiential phenomena, intended actions and behaviours that they do. This simply is not possible in large scale, quantitative, nomothetic research. One needs to see the qualitative fine detail of such interactions embodied in the life of an individual person. Non-trivially this also brings theories alive, shows how different levels of description dovetail together and allows the ideas therein to live in the world.

The individual case, when reported by patients or service users themselves, is also increasingly coming to be seen as providing valuable insights into serious mental illness as well as providing helpful reflection on mental health services (Hirsch and Weinberger 2003, p. 701).

Like all the contributors to this volume I am a seeker after knowledge (Latin *scientia*) but it is my personal belief that the rational–empirical way of positivistic mainstream science is only one route to this end. As a professional writer as well as psychologist (and indeed former patient) I explore the intersection of science, art and spirituality (Chadwick 2003a); these three endeavours constitute a nourishing blend, informing the ideology and view of reality in which I believe. Like any artist, a writer must be able to transcend his or her own experience and address wider, hopefully universal, concerns. One sees the achievement of this goal in painters such as Edward Hopper and Frida Kahlo. Kahlo's husband Rivera, like commentators on Hopper, saw her art not simply as narcissistic or egocentric self-indulgence but as 'collective–individual' in that it reached a universal dimension via 'monumental realism' and via the way in which she painted the outside, the inside, and the very depths of herself and the world (see Kettenmann 2002; Herrera 2003). In a similar vein both Carl Rogers and Oscar Wilde independently argued that one could more accurately know others, not via standardized methods, applied formally and impersonally to large samples of individuals, but via the intensification of one's own individuality (Chadwick 1997a). Doubtless George Kelly (1955) would sympathize with this to some degree as a likely outcome of achieving a more complex personal construct system with which to interpret events in social life, while psychoanalysts might also mirror Rogers and Wilde on this point, seeing their proposition as reflecting the benefit of greater general self-knowledge and trained acuity of perception and insight. How indeed, they might say, can one know others if one doesn't know oneself?

In this chapter I intend to bring the singular style that eventuates from a blend of science, art and spirituality to bear in the rendering of my own 1979 paranoid psychotic crisis and also use it to show how I recovered fully from the dreadful predicament that overcame me. It may be that the way I interpret this catastrophe in my life will give useful guidance to service users and professionals regarding the problems of how psychosis itself is to be evaluated, prevented and, if necessary, cured.

Paranoid consciousness

When looking on Hopper's forlorn paintings one has the feeling that no moment in life need be wasted. Hopper captures a barman putting a glass or cup on a shelf; a woman looking at her nails, another woman lost in thought in a cafe. Little things, things one wouldn't usually notice or think about, let alone render on canvas, are there to be appreciated. Some of the experiential moments which built the network of emotionally charged ideas that mediated my own psychosis were trivial in themselves. A remark from my mother; an insult from a bully at school; a strange expression on a shop assistant's face. But all were eventually collected up, knitted together and turned into a delusional web of thoughts and feelings that in the end drove me to multiple suicide attempts that very nearly succeeded in killing me. In madness, no moment of one's existence seems to be wasted; it is as if one's whole life, and the depths of one's very being in selective perspective, have been made magically clear in their awful and portentous significance. One's past comes hauntingly back, in a kind of near-death experience while one is still physically fully alive. '*This* is what it's all been leading up to!' I remember often thinking in the blazing hot, mad hot summer of 1979.

Like many people, if not all, who suffer from paranoia I was a member of a stigmatized minority group. This is a terrible vulnerability. People often would scorn individuals like me as they do Pakistanis and Afro-Caribbeans (at least in the West) in casual conversation. We were even represented on television in the 1960s by reactions such as 'a very killable man' and 'sickening'. I learned by an early age that to be bisexual and transvestite in the provinces of Britain, or America, was to have been born into hatred. I might just as well have been a Nazi war criminal. The contempt and loathing was total. 'Queerdom' was bad enough but queerdom in drag put one totally beyond Christian mercy. American men's magazines in the 1960s described people such as myself as 'deep down sickies' and 'the worst kind of queer' and so on. Sadly the language of psychoanalysts (e.g. Stoller 1975) was little better. I also could not have been born in a place (Manchester, England) further removed in its style of man than what I organismically was. The post-war standard model, so to speak, of 'Manchester Man' was utterly cynical, tough, callous, loud; aggressive, very easily angered; utterly homophobic and so 'transvestophobic' that the topic was not only unmentionable but (even worse) hardly thinkable. 'Manchester Man' behaved as if a line in his programming was 'If any conflict: escalate to verbal abuse or violence immediately.' I knew from a tender age that I was in very great danger. The training of the neural networks of my young brain in Manchester taught me that (though my mother knew) if I ever was discovered or revealed, wherever I was, to outsiders the consequences would be dire and might even be fatal. Indeed the 'model of Man' I received was so revolting it actually intensified my transvestic desires. In the summer of 1974 my private cross-dressing activities were overheard by neighbours in poorly soundproofed flats in Bristol and I was (of course) outed. Five years later I was insane.

Before 1979 I did have my own susceptibilities. I was (and had been since a toddler) highly fearful and threat sensitive; very poor at containing my emotions (both indicated also by my scores on Cattell's (1965) 16PF question-naire in 1973), oversensitive generally, poor on gist and context processing and highly analytical; my emotional life was brightly coloured, too brightly coloured; and the world had effectively been presented to me as I was growing up as being a totally unsupportive, back-stabbing place where it was better to be on one's guard and to trust nobody (even if one was psychologically and sexually 'normal'). The Chadwick family had indeed almost totally deserted us after my father died in 1953 when I was 7 years old and my experiences at the hands of a gang of bullying homophobic schoolboys (all school team foot-ballers) at my grammar school, as well as several beatings in the street and (later) in pubs, pretty well stamped in this cynical, mistrustful and wary perception I had been brought up to have of people (particularly men) and life. When my mother (all her life a hater of the Chadwick family) died in 1971 I was still only 25, had no family on either side left at all, other than my dog Penny, felt personally wretched and had to face the world, a suppressed bisex-ual transvestite, with a headful of expectations that discovery would mean my own destruction. I dared confide in nobody in my social circle the true nature of my sexual identity, nothing could be lower in northern England, at least in those days, than what I was. Getting married and raising a family were out of the question, my whole existence was perpetually, as Dylan Thomas would say, 'like laying eggs by tigers'. The very foundations of my life were *unsafe*. For me this was a very perilous world. How might I inadvertently give myself away? I had to think of such things. Often I would say to myself, 'Can people see the truth in my eyes? I'd better avoid 'poofy' arts subjects, take no interest in really sensitive things like poetry. After all I daren't weaken; rather I should keep watchful and give nothing away. How should I dress even as a man so as to give no clue? Are there hints in my walk or body language? Perhaps it would be useful to take up boxing and weightlifting?' Obviously I had to live very care-fully; in fact this—let's face it—was hardly a *life* at all.

The build-up to psychotic paranoia

'We're going to take photographs of him' said a very macho broken-nosed neighbour in Bristol to his girlfriend Wendy. The cardboard-thin ceilings and floors of the flats we were living in made everything audible. I knew that my cross-dressing had been rumbled weeks before. It was no hallucination. They were downstairs, chatting about me and discussing 'what they should do'—as if it was any of their business anyway. I might have known my game was up living in a place of so little real privacy. My own girlfriend of those days in the mid-1970s, Denise, informed me that the neighbours had indeed told her 'all about me'. She said that they'd described me as 'known for it' in the district where I lived. Bisexuality and transvestism she thought were 'vile and despicable'. This obviously was a relationship that couldn't last. I was sleeping with the enemy, and of course behind enemy lines you don't trust *people*, you trust 'only your heart'.

My friends of those days in Bristol (1974–75) were mainly geologists; they too were 'suitably informed' but it was clear that they thought bisexuality and transvestism were pretty pathetic and disgusting activities. 'Countryside types', as Denise also was, are generally scornful of transvestism; it is well known in the sexual underground that it is a very urban or city activity. One needs anonymity, a wide catchment area of people and always to be near the shops, the stores, the fashion houses, clubs, etc. In other words a life of opportunity and temptations. A life in rolling hills and dales is anathema to most transvestites.

Once I thought photographs of me were circulating: the world became my prison. I went back several times, after I'd moved, to the flat where the outing all started and hammered angrily on their door (ready to put my boxing to use), but it was never opened. I was very noticeable in those days because I always was to be seen (as a man) with Penny, my black labrador dog, who indeed was fast becoming my only real, trustworthy friend. This made me feel very perceptually salient—I stood out from the crowd. People across the street would look at me, say something to the person who was with them and then that person would also look, always with a cold, staring expression. A man looked at me from a doorway, stared at me and then shook his head as if he was thinking, 'I don't believe it, it can't be true.' A woman in a main street took a very long hard look at my face as she was walking towards me, ran ahead, with urgency, to catch up with her partner and said loudly, 'Hey!' I didn't hear the rest of what she said but it must have been about me. Surely she'd seen 'the photographs'? As Denise had told me was the case, it became obvious that word really was getting around—and this was in the days when I practised privately. Once I started, after 1977, to go *out* cross-dressed the gossip seemed to spread like wildfire. Such was life in Britain in the early 1970s if you were bisexual and bi-gender. I might just as well have been living on the wrong planet.

No-one can get away from their own paranoia; you take it with you there in your head wherever you move to. I fled Bristol in 1975 to Liverpool, then in 1976 to Glasgow and finally, in 1978, I moved to London. Everywhere I felt that 'the photographs', perhaps in leaflet form, had been seen. 'It's him on that piece of paper' a woman seemed to say to her friend in a shop in Wimbledon. 'Isn't that that bloke who…?'; 'Isn't this the one who dresses?'; 'It does look like 'im'; 'This bloke dresses up, I've seen photographs of 'im'; 'Yes it's him, by rights it was none of their business'; all the time I would pick up overheard confirmatory instances of the idea that I had been revealed and was known about, wherever I went. It did indeed seem that something was going around. A startled expression from a shop assistant; a lorry driver honking his horn as he went past; a wolf whistle from a gang of youths as they sped past in a car; a smirk on the face of a man walking towards me: those more ambiguous things I now started counting as 'confirming instances'. By 1976/77, in signal detection terms (McNicol 1972) my criterion for acceptance of 'reasonable quality data' before I made a decision—'a signal is there' (in the sense 'they know all about me') —was starting to go down. My false alarm rate therefore was starting to go up. Under the pressures of uncertainty stress I *had* to know what was going on and how many people 'knew'; it was vital to maximize the hit rate. I needed to *know*.

As the months went by, my mind was getting riskier and riskier in decisional style. My thinking also was getting increasingly loose because many more *remote* things were now seen as 'fitting'. By 1978/79 I was actually walking past people *listening* almost masochistically for 'comments at my expense'. Every 'him' or 'he' was now a hit. The photographs/leaflets assumed to be in circulation became by 1979 an absolute self-engrossing preoccupation. They were the very first thing I thought of every single morning when I awoke. The uncertainty stress in itself, like a cat chasing its own tail, was weakening the very fabric of my psyche. In effect the whole business of the leaflets, what I came to call 'the scandal sheet', was now an obsession. The only way I could achieve 'the inner peace of *certainty*', and maybe protect myself from total cerebral disintegration, was to manufacture it myself from the innards of my unconscious.

By the summer of 1979 even things said on television seemed vaguely to confirm that the scandal sheet had circulated, perhaps even internationally. I wrote to a colleague to complain of this 'terrible persecution'. But when the disc-jockey Pete Murray made a mocking, scornful remark a few days later about 'a cherub girl', a phrase I had actually used in my letter to my colleague, I assumed that the letter had been passed to the radio media in amusement and that now it was definitely presenters and disc-jockeys on the airwaves who were persecuting me and 'sending me messages'. At this point, as we say in England: I 'lost the plot' of life. Desperate for something *definite* I clutched at it—at the cost of paranoid insanity. What had started as veridical, as 'rational paranoia' had first become an obsession but was now a paranoid delusion. But it had all happened via a hundred confirmatory or seemingly confirmatory increments over a period of five years. Incrementally encroaching madness. I was now actually insane but, on the inside, I assumed I was perfectly normal. To me 'it really was happening'. In present day street slang I might have said,

'What's new?' After all, this had been my *life*, things had always been like this. If I'd been sleeping with the enemy all my life, obviously the time had now come for the enemy to kick me out of bed. As the reader also can guess, I was the victim of my own metaphors.

Psychotic paranoia

Once I had come to believe firmly that I was on the receiving end of com-ments, messages and scornful jokes from the radio, it is likely that any psychiatrist would have diagnosed me as paranoid. But to me the shift from being the talk of neighbourhoods (and of course the sixth forms at school) to the talk of the radio was smooth and perhaps quite inevitable. In fact if any-thing it was a welcome release from the tail-chasing agony of Conrad's (1968) 'delusional mood'. At least I could now get clear, unambiguous 'information', not snatches of conversation in the street or in bars or ambiguous things like wolf-whistles from passing cars. After the 'cherub girl' remark the portable radio in my bedsitter in Hackney, east London where I was living, became the star of the show. I listened to it for hours for 'messages' and 'clues' to build up my schemata of what people were thinking, doing and perhaps planning in respect of myself. It was, after all, what *really had* happened with the homo-phobic bullying ring at school in Manchester and with the neighbours in Bristol (so a proto-schema of this kind of thing already was in place); it seemed perfectly sensible to me that it was simply happening again. 'What's new?' It never for a moment occurred to me that I was mad. In a way the psychic air had cleared and I had a definite strategy and plan in my life. I now 'knew' what *really* was going on. If anything I felt better!

The descriptive narrative that I could produce from that moment would be merely a rendering of the twists and turns my thinking took as a result (mainly) of 'confirmatory' comments I gleaned from my radio over the weeks that followed plus remarks I overheard in the street and in temporary jobs I did to scrape a living. (Unemployment benefit in those days was even more pitiful than it is now—after rent and Penny's food I was left with a mere £2 a week on which to live, an awful stress at times in itself.)

Basically the jolts and jogs to my thinking produced by 'radio messages' and overheard remarks (plus even the headlines of newspapers trapped on rain-sodden pavements) led me from temporary relief into torment. There now was indeed (as there had been at school on a smaller scale) an organization of people seeking to discredit, ridicule and humiliate me. I referred to this outfit as 'The Organization'. They were doing this to make me change, clean up my 'vile and despicable' act and start living as a decent, normal person. It was manifest to them that I was 'possessed of the devil' (as I'd overheard a woman clearly and loudly say of me, to her daughter, on Hackney Downs). Should I *fail* in this effort at self-reform (God being, to me, a savage entity), the only alternative was death, and death by suicide, in order to cast Satan out of myself, as indeed I'd seen happen to a character at the end of the film *The Exorcist* in 1974.

A comment here, a memory of a film there, multiple 'messages' from the radio plus knowledge of the everyday scripts via which British people lived their lives in those days and the whole patchwork of threads and 'bits and pieces' from the present and the past all came together as if a giant schema of my whole decadent, sybaritic *life* was now cast before me. My past indiscretions were now known about by 'everybody'. I was perhaps 'the antichrist' himself. *That* would at least explain the *scale* of what was going on and the obsessive motivation of The Organization for doing it. Nothing less— in my increasingly unrestrained imagination—than a threat to the very integrity of the world would justify an operation like this! As inference built on inference as the weeks went by, my thinking soared to evermore outlandish levels—but still the confirmatory events and remarks kept coming.

Even when I moved to Fulham, west London, to live with a transsexual, the ever-so meaningful events and comments (now from pretty well everything going on around me) did not cease. Now there was meaning in *every* trivial event; the feeling of meaning totally pervaded my waking consciousness. But as I say: no-one can run from paranoia. Pondering in the office of my employer 'how I should kill myself', a man shouted to the manager at the end of a conversation, as he was walking out of a side-office, 'So he's got to do it by bus then?!'; 'Yes!' came the reply. Again the perfect, uncanny timing of the coincidences. In reality it was almost certainly about a delivery, but not to my way of thinking. A couple of days later I threw myself under a double decker London bus on New King's Road in Fulham so as to thrust Satan, the 'old king', out of myself thence allowing 'the new King' (Jesus) to come into the world to reign. I expected after death to be cast into Outer Darkness—clearly I felt a totally expendable being. Somehow it all fitted, it always did, thousands of 'coincidences' over three months had led me to my nemesis; relentless perfectly timed coincidences, surely it *had* to be true? These were not ordinary coincidences, they were *messages*. This was not madness—this, surely, was *really happening*!?!

Obviously the suicide attempt (very narrowly) failed, as did three further attempts in hospital before I was injected with antipsychotic drugs. Even as the nurse approached me with the (large) syringe I automatically assumed she was going to kill me, not help me. Such had been my delusion and my life.

I fell asleep instantly and, in a way, that injection and the years of medication did 'kill' my 'First Mind'. I have never, thank God, been the same again.

Reflections on the episode

Reasonably fine-grained details of this psychotic crisis have been published previously (Chadwick 1992, 1993, 1997b, 2001b,c, 2003b). For years after this personal catastrophe I was not entirely sure that the incredible tirade of perfectly timed coincidences that came my way was not in some respects paranormal or even supernatural in essence. My mystical state of mind just before the 'cherub girl' remark (Chadwick 1992) puts a very sinister perspective on the crisis (relevant at least to the first two weeks of it when the 'coincidences' were raining down on me). It is now more than twenty-five years ago and I write in a calm, stable frame of mind. But the ambience of Chapter 4 in *Borderline* (Chadwick 1992), some of which was written in 1986 with the aid of diaries from the actual crisis, does capture, close to the event, the real flavour of paranoid insanity. It shows how one *really could* believe that a saga, occult in ambience, was taking place. Many people who have written to me over the years do see it this way, but of course no qualified psychologists or psychiatrists. Is it possible that certain rare states of mind, where the experiential boundary between within and without has dissolved, can in some way permit or facilitate the genuinely uncanny? Is it possible that events, as Jung (1955) believed, can 'transgress' their usual causal framework and be instantiated in the world, guided by *meaning*? Do some states of mind genuinely amplify the truly synchronistic? This domain of experience between sanity and madness I call 'The Borderline' (Chadwick 1992, 1997b) and it may be, like hypnopompic and hypnogogic states, that this is a thin slice of our experiential realm where we have so far searched relatively little (Chadwick 2004). Certainly the *capacities* of the psychotic and near-psychotic mind are underresearched. It may be inferred that if the ontic status of The Borderline realm is veridical, it is a zone not only of The Divine but also of the infernal, and those who venture there do so at their peril (see also Greenberg *et al.* 1992 for warnings on this).

Psychological reflections on the narrative

There are numerous constructions one could put on a window of human experience such as that briefly described above. Since it has never been possible to publish the full story of the crisis—its twists and turns and psychological fine detail would fill hundreds of pages—I refer readers to the References for further material.

Most psychiatrists (and probably most psychologists) do not, unlike myself, believe in God (Neeleman and King 1993; Neeleman and Persaud 1995) but most people in the general population, even in such a secular nation as Britain, at least in fairly recent times, do so believe (Cox and Cowling 1989; Church 1997). Indeed about a quarter also believe in the existence of Satan—a name bestowed on me half-seriously both by my own mother ('They used to tar and feather your kind') and a Roman Catholic girlfriend. As an offspring and member of the Chadwick family (which she loathed) my mother had not an ounce of respect for me and she often showed it.

Though psychiatrists and psychologists might find it amusing, one distinguished British psychotherapist was just as disrespectful. Reviewing a manuscript of mine submitted for publication to Routledge in 1991, he came very close indeed to accusing me of actually *being* Satan incarnate. His review was not published.

When one carefully renders detailed accounts of experiences at the outer limits of what a human being can experience, as in some cases of psychotic paranoia, one reveals phenomena that can shock, amaze, puzzle and disturb both lay people and professionals.

In the twenty years or so since I have been writing, publishing and giving public lectures on this and related experiences, professionals may be surprised to learn that people have variously interpreted me as—and I quote—'a shaman'; 'a guru'; 'a messenger'; 'possessed by an imp'; 'a man of God'; 'a physical medium'; 'a psychic'; 'a recovered psychotic'; 'a person who people see as having been mad but who never was really'; 'a victim of a paranormal attack'; 'maybe you *were* Satan but became Jesus after the first suicide attempt?'; 'a psychokineticker'; 'a healer-teacher'; 'a deeply abused feminine man'; 'a living embodiment of Yin and Yang'; 'victim of your own conscience'; 'thought disordered'; 'a person who brought it all on himself'; 'a schizophrenic'; 'a schizoaffective'; 'a hypomanic'; 'a psychologist who should have been a priest'; 'someone who just needed a lot of loving'; 'deserved all he got'; 'male and female in one body'; ... and so it goes on. If one ever needed evidence that this is a postmodern world in which multiple perspectives vie for supremacy in an evolutionary setting—each perspective trying to 'discredit contenders for intelligibility' (Gergen 1985)—a detailed rendering of a psychotic crisis will certainly provide it!

One must also remember that at the time of this psychosis I actually was 2½ stones (35 lbs) underweight through having insufficient money to buy food for both myself and Penny. I was agitated, overaroused, hypervigilant and undernourished. This cannot have encouraged optimum brain functioning. My ribcage was fully visible when I was stripped off; I had no permanent job, no secure income, and was £500 overdrawn at the bank (equivalent to £5000 in 2006/7); I had no secure home, being a guest in a boarding house; all my family were dead ... and I was frightened, unhappy and terribly bored living in Hackney because there was no-one in my circle of contacts, even in the London transvestite underground, with whom I could hold a half-decent conversation. Abstract thought and complex ideas were simply 'not wanted here'. I could rarely complete more than one sentence without being interrupted and effectively 'shut up'.

It hardly is surprising that I moved from an unbearable past and an equally unbearable present into mysticism (or 'supersanity' as I would claim: Chadwick 1992, 2001c) and then into insanity. I was conflicted and guilt-ridden about my sexual identity, expected punishment for it, and, in psychoanalytic terms, projected not my id but my ('Manchester Man') super-ego out into the world. There was definitely narrative sense in my psychosis. 'The Organization' of my delusions was an existential gestalt of all the homo-phobic, transvestophobic self-righteous people I had ever known in my life—all bearing down on me (like the wheels of a ten-ton bus) and, as at school, ridiculing and trying to scorn me into non-existence. My persecution at school in northern England was a kind of mini-rehearsal of the whole event. It was the lock that the 'outing' in Bristol turned like a key, opening the door to paranoid insanity. This delusion wasn't a 'cognitive error' so much as my whole life experience demonstrating the moral sadism of '1950s and 1960s Manchester Man'. My existence had taught me that people *really would* be likely to do such things as I imagined—and at the same time feel pleased with themselves for doing so (Chadwick 1997c). My probability judgements had been skewed by abuse and betrayal.

Our long-term memories consist not just of words, objects and events, but of representations of our relations with other people (Thomas 1996, p. 326). In the relatively macho environment of post-war provincial Britain I could never (like a fish in water) escape from a relational model of myself likely to be seen as a 'worthless, perverted, inferior excuse for a man' were my bisexual, bigender proclivities ever fully or widely known. At school I was merely mis-read as 'homosexual' because of my ornate hairstyle. But in 1979 I came face to face with the horrific reality of my own worst nightmares and my own imagination took me 90% of the way there. To this day, no-one I have ever asked or confronted has ever seen or heard anything about me in the form of a leaflet or a scandal sheet. There is nothing on the internet on my transvestism other than my own writings. 'The photographs', if they were ever taken (it's possible that the remark was made just to intimidate me), may have been a prank to illustrate the local gossip at the time. I made a Hollywood-style movie script out of just one sentence of conversation. Back in 1970, while still in my previous career as a geologist, I had given a lecture at Imperial College entitled, 'Some implications of single and multilayer theories' to a conference audience in structural geology. In 1979 I adapted this approach to create 'A lot of implications of hearing a transvestophobe say, "We're going to take photographs of him."' One was productive inventiveness, the other unproductive. One led to a Royal Society research fellowship, the other to a psychiatric unit. Such is life, there are no prizes in this world for imaginative psychotic delusions.

Treatment and recovery

Neuroleptic medication, at first chlorpromazine, later changed to haloperidol, completely prevented any reactivation of the delusions and delusional perceptions of my psychotic state. Many other patients have told me that medication is not for them but in my case it was wonderfully helpful. In terms of the illness model, I have had no 'relapses' in 27 years. The medication also 'turned the volume down' on my basic affects of anger, fear and sex (making everyday life a lot more liveable) and improved my attentional style by substantially enhancing my processing of gist and context, something vital in social situations. Although it is not of assistance to everybody, in my case the illness model was appropriate and helpful. In effect the medication gave me a rather different personality but I never felt that haloperidol turned me into somebody I wasn't, only that it totally removed the barriers and distractions that had been preventing me from being who I am. Paradoxically I feel infinitely more my 'Real Self' while on haloperidol than I ever felt before I began taking it, or when I'm currently not taking it. This Real Self, however, has had to receive social feedback, in the sense of receiving reactions so as to validate my identity and self-image—a process taking many years.

My attentional style and 'emotion volume' really reflected cognitive and brain 'hardware' factors that could not, and were not, eased by software approaches such as psychotherapy and psychoanalysis. Neither of those endeavours had any effect on my sexual orientation either, indeed my mother noticed my fetishistic interests when I was an infant and only a few days old. Psychodynamic theorists seriously neglect the massive sensory attractions of women's clothes to some males. However, the obnoxious 'models of man' that I had been exposed to as a child and teenager did turn me away from valuing masculinity and maleness in myself and did, as I said earlier, intensify my interest in and (later) obsession with femininity that fuelled the transvestism. 'Why should I be a man?' I cryptically thought to myself, 'Men are vile.'

Moving to west London, just round the corner from the sexually liberal area of Earls Court, meeting my wife Jill (who thought transvestism was 'a laugh') and building up a circle of totally accepting friends (including infinitely nicer and kinder men) also did much to dispel my negative self-concept and low self-esteem. It helped me to accept myself as I really am and to accept and own—not disown—my own maleness.

It was obvious to priests I talked to that in 1979 my perception of God was totally distorted and my capacity to see my own inner beauty minuscule. (Years of reading cynical psychoanalytic texts had not helped in this latter respect.) The crisis had, however, definitely planted seeds which later I cultivated in the service of my own spiritual development. Sadly this was something that had also been blocked by psychoanalysis and years of 1970s positivistic Western academic psychology—where any mention of the spiritual was reduced to 'regression' or 'aberrant brain processes'. A psychotic episode gives one a very profound and intense experience of feeling open as if to forces from beyond oneself. After the crisis it is still possible to cultivate the very same kind of quality or 'music' to one's experiential life but turn it to productive and hopefully beautiful and loving outcomes. To scorn or reduce the spiritual via 'nothing buttery' thinking is to miss totally its vital function in enhancing creativity, openness to experience, kindling one's general sense of wonder about the cosmos and improving one's general quality of life. Are not spiritual experiences a natural part of the mind's operation? The latter should surely not be dismissed as 'psychic gas' (see Clarke 2001).

With the gradual elimination of the self-loathing I had acquired in Manchester in the 1950s and 1960s, my moral masochism ('I'm to blame, I'm no good, I have no right to exist') and existential fragility subsided, along with my internal justifications for them. Spending 18 months in the kind and accepting atmosphere of a psychiatric aftercare hostel also helped dissolve the horrifically negative self-schema that I had developed since a child. In a sense I was effectively cured 'from below' by medication and 'from above' by spiritual and social interventions.

It was difficult to do productive work only at the level of my cognitions. The remaining 'scandal sheet worry' (even after medication) was a contrascientific proposition. Unlike Karl Popper's (1959) 'All swans are white' example of a *scientific* proposition (refutable by finding one black swan), the scandal sheet worry was totally irrefutable. One example of the scandal sheet would *confirm* it, but a thousand disclaimers: 'No, I've never seen it' would not refute it. It provoked an ideal situation for Peter Wason's (1960) 'confirmation bias' to run rampant. I had a logical problem as much as a psychological one, but being mindful of this was helpful. I have been wary of confirmation bias and jumping to conclusions (see Garety and Freeman 1999) ever since. Eventually, by September 1980, the scandal sheet worry, which previously had dominated my life, became boring and I totally lost interest in it. After all, its only damage to me had been of my own making. There were other things in life. In the aftercare hostel where I was living at the time, another scientifically trained resident with a similar concern also lost his vitality for the cognition; he too became quite bored with his own delusion, realizing that there was more to life. Delusion thrives in a bored mind with an aimless life.

In Hackney in 1979 my life seemed to be over. It was a pity that I had had to live there but there was no other accommodation in London where I could keep Penny. London was not 'dog friendly'. But certainly in those days I had nothing to lose by soaring to the limits of my own imagination—cramped and stifled as it was by years of positivism. At least I became, in my own mind, a person of consequence in the middle of a spectacularly interesting saga who simultaneously atoned for 'a lifetime of transgressions'. In a way my delusions also released an artistic fiction-making ability and simultaneously satisfied my need for magic (Chadwick 2005). My cognitive processes were in many ways pawns to these deeper moral, motivational and even spiritual concerns. What one fears, one also longs for—full atonement and complete confrontation with that which one dreads can end a life of tension, guilt and fear. Peace has a beckoning quality.

It is fairly clear that actually to move into a psychotic state is the outcome of a life process—and recovery is rather similar. It is not something to be hurried. But recovery is far more than merely being delusion- and hallucination-free (Marland 2000): it means a total readjustment to life and sometimes rearrangement *of* one's life and an improvement in one's capacity to love and to work (and to manage money!). By far the most common interpretations of my 'dark night of the soul', from the long list given earlier, are that I am both a recovered psychotic and a shaman. Undoubtedly my journey to the furthest reaches of human experience and back is very much in the spirit of the shaman model, but the journey truly has enriched my life in the long term immeasurably and made me a better psychologist, a better teacher and a better healer of minds and souls. I remarked earlier that one cannot know others if one does not know oneself—both the light and the dark sides of one's being. A person afraid or avoidant of their own Jungian shadow (that which they disapprove of or disown in themselves (Wolman 1973, p. 347)) is not self-knowing. But by knowing one's own essence to its very core, one's empathy and understanding of others can become embracing, full, fair and genuinely insightful. This is the product, at least in my own understanding, of the blending of science, art and spirituality as a product of human questing. I hope that it can enlighten us about the 'common clay' of humanity more than tables of statistics.

Conclusion

I believe the example of my own case shows that psychosis has both meaning and narrative sense. The insights and understandings into one's own crisis play a critical part in recovery. Seeing it in the context of one's whole life development process also is constructive.

However, there was no 'magic bullet' to solve my 1979 psychosis and no single reason for its onset. The inducing and ameliorating factors were all reticular with many recursive loops. To recover permanently I had to change my town, my job, the kind of work I did, my circle of friends and contacts, the chemical state of my brain, my partner, my self-concept, style of thinking, even my attitude to psychology itself and of course my attitude to God. I had to re-take an interest in 'poofy arts subjects' and 'sensitive things like poetry' to release 'the artist within' and so learn to express, not deny, the artistic and spiritual sides of my own being which had been stifled by so many years of rational empiricism. By 1990/91 my bisexuality and transvestism were dead. I had thought I was a 'half woman' but in fact I was another man, a feminine man (an unthinkable identity in 1950s and 1960s Manchester). Transvestism and the creation of an alternative personality were no longer needed because I expressed my femininity perfectly adequately in the kind of work I did, felt secure in my identity and (importantly) in my right to exist, and my lifestyle was free from guilt. The nearest I approach to transvestism now is wearing satin dressing gowns from time to time or watching Fashion TV with my wife—both the kinds of things a feminine man would do. As the Taoists say a man should do: I have known the masculine but hold to the feminine (Burke 2004, p. 167). Without a really blatant feminine self-perception, however, my particular style of bisexuality also evaporated. I went from 'bi-transvestite' to 'teddy bear man'.

A psychoanalyst might be more idealistic and say that I am not really cured because I have to take a couple of milligrams of haloperidol every night; surely that is not good enough? But that is not the point. The point is that the problem is solved. The vulnerabilities biochemically, cognitively, emotionally and motivationally, existentially, socially and spiritually that led to the 1979 episode have all been corrected or eliminated—this is a triumph of what I call 'total psychology'. I admit that I felt I had been genuinely ill—my galloping confirmation-seeking became something I just couldn't stop. Perhaps my undernourished, over-aroused brain was temporarily malfunctioning; but biochemistry and physiology with no mind and mentalism, and spirituality with no brain, supply no professional solution to the problem of paranoid psychosis. If we accept that we have to work with the totality of the person-in-the-world (and indeed sometimes person in the context of their own total spiritual perspective (Clarke 2001)), not just with their dopamine pathways, cognitive biases or disrespectful parents, we will have at least the right attitude to solving the enigma of paranoia.

References

Burke, T.P. (2004) *The Major Religions*. Oxford: Blackwell.

Cattell, R.B. (1965) *The Scientific Analysis of Personality*. Harmondsworth: Penguin.

Chadwick, P.K. (1992) *Borderline: A Psychological study of Paranoia and Delusional Thinking*. London and New York: Routledge.

Chadwick, P.K. (1993) The stepladder to The Impossible: a first hand phenomenological account of a schizoaffective psychotic crisis. *Journal of Mental Health*, 2, 239–250.

Chadwick, P.K. (1997a) Oscar Wilde: psychologist. *Changes*, 15, 163–174.

Chadwick, P.K. (1997b) *Schizophrenia—The Positive Perspective: In Search of Dignity for Schizophrenic People*. London and New York: Routledge.

Chadwick, P.K. (1997c) Recovery from psychosis: Learning more from patients. *Journal of Mental Health*, 6, 577–588.

Chadwick, P.K. (2001a) *Personality as Art: Artistic Approaches in Psychology*. Ross-on-Wye: PCCS Books.

Chadwick, P.K. (2001b) Psychotic consciousness. *International Journal of Social Psychiatry*, 47, 52–62.

Chadwick, P.K. (2001c) Sanity to supersanity to insanity: a personal journey. In Clarke, I. (ed.) *Psychosis and Spirituality: Exploring the New Frontier*. London and Philadelphia: Whurr.

Chadwick, P.K. (2003a) Positivism, materialism and scientific psychology: the illusions of truth and certainty. *Journal of Critical Psychology, Counselling and Psychotherapy*, 3, 185–189.

Chadwick, P.K. (2003b) The stream of psychotic consciousness. *Open Mind*, 124, 22–23.

Chadwick, P.K. (2004) Paranormal, spiritual and metaphysical aspects of madness: an essay on love and cognition. *Paranormal Review*, 31, 13–16.

Chadwick, P.K. (2005) The other side of delusions: magic, fiction making and personal growth. *Journal of Critical Psychology, Counselling and Psychotherapy*, 5, 85–88.

Clarke, I. (2001) (ed.) *Psychosis and Spirituality: Exploring the New Frontier*. London and Philadelphia: Whurr.

Conrad, K. (1968) *Die beginnende Schizophrenie: Versuch einer Gestaltanalze des Wahns* (Commencing schizophrenia: an attempt at a gestalt analysis of delusion). Stuttgart: Thieme.

Cox, D. and Cowling, P. (1989) *Are You Normal?* London: Tower Press.

Garety, P.A. and Freeman, D. (1999) Cognitive approaches to delusions: a critical review of theories and evidence. *British Journal of Clinical Psychology*, 38, 113–154.

Gergen, K.J. (1985) The social constructionist movement in modern psychology. *American Psychologist*, 40, 266–275.

Greenberg, D., Witzum, E. and Buchbinder, J.T. (1992) Mysticism and Psychosis: the fate of Ben Zoma. *British Journal of Medical Psychology*, 65, 223–236.

Herrera, H. (2003) *Frida*. London: Bloomsbury.

Hirsch, S.R. and Weinberger, D.R. (eds) (2003) *Schizophrenia*, 2nd edn. Oxford and Massachusetts: Blackwell.

Jung, C.G. (1955) *Synchronicity: An Acausal Connecting Principle*. London: Ark.

Kelly, G. (1955) *The Psychology of Personal Constructs*. New York: Norton.

Kettenmann, A. (2002) *Kahlo*. Cologne: Taschen.

Marland, G. (2000) Cognitive deficits in schizophrenia. *Nursing Times*, 96 (16), 43–44.

McNicol, D. (1972) *A Primer of Signal Detection Theory*. London: Allen & Unwin.

Neeleman, J. and King, M.B. (1993) Psychiatrists' religious attitudes in relation to their clinical practice. *Acta Psychiatrica Scandinavica*, 88, 420–424.

Neeleman, J. and Persaud, R. (1995) Why do psychiatrists neglect religion? *British Journal of Medical Psychology*, 68, 169–178.

Parker, I. (1994) Qualitative Research. In: Banister, P., Burman, E., Parker, I., Taylor, M. and Tindall, C. (eds), *Qualitative Methods in Psychology: A Research Guide*. Buckingham and Philadelphia: Open University Press.

Popper, K.R. (1959) *The Logic of Scientific Discovery*. London: Hutchinson.

Church J. (ed.) (1997) *Social Trends*, Office for National Statistics, No. 27. London: HMSO.

Stoller, R.J. (1975) *Perversion: The Erotic Form of Hatred*. New York: Dell Publishing.

Thomas, K. (1996) The defensive self: a psychodynamic perspective. In: Stevens, R. (ed.), *Understanding the Self*. Milton Keynes: Open University.

Wason, P.C. (1960) On the failure to eliminate hypotheses in a conceptual task. *Quarterly Journal of Experimental Psychology*, 12, 129–140.

Wolman, B.V. (ed.) (1973) *Dictionary of Behavioural Science*. London and New York: Macmillan Press.

Part 2

Assessment, epidemiology, and prognosis

Chapter 2

The assessment of persecutory ideation

Daniel Freeman

Introduction

If you put several researchers or clinicians in a room to decide the best assessment instrument for a psychological disorder, do not expect agreement. The reason is simple: the choice depends upon the particular question to be answered and the conditions in which assessment is taking place. The assessment of paranoid thinking is no exception. For instance, a clinician may be keen to choose a measure that detects change in the distress associated with paranoia, while a researcher may choose to focus on why a person believes paranoid thoughts so strongly. The assessment may be for repeated detailed monitoring of a single case or for rapid screening of a large cohort of people in an epidemiological study. So there will be disagreement in a room of researchers or clinicians not only because of personal preferences (or idiosyncrasies), but because each is likely to have a different requirement in mind. In choosing measures, the researcher or clinician needs to be very clear about the aims of the assessment. Equally, it is important to consider what is acceptable for the client or research participant. In this chapter key issues to consider when choosing a measure of persecutory ideation are highlighted, the instruments for assessing persecutory ideation are reviewed, and recommendations are made.

Theory informing assessment

Accurate assessment depends on knowledge of the composition of the experience of interest. Recent psychosis research has put the experience of individuals at centre stage. This has led to a better understanding of the nature of persecutory thinking. However, there is wide variation in the degree to which developments in understanding paranoia have been incorporated into assessment instruments. Phenomenological examinations of paranoia also have much more to yield (Freeman *et al.* 2001; Boyd and Gumley 2007; Campbell and Morrison 2007; Freeman 2007).

Definitions and dimensionality

The starting point for the development of a measure should be a definition of the phenomenon of interest. Consideration of the definition of delusional beliefs—the broader category of which persecutory ideation is a sub-type—reveals the inherently complex multi-dimensional nature of the experience. Many commentaries point out the limitations of definitions of delusional beliefs in general (e.g. Strauss 1969; Jones 1999), in that most criteria do not apply to all delusions. The most sustainable position is that of Oltmanns (1988). Assessing the presence of a delusion may best be accomplished by considering a list of characteristics or dimensions, none of which is necessary or sufficient, that with increasing endorsement produces greater agreement on the presence of a delusion. For instance, the more a belief is implausible, unfounded, strongly held, not shared by others, distressing and preoccupying, the more likely it is to be considered a delusion. So it is not simply the content of a delusion that needs to be explained, but also the other elements that make up the experience, each of which is dimensional (see Table 2.1). For example, the degree of belief conviction differs both across individuals with delusions and within individuals across time (e.g. Strauss 1969; Brett-Jones *et al.* 1987). A multi-dimensional view of delusions is supported by a number of empirical studies (e.g. Kendler *et al.* 1983; Brett-Jones *et al.* 1987; Harrow *et al.* 1988; Garety and Hemsley 1994; Harrow *et al.* 2004). It is plausible that different factors are involved in the various dimensions of delusional experience. For example, the factors that lead a person to have a particular thought may be different from those that lead to strong belief conviction, which may in turn differ from the factors that make the thought preoccupying and distressing. Researchers and clinicians may wish to focus on different dimensions. Researchers may be particularly interested in why a strong belief has developed, while clinicians may prefer to focus on the factors that have caused the beliefs to become distressing. There needs to be a clear recognition of the element of delusional experience an assessment instrument is trying to capture.

The focus in this book is on one type of delusional thought: persecutory. Defining the persecutory sub-type has rarely been a topic of comment. This is perhaps because the issue is thought to be self-evident, but in fact it is more complex than might appear at first sight. There is great variety in the content of persecutory thoughts—for instance, in the type and timing of threat, the target of the harm, and the identity and intention of the persecutor (Freeman *et al.* 2001; Freeman *et al.* 2006; Freeman and Freeman 2008). Furthermore, terms such as paranoia, delusions of persecution, and delusions of reference have been used both interchangeably and to refer to different concepts. As will be seen, concepts of mistrust, suspicion, and hostility also feature in discussion of paranoia. Freeman and Garety (2000) therefore clarified the definition

Table 2.1 The multi-dimensional nature of delusions (Freeman 2007)

Characteristic of delusions	Variability in characteristic
Unfounded	For some individuals, the delusions reflect a kernel of truth that has been exaggerated (e.g. the person had a dispute with the neighbour, but now believes that the whole neighbourhood is monitoring them and will harm them). It can be difficult to determine whether the person is actually delusional. For others, the ideas are fantastic, impossible and clearly unfounded (e.g. the person believes that s/he was present at the time of the Big Bang and is involved in battles across the universe and heavens).
Firmly held	Beliefs can vary from being held with 100% conviction to only occasionally being believed when the person is in a particular stressful situation.
Resistant to change	An individual may be certain that they could not be mistaken and will not countenance any alternative explanation for their experiences. Others feel very confused and uncertain about their ideas and readily want to think about alternative accounts of their experiences.
Preoccupying	Some people report that they can do nothing but think about their delusional concerns. For other people, although they firmly believe the delusion, such thoughts rarely come into their mind.
Distressing	Many beliefs, especially those seen in clinical practice, are very distressing (e.g. persecutory delusions) but others (e.g. grandiose delusions) can actually be experienced positively. Even some persecutory delusions can be associated with low levels of distress (e.g. the individual believes that the persecutor hasn't the power to harm them).
Interferes with social functioning	Delusions can stop people interacting with others and lead to great isolation and abandonment of activities. Other people can have a delusion and still function at a high level including maintaining relationships and employment.
Involves personal reference	In many instances, the patient is at the centre of the delusional system (e.g. 'I have been singled out for persecution'). However, friends and relatives can be involved (e.g. 'They are targeting my whole family') and some people believe that everybody is affected equally (e.g. 'Everybody is being experimented upon').

of persecutory ideation: the individual believes both that harm is occurring, or is going to occur, to him or her, and that the persecutor has the intention to cause harm (see Table 2.2). The second element of the definition distinguishes persecutory from anxious thoughts.

The continuum of paranoia

An issue connected to the dimensionality of delusions is the relationship of clinical to non-clinical paranoid thought. As is seen throughout this book and elsewhere (Myin-Germeys *et al.* 2003), it is increasingly accepted that clinical persecutory delusions are related to more everyday persecutory thoughts. But, although complete discontinuity between clinical and non-clinical experiences is unlikely, the exact nature of the relationship remains to be established and may be one of a number of different types.

In providing a description of the development of the concept of schizotypal personality disorder, Kendler (1985) notes two traditions: descriptions of unusual *personality* characteristics in non-clinical relatives of people with schizophrenia and descriptions of attenuated *symptoms* of schizophrenia in patients. Claridge (1994, 1997) expands on this difference. He notes a quasi-dimensional (disease-based) perspective in which researchers focus on degrees of expression of an illness. So, for example, schizotypal personality disorder is considered a *forme fruste* of schizophrenia. This approach is particularly associated with the measurement of clinical signs and symptoms. Claridge also notes a fully dimensional (personality-based) perspective, in which psychotic symptoms are associated with a personality trait. In other words, there is a distribution of the trait or vulnerability or psychosis-proneness across the population and diagnoses

Table 2.2 Criteria for a delusion to be classified as persecutory (Freeman and Garety 2000)

Criteria A and B must be met:

  A. The individual believes that harm is occurring, or is going to occur, to him or her.

  B. The individual believes that the persecutor has the intention to cause harm.

There are a number of points of clarification:

  ♦ Harm concerns any action that leads to the individual experiencing distress.

  ♦ Harm only to friends or relatives does *not* count as a persecutory belief, unless the persecutor also intends this to have a negative effect upon the individual.

  ♦ The individual must believe that the persecutor, at present or in the future, will attempt to harm him or her.

  ♦ Delusions of reference do *not* count within the category of persecutory beliefs.

---

such as schizophrenia are at the extreme end of such variation (albeit that in many of these accounts there may still be discontinuity in shifts from traits to disorder). Scales associated with this approach would assess much less severe personality characteristics and related experiences compared with clinical symptoms. From a continuum perspective, it is of interest to assess the types of prominent paranoid symptoms present in severe mental illness, paranoid experiences present in less severe disorder, normal suspicious experience, and personality characteristics such as wariness and mistrust.

This clearly raises the central issue of the content of the questions used in assessment instruments. Some items may be clearly concerned with persecutory thoughts (meeting the criteria in Table 2.2), while others may instead concern related concepts such as mistrust. But, even within the category of thoughts that are clearly persecutory, there are important differences. Epidemiological research finds that plausible-sounding paranoid thoughts (e.g. my neighbours are trying to irritate me) are more common than odder-sounding ideas (e.g. there is a government conspiracy against me). Further, particular aspects of the content of paranoid thoughts (e.g. how powerful the persecutor is, how severe the outcome) are associated with distress (Birchwood et al. 2000; Freeman et al. 2001; Chisholm et al. 2006; Green et al. 2006). Depending on the content of the actual items, even an assessment instrument explicitly focusing on persecutory thoughts could easily have more of a clinical (severe) or non-clinical (mild) focus.

The assessment of persecutory ideation

The paranoia problem: justified suspicions

There is a spectre that accompanies the study of paranoia: the difficulty of ruling out the accuracy of paranoid thoughts. The interest of this book is the presence of unfounded or exaggerated paranoid thinking, but in most cases one cannot completely rule out the possibility that a thought is realistic. To confuse the issue further, unfounded paranoid thinking is more likely given a real victimization experience (e.g. Johns et al. 2004; Fowler et al. 2006a), and paranoid thinking may lead others into conspiratorial-type reactions, such as exclusion (Lemert 1962). Though some suggest that all clinicians have, on some occasions, misdiagnosed experiences as delusional (Maher and Ross 1980), actual reports of misdiagnosis are—unsurprisingly—rare in the literature (but see Mayerhoff et al. 1991). There has been no good systematic examination of the issue. Clearly, the reporting of justified suspicions is a particular problem for self-report assessments. But interview methods are also not without problems in establishing the true nature of events, since they can only rely on a judgement based upon the content of the belief, the evidence given, and the context. Spitzer (1992) goes as far to suggest that 'a delusion is not a delusion because it is a false statement, but because it is a statement made in an inappropriate context and, most importantly, with inappropriate justification.'

The accuracy of measures will be related to the actual content of persecutory thoughts assessed. Physically impossible beliefs (e.g. there is a persecutor who has killed or removed the whole brain of the individual) are evidently less likely to be true than more plausible beliefs (e.g. the neighbours are trying to get the individual to move away). Therefore the capability of an assessment to record real events depends on the content of the beliefs assessed. Scales that assess more bizarre clinical presentations are less likely to record justified suspicions than scales assessing paranoid thoughts of more plausible everyday content. It should certainly always be kept in mind that assessment of paranoia by self-report questionnaire will overestimate the presence of unfounded paranoid thinking. However, self-report positive symptom measure scores are correlated with those from interviewer assessments (e.g. Preston and Harrison 2003; Liraud *et al.* 2004; Watson *et al.* 2006) and self-report measures of paranoid thinking have been found to be associated with the occurrence of unfounded paranoid thinking in experimental conditions (Freeman *et al.* 2005a, 2007b, 2008; Valmaggia *et al.* 2007).

General measures of delusions

The most commonly used measures of persecutory ideation have been items from psychiatric measures such as the Positive and Negative Syndrome Scale (PANSS; Kay 1991), the Brief Psychiatric Rating Scale (Overall and Gorham 1962) and the Scale for the Assessment of Positive Symptoms (SAPS; Andreasen 1984). It should be emphasized that these scales have been used to assess persecutory delusions in clinical groups. The scales rely on single items and provide a unidimensional assessment, which means that the scales are often more useful than presence/absence interviews such as the Present State Examination—10 (PSE; World Health Organization 1992); but it should be remembered that diagnostic interview schedules such as the PSE, which are used especially in epidemiological research (see Freeman 2006), provide much better clarity in definitions and are therefore an excellent training experience. Besides their brevity and interview format, the main advantage of the unidimensional measures is that the other scale items assess important co-occurring symptoms such as hallucinations and grandiosity. This provides important descriptive information on clinical groups. In clinical settings there is often co-occurrence of symptoms (Maric *et al.* 2004) and a focus on single symptom research can overlook this confounding factor. Nonetheless, there are clear difficulties with the unidimensional scales: they mainly capture levels of conviction in the belief and are less sensitive in assessing distress (Steel *et al.* 2007); little belief content is specified, mainly relying on the judgment of the interviewer; and suspicion, ideas of reference, and persecution are often considered together.

An improvement on these measures is the Psychotic Symptom Rating Scales (PSYRATS; Haddock *et al.* 1999; Drake *et al.* 2007), which provides an explicitly multi-dimensional assessment of delusions. The delusions scale has six items assessing delusion conviction, preoccupation, distress and disruption. There are still considerable weaknesses, however: no guidance is given on the content of delusions; the scale is uneven in the assessment of different dimensions; the frequency and different types of delusional thoughts are not assessed; and the setting of the ordinal item points is rather arbitrary. In summary, for a study of persecutory delusions in a clinical group, ideally the PSYRATS should be used to provide information on different aspects of the experience such as conviction, distress and preoccupation. Dimensions on this scale should be reported separately. The use of this scale often needs to be combined with a measure such as the PANSS or SAPS or a diagnostic interview such as the PSE in order adequately to describe the presentation of the case or group. If there is a particular focus on persecutory ideation, one of the measures discussed in the next section will also need to be included.

Mention is also needed of a popular measure used with non-clinical populations: the Peters *et al.* Delusions Inventory (PDI) (Peters *et al.* 1999). Despite its name, it needs to be remembered that the PDI does *not* measure clinical delusions. In the questionnaire, item content is taken from the traditional psychiatric measure, the Present State Examination (Wing *et al.* 1974). But the items are attenuated, typically by inserting the words 'as if' (e.g. Do you ever feel as if someone is deliberately trying to harm you?), so that clinical symptom content is not actually depicted. The design of the questionnaire is deliberately based upon a continuum view of delusional ideation and does not facilitate direct comparison with clinical symptoms. The questionnaire aims to capture experiences over a lifetime and assesses conviction, preoccupation, and distress associated with the delusion-like ideas. The 40-item questionnaire has only four items of strict persecutory content (i.e. including harm and intent). In essence, it is a self-report questionnaire assessing delusion-like ideas including a few of a persecutory nature.

Persecutory ideation measures

Issues to consider when thinking about the merits of questionnaires assessing persecutory ideation include: the definition of the phenomena used; whether the scale has been developed for non-clinical and clinical groups; the extent of the psychometric evaluation; and the dimensions of the experience being assessed. Highlighted in this chapter will be two measures from the 1990s (Paranoia Scale, Paranoia/Suspicious Questionnaire) and three measures more recently developed (Green *et al.* Paranoid Thought Scales, Persecutory Ideation Questionnaire, Persecution and Deservedness Scale). It is of note that all the paranoid thought measures are self-report. The measures are included in an Appendix at the end of the chapter. Finally, a recent state measure (State Social Paranoia Scale), a content measure (Details of Threat Questionnaire) and two process measures (Safety Behaviours Questionnaire, Beliefs about Paranoia Scale) will be outlined.

The Paranoia Scale

The most widely used measure, the Paranoia Scale (PS; Fenigstein and Vanable 1992), was designed to assess non-clinical paranoid thoughts in college students. The authors describe aiming to assess experiences that are 'reminiscent' of clinical paranoia. The aspect of paranoia highlighted is that of an 'exaggerated and unwarranted tendency to regard the behaviour of others as if it were related to or targeted toward the self'. The questionnaire items were derived from the Minnesota Multiphasic Personality Inventory (MMPI) (Dahlstrom *et al.* 1975). The questions chosen to form the pool of items in the instrument development had to relate to the following categories: '(a) a belief that people or external forces are trying to influence one's behaviour or control one's thinking; (b) a belief that people are against one in various ways; (c) a belief that some people talk about, refer to, or watch one; (d) suspicion or mistrust of others' motives; and (e) feelings of ill will, resentment, or bitterness.' The scale was developed with ~600 students. Twenty items, scored on a five-point scale, were selected from the pool. The scale demonstrated good internal reliability (alpha = 0.84). Test–retest reliability was assessed by correlation of scores over six months ($r = 0.70$). Convergent validity was established by finding associations with measures of trust and anger and feelings of being observed in an experimental situation. More recently, in a study of 1200 students the scale was found to correlate highly with a 'paranoia checklist' that assesses the frequency of a range of paranoid thoughts (Freeman *et al.* 2005b). Looking at the item content of the PS, it is clear that the scale contains items mainly concerning mistrust (6/20), resentment (5/20), and ideas of reference (4/20). There is much less content concerning ideas of harm (4/20) and only one item includes both harm and intent ('Someone has it in for me'), thereby meeting the Freeman and Garety (2000) criteria. It is notable that there is a depressive element to several items (e.g. 'No one really cares much what happens to you',

'I am sure I get a raw deal from life') (Freeman *et al.* 2005c). The PS assesses mistrust and resentment, which are at the mild end of paranoid thinking, and not thoughts that are clearly persecutory.

Paranoia/Suspiciousness Questionnaire

The Paranoia/Suspiciousness Questionnaire (PSQ; Rawlings and Freeman 1996) was developed by researchers interested in the concept of schizotypy (Rawlings and Freeman 1997). The authors aimed to measure a 'broad concept of paranoid/suspiciousness in normal individuals'. No clear definition was used, but the five sub-scales were labelled: Interpersonal Suspiciousness/Hostility, Negative Mood/Withdrawal, Anger/Impulsiveness, Mistrust/Wariness, and Perceived Hardship/Resentment. The PSQ items were taken from several older questionnaires, including the MMPI and the Schizotypal Personality Scale (STA) paranoid ideation sub-scale (Hewitt and Claridge 1989). The 47-item PSQ has a Yes/No response format. The development sample was 561 psychology students. The total scale showed good internal consistency (alpha = 0.89) and the sub-scale internal consistencies were adequate. Seventy-four participants repeated the questionnaire after three months and 'a test–retest reliability of 0.82 was achieved'. There is little validity testing of the scale, although a significant association with the Psychoticism sub-scale of the Eysenck Personality Questionnaire—Revised (Eysenck *et al.* 1985) is reported (Rawlings and Freeman 1996). It is clear that the PSQ is not just assessing paranoid thoughts. It reflects an even broader conceptualization of paranoia than the PS—for instance, an anger sub-scale is included. Out of 47 items, only two contain the idea of deliberate intent and harm ('Do you often feel that people have it in for you?', 'Do people mean to do and say things to annoy you?'). Five items concern ideas of reference. Therefore the PSQ is weighted to anger, resentment, and mistrust. The absence of substantial validity data makes it difficult to recommend the use of this scale.

Green *et al.* Paranoid Thoughts Scales (G-PTS)   ✗

In summary, the PS and PSQ focus on the lower end of a hypothesized paranoia continuum. Resentment, mistrust, and ideas of reference tend to make up the scales and only a few thoughts of clear persecutory content are included. Alternatively, clinical measures are typically brief (the range of scores therefore being minimal) and focused upon persecutory delusion conviction assessment in clinical samples. Therefore the author and colleagues (Green *et al.* 2008) set out to devise a self-report questionnaire that: was based upon the definition of persecutory ideation by Freeman and Garety (2000); contained content that was all persecutory but included clinical ('I was convinced there was a conspiracy against me') and non-clinical ('I was sure certain people did things in order to annoy me') type ideas; assessed several dimensions of paranoid experience; was validated in clinical and non-clinical populations; and was sensitive to change.

The questionnaire was developed with a student sample of 353 individuals, a replication group of 306 students, and 50 individuals with current persecutory delusions. The 16-item persecutory scale (G-PTS Part B) comprises four-item sub-scales of conviction, preoccupation, and distress and four items reflecting a paranoid thought only (see Appendix). The total score for the 16-item scale or the sub-scale scores can be used. The internal consistency of the scale is high (alpha = 0.90) and that of the sub-scales adequate. The clinical group scored significantly higher on the scale than the non-clinical group, establishing criterion validity. Convergent validity with the Paranoia Scale, PSYRATS and paranoia items of the PDI was shown. The scale has also been shown to be associated with unfounded persecutory ideation assessed in an experimental situation (Freeman *et al.* 2007b; Valmaggia *et al.* 2007). Good test–retest reliability over a fortnight with 164 of the student sample was shown (intra-class $r = 0.81$). Sensitivity to change was established with 30 individuals with persecutory delusions assessed after a further six months. The persecutory thoughts questionnaire has an accompanying, highly correlated, 16-item questionnaire (Part A of the G-PTS) assessing social ideas of reference. The two questionnaires can be combined to produce a total G-PTS score. Overall, the G-PTS draws upon the developments in understanding paranoia, contains items that are clearly persecutory (but vary somewhat in severity), and is the most psychometrically evaluated of the measures.

Persecutory Ideation Questionnaire

McKay *et al.* (2006) have also produced a measure of persecutory ideation based upon the Freeman and Garety (2000) definition. The ten items of the Persecutory Ideation Questionnaire (PIQ), each rated on a five-point scale, were selected from a pool on the basis that they met the definition for persecutory ideation. This questionnaire has been less evaluated psychometrically. Ninety-eight psychology students participated and it was shown that the scale has good internal consistency (alpha = 0.87) and correlated highly with the PSQ ($r = 0.85$). Twenty-five participants with current or a history of persecutory delusions also completed the questionnaire. It was again found that the questionnaire had good internal consistency (alpha = 0.90) and was associated with PSQ scores ($r = 0.85$) and with the SAPS persecution item ($r = 0.61$). No data on test–retest reliability or sensitivity to clinical change are reported. The developers of the scale did not take a multi-dimensional approach, but from inspection of the items and the scaling it is likely to be assessing degree of belief conviction. At present this scale requires further testing, but it does have the advantage of containing mainly persecutory items.

Persecution and Deservedness Scale

The impetus for the development of the Persecution and Deservedness Scale (PaDS; Melo *et al.* in press) was the theoretical idea that there are two types of paranoia: 'bad me' (deserving harm) and 'poor me' (unjustly persecuted) (Trower and Chadwick 1995). An important aspect of the questionnaire design is that if a person endorses a paranoia item then a further question is rated concerning deservedness. Persecutory thoughts are defined as 'explicitly stated or implied that the individual is at risk as a consequence of the untrustworthiness and malevolence of others'. The content of the ten-item persecution scale indicates a broad conceptualization of paranoia. A few items are clearly persecutory (e.g. 'There are times when I worry that others might be plotting against me'), some are ideas of reference ('Sometimes I just know that people are talking about me') and others concern general mistrust (e.g. 'You should only trust yourself') or arguably depression (e.g. 'I often find it hard to think of anything other than the negative ideas others have about me.'). The development sample was 608 undergraduate students and 45 patients with persecutory delusions. In the non-clinical sample the persecution scale had good internal reliability (Cronbach's alpha = 0.84) and a high correlation with the Paranoia Scale. In the clinical group the internal reliability of the persecution scale was lower (Cronbach's alpha = 0.68) but criterion validity was established by their scores being higher than the student group. No test–retest data for the scale are reported. The clear advantage of this scale is the addition of the separate dimension of deservedness, which taps an affect-related content aspect of paranoia that may be of theoretical interest.

Other persecutory-ideation-specific measures

The paranoia questionnaires seldom specify time scales. They are designed to assess persecutory ideation over weeks or months and are not state assessments. There is a need for state measures of persecutory ideation for experimental studies. Progress in understanding paranoia is likely to depend upon experimental studies that, for example, manipulate hypothesized causal factors and assess the immediate impact on delusional thinking. As part of a programme using virtual reality to study paranoia, a measure to assess paranoid thoughts in a recent social situation has been developed (Freeman *et al.* 2007b). The State Social Paranoia Scale (SSPS) has ten persecutory items (e.g. 'Someone stared at me in order to upset me', 'Someone was trying to isolate me',

'Someone was trying to make me distressed') (see Appendix). It has been psychometrically tested with 164 non-clinical participants and 21 individuals at high risk of psychosis with attenuated positive symptoms. The SSPS has excellent internal reliability, adequate test–retest reliability, convergent validity with both independent interviewer ratings and self-report measures, and divergent validity in regards to measures of positive and neutral thinking. In summary, it has good psychometric properties.

Three questionnaires have been developed to understand factors that may contribute to paranoid experience. Morrison *et al.* (2005) have tested the Beliefs about Paranoia Scale with 300 students to investigate the idea that meta-cognitive beliefs contribute to the maintenance of paranoia (e.g. 'If I were not paranoid others would take advantage of me'). Two questionnaires have been developed for individuals with persecutory delusions. The Details of Threat Questionnaire assesses the content of persecutory thoughts to identify the most distressing aspects of the experience (Freeman *et al.* 2001; Chisholm *et al.* 2006). The Safety Behaviours Questionnaire—Persecutory Beliefs (SBQ) assesses the strategies that individuals use to protect themselves but that prevent the fears from being disconfirmed (Freeman *et al.* 2001, 2007a).

Associated and linked phenomena

Clinically and theoretically important is the co-occurrence of paranoid thinking with anxiety, worry, and depression (e.g. Fowler *et al.* 2006b; Startup *et al.* 2007). There is a close relationship of paranoia with affect. Clinicians will therefore wish to look at recovery in emotional symptoms and researchers will need to examine or control for the link between the experiences. In the author's clinical practice, the Beck Depression Inventory (Beck *et al.* 1996), Beck Anxiety Inventory (Beck *et al.* 1988) and Penn State Worry Questionnaire (Meyer *et al.* 1990) are routinely used at regular intervals throughout the provision of cognitive behaviour therapy for persecutory delusions. Clinicians will also need to consider the addition of consumer-based perspectives on recovery (see Resnick *et al.* 2005; Andresen *et al.* 2006; Bellack 2006) and assessments of social functioning and quality of life (e.g. Brazier *et al.* 1993; Jolley *et al.* 2006).

Summary

A single, easily administered measure is unlikely to serve everybody's purpose because of the complexity of paranoid experience and the variety of questions to be addressed in this area. No measure is ideal in all cases and a room full of researchers and clinicians will still create debate on the topic. Nonetheless, the G-PTS looks promising for many purposes, although a self-report measure will be particularly vulnerable to the problem of differentiating between realistic and unrealistic suspicions. The PSYRATS appears the best measure when the focus is on a clinically important single persecutory delusion. Ideally, these measures should be used with instruments that assess other delusional ideas, hallucinatory experiences, and emotional disorder. It is notable that both of the recommended measures have evolved from the recent developments in understanding delusional experience. The review in this chapter highlights that, although symptom-based research has brought paranoid experience into greater focus and made it clearer which elements a researcher and/or clinician may be interested in assessing, there is still much development work needed on measurement. No questionnaire fully captures both the variety in the content of paranoid thoughts and the different ways that these thoughts are experienced. The issue of how to deal with the difficulties of the entanglement of real, exaggerated, and unfounded suspiciousness merits much greater attention than has been given up till now. In the emerging research area of persecutory delusions, theory has undoubtedly proceeded at a faster pace than measurement development.

Acknowledgements

The author is supported by a Wellcome Trust Fellowship, and is grateful to all the questionnaire developers for permission to include their measures.

References

Andreasen, N.C. (1984) *The Scale for the Assessment of Positive Symptoms (SAPS)*. Iowa City: University of Iowa.

Andresen, R., Caputi, P. and Oades, L. (2006) Stages of recovery instrument: development of a measure of recovery from serious mental illness. *Australian and New Zealand Journal of Psychiatry*, 40, 972–980.

Beck, A.T., Epstein, N., Brown, G. and Steer, R. (1988) An inventory for measuring clinical anxiety: psychometric properties. *Journal of Consulting and Clinical Psychology*, 56, 893–897.

Beck, A.T., Steer, R.A. and Brown, G.K. (1996) *BDI-II Manual*. The Psychological Corporation: San Antonia.

Bellack, A.S. (2006) Scientific and consumer models of recovery in schizophrenia. *Schizophrenia Bulletin*, 32, 432—442.

Birchwood, M., Meaden, A., Trower, P., Gilbert, P. and Plaistow, J. (2000) The power and omnipotence of voices: subordination and entrapment by voices and significant others. *Psychological Medicine*, 30, 337–344.

Boyd, T. and Gumley, A. (2007) An experiential perspective on persecutory paranoia. *Psychology and Psychotherapy*, 80, 1–22.

Brazier, J., Jones, N. and Kind, P. (1993) Testing the validity of the EuroQol and comparing it with the SF-36 health survey questionnaire. *Quality of Life Research*, 2, 169–180.

Brett-Jones, J., Garety, P. and Hemsley, D. (1987) Measuring delusional experiences: a method and its application. *British Journal of Clinical Psychology*, 26, 257–265.

Campbell, M.L.C. and Morrison, A.P. (2007) The subjective experience of paranoia: comparing the experiences of patients with psychosis and individuals with no psychiatric history. *Clinical Psychology and Psychotherapy*, 14, 63–77.

Chisholm, B., Freeman, D. and Cooke, A. (2006) Identifying potential predictors of PTSD reactions to psychotic episodes. *British Journal of Clinical Psychology*, 45, 545–559.

Claridge, G. (1994) Single indicator of risk for schizophrenia: probable fact or likely myth. *Schizophrenia Bulletin*, 20, 151–168.

Claridge, G. (1997) Theoretical background and issues. In: Claridge G. (ed.), *Schizotypy: Implications for Illness and Health*, pp. 3–18. Oxford: Oxford University Press.

Dahlstrom, W.G., Welsh, G.S. and Dahlstrom, L.F. (1975) *An MMPI Handbook: Volume 2. Research Applications*. Minneapolis: University of Minnesota.

Drake, R., Haddock, G., Tarrier, N., Bentall, R. and Lewis, S. (2007) The Psychotic Symptom Rating Scales (PSYRATS): their usefulness and properties in first episode psychosis. *Schizophrenia Research*, 89, 119–122.

Eysenck, S.B.G., Eysenck, H.J. and Barrett, P. (1985) A revised version of the psychoticism scale. *Personality and Individual Differences*, 6, 21–29.

Fenigstein, A. and Vanable, P.A. (1992) Paranoia and self-consciousness. *Journal of Personality and Social Psychology*, 62, 129–138.

Fowler, D., Freeman, D., Steel, C. *et al.* (2006a) The catastrophic interaction hypothesis: How does stress, trauma, emotion and information processing abnormalities lead to psychosis? In Morrison, A. and Larkin, W. (eds), *Trauma and Psychosis*. pp. 101–124. Chichester: Wiley.

Fowler, D., Freeman, D., Smith, B. *et al.* (2006b) The Brief Core Schema Scales (BCSS): Psychometric properties and associations with paranoia and grandiosity in non-clinical and psychosis samples. *Psychological Medicine*, 36, 749–759.

Freeman, D. (2006) Delusions in the non-clinical population. *Current Psychiatry Reports*, 8, 191–204.

Freeman, D. (2007) Suspicious minds: the psychology of persecutory delusions. *Clinical Psychology Review*, 27, 425–457.

Freeman, D. and Freeman, J. (2008) *Paranoia: The 21st Century Fear*. Oxford: Oxford University Press.

Freeman, D. and Garety, P.A. (2000) Comments on the content of persecutory delusions: does the definition need clarification? *British Journal of Clinical Psychology*, 39, 407–414.

Freeman, D., Garety, P.A. and Kuipers, E. (2001) Persecutory delusions: developing the understanding of belief maintenance and emotional distress. *Psychological Medicine*, 31, 1293–1306.

Freeman, D., Garety, P.A., Bebbington, P. *et al.* (2005a) The psychology of persecutory ideation. II: A virtual reality experimental study. *Journal of Nervous and Mental Disease*, 193, 309–315.

Freeman, D., Garety, P.A., Bebbington, P.E. *et al.* (2005b) Psychological investigation of the structure of paranoia in a non-clinical population. *British Journal of Psychiatry*, 186, 427–435.

Freeman, D., Dunn, G., Garety, P.A. *et al.* (2005c) The psychology of persecutory ideation. I: A questionnaire study. *Journal of Nervous and Mental Disease*, 193, 302–308.

Freeman, D., Freeman, J. and Garety, P. (2006) *Overcoming Paranoid and Suspicious Thoughts*. London: Robinson Constable.

Freeman, D., Garety, P., Kuipers, E., Fowler, D., Bebbington, P.E. and Dunn, G. (2007a) Acting on persecutory delusions: the importance of safety seeking. *Behaviour Research and Therapy*, 45, 89–99.

Freeman, D., Pugh, K., Green, C., Valmaggia, L., Dunn, G. and Garety, P. (2007b) A measure of state persecutory ideation for experimental studies. *Journal of Nervous and Mental Disease*, 195, 781–784.

Freeman, D., Pugh, K., Antley, A., Slater, M., Bebbington, P., Giffins, M., Dunn, G., Kuipers, E., Fowler, D., Garety, P. (2008) A virtual reality study of paranoid thinking in the general population. *British Journal of Psychiatry*, 192, 258–263.

Garety, P.A. and Hemsley, D.R. (1994) *Delusions: Investigations into the Psychology of Delusional Reasoning*. Oxford: Oxford University Press.

Green, C., Garety, P.A., Freeman, D. *et al.* (2006) Phenomenology and affect in persecutory delusions. *British Journal of Clinical Psychology*, 45, 561–577.

Green, C., Freeman, D., Kuipers, E. *et al.* (2008) Measuring ideas of persecution and reference: the Green *et al*. Paranoid Thought Scales (G-PTS). *Psychological Medicine*, 38, 101–111.

Haddock, G., McCarron, J., Tarrier, N. and Faragher, E.B. (1999) Scales to measure dimensions of hallucinations and delusions: the psychotic symptom rating scales (PSYRATS). *Psychological Medicine*, 29, 879–889.

Harrow, M., Rattenbury, F. and Stoll, F. (1988) Schizophrenic delusions: an analysis of their persistence, of related premorbid ideas, and of three major dimensions. In: Oltmanns, T.F. and Maher, B.A. (eds), *Delusional Beliefs*, pp. 184–211. New York: Wiley.

Harrow, M., Herbener, E.S., Shanklin, A., Jobe, T.H., Rattenbury, F. and Kaplan, K.J. (2004) Followup of psychotic outpatients: dimensions of delusions and work functioning in schizophrenia. *Schizophrenia Bulletin*, 30, 147–161.

Hewitt, J.K. and Claridge, G.S. (1989) The factor structure of schizotypy in a normal population. *Personality and Individual Differences*, 10, 323–329.

Johns, L.C., Cannon, M., Singleton, N. *et al.* (2004) The prevalence and correlates of self-reported psychotic symptoms in the British population. *British Journal of Psychiatry*, 185, 298–305.

Jolley, S., Garety, P.A., Ellett, L. *et al.* (2006) A validation of a new measure of activity in psychosis. *Schizophrenia Research*, 85, 288–295.

Jones, E. (1999) The phenomenology of abnormal belief: a philosophical and psychiatric inquiry. *Philosophy, Psychiatry and Psychology*, 6, 1–16.

Kay, S. R. (1991) *Positive and Negative Syndromes in Schizophrenia: Assessment and Research*. New York: Brunner/Mazel.

Kendler, K.S. (1985) Diagnostic approaches to schizotypal personality disorder: a historical perspective. *Schizophrenia Bulletin*, 11, 538–553.

Kendler, K.S., Glazer, W.M. and Morgenstern, H. (1983) Dimensions of delusional experience. *American Journal of Psychiatry*, 140, 466–469.

Lemert, E.M. (1962) Paranoia and the dynamics of exclusion. *Sociometry*, 25, 2–20.

Liraud, F., Droulout, T., Parrot, M. and Verdoux, H. (2004) Agreement between self-rated and clinically assessed symptoms in subjects with psychosis. *Journal of Nervous and Mental Disease*, 192, 32–356.

Maher, B. and Ross, J.S. (1984) Delusions. In: Adams, H.E. and Sutker, P.B. (eds), *Comprehensive Handbook of Psychopathology*, pp. 383–409. New York: Plenum Press.

Maric, N., Myin-Germeys, I., Delespaul, P., de Graaf, R., Vollebergh, W. and van Os, J. (2004) Is our concept of schizophrenia influenced by Berkson's bias? *Social Psychiatry and Psychiatric Epidemiology*, 39, 600–605.

Mayerhoff, D., Pelta, E., Valentino, C. and Chakos, M. (1991) Real-life basis for a patient's paranoia [Letter]. *American Journal of Psychiatry*, 148, 682–683.

McKay, R., Langdon, R. and Coltheart, M. (2006) The Persecutory Ideation Questionnaire. *Journal of Nervous and Mental Disease*, 194, 628–631.

Melo, S., Corocan, R. and Bentall, R.P. (in press). The Persecution and Deservedness Scale (PaDS). *Psychology and Psychotherapy*.

Meyer, T.J., Miller, M.L., Metzger, R.L. and Borkovec, T.D. (1990) Development and validation of the Penn State Worry Questionnaire. *Behaviour Research and Therapy*, 28, 487–495.

Morrison, A.P., Gumley, A.I., Schwannauer, M. *et al.* (2005) The Beliefs about Paranoia Scale. *Behavioural and Cognitive Psychotherapy*, 33, 153–164.

Myin-Germeys, I., Krabbendam, L. and van Os, J. (2003) Continuity of psychotic symptoms in the community. *Current Opinion in Psychiatry*, 16, 443–449.

Oltmanns, T.F. (1988) Approaches to the definition and study of delusions. In: Oltmanns, T.F. and Maher, B.A. (eds), *Delusional Beliefs*, pp. 3–12. New York: Wiley.

Overall, J.E. and Gorham, D.R. (1962) The Brief Psychiatric Rating Scale. *Psychological Reports*, 10, 799–812.

Peters, E.R., Joseph, S.A. and Garety, P.A. (1999) The measurement of delusional ideation in the normal population: introducing the PDI (Peters *et al.* Delusions Inventory). *Schizophrenia Bulletin*, 25, 553–576.

Preston, N.J. and Harrison, T.J. (2003) The Brief Symptom Inventory and the Positive and Negative Syndrome Scale: discriminate validity between a self-reported and observational measure of psychopathology. *Comprehensive Psychiatry*, 44, 220–226.

Rawlings, D. and Freeman, J.L. (1996) A questionnaire for the measurement of paranoia/suspiciousness. *British Journal of Clinical Psychology*, 35, 451–462.

Rawlings, D. and Freeman, J.L. (1997) Measuring paranoia/suspiciousness. In: Claridge, G. (ed.), *Schizotypy: Implications for Illness and Health*, pp. 38–60. Oxford: Oxford University Press.

Resnick, S.G., Fontana, A., Lehman, A.F. and Rosenheck, R.A. (2005) An empirical conceptualisation of the recovery orientation. *Schizophrenia Research*, 75, 119–128.

Spitzer, M. (1992) The phenomenology of delusions. *Psychiatric Annals*, 22, 252–259.

Startup, H., Freeman, D. and Garety, P.A. (2007) Persecutory delusions and catastrophic worry in psychosis: developing the understanding of delusion distress and persistence. *Behaviour Research and Therapy*, 45, 523–537.

Steel, C., Garety, P., Freeman, D. *et al.* (2007) The measurement of the positive symptoms of psychosis. *International Journal of Psychiatric Research Methods*, 16, 88–96.

Strauss, J.S. (1969) Hallucinations and delusions as points on continua function. *Archives of General Psychiatry*, 20, 581–586.

Trower, P. and Chadwick, P. (1995) Pathways to defense of the self: a theory of two types of paranoia. *Clinical Psychology: Science and Practice*, 2, 263–278.

Valmaggia, L., Freeman, D., Green, C. *et al.* (2007) Virtual reality and paranoid ideations in people with an 'at risk mental state' for psychosis. *British Journal of Psychiatry*, 191 (Suppl. 51), s63–68.

Watson, P.W.B., Garety, P.A., Weinman, J. *et al.* (2006) Emotional dysfunction in schizophrenia spectrum psychosis: the role of illness perceptions. *Psychological Medicine*, 36, 761–770.

Wing, J.K., Cooper, J.E. and Sartorius, N. (1974) *Measurement and Classification of Psychiatric Symptoms*. Cambridge: Cambridge University Press.

World Health Organization (1992) *SCAN: Schedules for Clinical Assessment in Neuropsychiatry*. Geneva: World Health Organization.

Appendix

Paranoia Scale (Fenigstein and Vanable 1992)

Please rate how applicable each belief is to you by circling a number between 1 (not at all applicable to me) and 5 (extremely applicable to me).

		Not at all applicable to me			Extremely applicable to me
1	Someone has it in for me	1	2	3	4	5
2	I sometimes feel as if I'm being followed	1	2	3	4	5
3	I believe that I have often been punished without cause	1	2	3	4	5
4	Some people have tried to steal my ideas and take credit for them	1	2	3	4	5
5	My parents and family find more fault with me than they should	1	2	3	4	5
6	No one really cares much what happens to you	1	2	3	4	5
7	I am sure I get a raw deal from life	1	2	3	4	5
8	Most people will use somewhat unfair means to gain profit or advantage, rather than lose it	1	2	3	4	5
9	I often wonder what hidden reason another person may have for doing something nice for you	1	2	3	4	5
10	It is safer to trust no one	1	2	3	4	5
11	I have often felt that strangers were looking at me critically	1	2	3	4	5
12	Most people make friends because friends are likely to be useful to them	1	2	3	4	5
13	Someone has been trying to influence my mind	1	2	3	4	5
14	I am sure I have been talked about behind my back	1	2	3	4	5
15	Most people inwardly dislike putting themselves out to help other people	1	2	3	4	5
16	I tend to be on my guard with people who are somewhat more friendly than expected	1	2	3	4	5
17	People have said insulting and unkind things about me	1	2	3	4	5

		Not at all applicable to me				Extremely applicable to me
18	People often disappoint me	1	2	3	4	5
19	I am bothered by people outside, in cars, in stores, etc., watching me	1	2	3	4	5
20	I have often found people jealous of my good ideas just because they had not thought of them first	1	2	3	4	5

Paranoia/Suspiciousness Questionnaire (Rawlings and Freeman 1997)

Instructions: Please answer each question by putting a Y (for 'YES') or an N (for 'NO') on the line to the left of the question. There are no right or wrong answers and no trick questions. Be as honest as you can, but don't think too long about the exact meaning of each question.

_____ Do people generally seem to take offence easily?

_____ Do you sometimes feel that no one understands you?

_____ Are you sometimes eaten up with jealousy?

_____ Do you feel that it is other people who always seem to get the breaks?

_____ Do you feel that you have often been punished without cause?

_____ Would you have been more successful if others around you had not put difficulties in your way?

_____ Do you tend to assume that all people have a vicious streak and it will come out when they are given a chance?

_____ Are you sure you are being talked about?

_____ Do you often get into a jam because you do things without thinking?

_____ Have you had an awful lot of bad luck?

_____ Do you wonder why sometimes you feel so bitter about things?

_____ Do you believe you will never be satisfied?

_____ Do you think that you feel more intensely than other people?

_____ Do people you are with have a strong influence on your moods?

_____ Do you tend to be envious of other people's good fortune?

_____ Do you feel that you have had more than your share of things to worry about?

_____ Do you sometimes feel 'like a powder keg ready to explode'?

_____ Are you more sensitive than most people?

_____ Do you believe in never trusting anyone who has a grudge against you?

_____ Do people sometimes say insulting things about you?

_____ Do people mean to do and say things to annoy you?

_____ Do you suspect that people who act friendly to you can be disloyal to you behind your back?

_____ Are you an 'even tempered' person?

_____ Do you feel at times that you've got a raw deal out of life?

_____ Do you get suspicious of over-friendly strangers?

_____ Are you happy most of the time?

_____ Do you often get involved in things you later wish you could get out of?

_____ Have you had more trouble than most?

_____ Do you get so 'carried away' by new and exciting ideas that you never think of the possible snags?

_____ Do you often notice your ears ringing or buzzing?

_____ When put in charge of something, do you insist that your instructions are followed, or else you resign?

_____ When people are especially nice, do you wonder what they want?

_____ Do you sometimes feel that people are laughing at you behind your back?

_____ Do you doubt the honesty of people who are more friendly than you would expect them to be?

_____ Do some of your friends think that you are a hothead?

_____ Do you find that you can't help getting into arguments when people disagree with you?

_____ Do you sometimes fly off the handle for no good reason?

_____ Do you agree that there are really more nice people than objectionable people in the world?

_____ Do you get upset when people don't notice how you look when you go out in public?

_____ Do you have trouble controlling your temper?

_____ Would you like to be in a position where people were frightened to defy you?

_____ Do you often feel that people have it in for you?

_____ Do you feel at times that people are talking about you?

_____ Do you feel that you have to be on your guard even with your friends?

_____   Do you feel that it is safer to trust nobody?

_____   Do you feel lonely most of the time, even when you're with people?

_____   Are you often bothered by the feeling that people are watching you?

Scoring:
Items 23, 26, 38 are reversed.
Sub-scales:

Green *et al.* Paranoid Thoughts Scale (Green, Freeman, Kuipers *et al.* 2008)

Please read each of the statements carefully.

They refer to thoughts and feelings you may have had about others over the last month.

Think about the last month and indicate the extent of these feelings from 1 (Not at all) to 5 (Totally). Please complete both Part A and Part B.

(N.B. Please do not rate items according to any experiences you may have had under the influence of drugs.)

Part A	Not at all				Totally
1 I spent time thinking about friends gossiping about me	1	2	3	4	5
2 I often heard people referring to me	1	2	3	4	5
3 I have been upset by friends and colleagues judging me critically	1	2	3	4	5
4 People definitely laughed at me behind my back	1	2	3	4	5
5 I have been thinking a lot about people avoiding me	1	2	3	4	5
6 People have been dropping hints for me	1	2	3	4	5
7 I believed that certain people were not what they seemed	1	2	3	4	5
8 People talking about me behind my back upset me	1	2	3	4	5
9 I was convinced that people were singling me out	1	2	3	4	5
10 I was certain that people have followed me	1	2	3	4	5
11 Certain people were hostile towards me personally	1	2	3	4	5
12 People have been checking up on me	1	2	3	4	5
13 I was stressed out by people watching me	1	2	3	4	5
14 I was frustrated by people laughing at me	1	2	3	4	5
15 I was worried by people's undue interest in me	1	2	3	4	5

16 It was hard to stop thinking about people   1   2   3   4   5
    talking about me behind my back

Part B

1   Certain individuals have had it in for me   1   2   3   4   5
2   I have definitely been persecuted   1   2   3   4   5
3   People have intended me harm   1   2   3   4   5
4   People wanted me to feel threatened,   1   2   3   4   5
    so they stared at me
5   I was sure certain people did things in   1   2   3   4   5
    order to annoy me
6   I was convinced there was a conspiracy   1   2   3   4   5
    against me
7   I was sure someone wanted to hurt me   1   2   3   4   5
8   I was distressed by people wanting to harm   1   2   3   4   5
    me in some way
9   I was preoccupied with thoughts of people   1   2   3   4   5
    trying to upset me deliberately
10 I couldn't stop thinking about people   1   2   3   4   5
    wanting to confuse me
11 I was distressed by being persecuted   1   2   3   4   5
12 I was annoyed because others wanted to   1   2   3   4   5
    deliberately upset me
13 The thought that people were persecuting   1   2   3   4   5
    me played on my mind
14 It was difficult to stop thinking about people   1   2   3   4   5
    wanting to make me feel bad
15 People have been hostile towards me on purpose   1   2   3   4   5
16 I was angry that someone wanted to hurt me   1   2   3   4   5

Persecutory Ideation Questionnaire (McKay *et al.* 2006)

This questionnaire provides information about your beliefs about and perceptions of yourself, others and the world. Please read each of the statements carefully. Using the scale provided, please circle a number to show how much you agree with it.

1 I sometimes feel as if there is a conspiracy against me.

0	1	2	3	4
very untrue	mostly untrue	true half the time	mostly true	very true

2 I feel at times that I am deliberately ill-treated by others.

0	1	2	3	4
very untrue	mostly untrue	true half the time	mostly true	very true

3 I often feel that others have it in for me.

0	1	2	3	4
very untrue	mostly untrue	true half the time	mostly true	very true

4 People mean to do and say things to annoy me.

0	1	2	3	4
very untrue	mostly untrue	true half the time	mostly true	very true

5 I sometimes feel that people are plotting against me.

0	1	2	3	4
very untrue	mostly untrue	true half the time	mostly true	very true

6 I sometimes feel that people are laughing at me behind my back.

0	1	2	3	4
very untrue	mostly untrue	true half the time	mostly true	very true

7 Some people try to steal my ideas and take credit for them.

0	1	2	3	4
very untrue	mostly untrue	true half the time	mostly true	very true

8 I sometimes feel that I am being persecuted in some way.

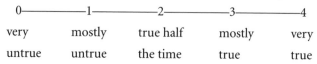

0	1	2	3	4
very untrue	mostly untrue	true half the time	mostly true	very true

9 I often pick up hidden threats or put-downs from what people say or do.

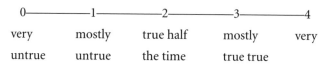

0	1	2	3	4
very untrue	mostly untrue	true half the time	mostly true true	very

10 Some people harass me persistently.

0	1	2	3	4
very untrue	mostly untrue	true half the time	mostly true	very true

Persecution and Deservedness Scale (Melo *et al.* in press)

Please read each of the following statements carefully and indicate the extent to which they are true or false by circling a number on the scale.

1	There are times when I worry that others might be plotting against me.	Certainly false	Possibly false	Unsure true	Possibly true	Certainly
		0	1	2	3	4

If you've answered 2 or above to the last question, please answer to the following question:

1.1	Do you feel like you deserve others to plot against you?	Not at all	Possibly not	Unsure	Possibly	Very much
		0	1	2	3	4

2.	I often find it hard to think of anything other than the negative ideas others have about me.	Certainly false	Possibly false	Unsure	Possibly true	Certainly true
		0	1	2	3	4

If you've answered 2 or above to the last question, please answer to the following question:

2.1	Do you feel like you deserve people to have negative ideas about you?	Not at all	Possibly not	Unsure	Possibly	Very much
		0	1	2	3	4

3	My friends often tell me to relax and stop worrying about being deceived or harmed.	Certainly false	Possibly false	Unsure	Possibly true	Certainly true
		0	1	2	3	4

If you've answered 2 or above to the last question, please answer to the following question:

3.1	Do you feel like you deserve being deceived or harmed?	Not at all	Possibly not	Unsure	Possibly	Very much
		0	1	2	3	4

4	Every time I meet someone for the first time, I'm afraid they've already heard bad things about me.	Certainly false	Possibly false	Unsure true	Possibly true	Certainly
		0	1	2	3	4

If you've answered 2 or above to the last question, please answer to the following question:

4.1	Do you feel like you deserve to have people hearing bad things about you?	Not at all	Possibly not	Unsure	Possibly	Very much
		0	1	2	3	4

5	I'm often suspicious of other people's intentions towards me.	Certainly false	Possibly false	Unsure	Possibly true	Certainly true
		0	1	2	3	4

If you've answered 2 or above to the last question, please answer to the following question:

5.1	Do you feel like you deserve people having bad intentions towards you?	Not at all	Possibly not	Unsure	Possibly	Very much
		0	1	2	3	4

6	Sometimes, I just know that people are talking critically about me.	Certainly false	Possibly false	Unsure	Possibly true	Certainly true
		0	1	2	3	4

If you've answered 2 or above to the last question, please answer to the following question:

6.1	Do you feel like you deserve people to talk critically about you?	Not at all	Possibly not	Unsure	Possibly	Very much
		0	1	2	3	4

7	There are people who think of me as a bad person.	Certainly false	Possibly false	Unsure	Possibly true	Certainly true
		0	1	2	3	4

If you've answered 2 or above to the last question, please answer to the following question:

7.1	Do you feel like you deserve people to think of you as a bad person?	Not at all	Possibly not	Unsure	Possibly	Very much
		0	1	2	3	4

8	People will almost certainly lie to me.	Certainly false	Possibly false	Unsure	Possibly true	Certainly true
		0	1	2	3	4

If you've answered 2 or above to the last question, please answer to the following question:

8.1	Do you feel like you deserve people to lie to you?	Not at all	Possibly not	Unsure	Possibly	Very much
		0	1	2	3	4

9	I believe that some people want to hurt me deliberately.	Certainly false	Possibly false	Unsure	Possibly true	Certainly true
		0	1	2	3	4

If you've answered 2 or above to the last question, please answer to the following question:

		Not at all	Possibly not	Unsure	Possibly	Very much
9.1	Do you feel like you deserve people to hurt you deliberately?					
		0	1	2	3	4

		Certainly false	Possibly false	Unsure	Possibly true	Certainly true
10	You should only trust yourself.					
		0	1	2	3	4

If you've answered 2 or above to the last question, please answer to the following question:

		Not at all	Possibly not	Unsure	Possibly	Very much
10.1	Do you feel like you deserve to have no one you can trust?					
		0	1	2	3	4

State Social Paranoia Scale (SSPS) (Freeman *et al*. 2007)

Please circle **how much you agree or disagree** with following statements:

1 = Do not agree
2 = Agree a little
3 = Agree moderately
4 = Agree very much
5 = Totally agree

1	**Someone was hostile towards me**	1	2	3	4	5
2	No-one had any particular feelings about me	1	2	3	4	5
3	**Someone had bad intentions towards me**	1	2	3	4	5
4	Someone was friendly towards me	1	2	3	4	5
5	**Someone was trying to make me distressed**	1	2	3	4	5
6	I felt very safe in their company	1	2	3	4	5
7	**Someone stared at me in order to upset me**	1	2	3	4	5
8	Everyone was trustworthy	1	2	3	4	5
9	**Someone wanted me to feel threatened**	1	2	3	4	5
10	I wasn't really noticed by anybody	1	2	3	4	5
11	Someone had kind intentions toward me	1	2	3	4	5
12	**Someone would have harmed me in some way if they could**	1	2	3	4	5
13	**Someone had it in for me**	1	2	3	4	5
14	Everyone was neutral towards me	1	2	3	4	5
15	**Someone was trying to intimidate me**	1	2	3	4	5
16	Everyone was pleasant	1	2	3	4	5
17	**Someone was trying to isolate me**	1	2	3	4	5
18	No-one had any intentions towards me	1	2	3	4	5
19	Everyone seemed unconcerned by my presence	1	2	3	4	5
20	**Someone was trying to irritate me**	1	2	3	4	5

[Persecution items in bold.]

Chapter 3

Epidemiology and social factors: findings from the Netherlands Mental Health Survey and Incidence Study (NEMESIS)

Bart P. F. Rutten, Jim van Os, Mari Dominguez, and Lydia Krabbendam

Introduction

The core symptoms of psychosis, delusions and hallucinations, are much more prevalent in the general population than their clinical counterparts (Eaton *et al.* 1991; Tien 1991; Verdoux *et al.* 1998; Peters *et al.* 1999; Van Os *et al.* 2000; Johns *et al.* 2004), suggesting that psychosis can be seen as a distribution of experiences that are not necessarily associated with disability. General population studies have reported prevalence rates of 5–10% for hallucinations around 15% for delusions, with a prevalence of persecutory delusions up to 8% (Johns and van Os 2001).

Established demographic, social and environmental risk factors for schizophrenia also affect the occurrence of non-clinical psychosis-like experiences, providing support for the continuity between the clinical and non-clinical expression of the psychosis phenotype. Examples of these are victimization (Janssen *et al.* 2003; Spauwen *et al.* 2006b), cannabis (van Os *et al.* 2002; Henquet *et al.* 2005) or urbanicity (van Os *et al.* 2001; Spauwen *et al.* 2004, 2006a). According to cognitive models of psychosis, social risk factors such as victimization and urbanicity act by influencing the formation of negative schematic models of the self and the world (Bentall *et al.* 2001; Garety *et al.* 2001). Conceivably, formation of such cognitive schemas may be expressed predominantly in the form of paranoid ideation. However, the specificity of any association with social risk factors for persecutory delusions has not been assessed.

Studies investigating the aetiology of persecutory delusions in non-clinical populations have highlighted the role of affective and cognitive biases. In a group of 324 college students, of whom 47.2% reported an experience of paranoia, greater levels of paranoid symptoms were associated with lower self-esteem (Ellett *et al.* 2003). Similarly, Martin and Penn (2001) found evidence that higher levels of paranoid symptoms in college students were associated with greater depressed mood, higher social anxiety and greater attention to public aspects of the self, as well as lower self-esteem. A low level of self-esteem and unstable self-esteem were found to be associated with persecutory delusions in the Netherlands Mental Health Survey and Incidence Study (NEMESIS), a large general population sample which was also used for the present study (Thewissen *et al.* 2006). In a virtual reality experiment, Freeman *et al.* (2005) showed that non-clinical paranoid ideation was associated with emotional disturbances, and with anomalous experiences. The cognitive hypothesis would suggest that social adversities act by influencing these affective and cognitive factors in the development of persecutory delusions.

We have recently suggested that the environmental risk factors may act to modify the generally good (because the symptoms are only transitory) outcome of subclinical psychotic experiences to poorer outcomes of persistence and clinical need for care (Cougnard *et al.* 2007). In other words, transitory developmental expression of psychosis may become abnormally persistent and clinically relevant depending on the degree of environmental risk the person is additionally exposed to.

There is very little empirical work in representative populations regarding the distribution and course of paranoid experiences. Therefore, the aims in the chapter are to examine, for the first time, (i) the prevalence and incidence of persecutory delusions in the general population, (ii) their association with established social risk factors for psychosis, namely perceived discrimination, childhood trauma, and urbanicity, as well as the extent to which these associations are mediated by cognitive/affective bias (i.e. neuroticism), and (iii) the effect of these risk factors on the persistence of persecutory delusions and their transition into clinical outcomes.

Methods

Sample

NEMESIS is a study of the prevalence, incidence, course and consequences of psychiatric disorders in the Dutch general population. The overall design of the study is prospective (three years), consisting of a T0 baseline survey in 1996, and two follow-up surveys at T1 (assessing the period between T0 and T1) in 1997, and at T2 (assessing the period between T1 and T2) in 1999 (Fig. 3.1). A comprehensive description of the project objectives, sample procedure,

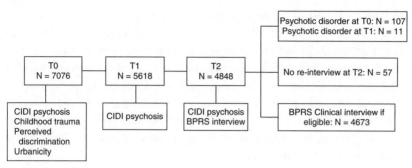

Fig. 3.1 The NEMESIS sample at T0, T1 and T2.

response, diagnostic instruments, quality control procedures and analyses is provided in previous publications (Bijl *et al.* 1998a,b). NEMESIS is based on a multi-stage, stratified, random sampling procedure, in 90 municipalities. A sample of private households within each municipality and members with the most recent birthday within each household were selected. Subjects were aged 18–64 years and sufficiently fluent in Dutch to be interviewed. Individuals living in institutions were not eligible for interview. A total of 7076 individuals provided informed consent and were interviewed at T0, representing a response rate of 69.7%. Previous analyses have shown that psychopathology had only weak effects on attrition rate over the follow-up periods and was mainly related to failure to locate individuals and morbidity/mortality rather than refusal (de Graaf *et al.* 2000).

Instruments

Subjects were interviewed at home by using the Composite International Diagnostic Interview (CIDI), version 1.1 (Smeets and Dingemans 1993), at T0 ($n = 7076$), T1 ($n = 5618$) and T2 ($n = 4848$). The CIDI is a structured interview developed by the World Health Organization, and generates diagnoses pertaining to the *Diagnostic and Statistical Manual of Mental Disorders*, 3rd edn, revised (*DSM-III-R*) (American Psychiatric Association 1994). It was designed for use by trained interviewers who are not clinicians. Interviewers read the questions and recorded the answers of respondents, making the CIDI essentially a self-report instrument (Eaton *et al.* 2000). At T0, the lifetime version of the CIDI was used. At each of the follow-up assessments, the CIDI interval version was applied, which refers to the period of assessment from the last interview until the present. Data on the CIDI-G-section about psychosis were collected at each assessment (T0, T1, T2). At T0 and T2, telephone clinical re-interviews were held with individuals endorsing psychotic experiences as reported previously, in order to correct false-positive reports (Van Os *et al.* 2000; Hanssen *et al.* 2005). At T1, no clinical re-interviews were held, but interviewers were allowed to probe with clinical follow-up questions if individuals endorsed psychotic experiences and discussed these items later with a psychiatrist. At T2, clinical re-interviews additionally consisted of the two positive psychosis items from the Brief Psychiatric Rating Scale (BPRS) (Overall and Gorham 1962) for all individuals who had a rating of 2, 5, or 6 on any CIDI psychosis item. Telephone re-interviews were completed on 74.4% of the subjects eligible for re-interview.

Assessment of T0 persecutory delusions

The G-section of the CIDI psychosis section was used to measure persecutory delusions at T0. The G-section of the CIDI psychosis section consists of four psychosis items concerning persecutory delusions, as follows. G1: 'Have you ever been convinced that people were spying on you?'; G2: 'Has there ever been a period in which you were convinced that you were persecuted by people?'; G3: 'Have you ever been convinced that you were secretly tested on or that experiments were carried out on you?'; G4: 'Have you ever been convinced that someone was conspiring against you, wanted to cause you harm or poisoning you?'. These items are scored in six categories: 1, no symptom; 2, psychotic symptom present but not clinically relevant (not bothered by it and not seeking help for it); 3, symptom is always the result of substance use; 4, symptom is always the result of somatic disorders or conditions; 5, true psychotic symptom; 6, interviewer is in doubt because there appears to be some plausible explanation for what appears to be a psychotic experience. Clinically relevant persecutory delusions were defined as a rating of 5 on any of the four items (hereafter: narrowly defined persecutory delusions). Possible persecutory delusions were defined as any rating of 2–6 on any of the four items (hereafter: broadly defined persecutory delusions). Other positive psychotic symptoms were defined dichotomously as a CIDI rating of 5 on any of the CIDI psychosis items, in the absence of a rating of 5 on any of the four items on persecutory delusions. Other possible positive psychotic symptoms were defined dichotomously as a CIDI rating of 2–6 on any of the CIDI psychosis items, in the absence of a rating of 2–6 on any of the four items on persecutory delusions.

The justification for these broad ratings was derived from a previous study, where it was shown that the five different ratings on the CIDI psychosis items were strongly associated with each other (van Os *et al.* 2000). In addition, the five different ratings independently showed a similar pattern of associations with known risk factors for psychosis (van Os *et al.* 2000 2001). As they therefore appear to reflect the same underlying latent dimension of 'positive psychosis', they were joined together into single broad ratings of persecutory delusions and other positive psychotic symptoms, respectively.

Assessment of the delusion outcome

The delusion outcome at T2 was specified at three levels: (i) any rating of 5 on any of the four CIDI persecutory delusion outcomes; (ii) any rating >0 on the BPRS item 'unusual thought content' (BPRS delusion); (iii) any rating >3 on the BPRS item 'unusual thought content' (BPRS clinical delusion).

Urbanicity exposure

Consistent with previous work, the original five-level classification of the urbanization measure expressed as density of addresses per km^2 (Van Os et al. 2001, 2003) was dichotomized as follows: levels 1 (<500), 2 (500–900), and 3 (1000–1499) were coded as 0 and levels 4 (1500–2499) and 5 (≥2500) as 1.

Discrimination

At T0, subjects were asked if they had experienced discrimination over the last year because of their: (i) skin colour or ethnicity, (ii) sex, (iii) age, (iv) appearance, (v) handicap, or (vi) sexual orientation (Janssen et al. 2003). Participants answered 'yes' or 'no' to each of the six questions. Perceived discrimination was defined dichotomously as a 'yes' on any of the six questions.

Trauma

At T0, subjects were asked, using a semi-structured interview, whether they had experienced any kind of emotional, physical, psychological or sexual abuse before age 16 years, providing an example of each type of trauma (Janssen et al. 2004). Subjects answered 'yes' or 'no' to each of the questions and were asked to give an indication about the frequency on a six-point scale: 1, never; 2, once; 3, sometimes; 4, regular; 5, often; and 6, very often. Consistent with previous work (Janssen et al. 2004; Bak et al. 2005), in the analyses, experience of trauma was a priori dichotomized as follows: 'no early trauma' if the score on any item was 3 and 'early trauma' if the score on any item was >3.

Neuroticism

At T0, subjects completed the 14-item Groningen Neuroticism Scale (Ormel 1980; Krabbendam et al. 2002). Neuroticism is related to stress reactivity and anxiety proneness. Cronbach's alpha for this scale was 0.8, suggesting that the set of items measures a single unidimensional latent construct.

Analyses

All statistical analyses were done using the STATA statistical package version 9.2.

Associations between persecutory delusions and other psychotic experiences at T0 were assessed using logistic regression analyses for hallucinations and other delusions, adjusted for each other.

Logistic regression analysis was used to assess associations with social risk factors, adjusted for each other and for the a priori confounding variables age, gender, marital status, employment status, education, and lifetime psychiatric diagnosis. The extent to which any associations were mediated by neuroticism was investigated by additional adjustment for neuroticism. In order to examine the extent to which any association was independent from the presence of other psychotic experiences, a separate analysis was run additionally adjusting for hallucinations and other delusions. Lifetime prevalence of persecutory delusions was used as the outcome variable in these analyses. The analysis was repeated using incident persecutory delusions as the outcome variable in order to make sure the exposure to discrimination and childhood abuse preceded onset of the persecutory delusions and recall of these exposures could not be biased by the presence of persecutory delusions.

In order to examine the specificity of any association for persecutory delusions, the analyses were also run using other psychotic experiences as the outcome variable.

Persistence and transition of persecutory delusions were expressed as post-test probabilities (PP), calculated as the proportion of individuals with (possible) persecutory delusions at T1 who had the delusion outcome at T2.

In order to test the hypothesis that the social risk factors would interact with persecutory delusions at T1 in the risk for persistence and transition at T2, an interaction was fitted between the social risk factors and presence of persecutory delusions at T1, adjusted for each other, as well as for neuroticism and baseline presence of persecutory delusions. The coefficient of this interaction reflects the difference in risk for the T2 delusion outcome between individuals with persecutory delusions at T1 who were also exposed to the social risk factor compared to individuals with persecutory delusions at T1 who had not been exposed to the social risk factor. In order to calculate the statistical interaction under an additive model, the BINREG procedure in the STATA statistical programme was used. This procedure fits generalized linear models for dependent variables with a binomial distribution.

Risk set

The prevalence of persecutory delusions (narrow and broad definitions) was assessed for the entire sample at T0 ($n = 7075$), for the group of individuals who had received no lifetime diagnosis of any DSM-III-R affective or non-affective psychotic disorder at T0 ($n = 6968$) and for the group of individuals who had received such a diagnosis at T0 ($n = 107$). All other analyses in which lifetime prevalence of persecutory delusions was the outcome variable were done in the group of individuals who had received no lifetime diagnosis of any DSM-III-R affective or non-affective psychotic disorder at the T0 interview.

The analysis of the incidence of persecutory delusion (narrowly and broadly defined) at T1 or T2 was done in the group of individuals who had received no lifetime diagnosis of any *DSM-III-R* affective or non-affective psychotic disorder at T0 and at T1, and additionally with lifetime absence of persecutory delusions, narrowly defined (T1 only: $n = 5498$; T1 and T2: $n = 4700$) or broadly defined (T1 only: $n = 5041$; T1 and T2: 4317), at T0.

The analysis of the outcome of the persecutory delusions at T2 was done in the group of individuals who had received no lifetime diagnosis of any DSM-III-R affective or non-affective psychotic disorder at the T0 and T1 interview, had had a CIDI interview at T2, and had not missed re-interview by clinicians about the presence of psychotic symptoms if they had been eligible for this clinical re-interview ($n = 4673$).

Results

Prevalence and incidence

Mean age for the entire sample was 41.2 (SD 12.2), 46.6% were male. The lifetime prevalence of narrowly defined persecutory delusion was 0.9% ($n = 65$) for the entire sample, 0.4% ($n = 31$) for the sample of individuals without a lifetime diagnosis of psychotic disorder, and 31.8% ($n = 34$) for the sample of individuals with a lifetime diagnosis of psychotic disorder at T0. The lifetime prevalence of broadly defined persecutory delusion was 10.0% ($n = 705$) for the entire sample, 9.1% ($n = 636$) for the sample of individuals without a lifetime diagnosis of psychotic disorder, and 64.5% ($n = 69$) for the sample of individuals with such a diagnosis at T0.

With respect to the answer on question G1 'Have you ever been convinced that people were spying on you?', 6591 individuals of the entire sample were classified in category 1 (no symptom, 93.19%), 284 individuals in category 2 (psychotic symptom present but not clinically relevant, 4.01%), 11 individuals in category 3 (symptom is always the result of substance use, 0.16%), 0 individuals in category 4 (symptom is always the result of somatic disorders or conditions, 0.0%), 40 individuals in category 5 (true psychotic symptom, 0.57%), and 147 individuals in category 6 (interviewer is in doubt because there appears to be some plausible explanation for what appears to be a psychotic experience, 2.08%).

With respect to the answer on question G2 'Has there ever been a period in which you were convinced that you were persecuted by people?', 6853 individuals of the entire sample were classified in category 1 (no symptom, 96.86%),

111 individuals in category 2 (psychotic symptom present but not clinically relevant, 1.57%), three individuals in category 3 (symptom is always the result of substance use, 0.04%), 0 individuals in category 4 (symptom is always the result of somatic disorders or conditions, 0.0%), 28 individuals in category 5 (true psychotic symptom, 0.40%), and 80 individuals in category 6 (interviewer is in doubt because there appears to be some plausible explanation for what appears to be a psychotic experience, 1.13%).

With respect to the answer on question G3 'Have you ever been convinced that you were secretly tested on or that experiments were carried out on you?', 6985 individuals of the entire sample were classified in category 1 (no symptom, 98.73%), 63 individuals in category 2 (psychotic symptom present but not clinically relevant, 0.89%), 1 individual in category 3 (symptom is always the result of substance use, 0.01%), 0 individuals in category 4 (symptom is always the result of somatic disorders or conditions, 0.0%), 14 individuals in category 5 (true psychotic symptom, 0.20%), and 12 individuals in category 6 (interviewer is in doubt because there appears to be some plausible explanation for what appears to be a psychotic experience, 0.17%).

With respect to the answer on question G4 'Have you ever been convinced that someone was conspiring against you, wanted to cause you harm or poisoning you?', 6894 individuals of the entire sample were classified in category 1 (no symptom, 97.44%), 59 individuals in category 2 (psychotic symptom present but not clinically relevant, 0.83%), two individuals in category 3 (symptom is always the result of substance use, 0.03%), 0 individuals in category 4 (symptom is always the result of somatic disorders or conditions, 0.0%), 32 individuals in category 5 (true psychotic symptom, 0.45%), and 88 individuals in category 6 (interviewer is in doubt because there appears to be some plausible explanation for what appears to be a psychotic experience, 1.24%).

The prevalence of persecutory delusions (narrowly defined) was significantly associated with hallucinatory experiences (narrowly defined; OR 7.9, 95% CI 2.6–24.2) and other delusions (narrowly defined; OR 16.0, 95% CI 6.5–39.3). Eight individuals (0.2%) reported onset of a persecutory delusion (narrowly defined) at T1 and 49 individuals (1.0%) reported onset of a persecutory delusion (broadly defined) at T1.

Factors associated with the lifetime prevalence of persecutory delusions

In the group of individuals with no lifetime diagnosis of psychotic disorder, perceived discrimination was reported by 1093 (15.7%) individuals and childhood trauma was reported by 890 (12.8%) individuals. A total of 2677 (38.4%)

lived in an urban area according to our a priori dichotomization. Mean score on the neuroticism scale was 38.1 (SD 4.3).

Both types of victimization experiences were significantly associated with the presence of lifetime persecutory delusions (both narrowly and broadly defined) in individuals with no lifetime diagnosis of psychotic disorder (Table 3.1). Adjustment for neuroticism reduced the associations to some extent (Table 3.1), the reduction being in the order of 35% for the associations with childhood trauma, and 15–25% for perceived discrimination. Adjustment for the lifetime presence of hallucinations and other delusions reduced but did not nullify the association with childhood trauma (narrowly defined: OR 2.08, 95% CI 0.91–4.76; broadly defined: OR 1.59, 95% CI 1.28–1.97) nor with discrimination (narrowly defined: OR 1.95, 95% CI 0.87–4.33; broadly defined: OR 1.71, 95% CI 1.39–2.09). The association with the urban exposure was only evident in the model of broadly defined persecutory delusions (Table 3.1), and this association was reduced after adjustment for other psychotic experiences (OR after adjustment 1.13, 95% CI 0.95–1.36).

All three social risk factors were associated with the lifetime prevalence of other psychotic experiences, both narrowly (present in 170 individuals) and broadly (present in 486 individuals) defined (Table 3.2).

Factors associated with the incidence of persecutory delusions

Perceived discrimination and childhood trauma also increased the risk for incident persecutory delusions at T1 or T2 (Table 3.3), although in the model of broadly defined persecutory delusions, the association with discrimination lacked statistical precision. Adjustment for neuroticism reduced the effect sizes to some extent, but again the associations were partly independent of the effect of neuroticism (Table 3.3). The association with childhood trauma was independent of the presence of hallucinations and other delusions (narrow outcome: OR after adjustment 6.75, 95% CI 1.99–22.94; broad outcome OR after adjustment 4.23, 95% CI 2.32–7.70). The association with discrimination, however, decreased substantially after adjustment for hallucinations and other delusions (narrow outcome: OR 1.64, 95% CI 0.80–3.36; broad outcome: OR 1.21, 95% CI 0.75–1.94). Urbanicity did not increase the risk for incident persecutory delusions (Table 3.3).

Persistence and transition to clinical delusions

In the group with lifetime absence of psychotic disorder at T0 and T1, two out of eight individuals with persecutory delusions (narrowly defined) at T1 again

Table 3.1 Associations between social risk factors and persecutory delusions at T0 in the group of individuals with lifetime absence of psychotic disorder (N = 6968)

	Persecutory delusions (narrow)						Persecutory delusions (broad)					
	Presence		Absence		OR	P (95% CI)	Presence		Absence		OR	P (95% CI)
	n	%	n	%			n	%	n	%		
Discrimination	0	19	0.3	5846	99.7			457	7.8	5408	92.2	
	1	11	1.0	1082	99.0	2.17	0.05 (1.00–4.70)	175	16.0	918	84.0	1.83	0.00 (1.50–2.24)
+ neuroticism						1.85	0.12 (0.85–4.05)					1.69	0.00 (1.38–2.07)
Childhood trauma	0	18	0.3	6060	99.7			480	7.9	5598	92.1	
	1	13	1.5	877	98.5	2.93	0.01 (1.36–6.32)	156	17.5	734	82.5	1.81	0.00 (1.47–2.23)
+ neuroticism						2.22	0.05 (1.00–4.94)					1.52	0.00 (1.22–1.89)
Urbanicity	0	18	0.4	4273	99.6			349	8.1	3942	91.9	
	1	13	0.5	2664	99.5	0.90	0.79 (0.43–1.91)	287	10.7	2390	89.3	1.23	0.02 (1.03–1.46)
+ neuroticism						0.87	0.73 (0.41–1.86)					1.20	0.04 (1.01–1.43)

OR, odds ratio; CI, confidence interval.

Table 3.2 Associations between social risk factors and other psychotic experiences at T0 in the group of individuals with lifetime absence of psychotic disorder (N = 6968)

		Other psychotic experiences (narrow)						Other psychotic experiences (broad)					
		Presence		Absence		OR	P (95% CI)	Presence		Absence		OR	P (95% CI)
		n	%	n	%			n	%	n	%		
Discrimination	0	120	2.1	5745	98.0			457	7.8	5408	92.2		
	1	50	4.6	1043	95.4	1.58	0.01 (1.108–2.27)	132	12.1	961	87.9	1.70	0.00 (1.36–2.12)
+ neuroticism						1.41	0.06 (0.98–2.04)					1.61	0.00 (1.29–2.02)
Childhood trauma	0	109	1.8	5969	98.2			372	6.1	5706	93.9		
	1	61	6.9	829	93.2	2.73	0.00 (1.93–3.85)	114	12.8	776	87.2	1.70	0.00 (1.34–2.15)
+ neuroticism						2.23	0.00 (1.55–3.19)					1.54	0.00 (1.21–1.97)
Urbanicity	0	85	2.0	4206	98.0			248	5.8	4043	94.2		
	1	85	3.2	2592	96.8	1.43	0.03 (1.04–1.98)	238	8.9	2439	91.1	1.44	0.00 (1.18–1.74)
+ neuroticism						1.40	0.04 (1.01–1.93)					1.41	0.00 (1.16–1.71)

OR, odds ratio; CI, confidence interval.

Table 3.3 Associations between social risk factors and incident persecutory delusions at T1 or T2 in the group of individuals with lifetime absence of psychotic disorder at T0 and T1 and lifetime absence of persecutory delusions (N = 4700 for narrow persecutory delusions; N = 4317 for broad persecutory delusions)

		Persecutory delusions (narrow)						Persecutory delusions (broad)					
		Presence		Absence		OR	P (95% CI)	Presence		Absence		OR	P (95% CI)
		n	%	n	%			n	%	n	%		
Discrimination	0	6	0.2	3965	99.9			41	1.1	3651	98.9		
	1	6	0.8	722	99.2	3.78	0.03 (1.16–12.36)	14	2.2	610	97.8	1.69	0.12 (0.88–3.26)
+ neuroticism						3.47	0.04 (1.05–11.5)					1.46	0.27 (0.75–2.84)
Childhood trauma	0	6	0.2	4118	99.9			36	0.9	3794	99.1		
	1	6	1.0	570	99.0	5.42	0.01 (1.65–17.80)	19	3.9	468	36.1	4.36	0.00 (2.40–7.90)
+ neuroticism						4.77	0.01 (1.40–16.23)					3.41	0.00 (1.84–6.32)
Urbanicity	0	7	0.2	2939	99.8			34	1.2	2708	98.8		
	1	5	0.3	1749	99.7	0.84	0.78 (0.25–2.80)	21	1.3	1554	98.7	0.92	0.79 (0.52–1.65)
+ neuroticism						0.82	0.75 (0.25–2.76)					0.90	0.71 (0.50–1.61)

OR, odds ratio; CI, confidence interval.

reported persecutory delusions at T2 (PP = 25.0%). Broadly defined persecutory delusions were persistent in 15 out of 99 individuals (PP = 15.2%). In two out of the seven individuals with narrowly defined persecutory delusions, transition occurred to the BPRS delusion outcome at T2 (PP = 28.7%), whereas none of these individuals developed the (more severe) BPRS clinical delusion outcome.

Discrimination increased the risk for persistence of persecutory delusions (broadly defined); the risk difference between those with presence versus absence of persecutory delusions at T1 in the group of non-exposed individuals was 8.9%, whereas this risk difference in the group with self-reported experience of discrimination was 24.1% (risk difference: 15.2%, interaction: $\chi^2 = 3.41$, $P = 0.065$). Adjustment for the other social risk factors, neuroticism, and baseline presence of broadly defined persecutory delusions did not change the results (adjusted interaction: $\chi^2 = 3.68$, $P = 0.055$). Childhood abuse similarly increased the risk for persistence of persecutory delusions (broadly defined); the risk difference between those with presence versus absence of persecutory delusions at T1 in the group of non-exposed individuals was 9.2%, whereas this risk difference in the group with self-reported childhood abuse was 28.0% (risk difference: 18.8%; interaction: $\chi^2 = 3.93$; $P = 0.047$). Adjustment for the other social risk factors, neuroticism, and baseline presence of broadly defined persecutory delusions again did not change the results (adjusted interaction: $\chi^2 = 4.07$; $P = 0.044$). Urbanicity did not influence the risk for persistence of broadly defined persecutory delusions, the risk differences for the exposed versus the non-exposed group of individuals being 15.1% and 14.1% respectively (risk difference: 1.0%; interaction: $\chi^2 = 0.02$; $P = 0.89$).

Risk factors for persistence of narrowly defined persecutory delusions and for transition into clinical delusion outcomes could not be determined due to the small numbers (i.e. two out of eight individuals had persistent persecutory delusions, and two out of seven developed the BPRS delusion outcome).

Discussion

Prevalence and incidence

The lifetime prevalence of persecutory delusions defined narrowly, i.e. causing distress and triggering help-seeking behaviour, in the general population was very low at 0.4%. However, the broad category of persecutory delusions, including non-distressing experiences as well as experiences with a plausible origin or secondary to other causes, was much more frequent, occurring in 9.1% of the sample. New onset of persecutory delusions over a period of one year occurred in 0.2% using the narrow criteria and in 1.0% of the sample when the broad definition was used.

Compared to the prevalence figures for psychotic experiences in non-clinical population samples in general (for example 17.5% broadly defined and 4.2% narrowly defined psychosis in the NEMESIS study (van Os *et al.* 2000, 2001), the discrepancy between the narrow and broad categories of experiences is more substantial, suggesting that persecutory experiences are more likely to occur in a benign mode.

Risk factors for prevalence, incidence, and persistence

In accordance with our hypothesis, all three social risk factors were associated with the lifetime prevalence of persecutory delusions. The associations, however, were not specific for the outcome of persecutory delusions, as the effect sizes for the other psychotic experiences were of similar magnitude and statistical precision. The results were most robust for the effect of victimization experiences (i.e. self-reported childhood trauma and perceived discrimination), which were evident in the models of the broad and narrow definitions of persecutory delusions, and were largely independent of the presence of other psychotic experiences. Part of the association between self-reported victimization experiences and persecutory delusions was mediated by neuroticism.

The effect of the urban exposure was evident in the model of the broad persecutory delusion outcome only and this association was partly due to the overlap with other psychotic experiences.

Importantly, perceived discrimination and self-reported childhood abuse also increased the risk for incident persecutory delusions, although again the association with discrimination was less robust and lacked precision for the narrow definition of persecutory delusions. The finding of a significant association with new onset of persecutory delusions indicates that the self-reported experiences of victimization preceded the emergence of the delusions, adding credibility to a causal interpretation of the findings. Both types of victimization experiences also increased the risk for persistence of persecutory delusions, the risk differences between the exposed and the unexposed groups of individuals being in the order of 15–19%.

Limitations

There are several methodological limitations. First, as in all longitudinal population surveys, there was substantial attrition between baseline and T2. However, detailed analyses of attrition in this sample suggest that it was largely random as far as baseline psychopathology is concerned (de Graaf *et al.* 2000).

Second, the measurements of perceived discrimination and childhood trauma were not very refined. Respondents were not able to report qualitative aspects of the perceived victimization experiences. Yet, the use of a direct semi-structured interview to assess childhood trauma is one of the strengths of the current study, because the relationship between childhood trauma and psychiatric disorders is frequently underestimated by researchers' reliance on records rather than direct questioning (Briere and Zaidi 1989; Read 1997). In addition, perceived victimization does not have to be proved to reflect identifiable events. For the argument by which cognitive mechanisms result in delusions this may not be relevant, as subjective perception of victimization alone is the prerequisite for the development of a paranoid attributional style.

Third, the statistical resolution of the analyses of incidence and persistence of persecutory delusions was limited, with only 49 onsets of broadly defined persecutory delusions and eight onsets of narrowly defined persecutory delusions at T1. Only 15 out of 99 individuals with current persecutory delusions (broadly defined) at T1 continued to report persecutory delusions at T2; for the narrow definition this was true for two out of eight individuals. However, the results for self-reported childhood trauma, and to a lesser extent for perceived discrimination, were robust in the analyses of prevalence, incidence and persistence, and remained after adjustment for possible confounders, including the presence of other psychotic experiences.

Mechanism of risk

There is increasing evidence that cognitive attributions contribute to the development of psychotic symptoms such as delusions (Bentall *et al.* 2001; Garety *et al.* 2001). As proposed earlier by Garety and colleagues it can be hypothesized that 'earlier adverse experience, such as social marginalization, childhood loss or severe childhood trauma, may create an enduring cognitive vulnerability, characterized by negative schematic models of the self and the world (e.g. beliefs about the self as vulnerable to threat, or about others as dangerous) that facilitate external attributions and low self-esteem' (Garety *et al.* 2001, p. 190). This tendency to externally attribute events may lie beneath paranoid ideation (Bentall *et al.* 2001; Janssen *et al.* 2006). Similarly, perceived discrimination may have effects on attributions of daily events (Gilvarry *et al.* 1999), facilitating an understandably paranoid attributional style. The mediating effect of neuroticism fits within this cognitive framework, as neuroticism can be conceived of as a cognitive style characterized by a selective attentional focus on external threats, a tendency to worry, and beliefs about uncontrollability of anomalous experiences, which will increase the risk of undergoing these experiences as well as the distress caused by them (Baker and Morrison 1998; Freeman and Garety 1999; Freeman *et al.* 2000).

Current ideas about biological consequences of early adversities lend credibility to the notion of an enduring psychological vulnerability. Recent studies have reported that neurotoxicity may be on the pathway between childhood trauma and psychosis (Walker and Diforio 1997). Childhood trauma may lead to neurodevelopmental abnormalities and, in particular, produce permanent damage in the stress regulation mechanism in the hypothalamic–pituitary–adrenal (HPA) axis (Bremner 2005). The persistence of exposure to stressors and heightened glucocorticoid release for extended periods can induce permanent changes in the HPA axis, and, through this, affect the dopamine system (Walker and Diforio 1997). Thus, exposition to stressors increases both cortisol release and dopamine, the latter being known as a neurotransmitter associated with the expression of psychosis (Kapur 2003). In subjects with a liability to delusion formation, as evidenced by delusional experiences, exposure to these environmental risk factors may result in changes in the functioning of the dopamine system, possibly affecting the persistence of developmental psychotic features.

References

American Psychiatric Association (1994) *Diagnostic and Statistic Manual of Mental Disorders*, 3rd edn, revised. Washington, DC: American Psychiatric Press.

Bak, M., Krabbendam, L., Janssen, I., de Graaf, R., Vollebergh, W. and van Os, J. (2005) Early trauma may increase the risk for psychotic experiences by impacting on emotional response and perception of control. *Acta Psychiatrica Scandinavica*, 112, 360–366.

Baker, C.A. and Morrison, A.P. (1998) Cognitive processes in auditory hallucinations: attributional biases and metacognition. *Psychological Medicine*, 28, 1199–1208.

Bentall, R.P., Corcoran, R., Howard, R., Blackwood, N. and Kinderman, P. (2001) Persecutory delusions: a review and theoretical integration. *Clinical Psychology Review*, 21, 1143–1192.

Bijl, R.V., Ravelli, A. and van-Zessen, G. (1998a) Prevalence of psychiatric disorder in the general population: results of The Netherlands Mental Health Survey and Incidence Study (NEMESIS). *Social Psychiatry and Psychiatric Epidemiology*, 33, 587–595.

Bijl, R.V., van-Zessen, G., Ravelli, A., de-Rijk, C. and Langendoen, Y. (1998b) The Netherlands Mental Health Survey and Incidence Study (NEMESIS): objectives and design. *Social Psychiatry and Psychiatric Epidemiology*, 33, 581–586.

Bremner, J.D. (2005) Effects of traumatic stress on brain structure and function: relevance to early responses to trauma. *Journal of Trauma & Dissociation*, 6, 51–68.

Briere, J. and Zaidi, L.Y. (1989) Sexual abuse histories and sequelae in female psychiatric emergency room patients. *American Journal of Psychiatry*, 146, 1602–1606.

Cougnard, A., Marcelis, M., Myin-Germeys, I. *et al.* (2007) Does normal developmental expression of psychosis combine with environmental risk to cause persistence of psychosis? A psychosis proneness-persistence model. *Psychological Medicine*, 37, 1–15.

de Graaf, R., Bijl, R.V., Smit, F., Ravelli, A. and Vollebergh, W.A. (2000) Psychiatric and sociodemographic predictors of attrition in a longitudinal study: the Netherlands Mental Health Survey and Incidence Study (NEMESIS). *American Journal of Epidemiology*, 152, 1039–1047.

Eaton, W.W., Romanoski, A., Anthony, J.C. and Nestadt, G. (1991) Screening for psychosis in the general population with a self-report interview. *Journal of Nervous and Mental Disease*, 179, 689–693.

Eaton, W.W., Neufeld, K., Chen, L.S. and Cai, G. (2000) A comparison of self-report and clinical diagnostic interviews for depression: diagnostic interview schedule and schedules for clinical assessment in neuropsychiatry in the Baltimore epidemiologic catchment area follow-up. *Archives of General Psychiatry*, 57, 217–222.

Ellett, L., Lopes, B. and Chadwick, P. (2003) Paranoia in a nonclinical population of college students. *Journal of Nervous and Mental Disease*, 191, 425–430.

Freeman, D. and Garety, P.A. (1999) Worry, worry processes and dimensions of delusions: an exploratory investigation of a role for anxiety processes in the maintenance of delusional distress. *Behavioural and Cognitive Psychotherapy*, 27, 47–62.

Freeman, D., Garety, P.A. and Phillips, M.L. (2000) An examination of hypervigilance for external threat in individuals with generalized anxiety disorder and individuals with persecutory delusions using visual scan paths. *Quarterly Journal of Experimental Psychology*, 53, 549–567.

Freeman, D., Garety, P.A., Bebbington, P. *et al.* (2005) The psychology of persecutory ideation. II: a virtual reality experimental study. *Journal of Nervous and Mental Disease*, 193, 309–315.

Garety, P.A., Kuipers, E., Fowler, D., Freeman, D. and Bebbington, P.E. (2001) A cognitive model of the positive symptoms of psychosis. *Psychological Medicine*, 31, 189–195.

Gilvarry, C.M., Walsh, E., Samele, C. *et al.* (1999) Life events, ethnicity and perceptions of discrimination in patients with severe mental illness. *Social Psychiatry and Psychiatric Epidemiology*, 34, 600–608.

Hanssen, M., Bak, M., Bijl, R., Vollebergh, W. and van Os, J. (2005) The incidence and outcome of subclinical psychotic experiences in the general population. *British Journal of Clinical Psychology*, 44, 181–191.

Henquet, C., Krabbendam, L., Spauwen, J. *et al.* (2005) Prospective cohort study of cannabis use, predisposition for psychosis, and psychotic symptoms in young people. *British Medical Journal*, 330(7481), 11.

Janssen, I., Hanssen, M., Bak, *et al.* (2003) Discrimination and delusional ideation. *British Journal of Psychiatry*, 182, 71–76.

Janssen, I., Krabbendam, L., Bak, M. *et al.* (2004) Childhood abuse as a risk factor for psychotic experiences. *Acta Psychiatrica Scandinavica*, 109, 38–45.

Janssen, I., Versmissen, D., Campo, J.A., Myin-Germeys, I., van Os, J. and Krabbendam, L. (2006) Attribution style and psychosis: evidence for an externalizing bias in patients but not in individuals at high risk. *Psychological Medicine*, 36, 771–778.

Johns, L.C. and van Os, J. (2001) The continuity of psychotic experiences in the general population. *Clinical Psychology Review*, 21, 1125–1141.

Johns, L.C., Cannon, M., Singleton, N. *et al.* (2004) Prevalence and correlates of self-reported psychotic symptoms in the British population. *British Journal of Psychiatry*, 185, 298–305.

Kapur, S. (2003) Psychosis as a state of aberrant salience: a framework linking biology, phenomenology, and pharmacology in schizophrenia. *American Journal of Psychiatry*, 160, 13–23.

Krabbendam, L., Janssen, I., Bak, M., Bijl, R.V., De Graaf, R. and Van Os, J. (2002) Neuroticism and low self-esteem as risk factors for psychosis. *Social Psychiatry and Psychiatric Epidemiology*, 37, 1–6.

Martin, J.A. and Penn, D.L. (2001) Social cognition and subclinical paranoid ideation. British *Journal of Clinical Psychology*, 40, 261–265.

Ormel, J. (1980) *Moeite met Leven of een Moeilijk Leven?* Groningen: University of Groningen.

Overall, J.E. and Gorham, D.E. (1962) The brief psychiatric rating scale. *Psychological Reports*, 10, 799–812.

Peters, E.R., Joseph, S.A. and Garety, P.A. (1999) Measurement of delusional ideation in the normal population: introducing the PDI (Peters *et al.* Delusions Inventory). *Schizophrenia Bulletin*, 25, 553–576.

Read, J. (1997) Child abuse and psychosis: a literature review and implications for professional practice. *Professional Psychology: Research and Practice*, 28, 448–456.

Smeets, R.M.W. and Dingemans, P.M.A.J. (1993) *Composite International Diagnostic Interview (CIDI) Version 1.1.* Amsterdam/Geneva: World Health Organization.

Spauwen, J., Krabbendam, L., Lieb, R., Wittchen, H.U. and Van Os, J. (2004) Does urbanicity shift the population expression of psychosis? *Journal of Psychiatric Research*, 38, 613–618.

Spauwen, J., Krabbendam, L., Lieb, R., Wittchen, H.U. and van Os, J. (2006a) Evidence that the outcome of developmental expression of psychosis is worse for adolescents growing up in an urban environment. *Psychological Medicine*, 36, 407–415.

Spauwen, J., Krabbendam, L., Lieb, R., Wittchen, H.U. and van Os, J. (2006b) Impact of psychological trauma on the development of psychotic symptoms: relationship with psychosis proneness. *British Journal of Psychiatry*, 188, 527–533.

Thewissen, V., Myin-Germeys, I., Bentall, R., de Graaf, R., Vollebergh, W. and van Os, J. (2006) Instability in self-esteem and paranoia in a general population sample. *Social Psychiatry and Psychiatric Epidemiology*, 42, 1–5.

Tien, A.Y. (1991) Distributions of hallucinations in the population. *Social Psychiatry and Psychiatric Epidemiology*, 26, 287–292.

van Os, J., Hanssen, M., Bijl, R.V. and Ravelli, A. (2000) Strauss (1969) revisited: a psychosis continuum in the general population? *Schizophrenia Research*, 45(1–2), 11–20.

van Os, J., Hanssen, M., Bijl, R.V. and Vollebergh, W. (2001) Prevalence of psychotic disorder and community level of psychotic symptoms: an urban–rural comparison. *Archives of General Psychiatry*, 58, 663–668.

van Os, J., Bak, M., Hanssen, M., Bijl, R.V., de Graaf, R. and Verdoux, H. (2002) Cannabis use and psychosis: a longitudinal population-based study. *American Journal of Epidemiology*, 156, 319–327.

van Os, J., Hanssen, M., Bak, M., Bijl, R.V. and Vollebergh, W. (2003) Do urbanicity and familial liability coparticipate in causing psychosis? *American Journal of Psychiatry*, 160, 477–482.

Verdoux, H., Maurice-Tison, S., Gay, B., Van Os, J., Salomon, R. and Bourgeois, M.L. (1998) A survey of delusional ideation in primary-care patients. *Psychological Medicine*, 28, 127–134.

Walker, E.F. and Diforio, D. (1997) Schizophrenia: a neural diathesis-stress model. *Psychological Review*, 104, 667–685.

Chapter 4

Prognosis of persecutory delusions in schizophrenia: a 20-year longitudinal study

Martin Harrow, Thomas Jobe, and Ellen B. Astrachan-Fletcher

Introduction

How different are persecutory delusions from other types of delusions? The research which we will describe in this chapter was designed to provide longitudinal data on the consistency and uniqueness of persecutory delusions in schizophrenia over an extended period of time. Longitudinal data for persecutory delusions has been relatively scant. Only a few investigators have provided such data on patients with these kinds of beliefs (e.g. Astrup 1962, 1966).

In general, persecutory delusions have been a source of special interest to a number of theorists who have proposed specific mechanisms which, they have believed, are responsible for them. Freud's theory of paranoia was formulated, in part, on the Schreber case. It provided an explanation of several of the key features which distinguish persecutory delusions from non-persecutory delusions. Freud tried to account for the major features of persecutory delusions by combining the 'defence' mechanism of projection with the defence mechanism of reaction formation. Using his dynamic formulation, Freud linked paranoia to homosexuality, specifically the projection of denied homosexual conflict (Freud 1911/1959).

Although later empirical studies found mixed or negative results on the relationship between 'homosexual signs' and paranoia (Klaf and Davis 1960; Planansky and Johnson 1962), the defensive aspect of Freud's theory was an important contribution. This emphasis on the defensive aspect of persecutory delusions remains cogent in current times as cognitive psychology has developed a series of empirically testable hypotheses.

Among the major cognitive investigators in this area, Bentall *et al.* (1994, 2001) emphasized the usefulness of attributional theory in explaining persecutory delusions. Bentall's view, and that of many other major theorists, notes the potential defensive function of persecutory delusions in preventing loss of self-esteem. Bentall's theory is a sophisticated one which includes poor self-esteem, but would not automatically expect *overt* signs of poor self-esteem in all patients with persecutory delusions. Some investigators such as Zigler and Glick (2001) have hypothesized about the role of persecutory delusions in defending against dysphoria and depression. Drake *et al.* (2004) and Freeman *et al.* (1998) have found evidence of more complicated relationships between these variables. Major theorists such as Freeman and Garety (1999, 2004), instead of viewing persecutory delusions as defensive against negative emotional states, see them as resulting from the worsening of already biased appraisal processes related to negative emotional states such as anxiety, depression, and anger, as well as other variables with attributional factors and other cognitive variables playing a key role.

Running through much of this diverse thinking about factors involved in persecutory delusions (partly dated back to Freud's formulations, and emphasized by modern theorists) are (a) the misinterpretation of other people's intentions, and (b) false causal inferences of potential and often imminent harm to the delusional individual, arising in conjunction with these misinterpreted intentions.

The current report uses longitudinal data from the Chicago Follow-up Study, extending over 20 years, to address the following important questions:

1 Over an extended period of time, are persecutory delusions found in some, many, or almost all patients with schizophrenia?
2 Do many patients with schizophrenia who have persecutory delusions also experience non-persecutory delusions at some point in time?
3 How consistent and continuous are persecutory delusions over time?
4 Do schizophrenia patients with persecutory delusions, or with paranoid delusions, have better outcomes and more subsequent periods of recovery than other types of schizophrenia patients?
5 Do patients who have other types of psychotic disorders also experience persecutory delusions?
6 Are the risk and protective factors involved in persecutory delusions unique and different from the risk and protective factors involved in non-persecutory delusions?

Patient sample

The present research is based on data from the Chicago Follow-up Study, a prospective multi-follow-up research programme investigating schizophrenia and mood disorders longitudinally. The study was designed to provide data on functioning, adjustment, potential recovery, and major symptoms, with a special focus on factors involved in positive and negative symptoms (Harrow *et al.* 1983, 1989, 1990, 2000, 2004, 2005; Jobe and Harrow 2000).

The present sample of 97 patients, diagnosed using the classification system of the Research Diagnostic Criteria (RDC; Spitzer *et al.* 1978), includes 55 patients with schizophrenia, and 42 patients with other types of psychotic disorders (including 24 bipolar patients) at index hospitalization. The participants were assessed prospectively at index hospitalization and then reassessed for functioning and adjustment in six successive follow-up interviews over 20 years. These interviews occurred at 2 and 4.5 years post-hospital, and then again at 7.5, 10, 15, and 20 years post-hospital. Diagnoses were based on the administration of structured research interviews and other clinical material at index hospitalization (Grinker and Harrow 1987).

The research was designed to study patients who, at index hospitalization, were relatively young, non-chronic patients, in order to reduce the confounding effects of long-term treatment. The mean age of the patient sample was 23 years at index hospitalization; 56% of the patients were male. Of the overall sample, 46% were first-admission patients on entry to the study. The mean educational level of this sample was 13 years at this point in time.

Follow-up assessments

Follow-ups were conducted by trained interviewers who were blind to diagnosis and, after the first wave of follow-ups, were blind to the results of previous follow-ups. Informed written consent was obtained at each assessment.

At each follow-up, the patients were given structured interviews to assess different types of delusions, other types of positive symptoms and functioning in multiple areas (e.g. work, social functioning, potential rehospitalization, treatment, etc.). The interview included an assessnent of functioning and the SADS (Schedule for Affective Disorders and Schizophrenia) (Endicott and Spitzer 1978) to assess major symptoms, such as persecutory and non-persecutory delusions and depression. The SADS covers the occurrence within the past month and past year of 16 individual types of delusions including persecutory delusions and first-rank symptoms (Silverstein and Harrow 1981). These were rated on three-point scales as follows: 1, delusion absent; 2, weak or equivocal delusion; 3, full delusion present. To assess global outcome at each follow-up, we used the eight-point Levenstein, Klein and Pollock Scale (Levenstein *et al.* 1966).

Operational definition of recovery

Our operational criteria for a *period* of recovery requires: (1) the absence of major symptoms throughout the year (absence of psychosis and absence of negative symptoms); (2) no rehospitalization during the follow-up year; and (3) adequate work and social functioning. Our scale for recovery has been used successfully in previous research (Harrow *et al.* 2005; Grossman *et al.* 2006). The recovery index provides data on recovery during the year and also the cumulative percentage of patients who, over the 20 years of follow-ups, ever show an interval or period of recovery.

Medications

As is typical in the natural course of schizophrenia and other major disorders over many years, no single uniform treatment plan emerged for all patients in this naturalistic multi-year study, and some patients left treatment altogether. At each of the six follow-ups over the 20 years, between 55% and 65% of the patients with schizophrenia were being treated with antipsychotic medications, and between 18% and 30% of the schizophrenia patients were not in treatment. The patients with schizophrenia who were not in treatment had fewer persecutory and fewer non-persecutory delusions than those on antipsychotics at each of the follow-ups ($P <0.05$). As in many other medical disorders, patients who see themselves as functioning well over time, sometimes feel that they do not need help and then leave treatment (Harrow and Jobe 2007).

Results on the frequency of persecutory delusions and of delusional activity over time

The multiple follow-up data indicate that more than 75% of the patients with schizophrenia had at least some delusional activity over the 20 years after the acute phase of hospitalization. The majority had some persecutory delusions as well as some non-persecutory delusions (see Figs 4.1 and 4.2). A similar high rate of both persecutory delusions and non-persecutory delusions was found among psychotic patients by Appelbaum *et al.* (1999) in a study of acutely hospitalized patients.

Less than 25% of the schizophrenia patients experienced delusional activity at all six follow-ups over the 20 years and slightly less than 5% showed persecutory delusions at all the follow-ups. This was because many of the schizophrenia patients who had continuous delusional activity had some interchangeability of persecutory and non-persecutory delusions. Clearly, the presence of continuous persecutory delusions over the full 20-year period was not a frequent occurrence.

Do schizophrenia patients with persecutory delusions also have non-persecutory delusions?

Since a delusion with persecutory content may also have non-persecutory content linked to it, we looked at whether some or many schizophrenia patients

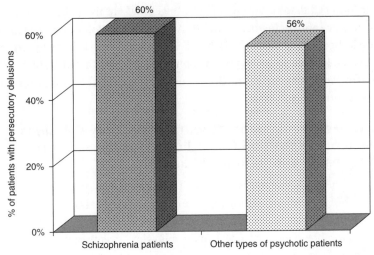

Fig. 4.1 Patients with persecutory delusions at some point over the 20-year period.

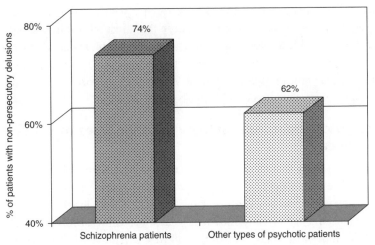

Fig. 4.2 Patients with non-persecutory delusions at some point over the 20-year period.

with persecutory delusions also have other separate non-persecutory delusions at the same time. A more detailed analysis was conducted with ten schizophrenia patients who had persecutory delusions at the 10-year follow-ups. Seven of these patients also had separate non-persecutory delusions at the same time. The picture is similar at the other follow-ups. Two examples of this are as follows. At the 2-year follow-ups, R.P., a 28 year-old male with schizophrenia, was concerned that his family was 'out to get me.' He also believed that laser beams were influencing his thoughts. At the 7.5-year follow-up, he felt that electric bolts shot out of his head. At the 10-year follow-ups, D.M., a 29-year-old male patient with schizophrenia, reported that 'the FBI is trying to harm me.' Independent of this delusion, the patient also reported that 'I have control over the seas.'

Do schizophrenia patients with persecutory delusions have a predisposition toward continual persecutory delusions on a longitudinal basis?

Our data indicate some consistency, albeit limited, in delusion content over time for most of the patients with persecutory delusions. Analysis of the original content of the records of a sub-sample of 21 patients with delusional activity at three or more follow-ups indicated the following. Twenty of these 21 patients who had delusions at three or more follow-ups had persecutory delusions at one or more of these follow-ups. All 20 of these patients also had non-persecutory delusions at one or more follow-ups. In addition, 16 of these patients had one or more follow-ups in which they had a non-persecutory delusion, and no persecutory delusions. These data indicate that most schizophrenia patients who are vulnerable to persecutory delusions are also vulnerable to other non-persecutory delusions. The variation in the content of persecutory and other delusions over time in psychotic patients has also been reported in other studies using a shorter follow-up period (Appelbaum *et al.* 2004).

Persecutory delusional activity in other types of psychotic disorders

The data indicate that most of the patients who had been hospitalized at the acute phase with other types of psychotic disorders also showed a mixture of persecutory and non-persecutory delusions during their longitudinal course. These patients had already shown at least some vulnerability to psychotic episodes at the acute phase, in that they all were psychotic at index hospitalization. While the majority (>65%) of these patients had some subsequent delusional activity over the 20-year follow-up period, their psychotic activity was less frequent, often involved less severe delusions, and was of shorter duration than those found in the patients with schizophrenia.

In regard to the content of their delusions, over half of them experienced persecutory delusions at some point during the follow-ups (Fig. 4.1). However, a large number of these patients also experienced non-persecutory delusions (Fig. 4.2), with the main difference from the schizophrenia patients being their less frequent and less severe nature of the delusional activity.

In regard to frequency, 44% of the schizophrenia patients experienced persecutory delusions during more than one follow-up year; by contrast, only 17% of the patients with other types of psychotic disorders experienced persecutory delusions during more than one follow-up year ($P <0.05$). Looked at from one point of view, like the schizophrenia patients these other patients were vulnerable to both persecutory and non-persecutory delusions, but less vulnerable than the patients with schizophrenia. Our previous research has indicated that, when other types of psychotic patients with affective disorders have positive symptoms, these are often associated with the recurrence of affective syndromes (Grossman *et al.* 1986; Harrow *et al.* 1986).

Do schizophrenia patients with persecutory delusions have better outcomes and more periods of recovery than schizophrenia patients with non-persecutory delusions?

Some researchers have observed that schizophrenia patients with paranoid schizophrenia, or those with persecutory delusions, have better outcomes and better prognoses than patients with other types of schizophrenia. Longitudinal multiple follow-up research on the long-term course of patients with persecutory delusions is best suited to providing data bearing on this issue.

Using diagnosis at the acute phase of hospitalization, patients with a diagnosis of paranoid schizophrenia (which has some limited overlap, but not complete overlap with persecutory delusions) were compared to the patients with undifferentiated schizophrenia on later outcome and recovery. The results were mixed with some, but inconsistent, support for the view of better outcome for paranoid patients. There was no relationship between paranoid schizophrenia and better global outcome at most follow-ups. However, at the 10-year follow-up there was a non-significant trend ($P = 0.065$), and at the 20-year follow-up there were significant differences ($P = 0.01$) towards better outcome for the patients with paranoid schizophrenia. In regard to recovery, there were minor non-significant trends towards more later periods of recovery for the paranoid schizophrenia patients ($P < 0.15$).

An important issue for which data has not been presented before is whether, *after* the acute phase, the presence of persecutory delusions predicts better outcome, and whether it predicts subsequent recovery many years later. Figure 4.3 presents data addressing this issue.

Poorer subsequent outcome and fewer subsequent periods of reovery were evident when the patients with persecutory delusions were compared to schizophrenia patients who were no longer delusional at the 2-year follow-up ($\chi^2 = 5.66$, 1 df, $P < 0.02$). However, the presence of non-persecutory delusions also predicted fewer subsequent periods of recovery when these patients were

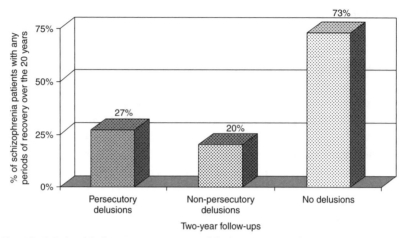

Fig. 4.3 Relationship between persecutory delusions at 2-year follow-ups and subsequent recovery.

compared to schizophrenia patients who were no longer delusional ($\chi^2 = 8.29$, 1 df, $P < 0.01$). Hence, the presence of both types of delusions after the most acute phase predicts poorer subsequent outcome and less recovery over the next 18 years. The important variable here appears to be whether or not the schizophrenia patient is delusional, with the distinction between persecutory and non-persecutory delusions not being as important in terms of subsequent functioning, outcome, and recovery.

We believe that our data indicate that the presence of *any* delusions after the acute phase in schizophrenia is a sign of greater vulnerability to subsequent psychopathology, with the extent of this type of vulnerability increasing the chances for poorer subsequent outcome for many years.

Select risk and protective factors which may be involved in persecutory delusions in schizophrenia

An issue of considerable importance is identifying the risk and protective factors involved in the generation and maintenance of persecutory delusions in schizophrenia. Our preliminary analyses and the research of others have identified a number of factors, and we briefly outline our results concerning two of these factors.

We view the issue of risk and protective factors in terms of a stress-diathesis vulnerability model (Nuechterlein 1984; Norman and Malla 1993; Walker and Diforio 1997). Using this model in relation to persecutory delusions, we assume that, for patients with schizophrenia and also for patients with other types of psychotic disorders, there is an underlying biological vulnerability (diathesis) either to persecutory delusions or to delusions in general. In addition, a group of external risk factors dramatically increase the chances of this diathesis being expressed overtly over time.

Anxiety as a factor in persecutory delusions

One example is a *combination* of high *internal* vulnerability to psychosis and to anxiety (part of the diathesis) coupled with *external* stress. The research and reviews of a number of major investigators have emphasized the importance of anxiety and stress as potential factors involved in psychosis (Norman and Malla 1993; Walker and Diforio 1997; Freeman and Garety 1999, 2004; Garety *et al.*, 2001; Freeman *et al.* 2002; Corcoran 2003). There has been research supporting these views on the tentative importance of anxiety for delusions. However, longitudinal research in this area has been relatively scarce (Krabbendam *et al.* 2002).

Our multiple follow-up research design has allowed us to begin to explore this issue on a longitudinal basis. We have used a slightly shortened version of the SCL-90 (Symptom Check List) scale for anxiety (Derogatis and Lazarus 1994), administered to a sub-sample of our patients at the 2-year, 4.5-year, and 10-year follow-ups. Our research suggests that some, but not all, patients with schizophrenia are vulnerable to high anxiety. Our longitudinal data indicate a significant relationship between high anxiety at the 4.5-year follow-ups and the presence of concurrent persecutory delusions ($r = 0.45$, 30 df, $P < 0.01$) for patients with schizophrenia. There also was a trend for highly anxious schizophrenia patients at the 4.5-year follow-ups to have more subsequent persecutory delusions at the 7.5-year, 10-year, and 15-year follow-ups ($P < 0.10$). The data for schizophrenia patients showed a significant relationship between anxiety at the 10-year follow-ups and both the concurrent presence ($r = 0.57$, 23 df, $P < 0.01$), and the subsequent presence of persecutory delusions at the 15-year follow-ups ($r = 0.72$, 22 df, $P < 0.001$). Looking at vulnerability to anxiety as a trait-like feature, a high score on this trait was a risk factor, predicting both concurrent and subsequent persecutory delusions many years later for schizophrenia patients.

However, the presence of anxiety at the 4.5-year follow-ups also predicted, significantly, the presence of *overall* delusional activity at the 4.5-year follow-ups ($P < 0.001$), and predicted the subsequent presence of delusional activity at the 7.5-year, 10-year, and 15-year follow-ups ($P < 0.05$). The presence of anxiety at the 10-year follow-ups was also associated with overall delusional activity at the 10-year follow-ups ($P = 0.001$) and at the 15-year follow-ups ($P < 0.001$). Thus, while vulnerability to anxiety may be a risk factor for persecutory delusions, it is a risk factor for delusional activity in general, regardless of whether this involves persecutory or non-persecutory content.

These data could fit with and support the stress-diathesis model noted above for schizophrenia, either through neurochemical processes such as the HPA axis (Corcoran *et al.* 2003), and/or through neural circuits (Benes 2000). One of the frequent products of external stress, linked to increases in both norepinephrine and cortisol, is anxiety. Our longitudinal data on anxiety could be consistent with the view, advanced by some, that dopamine release is differentially increased by exposure to stress and anxiety in schizophrenia patients (LaRuelle *et al.* 1999). It has been proposed that the biological response to stress, which is linked to activation of the HPA axis, can trigger a downstream cascade of neurochemical events that can exacerbate psychosis (Corcoran *et al.* 2003). We therefore suggest that, in vulnerable patients, a combination of high biological vulnerability to anxiety, combined with external stress, triggers increased HPA axis and neurochemical activity, leading to psychosis. In our view, data from other studies on expressed emotion (EE) could indicate a relationship between anxiety (easily generated in high-EE families) and increased delusional activity.

Poor overt self-esteem as a factor in persecutory delusions

There are a number of hypotheses by major investigators (Bentall *et al.* 1994; Krabbendam *et al.* 2002) about delusions as compensation for low self-esteem in schizophrenia. Bentall *et al.* (2001) have suggested a sophisticated formulation concerning the defensive function of persecutory delusions as protective against the exposure of hidden layers of negative self-esteem.

Using a slightly shortened version of the Rosenberg (1965) Self-Esteem Scale, our longitudinal data on the relationship between low self-esteem and persecutory delusions for the patients with schizophrenia produced some mixed and some positive results. Poor self-esteem at the 4.5-year follow-ups was not significantly associated with persecutory delusions, but poor self-esteem at the 10-year follow-ups was significantly associated with concurrent persecutory delusional activity ($P < 0.01$). Poor self-esteem at the 10-year follow-ups also predicted the presence of subsequent persecutory delusions at the 15-year and 20-year follow-ups ($P = 0.01$). However, the presence of poor self-esteem at the 10-year follow-ups was also related to concurrent overall delusional activity at the 10-year follow-ups ($P < 0.01$) and also predicted, significantly, overall delusional activity at the 15-year and 20-year follow-ups ($P < 0.05$). Poor self-esteem and negative reactions to the presence of delusions may have reciprocal effects, with each interacting and influencing the other, and this could be a factor in the significant correlations which did emerge. Overall, while there was some, limited, association between poor overt self-esteem and persecutory delusions, the overall pattern of relationships was weaker than that found for anxiety and, similar to anxiety, the relationships discovered were not specific to persecutory delusions but rather were present for all types of delusions.

Conclusions

Frequency of persecutory and non-persecutory delusions and their co-occurrence over time

The analysis of persecutory delusions in a sample studied longitudinally over a prolonged period (20 years) provides information on the uniqueness and the consistency of these types of beliefs in schizophrenia, which has not previously been available to the field. One of the most important aspects of these data is that the same patients with schizophrenia, when studied longitudinally, showed considerable interchangeability over time, between persecutory and non-persecutory delusions. Among schizophrenia patients who were vulnerable to delusional activity after the initial acute phase, very few had *only* persecutory delusions during the 20-year period studied. Over the 20-year period, a large percentage of the patients with schizophrenia experienced both persecutory and non-persecutory delusions.

Often when they showed persecutory delusions, they also had accompanying non-persecutory delusions. However, some had persecutory delusions more frequently. Also, while there are many similarities, select patients with persecutory delusions sometimes present increased risk of violence (Cheung *et al.* 1997). In addition, it is possible that in a sample of patients with late-onset psychosis, one might find a larger percentage of patients with only persecutory delusions, although this issue has not been resolved definitively. Recent genetic research suggests the possibility of a unique genetic vulnerability to persecutory delusions for patients with bipolar disorder (Schulze *et al.* 2005). However, the current data indicating the frequent presence of both types of delusions suggest that persecutory delusions do not substantially set themselves apart from other types of delusions. They probably involve most of the same basic mechanisms as other non-persecutory delusions. Also, schizophrenia patients with persecutory delusions and those with non-persecutory delusions at the 2-year follow-ups showed similar prognostic patterns, with both groups showing significantly fewer periods of recovery than schizophrenia patients who were not delusional at the 2-year follow-ups.

Factors involved in persecutory delusions

From our data, we propose that the same basic underlying factors are prominent in leading to many different types of delusions in patients with schizophrenia. Thus, factors which increase the chances for the overt expression of both persecutory and non-persecutory delusions in schizophrenia patients who have an underlying diathesis for delusional activity include anxiety (providing strong support for the views of Freeman and Garety), poor overt self-esteem to a limited extent, and a host of other factors. However, a number of specific cognitive and other factors may be involved in shaping the content of the delusions (for some, in the direction of persecutory delusions).

Our previous research has investigated background factors that might influence the content of patients' delusions. The results indicated that the content of the delusions of over half of our patients with schizophrenia and our patients with other types of psychotic disorders was related to the content of non-delusional ideas or concerns of theirs that predated the onset of the delusions being studied (Harrow *et al.* 1988). Chapman and Chapman (1988) and others have reported similar results. Some of these non-delusional ideas or concerns were present years before the onset of psychosis and others were relatively recent. Data indicating that prior non-delusional material may shape the subsequent persecutory delusion is consistent with neural network theories of delusions that rely on 'parasitic foci' such as proposed by Hoffman (1987), Blackwood *et al.* (2001), and others, although further research is needed to support this outlook.

The reason that patients select some concerns and not others as the basis of their delusions remains unknown, and leaves room for many other important factors that may be involved in delusion formation. Among the specific factors which may be involved in shaping the persecutory content, investigators such as Bentall *et al.* (1994, 2001) and others have proposed the importance of attributional biases, such as self-serving bias, externalizing bias, and personalizing bias. There are considerable additional data supporting this hypothesis (Sharp *et al.* 1997; Martin and Penn 2002) and some data that question it (McKay *et al.* 2005). The mostly positive, but still mixed, evidence in this area points to the need for further study and analysis of the factors involved in delusions in general, and also to factors involved in some specific types of delusions, such as persecutory delusions and first-rank symptoms. However, the current longitudinal evidence, and the evidence on the co-occurrence of different types of delusions, would suggest that an important task in this area is increasing knowledge with regard to factors involved in delusions in general.

Vulnerability to persecutory delusions in patients with other types of psychotic disorders

The data suggest that patients with other types of psychotic disorders also have some vulnerability to both persecutory and non-persecutory delusions, or towards delusions in general, but that they are less frequent and less severe in these patients. In addition, a slightly larger percentage of their delusions were non-persecutory. Their psychosis at index hospitalization, followed by psychosis at some of the six follow-ups, supports an overall view of their having some vulnerability to delusional activity. However, the current data, and other data we have collected (Harrow *et al.* 1995), suggest that their underlying vulnerability to delusional activity is less severe than that of patients with schizophrenia. Since a number of these patients with other types of psychotic disorders eventually re-experience delusional activity, often in a milder form, consideration of factors involved in their abnormal beliefs is also of some importance. Our previous research on patients with unipolar depressive disorders, together with research on differences between unipolar non-psychotic depression and unipolar psychotic depression, has suggested that delusional activity is not just a consequence of the severity of affective syndromes (Sands and Harrow 1994, 1995; Harrow *et al.* 1995).

The current results on patients with other types of psychotic disorders, when combined with the data on the patients with schizophrenia, fit the stress-diathesis model for vulnerability to delusions and psychosis. Using this type of model, both schizophrenia patients and patients with other types of psychotic disorders have an underlying diathesis or vulnerability to delusional activity, and this underlying vulnerability is more likely to be expressed overtly under conditions of heightened cognitive arousal. The data on the frequency and severity of symptoms, together with evidence of slower recoverability in schizophrenia patients after psychotic episodes (Harrow *et al.* 1995), suggests a spectrum of vulnerability to the psychosis along which the diagnostic groups lie, and with schizophrenia occupying the most vulnerable end.

Other factors involved in delusions

Previous research of ours and others has indicated that one of the important factors involved in both persecutory and non-persecutory delusions is disordered self-monitoring (Frith and Done 1988; Harrow *et al.*, 1988, 1989, 2004; Frith *et al.* 1998). Adequate self-monitoring of one's ideas, thinking, and behaviour is linked, in part, to effective and usually routine accessing of stored knowledge in long-term memory, concerning normative standards of social appropriateness (Harrow *et al.* 1989). Under normal circumstances, this helps to keep ideas and beliefs 'on track' and consonant with socially accepted standards.

All people have incorporated normative standards of behaviour concerning what is appropriate and what is 'real.' Under normal circumstances, those standards of behaviour, stored in long-term memory, help to self-monitor one's own ideas and beliefs (Harrow *et al.* 1989, 2004; Jobe and Harrow 2000). Faulty self-monitoring that is based on ineffective use of stored knowledge about what types of ideas are socially appropriate may be an important component of almost all psychotic symptoms, including delusions, although other unknown factors are also involved.

Our evidence has suggested that the impaired self-monitoring is not a general factor that cuts across all aspects of a patient's thinking. Rather, it is content-specific, with psychotic patients being better able to monitor the appropriateness of their thinking in non-delusional content areas and better able to monitor other patients' ideas than their own ideas (Harrow *et al.* 1989). Ordinary people in the midst of intense heated debates (during heightened cognitive arousal) with people they are affectively involved with sometimes show diminished self-monitoring on the 'hot' topic and say derogatory or socially unacceptable things (e.g. 'You're lazy' or worse). Unlike most psychotic patients, a few hours later, when self-monitoring is restored, they will regret this lapse. Delusions and thought disorder are not due solely to impaired self-monitoring, but it is one important factor, and this impairment is almost necessary for full psychosis to occur.

The greater vulnerability among schizophrenia patients to delusional activity may reflect differences at the genetic and brain circuitry level. Yui *et al.* (1999) have hypothesized that the greater vulnerability to psychosis seen in patients with schizophrenia may result from the underlying biological mechanism of increased endogenous sensitization of dopamine, thus linking risk factors such as increased anxiety and low self-esteem with exacerbation of psychosis and manifestation of positive symptom psychopathology. Recent evidence provides some support for this view (Boileau, 2006).

According to the stress-diathesis and vulnerability model, among these patients with vulnerability to delusional activity, only some will express it overtly. The probability of the overt appearance of delusions by these patients will depend on multiple factors. The extent of their underlying vulnerability to delusions will be the most important factor, with the current data suggesting that patients with schizophrenia have a greater vulnerability than patients with other types of psychotic disorders. However, a host of other factors, among which are external stress and vulnerability to anxiety, which can alter neurochemical processes and may be linked to heightened cognitive arousal, also play a role in increasing the frequency of the overt appearance of delusional activity. The present data suggest that poor self-esteem may also play some role, though perhaps limited. While the latter two factors (anxiety and poor self-esteem) were explored in the current study, the research of ourselves and others is beginning to suggest a number of other risk factors which increase the chances of the overt appearance of delusions and other positive symptoms in patients with an underlying diathesis.

Acknowledgements

Supported, in part, by USPHS Grants MH-26341 and MH-068688 from the National Institute of Mental Health, USA (M.H.). The authors are indebted to Robert Faull for his assistance with data preparation and statistical analysis.

References

Appelbaum, P., Robbins, P. and Roth, L. (1999) Dimensional approach to delusions: comparison across types and diagnoses. *American Journal of Psychiatry*, 156, 1938–1943.

Appelbaum, P., Robbins, P. and Vesselinov, R. (2004) Persistence and stability of delusions over time. *Comprehensive Psychiatry*, 45, 312–324.

Astrup, C., Fossum, A. and Holmboe, R. (1962) *Prognosis in Functional Psychoses.* Springfield, IL, Charles C. Thomas.

Astrup, C., Noreik, K. and Elkes, J. (1966) *Functional Psychoses: Diagnostic and Prognostic Models.* Springfield, IL: Charles C. Thomas.

Benes, F. (2000) Emerging principles of altered neural circuitry in schizophrenia. *Brain Research Reviews*, 31, 251–269.

Bentall, R., Kinderman, P. and Kaney, S. (1994) The self, attributional processes and abnormal beliefs: towards a model of persecutory delusions. *Behavior Research and Therapy*, 32, 331–341.

Bentall, R., Corcoran, R., Howard, R., Blackwood, N. and Kinderman, P. (2001) Persecutory delusions: a review and theoretical integration. *Clinical Psychological Review*, 21, 1143–1192.

Blackwood, N.J., Howard, R.J., Bentall, R.P. and Murray, R.M. (2001) Cognitive neuropsychiatric models of persecutory delusions. *American Journal of Psychiatry*, 158, 527–539.

Boileau, I., Dagher, A., Leyton, M. *et al.* (2006) Modeling sensitization to stimulants in humans. *Archives of General Psychiatry*, 63, 1386–1395.

Chapman, L.J. and Chapman, J.P. (1988) The genesis of delusions. In: Oltmanns, T. F. and Maher, B.A. (eds), *Delusional Beliefs*, pp. 167–183. New York: Wiley.

Cheung, P., Schweitzer, I., Crowley, K. and Tuckwell, V. (1997) Violence in schizophrenia: role of hallucinations and delusions. *Schizophrenia Research*, 26, 181–190.

Corcoran, C., Walker, E., Huot, R. *et al.* (2003) The stress cascade and schizophrenia: etiology and onset. *Schizophrenia Bulletin*, 29, 671–692.

Derogatis, L. and Lazarus, L. (1994) SCL-90-R, Brief Symptom Inventory, and matching clinical rating scales. In: Maruish, M. (ed.), *The Use of Psychological Testing for Treatment Planning and Outcome Assessment*, pp. 217–248. Hillsdale, NJ: Lawrence Erlbaum.

Drake, R., Pickles, A., Bentall, R., Kinderman, P., Haddock, G.N.T. and Lewis, S. (2004) The evolution of insight, paranoia and depression during early schizophrenia. *Psychological Medicine*, 34, 285–292.

Endicott, J. and Spitzer, R. (1978) A diagnostic interview. *Archives of General Psychiatry*, 35, 837–844.

Freeman, D. and Garety, P. (1999) Worry, worry processes and dimensions of delusions: an exploratory investigation of a role for anxiety processes in the maintenance of delusional distress. *Behavioural and Cognitive Psychotherapy*, 27, 47–62.

Freeman, D. and Garety, P.A. (2004) *Paranoia: The Psychology of Persecutory Delusions.* New York: Psychology Press.

Freeman, D., Garety, P., Fowler, D. *et al.* (1998) The London-East Anglia randomized controlled trial of cognitive-behaviour therapy for psychosis. IV: Self-esteem and persecutory delusions. *British Journal of Clinical Psychology*, 37, 415–430.

Freeman, D., Garety, P., Kuipers, E., Fowler, D. and Bebbington, P. (2002) A cognitive model of persecutory delusions. *British Journal of General Psychology*, 41, 331–347.

Freud, S. (1911/1959) Psycho-analytic notes upon an autobiographical account of a case of paranoia (Dementia Paranoides). In: Strachey, A. and Strachey, J. (eds), *Collected Papers*, pp. 387–470. New York: Basic Books.

Frith, C. and Done, D. (1988) Towards a neuropsychology of schizophrenia. *British Journal of Psychiatry*, 153, 437–443.

Frith, C., Geraint, R. and Friston, K. (1998) Psychosis and the experience of self: brain systems underlying self-monitoring. *Annals of the New York Academy of Sciences*, 843, 170–178.

Garety, P., Kuipers, E., Fowler, D., Freeman, D. and Bebbington, P. (2001) A cognitive model of the positive symptoms of psychosis. *Psychological Medicine*, 31, 189–195.

Grinker, R. and Harrow, M. (eds) (1987) *Clinical Research in Schizophrenia: A Multidimensional Approach.* Springfield, IL: Charles C. Thomas.

Grossman, L., Harrow, M. and Sands, J. (1986) Features associated with thought disorder in manic patients at 2–4 year follow-up. *American Journal of Psychiatry*, 143, 306–311.

Grossman, L., Harrow, M., Rosen, C. and Faull, R. (2006) Sex differences in outcome and recovery for schizophrenia and other psychotic disorders: 5 followups over 15 years. *Psychiatric Services*, 57, 844–850.

Harrow, M. and Jobe, T. (2007) Factors involved in outcome and recovery in schizophrenia patients not on antipsychotic medications: a 15-year multi-followup study. *Journal of Nervous and Mental Disease*, 145, 406–414.

Harrow, M., Lanin-Kettering, I., Prosen, M. and Miller, J. (1983) Disordered thinking in schizophrenia: intermingling and loss of set. *Schizophrenia Bulletin*, 9, 354–367.

Harrow, M., Grossman, L., Silverstein, M., Meltzer, H. and Kettering, R. (1986) A longitudinal study of thought disorder in manic patients. *Archives of General Psychiatry*, 43, 781–785.

Harrow, M., Rattenbury, F. and Stoll, F. (1988) Schizophrenic delusions: an analysis of their persistence, of related premorbid ideas, and of three major dimensions. In: Oltmanns, T. and Maher, B. (eds), *Delusional Beliefs: Interdisciplinary Perspectives*, pp. 184–211. New York: Wiley.

Harrow, M., Lanin-Kettering, I. and Miller, J. (1989) Impaired perspective and thought pathology in schizophrenic and psychotic disorders. *Schizophrenia Bulletin*, 15, 605–623.

Harrow, M., Goldberg, J., Grossman, L. and Meltzer, H. (1990) Outcome in manic disorders: a naturalistic followup study. *Archives of General Psychiatry*, 47, 665–671.

Harrow, M., Mcdonald, A., Sands, J. and Silverstein, M. (1995) Vulnerability to delusions over time in schizophrenia, schizoaffective and bipolar and unipolar affective disorders: a multi-followup assessment. *Schizophrenia Bulletin*, 21, 95–109.

Harrow, M., Grossman, L., Herbener, E. and Davis, E. (2000) Ten-year outcome: patients with schizoaffective disorders, schizophrenia, affective disorders, and mood-incongruent psychotic symptoms. *British Journal of Psychiatry*, 177, 421–426.

Harrow, M., Herbener, E., Shanklin, A., Jobe, J., Rattenbury, F. and Kaplan, K. (2004) Followup of psychotic outpatients: dimensions of delusions and work functioning in schizophrenia. *Schizophrenia Bulletin*, 30, 147–161.

Harrow, M., Grossman, L., Jobe, T. and Herbener, E. (2005) Do patients with schizophrenia ever show periods of recovery? A 15 year multi-followup study. *Schizophrenia Bulletin*, 31, 723–734.

Hoffman, R.E. (1987) Computer simulations of neural information processing and the schizophrenia-mania dichotomy. *Archives of General Psychiatry*, 44, 178–188.

Jobe, T. and Harrow, M. (2000) Delusions. In: Kadzin, A. (ed.), *Encyclopedia of Psychology*. New York, Oxford University Press, 467–469.

Klaf, F. and Davis, C. (1960) Homosexuality and paranoid schizophrenia: a study of 150 cases and controls. *American Journal of Psychiatry*, 40, 1070–1075.

Krabbendam, L., Janssen, I., Bak, M., Bijl, R., De Graaf, R. and Van Os, J. (2002) Neuroticism and low self-esteem as risk factors for psychosis. *Social Psychiatry and Psychiatric Epidemiology*, 37, 1–6.

Laruelle, M., Abi-Dargham, A., Gil, R., Kegeles, L. and Innis, R. (1999) Increased dopamine transmission in schizophrenia: relationship to illness phases. *Biological Psychiatry*, 46, 56–72.

Levenstein, D., Klein, D. and Pollack, M. (1966) Follow-up study of formerly hospitalized voluntary psychiatric patients: the first two years. *American Journal of Psychiatry*, 122, 1102–1109.

Martin, J.A. and Penn, D.L. (2002) Attributional style in schizophrenia: an investigation in outpatients with and without persecutory delusions. *Schizophrenia Bulletin*, 28, 131–142.

McKay, R., Langdon, R. and Coltheart, M. (2005) Paranoia, persecutory delusions, and attributional biases. *Psychiatry Research*, 136, 233–245.

Norman, R. and Malla, A. (1993) Stressful life events and schizophrenia. 1: A review of the research. *British Journal Psychiatry*, 162, 161–166.

Nuechterlein, K. and Dawson, M. (1984) A heuristic vulnerability/stress model of schizophrenic episodes. *Schizophrenia Bulletin*, 10, 300–312.

Planansky, K. and Johnson, R. (1962) The incidence and relationship of homosexual and paranoid features in schizophrenia. *Journal of Mental Science*, 108, 604–615.

Rosenberg, M. (1965) *Society and the Adolescent Self-Image*. Princeton, NJ: Princeton University Press.

Sands, J. and Harrow, M. (1994) Psychotic unipolar depression at follow-up: factors related to psychosis in the affective disorders. *American Journal of Psychiatry*, 151, 995–1000.

Sands, J. and Harrow, M. (1995) Vulnerability to psychosis in unipolar major depression: Is premorbid functioning involved. *American Journal of Psychiatry*, 152, 1009–1015.

Schulze, T.G., Ohlraun, S., Czerski, P.M. *et al.* (2005) Genotype-phenotype studies in bipolar disorder showing association between the DAOA/G30 locus and persecutory delusions: a first step toward a molecular genetic classification of psychiatric phenotypes. *American Journal of Psychiatry*, 162, 2101–2108.

Sharp, H.M., Fear, C.F. and Healy, D. (1997) Attributional style and delusions: an investigation based on delusional content. *European Psychiatry*, 12, 1–7.

Silverstein, M. and Harrow, M. (1981) Schneiderian first rank symptoms in schizophrenia. *Archives of General Psychiatry*, 38, 288–293.

Spitzer, R., Endicott, J. and Robins, E. (1978) Research diagnostic criteria: rationale and reliability. *Archives of General Psychiatry*, 35, 773–782.

Walker, E. and Diforio, D. (1997) Schizophrenia: a neural diathesis-stress model. *Psychological Review*, 104, 667–685.

Yui, K., Goto, K., Ikemoto, S. *et al.* (1999) Neurobiological basis of relapse prediction in stimulant-induced psychosis and schizophrenia: the role of sensitization. *MOI Psychiatry*, 4, 512–523.

Zigler, E. and Glick, M. (2001) The developmental approach to adult psychopathology. *Clinical Psychologist*, 54, 2–11.

Chapter 5

Violence and persecutory delusions

Jayne L. Taylor

Introduction

Although there is an increasing sophistication in our understanding of the cognitive and emotional processes which underpin persecutory delusions, there is to date a relative paucity of research on the behaviour associated with such ideation—in other words, why and how people choose to act upon their delusional beliefs. The issue is particularly pertinent in relation to those people who react violently to delusions of persecution. This chapter seeks to present a review of the current research base on the relationship between violence and psychosis by first reviewing the evidence for a link between both psychosis and, more specifically, persecutory delusions. Research on the factors believed to contribute to this relationship is then discussed, with a specific emphasis upon the role of threat, emotional processing, attributional bias, 'theory of mind' and early experience.

Violence and psychosis: evidence of a link

The relationship between psychosis and offending behaviour, particularly violence towards others, has remained a controversial area. Early research findings provided little evidence of a link in that the prevalence of mental disorder was found to be no higher in samples of people who had been arrested than in that of people from a comparable socio-economic background (Monahan and Steadman 1983). However, many early studies were criticized for poor methodological design such as the use of inappropriate samples and failure to control for confounding variables such as sociodemographic factors. Results were also difficult to compare due to varying definitions and measures of violence.

Notwithstanding this, the move towards de-institutionalization, twinned with a politically driven emphasis upon risk assessment and reduction, has resulted in a renewed interest in the area. The demise of institutionalization has enabled study of the relationship between violent offending and the symptoms of psychosis in more natural environments where people have fewer restrictions and greater exposure to trigger factors and potential mediating factors such as substance misuse. This was demonstrated by Swanson *et al.* (2002) who examined epidemiological risk factors for violent behaviour in a sample of 802 adults with mental health difficulties. Violence was independently associated with a range of factors including exposure to community violence, homelessness, history of violent victimization and substance abuse. Thus, a growing body of research using numerous methods has demonstrated that people with psychosis are at increased risk of committing violent acts towards others (O'Kane and Bentall, 2000; Bjorkly, 2002a,b; Walsh *et al.* 2002). This has included epidemiological studies examining the prevalence of both violence and schizophrenia in unselected community samples (Link and Stueve, 1994; Hodgins *et al.* 1996), studies of the prevalence of violence by people with psychosis within the community (Karson and Bigelow, 1987) and studies of the prevalence of psychosis within prison or offending samples (Hodgins and Cote, 1993; Tiihonen *et al.* 1997).

Although it is now largely accepted that people who present with symptoms of psychosis are more at risk of committing violent acts towards others, the literature base has continued to attract criticism relating to the strength of the relationship. Each of the methodological strategies has inherent weaknesses. For example, large epidemiological studies necessitate the use of crude measures such as frequency of hospitalization and arrest or conviction rates. Prevalence studies in offending samples may be biased by those who fabricate symptoms as a way of achieving a lesser sentence or hospital transfer or, conversely, by those who attempt to hide symptoms due to the stigma attached to mental health problems and associated fear of victimization within the prison setting. In studies of violence in community samples of people with psychosis, it is possible that an offending history makes one more likely to receive treatment through the imposition of community treatment orders and may miss those who have not come into contact with services. Some have argued that this provides even stronger evidence of the strength of the relationship as repeated positive findings appear to transcend issues of methodological design. However, in answer to this, Arboleda-Florez *et al.* (1998) argue the converse in that this only leads to a distorted and inaccurate representation of the relationship.

Importantly, most of the literature to date has focused upon whether a link between psychosis and violence exists and has used the concept of relative risk to explore this relationship. Relative risk refers to the amount of risk posed by an individual compared to other people and most studies to date have assessed the risk of violence posed by a person with psychosis compared to people without psychosis. This approach has been widely criticized for being overly simplistic and stigmatizing. In recent years, a number of alternative strategies of investigation have been suggested. For example, Walsh *et al.* (2002) advocate the use of population attributable risk, i.e. the degree of risk within a population attributable to one factor such as a diagnosis of schizophrenia. In a re-examination of the violence rates of a Finnish cohort study (Tiihonen *et al.* 1997), the population risk of violence attributable to people with schizophrenia was only 4%. Walsh *et al.* (2002) argue that this demonstrates the small number of violent acts within society that can be attributed to people with psychosis. This point is also supported when one compares the risk of future violence in psychotic and non-psychotic offenders. In a meta-analysis of recidivism, Bonta *et al.* (1998) found that people with psychosis were less likely to re-offend in the future. However, although attributable risk is useful in reducing stigma, it does not allow us to identify the specific groups of individuals who may be at risk of committing violent acts in response to persecutory delusions nor to identify those points in time at which people may be particularly vulnerable. In order to address these questions we need to understand the mechanisms underpinning the relationship.

Violence and delusional beliefs

In the search for more refined predictors of violence in people with psychosis and as a first step towards understanding the psychological processes which contribute to this, some have argued that a more fruitful line of enquiry is to focus upon individual symptoms as opposed to large diagnostic categories (O'Kane and Bentall 2000). The importance of this was demonstrated in a study by Link *et al.* (1992) who compared both self-reported violence and arrest rates in a community sample who had never had contact with psychiatric service in addition to three patient groups. Interestingly, current psychotic symptoms were associated with violence in all groups, including the community sample. Although the patient groups were found to be more violent than the community sample, these differences were not evident when psychotic symptoms were specifically controlled.

Although both command hallucinations (Rogers *et al.* 1990) and passivity delusions (Taylor, 1993) have been associated with increased risk of violence, the most robust finding comes from studies focusing upon persecutory delusions (Cheung *et al.* 1997). Furthermore, as indicated by the findings of Link *et al.* (1992), the relationship between feelings of persecution and violence does not appear to be specific to people with psychosis. In 38 132 participants in the US National Household Survey on Drug Abuse, Mojtabai (2006) found that the risk of violence increased with the frequency of psychotic-like experiences. Paranoid ideation and unusual perceptual experiences were most consistently linked to violence.

However, within the current climate of risk assessment and prediction, there has been increasing pressure on clinicians to provide even more refined formulations of risk. In recent years, this approach has entailed not just actuarial assessments of risk based on those factors known to be statistically associated with future violence, such as previous violence, but also of phenomenological aspects based on structured clinical judgement. Clinicians are required to provide a risk formulation detailing factors such as potential targets of violence or specific triggers to violence.

In view of this, and going one step beyond the symptom approach, Junginger (2006) argues that a subgroup of people with persecutory delusions may respond violently to the same specific delusional content throughout the course of their illness. Junginger refers to this as 'stereotypic' delusional offending, the basic premise being that people are motivated to violence by specific delusional content which is over and above basic typologies of delusion. In support of this, Junginger *et al.* (1998) found that 17% of a sample of 54 people with delusional beliefs accounted for 41% of the violent incidents reported across the sample, suggesting that a small minority of patients may be responsible for a disproportionate amount of the violent acts that are committed by people with delusional beliefs. With regards to motivation for violence, 40% of the sample described incidents of violence that were motivated by a delusion and 18% reported that this had motivated at least one act of 'extreme' violence. Furthermore, 15% were classified as stereotypic delusional offenders in that the same delusion had motivated at least two acts of violence that were significantly separated in time.

Although the study was based on semi-structured interviews and the sample size was small, the study demonstrates the importance of the content of the delusional beliefs in relation to motivated acts of violence and the potential stability of this over time.

This has significant implications for risk prediction but the question remains as to how content of delusional beliefs relates to motivated violence. Unsurprisingly, research appears to suggest that violence may actually reflect an extreme safety behaviour. For example, Staznickas *et al.* (1993) found that the link between delusions and violence was particularly evident when the violent act was perceived as a protection against a perceived threat. Interestingly, Aziz *et al.* (2005) presented case studies of people with delusional misidentification syndrome who had acted violently in response to their delusional beliefs. The authors suggest that although alcohol and substance intoxification facilitated the acting out of the belief, it was the degree of threat perceived from the delusionally misidentified object that was the crucial factor in influencing the response to the delusional belief.

The importance of social context, particularly interpersonal relationships, is highlighted by Nordstrom and Kullgren (2003) who examined the court convictions of a cohort of people diagnosed with schizophrenia over a two-year period. From a total of 588 victims identified, the majority were unacquainted with the offender ($n = 328$). However, although only 77 victims were members of the offender's family, death was most likely in female family members, particularly mothers. This concurs with Estroff et al. (1998) who found that mothers who reside with adult children with schizophrenia and co-occurring substance abuse are at an elevated risk of being a target of violence compared with other members of the social network. The authors additionally observe that violent acts were most apparent in those families with multiple psychosocial challenges.

In discussing the mechanisms underpinning this, Estroff and Zimmer (1994) conducted a series of interviews over an 18-month period with 169 people with severe and enduring mental health difficulties. Where possible, interviews were also conducted with significant others. During this period, approximately one-third of the sample engaged in threats or violent acts towards others and those with delusional beliefs and beliefs of thought insertion or broadcasting were more likely to be assaultative. Content analysis of the interviews revealed that many respondents reported residing in environments which they perceived as threatening and hostile. Furthermore, respondents who made violent threats perceived themselves to be less hostile than the sample in general, but perceived their significant others as more attacking.

Overall, it would seem that violence in people with persecutory delusions may be related to recurrent beliefs involving specific relationships where there is a high degree of perceived threat by another. Freeman et al. (2007) suggest that acting upon delusions reflects anxious attempts to prevent the occurrence of the perceived threat. In support of this, they found that the use of safety behaviours was associated with both acting on delusions and a history of violence in people with persecutory delusions.

Factors underpinning the relationship

In a discussion of the relationship between violence and psychosis, Taylor (1998) argues that, as delusions are common symptoms of psychosis and violence in this group is rare, other factors must be operating to mediate the relationship. In accordance with this, a small but growing body of research has focused upon five main strands of enquiry. Whereas the first of these has addressed the specific role of perceived threat, other investigators have focused not on the association of symptom profiles with violence but rather on the psychological factors that differentiate those who act violently upon persecutory delusions from those who do not. This research has focused on key areas already known to be implicated in the psychological underpinnings of persecutory delusions, namely emotional processing, appraisal biases, theory of mind deficits and the role of early experience.

Threat/control over-ride

The role of threat as a potential mediator between delusions of persecution and violent behaviour was demonstrated by Link et al. (1998). They found that it was those symptoms which specifically related to the individual feeling threatened or controlled by external forces (Threat/Control Override symptoms: TCO) which were associated with increased risk of physical violence towards others. This would explain why command hallucinations, passivity delusions and persecutory delusions have all been found to be linked with an increased risk of violence. Although some studies have found no difference in the prevalence of TCO symptoms between those people with a diagnosis of schizophrenia who have violently offended and those who have not (Stompe et al. 2004), there is growing evidence for the importance of the concept. Hodgins et al. (2003) followed 128 men from both general and forensic mental health units with a diagnosis of schizophrenia during two 6-month periods following discharge into the community. Within the first 6-month period, a severe positive symptom increased the risk of aggressive behaviour. During the second 6-month period, the presence of a severe positive symptom and an increase in TCO symptoms specifically increased the risk of aggressive behaviour. This finding remained even after controlling for the effects of antisocial personality disorder and previous substance abuse. The authors suggest that TCO symptoms may be important antecedents of aggressive behaviour amongst males being treated in the community. They also state that contradictions in the findings relating to the TCO concept may reflect inadequate control of co-morbid affective symptoms, arguing that violence may only be associated with TCO symptoms when accompanied by low affect.

This was supported by Buchanan et al. (1993) in a study examining the phenomenological correlates of actions emanating from delusions.

They found that it was those beliefs that resulted in depression, anxiety or fear which were associated with acting upon the belief, as opposed to those which resulted in anger. The role of affect in this process was highlighted by Kennedy *et al.* (1992). They hypothesized that the content of delusional beliefs in people with psychosis following a violent act would be congruent with fear and anger. In a test of this, they reviewed the case notes of 126 people admitted to a regional secure unit. Of these, 15 people were identified as fulfilling DSM-III-R criteria for delusional disorder and also had a violent or threatening index offence. They found that defensive fear and projective anger were congruent with delusional beliefs in all cases, both during the offence and within the previous month.

As a caveat to this, Swanson *et al.* (1997) found that only moderate levels of psychotic symptoms increased the risk of physical violence. Higher levels of positive symptom severity resulted in lower risk, implying that severe dysfunction impedes violence. This highlights the importance of also controlling for disorganization and may imply that there is a critical time period in which people are most vulnerable to acting violently upon their beliefs. As further evidence of this, Gardner *et al.* (1996) found that thought disorder was negatively associated with violent offending.

The symptom-based approach provides a first step in advancing our understanding of the relationship between violence and psychosis, demonstrating that it is those symptoms which are specifically related to feeling threatened which confer the most risk as well as highlighting the importance of secondary symptoms such as low mood. However, even if one considers Junginger's refinement with the concept of stereotypic delusional offending, the fact remains that the majority of people who experience such beliefs do not act upon their beliefs in a violent manner.

Emotional processing

It would seem that if violence in people with persecutory delusions reflects a response to an excessive perception or preoccupation with threat, then this might be apparent in attentional processes. Freeman *et al.* (2001) suggest that persecutory delusions reflect threat beliefs which involve the anticipation of danger and it might be concluded therefore that people with delusional beliefs may display attentional biases characterized by either a hypervigilance for threat-related stimuli or even a difficulty in detecting 'escape-related' cues within their environment. This would also concur with models of anger and aggression which have indicated that an attentional bias for hostile stimuli and cues within the environment develops as an automatic process, thereby maintaining any underlying threat-related schemata (Berkowitz 1990).

Certainly, violent offenders have been found to display an attentional bias for aggression-related words on probe-detection tasks (Smith and Waterman 2003). However, interesting results were obtained by Silver *et al.* (2005) in a study investigating a range of cognitive functions in people with a diagnosis of schizophrenia and a history of severe violent behaviour. Tests of identification and differentiation of facial emotions were administered in addition to tests of executive functioning, working memory, attention, visual orientation and motor function. Performance on the cognitive tasks was not found to discriminate between those with a history of violence and those without. However, those with a history of violence demonstrated a superior ability to identify facial emotional expressions but were less able to discriminate between the intensity of emotions than those without a history of violence. The authors conclude that this may contribute to conflict generation in that people are able to detect anger and aggression in others but may be less able to detect the moderation of these emotions and, hence, may miss important resolution signals. Notwithstanding this, previous studies on attentional processes in people with persecutory delusions have demonstrated that the mechanisms underlying threat perception are more complex than a simple hypervigilance for threat-related stimuli. In a review of this area, Green and Phillips (2004) suggest that the attentional bias for threat-related stimuli in people with persecutory delusions varies across the stages of processing, with an initial vigilance for threat at earlier pre-attentive stages, followed by avoidance during later controlled stages of processing. It is possible that people with persecutory delusions with a history of violence do not demonstrate this latter stage of active avoidance which may alternatively be characterized as a 'flight' or escape response. Therefore, unable to avoid the threat, their only alternative course of action may be to act upon this or to 'fight'.

Attributional bias

Research has consistently demonstrated that persecutory delusions are associated with an attributional style characterized by externalising the cause of negative events to other people (Bentall *et al.* 2001). It is argued that this reflects an exaggerated form of the self-serving bias in which self-esteem is maintained by attributing the causes of positive events to the self and negative events to others or to circumstances. However, as self-esteem in people with persecutory delusions has often been found to be low (Freeman *et al.* 1998), the role of attributional biases in people with paranoia may not function directly as a means of maintaining self-esteem but as a factor which serves to maintain underlying core beliefs that the world is hostile and threatening. This would suggest that people who respond violently to delusional beliefs may have an excessive externalising attributional style compared to people who do not act upon their beliefs and, moreover, that their attributional style is characterized by further distortions related to the intent of others.

In a test of this, McNiel *et al.* (2003) administered a specific measure of 'aggressive' cognitive style to 110 psychiatric inpatients. The measure included not only attributions relating to the hostile intent of others, but also beliefs regarding the perception of threat and permissive beliefs regarding the use of violence. They found that permissive views regarding the use of physical violence, in addition to the excessive perception of threat, may be additive factors which precipitate violence in people with paranoia. This study indicates that additional personality characteristics may be important in distinguishing people who react violently to delusions of persecution from those who do not.

Theory of mind

The additive role of personality factors has also been found in the literature relating to mentalizing abilities in people with persecutory delusions and a history of violence. Deficits in 'theory of mind' (the ability to understand the mental states of others) have been found to play a role in persecutory delusions (Corcoran *et al.* 1997; Craig *et al.* 2004) and there is some evidence that they may also have a role in violent responses to persecutory delusions. Murphy (1998) found that people with a diagnosis of schizophrenia and convictions for serious offences had a deficit in their ability to understand theory-of-mind problems requiring the ability to understand that a person may hold a false belief about the mental state of another individual (second-order theory of mind), despite being able to make normal inferences about the world that did not involve the mental states of others. Abu-Akel and Abushua'leh (2004) expanded upon this by investigating the role of both theory of mind, empathy and hostility in people with schizophrenia and a history of violence. They found that people with a history of violence actually performed better on those tasks requiring higher-order mentalizing abilities than those people with a diagnosis of schizophrenia but no history of violence. However, they found that the violent group was significantly impaired on tasks that required the ability to understand the feelings of others. Moreover, hostility appeared to increase the predictive value of the model. The authors concluded that ersonality traits may have a central role in the development of violence in people with persecutory delusions.

Early experience

In addition to cognitive factors, evidence has suggested that adverse experiences in childhood may confer vulnerability for violence in people with psychosis. There is extensive research demonstrating that people with a history of violence and psychosis have histories characterized by trauma in early life. This was supported by Heads *et al.* (1997) in a study of childhood experiences in people with schizophrenia and a history of violence. In an examination of 102 people with schizophrenia in a special hospital, two-thirds were found to have experienced childhood difficulties prior to illness onset, including parental neglect/rejection, physical abuse, parental conflict, criminality and sexual abuse. Fresnan *et al.* (2004) also found that people with a diagnosis of schizophrenia and a history of violence demonstrated worse premorbid adjustment than those without a history of violence and demonstrated difficulties within peer relationships across childhood, early and late adolescence.

Although it could be argued that such early adverse experiences are non-specific risk factors which may predispose individuals to a range of difficulties in adulthood, there is some indication that exposure to these factors is specifically related to violence in people with psychosis. In support of this, Yesavage *et al.* (1983) found that frequency of assaults by male inpatients with a diagnosis of schizophrenia was positively associated with parental discipline and physical parental conflict. Furthermore, Addad *et al.* (1981) also found evidence that criminality in schizophrenia was associated not only with frequent parental conflict but also with an adversarial relationship with mothers. The role of disrupted attachments in early childhood has consistently been found to be associated with violence in later life, particularly when characterized by maternal rejection. Raine *et al.* (1994, 1997) found that maternal rejection as represented by attempts to abort a fetus or institutionalizing the infant for the first 12 months of life interacted with birth complications to increase the risk of violence when assessed at 18 and 34 years of age. Moreover, the interaction effect was specific to early-onset, severe violence as opposed to less severe, late-onset acts or threats of violence. In an attempt to explain this relationship, Bjorkly (1995) posits that aggression in people with persecutory delusions serves as a defence against a perceived threat which only exists within the inner world of the individual. As such Bjorkly argues that severe abuse early in life impacts upon self-image. Aggression is therefore the result of protective, paranoid projections.

Conclusion

Despite earlier research findings suggesting that there is no relationship between mental disorder and violence, recent research has indicated that there is a relationship and that this is particularly evident with those symptoms involving the perception of threat to the self. Furthermore, there is increasing evidence that psychological factors may contribute to the likelihood of acting violently upon these beliefs. To date, the research base suggests that early adverse experiences may contribute both to the development of threat-related beliefs regarding the hostility of others and, importantly, the degree of protection that one can expect from others. Exposure to violence and aggression at a young age may also contribute to permissive views about the use of violence and additional personality traits in adulthood which confer further vulnerability to reacting violently to threatening situations. Cognitive processes such as biases in attention and appraisal may serve to maintain underlying beliefs.

The emerging research base demonstrates the importance of psychological processes as well as highlighting further areas for exploration. These include the possibility of a 'critical period' in which delusions are active yet not debilitating nor moderated by the effects of negative symptoms. The role of personality variables remains an area yet to be fully explored particularly in relation to cognitive processes. The literature also suggests that a focus upon escape as opposed to threat may be warranted. However, evidently violence occurs within a social context. In considering the degree of victimization that people with psychosis continue to encounter within society, it is equally possible that the increased risk of violence within this group also reflects social pressures such as a history of stigmatization, rejection and experiences of violent crime. In order to fully explore the relationship between delusions of persecution and violence, further research also needs to consider this group as the victim as well as the perpetrator.

References

Abu-Akel, A., and Abushua'leh, K. (2004) Theory of mind in violent and non-violent patients with schizophrenia. *Schizophrenia Research*, 69, 45–53.

Addad, M., Benezech, M., Bourgeios, M. and Yesavage, J. (1981) Criminal acts among schizophrenics in French mental hospitals. *Journal of Nervous and Mental Disease*, 169, 289–293.

Arboleda- Florez, J., Holley, H. and Crisanti, A. (1998) Understanding causal paths between mental illness and violence. *Social Psychiatry and Psychiatric Epidemiology*, 33, S38–S46.

Aziz, M.A., Razik, G.N. and Donn, J.E. (2005) Dangerousness and management of Delusional Misidentification Syndrome. *Psychopathology*, 38, 97–102.

Bentall, R.P.,Corcoran, R.,Howard, R., Blackwood, R. and Kinderman, P. (2001) Persecutory delusions: a review and theoretical integration. *Clinical Psychology Review*, 21, 1143–1192.

Berkowitz, L. (1990) On the formation and regulation of anger and aggression: a cognitive-neoassociationistic analysis. *American Psychologist*, 45, 494–503.

Bjorkly, S. (1995) Trauma and violence: the role of early abuse in the aggressive behaviour of two violent psychotic women. *Bulletin of the Menninger Clinic*, 59, 205–220.

Bjorkly, S. (2002a) Psychotic symptoms and violence toward others—a literature review of some preliminary findings. Part 1. Delusions. *Aggression and Violent Behaviour*, 7, 617–631.

Bjorkly, S. (2002b) Psychotic symptoms and violence toward others—a literature review of some preliminary findings. Part 2. Hallucinations. *Aggression and Violent Behaviour*, 7, 605–615.

Bonta, J., Law, M. and Hanson, K. (1998) The prediction of criminal and violent recidivism among mentally disordered offenders. *Psychological Bulletin*, 123, 123–142.

Buchanan, A., Reed, A., Wessely, S., Garety, P., Taylor, P. and Grubin, D.G. (1993) Acting on delusions: II. The phenomenological correlates of acting on delusions. *British Journal of Psychiatry*, 163, 77–81.

Cheung, P., Schweitzer, I., Crowley, K. and Tuckwell, V. (1997) Violence in schizophrenia: role of hallucinations and delusions. *Schizophrenia Research*, 26, 181–190.

Corcoran, R., Cahill, C. and Frith, C.D. (1997) The appreciation of visual jokes in people with schizophrenia: a study of 'mentalizing' ability. *Schizophrenia Research*, 24, 319–327.

Craig, J.S., Hatton, C., Craig, F.B. and Bentall, R. (2004) Persecutory beliefs, attributions and Theory of Mind: comparison of patients with paranoid delusions, Asperger's Syndrome and health controls. *Schizophrenia Research*, 69, 29–33.

Estroff, S.E. and Zimmer, C. (1994) Social networks, social support and violence among persons with severe, persistent mental illness. In; Monahan, J. and Steadman, H. (eds), *Violence and Mental Disorder: Developments in Risk Assessment*, pp. 259–295. Chicago: University of Chicago Press.

Estroff, S.E., Swanson, J.W., Lachiotte, W.S., Swartz, M. and Bolduc, M. (1998) Risk reconsidered: targets of violence in the social networks of people with serious psychiatric disorders. *Social Psychiatry and Psychiatric Epidemiology*, 33 (Suppl. 1), S95–101.

Freeman, D., Garety, P., Fowler, D. et al. (1998) The London–East Anglia randomized controlled trial of cognitive-behaviour therapy for psychosis IV: self-esteem and persecutory delusions. *British Journal of Clinical Psychology*, 37, 415–430.

Freeman, D. Garety, P.A. and Kuipers, E. (2001) Persecutory delusions: developing the understanding of belief maintenance and emotional distress. *Psychological Medicine*, 31, 1293–1306.

Freeman, D., Garety, P.A., Kuipers, E., Fowler, D., Bebbington, P.E. and Dunn, G. (2007) Acting on persecutory delusions: The importance of safety seeking. *Behaviour Research and Therapy*, 45, 89–99.

Fresnan, A., Apiquian, R., de la Fuente-Sandoval, C. et al. (2005) Violent behaviour in schizophrenic patients: Relationship with clinical symptoms. *Aggressive Behaviour*, 31, 511–520.

Gardner, W., Lidz, C.W., Mulvey, E.P. and Shaw, E.C. (1996) Clinical versus actuarial predictions of violence in patients with mental illness. *Journal of Consulting and Clinical Psychology*, 64, 602–609.

Green, M.J. and Phillips, M.L. (2004) Social threat perception and the evolution of paranoia. *Neuroscience and Biobehavioural Reviews*, 28, 333–342.

Heads, T.C., Taylor, P. and Leese, M. (1997) Childhood experiences of patients with schizophrenia and a history of violence: a special hospital sample. *Criminal Behaviour and Mental Health*, 7, 117–130.

Hodgins, S. and Cote, G. (1993) Major mental disorder and antisocial personality disorder: a criminal combination. *Bulletin of the American Academy of Psychiatry and Law*, 21, 155–160.

Hodgins, S., Mednick, S.A., Brennan, P.A.,Schulsinger, F. and Engberg, M. (1996) Mental disorder and crime: evidence from a Danish birth cohort. *Archives of General Psychiatry*, 53, 489–496.

Hodgins, S., Hiscoke, U.L. and Freese, R. (2003) The antecedents of aggressive behaviour among men with schizophrenia: a prospective investigation of patients in community treatment. *Behavioural Science and the Law*, 21, 523–546.

Junginger, J. (2006) "Stereotypic" delusional offending. *Behavioral Sciences and the Law*, 24, 295–311.

Junginger, J., Parks-Levy, J. and McGuire, L. (1998) Delusions and symptom-consistent violence. *Psychiatric Services*, 49, 218–220.

Karson, C. and Bigelow, L.B. (1987) Violent behaviour in schizophrenic patients. *Journal of Nervous and Mental Disease*, 175, 161–164.

Kennedy, H.G., Kemp, L.I. and Dyer, D.E. (1992) Fear and anger in delusional (paranoid) disorder: The association with violence. *British Journal of Psychiatry*, 160, 488–492.

Link, B.G. and Stueve, A. (1994) Psychotic symptoms and the violent/illegal behaviour of mental patients compared to community controls. In: Monahon, J. and Steadman, H. (eds), *Violence and Mental Disorder: Developments in Risk Assessment*, pp. 137–160. Chicago: Chicago University Press.

Link, B.G., Andrews, H. and Cullen, F.T. (1992) The violent and illegal behaviour of mental patients reconsidered. *American Sociological Review*, 57, 275–292.

Link, B.G., Stueve, A. and Phelan, J. (1998) Psychotic symptoms and violent behaviours: probing the components of "threat/control-override" symptoms. *Social Psychiatry and Psychiatric Epidemiology*, 22, S55–S60.

McNiel, D., Eisner, J.P. and Binder, R.L. (2003) The relationship between aggressive attributional style and violence by psychiatric patients. *Journal of Consulting and Clinical Psychology*, 71, 399–403.

Mojtabai, R. (2006) Psychotic-like experiences and interpersonal violence in the general population. *Social Psychiatry and Psychiatric Epidemiology*, 41, 183–190.

Monahan, J. and Steadman, H.J. (1983) Crime and mental disorder: an epidemiological approach. In Tonry, M. and Morris, N. (eds), *Crime and Justice: An Annual Review of Research*. Chicago: Chicago University Press.

Murphy, D. (1998) Theory of mind in a sample of men with schizophrenia detained in a special hospital: its relationship to symptom profiles and neuropsychological tests. *Criminal Behaviour and Mental Health*, 8, 13–26.

Nordstrom, A. and Kullgren, G. (2003) Victim relations and victim gender in violent crimes committed by offenders with schizophrenia. *Social Psychiatry and Psychiatric Epidemiology*, 38, 326–330.

O'Kane, A. and Bentall, R. (2000) Psychosis and offending. In: McGuire J., Mason, T. and O'Kane, A. (eds), *Behaviour, Crime and Legal Processes*, pp. 161–176. New York: Wiley.

Raine, A., Brennan, P. and Mednick, S. (1994) Birth complications combined with early maternal rejection at age 1 year predispose to violent crime at age 18 years. *Archives of General Psychiatry*, 51, 984–988.

Raine, A., Brennan, P. and Mednick, S. (1997) Interaction between birth complications and early maternal rejection in predisposing individuals to adult violence: specificity to serious, early-onset violence. *American Journal of Psychiatry*, 154, 1265–1271.

Rogers, R., Gillis, J., Turner, E.R. and Frise-Smith, T. (1990) The clinical presentation of command hallucinations in a forensic population. *American Journal of Psychiatry*, 147, 1304–1307.

Silver, H., Goodman, C., Knoll, G., Isakov, V. and Modai, I. (2005) Schizophrenia patients with a history of severe violence differ from non-violent schizophrenia patients in perception of emotions but not cognitive function. *Journal of Clinical Psychiatry*, 66, 300–308.

Smith, P. and Waterman, M. (2003) Processing bias for aggression words in forensic and nonforensic samples. *Cognition and Emotion*, 17, 681–701.

Staznickas, K., McNiel, D. and Binder, R. (1993) Violence towards family caregivers by mentally ill relatives. *Hospital and Community Psychiatry*, 44, 385–387.

Stompe, T., Ortwein-Swoboda, G. and Schanda, H. (2004) Schizophrenia, delusional symptoms and violence: The threat/control over-ride concept re-examined. *Schizophrenia Bulletin*, 30, 31–44.

Swanson, J,W., Holzer, C.E.III, Ganju, V.K. *et al.* (1990) Violence and psychiatric disorder in the community: evidence from the Epidemiologic Catchment Area surveys. *Hospital and Community Psychiatry*, 41, 761–770.

Swanson, J.W., Swartz, M.E., Essock, S.M. *et al.* (2002) The social–environmental context of violent behaviour in persons treated for severe mental illness. *American Journal of Public Health*, 92, 1523–1531.

Taylor, P. (1993) Schizophrenia and crime: distinctive patterns in association. In Hodgins, S. (ed.), *Crime and Mental Disorder*. Newbury Park, CA: Sage.

Taylor, P. (1998) When symptoms of psychosis drive serious violence. *Social Psychiatry and Psychiatric Epidemiology*, 33, S47–54.

Tiihonen, J., Isohanni, M., Rasanen, P., Koiranen, M. and Moring, J. (1997) Specific major mental disorders and criminality: a 26-year prospective study of the 1966 northern Finland birth cohort. *American Journal of Psychiatry*, 154, 840–845.

Walsh, E., Buchanan, A. and Fahy, T. (2002) Violence and schizophrenia: examining the evidence. *British Journal of Psychiatry*, 180, 490–495.

Yesavage, J.A., Becker, J.M.T., Werner, P.D. *et al.* (1983) Family conflict, psychopathology, and dangerous behaviour by schizophrenic inpatients. *Psychiatry Research*, 8, 271–280.

Chapter 6

Aspects of persecutory delusions in the setting of delusional disorder

Alistair Munro

Introduction

Many practical difficulties beset research on delusions, including the recruitment of suitable participants. This chapter deals with aspects of the clinical situation which may be relevant to investigators and it addresses four topics:

1 The importance of surrounding clinical features in determining whether or not an abnormal belief is delusional.

2 Consideration of the diagnostic approach to delusional disorder in the clinical setting.

3 Difficulties in studying delusions because of rapid treatment interventions.

4 A proposal that delusional disorder (formerly paranoia) be utilized for its suitability in studies on delusions.

My interest in delusional disorder began with observations on individuals with encapsulated hypochondriacal delusions and gradually extended to monodelusional illnesses with other contents, including delusions of persecution.

Delusions are cited both by the *DSM-IV-TR* (American Psychiatric Association 2000) and *ICD-10* (World Health Organization 1993) as one of the symptoms most indicative of schizophrenia and delusional disorder; although delusions are also found in organic mental disorders, psychoactive substance-induced mental disorders and withdrawal disorders, and severe mood disorders.

It is usually assumed by psychiatrists that delusions are qualitatively different from normal beliefs with an all-or-nothing nature, and the *DSM-IV-TR* definition of delusion largely encourages this viewpoint. However, the manual goes on to say that it is often difficult to distinguish between a delusion and an overvalued idea, which implies a less black-and-white concept of delusion and it uses the phrase occurring 'on a continuum', suggesting that there is no sharp division between delusional and non-delusional thinking.

DSM-IV-TR also states that delusions are sometimes inferred from the individual's behaviour and certainly clinicians often decide on the delusionality of an idea by taking into account symptoms that lie outside the idea itself.

In studies on delusions, inconsistency of definition is widespread. Experts point to difficulties in conceptualization (Butler and Braff 1991), heterogeneity of data (Flint 1991) and fallibility of criteria (Garety and Hemsley 1994). It is still impossible to characterize delusions so as to align them with specific mental illnesses (Butler and Braff 1991), and this is made even more difficult by ongoing changes in diagnostic concepts and nomenclature.

Many psychiatrists still pay lip-service to the psychopathological theories of Jaspers (1883–1969) when they formulate their findings on delusions. In fact, in present-day circumstances his descriptions of autochthonous delusion, differences between primary and secondary delusions, and delusional perceptions (Jaspers 1963) are of little current value in research or practice because they rely on outmoded theory and on observation greatly influenced by personal ideology. The one concept of Jaspers which has actually gained in relevance is that of delusional memory, where the individual claims to remember something which never happened and will attest to it with profound conviction. Especially in the legal field this can cause serious problems.

It should be noted that the specific content of a delusion is not part of the primary definition but is an important associated phenomenon which largely determines how the delusion will be expressed. Of course the content of some delusions is relatively characteristic such as the nihilistic beliefs of the severe depressive, but it is not pathognomonic. The expression of unfounded persecutory ideas is not, of itself, evidence of delusion but when an accumulation of evidence suggests that persecutory delusions are present then the presence of a mental illness is virtually certain and the existence of the delusion aids in deciding the type of the illness.

The clinical recognition of delusions

Despite unsatisfactory definitions of both delusions and of mental illness the clinician must have reasonable working criteria and must be able to relate the presence of delusions to a substantive diagnostic formulation. When a patient expresses a belief that is unusual enough to be regarded as delusional we try to confirm the delusionality by considering the usually accepted core features of delusion (Jaspers 1963; Mullen 1979):

1 The belief is held with extraordinary conviction.
2 It is associated with excessive subjective certainty.

3　It is maintained against contrary experience or convincing argument.

4　The content is unlikely and may even be fantastic.

5　It is not shared by others from a similar background (but see 'Shared delusional disorder' below).

6　It is confirmed by a knowledgeable observer to be qualitatively different from the individual's usual beliefs (such corroborative evidence is of the essence).

These factors, though highly suggestive of delusion, are often not conclusive. Thus, in clinical work we seek out accompanying features, an accumulation of which will make the presence of delusion increasingly likely. These additional features include:

(a)　There is an accompanying mental illness of psychotic intensity.

(b)　The way of life is altered to an unconscionable degree.

(c)　Despite the profound conviction there is often an air of evasiveness and suspicion when details are sought.

(d)　There is a quality of 'centrality'; no matter how unlikely it is that such strange experiences are happening to this person, he/she accepts them more-or-less unquestioningly.

(e)　The individual is guarded and oversensitive about the belief.

(f)　Emotional overinvestment in the idea overshadows other aspects of the psyche.

(g)　There may be abnormal behaviours which are out of character though perhaps explainable in light of the delusion. These behaviours sometimes include violence.

(h)　Other associated elements include eccentricity, hauteur and grandiosity as well as hallucinations, thought disorder and abnormal mood. Tension and over-alerting are common though apathy may be present in chronic cases.

With information from these two lists, the clinician should be able to make a reasonable estimate as to the presence or not of delusion and should be well on the way to diagnosing a particular syndrome. Nowadays, in cases in a therapeutic setting, treatment will rapidly ensue.

Delusional disorder: a description

It is possible to study delusions in any of the mental disorders in which they occur, schizophrenia being the favourite, but it is always difficult to tease out the delusional features from the mass of other psychopathology.

In delusional disorder the central abnormality is a delusional belief which stands out in relief from the illness's other features and the individual is usually very able to articulate this belief, with justifications that are illogical but not confused. Hence it is easier to study the delusion in relative isolation.

Delusional disorder was conceptualized in its present form when *DSM-III-R* was published (American Psychiatric Association 1987) but in fact this was largely a re-statement of the work of Emil Kraepelin (1856–1926) who, in successive editions of his *Textbook of Psychiatry*, refined a description of para-noia, clearly differentiating it from schizophrenia and showing that it had subtypes characterized by their predominating delusional content. He also emphasized the relative sparing of the surrounding personality. The modern transition from 'paranoia' to 'delusional disorder' was therefore largely one of name.

Kendler (1982) believed that 'The paranoid disorders may be the third great group of functional psychoses, along with affective disorder and schizophrenia'. Since *DSM-III-R* re-conceptualized 'paranoia' as 'delusional disorder' the illness has gained greater recognition but still remains a somewhat elusive concept to many investigators and clinicians unfamiliar with its characteristics.

Features of the illness

Delusional disorder is a psychotic illness that does not satisfy the principal criteria for schizophrenia and its features are as follows (Munro 1999):

1 It is not secondary to another psychiatric condition (though a background history of alcohol- or substance abuse and/or head-injury is relatively common and in some cases the aging brain may be a factor).

2 It is a stable disorder characterized by delusions to which the patient clings tenaciously.

3 The illness occurs in clear consciousness, with heightened self-awareness.

4 It is chronic and, without treatment, probably lifelong.

5 The delusions are internally consistent and appear superficially logical but there is usually some degree of bizarreness in the belief itself or in the way it is presented.

6 There is a predominant, persistent theme to the delusion though in some cases more than one theme may be intertwined (e.g. delusions of persecu-tion and jealousy).

7 The content of the delusion differs from patient to patient but a small number of themes predominates, namely, persecution, hypochondriasis, jealousy, erotomania and grandiosity (possibly also misidentification).

8 The delusions interfere relatively little with general logical reasoning but within the delusional system logic is perverted. There is no general

disintegration of behaviour: if overtly disturbed behaviour does occur it is directly related to the delusional beliefs.

9 It is usual to say that many cases arise in the setting of a markedly abnormal personality but this is uncertain because the onset of the illness is often insidious and early symptoms may be mild enough to be mistaken for aberrant personality features.

10 Hallucinations may or may not be present but are usually non-prominent.

11 The individual has a heightened sense of self-reference. Events which appear trivial to others are of great significance to him/her and the atmosphere surrounding the delusions is emotionally highly charged.

12 The delusional system is 'encapsulated', sparing much of the rest of the personality: despite this the patient's way of life typically is driven by the dominating influence of the abnormal beliefs.

13 A unique feature of the illness is that many patients alternate between delusional and relatively normal 'modes' of thought and behaviour, the shift sometimes occurring quite sharply. In the delusional mode the individual is over-alerted, preoccupied with delusional ideas, appears emotionally driven and is scornful of argument or attempted intervention. Conversely, in the normal mode there is relatively calm mood, reasonable range of affect, some interest in everyday topics and some ability to pursue normal activities. If one encounters the person in this latter state it is quite easy to be misled about the seriousness of the illness, which emphasizes the need for longitudinal observation in the diagnostic process.

14 Despite the illogicality of the delusional beliefs, many patients with delusional disorder are capable of intense focusing of attention and since they are constantly rehearsing these beliefs they can present them with vehemence, so much so that others are quite likely to believe them.

15 Males and females are probably equally liable to develop the illness but there seems to be a tendency for the illness to occur earlier in males (Munro 1982). Contrary to given wisdom it is not confined to middle and old age and cases can arise in adolescence and early adulthood.

Delusional content in delusional disorder

As already noted there seems to be a relatively limited repertoire of contents, one of the most prominent being the theme of persecution. It is important to note that, whatever the theme, the form of the illness is remarkably similar from one case to another and, so far as is known, the basic treatment is the same for all.

Nevertheless the content of the delusion will largely determine the path by which individuals come to official notice. For example, persecutory delusions lead the person to complain unreasonably to the authorities or to get into brushes with the law if socially unacceptable views are aired or if some form of 'retaliation' is carried out. Hypochondriacal delusions usually lead to over-attendance at medical or surgical (but rarely psychiatric) clinics. Jealousy may provoke assault and even murder and erotomania may result in stalking of victims and consequently police involvement.

Persecutory delusional presentations in delusional disorder

The archetype of paranoia/delusional disorder is the individual who is convinced that he or she is being persecuted or harmed, sometimes by 'them' but often with very specific attributions against persons or organizations. Many people believe that this is the commonest form of delusional disorder, so one might expect an extensive psychiatric literature on the topic. Indeed it forms the basis of psychoanalytic theories on the origin of paranoia but these have not led to worthwhile systematic investigation. Attributions in the psychiatric literature are conjectural and largely relate to anecdotal case analyses. Even Jaspers (1963), despite his longstanding reputation in the field, has failed to pass on much of relevance to present-day practice.

Currently the neo-Kraepelinian descriptions of delusional disorder in *DSM-IV* and *ICD-10* are the accepted benchmarks for diagnosing all the variants of delusional disorder, though neither system presents a very nuanced picture of the illness. Thus an individual with delusional disorder, persecutory sub-type, would by definition have a chronic and unremitting illness characterized by an encapsulated delusional system and a relatively well-preserved personality. The persecutory beliefs are often well-formulated and the complaints made with clarity and extraordinary persistence. 'Evidence' is cited to support the complaints and there may be voluminous writings and collections of articles from journals, etc., but when attempts are made to establish verifiable facts there is evasiveness and promises to produce supportive data which never materialize.

The persecutory beliefs are associated with querulousness and anger, often underlaid by considerable fear and anxiety. Acting out of the delusion may consist of public accusations against a supposed persecutor, harassing telephone calls, carrying defamatory placards or seeking recourse through the legal system (see below). There is usually an overbearing refusal to enter into reasonable negotiations and the campaign is waged far beyond any reasonable limits.

Even in the face of restrictions or punishment there is no let-up. In some cases (probably a relatively small minority) assaultive and even homicidal behaviours may occur, often on an ascending scale. Usually the motivation for violence is the belief that it is pre-empting assault against himself or else there is a desire for revenge.

The presence of persecutory delusions makes the sufferer pathologically wary: at the same time there is total denial that psychiatric illness could possibly be at the root of his problems. Naturally this makes engagement with helping agencies very difficult and often means that no-one is truly aware of the severity of the illness or its degree of escalation. To make matters worse the individual will often incorporate into his delusional system people who are trying to help (Cameron 1959) including therapists, social workers and members of the legal profession. Psychiatrists and psychologists are especially at risk here, especially if they have been involved in a patient's involuntary commitment to an institution. It is essential to avoid confrontation, which is difficult in the face of highly provocative behaviour. It is also vital that each transaction with the person be carefully documented at the time so that false recollections and accusations can later be refuted.

Litigious paranoid states

There is an important variant of delusional disorder, persecutory subtype, known by a variety of terms such as querulous paranoia, litigious delusional state, etc. Here we see people who have a profound and unremitting sense of having been wronged and endlessly seek redress through the legal system (Goldstein 1995). Not all overly persistent litigants have delusional disorder (Lester *et al.* 2004) but those who do are a particular thorn in the side of the court system because they present their cases in a quasi-rational manner, with great intensity and perseverance, and will never accept a decision which does not totally accord with their demands. Even if they do achieve satisfaction the process usually begins again, perhaps on a slightly different tack.

These individuals take up an inordinate amount of legal time (Goldstein 1995) and British, Canadian and American courts do not have a satisfactory method of short-circuiting the unreasonable client. As Astrup (1984) has noted, some relatively high-functioning individuals with psychosis can pursue their disruptive activities for long periods without the law perceiving them as ill. On the other hand, in Scandinavia and Germany there is a legal 'diagnosis' of 'querulent paranoia' which, once made, allows a judge to divert cases to more appropriate avenues of help.

Freckelton (1988) has given several pointers to early recognition of deluded litigants as follows:

1 A determination to succeed against all odds.

2 A ready tendency to identify barriers as conspiracies.

3 An endless crusading spirit to right a wrong (sometimes the original wrong being real).

4 A driven quality, getting 'agonising' pleasure from pursuing the cause.

5 Unsociability and quarrelsomeness.

6 The 'blunderbuss' or 'scatter-gun' approach, saturating the field with multiple complaints.

7 Suspiciousness in interviews.

These individuals readily fall out with their lawyers, summarily dismissing them and refusing to pay their fees, and threatening to complain to higher authority (which they often do). If thwarted they may resort to unpleasant harassment of witnesses or authority. They become expert at exploiting loopholes in rules of procedure and will pursue cases far beyond the bounds of reasonableness, not uncommonly losing sight of the original motivation.

Shared delusional disorder (*folie á deux*)

It is not uncommon for persons with persecutory delusions (including the litigious group just described) to produce corroborative witnesses to their complaints and sometimes the persuasiveness of the latter may convince observers that the beliefs are true, despite all commonsense evidence to the contrary. It is here that one must be aware of the phenomenon of shared delusional disorder in which a deluded individual imposes his/her abnormal belief on another person (or persons) who accepts it unreservedly as true. The two people are usually closely associated, especially spouses, siblings or parent–child, but can include colleagues at work and religious congregations. The second person (s) is usually not psychotic but is highly impressionable and the effect is exaggerated if the two people are socially isolated (Silveira and Seeman 1995).

Folie á deux (the older term) in relation to delusions of persecution is well documented (Fernando and Frieze 1985; Kendler *et al*. 1986; Brooks 1987), and Myers (1988) has described the phenomenon of shared delusional beliefs in a cult setting where large numbers of individuals accept the delusions of a disturbed but charismatic leader.

It is important to be aware of shared delusional disorder in assessing the apparently delusional case. It can be extremely perplexing when, for example, a close relative confirms the unlikeliest complaints of harassment in a seemingly rational way. Failure to diagnose folie á deux can lead to a total misunderstanding of the true situation.

Separation of the two people, as when the patient is committed to prison or admitted to hospital, makes little difference to the deluded person's beliefs and may aggravate their expression. On the other hand, removal from the source often produces a gradual waning of the abnormal beliefs in the other individual.

Aetiological factors and treatment

Despite an increasing volume of relevant research we are still unable to pin-point the underlying pathognomic factors which lead to delusions or to delusional disorder. The latter seems to have much less of a genetic background than schizophrenia (Farmer et al. 1987) and, as previously mentioned, there is evidence that a past history of alcohol or substance abuse and/or brain impairment may act as provocative factors. Since the illness appears to respond best to antidopaminergic agents a case has been made for overactivity in brain dopaminergic systems in its origins (Munro and Mok 1994)

Since our knowledge of aetiology in delusional disorder is so sparse, treatment has to be by analogy to that of other psychotic disorders. There seems no doubt that cognitive/behavioural approaches have a role in modifying delusional beliefs and diminishing their associated distress and over-alerting (Jakes et al. 1999; Birchwood and Trower 2006).

In the psychiatric treatment of delusional disorder, theory has largely been abandoned and delusions are expected to respond to the present-day treatment of functional psychoses. Empirical evidence suggests that neuroleptic drugs can be effective in delusional disorder, some more than others (Munro and Mok 1994; Manschreck et al. 2006).

An unfortunate canard exists that delusional disorder is essentially untreatable and that the patients cannot be engaged in meaningful therapy. In fact, if patients can be persuaded to accept appropriate drug treatment it can be shown that approximately half will markedly improve with a lesser degree of improvement in 50% of the remainder (Munro 1982). What is more, failure to respond is often found to be related to non-compliance and/or inadequate treatment.

Because many individuals with delusional disorder are sufficiently well-retained to stay in the community they can continue to express their delusions while refusing all offers of help, unless that help exactly matches their unreasonable demands. Often it is only when a crisis occurs, when someone is brought before the law for uttering threats, behaving in an outrageous way, committing assault, attempting suicide, etc., that he or she can be brought within the legal or medical systems and an adequate mental assessment be carried out.

Once there, many continue to resist help, often because the situation, especially the forensic one, is inherently confrontational. If a potential caregiver can adopt a low-key, non-provocative approach, in a proportion of cases there is gradual reduction of hostility and an acceptance of help and even treatment. Several contact sessions are usually necessary to establish some basic trust and rapport, during which the person will use every kind of sophistry to avoid treatment while, strangely enough, not always refusing psychological—as opposed to psychiatric—assessment.

If the patient does accept a neuroleptic, the drug has to be started in very low dosage to avoid inadvertent side-effects which are likely to be incorporated into the delusional beliefs. If the individual is faithfully taking his medication there is often a reduction of over-alerting and anxiety in a few days and, as the dose is optimized, the intensity of the delusion is likely to fade over the next several weeks, though a fuller degree of recovery may take months.

At this point many patients insist on stopping the drug because they feel better, though most will deny that this indicates any kind of relief from illness. Within a relatively short time the symptoms and the severe tension return; if good supervision has been maintained it is now much easier to persuade the person to resume the medication. Then a maintenance dosage is established and the patient should continue on this indefinitely. Subsequently many of them learn that cheating on their treatment leads to fairly rapid return of severe anxiety and, even worse, this has a strong behavioural effect in promoting co-operativeness. Even at this point many continue to deny that they had a psychiatric illness, but some do achieve a measure of insight.

Strikingly, some of the successfully treated sufferers return to a surprisingly normal lifestyle and from being recalcitrant non-cooperators become pleasant and compliant patients. This contradicts the stereotype that delusional disorder usually arises in a setting of severe personality disorder.

Implications for research

Delusional disorder may have some inherent advantages for the investigation of delusional features, namely:

1 Because the basic personality is well-preserved, delusional disorder presents a 'purer' picture than do many other psychoses, with its delusions standing out from a surrounding confusion of psychopathology.

2   Those individuals who refuse treatment while within the legal or medical systems provide an opportunity—if co-operation is obtained—to observe delusions which are not being rapidly modified by neuroleptics.

3   If the individual does accept treatment it is possible to observe a relatively quick normalization of thinking and behaviour with possibilities for serial measurement.

4   Since many patients/clients renege at least once during treatment this gives the chance to observe the process of relapse as well as, one hopes, subsequent re-recovery.

5   Even if the person refuses treatment, as previously noted he/she can alternate between a delusional and a normal 'mode'. This presents the intriguing opportunity to observe subject and control within the same individual.

6   There should be very considerable scope for simultaneous psychological and physiological studies in observing the alternating modes, something which has largely been ignored until now.

Obtaining experimental participants

Any of the delusional disorders, and especially the persecutory subtype, should be an attractive field of research but how does one set about collecting participants and persuading them to collaborate? In this author's experience the question of source is fairly easily answered if one establishes good rapport with a system that deals with relatively large numbers of cases of delusional disorder. For example, if a psychiatrist informs colleagues in certain physical specialties that one is interested in patients with delusional hypochondriasis, a steady flow of them will result.

Similarly, if one presents criteria to police, criminal lawyers, community workers, parole officers, etc., indicating an interest in cases of persecutory preoccupation, querulent litigiousness or stalking carried out by psychotic individuals, there will be no shortage of referrals, especially if the possibility of a treatment element is held out.

And, of course, in research within a forensic setting the investigator may have an enhanced opportunity to carry out longitudinal studies.

Conclusion

The researcher will have to accept that it is impossible to see the great majority of cases of delusional disorder which go unrecognized in the community because the individuals have sufficient self-control to avoid detection. This makes generalized epidemiological studies of this illness impossible to carry out.

Even when cases are identified, the investigator who approaches them will meet with scornful rejection in a considerable proportion and it will demand tact, compassion and persistence to persuade most of the remainder to co-operate. In this author's experience the effort is well worthwhile.

We need much more information on the general and group characteristics of delusional disorder, but it should be stressed once more that this illness has the fascinating potential for observation of normative and pathological data within the same participant and to observe that participant in various phases of recovery and relapse. Thus the vexed question of finding suitable control material is virtually by-passed. And, as the study of the brain increases in sophistication—as is already happening—delusional disorder could well provide a quite unique opportunity to match psychological with psychobiological findings, perhaps allowing us at last to achieve the goal of verifiable data in the field of delusions and delusional illnesses.

References

American Psychiatric Association (1987) Delusional (paranoid) disorder. In: *Diagnostic and Statistical Manual of Mental Disorders*, 3rd edition, revised (*DSM-III-R*), pp. 199–203. Washington, DC: American Psychiatric Association.

American Psychiatric Association (2000) *Diagnostic and Statistical Manual of Mental Disorders*, 4th edn, text revision (*DSM-IV-TR*), pp. 323–328. Washington, DC: American Psychiatric Association.

Astrup, C. (1984) Querulent paranoia: a follow-up. *Neuropsychobiology*, 11, 149–154.

Birchwood, M. and Trower, P. (2006) The future of cognitive-behavioural therapy for psychosis: not a quasi-neuroleptic. *British Journal of Psychiatry*, 188, 107–108.

Brooks, S. (1987) Folie á deux in the aged: variations in psychopathology. *Canadian Journal of Psychiatry*, 32, 61–63.

Butler, R.W. and Braff, D.L. (1991) Delusions: a review and integration. *Schizophrenia Bulletin*, 17, 633–647.

Cameron, N. (1959) The paranoid pseudocommunity revisited. *American Journal of Sociology*, 65, 57–61.

Farmer, A.E., McGuffin, P. and Gottesmann, I.I. (1987) Searching for the split in schizophrenia: a twin perspective. *Psychiatric Research*, 13, 109–118.

Fernando, F.P. and Frieze, M. (1985) A relapsing folie à trois. *British Journal of Psychiatry*, 146, 315–324.

Flint, A.J. (1991) Delusions in dementia: a review. *Neuropsychiatry and Clinical Neurosciences*, 3, 121–130.

Freckelton, I. (1988) Querulent paranoia and the vexatious complainant. *International Journal of Law and Psychiatry*, 11, 127–143.

Garety, P.A. and Hemsley, D.R. (1994) Theories of the formation and maintenance of delusions. In *Delusions: Investigations into the Psychology of Delusional Reasoning*. Maudsley Monograph No. 36, pp. 67–85, Oxford: Oxford University Press.

Goldstein, R.L. (1995) Paranoids in the legal system: the litigious paranoid and the paranoid criminal. *Psychiatric Clinics of North America*, 18, 303–315.

Jakes, S., Rhodes, J. and Turner, T. (1999) Effectiveness of cognitive therapy for delusions in routine clinical practice. *British Journal of Psychiatry*, 175, 331–335.

Jaspers, K. (1963) Individual performances. In: Hoenig, J. and Hamilton, M. (transl.), *General Psychopathology*, pp. 168–198. Manchester: Manchester University Press.

Kendler, K.S. (1982) Demography of paranoid psychosis (delusional disorder): a review and comparison with schizophrenia and affective illness. *Archives of General Psychiatry*, 39, 890–902.

Kendler, K.S., Robinson, G., McGuire, M. and Spellman, M.P. (1986) Late-onset folie simultanèe in a pair of monozygotic twins. *British Journal of Psychiatry*, 148, 463–465.

Lester, G., Wilson, B., Griffin, I. and Mullen, P.E. (2004) Unusally persistent complaints. *British Journal of Psychiatry*, 184, 352–356.

Manschreck, T.C. Khan, N.L. and Corrigan, J.C. (2006) Recent advances in the treatment of delusional disorder. *Canadian Journal of Psychiatry*, 51, 114–119.

Mullen, P. (1979) Phenomenology of disordered mental function. In Hill, P., Murray, R. and Thorley, G. (eds), *Essentials of Postgraduate Psychiatry*, pp. 25–54. London: Academic Press.

Munro, A. (1982) The Findings (Chapter 15). In: *Delusional Hypochondriasis*, pp. 210–229. Toronto: Clarke Institute of Psychiatry Monograph Series No. 5.

Munro, A. (1999) Descriptive and clinical aspects of paranoia/delusional disorder. In: *Delusional Disorder: Paranoia and Related Illnesses*, pp. 43–70. Cambridge: Cambridge University Press.

Munro, A. and Mok, H. (1995) An overview of treatment in paranoia/delusional disorder. *Canadian Journal of Psychiatry*, 40, 616–622.

Myers, P.L. (1988) Paranoid pseudocommunity beliefs in a sect milieu. *Social Psychiatry and Psychiatric Epidemiology*, 23, 252–255.

Silveira, J.M. and Seeman, M.V. (1995) Shared psychotic disorder: a critical review of the literature. *Canadian Journal of Psychiatry*, 40, 389–395.

World Health Organization (1993) *International Statistical Classification of Mental and Behavioural Disorders*, 10th edn (*ICD-10*), Diagnostic criteria for research, Delusional disorder, p. 70. Geneva: World Health Organization.

Part 3

Psychological processes

Chapter 7

The puzzle of paranoia

Daniel Freeman, Philippa Garety, and
David Fowler

You can look at a piece of a puzzle for three whole
days, you can believe that you know all there is to
know about its colouring and shape, and be no
further on than when you started. The only thing
that counts is the ability to link this piece to other
pieces. The pieces are readable, take on a sense, only
when assembled; in isolation, a puzzle piece means
nothing—just an impossible question, an opaque
challenge.

G. Perec (1978), p. xv

Introduction

The first commercial jigsaw puzzle, created in the eighteenth century, was of a map of the world. There is no such guide picture for helping to understand paranoid experience. Therefore we will begin this chapter by describing the puzzle that needs to be solved. Then we will lay out the pieces which have been found so far. Implicit in this approach is the idea that paranoid thinking needs to be understood in terms of multiple factors. No single cause of paranoia will be found. Our initial attempt to assemble the pieces—the 'threat anticipation cognitive model'—will be presented. However, this model only identifies the corner pieces of the puzzle, at best. We therefore also outline potential pieces worthy of inspection, promising methodologies, and key questions to guide future research.

The complexity of the paranoid picture

Delusional experience is clearly multi-dimensional. This has been learned from debates on defining delusions (e.g. Strauss 1969; Garety 1985; Oltmanns 1988), factor analytic studies of patients' experiences (e.g. Kendler *et al.* 1983; Harrow *et al.* 1988; Garety *et al.* 1988), and evidence that response to treatment varies across the different dimensions (e.g. Trower *et al.* 2004; Mizrahi *et al.* 2006). Key dimensions include level of belief conviction, degree of preoccupation, and extent of distress. The important implication is that multiple questions should be asked about paranoid experience: what causes thoughts of an unfounded paranoid content, when does a paranoid thought capture a person's attention, what causes the thought to become held as a belief, why does resistance to change occur, how does the thought become distressing, and why does it impact on day-to-day life? Many of these questions may sub-divide when brought into focus. For example, persecutory thinking contains two key elements: the individual believes that harm is occurring, or is going to occur, to him or her, and that the persecutor has the intention to cause harm (Freeman and Garety 2000). Therefore it is reasonable to ask: are there separate processes involved in the development of ideas about threat and of ideas about others' intentions? In other words, how does an anxious thought turn into a paranoid thought? But it is also important to stand back from the detail and view the wider picture. The most striking findings here are the relatively high frequency in the general population of paranoid thoughts and their continuous distribution across the population (e.g. van Os *et al.* 2000; Freeman *et al.* 2005a). This raises two questions: what is the function of paranoid thought and what is the relationship between clinically severe and non-clinical everyday paranoid experience? The number of questions listed illustrates the complexity of the paranoid picture and points towards the likelihood that multiple factors will be invoked in answering them.

(Some of the) pieces of the puzzle: psychological factors and persecutory ideation

The recent psychological approaches to paranoia make plausible connections to the experiences reported by patients. The explanations often have face validity. This is a helpful step before empirical testing. We highlight the plausible factors that have research evidence to support them. For a detailed review of this literature see Freeman (2007). There are caveats to keep in mind: the psychological processes have not been evaluated equally; some factors have been investigated in relation to delusions in general rather than persecutory ideation specifically; and most studies do not control for the common co-occurrence of symptoms found in clinical settings (Maric *et al.* 2004) so that spurious associations with paranoia might have been found.

Anxiety

Our contention has been that a key piece of the puzzle is anxiety, since paranoia concerns fear. Persecutory and anxious thoughts both concern the anticipation of threat; fears of physical, social or psychological harm are apparent both in anxious thoughts (e.g. Eysenck and van Berkum 1992; Wells 1994) and in persecutory thoughts (Freeman and Garety 2000; Freeman *et al.* 2001). It is argued that anxiety helps to create thoughts of a paranoid content. Anxiety has repeatedly been found to be associated with paranoid thoughts (e.g. Martin and Penn 2001; Johns *et al.* 2004) and persecutory delusions (e.g. Freeman and Garety 1999; Startup *et al.* 2007) and it is predictive of the occurrence of paranoid thoughts (Freeman *et al.* 2003, 2005b, 2008; Valmaggia *et al.* 2007) and of the persistence of persecutory delusions (Startup *et al.* 2007). Moreover, it has been shown in non-clinical groups that paranoid thoughts build upon common interpersonal anxieties and worries such as fears of rejection (e.g. Freeman *et al.* 2005a,b). Anxiety is apparent in many patient accounts, for example, Kristen Fowler's (2007) description of the early stages of her psychosis: 'In darkened spaces, I feel a presence is lurking; I fear that it is watching me. I don't like to think about what it might be, but I think it's something dead, something that is alive and yet shouldn't be alive. Something silent, stealthy, evil, made of bones, or bloody, decaying body parts. I am terrified to look in the closets, or behind doors, or in the garage. I am constantly turning my head to look behind me. Even a familiar sound such as the cat jumping off the counter startles me. My heart pounds while the water sprays over me in the shower, for fear that my eyes might be closed or my back turned and my body vulnerable as something advances toward me.'

Paranoid thinking and anxiety-related *processes* have been linked. Initial evidence indicates that almost two-thirds of individuals with persecutory delusions have a thinking style characterized by worry (even about matters unrelated to paranoia) (Freeman and Garety 1999; Startup *et al.* 2007). Worry in individuals with paranoia is associated with more catastrophic delusion content, higher levels of distress and with delusion persistence. Worry is likely to be an important process in understanding paranoia (Freeman *et al.* in press). Other anxiety-related processes are also apparent in people with persecutory delusions. An example is safety behaviour (Freeman *et al.* 2001, 2007). Individuals who feel threatened often carry out actions designed to prevent their feared catastrophe from occurring; this has been termed 'safety behaviour' (Salkovskis 1991). When the perceived threat is a misperception, such as in anxiety disorders and paranoia, there are important consequences. Individuals fail to attribute the absence of catastrophe to the incorrectness of their threat beliefs. Rather, they believe that the threat was averted only by their safety behaviours (e.g. 'The reason I wasn't attacked was because I left the street in time and made it back home'). Conviction in threat beliefs is likely to persist partly due to this failure to obtain and process disconfirmatory evidence.

Negative beliefs about self and others

It is a reasonably common concern to have ideas that the self is weak, foolish, unloved, different or misunderstood. Paranoid thoughts may be an anxious extension of such ideas. Negative beliefs about the self may be a first step to thinking about being a vulnerable target for others to mock, exploit or harm. This may be especially likely when negative ideas about others are also held, for example, that people are generally bad, selfish, or devious. In what is likely to prove a key paper, Fowler *et al.* (2006a) found that in a non-clinical population of more than 700 students paranoia was associated with negative beliefs about the self, negative beliefs about others, less positive beliefs about others, and anxiety. Self-esteem as traditionally measured was not as good a predictor of paranoia and, unlike schematic beliefs, did not discriminate between the non-clinical group and a group of 250 patients with psychosis. A related study of 100 patients with psychosis found that the severity, preoccupation and distress of persecutory delusions were associated with negative beliefs about the self, negative beliefs about others, low self-esteem and depression (Smith *et al.* 2006). These findings are consistent with a wider literature indicating an association of affective problems with the positive symptoms of psychosis (e.g. Norman and Malla 1994; Guillem *et al.* 2005) and evidence that low self-esteem predicts the later development of positive symptoms of psychosis (Krabbendam *et al.* 2002). The view that paranoid thoughts build on conscious negative thoughts about the self is the opposite of delusion-as-defence accounts in which paranoid thoughts are believed to suppress unconscious low self-esteem.

Adverse events and trauma

An obvious potential factor is past experience: previous experience of negative intent from others is likely to mean that explanations concerning hostility are more forthcoming in the future. The unfortunate implication is that being bullied or victimized may bias towards the negative future interpretations of others' behaviour. There has been renewed interest in the topic of trauma and psychosis, following repeated reports of an association (e.g. Fowler 1997; Fowler *et al.* 2006b; Read *et al.* 2005; Larkin and Morrison 2006). For example, in the 2000 British National Survey of Psychiatric Morbidity of more than

8000 respondents, a history of victimization experiences was significantly associated with paranoid thoughts (Johns *et al.* 2004). In a survey of more than 10 000 Australians, all types of trauma, but especially rape, were associated with delusional ideation, and a dose–response relationship was found (i.e. those who had been exposed to a greater number of different types of trauma were more likely to report delusions) (Scott *et al.* 2007). In a cross-sectional study of 200 students, Gracie *et al.* (2007) found that a history of childhood trauma, sexual abuse or physical assault was associated with raised levels of paranoid thinking. Further, analysis indicated that negative beliefs about the self and others may be a mediating factor between traumatic reactions and paranoid thinking. Selten and Cantor-Graae (2005) argue, on the basis of findings of higher rates of psychosis in those brought up in urban areas and migrant groups, that chronic and long-term experience of 'social defeat' is a risk factor for schizophrenia. It seems plausible that negative past experience—via its affective impact—is a piece in the puzzle of understanding paranoid experience.

Puzzling experiences

Maher (1974, 1988) emphasizes that delusional ideas spring from unusual internal experiences. This is consistent with findings that many people with psychosis have clear anomalous experiences such as hallucinations, thought insertion, and replacement of will, and also a range of more subtle perceptual and attentional alterations in experience (e.g. McGhie and Chapman 1961; Bunney *et al.* 1999) and, often, periods of arousal (e.g. Docherty *et al.* 1978; Hemsley 1994). There are two key points here. The first point is that delusions are explanations of experiences, attempts by individuals to make sense of their experiences. The second point is that odd experiences may lead to odd ideas. Other theorists have speculated similarly. Kapur (2003) has highlighted the importance of aberrant feelings of salience in delusion formation, which is particularly of note since in this account the abnormal experience itself concerns processes of meaning ascription. A tradition in German psychiatry is to study anomalies of experience ('basic symptoms') for which 'delusions may provide new elaborative contexts to understand the dislocated or overly salient perceptual fragments' (Uhlhaas and Mishara 2007). Explanations for anomalies of experience include core cognitive dysfunction (e.g. Hemsley 1994), impairment in early stage sensory processing (e.g. Butler and Javitt 2005), illicit drug use (e.g. D'Souza *et al.* 2004), and hearing impairment (e.g. Zimbardo *et al.* 1981). In one study it has been found that predisposition to hallucinatory experience differentiated the prediction of paranoid from anxious thoughts (Freeman *et al.* 2005b).

Reasoning

If delusions are incorrect—or perhaps, more importantly, *uncorrected*—beliefs, then judgemental or reasoning processes are inherently implicated in their cause. A number of researchers have therefore tried to identify biases or deficits in reasoning in individuals with paranoia. The most convincing empirical evidence is that a significant proportion of individuals with delusions are hasty in their data-gathering ('jump to conclusions'), which is hypothesized to lead to the rapid acceptance of beliefs even if there is limited evidence to support them (e.g. Garety and Freeman 1999; Garety *et al.* 2005; van Dael *et al.* 2006; Fine *et al.* 2007). There is also evidence that the biases in reasoning may be much more subtle outside of acute delusional states (Freeman *et al.* 2005b; van Dael *et al.* 2006). Probabilistic reasoning has rarely been studied in relation to delusion sub-type. Only the limited conclusion can be made that jumping to conclusions is often present in people with persecutory delusions (Freeman 2007). In clinical groups there is also evidence that individuals with delusions have 'belief inflexibility', defined as difficulties in reflecting on one's own beliefs and to consider alternative ideas, which may lead to delusion persistence (Garety *et al.* 1997, 2005; Freeman *et al.* 2004). Interestingly, Chapman (2002) describes how he reversed such reasoning biases to quell his delusions: 'The belief stayed fixed until I researched and found sceptical debunking counterarguments and disconfirming evidence. Overcome by the stranglehold of delusions, I fought almost unceasingly for the troops of reality to save me. If reality was a door, I could say I knocked on it 10 000 times while I trembled in fear, unshielded from the barrage of imaginary horrors that surrounded me.'

Phenomenology

Frequently, when talking to patients, a richness in the content of their persecutory fears is obviously apparent. Some aspects of the situation seem to cause more distress than others. The basic cognitive model in which emotion is linked to beliefs provides an ideal way to understand this. Chadwick and Birchwood took such an approach to show that there are commonalities in the most distressing aspects of hallucinatory experience (e.g. Chadwick and Birchwood 1994; Birchwood *et al.* 2000). Following this work, we examined whether there were particular parts of the content of persecutory delusions that are most distressing (Freeman *et al.* 2001). Higher levels of depression were associated with higher ratings of the power of the persecutor, a lower sense of control over the situation, ideas about the inability to cope if the threat materialized, and believing that the persecution was deserved. There were indications that higher levels of anxiety may be associated with feeling

under constant threat and that there was no chance of rescue from the threatening situation. We postulated that prior emotional distress influences the
content of delusions and that delusion content in turn influences level of
emotional distress. Subsequent studies have confirmed content and distress
links in paranoid experiences (Chisholm *et al.* 2006; Green *et al.* 2006).
An alternative account of Trower and Chadwick's (1995) distinction between
'poor me' and 'bad me' paranoia is that the concept of deservedness is a
(dimensional) aspect of the content of paranoia associated with distress, but
not an indicator of discrete categories with opposite causes. It is also likely that
further reflection about what is happening—how people understand their
difficulties—influences the emotional reaction. There is an emerging and
important literature in which self-appraisals of illness/problems—concerning,
for example, cause, course, outcome, loss, entrapment, and humiliation—are
associated with levels of depression, anxiety and self-esteem in schizophrenia
(e.g. Rooke and Birchwood 1998; Lobban *et al.* 2003; Watson *et al.* 2006).

Pieces of other puzzles?

There are two psychological processes well-researched in regard to paranoia
that, in our view, have equivocal empirical support: attributional style and
'theory of mind' (ToM). Different evaluations of the literature are provided in
Chapters 8 and 10 of this book. We therefore describe the evidence base here
in a little more detail.

If a person tends to explain negative events in terms of other people (i.e. has
a particular attributional style) then this would certainly be a plausible factor
in the creation of paranoid thoughts. Most attribution studies have used either
the Attributional Style Questionnaire (ASQ) (Peterson *et al.* 1982) or the
Internal, Personal and Situational Attributions Questionnaire (IPSAQ)
(Kinderman and Bentall 1996a). Three ASQ studies (Lyon *et al.* 1994; Fear *et al.*
1996; Krstev *et al.* 1999) show clear evidence of an externalizing bias for negative events in people with persecutory delusions compared with non-clinical
controls and two ASQ studies find no differences between persecutory delusion and non-clinical control groups (Kinderman *et al.* 1992; Martin and Penn
2002). None of the four IPSAQ studies find evidence of an externalizing bias
for negative events in persecutory delusion groups compared with non-clinical
controls (Kinderman and Bentall 1996b; Martin and Penn 2002; Randall *et al.*
2003; McKay *et al.* 2005). In the first clinical study using the IPSAQ, Kinderman
and Bentall (1996b) found that, when external attributions were made,
individuals with persecutory delusions were more likely to make external–
personal attributions compared with non-clinical controls. However, in three
further clinical studies this has not been replicated (Martin and Penn 2002;

Randall *et al.* 2003; McKay *et al.* 2005). Therefore, the empirical case for persecutory delusions being associated with an excessive externalizing style for negative events is unconvincing at present. Attributional style may be more closely tied with affective state (see Jolley *et al.* 2006).

Individuals with persecutory ideation are by definition sometimes misreading the intentions of other people. Therefore Frith (1992, 2004) proposes that symptoms of schizophrenia develop from newly acquired difficulties in ToM abilities, the mechanism of determining others' mental state. Persecutory delusions are hypothesized to arise because the person notices that other peoples' actions have become opaque and surmises that a conspiracy exists. The empirical evidence indicates that ToM difficulties are apparent in people with a diagnosis of schizophrenia, but may be most severely present in individuals with negative symptoms and incoherent speech (Sarfati *et al.* 1997; Garety and Freeman 1999; Brüne 2005; Harrington *et al.* 2005a; Freeman 2007). Indeed, this association with negative symptoms may be expected from the neuropsychological literature; ToM tasks and executive functioning have been found to be linked in the developmental psychology literature (e.g. Hughes 2002) and executive functioning difficulties have been found to be associated with negative symptoms and thought disorder but not the positive symptoms of psychosis (e.g. O'Leary *et al.* 2000). Six studies have examined correlations with paranoid symptom assessments. Four found no association of paranoia and ToM abilities (Langdon *et al.* 1997, 2001; Blackshaw *et al.* 2001; Greig *et al.* 2004) and two studies did find an association (Craig *et al.* 2004; Harrington *et al.* 2005b). The study of Greig *et al.* (2004) is the largest study of ToM in schizophrenia and best addresses the question of ToM and psychotic symptoms. A sample of 128 outpatients with schizophrenia were assessed on the ability to understand hints. It was found that ToM performance was associated with thought disorder. An interesting study by McCabe *et al.* (2004) also merits note. They argue that if ToM difficulties are present in individuals with schizophrenia then they should be detectable in real-life social interactions. These researchers found that outpatients with positive and negative symptoms of schizophrenia actually showed intact ToM skills in conversations with mental health professions.

The threat anticipation model of persecutory delusions

The pieces of the puzzle that we judge important to the psychological understanding of persecutory ideation are: *anomalous experiences*, such as hallucinations and perceptual anomalies, which may be caused by core cognitive dysfunction and street drug use; *affective processes*, especially anxiety, worry, and interpersonal sensitivity; *reasoning biases*, particularly jumping to conclusions, and belief inflexibility; and *social factors*, such as adverse events and environments. These have been assembled into the threat anticipation model of paranoia (Fowler 2000; Garety *et al.* 2001; Freeman *et al.* 2002; Freeman and Garety 2004; Freeman 2007; Freeman and Freeman 2008). The model is explicitly built on the idea that there are multiple factors responsible for the development and maintenance of paranoia. Further, the model addresses the multi-dimensional nature of persecutory experience, highlighting specific factors for the development of delusion content, conviction, persistence, and distress (see Figures 7.1 and 7.2).

Delusion formation

Following the influential work of Maher (1974), delusional beliefs are considered as explanations of experience. The sorts of experiences considered as the proximal source of evidence for persecutory delusions are:

- Internal feelings. Unusual or anomalous experiences are frequently key to delusional ideation. These include: being in a heightened state/aroused; having feelings of significance; perceptual anomalies (e.g. things may seem vivid or bright or piercing, sounds may feel very intrusive); having feelings as if one is not really there (depersonalization); and illusions and hallucinations (e.g. hearing voices). These sorts of experiences can be caused by

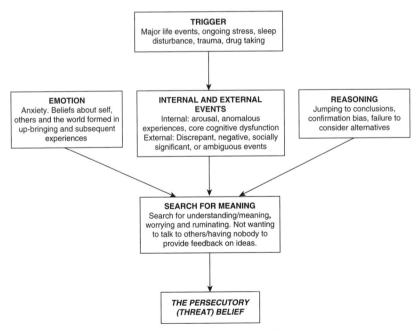

Fig. 7.1 Outline of factors involved in persecutory delusion development.

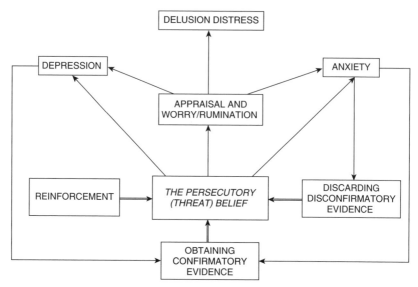

Fig. 7.2 Outline of the maintenance of a persecutory delusion.

the processes hypothesized by theorists such as Hemsley (1994) or Kapur (2003), by the use of street drugs or by high levels of affect.

- External events. Ambiguous social information is particularly important. This includes both non-verbal information (e.g. facial expressions, people's eyes, hand gestures, laughter/smiling) and verbal information (e.g. snatches of conversation, shouting). Coincidences and negative or irritating events also feature in persecutory ideation.

In essence, the person feels *different* and this needs an explanation. Typically, individuals vulnerable to paranoid thinking try to make sense of internal unusual states by drawing in negative, discrepant, or ambiguous external information. For example, a person may go outside feeling in an unusual state and, rather than label this experience as such (e.g. 'I'm feeling a little odd and anxious today, probably because I've not been sleeping well'), the feelings are instead used as a source of evidence, together with the facial expressions of strangers in the street, that there is a threat (e.g. 'People don't like me and may harm me').

But why a suspicious interpretation of experiences? The internal and external events are interpreted in line with previous experiences, knowledge, emotional state, memories, personality, and decision-making processes and therefore the origin of persecutory explanations lies in such psychological processes.

Emotion is key, especially anxiety. Suspicious thoughts often occur in the context of emotional distress, frequently triggered by stressful events (e.g. difficult interpersonal relationships, bullying, isolation). The stresses will have a greater impact if they occur against a background of previous adverse experiences that have led the person to have negative beliefs about the self (e.g. as vulnerable), others (e.g. as potentially dangerous), and the world (e.g. as bad). Negative beliefs about the self and others are associated with anxiety and depression, but anxiety may be especially important in the generation of persecutory ideation. The theme of anxiety is the anticipation of danger and it is the origin of the threat content in persecutory ideation. Paranoid thoughts are an anxious extension of the negative ideas about the self and others. Moreover, it is unsurprising that paranoid thoughts pass through the mind, since the decision whether to trust or mistrust is at the heart of all social interactions, and is often a difficult judgement to make and therefore prone to errors. Anxiety may be fleeting in the generation of a paranoid thought, but paranoid thoughts will be more significant in the context of higher levels of trait anxiety. Paranoid thoughts are hypothesized to have close links with anxiety *processes*. For example, worry may keep the suspicions in mind and develop the content in a catastrophizing manner. Hence in the model emotion is given a direct role in delusion formation.

The persecutory ideas are most likely to become of a delusional intensity when there are accompanying biases in reasoning such as reduced data gathering ('jumping to conclusions') (Garety and Freeman 1999), a failure to generate or consider alternative explanations for experiences (Freeman *et al.* 2004), and a strong confirmatory reasoning bias (Freeman *et al.* 2005c). Social isolation may also contribute to a failure to fully review paranoid thoughts. When reasoning biases are present, the suspicions are more likely to become near certainties; the threat beliefs become held with a conviction unwarranted by the evidence and may then be considered delusional.

Delusion maintenance

Maintaining factors can be divided into two types: those that result in the obtaining of confirmatory evidence and those that lead to disconfirmatory evidence being discarded. There are a number of ways in which confirmatory evidence is obtained. The normal belief confirmation bias will operate: individuals will look for evidence consistent with their beliefs. The confirmation bias may be particularly strong in individuals with delusions. Persecutory delusions are viewed as explanations that contain threat beliefs about physical, social, or psychological harm. Therefore, attentional biases will come on-line, as is found in emotional disorders: threat will be preferentially processed (Bentall and Kaney 1989); threatening interpretations of ambiguous events will be made; and such biases are likely to be enhanced by a self-focused cognitive style (Freeman *et al.* 2000). Memory biases will lead to frequent presentations of the evidence for the delusion in the mind of the individual. Continuing anomalous experiences (often triggered by anxiety) will also provide powerful evidence consistent with the threat belief. Finally, the person's interactions with others may become disturbed. The person may act upon their delusion in a way that elicits hostility or isolation (e.g. by being aggressive, or treating others suspiciously), and they may suffer stigma (Wahl 1999). In essence, others may act differently around the person, or break contact with them, thus confirming persecutory ideas.

But why does the persecutory belief remain for such a length of time when the predicted harm has not actually happened? Potentially disconfirmatory evidence is discarded in two main ways. The first main way is by the use of safety behaviours. Individuals with persecutory delusions take actions designed to reduce the threat, but which actually prevent disconfirmatory evidence being received or fully processed. The second way in which disconfirmatory evidence may be discarded is by incorporating the failure of predicted harm events into the delusional system. Attributes of the persecutor (e.g. the deviousness of the persecutors, their cruelty, occasionally their limited powers) or the situation (e.g. others are protecting them, luck has been on their side) may be considered as explaining the non-occurrence of harm. As well as this accommodation within the delusional system, disconfirmatory evidence may simply be disregarded because no alternative explanation for the delusional experiences is available.

Delusion distress

At the simplest level, emotional experiences are directly associated with the content of delusional beliefs. The cognitive content of emotions will have been expressed in the delusions and, in turn, the content of the delusions will contribute to the maintenance and exacerbation of the emotion. So, for example, anxiety will directly result from the threat belief. The threat belief will re-affirm and exacerbate previously held ideas about vulnerability and hostility. Levels of anxiety and distress will be higher for individuals who believe that the harm will be extremely awful, that it is very likely to occur, and who feel under constant threat (24 h a day). Depression will be associated with delusion content about the power of the persecutors and whether the persecution is deserved punishment. If persecutors are believed to be extremely powerful, this will reinforce and increase depression.

Emotion is also generated from further appraisal, in relation to the self, of the contents of the delusional belief and of the actual delusional experience itself. Depression will result from negative appraisals of the delusion or delusional thoughts (e.g. that the persecution or persecutory thoughts are a sign of failure or badness). For some individuals, the negative beliefs about the self are long-term, precede delusion formation, and were already reflected in the contents of the delusion. However, for other individuals appraisal of the delusion can trigger such negative beliefs. Depression will also occur if individuals believe upon reflection that they have no control over the persecutory situation, and that this seems to be true of many areas of their lives. Additional anxiety may result from appraisals concerning vulnerability, hostility, and danger. Delusional distress will be associated with appraisals of the experience of delusional thoughts. Higher levels of delusional distress are associated with worries about a lack of control of persecutory thoughts. Contributing to these feelings of uncontrollability will be the counter-productive use of thought-control strategies. Finally, negative appraisal of the problems (or of illness) will lead to greater emotional distress. For example, individuals who appraise their problems as completely uncontrollable, likely to last a long time, a significant impediment to work, and as embarrassing, are likely to feel depressed.

Future research

The research area is at an early stage of development. Even the pieces of the puzzle identified so far require further empirical scrutiny. Can it be shown that the psychological factors are causal in paranoid thinking? Can it be shown that the factors explain significant amounts of the variance in paranoid thoughts (i.e. that the factors are important)? Do these factors interact in the development of paranoia? There are then questions to further the theoretical understanding: What factors distinguish the development of persecutory ideation from the development of grandiose (or other types of) delusional ideation? What distinguishes the development of paranoid from anxious fears? How do the psychological processes relate to social and biological factors (see Garety et al. 2007)?

Taking the last of these questions, there is the possibility of an exciting line of research into the understanding of the psychological impact of social factors. McGrath (2007) has recently highlighted 'the surprisingly rich contours of schizophrenia epidemiology'. There is robust evidence of increased rates of psychosis being associated with social factors such as urban environments (e.g. Marcelis et al. 1998), lower socio-economic status (e.g. Wicks et al. 2005) and migrant status (e.g. Kirkbride et al. 2006). Their impact on paranoid experiences or on psychological processes is much less established. In the Camberwell Walk Study, we examined the clinical and psychological impact on people with persecutory delusions of entering a deprived urban area (Ellett et al. 2008). Thirty patients with persecutory delusions were randomized to exposure to a deprived urban environment or to a brief mindfulness relaxation task.

After exposure, assessments of symptoms, reasoning, and affective processes were taken. Spending time in an urban environment made the participants more paranoid and anxious. Compared with relaxation, walking in the main shopping street of Camberwell made patients think more negatively in general about other people and increased the jumping-to-conclusions reasoning bias. There are methodological challenges in this area, but the study indicates that a number of processes hypothesized to lead to paranoid thoughts are exacerbated by entering a deprived urban environment.

Innovative methodologies are clearly needed. We have recently developed an experimental method, using virtual reality, to study unfounded persecutory ideation (Freeman *et al.* 2003, 2005b, 2008; Valmaggia *et al.* 2007; Freeman in press). The key to this work is that virtual reality enables individuals to experience an identical controlled situation. This provides a means of investigating variation in interpretations. In applying this method to the study of persecutory ideation, participants experience a neutral social event (e.g. tube train, library). The computer characters ('avatars') are programmed to exhibit only behaviour that most people would assess as neutral (and the avatars certainly have no hostile intentions). Individuals' appraisals of the avatars are then assessed. Most people have positive or neutral appraisals of the characters. However, a significant minority have paranoid interpretations, which are clearly unfounded. Not only is it known that paranoid thinking in the virtual environment is unfounded but the person's behaviour cannot elicit hostile or negative reactions from the characters. This methodology is likely to prove crucial not only in establishing predictors of paranoid thinking but in establishing causal roles of psychological variables. In the longer term, virtual reality may even be used in treatments.

It should be recognized that a multi-factorial perspective provides difficulties for empirical investigations. If a factor is neither necessary nor sufficient, then it may be infrequent. As such, empirical evidence for its importance may not be easily obtained (false negative). If multiple factors are assessed, there is an increased risk of obtaining a statistically significant result by chance (false positive). If interactions are hypothesized between factors, large data-sets are needed to achieve statistical power. There is also the danger that multi-factorial models become over-inclusive in order that any results can be accommodated. The models can be difficult to disprove. Our strategy has been to investigate factors that we think are of particular importance (i.e. occur in a significant proportion of individuals). Another strategy is to conduct stepwise investigations of the cognitive processes in a multi-factorial model by choosing control groups matched for some of the identified factors (see Table 7.1). We also note that studies of delusions dimensionally in non-clinical groups enable recruitment of a larger number of participants than is possible for studies of clinical

Table 7.1 Control groups that can strengthen study designs (Freeman and Garety 2004)

Topic addressed	Comparison groups	Comments
Maintenance factors	Persistent vs acute groups	Cognitive processing can be compared between individuals whose symptoms are known to persist and individuals whose symptoms naturally recover quickly. This is informative about maintenance factors. Previous studies have tended to group these individuals together which might have obscured identification of maintenance factors.
State/Trait factors	Delusion vs recovered group	Whether factors are state or trait variables can be examined with this study design. However, it is possible that key processes are latent, in which case mood induction procedures may also be necessary.
Factors specific to delusions	Delusions in disorders other than non-affective functional psychosis vs individuals with the same diagnosis but no delusions	Studying delusions in, for example, affective psychosis enables recruitment of a closely matched control group (e.g. individuals with depression but no delusions). Factors that are specifically associated with the delusion presentation can be identified. Ideally this should be carried out across affective, non-affective, and organic conditions so that the relevant importance of factors can be assessed.
Factors specific to persecutory delusions	Persecutory delusions vs other delusions group	Cognitive processing by individuals with persecutory delusions could be compared with individuals with grandiose delusions. Factors specific to persecutory delusions, rather than delusions in general, could be identified.
Similarities and differences with neurosis	Delusions vs emotional disorder	Cognitive processing can be compared between groups with neurotic and psychotic disorders to identify shared and distinct maintenance factors.

Table 7.1 (continued) Control groups that can strengthen study designs (Freeman and Garety 2004)

Topic addressed	Comparison groups	Comments
Testing the importance of single factors in a multi-factorial model	Delusions vs similar cognitive processing but no delusions group.	Individuals who have cognitive processing identified by the model as involved in delusion development but do not have delusions can form an interesting control group. For instance, individuals who have anomalous experiences or individuals who have a jumping-to conclusions reasoning bias. Differences from a delusion group can identify the additional factors needed for a delusion to develop.

populations and therefore provide a better means of testing complex models. Furthermore, studying single dimensions of delusional experience will simplify the theoretical and practical challenges.

There also needs to be a search for other pieces of the puzzle. For example, are loneliness and social isolation (Heinrich and Gullone 2006; Freeman *et al.* 2008) important to paranoia? Are everyday processes of trust formation (Crouch and Jones 1997) implicated? And there is still much more to learn about reasoning and delusions. Experimental work is needed on the interaction of the production of potential explanations, data gathering, the processing of confirmatory and disconfirmatory reasoning, the acceptance of explanations, and how beliefs change. Further, how these reasoning elements are modified by current goals, emotional state, and interactions with others needs to be examined. Finally, of course, still remaining is the significant challenge of translating advances in understanding persecutory ideation into improved clinical treatments (Freeman *et al.* 2006). Once causal roles of psychological variables have been established, it needs to be demonstrated that therapeutic techniques can make an impact on such processes and thereby effect lasting change in paranoid experience. Such work is only now beginning.

Acknowledgement

Daniel Freeman is supported by a Wellcome Trust Fellowship.

References

Bentall, R.P. and Kaney, S. (1989) Content specific processing and persecutory delusions: an investigation using the emotional Stroop test. *British Journal of Medical Psychology*, 62, 355–364.

Birchwood, M., Meaden, A., Trower, P., Gilbert, P. and Plaistow, J. (2000) The power and omnipotence of voices. *Psychological Medicine*, 30, 337–344.

Blackshaw, A.J., Kinderman, P., Hare, D.J. and Hatton, C. (2001) Theory of mind, causal attribution and paranoia in Asperger syndrome. *Autism*, 5, 147–163.

Brüne, M. (2005) "Theory of Mind" in schizophrenia. *Schizophrenia Bulletin*, 31 21–42.

Bunney, W.E., Hetrick, W.P., Bunney, B.G. *et al.* (1999) Structured interview for assessing perceptual anomalies (SIAPA). *Schizophrenia Bulletin* 25, 577–592.

Butler, P.D. and Javitt, D.C. (2005) Early-stage visual processing deficits in schizophrenia. *Current Opinion in Psychiatry* 18 151–157.

Chadwick, P.D.J. and Birchwood, M.J. (1994) The omnipotence of voices: a cognitive approach to hallucinations. *British Journal of Psychiatry*, 164 190–201.

Chapman, R.K. (2002) First person account: eliminating delusions. *Schizophrenia Bulletin* 28, 545–553.

Chisholm, B., Freeman, D. and Cooke, A. (2006) Identifying potential predictors of PTSD reactions to psychotic episodes. *British Journal of Clinical Psychology*, 45, 545–559.

Craig, J.S., Hatton, C., Craig, F.B. and Bentall, R.P. (2004) Persecutory beliefs, attributions and theory of mind. *Schizophrenia Research*, 69 29–33.

Crouch, L.L. and Jones, W.H. (1997) Measuring levels of trust. *Journal of Research in Personality*, 31, 319–336.

D'Souza, D.C., Perry, E., MacDougall, L. *et al.* (2004) The psychotomimetic effects of intravenous delta 9-tetrahydrocannabinol in healthy individuals: implications for psychosis. *Neuropsychopharmacology*, 29 1558–1572.

Docherty, J.P., Van Kammen, D.P., Siris, S.G. and Marder, S.R. (1978) Stages of onset of schizophrenic psychosis. *American Journal of Psychiatry*, 135, 420–426.

Ellett, L., Freeman, D. and Garety, P. (2008) The psychological effect of an urban environment on individuals with persecutory delusions: the Camberwell walk study. *Schizophrenia Research*, 99, 77–84.

Eysenck, M.W. and Van Berkum, J. (1992) Trait anxiety, defensiveness and the structure of worry. *Personality and Individual Differences*, 13 1285–1290.

Fear, C., Sharp, H. and Healy, D. (1996) Cognitive processes in delusional disorders. *British Journal of Psychiatry*, 168 1–8.

Fine, C., Gardner, M., Craigie, J. and Gold, I. (2007) Hopping, skipping or jumping to conclusions? Clarifying the role of the JTC bias in delusions. *Cognitive Neuropsychiatry*, 12, 46–77.

Fowler, D. (1997) Direct and indirect links between the content of psychotic symptoms and past traumatic experience. Paper presented at the British Association of Behavioural and Cognitive Psychotherapy Annual Conference. Southport, UK.

Fowler, D. (2000) Psychological formulation of early episodes of psychosis: a cognitive model. In: Birchwood, M., Fowler, D. and Jackson, C. (eds), *Early Intervention in Psychosis: A Guide to Concepts, Evidence and Interventions*, pp. 101–127. Chichester: Wiley.

Fowler, D., Freeman, D., Smith, B. *et al.* (2006a) The Brief Core Schema Scales (BCSS): psychometric properties and associations with paranoia and grandiosity in non-clinical and psychosis samples. *Psychological Medicine*, 36, 749–759.

Fowler, D., Freeman, D., Steel, C. *et al.* (2006b) The catastrophic interaction hypothesis: how does stress, trauma, emotion and information processing abnormalities lead to psychosis? In: Morrison, A. and Larkin, W. (eds), *Trauma and Psychosis*, pp. 101–124. Hove: Routledge.

Fowler, K.B. (2007) Snapshots: the first symptoms of psychosis. *Schizophrenia Bulletin*, 33 16–18.

Freeman, D. (2007) Suspicious minds: the psychology of persecutory delusions. *Clinical Psychology Review*, 27, 425–457.

Freeman, D. (in press) Studying and treating schizophrenia using virtual reality (VR): a new paradigm. *Schizophrenia Bulletin*.

Freeman, D. and Freeman, J. (2008) *Paranoia: The 21st Century Fear*. Oxford: Oxford University Press.

Freeman, D. and Garety, P.A. (1999) Worry, worry processes and dimensions of delusions: an exploratory investigation of a role for anxiety processes in the maintenance of delusional distress. *Behavioural and Cognitive Psychotherapy*, 27, 47–62.

Freeman, D. and Garety, P.A. (2000) Comments on the content of persecutory delusions: Does the definition need clarification? *British Journal of Clinical Psychology*, 39, 407–414.

Freeman, D. and Garety, P.A. (2004) *Paranoia: The Psychology of Persecutory Delusions*. Hove: Psychology Press.

Freeman, D., Garety, P.A. and Phillips, M.L. (2000) An examination of hypervigilance for external threat in individuals with generalised anxiety disorder and individuals with persecutory delusions using visual scan paths. *Quarterly Journal of Experimental Psychology*, 53A, 549–567.

Freeman, D., Garety, P.A. and Kuipers, E. (2001) Persecutory delusions: developing the understanding of belief maintenance and emotional distress. *Psychological Medicine*, 31, 1293–1306.

Freeman, D., Garety, P.A., Kuipers, E., Fowler, D. and Bebbington, P.E. (2002) A cognitive model of persecutory delusions. *British Journal of Clinical Psychology*, 41, 331–347.

Freeman, D., Slater, M., Bebbington, P.E. *et al.* (2003) Can virtual reality be used to investigate persecutory ideation? *Journal of Nervous and Mental Disease*, 191, 509–514.

Freeman, D., Garety, P.A. Fowler, D., Kuipers, E., Bebbington, P., Dunn, G. (2004) Why do people with delusions fail to choose more realistic explanations for their experiences? An empirical investigation. *Journal of Consulting and Clinical Psychology*, 72, 671–680.

Freeman, D., Garety, P.A., Bebbington, P.E. *et al.* (2005a) Psychological investigation of the structure of paranoia in a non-clinical population. *British Journal of Psychiatry* 186, 427–435.

Freeman, D., Garety, P.A., Bebbington, P. *et al.* (2005b) The psychology of persecutory ideation II: A virtual reality experimental study. *Journal of Nervous and Mental Disease*, 193, 309–315.

Freeman, D., Freeman, J. and Garety, P. (2006) *Overcoming Paranoid and Suspicious Thoughts*. London: Robinson Constable.

Freeman, D., Garety, P., Kuipers, E., Fowler, D., Bebbington, P.E. and Dunn, G. (2007) Acting on persecutory delusions: the importance of safety seeking. *Behaviour Research and Therapy*, 45, 89–99.

Freeman, D., Garety, P.A., McGuire, P. and Kuipers, E. (2005c) Developing a theoretical understanding of therapy techniques: reasoning, therapy and symptoms. *British Journal of Clinical Psychology*, 44 241–254

Freeman, D., Pugh, K., Antley, A. *et al.* (2008) A virtual reality study of paranoid thinking in the general population. *British Journal of Psychiatry*, 192, 258–263.

Frith, C.D. (1992) *The Cognitive Neuropsychology of Schizophrenia*. Hove: LEA.

Frith, C.D. (2004) Schizophrenia and theory of mind. *Psychological Medicine*, 34, 385–389.

Garety, P.A. (1985) Delusions: problems in definition and measurement. *British Journal of Medical Psychology*, 58 25–34.

Garety, P.A. and Freeman, D. (1999) Cognitive approaches to delusions: a critical review of theories and evidence. *British Journal of Clinical Psychology*, 38 113–154.

Garety, P.A., Everitt, B.S. and Hemsley, D.R. (1988) The characteristics of delusions. *European Archives of Psychiatry and Neurological Sciences*, 237, 112–114.

Garety, P.A., Fowler, D., Kuipers, E. *et al.* (1997) The London–East Anglia Randomised Controlled Trial of Cognitive Behaviour Therapy for Psychosis II: predictors of outcome. *British Journal of Psychiatry*, 171, 420–426.

Garety, P.A., Kuipers, E., Fowler, D., Freeman, D. and Bebbington, P.E. (2001) A cognitive model of the positive symptoms of psychosis. *Psychological Medicine*, 31, 189–195.

Garety, P.A., Freeman, D., Jolley, S. *et al.* (2005) Reasoning, emotions and delusional conviction in psychosis. *Journal of Abnormal Psychology*, 114, 373–384.

Garety, P.A., Bebbington, P., Fowler, D., Freeman, D. and Kuipers, E. (2007) Implications for neurobiological research of cognitive models of psychosis. *Psychological Medicine*, 37, 1377–1391.

Gracie, A,. Freeman, D., Green, S. *et al.* (2007) The association between traumatic experience, paranoia and hallucinations: a test of the predictions of psychological models. *Acta Psychiatrica Scandinavica*, 116, 280–289.

Green, C., Garety, P.A., Freeman, D. *et al.* (2006) Phenomenology and affect in persecutory delusions. *British Journal of Clinical Psychology*, 45, 561–577.

Greig, T.C., Bryson, G.J. and Bell, M.D. (2004) Theory of mind performance in schizophrenia. *Journal of Nervous and Mental Disease*, 192 12–18.

Guillem, F., Pampoulova, T., Stip, E., Lalonde, P. and Todorov, C. (2005) The relationships between symptom dimensions and dysphoria in schizophrenia. *Schizophrenia Research*, 75, 83–96.

Harrington, L., Siegert, R.J. and McClure, J. (2005a) Theory of mind in schizophrenia. *Cognitive Neuropsychiatry*, 10, 249–286.

Harrington, L., Langdon, R., Seigert, R.J. and McClure, J. (2005b) Schizophrenia, theory of mind and persecutory delusions. *Cognitive Neuropsychiatry*, 10, 87–104.

Harrow, M., Rattenbury, F. and Stoll, F. (1988) Schizophrenic delusions: an analysis of their persistence, of related premorbid ideas and of three major dimensions. In: Oltmanns, T.F. and Maher, B.A. (eds), *Delusional Beliefs*, pp. 184–211. New York: Wiley.

Heinrich, L.M. and Gullone, E. (2006) The clinical significance of loneliness. *Clinical Psychology, Review*, 26, 695–718.

Hemsley, D.R. (1994) Perceptual and cognitive abnormalities as the bases for schizophrenic symptoms. In: David, A.S. and Cutting, J.C. (eds), *The Neuropsychology of Schizophrenia*. pp. 97–116. Hove: Erlbaum.

Hughes, C. (2002) Executive functions and development: emerging themes. *Infant and Child Psychology*, 11, 201–209.

Johns, L.C., Cannon, M., Singleton, N. *et al.* (2004) The prevalence and correlates of self-reported psychotic symptoms in the British population. *British Journal of Psychiatry*, 185, 298–305.

Jolley, S., Garety, P.A., Bebbington, P.E. *et al.* (2006) Attributional style in psychosis—the role of affect and belief type. *Behaviour Research and Therapy*, 44 1597–1607.

Kapur, S. (2003) Psychosis as a state of aberrant salience: a framework linking biology, phenomenology and pharmacology. *American Journal of Psychiatry*, 160, 13–23.

Kendler, K.S., Glazer, W.M. and Morgenstern, H. (1983) Dimensions of delusional experience. *American Journal of Psychiatry*, 140, 466–469.

Kinderman, P. and Bentall, R.P. (1996a) A new measure of causal locus: the internal, personal and situational attributions questionnaire. *Personality and Individual Differences*, 20, 261–264.

Kinderman, P. and Bentall, R.P. (1996b) Self-discrepancies and persecutory delusions. *Journal of Abnormal Psychology*, 105, 106–113.

Kinderman, P., Kaney, S., Morley, S. and Bentall, R.P. (1992) Paranoia and the defensive attributional style. *British Journal of Medical Psychology*, 65, 371–383.

Kirkbride, J.B., Fearon, P., Morgan, C. *et al.* (2006) Heterogeneity in incidence rates of schizophrenia and other psychotic syndromes. *Archives of General Psychiatry*, 63, 250–258.

Krabbendam, L., Janssen, I., Bijl, R.V., Vollebergh, W.A.M. and van Os, J. (2002) Neuroticism and low self-esteem as risk factors for psychosis. *Social Psychiatry and Psychiatric Epidemiology*, 37, 1–6.

Krstev, H., Jackson, H. and Maude, D. (1999) An investigation of attributional style in first-episode psychosis. *British Journal of Clinical Psychology*, 38, 181–194.

Langdon, R., Michie, P.T., Ward, P.B., McConaghy, N., Catts, S.V. and Coltheart, M. (1997) Defective self and/or other mentalising in schizophrenia. *Cognitive Neuropsychiatry*, 2, 167–193.

Langdon, R., Coltheart, M., Ward, P.B. and Catts, S.V. (2001) Mentalising, executive planning and disengagement in schizophrenia. *Cognitive Neuropsychiatry*, 6, 81–108.

Larkin, W. and Morrison, A.P. (eds) (2006) *Trauma and Psychosis*. Hove: Routledge.

Lobban, F., Barrowclough, C. and Jones, S. (2003) A review of the role of illness models in severe mental illness. *Clinical Psychology Review*, 23, 171–196.

Lyon, H.M., Kaney, S. and Bentall, R.P. (1994) The defensive function of persecutory delusions: evidence from attribution tasks. *British Journal of Psychiatry*, 164, 637–646.

Maher, B.A. (1974) Delusional thinking and perceptual disorder. *Journal of Individual Psychology*, 30, 98–113.

Maher, B.A. (1988) Anomalous experience and delusional thinking: the logic of explanations. In: Oltmanns, T.F. and Maher, B.A. (eds), *Delusional Beliefs*, pp. 15–33. New York: Wiley.

Marcelis, M., Navarro-Mateu, F., Murray, R., Selten, J.P. and van Os, J. (1998) Urbanisation and psychosis. *Psychological Medicine*, 28, 871–879.

Maric, N., Myin-Germeys, I., Delespaul, P., de Graaf, R., Vollebergh, W., van Os, J. (2004) Is our concept of schizophrenia influenced by Berkson's bias? *Social Psychiatry and Psychiatric Epidemiology*, 39, 600–605.

Martin, J.A. and Penn, D.L. (2001) Brief report: social cognition and subclinical paranoid ideation. *British Journal of Clinical Psychology*, 40 261–265.

Martin, J.A. and Penn, D.L. (2002) Attributional style in schizophrenia. *Schizophrenia Bulletin*, 28, 131–141.

McCabe, R., Leudar, I. and Antaki, C. (2004) Do people with schizophrenia display theory of mind deficits in clinical interactions? *Psychological Medicine*, 34, 401–412.

McGhie, A. and Chapman, J. (1961) Disorders of attention and perception in early schizophrenia. *British Journal of Medical Psychology*, 34, 103–116.

McGrath, J.J. (2007) The surprisingly rich contours of schizophrenia epidemiology. *Archives of General Psychiatry*, 64, 14–16.

McKay, R., Langdon, R. and Coltheart, M. (2005) Paranoia, persecutory delusions and attributional biases. *Psychiatry Research*, 136, 233–245.

Mizrahi, R., Kiang, M., Mamo, D.C. *et al.* (2006) The selective effect of antipsychotics on the different dimensions of the experience of psychosis in schizophrenia spectrum disorders. *Schizophrenia Research*, 88, 111–118.

Norman, R.M. and Malla, A.K. (1994) Correlations over time between dysphoric mood and symptomatology in schizophrenia. *Comprehensive Psychiatry*, 35, 34–38.

O'Leary, D.S., Flaum, M., Kesler, M.L., Flashman, L.A., Arndt, S. and Andreasen, N.C. (2000) Cognitive correlates of the negative, disorganized and psychotic symptom dimensions of schizophrenia. *Journal of Neuropsychiatry and Clinical Neurosciences* 12, 4–15.

Oltmanns, T.F. (1988) Approaches to the definition and study of delusions. In: Oltmanns T.F. and Maher B.A. (eds), *Delusional Beliefs*, pp. 3–12. New York: Wiley.

Perec, G. (1978) *Life: A User's Manual*. Harvill Press, London.

Peterson, C., Semmel, A., Von Baeyer, C. *et al.* (1982) The Attributional Style Questionnaire. *Cognitive Therapy and Research*, 3, 287–300.

Randall, F., Corcoran, R., Day, J.C. and Bentall, R.P. (2003) Attention, theory of mind and causal attributions in people with persecutory delusions. *Cognitive Neuropsychiatry*, 8, 287–294.

Read, J, van Os, J., Morrison, A.P. and Ross, C.A. (2005) Childhood trauma, psychosis and schizophrenia. *Acta Psychiatrica Scandinavica*, 112, 330–350.

Rooke, O. and Birchwood, M. (1998) Loss, humiliation and entrapment as appraisals of schizophrenic illness. *British Journal of Clinical Psychology*, 37, 259–268.

Salkovskis, P.M. (1991) The importance of behaviour in the maintenance of anxiety and panic: a cognitive account. *Behavioural Psychotherapy*, 19, 6–19.

Sarfati, Y., Hardy-Baylé, M., Besche, C. and Widlöcher, D. (1997) Attribution of intentions to others in people with schizophrenia. *Schizophrenia Research*, 25, 199–209.

Scott, J., Chant, D. andrews, G., Martin, G. and McGrath, J. (2007) Association between trauma exposure and delusional experiences in a large community-based sample. *British Journal of Psychiatry*, 190, 339–343.

Selten, J.-P. and Cantor-Graae, E. (2005) Social defeat: risk factor for schizophrenia? *British Journal of Psychiatry*, 187, 101–102.

Smith, B., Fowler, D., Freeman, D. *et al.* (2006) Emotion and psychosis: direct links between schematic beliefs, emotion and delusions and hallucinations. *Schizophrenia Research*, 86, 181–188.

Startup, H., Freeman, D. and Garety, P.A. (2007) Persecutory delusions and catastrophic worry in psychosis: developing the understanding of delusion distress and persistence. *Behaviour Research and Therapy*, 45, 523–537.

Strauss, J.S. (1969) Hallucinations and delusions as points on continua function. *Archives of General Psychiatry*, 20, 581–586.

Trower, P. and Chadwick, P. (1995) Pathways to defense of the self: a theory of two types of paranoia. *Clinical Psychology: Science and Practice*, 2, 263–278.

Trower, P., Birchwood, M., Meaden, A., Byrne, S., Nelson, A. and Ross, K. (2004) Cognitive therapy for command hallucinations. *British Journal of Psychiatry*, 184, 312–320.

Uhlhaas, P.J. and Mishara, A.L. (2007) Perceptual anomalies in schizophrenia. *Schizophrenia Bulletin*, 33, 142–156.

Valmaggia, L., Freeman, D., Green, C. *et al.* (2007) Virtual reality and paranoid ideations in people with an 'at risk mental state' for psychosis. *British Journal of Psychiatry*, 191 (Suppl 51), s63–68.

van Dael, F., Versmissen, D., Janssen, I., Myin-Germeys, I., van Os, J. and Krabbendam, L. (2006) Data gathering: biased in psychosis? *Schizophrenia Bulletin*, 32, 341–351.

van Os, J., Hanssen, M., Bijl, R.V. and Ravelli, A. (2000) Strauss (1969) revisited: a psychosis continuum in the general population. *Schizophrenia Research*, 45 11–20.

Wahl, O.F. (1999) Mental health consumers' experience of stigma. *Schizophrenia Bulletin*, 25, 467–478.

Watson, P.W.B., Garety, P.A., Weinman, J. *et al.* (2006) Emotional dysfunction in schizophrenia spectrum psychosis: the role of illness perceptions. *Psychological Medicine*, 36, 761–770.

Wells, A. (1994) A multi-dimensional measure of worry: development and preliminary validation of the anxious thoughts inventory. *Anxiety, Stress and Coping*, 6 289–299.

Wicks, S., Hjern, A., Gunnell, D., Lewis, G. and Dalman, C. (2005) Social adversity in childhood and the risk of developing psychosis. *American Journal of Psychiatry*, 162, 1652–1657.

Zimbardo, P.G., Andersen, S.M. and Kabat, L.G. (1981) Induced hearing deficit generates experimental paranoia. *Science*, 212, 1529–1531.

Chapter 8

The role of self-esteem in paranoid delusions: the psychology, neurophysiology, and development of persecutory beliefs

Richard P. Bentall, Peter Kinderman, and Michael Moutoussis

Introduction

Studies in the developed world (Garety and Hemsley 1987; Jorgensen and Jensen 1994) and elsewhere (Ndetei and Vadher 1984; Stompe *et al.* 1999) have consistently reported that paranoid (persecutory) beliefs are the most common type of delusion observed in psychiatric patients. For example, in a large, first-episode sample, we found that paranoid beliefs were experienced by more than 90% of patients meeting the diagnostic criteria for schizophrenia spectrum disorder (schizophrenia, schizoaffective disorder and delusional disorder) (Moutoussis *et al.* 2007). Paranoid delusions have also been reported in people diagnosed with bipolar disorder (Goodwin and Jamison 1990) and major depression (Haltenhof *et al.* 1999) and in a substantial minority of the general population (Poulton *et al.* 2000; van Os *et al.* 2000). The fact that sub-clinical paranoia is detectable in even larger numbers of ordinary people (Fenigstein and Vanable 1992; Freeman *et al.* 2005) raises the possibility that fears about the malevolent intentions of others are an almost universal experience. In this chapter we will argue that paranoid thinking is so ubiquitous because it reflects common preoccupations about self-worth, and that self-esteem therefore plays a central role in this kind of experience. On this argument, abnormal self-esteem plays a causal role in the extreme forms of paranoia observed in psychiatric patients. Before proceeding to examine the evidence for this proposition, however, we must first address some definitional issues.

Freeman and Garety (2000) have proposed operational criteria for paranoia, arguing that a delusion should only be considered persecutory if the individual believes that harm is directed at him or herself, and is perceived as either ongoing or anticipated in the future (reports of past persecution, or the belief that the Earth is about to be struck by a meteorite would not qualify on this basis). This definition suggests that the anticipation of future negative events is a central feature of paranoia, and has some empirical support in studies that have measured threat-anticipation in paranoid patients and control groups (Kaney *et al.* 1997; Corcoran *et al.* 2006). In a recent study (to be described in more detail below) in which a wide range of psychological measures were administered to people with paranoid delusions but who had a range of diagnoses, a measure of anticipated future negative events was found to correlate so strongly with a clinical measure of paranoia that we considered threat-anticipation part of the core phenomenon (R.P. Bentall *et al.* in press *a*). The challenge is to explain how this exaggerated perception of threat comes about.

We have already mentioned evidence that paranoid beliefs are often experienced outside of the psychiatric clinic. This observation suggests a continuum of paranoid thinking, running from extreme fears of persecution to more mundane suspiciousness (Freeman *et al.* 2005). However, Trower and Chadwick (1995) have suggested that there are at least two different kinds of paranoia: 'poor me' paranoia in which persecution is believed to be undeserved and in which self-esteem is relatively high, and 'bad me' paranoia in which persecution is believed to be deserved (perhaps because of some severe personal defect or sin) and in which self-esteem is relatively low. Trower and Chadwick argue that this distinction is categorical, which implies that there may be some kind of discontinuity within the paranoid spectrum.

Other investigators have reported that 'bad me' paranoia is extremely rare in people experiencing acute episodes of psychosis (Fornells-Ambrojo and Garety 2005). In our own work we have found that, if asked to rate the degree to which they feel they deserve to be persecuted using a simple analogue scale, people receiving psychiatric care make ratings across the entire range of the scale, with the ratings of people diagnosed as suffering from schizophrenia being highly skewed towards the 'poor me' end, and people with a primary diagnosis of major depression returning higher (but by no means always 'bad me') deservedness scores (Bentall *et al.* in press *b*). Moreover, in a longitudinal study of people in acute psychotic episodes and experiencing paranoid delusions, we found that, although most rated their beliefs at the 'poor me' end of the spectrum of deservedness, many people changed their ratings from 'poor me' to 'bad me' and/or vice versa over a period of a few weeks (Melo *et al.* 2006).

These observations suggest that the distinction between 'poor me' and 'bad me' beliefs is not simply categorical and that complex dynamic processes may underlie this phenomenon.

To address this issue further, we recently developed the Persecution and Deservedness Scale (PADS; Melo *et al.* in press), which allows both people in receipt of psychiatric care and people in the general population to give theoretically independent ratings of perceived persecution and perceived deservedness. Figure 8.1 shows a graph summarizing the relationship between the two measures in a large sample of students and a smaller group of people experiencing acute psychosis. It can be seen that the two scores are clearly correlated in the student sample, so that severe non-psychotic paranoia is nearly always 'bad me'. In the people experiencing psychosis, on the other hand, deservedness scores are suppressed, so that clinical paranoia appears to be largely 'poor me'.

This finding raises the possibility that the transition from subclinical to clinical paranoia (which, presumably, often marks the beginning of a first episode of psychosis) is also a point of transition between the 'bad me' and 'poor me' forms, perhaps accompanied by a relative improvement in self-esteem,

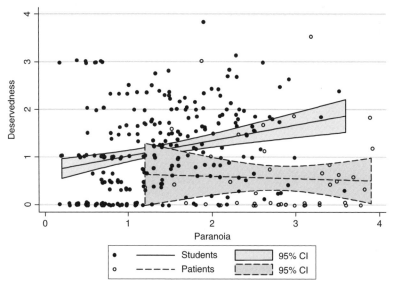

Fig. 8.1 Scatterplot showing the relationship between deservedness and perceived persecution (both scored 0–4) on the Persecution and Deservedness Scale (PADS; Melo *et al.* in press). Black circles show scores for student participants; white circles show scores for acutely ill patients. Boxes show 95% confidence intervals around the regression lines for the two samples.

after which deservedness beliefs become unstable (see Fig. 8.2). Whether or not this is indeed the case can only be determined by longitudinal investigation. However, consistent with this hypothesis, in a recent study of individuals who were judged to be at ultra-high risk of a first psychotic breakdown we found that severity of subclinical psychotic symptoms was associated with increasing satisfaction with the self (Morrison *et al.* 2006).

Causal attributions and paranoid beliefs

The term 'attribution' is used to indicate a statement about the cause of a particular event; that is, a statement that either includes or implies the word 'because'. Human beings make an extraordinary number of attributions every day; as much as one for every one hundred words of speech (Zullow *et al.* 1988). It seems that we constantly try to explain why things are happening, either in what we say to other people or when talking to ourselves. It is very likely, therefore, that, at some level, attributional processes are implicated in the persecutory beliefs of both people in receipt of psychiatric care and ordinary people. Indeed, most accounts of delusions in general and paranoia in particular make this assumption in one way or another, for example by claiming that these beliefs arise as a consequence of attempts to explain anomalous experiences (Maher 1988) or emotional disturbance (Freeman *et al.* 2002). However, specifying the precise role of attributions has proved difficult for a number of reasons.

Our initial research in this area was inspired by models of depression based on a typology of attributions which categorized them along three bipolar

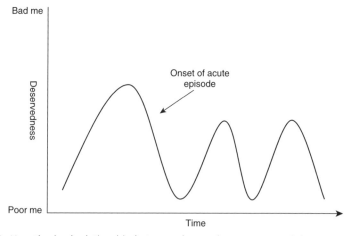

Fig. 8.2 Hypothesized relationship between deservedness scores and the onset of acute paranoid psychosis.

dimensions: *internality–externality* (whether the event being explained is believed to be mostly caused by something about the person making the attribution or, conversely, by other people or circumstances); *stability–instability* (whether the cause is likely to persist and be present in the future); and *globalness–specificity* (whether the cause will affect all areas of life or just this particular kind of event). According to these models, depression is caused when an individual with a pessimistic attributional style (a dispositional tendency to explain negative events in terms of causes that are internal, stable and global) experiences a negative event (Abramson *et al.* 1978). [In later versions of this theory, the pessimistic style was defined in terms of a tendency to make stable and global attributions for negative events, which was presumed to cause hopelessness in response to adversity, which in turn was assumed to be the proximal cause of a cognitive sub-type of depression; c.f. Abramson *et al.* (1989). These versions of the theory therefore downgraded the importance of the internality dimension.] Note that, in all models of this kind, attributional style is conceived of as a relatively enduring trait. Research has generally supported the predicted association between the pessimistic attributional style and depression (Mezulis *et al.* 2004) and there is some evidence that, when present in non-depressed individuals, a pessimistic style predicts later depressive episodes (Alloy *et al.* 1999).

In an initial study (Kaney and Bentall 1989) it was observed that paranoid people, like depressed people, made excessively stable and global attributions for negative events. (Hence, within the definitional framework of later versions of the attributional model of depression, they made pessimistic attributions in a similar way to depressed patients.) However, in contrast to both depressed participants and psychologically healthy control participants, they made excessively *external* attributions for negative events, and excessively *internal* attributions for positive events. The participants in the study also completed Levenson's (1974) multi-dimensional questionnaire measure of locus of control—a construct obviously closely related to attributional style—which has three sub-scales: internality (the general tendency to assume that events are caused by oneself), belief in powerful others and belief in chance. Not surprisingly, the paranoid participants, compared to both comparison groups, scored highly on the subscale measuring the tendency to believe that life is under the control of powerful others.

This apparent tendency to attribute the cause of unpleasant events to forces external to the self seemed to be an exaggeration of what social psychologists have termed the self-serving bias, the general tendency to make more internal attributions for positive events than for negative events ('If I pass an exam, it's because I'm very clever; if I fail its because there have been a lot of distractions in my life lately'). As the self-serving bias is widely believed to have a self-protective function, buffering self-esteem against adversity (Campbell and Sedikides 1999), this observation seems consistent with the idea that persecutory delusions are defensive, that is, that they function help to protect individuals under threat against low self-esteem.

The 1989 study has provoked a number of further studies measuring either attributional style or locus of control, using a variety of methods, and these are listed in Table 8.1. This table also includes three studies, one of locus of control (Rosenbaum and Hadari 1985) and two of attributional style (Rossler and Lackus 1986; Zimmerman *et al.* 1986) that pre-dated Kaney and Bentall (1989), but which we were unaware of at the time.

It is notable that there is a considerable amount of variability in the findings. The most consistent data are for locus of control, with all three available studies reporting that paranoia is associated with a belief in powerful others. In the case of attributional style, some studies have broadly replicated the earlier observations of a defensive style (e.g. Fear *et al.* 1996) whereas others have clearly failed to do so (e.g. Humphreys and Barrowclough 2006). A number of methodological issues may help to account for some of these discrepancies.

First, studies have varied in the way in which they have defined paranoia and recruited participants for investigation. Three separate research groups in the USA (Martin and Penn 2001, 2002), Australia (McKay *et al.* 2005) and The Netherlands (Janssen *et al.* 2006) have reported some degree of attributional abnormality in psychotic patients experiencing paranoid delusions but not in non-psychotic individuals with high paranoia scores. Jolley *et al.* (2006) reported that only psychotic patients with both grandiose and paranoid beliefs made excessively external attributions for negative events. In a longitudinal study of people experiencing acute paranoia, we recently found that our participants only made excessively external attributions for negative events when reporting 'poor me' (as opposed to 'bad me') delusions (Melo *et al.* 2006). Given that only 'poor me' patients are likely to be grandiose, these last two findings are probably consistent.

Second, the measurement of attributional processes is not without difficulty. Most studies have used Peterson *et al.*'s (1982) Attributional Style Questionnaire (ASQ), in which participants are presented with a hypothetical event (e.g. 'You fail an exam') and have to state the most likely cause of the event, before rating the cause for internality, stability and globalness. However, the ASQ has been repeatedly criticised because of its poor psychometric properties, especially in the case of the internality subscale (Reivich 1995). (Some commentators have also noted that the very concept of internality is poorly specified, so that individuals are often confused while attempting to make judgements in this domain; White 1991). It was partly in recognition of these problems that we devised the Internal, Personal and Situational Attributions Questionnaire (IPSAQ), which does not measure stability and globalness judgements but which, unlike the ASQ, distinguishes between external personal attributions (in which events are attributed to the actions of others) and external situational attributions (in which events are attributed to chance or circumstance). The IPSAQ has much better reliability than the ASQ (Kinderman and Bentall 1996b; Day and Maltby 2000) and, in a study using this scale, we found that paranoid patients made excessively external–personal attributions for negative events (Kinderman and Bentall 1997), a finding which was in harmony with the more consistent locus of control data.

Other approaches to measuring attributional processes in people suffering from paranoia have included experimental measures (Kaney and Bentall 1992), structured interviews (Craig *et al.* 2004) and extracting spontaneous attributions from recorded speech (Lee *et al.* 2004). It might be argued that, although identifying attributions in natural discourse is arduous and difficult to achieve reliably, the last approach is the most ecologically valid. However, a complication that arises when these different methods are compared concerns the identity of the person who classifies the attributional statements. When completing the ASQ and the IPSAQ, participants classify their own causal statements, rating them along scales of internality, stability and globalness in the case of the ASQ, or choosing whether they are classified as internal, personal or situational in the case of the IPSAQ. However, when attributions are extracted from spontaneous speech it is the researcher who must do the classifying. It is possible to construct arguments for either approach—perhaps classification by an independent judge is less subject to social desirability biases but, on the other hand, perhaps the generator of the attribution has background knowledge (for example, memories of his or her own thinking processes) which will make the classification more accurate. It would not be necessary to resolve this debate if those making attributions and independent judges always agreed, but it is clear that they do not. When we compared the two approaches in one of our earliest studies (Kinderman *et al.* 1992), we found that paranoid patients often made attributions for negative events which they classified as external but which judges classified as internal. We interpreted this as evidence of an implicit negative view of the self (as evidenced by the kinds of factors the patients said were likely causes of their misfortunes, as rated by the judges) and defensiveness (as evidenced by the patients' own ratings of the identified causes). More recently, Martin and Penn (2002) found no relationship between attributions as measured by the IPSAQ and paranoia when psychotic patients classified their own attributions, but paranoia was associated with highly external–personal

Table 8.1 Summary of research on attributional style and paranoia

Author(s) and date	Variables investigated and measures used	Participant groups and numbers	Summary of findings
Rosenbaum and Hadari (1985)	Locus of control: Levenson's (1974) multi-dimensional locus of control scale	Participants drawn from the general ($n = 200$) and student ($n = 161$) populations	Paranoid participants ascribed greater control to the influence of powerful others
Rossler (1986)	Attributional style: bespoke ratings of verbatim attributional responses to hypothetical social situations	People with a diagnosis of 'paranoid-hallucinatory schizophrenia in remission' ($n = 25$) Control participants ($n = 25$)	Paranoid participants made more 'incorrect' attributions, and fewer 'circumstantial' attributions than control participants
Zimmerman et al. (1986)	Attributional style: Attributional Style Questionnaire (ASQ)	People with a diagnosis of schizophrenia ($n = 37$) People with a diagnosis of psychotic depression ($n = 87$) People with a diagnosis of non-psychotic depression ($n = 118$) Control participants ($n = 53$)	Depressed participants made more internal attributions for negative events than both the control participants and participants with a diagnosis of schizophrenia
Kaney and Bentall (1989)	Causal attributions; Attributional Style Questionnaire (ASQ)	People with persecutory delusions ($n = 17$) People with depressed mood ($n = 16$) Control participants ($n = 17$)	Paranoid participants made excessively external, global and stable attributions for negative events
Candido and Romney (1990)	Attributional style: Attributional Style Questionnaire (ASQ)	Participants experiencing persecutory delusions who were not also depressed ($n = 15$), participants experiencing depressed mood who were not also experiencing persecutory delusions ($n = 15$), participants experiencing both persecutory delusions and depressed mood ($n = 15$)	Paranoid individuals attributed good events to themselves and bad events to others or to chance, depressed individuals attributed bad events to themselves and good events to others or to chance. Participants who were both paranoid and depressed fell in between the two other groups with respect to their attributions of good events but did not differ from the paranoid group in their attribution of bad events

Study	Measures	Participants	Findings
Kaney and Bentall (1992)	Perceived control: computerized judgement task, disguised as two computer games with success and failure outcomes	People with persecutory delusions (n = 14); People with depressed mood (n = 14); Control participants (n = 14)	Paranoid patients showed a greater self-serving bias towards attributing more control when apparently winning than when apparently losing
Kinderman et al. (1992)	Causal attributions. Quantitative data and raters' blind judgements of participants' qualitative responses on ASQ	People with persecutory delusions (n = 23); People with depressed mood (n = 21); Control participants (n = 28)	Paranoid participants' internality ratings showed an exaggerated self-serving bias and an absence of such a bias in depressed participants, but independent raters' judgements showed no such group differences
Fear et al. (1996)	Attributional style: ASQ	People with a diagnosis of delusional disorder (n = 29); People with depressed mood (n = 20); Control participants (n = 20)	Deluded participants showed exaggerated self-serving attributional style
Kinderman and Bentall (1997)	Causal attributions for positive and negative hypothetical social events, the Internal, Personal and Situational Attributions Questionnaire (IPSAQ)	People with persecutory delusions (n = 20); People with depressed mood (n = 20); Control participants (n = 20)	Depressed participants had a self-blaming attributional style compared to paranoid participants. In addition, paranoid participants chose external attributions that located blame in other persons
Lasar (1997)	Locus of control: the Locus of Control Scale	Participants with a diagnosis of schizophrenia (n = 50)	Correlation between external locus of control and paranoid beliefs
Martin and Penn (2001)	Attributional style: ASQ	Undergraduate students (n = 193); correlational design	No significant associations between paranoid ideation and attributional biases

(continued)

Table 8.1 (continued) Summary of research on attributional style and paranoia

Author(s) and date	Variables investigated and measures used	Participant groups and numbers	Summary of findings
Martin and Penn, (2002)	Attributional style: ASQ	Participants with a diagnosis of schizophrenia and currently experiencing delusions ($n = 15$) Participants with a diagnosis of schizophrenia but not currently experiencing delusions ($n = 15$) Control participants ($n = 16$)	Self-serving and other blaming attributional biases in paranoid people
Craig et al. (2004)	Attributional Style: the Attributional Style Structured Interview (ASSI)	Participants with a diagnosis of schizophrenia or delusional disorder and currently experiencing delusions ($n = 16$) Participants with a diagnosis of Asperger's syndrome ($n = 17$) Control participants ($n = 16$)	Deluded participants made excessively self-serving and other-blaming attributions for negative events
Lee et al. (2004)	Coding of attributions in free speech using the Content Analysis of Verbatim Explanations (CAVE), as participants related positive and negative life experiences	Participants with acute paranoid delusions ($n = 12$) and healthy controls ($n = 12$)	Deluded patients made more attributions for negative events that were external-personal, stable and global; however, there was considerable variability within the paranoid group
McKay et al. (2005)	Attributional style: IPSAQ	First-year psychology undergraduates ($n = 40$); correlational design	No association between self-serving attributional biases and subclinical persecutory ideation. Marginal support for an association between paranoia and personalizing bias
Bentall and Kaney (2005)	Attributional Style (Extended ASQ) for negative events before and after a contrived failure experience		

Study	Measures	Participants / design	Findings
Humphreys and Barrowclough (2006)	Attributional style: ASQ, IPSAQ and the Pragmatic Inference Test	Participants receiving care for psychotic experiences (n = 35); correlational design	A self-serving bias on the ASQ was found in the total sample but not specifically in participants with persecutory delusions
Janssen et al. (2006)	Attribution style; IPSAQ	Participants with lifetime presence of non-affective pychosis (n = 23) First-degree relatives of people with non-affective psychosis (n = 36) Participants with sub-clinical psychotic experiences (n = 31) Control participants (n = 46)	Participants experiencing clinical psychosis exhibited an externalizing bias, with a dose–response association between externalizing bias and delusional beliefs No significant differences were found in personalizing bias
Jolley et al. (2006)	Attributional style; ASQ	Participants receiving care for psychotic experiences (n = 74); correlational design	Depression related to a reduced self-serving bias. Paranoia was not related to any attributional bias
Melo et al. (2006)	Attributional style (ASQ)	Participants with diagnoses of delusional disorder, schizophrenia or schizoaffective disorder in receipt of in-patient care (n = 66) Control participants (n = 21)	Greater externalising attributional bias for negative events in 'poor me' paranoia, where individuals believe they are undeserving victims of persecution than in 'bad me' paranoia
Merrin et al. (2007)	Causal attributions and information search strategies using a modified inductive reasoning task	People with persecutory delusions (n = 24) People with depressed mood (n = 24) Control participants (n = 24)	Depressed and particularly paranoid people 'jumped to conclusions' and sought information consistent with their belief systems. No significant differences between the groups in attributional style

attributions for negative events when independent judges classified the attribu-tions. We subsequently obtained a similar results in a study comparing acutely ill paranoid patients, remitted patients and healthy controls (Randall *et al.* 2003).

A third, related difficulty besetting attributional research on paranoia concerns the notion of an attributional *style* itself. Depression researchers have usually conceived of this as a relatively stable personality dimension, but it might be argued that attributions are better viewed as speech acts that are affected by numerous contextual factors. Indeed it is pretty obvious that the kinds of attributions we make in every day life vary enormously according to circumstances. This was demonstrated experimentally by Forgas *et al.* (1990), who found that healthy individuals showed a loss of the normal self-serving bias after induced negative mood, but an exaggeration of the bias after induced positive mood. Adapting their procedure, we measured attributions (using a variant of the ASQ) in paranoid patients, depressed patients and non-distressed control participants before and after exposing them to a con-trived failure experience (they were asked to solve a series of anagrams, some of which were insoluble) (Bentall and Kaney 2005). We found that, whereas the attributions made by the control participants were relatively unaffected by this process, those made by the paranoid and depressed patients shifted to becoming more internal for negative events after the failure experience. In the case of the paranoid group, this shift was sufficient to make their attributional style look much more like that of the depressed patients at the end of the experiment.

Finally, these latter findings point to the fact that very little is known about the cognitive mechanisms involved in attribution generation. It seems likely that the decision about where the cause of an event is attributed follows after some kind of cognitive search for likely candidate causes. In an attempt to investigate this search process, we recently presented paranoid, depressed and non-distressed participants with a task in which they could ask as many ques-tions as they liked before deciding the likely cause of a series of positive and negative hypothetical events (the experimenter answered the questions 'yes' or 'no' according to a predetermined random sequence) (Merrin *et al.* 2007). One interesting observation from this study was that the paranoid patients tended to ask fewer questions than the depressed or control participants—they tended to jump to an attribution. A further interesting observation was that the partic-ipants tended to ask questions which presupposed a certain kind of cause (e.g. 'Was it something I did?') and, when the questions were classified accordingly, it was found that, for negative events, the paranoid patients tended to ask exter-nal–personal questions, the depressed patients tended to ask internal questions, and the questions of the healthy controls more often implied situational causes. (In this study, no difference was observed between the groups in the final attributional decisions they reached, but this may partly have been an artefact of the procedure, and the way in which the experimenter responded to the participant's questions.)

It is clearly hazardous to attempt a short summary of such a range of findings collected with such different methods. However, three conclusions seem reasonable. First, it seems that attributional processes are highly dynamic and difficult to define and measure; people clearly do not show a consistent tendency to make one type of attribution rather than another. Secondly, despite this caveat, abnormal attributions do seem to be evident in people with 'poor me' and/or grandiose paranoid belief systems. However, people with 'bad me' delusions and non-psychotic but highly suspicious individuals do not show evidence of abnormal attributions. Baring in mind Melo *et al.*'s (2006) observation that people in acute psychotic episodes often switch between 'poor me' and 'bad me' beliefs, this observation is consistent with the idea that attributional processes in paranoid people (and perhaps in other people also) are highly dynamic.

The idea of a paranoid defence

In our first detailed attempt to explain our attributional findings, and with the social psychological research on the self-serving bias in mind, we emphasized the impact of attributions on self-esteem (Bentall *et al.* 1994). Our reasoning was that, if external attributions for negative events are protective in the case of ordinary people, the extreme external attributions made by people with paranoid delusions must reflect an excessive need to avoid negative self-esteem. This account was consistent with some previous psychodynamic formulations (Colby 1977) and with the suggestion that paranoia is a form of camouflaged depression (Zigler and Glick 1988).

The exact model we proposed was formulated in terms of Higgins' (1987) *self-discrepancy theory*, a complex model of self-representation. According to Higgins, it is a mistake to assume that our internal representations or models of the self can be adequately described by a one-dimensional construct of self-esteem; instead, we have many such representations that become differentially accessible according to circumstances. Higgins argued that the *actual self* (beliefs about how the self actually is), the *ought self* (the self we think we ought to be) and the *other–self* (our beliefs about how we are perceived by significant others) are particularly important. According to self-discrepancy theory, aversive affective states are elicited when these representations are discrepant with each other, *actual–ideal discrepancies* leading to depression and *actual–ought discrepancies* leading to anxiety and agitation. [Both experimental studies (e.g. Strauman and Higgins 1987) and clinical observations (e.g. Strauman 1989; Scott and O'Hara 1993) broadly support this aspect of the theory.] Applying this model to paranoia, we proposed that persecutory delusions arose as the consequence of making external attributions for threatening events, reducing the accessibility of actual–ideal discrepancies (because the events are attributed to an external cause, the individual is not prompted to feel a discrepancy between the actual self and ideals) but increasing the accessibility of discrepancies between the actual self and the perceived views of others (because others are assumed to be responsible for misfortunes) (Bentall *et al.* 1994).

A study of paranoid, depressed and healthy individuals yielded a pattern of self-discrepancies that was consistent with this model (Kinderman and Bentall 1996a). Furthermore, in a series of analogue studies in which self-discrepancies were assessed before and after healthy individuals made attributions for hypothetical negative events, it was found that self-discrepancies changed in the predicted manner: internal attributions tended to cause a worsening of actual–ideal discrepancies, external–situational attributions were psychologically benign, but external–personal attributions led to an increase in actual–other discrepancies (Kinderman and Bentall 2000; Kinderman *et al.* 2003).

With the psychodynamic conception of defence in mind, we attempted a more direct test of the defence hypothesis (Lyon *et al.* 1994). Paranoid, depressed and healthy control participants were administered an implicit measure of attributional style developed by Winters and Neale (1985). On this Pragmatic Inference Task (PIT), participants listen to self-referent stories depicting success and failure events before answering a series of questions. One question after each story requires the participant to choose between equally plausible internal or external causes for the described event, neither of which is explicitly signposted in the story. We reported that paranoid people tended to make internal attributions for negative events on the PIT, which we interpreted as evidence of implicit low self-esteem, in contrast to a robust self-serving bias on a conventional measure of attributional style, which we thought reflected defensiveness. However, other studies with the PIT failed to replicate our findings (Kristev *et al.* 1999; Martin and Penn 2002). Recently, Peters and Garety (2006) reported that only people with 'bad me' paranoid delusions showed a depressive cognitive bias on the PIT, and that this bias was no longer evident after recovery.

Paranoia and self-esteem

The idea that persecutory delusions might have a defensive function has provoked some controversy. One important objection to the model is that self-esteem is often poor in paranoid individuals whereas a defensive account seems to imply that it should be high (Freeman *et al.* 1998). However, as was the case with the attributional data, the data on self-esteem in paranoia is complex, and defies a simple summary.

One complicating factor is co-morbid depression, which is quite common in paranoid people. Candido and Romney (1990) compared self-esteem in depressed, paranoid but non-depressed people, and in people with so-called comorbid problems, finding that the scores of the co-morbid group fell midway between the low scores of the depressed people and the high scores of the pure paranoid group. In a recently completed and much larger study funded by the Wellcome Trust, we examined people with a diagnosis of schizophrenia who either were or were not currently paranoid, people with a diagnosis of major depression with and without paranoid delusions, and non-distressed controls, measuring negative self-esteem and positive self-esteem separately (one rationale for separating the two is that some people might hold highly negative and highly positive beliefs about themselves simultaneously; in practice, measures of positive and negative self-esteem are usually highly negatively correlated). Across the groups, negative self-esteem was highly predictive of paranoid symptoms, but the paranoid people with a diagnosis of schizophrenia had higher positive self-esteem and less negative self-esteem than the paranoid people with a diagnosis of depression (Bentall *et al.* in press *b*).

A second complication concerns the longitudinal progression of paranoid beliefs and the type of paranoia experienced. In a study of people in their first episode of psychosis, we found no relationship between self-esteem and severity of paranoia (Drake *et al.* 2004) and, indeed, in our Wellcome sample, negative self-esteem was not significantly correlated with paranoia within our paranoid schizophrenic group. Other researchers have reported, not surprisingly, that 'poor me' paranoia is associated with higher self-esteem than 'bad me' paranoia (Chadwick *et al.* 2005).

A third complication concerns the way in which self-esteem is assessed. The defence account of paranoia depends on identifying both explicit self-esteem (the person's overt acknowledged self-evaluative beliefs) and implicit self-esteem, which can be defined as an 'automatic, overlearned, and nonconscious evaluation of the self that guides spontaneous reactions to self-relevant stimuli' (Bosson *et al.* 2000, p. 631). This distinction is important for understanding defensive psychological processes, as the assumption is that defensive processes (in this case attributional biases) are dependent on the implicit self-esteem, but influence explicit self-esteem. However, different implicit self-esteem measures are poorly correlated and most have questionable reliability (Bosson *et al.* 2000).

Several research groups have sought to test the defence hypothesis by comparing the performance of paranoid people on implicit and explicit tests, Indeed, we construed our study of performance on the PIT (Lyon *et al.* 1994, see above) in this way. In a further study, we argued that Weissman and Beck's (1978) Dysfunctional Attitude Scale could be considered an implicit self-esteem measure, as it asks respondents about their standards for evaluating themselves rather than directly for self-descriptions (Bentall and Kaney 1996). Comparing paranoid patients who were also depressed, non-depressed paranoid patients, depressed patients and healthy controls, we found high DAS scores (indicative of perfectionist standards of self-evaluation and hence vulnerability to low self-esteem) not only in the depressed patients but in both paranoid groups. Two recent studies by other research groups have utilised the Implicit Association Test (IAT), which can be used to assess implicit self-esteem by measuring the ease with which associations can be made between the self-concept and positive and negative trait words. Moritz *et al.* (2006) reported that a group of schizophrenic patients showed low implicit self-esteem on the IAT, but that those with paranoid delusions scored higher than non-paranoid patients on an explicit test (the Rosenberg Scale), though not as high as healthy controls. McKay *et al.* (2007) carried out a similar study, again reporting that paranoid patients showed low self-esteem on the IAT. On two measures of overt self-esteem, however, the currently paranoid patients did not differ significantly from either remitted patients or healthy controls once the effects of co-morbid depression had been taken into account.

A final complication concerns the relationship between self-esteem and other psychological processes implicated in paranoid beliefs. To address this question, we have recently combined data from our Wellcome Trust study of people with a diagnosis of schizophrenia, people with a diagnosis of depression and control participants with a similar dataset collected from paranoid people diagnosed as suffering from late-onset schizophrenia-like psychosis (onset after the age of 60 years), depressed elderly people and elderly controls, yielding a total dataset of 173 people in receipt of psychiatric care and 65 controls (R.P. Bentall *et al.* in press *a*). The virtue of a dataset this size is that it is possible to use structural equation modelling to examine relationships between the different variables. Psychological constructs assessed in addition to self-esteem were anticipation of future threats (Corcoran *et al.* 2006), stability and globalness of attributions assessed using the ASQ (internality ratings were not included because of their inadequate reliability), anxiety and depression (the Hospital Anxiety and Depression Scale; Zigmond and Snaith 1983), two measures of the tendency to jump to conclusions (Dudley *et al.* 1997; Garety *et al.* 1991; see Chapter 7), two measures of 'theory of mind' (the ability to understand the mental states of other people; Moore *et al.* 2006; see Chapter 10), and the vocabulary and matrix reasoning subscales of the Wechsler Abbreviated Intelligence Scale (WAIS; Wechsler 1999). (Multiple measures were taken of some of the constructs as this allowed a better estimation of their 'latent' structure.)

In examining these data we tried to identify transdiagnostic processes that were specifically related to paranoia, regardless of patient diagnosis. For reasons outlined in the introduction to this chapter, we modelled severity of paranoia on the basis of both threat-anticipation and also a measure of paranoid beliefs (based on the Peters Delusion Inventory; Peters *et al.* 1999), which were very highly correlated. The model that best fitted the data, shown in Fig. 8.3, grouped the psychological processes into two relatively independent factors: an emotional factor comprising low self-esteem, negative affect and pessimistic attributions, and a cognitive factor comprising jumping to conclusions, poor theory of mind and poor performance on the intellectual tests. The emotional factor was much more closely related to paranoia than the cognitive factor, and it was not possible to single out any single cognitive test (e.g. jumping to conclusions or theory of mind) as more influential than the others. One plausible interpretation of these finding is that paranoia is very closely related to low self-esteem and related processes (pessimistic attributions and negative affect), but also influenced by poor executive functioning as indexed by the cognitive measures. This account would be consistent with the suggestion (Coltheart 2007; see Chapter 11) that delusions in general require two factors: processes leading to abnormal thought content (in this case related to low self-esteem) and processes impairing the adequate evaluation of abnormal thought content (executive impairment).

This model is probably an over-simplification, because it does not address the temporal, dynamic aspects of paranoia, which are revealed by the deservedness data we considered earlier. For this reason, we have recently conducted two longitudinal analyses of self-esteem in people with paranoid beliefs. In the first study, using data from a large Dutch epidemiological study, we found that paranoid beliefs were associated with self-esteem that was highly variable across assessments taken at intervals spanning five years (Thewissen *et al.* 2008). In the second study, we repeatedly assessed self-esteem over a six-day period by means of the experience sampling method (Myin-Germeys *et al.* 2003). Patients currently experiencing paranoid delusions, highly paranoid but non-psychotic people recruited from the community and control participants completed simple diaries when cued by a watch that bleeped at random intervals, ten times a day. Paranoia was associated with highly unstable self-esteem, even after levels of average self-esteem and depression had been

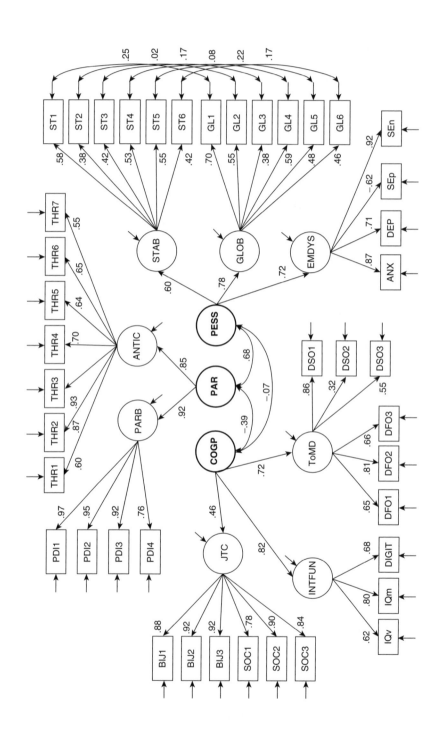

Fig. 8.3 Structural equation model describing the relationship between different psychological constructs and paranoid symptoms in a sample of schizophrenia patients with paranoid delusions aged 18–59 years ($n = 39$), schizophrenia patients whose paranoid delusions were in remission aged 18–59 years ($n = 29$), depressed patients with paranoid delusions aged 18–59 ($n = 20$), non-psychotically depressed patients aged 18–59 years ($n = 27$), patients aged ≥60 years with late-onset schizophrenia-like psychosis with paranoid delusions ($n = 29$), patients aged ≥60 years suffering from non-psychotic depression ($n = 29$), healthy controls aged 18–59 years ($n = 33$), and healthy controls aged ≥60 years ($n = 31$). Modelled latent traits are shown as circles, measured variables as squares. Paranoia (PAR) is modelled by four paranoid belief items from the Peters Delusions Inventory (PAR-B) and seven threat anticipation items (ANTIC). Cognitive performance (COGP) is modelled as a higher-order construct explained by Jumping to Conclusions (JTC; three items from Garety's beads test and three items from a similar test using meaningful materials), Theory of Mind (ToMD; three first-order and three second-order deception measures); and intellectual functioning (INTFUN; two Wechsler Abbreviated Intelligence Scale items and a digit span task). Pessimistic cognitive style (PESS) is modelled as a higher-order construct explained by stability of attributions for negative events items on the Attributional Style Questionnaire (STAB; six items), globalness of attributions for negative events (GLOB; six items), anxiety, depression (both measured by the Hospital Anxiety and Depression Scale), positive self-esteem (SEp) and negative self-esteem (SEn). The model fit statistics are: χ^2 [96] = 131.69, $P = 0.01$; CFI = 0.95; TLI = 0.96; RMSEA = 0.04. Free parameters: 133.

controlled for (Thewissen *et al.* 2008). In an unpublished analysis of data from the same study, we found that momentary increases in anxiety and, to a lesser extent, depression predicted temporary increases in paranoid thinking, but that decreases in self-esteem were even more closely associated with an exacerbation in paranoid thinking.

Summarising this evidence on self-esteem and paranoia is a challenging task. However, on the whole, paranoia seems to be robustly associated with representations of the self that are highly negative. Nonetheless, it is notable that self-esteem is relatively better in paranoid patients with a diagnosis of schizophrenia and/or who have 'poor me' delusions in comparison with those who are depressed and/or who have 'bad me' delusions. When self-esteem is observed longitudinally, an even more complex picture emerges, with paranoia associated with self-esteem that is highly unstable over time. It seems very likely that the fluctuations in deservedness judgements observed in acutely ill patients are related to this instability, so that patients shift from 'poor me' to 'bad me' as their self-esteem drops and from 'bad me' to 'poor me' as it temporarily improves.

Some studies have provided limited support for discrepancies between implicit and explicit self-esteem in paranoid patients, even when explicit self-esteem remains poor compared to that of healthy controls. Given that explicit self-esteem is higher in 'poor me' than 'bad me' patients it seems likely that these discrepancies will be particularly evident in the former group, but this prediction has yet to be tested empirically. Although perhaps not entirely consistent with the kind of impenetrable defence that might be expected from psychoanalytic theory, these findings suggest that, during 'bad me' paranoia, an underlying negative set of beliefs about the self is coupled with the assumption that others will have malevolent intentions and the anticipation of threat. During acute paranoid psychosis, however, the individual may be engaged in attempts to avoid negative beliefs about the self, resulting in increased average self-esteem coupled with extreme self-esteem fluctuations and shifts between the 'poor me' and 'bad me' belief systems.

Possible biological substrates of the avoidance of negative beliefs about the self in 'poor me' paranoia

We have suggested that, during the 'poor me' phase of paranoia, specific mechanisms are involved in the avoidance of negative representations of the self. Any attempt to explain how these mechanisms might be biologically implemented must, of course, draw on four classic observations from the research literature on the psychopharmacology of psychosis: first, that dopamine agonists such as amphetamine can provoke an acute, paranoid-type psychosis in previously healthy individuals (Angrist and Gershon 1970); second, that all effective antipsychotic drugs block dopamine D_2 receptors (Seeman *et al.* 1976); third, that the same drugs inhibit the avoidance of aversive stimuli in animals, but not the attempt to escape from aversive stimuli once experienced (Benninger *et al.* 1980); fourth, that acute psychosis is associated with the abnormal phasic release of dopamine in the mesolimbic system (Laruelle and Abi-Dargham 1999; Laruelle *et al.* 1999). In what follows, we attempt to elaborate on the significance of these observations for paranoia by taking advantage of recent developments in neurobiology of emotion and learning (see Moutoussis *et al.* 2007, for more details).

One of the most fruitful recent accounts of the neurobiology of psychosis is Kapur's (2003) aberrant-salience hypothesis, which states that positive symptoms arise as the consequence of attributing very high salience to relatively unimportant experiences. Kapur argues that the meso-limbo-cortical dopamine system normally mediates the attribution of salience necessary for affectively laden learning and that, in prodromal states, excessive dopamine is released causing salience to be attached to irrelevant events. Delusions are seen as a result of a cognitive effort to give meaning to these disparate, apparently salient experiences. This theory has implications for the mode of action of antipsychotic drugs, suggesting that they do not directly alter positive symptoms but, instead, that they reduce the sense of salience that has been inappropriately attached to specific contexts; this in turn allows for reality-testing and re-learning, which in turn leads eventually to a return to normal functioning.

The aberrant salience model has led to predictions about the time-course of the clinical response to antipsychotics, about animal behaviour in response to dopamine-blocking drugs, and about the neural activations associated with positive and negative affect, which have been supported by empirical studies (Smith *et al.* 2006; Li *et al.* 2007; Menon *et al.* 2007). As far as paranoid ideas are concerned, the theory might be applied as follows. Events in the social environment that do not have obvious causes can often be explained in terms of the action of powerful others (such as social groups, the government, etc.). Chaotic dopamine release might lead to the attachment of special salience to such events, causing them to have the greatest personal significance, and hence leading to the development of ideas of persecution. However, despite its substantial merits, the aberrant salience theory has some important limitations which make it, in our opinion, an inadequate explanation of paranoid states. Our critique is largely based on the emerging picture of the basic psychobiology of the brain systems involved in learning and motivation.

There is no doubt that the dopamine system is heavily involved in affect and motivation. Reviewing a large number of studies, Panksepp (1998) has described the meso-limbo-cortical system as mediating anticipation and seeking. Dopamine neurons in this region of brain appear to signal incentive value, or 'wanting' rather than hedonic value or 'liking' (Wyvell and Berridge 2000). These insights have been developed into quite a detailed understanding of how, during reward learning, the phasic release of dopamine in the nucleus accumbens helps the organism learn which rewards will follow which specific stimuli (Montague *et al.* 1996; Schultz *et al.* 1997). Tonic dopamine release, on the other hand, appears to have a major role in regulating how vigorously individuals take action (Niv *et al.* 2007).

However, the idea that dopamine is involved in the direct reporting of aversive stimuli (as the aberrant salience theory requires) has proved controversial. While there is microdialysis and imaging evidence of dopamine activity following aversive events (Horvitz 2000; Menon *et al.* 2007), individual dopamine neurons do not appear to respond directly to unconditioned aversive stimuli (Ungless 2004). Moreover, animal studies of conditioned avoidance have clearly shown that antipsychotic drugs do not stop animals from learning the value of aversive stimuli, as would be expected by the aberrant salience theory, but instead impair the acquisition of appropriate avoidance responses (Benninger *et al.* 1980). It is therefore likely that other neurotransmitter systems are involved in signalling negative events during aversive learning. There is evidence that serotonin is involved (Daw *et al.* 2002) although its role is quite complicated.

We argued at the outset that the anticipation of threat—which involves the adoption of inappropriate warning signs of highly aversive events—is the core feature of paranoia. The above review of the neurobiological evidence suggests a more subtle role for dopamine in the detection and avoidance of threat than that suggested by aberrant salience theory, and also points to how the dopamine system may be involved in the avoidance of negative beliefs about the self. First, it seems likely that a non-dopaminergic, possibly serotonergic system signals when events are aversive, and associates antecedent (warning) stimuli with the expectation of unpleasant outcomes (Benninger 1980; Daw *et al.* 2002). Second, we hypothesize that phasic-dopamine release mediates the experience of reinforcement (that things are better than expected) following the successful avoidance of predicted harm (Seymour *et al.* 2007). Finally, because tonic-dopamine release mediates response vigour (Niv *et al.* 2007), in paranoia, the individual will feel that he or she has the energy to invest in appropriate action to reduce the probability of negative events, such as overt (Freeman *et al.* 2001) or cognitive (Bach and Hayes 2002) avoidance behaviours.

Threats to self-esteem, such as becoming aware of discrepancies between beliefs about the self and ideals, would be expected to recruit the same aversive-processing mechanisms as any other serious threat. On this view, 'poor me' beliefs will be the consequence of dopamine-mediated avoidance of negative self-representations during acute psychosis, for example by making external attributions for negative events. Paranoid ideas therefore need not be rewarding in Berridge and Robinson's (2003) sense of being 'liked', but are likely to be rewarding in the sense of being 'wanted'. In this account, antipsychotic drugs would be expected to reduce both the vigour of avoiding and the reward internally signalled by successful avoidance.

Some research and clinical implications

In the preceding account we have tried to draw together the psychological and neurobiological literature to give a coherent account of paranoid beliefs. We think that there is compelling evidence that self-esteem plays a central but complex role in paranoid phenomena. However, beyond this observation much of the foregoing has been speculative, especially with respect to the neurobiological data. The model we have suggested may well need modifying as further evidence becomes available. However, as it stands, the model has a number of implications.

First, it is clear that it will be a great mistake to ignore temporal aspects of paranoia in future research. Paranoia is a dynamic phenomenon, as evidenced by fluctuations in self-esteem and deservedness judgements. Correlational studies, which simply take a snapshot of the relationships between symptoms and key psychological variables, may therefore present a partial or even misleading picture of the processes underlying persecutory beliefs. In those investigations that do not include a longitudinal element, it must be acknowledged that any findings may be specific to the population (healthy, acutely psychotic or chronically ill) and type of paranoia ('poor me' versus 'bad me') studied, and these should be carefully specified.

Second, our account of the neurobiological mechanisms involved in paranoia must be tested using appropriate methodologies. Menon *et al.* (2007) have recently shown that it is possible to use functional magnetic resonance imaging to measure mesolimbic activations during aversive learning. It would obviously be extremely interesting to carry out similar studies with drug-naïve psychotic patients varying in the extent to which they experience paranoid symptoms, but this is likely to be difficult for a variety of technical and practical reasons (not the least being the problem of finding drug-naïve people with acute paranoid delusions).

The developmental origins of paranoia must also be explored in future research, as all psychotic symptoms can be construed as the end points of developmental trajectories that are affected, not only by biological vulnerabilities, but also by adverse experiences (Bentall *et al.* 2007). Although there is not space here to discuss the likely developmental antecedents of paranoia in detail, two types of influences are worth briefly mentioning.

There is evidence that the risk of psychosis is increased by being unwanted at birth (Myhrman *et al.* 1996) and by early separation from parents (Morgan *et al.* 2006). Furthermore, psychotic patients (Dozier *et al.* 1991) and people living in the community who are experiencing psychotic symptoms (Mickelson *et al.* 1997; Cooper *et al.* 1998) tend to have insecure attachment styles. As insecure attachment is known to be related to mistrust and low self-esteem, it would not be surprising if disrupted attachment relations contributed to the development of paranoia. In a recent study with a student sample, we found that insecure attachment was specifically associated with low self-esteem and subsyndromal paranoia but not subsyndromal hallucinations (Pickering *et al.* 2008). Clearly this study needs to be replicated with a clinical sample.

Of course, insecure attachment on its own is unlikely to lead to paranoid beliefs. However, epidemiological studies (Mirowsky and Ross 1983; Janssen *et al.* 2003) and the retrospective reports of patients (Day *et al.* 1987; Harris 1987; Fuchs 1999) indicate that paranoia symptoms often emerge following genuine experiences of victimization and powerlessness. In this context, animal studies have shown that repeated victimization leads to sensitization of the mesolimbic dopamine system (Selten and Cantor-Graae 2005). Hence, it is possible that the dopamine abnormalities underlying acute paranoid symptoms reflect, at least in part, the brain's adaptation to victimization and sensitization to warnings of aversive events, rather than some endogenous biological dysfunction. In future developmental studies it will be important to determine whether the combination of victimization and insecure attachment creates the circumstances in which persecutory beliefs are particularly likely to flourish.

Finally, the account we have given has some implications for both pharmacological and the psychological treatment of paranoia. We would expect dopamine-blocking drugs to be less effective with 'bad me' delusions than with 'poor me' delusions and, consistent with this prediction, a recent Cochrane review has reported no advantage from adding antipsychotics to antidepressants in the treatment of psychotic depression (Wijkstra *et al.* 2005). Psychological interventions designed to increase tolerance of negative beliefs about the self and to decrease avoidance of aversive mental contents should, according to our model, be of therapeutic value. A psychological treatment approach that has been developed specifically with this goal in mind is Acceptance and Commitment Therapy (ACT; Hayes *et al.* 1999). The results of two small-scale trials of ACT have suggested that a very short course of therapy (four sessions) can markedly decrease the likelihood of relapse in recently hospitalised psychotic patients (Bach and Hayes 2002; Gaudiano and Herbert 2006). However, these findings require replication with larger samples.

References

Abramson, L.Y., Seligman, M.E.P. and Teasdale, J.D. (1978) Learned helplessness in humans: Critique and reformulation. *Journal of Abnormal Psychology*, 78, 40–74.

Abramson, L.Y., Metalsky, G.I. and Alloy, L.B. (1989) Hopelessness depression: a theory-based subtype of depression. *Psychological Review*, 96, 358–372.

Alloy, L.B., Abramson, L.Y., Whitehouse, W.G. *et al.* (1999) Depressogenic cognitive styles: predictive validity, information processing and personality characteristics, and developmental origins. *Behaviour Research and Therapy*, 37, 503–531.

Angrist, B.M. and Gershon, S. (1970) The phenomonenology of experimentally induced amphetamine psychosis—preliminary observations. *Biological Psychiatry*, 2, 95–107.

Bach, P. and Hayes, S.C. (2002) The use of Acceptance and Commitment Therapy to prevent the rehospitalization of psychotic patients: a randomized controlled trial. *Journal of Consulting and Clinical Psychology*, 70, 1129–1139.

Benninger, R., Mason, S., Phillips, A. and Fibiger, H. (1980) The use of extinction to investigate the nature of neuroleptic-induced avoidance deficits. *Psychopharmacology*, 69, 11–18.

Bentall, R.P. and Kaney, S. (1996) Abnormalities of self-representation and persecutory delusions. *Psychological Medicine*, 26, 1231–1237.

Bentall, R.P. and Kaney, S. (2005) Attributional lability in depression and paranoia. *British Journal of Clinical Psychology*, 44, 475–488.

Bentall, R.P., Kinderman, P. and Kaney, S. (1994) The self, attributional processes and abnormal beliefs: towards a model of persecutory delusions. *Behaviour Research and Therapy*, 32, 331–341.

Bentall, R.P., Fernyhough, C., Morrison, A.P., Lewis, S. and Corcoran, R. (2007) Prospects for a cognitive-developmental account of psychotic experiences. *British Journal of Clinical Psychology*.

Bentall, R.P., Rowse, G., Shryane, N.M. *et al.* (in press *a*) The cognitive and affective structure of paranoid delusions: a transdiagnostic investigation of patients with schizophrenia spectrum disorders and depression. *Archives of General Psychiatry*.

Bentall, R.P., Kinderman, P., Howard, R. *et al.* (in press *b*) Paranoid delusions in schizophrenia and depression: the transdiagnostic role of expectations of negative events and negative self-esteem. *Journal of Nervous and Mental Disease*.

Berridge, K.C. and Robinson, T.E. (2003) Parsing reward. *Trends in Neuroscience*, 9, 507–513.

Bosson, J.K., Swann, W.B. and Pennebaker, J.W. (2000) Stalking the perfect measure of implicit self-esteem: the blind men and the elephant revisited? *Journal of Personality and Social Psychology*, 79, 631–643.

Campbell, W.K. and Sedikides, C. (1999) Self-threat magnifies the self-serving bias: a meta-analytic integration. *Review of General Psychology*, 3, 23–43.

Candido, C.L. and Romney, D.M. (1990) Attributional style in paranoid vs depressed patients. *British Journal of Medical Psychology*, 63, 355–363.

Chadwick, P., Trower, P., Juusti-Butler, T.-M. and Maguire, N. (2005) Phenomenological evidence for two types of paranoia. *Psychopathology*, 38, 327–333.

Colby, K.M. (1977) Appraisal of four psychological theories of paranoid phenomena. *Journal of Abnormal Psychology*, 86, 54–59.

Coltheart, M. (2007) The 33rd Sir Frederick Bartlett Lecture: Cognitive neuropsychiatry and delusional beliefs. *Quarterly Journal of Experimental Psychology*, 60, 1041–1062.

Cooper, M.L., Shaver, P.R. and Collins, N.L. (1998) Attachment style, emotion regulation, and adjustment in adolescence. *Journal of Personality and Social Psychology*, 74, 1380–1397.

Corcoran, R., Ciummins, S., Rowse, G. *et al.* (2006) Reasoning under uncertainty: heuristic judgments in patients with persecutory delusions or depression. *Psychological Medicine*, 36, 1109–1118.

Craig, J., Craig, F., Hatton, C. and Bentall, R.P. (2004) Theory of mind and attributions in persecutory delusions and Asperger's syndrome. *Schizophrenia Research*, 69, 29–33.

Daw, N., Kakade, S. and Dayan, P. (2002) Opponent interactions between serotonin and dopamine. *Neural Networks*, 15, 603–616.

Day, L. and Maltby, J. (2000) Can Kinderman and Bentall's suggestion for a personal and situational attributions questionnaire be used to examine all aspects of attributional style? *Personality and Individual Differences*, 29, 1047–1055.

Day, R., Neilsen, J.A., Korten, A. *et al.* (1987) Stressful life events preceding the onset of acute schizophrenia: a cross-national study from the World Health Organization. *Culture, Medicine and Psychiatry*, 11, 123–206.

Dozier, M., Stevenson, A.L., Lee, S.W. and Velligan, D.I. (1991) Attachment organization and familiar overinvolvement for adults with serious psychopathological disorders. *Development and Psychopathology*, 3, 475–489.

Drake, R.J., Pickles, A., Bentall, R.P. *et al.* (2004) The evolution of insight, paranoia and depression during early schizophrenia. *Psychological Medicine*, 34, 285–292.

Dudley, R.E.J., John, C.H., Young, A.W. and Over, D.E. (1997) The effect of self-referent material on the reasoning of people with delusions. *British Journal of Clinical Psychology*, 36, 575–584.

Fear, C.F., Sharp, H. and Healy, D. (1996) Cognitive processes in delusional disorder. *British Journal of Psychiatry*, 168, 61–67.

Fenigstein, A. and Vanable, P.A. (1992) Paranoia and self-consciousness. *Journal of Personality and Social Psychology*, 62, 129–134.

Forgas, J.P., Bower, G.H. and Moylan, S. J. (1990) Praise or blame? Affective influences on attributions for achievement. *Journal of Personality and Social Psychology*, 59, 809–819.

Fornells-Ambrojo, M. and Garety, P. (2005) Bad me paranoia in early psychosis: a relatively rare phenomenon. *British Journal of Clinical Psychology*, 44, 521–528.

Freeman, D. and Garety, P.A. (2000) Comments on the contents of persecutory delusions: does the definition need clarification? *British Journal of Clinical Psychology*, 39, 407–414.

Freeman, D., Garety, P., Fowler, D. *et al.* (1998) The London–East Anglia randomized controlled trial of cognitive-behaviour therapy for psychosis. IV: self-esteem and persecutory delusions. *British Journal of Clinical Psychology*, 37, 415–430.

Freeman, D., Garety, P.A. and Kuipers, E. (2001) Persecutory delusions: developing the understanding of belief maintenance and emotional distress. *Psychological Medicine*, 31, 1293–1306.

Freeman, D., Garety, P.A., Kuipers, E., Fowler, D. and Bebbington, P.E. (2002) A cognitive model of persecutory delusions. *British Journal of Clinical Psychology*, 41, 331–347.

Freeman, D., Garety, P.A., Bebbington, P.E. *et al.* (2005) Psychological investigation of the structure of paranoia in a non-clinical population. *British Journal of Psychiatry*, 186, 427–435.

Fuchs, T. (1999) Life events in late paraphrenia and depression. *Psychopathology*, 32, 60–69.

Garety, P.A. and Hemsley, D.R. (1987) The characteristics of delusional experience. *European Archives of Psychiatry and Neurological Sciences*, 236, 294–298.

Garety, P.A., Hemsley, D.R. and Wessely, S. (1991) Reasoning in deluded schizophrenic and paranoid patients. *Journal of Nervous and Mental Disease*, 179, 194–201.

Gaudiano, B.A. and Herbert, J.D. (2006) Acute treatment of inpatients with psychotic symptoms using Acceptance and Commitment Therapy: pilot results. *Behaviour Research and Therapy*, 44, 415–437.

Goodwin, F.K. and Jamison, K.R. (1990) *Manic-depressive Illness*. Oxford: Oxford University Press.

Haltenhof, H., Ulrich, H. and Blanenburg, W. (1999) Themes of delusion in 84 patients with unipolar depression. *Krankenhauspsychiatrie*, 10, 87–90.

Harris, T. (1987) Recent developments in the study of life events in relation to psychiatric and physical disorders. In Cooper, B. (ed.), *Psychiatric Epidemiology: Progress and Prospects*, pp. 81–102. London: Croom Helm.

Hayes, S.C., Strosahl, K.D. and Wilson, K.G. (1999) *Acceptance and Commitment Therapy: An Experiential Approach to Behavior Change*. New York: Guilford.

Higgins, E.T. (1987) Self-discrepancy: a theory relating self and affect. *Psychological Review*, 94, 319–340.

Horvitz, J.C. (2000) Mesolimbocortical and nigrostriatal dopamine responses to salient non-reward events. *Neuroscience*, 96, 651–656.

Humphreys, L. and Barrowclough, C. (2006) Attributional style, defensive functioning and persecutory delusions: symptom-specific or general coping strategy? *British Journal of Clinical Psychology*, 45, 231–246.

Janssen, I., Hanssen, M., Bak, M. *et al.* (2003) Discrimination and delusional ideation. *British Journal of Psychiatry*, 182, 71–76.

Janssen, I., Versmissen, D., Campo, J. A., Myin-Germeys, I., van OS, J. and Krabbendam, L. (2006) Attributional style and psychosis: evidence for externalizing bias in patients but not individuals at high risk. *Psychological Medicine*, 27, 1–8.

Jolley, S., Garety, P., Bebbington, P. *et al.* (2006) Attributional style in psychosis: the role of affect and belief type. *Behaviour Research and Therapy*, 44, 1597–1607.

Jorgensen, P. and Jensen, J. (1994) Delusional beliefs in first admitters. *Psychopathology*, 27, 100–112.

Kaney, S. and Bentall, R.P. (1989) Persecutory delusions and attributional style. *British Journal of Medical Psychology*, 62, 191–198.

Kaney, S. and Bentall, R.P. (1992) Persecutory delusions and the self-serving bias. *Journal of Nervous and Mental Disease*, 180, 773–780.

Kaney, S., Bowen-Jones, K., Dewey, M.E. and Bentall, R.P. (1997) Frequency and consensus judgements of paranoid, paranoid-depressed and depressed psychiatric patients: subjective estimates for positive, negative and neutral events. *British Journal of Clinical Psychology*, 36, 349–364.

Kapur, S. (2003) Psychosis as a state of aberrant salience: a framework linking biology, phenomenology and pharmacology in schizophrenia. *American Journal of Psychiatry*, 160, 13–23.

Kinderman, P. and Bentall, R.P. (1996a) Self-discrepancies and persecutory delusions: evidence for a defensive model of paranoid ideation. *Journal of Abnormal Psychology*, 105, 106–114.

Kinderman, P. and Bentall, R.P. (1996b) The development of a novel measure of causal attributions: the Internal Personal and Situational Attributions Questionnaire. *Personality and Individual Differences*, 20, 261–264.

Kinderman, P. and Bentall, R.P. (1997) Causal attributions in paranoia: internal, personal and situational attributions for negative events. *Journal of Abnormal Psychology*, 106, 341–345.

Kinderman, P. and Bentall, R.P. (2000) Self-discrepancies and causal attributions: studies of hypothesized relationships. *British Journal of Clinical Psychology*, 39, 255–273.

Kinderman, P., Kaney, S., Morley, S. and Bentall, R.P. (1992) Paranoia and the defensive attributional style: deluded and depressed patients' attributions about their own attributions. *British Journal of Medical Psychology*, 65, 371–383.

Kinderman, P., Prince, S., Waller, G. and Peters, E.R. (2003) Self-discrepancies, attentional bias and persecutory delusions. *British Journal of Clinical Psychology*, 42, 1–12.

Kristev, H., Jackson, H. and Maude, D. (1999) An investigation of attributional style in first-episode psychosis. *British Journal of Clinical Psychology*, 88, 181–194.

Laruelle, M. and Abi-Dargham, A. (1999) Dopamine as the wind in the psychotic fire: new evidence from brain imaging studies. *Journal of Psychopharmacology*, 13, 358–371.

Laruelle, M., Abi-Dargham, A., Gil, R., Kegeles, L. and Innis, R. (1999) Increased dopamine transmission in schizophrenia: relationship to illness phases. *Biological Psychiatry*, 46, 56–72.

Lasar, M. (1997) Cognitive evaluation of action in chronic schizophrenia: locus of control beliefs in an inpatient group. *Psychologische Beitrage*, 39, 297–311.

Lee, D., Randall, F., Beattie, G. and Bentall, R.P. (2004) Delusional discourse: an investigation comparing the spontaneous causal attributions of paranoid and non-paranoid individuals. *Psychology and Psychotherapy—Theory, Research, Practice*, 77, 525–540.

Levenson, H. (1974) Activism and powerful others: distinctions within the concept of internal-external control. *Journal of Personality Assessment*, 38, 377–383.

Li, M., Fletcher, P. J. and Kapur, S. (2007) Time course of the antipsychotic effect and the underlying behavioural mechanisms. *Neuropsychopharmacology*, 32, 263–272.

Lyon, H.M., Kaney, S. and Bentall, R.P. (1994) The defensive function of persecutory delusions: evidence from attribution tasks. *British Journal of Psychiatry*, 164, 637–646.

Maher, B. A. (1988) Anomalous experience and delusional thinking: the logic of explanations. In: Oltmanns, T.F. and Maher, B.A. (eds), *Delusional Beliefs*, pp. 15–33. New York: Wiley.

Martin, J. A. and Penn, D. L. (2001) Social cognition and subclinical paranoid ideation. *British Journal of Clinical Psychology*, 40, 261–265.

Martin, J. A. and Penn, D.L. (2002) Attributional style in schizophrenia: an investigation in outpatients with and without persecutory delusions. *Schizophrenia Bulletin*, 28, 131–142.

McKay, R., Langdon, R. and Coltheart, M. (2005) Paranoia, persecutory delusions and attributional biases. *Psychiatry Research*, 136, 233–245.

McKay, R., Langdon, R. and Coltheart, M. (2007) The defensive function of persecutory delusions: an investigation using the implicit association test. *Cognitive Neuropsychiatry*, 12, 1–24.

Melo, S., Taylor, J. and Bentall, R.P. (2006) 'Poor me' versus 'bad me' paranoia and the instability of persecutory ideation. *Psychology and Psychotherapy: Theory, Research, Practice*, 79, 271–287.

Melo, S., Corcoran, R. and Bentall, R. P. (in press) The Persecution and Deservedness Scale. *Psychology and Psychotherapy: Theory, Research and Practice*.

Menon, M., Jensen, J., Vitcu, I. *et al.* (2007) Temporal difference modeling of the blood-oxygen level dependent response during aversive conditioning in humans: effects of dopaminergic modulation. *Biological Psychiatry*, 62, 765–772.

Merrin, J., Kinderman, P. and Bentall, R.P. (2007) 'Jumping to conclusions' and attributional style in patients with persecutory delusions. *Cognitive Therapy and Research*, 31(8), 741–758.

Mezulis, A.H., Abramson, L.Y., Hyde, J.S. and Hankin, B.L. (2004) Is there a universal positivity bias in attributions? A meta-analytic review of individual, developmental and cultural differences in the self-serving attributional bias. *Psychological Bulletin*, 130, 711–747.

Mickelson, K.D., Kessler, R.C. and Shaver, P.R. (1997) Adult attachment in a nationally representative sample. *Journal of Personality and Social Psychology*, 73, 1092–1106.

Mirowsky, J. and Ross, C.E. (1983) Paranoia and the structure of powerlessness. *American Sociological Review*, 48, 228–239.

Montague, P.R., Dayan, P. and Sejnowski, T.J. (1996) A framework for mesencephalic dopamine systems based on predictive Hebbian learning. *Journal of Neuroscience*, 16, 1936–1947.

Moore, R., Blackwood, N., Corcoran, R. *et al.* (2006) Misunderstanding the intentions of others: an exploratory study of the cognitive etiology of persecutory delusions in very late-onset schizophrenia-like psychosis. *American Journal of Geriatric Psychiatry*, 14, 410–418.

Morgan, C., Kirkbride, J., Leff, J. *et al.* (2006) Parental separation, loss and psychosis in different ethnic groups: a case–control study. *Psychological Medicine*, 37, 495–503.

Moritz, S., Werner, R. and von Collani, G. (2006) The inferiority complex in paranoia readdressed: a study with the Implicit Association Test. *Cognitive Neuropsychiatry*, 11, 402–415.

Morrison, A.P., French, P., Lewis, S.W. *et al.* (2006) Psychological factors in people at ultra-high risk of psychosis: comparisons with non-patients and associations with symptoms. *Psychological Medicine*, 36, 1395–1404.

Moutoussis, M., Williams, J., Dayan, P. and Bentall, R.P. (2007) Persecutory delusions and the conditioned avoidance paradigm: towards an integration of the psychology and biology of paranoia. *Cognitive Neuropsychiatry*, 12, 495–510.

Myhrman, A., Rantakallio, P., Isohanni, M. and Jones, P. (1996) Unwantedness of preganancy and schizophrenia in the child. *British Journal of Psychiatry*, 169, 637–640.

Myin-Germeys, I., Delespaul, P. and van Os, J. (2003) The experience sampling method in psychosis research. *Current Opinion in Psychiatry*, 16 (Suppl. 2), 33–38.

Ndetei, D.M. and Vadher, A. (1984) Frequency and clinical significance of delusions across cultures. *Acta Psychiatrica Scandinavica*, 70, 73–76.

Niv, Y., Daw, N.D., Joel, D. and Dayan, P. (2007) Tonic dopamine: opportunity costs and the control of response vigor. *Psychopharmacology*, 191, 507–520.

Panksepp, J. (1998) *Affective Neuroscience: The Foundations of Human and Animl Emotions.* Oxford: Oxford University Press.

Peters, E.R. and Garety, P. (2006) Cognitive functioning in delusions: a longitudinal analysis. *Behaviour Research and Therapy*, 44, 481–514.

Peters, E.R., Joseph, S.A. and Garety, P.A. (1999) Measurement of delusional ideation in the normal population: introducing the PDI (Peters *et al.* Delusions Inventory). *Schizophrenia Bulletin*, 25, 553–576.

Peterson, C., Semmel, A., Von Baeyer, C., Abramson, L., Metalsky, G.I. and Seligman, M.E.P. (1982) The Attributional Style Questionnaire. *Cognitive Therapy and Research*, 3, 287–300.

Pickering, L., Simpson, J. and Bentall, R.P. (2008) Insecure attachment predicts proneness to paranoia but not hallucinations. *Personality and Individual Differences*, 44, 1212–1224.

Poulton, R., Caspi, A., Moffitt, T.E., Cannon, M., Murray, R. and Harrington, H. (2000) Children's self-reported psychotic symptoms and adult schizophreniform disorder: a 15-year longitudinal study. *Archives of General Psychiatry*, 57, 1053–1058.

Randall, F., Corcoran, R., Day, J.C. and Bentall, R.P. (2003) Attention, theory of mind and causal attributions in people with paranoid delusions: a preliminary investigation. *Cognitive Neuropsychiatry*, 8, 287–294.

Reivich, K. (1995) The measurement of explanatory style. In: Buchanan, G.M. and Seligman, M.E. P. (eds), *Explanatory Style*, pp. 21–48. Hillsdale, NJ: Erlbaum.

Rosenbaum, M. and Hadari, D. (1985) Personal efficacy, external locus of control, and perceived contingency of parental reinforcement among depressed, paranoid and normal subjects. *Journal of Abnormal Psychology*, 49, 539–547.

Rossler, W. and Lackus, B. (1986) Cognitive disorders in schizophrenia viewed from the attribution theory. *European Archives of Psychiatry and the Neurological Sciences*, 235, 382–387.

Schultz, W., Dayan, P. and Montague, P. (1997) A neural substrate of prediction and reward. *Science*, 275, 1593–1599.

Scott, L. and O 'Hara, M.W. (1993) Self-discrepancies in clinically anxious and depressed university students. *Journal of Abnormal Psychology*, 102, 282–287.

Seeman, P., Lee, T., Chau-Wong, M. and Wong, K. (1976) Antipsychotic drug dose and neuroleptic/dopamine receptors. *Nature*, 261, 717–719.

Selten, J.-P. and Cantor-Graae, E. (2005) Social defeat: risk factor for psychosis? *British Journal of Psychiatry*, 187, 101–102.

Seymour, B., Daw, N., Dayan, P., Singer, T. and Dollan, R. (2007) Differential encoding of losses and gains in the human striatum. *Journal of Neuroscience*, 27, 4826–4831.

Smith, A., Li, M., Becker, S. and Kapur, S. (2006) Dopamine, prediction error and associative learning: a model-based account. *Network: Computation in Neural Systems*, 17, 61–84.

Stompe, T., Friedman, A., Ortwein, G. *et al.* (1999) Comparisons of delusions among schizophrenics in Austria and Pakistan. *Psychopathology*, 32, 225–234.

Strauman, T.J. (1989) Self-discrepancies in clinical depression and social phobia: cognitive structures that underlie emotional disorders? *Journal of Abnormal Psychology*, 98, 14–22.

Strauman, T.J. and Higgins, E.T. (1987) Automatic activation of self-discrepancies and emotional syndromes: when cognitive structures influence affect. *Journal of Abnormal Psychology*, 98, 14–22.

Thewissen, V., Myin-Germeys, I., Bentall, R.P., de Graaf, R., Vollenberg, W. and van Os, J. (2007) Instability in self-esteem and paranoia in a general population sample. *Social Psychiatry and Psychiatric Epidemiology*, 42, 1–5.

Thewissen, V., Bentall, R.P., Lecomte, T., van Os, J. and Myin-Germeys, I. (2008) Fluctuations in self-esteem and paranoia in the context of everyday life. *Journal of Abnormal Psychology* 117(1), 143–153.

Trower, P. and Chadwick, P. (1995) Pathways to defense of the self: a theory of two types of paranoia. *Clinical Psychology: Science and Practice*, 2, 263–278.

Ungless, M.A. (2004) Dopamine: the salient issue. *Trends in Neurosciences*, 27, 702–705.

van Os, J., Hanssen, M., Bijl, R.V. and Ravelli, A. (2000) Strauss (1969) revisited: a psychosis continuum in the normal population? *Schizophrenia Research*, 45, 11–20.

Wechsler, D. (1999) *Wechsler Abbreviated Scale of Intelligence*. San Antonio, TX: The Psychological Corporation.

Weissman, A.N. and Beck, A.T. (1978) Development and validation of the Dysfunctional Attitude Scale. Paper presented at the Annual Meeting of the Association for the Advancement of Behavior Therapy, Chicago.

White, P.A. (1991) Ambiguity in the internal/external distinction in causal attibution. *Journal of Experimental Social Psychology*, 27, 259–270.

Wijkstra, L., Lijmer, J., Balk, F., Geddes, J. and Nolen, W.A. (2005) Pharmacological treatment for psychotic depression. www.chochrane.org

Winters, K.C. and Neale, J.M. (1985) Mania and low self-esteem. *Journal of Abnormal Psychology*, 94, 282–290.

Wyvell, C.L. and Berridge, K.C. (2000) Intra-accumbens amphetamine increases the conditioned incentive salience of sucrose reward: enhancement of reward "wanting" without enhanced "liking" or response reinforcement. *Journal of Neuroscience*, 20, 8122–8130.

Zigler, E. and Glick, M. (1988) Is paranoid schizophrenia really camoflaged depression? *American Psychologist*, 43, 284–290.

Zigmond, A.S. and Snaith, R.P. (1983) The Hospital Anxiety and Depression Scale. *Acta Psychiatrica Scandinavica*, 67, 361–370.

Zimmerman, M., Coryell, W., Corenthal, C. and Wilson, S. (1986) Dysfunctional attitudes and attributional style in healthy controls and patients with schizophrenia, psychotic depression, and nonpsychotic depression. *Journal of Abnormal Psychology*, 95, 403–405.

Zullow, H.M., Oettingen, G., Peterson, C. and Seligman, M.E.P. (1988) Pessimistic explanatory style in the historical record: CAVing LBJ, Presidential candidates, and East versus West Berlin. *American Psychologist*, 43, 673–682.

Chapter 9

Social cognition in paranoia

Dennis R. Combs and David L. Penn

Introduction

Paranoia can be generally defined as the perception or belief that others have current or future malevolent or harmful intentions towards another person (Bentall *et al.* 2001; Freeman and Garety 2000). Although paranoia can be approached from a variety of perspectives (cognitive, neuropsychological, neural/imaging), it is the hostile perceptions of others and their intentions that places paranoia clearly in the domain of social cognition. For example, when a person with persecutory delusions engages in an ambiguous social interaction (e.g. person walks by without speaking) there are a host of perceptual and inferential processes that are actively processing the encounter, which may ultimately lead to a paranoid interpretation of the event. Thus, there seems to be some impairment in the way the person perceives the event and the conclusions drawn from those interactions. In a sense, paranoia is the ideal disorder to study from a social cognitive perspective.

In this chapter, first we will define what comprises the study of social cognition and why it is important to study this area. Second, we discuss whether paranoia exists on a continuum and specifically whether social cognitive biases are present in individuals with varying levels of paranoid ideation. Third, we will review the extant literature on paranoia and social cognition and focus on the domains of 'theory of mind' (ToM), attributional style, and social/emotion perception. Within this section, we will also comment on methodological issues that are important in social cognitive research. Finally we will provide a social cognitive model of paranoia and discuss a new group-based intervention (Social Cognition and Interaction Training; SCIT) that attempts to remediate the social cognitive biases present in paranoia.

Social cognition: definitions, domains, and importance

Before we proceed with a review of the research on paranoia and social cognition, we need to define what constitutes social cognition and why is it important to study this area. Social cognition can be generally defined as the 'mental operations underlying social interactions, which include the human ability and capacity to perceive the intentions and dispositions of others' (Brothers 1990, p. 28). Similarly, Adolphs (2001) identified social cognition as 'the ability to construct representations of the relation between oneself and others and to use those representations flexibly to guide social behavior' (p. 231). These definitions share the idea that social cognition is a set of related neurocognitive processes applied to the recognition, understanding, accurate processing, and effective use of social cues and information in real-world situations (Penn *et al.* 1997).

The construct of social cognition is vast and there are many methods to study these processes. However, in terms of schizophrenia and paranoia, there appear to be three primary social cognitive processes of interest (Penn *et al.* 1997, 2006). These domains include ToM, attributional style, and social and emotion perception (Table 9.1).

Once we have a working definition of social cognition and its major domains, it is imperative to ask why it is important to study this area. First, performance on neurocognitive (memory, language, etc.) and social cognitive tasks is dissociable. In some studies, participants can complete non-social

Table 9.1 Major domains of social cognition

Domain	Description	Representative measures
Theory of mind	Ability to represent the mental states of others or make inferences about others' intentions. This includes understanding hints, false beliefs, intentions, irony, metaphor, and *faux pas.*	Hinting Task Sally-Anne Test Brüne Cartoons
Attributional style	Assigning causality to positive and negative events	Internal Personal, and Situational Attributions Questionnaire (IPSAQ) Ambiguous Intentions Hostility Questionnaire (AIHQ)
Social/emotion perception	1. Perception or scanning of social details and scenes. 2. Identification or discrimination of emotional expressions. emotional expressions usually reflect both positive (happy and surprise) and negative emotional states (anger, fear, sadness, ashamed, disgust).	Social Perception Scale Face Emotion Identification Test (FEIT) Bell–Lysaker Emotion Recognition Test (BLERT)

tasks quite well and perform poorly on social cognition tasks. At the clinical level, individuals with frontal lobe damage (Anderson *et al.* 1999; Blair and Cipolotti 2000; Fine *et al.* 2001) or prosopagnosia (inability to recognize faces; Kanwisher 2000) show significantly impaired performance in varying areas of social cognition such as ToM and facial processing, but have intact discrimination of non-social stimuli (e.g. geometric designs). In contrast, individuals with Williams syndrome tend to show a relative strength in social cognitive abilities, such as the detection of basic emotions from faces and normal performance on some ToM tasks, but tend to have below-normal intelligence and have deficits in other aspects of neurocognition (Tager-Flusberg *et al.* 1998; Jones *et al.* 2000). Second, there is evidence in support of the presence of a 'social cognitive neural circuit', incorporating the amygdala, fusiform gyrus, superior temporal sulcus, and prefrontal cortices (Phillips *et al.* 2000b, 2003; Blackwood *et al.* 2001; Adolphs 2003; Pinkham *et al.* 2003; Blakemore and Frith, 2004; Lee *et al.* 2004). Finally, performance on social cognitive tasks tends to be only moderately associated with neurocognitive performance (e.g. Penn *et al.* 1993). In general, the correlations between affect recognition and attention, memory, and executive processing range from 0.20 to 0.60 (Schneider *et al.* 1995; Bryson *et al.* 1997; Kee *et al.* 1998; Kohler *et al.* 2000; Silver and Shlomo 2001; Sergi and Green 2002; Bozikas *et al.* 2004; Combs and Gouvier, 2004; Sachs *et al.* 2004; Sergi *et al.* 2006). Therefore, neurocognition and social cognition appear to represent related, but non-redundant constructs.

The study of social cognition, albeit interesting by itself, must relate to real-world functioning. Both emotion perception and ToM have a consistent relationship with functional outcomes (Appelo *et al.* 1992; Mueser *et al.* 1996; Toomey *et al.* 1997; Hooker and Park, 2002; Penn *et al.* 2002; Kee *et al.* 2003; Brüne 2005a; Schenkel *et al.* 2005; Pinkham and Penn 2006; reviewed in Couture *et al.* 2006). In fact, some studies have shown that social cognition has a stronger relationship with functional outcome than neurocognition (Penn *et al.* 1996; Roncone *et al.* 2002; Vauth *et al.* 2004; Pinkham and Penn 2006). As we discuss later, by improving social cognition perhaps the social functioning of persons with paranoia can also be enhanced.

Paranoia across the continuum

In this chapter, we will approach paranoia and social cognition from a continuum approach. It has been argued that clinical researchers begin to focus more on the study of symptoms instead of traditional diagnostic syndromes (Bentall *et al.* 1988; Costello 1994). A number of studies have found that delusions and hallucinations are present in normal individuals (Peters *et al.* 1999; van Os *et al.* 2000; Johns and van Os 2001; Verdoux and van Os 2002; Johns 2004).

Paranoia also appears to exist on a continuum ranging from sub-clinical to clinical levels. At the lower end of the paranoia continuum, sub-clinical paranoia is found in normal persons often in response to everyday situations or contexts that evoke suspicion or self-focused attention (i.e. self as the target of others; Fenigstein and Vanable 1992). In fact, paranoia appears to be relatively common among non-clinical samples. Recently, Ellett *et al.* (2003) reported that a sizeable number of adults ($n = 153$ out of 324) reported beliefs or experiences in which others were out to harm them intentionally (see also Freeman *et al.* 2005b). The origin of this type of sub-clinical paranoia may reflect environmental events such as racism, poverty, immigration, incarceration, or a diathesis (predisposition) towards paranoia (Newhill 1990; Bentall *et al.* 2001; Whaley 2001; Combs *et al.* 2006b). Little is known, however, about how to distinguish between these 'contextual' or 'cultural' forms of paranoia from the unfounded paranoia found in psychosis (Freeman *et al.* 2005b). At the more severe end of the paranoia continuum are clinical forms of paranoia such as persecutory delusions or paranoid personality disorder which are more extreme, based on less external evidence, and which have more functional and social impairment (e.g. behavioural avoidance).

Based on the continuum view of paranoia, we would expect that many of the same cognitive, social cognitive, and symptom characteristics of persons with persecutory delusions would also be present in analogue samples. A few illustrations from recent research studies will reflect the underlying similarity across the continuum. First, the theoretical relationships between paranoia and other symptoms such as anxiety, depression, abnormal sensory experiences, self-esteem, and self-monitoring are also found in sub-clinical samples (Martin and Penn 2001; Freeman *et al.* 2005a,c; Combs *et al.* 2007a). Second, there are similarities in social behaviours between sub-clinical and clinical participants. In two separate studies, we demonstrated that as the level of paranoia increased (from sub-clinical to clinical) so did social distance from the examiner and there was also a greater tendency to perceive others more negatively (Combs and Penn 2004; Gay and Combs 2005). In addition, persons high in sub-clinical paranoia show biases to threatening stimuli based on slower read times for paranoid words using the Emotional Stroop Task and poorer recognition of negative emotional expressions (Combs *et al.* 2003; Green *et al.* 2003a,b). Finally, we found evidence for Trower and Chadwick's two types of paranoia ('poor me' and 'bad me'; Trower and Chadwick 1995) in a sub-clinical sample of 114 college students who scored 1 standard deviation on the Paranoia Scale (Combs *et al.* 2007b). All of these studies support the idea that paranoia is present on a continuum and, more importantly, that the construct can be approached at any point on the continuum. Given the cost and difficulty in identifying persons with persecutory delusions, the use of analogue samples may lead to an explosion of research on social cognition and paranoia.

The continuum approach to the study of paranoia is not without its critics (e.g. few measures are available to measure the paranoia continuum) and encounters resistance from those who remain committed to the traditional approach to the study of schizophrenia and its clinical subtypes (e.g. paranoid and disorganized schizophrenia). However, the use of diagnostic categories such as paranoid schizophrenia is relatively heterogeneous (delusions and/or hallucinations) in terms of symptom patterns and may not contain individuals who have persecutory delusions (Corcoran 2001; Combs *et al.*, 2006a). Also, the use of paranoid schizophrenia as a diagnostic entity usually leads to the formation of a non-paranoid group, which contains persons with more severe symptoms and greater cognitive impairment, thus hindering comparisons. One of the major challenges in symptom-focused research is to demonstrate that the participants are actually paranoid, which necessitates a careful assessment of the level of paranoia. The use of a combination of self-report and interviewer-rated measures, which provide convergent data as to the presence of paranoia, is an especially strong methodology. Also, there appears to be emerging evidence that the persecutory ideation component of paranoia is the most valid aspect of the construct to measure (Freeman and Garety 2000; McKay *et al.* 2006). The impact of ethnicity on paranoia suggests that culturally validated measures be developed to provide a more sensitive examination of mistrust. Thus, a continuum approach would bring much-needed specificity to the study of paranoia and allow researchers to examine the impact of a single symptom on social cognition. We propose that a symptom-focused approach which spans the paranoia continuum provides the strongest evidence for the presence of social cognitive deficits in paranoia.

Paranoia and social cognition: research evidence

As we review the research literature on paranoia and social cognition, we pose several questions to consider as we proceed. To reflect the paranoia continuum, we will draw conclusions from studies using both clinical and sub-clinical participants.

1 What conclusions can we draw from research about social cognition and paranoia? For example, are the deficits specific to paranoia and are these deficits stable over time?

2 Is there evidence that these deficits are present across the paranoia continuum? For example, do persons with sub-clinical paranoia show similar deficits in social cognition to those with persecutory delusions?

3 What are the important methodological issues in research on social cognition and paranoia?

Theory of mind

A comprehensive review of ToM is presented by Corcoran in Chapter 10. However, since ToM falls under the construct of social cognition, we would like briefly to comment on this area of research as it pertains to paranoia. First, superficially it makes sense that individuals with paranoia have impairments in understanding the mental states, motives, or intentions of others. The belief that someone harbours ill will or malevolent intentions can be viewed as a type of 'mentalizing' deficit in which a false belief or motive about some other person or group is inferred. In his cognitive theory of schizophrenia, Frith (1992) argued that ToM deficits should be present in persons with disorders involving impaired willed action (e.g. negative and disorganized symptoms), self-monitoring (e.g. delusions of passivity and control), and others' beliefs and intentions (e.g. delusions of persecution). According to Frith (1992), persons with paranoia show a normal development of ToM, but these abilities become impaired during the acute paranoia. The ToM literature is complex and fraught with different methodologies, samples, and ToM tasks, which makes drawing conclusions difficult. However, there is consistent evidence that (i) persons with schizophrenia show impaired ToM performance compared to normal controls, and (ii) the most severe deficits in ToM are found in persons with negative symptoms and disorganization (see Brüne 2005b for a review). Also, it appears that persons in the acute phase of illness show more ToM impairment than those in remission, who show relatively intact ToM and perform similar to normal controls (Drury et al. 1998; Corcoran 2001). Thus, many consider ToM deficits a 'state' instead of a 'trait' deficit (Penn et al. 2006).

So, what can we conclude about the ToM abilities of persons with paranoia? Several recent reviews have concluded that the empirical link between paranoia and ToM is relatively weak, and that ToM deficits are not specific to paranoia, but found in a number of other disorders such as autism, Asperger syndrome, and even other subtypes of schizophrenia (Pilowsky et al. 2000; Craig et al. 2004; Brüne 2005b).

Studies supporting the presence of ToM deficits in paranoia are primarily found in early research conducted by Corcoran, Frith and colleagues (see Corcoran 2001 for a review). More recently, Harrington et al. (2005a) examined a sample of 25 persons classified as paranoid and non-paranoid and found that those with persecutory delusions showed ToM deficits for first- and second-order verbal tasks, but not non-verbal tasks. On average, ToM deficits in persons with paranoia appear to be less severe than in persons with negative symptoms and disorganization, but greater than those in remission, with passivity symptoms, and normal controls. In fact, some have asserted that only three studies have found clear evidence to support the ToM–paranoia link (Blackwood *et al.* 2001; Harrington *et al.* 2005b). In contrast, other studies are inconclusive (Brüne 2005b) or do not support a relationship between paranoia and ToM deficits (see Mazza *et al.* 2001). For example, Drury *et al.* (1998) did not find differences in ToM between persecutory deluded versus non-deluded participants on ToM tasks, but persons with schizophrenia showed significantly lower scores than psychiatric controls. Thus, the consensus is that paranoia has not been consistently linked to ToM deficits and largely depends on the comparison groups used in the study (Brüne 2005b; Penn *et al.* 2006).

There are several methodological issues that are important to note in this area of research. First, the method of symptom classification may be partially responsible for the mixed results. Studies have used a variety of classification schemes such as positive versus negative symptom dimensions, factor analytic classification systems (positive, negative, thought disorder) and paranoid versus non-paranoid schizophrenia (Harrington *et al.* 2005b). These symptom groupings do not allow clear conclusions about whether ToM is present or absent as it pertains to paranoia (Corcoran 2001). As we stated earlier, using clearly defined groups whose primary symptom is persecutory delusions can lead to clarification of whether ToM deficits are present (Walston 2000). Clearly, more attention is needed to symptom measurement and classification in this type of research.

Second, the types of tasks used in research needs to be addressed. Measurement considerations include the use of both first-order (false belief) and second-order (false belief about another person's belief; more difficult) tasks and whether to use control tasks that do not contain the mentalizing aspect such as physical, non-verbal, or mechanical-type tasks. It is important to match these tasks psychometrically or at least report the psychometric properties since verbal or social ToM tasks may be inherently more difficult (differential deficit model; see Penn *et al.* 1997 for a review). In many cases, ToM deficits are found for the verbal, but not the non-verbal, tasks and it needs to be demonstrated that this is not an artefact of the measurement.

Finally, the successful completion of ToM tasks can be affected by cognitive factors such as intellectual, abstraction/reasoning, memory, or language-processing deficits (Frith and Corcoran 1996; Pickup and Frith 2001;

Roncone *et al.* 2002; Brüne 2003, 2005b; Greig *et al.* 2004), but this is an issue for all psychological testing. For example, the most severe deficits in ToM are found in persons with autism due to the pervasive cognitive deficits found in this population. In schizophrenia, ToM appears partially influenced by cognitive factors. Thus, it is important to account for these characteristics in this area of research either by matching participants on IQ or cognitive ability or by measuring these areas with neuropsychological tests which can later be examined (account for variance). For paranoia, it has been suggested that paranoid individuals can pass first-order ToM tasks which are relatively easy and tend to fail the harder second-order tasks due to intact cognitive functioning (Pickup and Frith 2001). It is possible that when under greater cognitive load, such as during natural or in-vivo social interactions, these persons may show the expected ToM deficit, but this remains to be demonstrated (see Walston 2000).

What evidence can we draw from studies that use individuals at risk or at the lower end of the paranoia continuum in terms of ToM and paranoia? Unfortunately, no studies have assessed the ToM abilities of subjects with persecutory delusions compared with sub-clinical paranoid people. However, we can draw some inferences from studies using high-risk individuals (family history) and those with schizotypal symptoms. We found seven studies that have examined this issue and most involve whether ToM represents a 'state' or 'trait' deficit. Pickup and Frith (2001) showed that remitted participants performed as well as normal controls, while Herold *et al.* (2002) showed that the ToM deficits were persistent, trait-like, and found in remitted clients. In a study on non-clinical participants, Langdon and Coltheart (1999) showed that individuals who reported schizotypal symptoms performed more poorly on ToM tasks than low-schizotypal persons and the scores were related to the degree of positive symptoms reported by participants (Brüne 2005b). This link to specific symptoms at the time of testing, which is consistent with Frith's idea of a loss of ToM during acute illness, has been supported by Marjoram *et al.*'s (2006) study in which high-risk relatives with current transient positive symptoms were more impaired on a self-monitoring-type task than those who reported symptoms in the past. Pickup (2006) found that level of positive symptoms on a measure of schizotypy significantly predicted ToM scores, but there was no difference between high and low scorers on ToM tasks. Studies by Janssen *et al.* (2003) and Wykes *et al.* (2001) found evidence for ToM deficits in unaffected relatives with a family risk of schizophrenia. Janssen *et al.* (2003) suggested that there is a dose–response relationship between ToM impairment and schizophrenia risk.

Overall, it appears that deficits in ToM are found in persons at risk for schizophrenia such as family members and persons reporting schizotypal symptoms at the time of testing. The level of impairment is lower than in schizophrenia but is related to current level of positive symptoms. For non-clinical samples, there is little support for the role of negative symptoms in ToM and the impact of negative symptoms may only be relevant for persons with psychosis (Pickup 2006). However, ToM has not been examined across the paranoia continuum and the use of high-risk groups can only be considered a proxy for a direct examination of paranoia.

Attributional style

Attributions are generally defined as the manner in which one explains and assigns causality to positive (e.g. receiving a pay raise) and negative (e.g. getting fired) events. For example, if a friend does not show up for a movie, the person generates a reason as to why this occurred. Attributions usually assign causes to internal (something about me), personal (something about the other person), or situational factors (something about the situation or context). Historically, the work on attributional style has been largely centred on persons with depression, and it was found that depressed persons have a greater tendency to blame themselves for negative events while attributing positive events/success to others or external factors (Bentall *et al.* 2001). Most of the research on attributional style and paranoia has come from the work of Bentall and colleagues in the UK. There is consistent evidence that persons with paranoia and persecutory delusions show attributional abnormalities. Most commonly, these persons exhibit a type of 'personalizing' bias in which they blame others for negative events rather than themselves (Bentall and Kinderman 1997; Garety and Freeman 1999; Bentall *et al.* 2001). However, there is mixed evidence as to whether this personalizing bias is specific to paranoia as it may be found in persons with delusions in general (Fear *et al.* 1996; Martin and Penn 2002). This presence of a personalizing bias is found across the majority of studies, but the reason why this occurs remains unclear and hotly debated.

Theoretically, Bentall and colleagues have proposed several inter-related models to explain the attributional style of persons with persecutory delusions. The most current version of this theory is called the Attribution Self-Representation Cycle (ASRC). Bentall *et al.* (1994) in their original theory proposed that paranoia may be a defence that prevents negative information from reducing self-esteem (see Zigler and Glick 1988). Thus, by blaming others self-esteem is protected. More recently, it has been suggested that personalizing or external–personal attributions prevent self-discrepancies between the actual and ideal parts of the self (which maintain self-esteem) while open-ing up discrepancies between the self and others (Kinderman and Bentall 1996b, 1997). Evidence for the 'paranoia as a defence' model was initially derived from studies showing that persons with paranoia demonstrate an exaggerated self-serving bias (tendency to blame others for negative events and to take credit for positive events) compared to both normal controls and persons with depression (Kaney and Bentall 1989; Candido and Romey 1990). Several reviews (Garety and Freeman 1999; Bentall *et al.* 2001; Penn *et al.* 2006) have suggested that there is greater support for the presence of an external–personalizing bias for negative events, but less support for the inter-nalization for positive events (Fear *et al.* 1996; Won and Lee 1997; Kristev *et al.* 1999; Martin and Penn 2002; Humphreys and Barrowclough 2006). Furthermore, if the defence theory of paranoia is correct, then persons with persecutory delusions should show a depressive attributional style on covert or opaque attributional tasks (e.g. Pragmatic Inference Test) and show evidence of a discrepancy between overt and covert self-esteem. However, the research on self-esteem levels is inconsistent, with some studies showing high or normal levels of self-esteem and some showing low self-esteem (Kinderman 1994; Kinderman and Bentall 1996b; Peters *et al.* 1997; Humphreys and Barrowclough 2006; Moritz and Woodward 2005). In fact, only two studies have found a discrepancy between overt and covert self-esteem (Lyon *et al.* 1994; McKay *et al.* 2007). It is currently believed that the relationship between paranoia and self-esteem seems to be related to whether the sample contains persons with elevated levels of depression (Freeman *et al.* 1998; Peters and Garety 2006).

The finding that persons with paranoia make personalizing attributions poses the question as to why situational or contextual information is not used. According to Gilbert *et al.* (1988), most persons make automatic personal or dispositional attributions and subsequently correct these explanations for situational factors, but this seems to be absent in persons with paranoia. For example, we may blame our friend for not showing up to the movie, but we correct that attribution if we learn that she had a flat tyre *en route*. The failure to incorporate situational information may stem from impairments in ToM (Kinderman *et al.* 1998; Taylor and Kinderman 2002; Randall *et al.* 2003), which provides additional contextual information about the intentions or minds of others, or a greater need for closure (Colbert and Peters 2002; Bentall and Swarbrick 2003), which prematurely closes the search for situational information.

There are several methodological issues to consider in this area of research. First, most studies on attributions use paper-and-pencil self-report questionnaires such as the Attributional Style Questionnaire (ASQ; Peterson *et al.* 1982), and the Internal, Personal and Situational Attributions Questionnaire (IPSAQ; Kinderman and Bentall 1996a, 1997), which present a variety of hypothetical positive and negative situations. The ASQ, in particular, has been criticized for having poor internal consistency values for the internality index and has been supplanted by the IPSAQ. Second, it has been argued that coding natural social interactions may be a more valid method of studying attributions. A recent study by Lee *et al.* (2004) found that more external–personal attributions were identified from the speech samples of 24 persons classified as paranoid versus non-paranoid. Third, it is open to debate as to the best method to study attributions in terms of using self-ratings or having independent raters' code responses (Bentall *et al.* 2001). Some studies have found that comparing self versus independent ratings leads to different findings (Kinderman *et al.* 1998; Martin and Penn 2002; Randall *et al.* 2003). Fourth, current measures of attributional style do not address situations that differ in intentionality. Research by Crick and Dodge (1994) suggest that conduct-disordered children have a hostile attribution bias for ambiguous situations. Theoretical models of persecutory delusions posit that ambiguous situations are difficult to interpret and may be misperceived as hostile and threatening (Turkat *et al.* 1995; Freeman *et al.* 2002, 2005a; Freeman and Garety 2003; Green and Phillips 2004). That may be one reason why persons with persecutory delusions (or persecutory ideation) spend extra time looking at ambiguous scenes (Phillips *et al.* 2000a), and why they perceive neutral experimenter behaviour in a negative manner (Combs and Penn 2004).

To address this limitation in current attributional style measures, we developed a new measure of attributional style called the Ambiguous Intentions Hostility Questionnaire (AIHQ) which includes situations that are ambiguous, accidental, and intentional (Combs *et al.* 2007c). In a sample of 322 college students reflective of the paranoia continuum, there were significant correlations between several measures of paranoia [Paranoia Scale (PS) and the Structured Clinical Interview for *DSM-IV* (SCID-I) paranoia items] and AIHQ self-rated blame and hostility scores for ambiguous situations. More importantly, the AIHQ blame and hostility scores for ambiguous situations accounted for significant incremental variance in the prediction of paranoia scores as compared to the IPSAQ, which supports the usefulness of the scale in paranoia research. Finally, there are few studies on attributional style that involve longitudinal measurement, and, given the instability of attributions (Bentall *et al.* 2001; Bentall and Kaney 2005), this area needs additional research.

In terms of data from sub-clinical studies, there does not appear to be clear evidence for the presence of personalizing attributional biases when college student samples are used. Combs and Penn (2004) identified 29 persons with elevated scores on the PS (>1 SD on the PS) and compared them with 31 persons with low PS (<1 SD on the PS) scores on a variety of social cognition measures. There was no difference between the groups on the externalizing or personalizing bias scores from the IPSAQ. In addition, several studies have found that sub-clinical paranoia scores are not correlated with attributional style (Martin and Penn 2001; McKay et al. 2005); a finding which is supported in studies on clinical samples (Garety and Freeman 1999; Martin and Penn 2002). Despite the lack of findings in attributions style, there is some support for a relationship between ToM errors and a greater tendency to make personalizing attributions for negative events (Kinderman et al. 1998; Taylor and Kinderman 2002). Also several studies have found relationships between subclinical paranoia, self-discrepancies and self-concept (Chung and Lee 1998; Lee and Won 1998) and negative perceptions of others (Lee, 1999). Thus, it appears that some aspects of attributional style such as the presence of ToM impairments, self-discrepancies and lower self-concept are present in analogue studies, but it appears that personalizing attributions only appear when paranoia reaches delusional levels (McKay et al. 2005).

Social and emotion perception

It is believed that perceptions and other cognitive processes (attention, memory, learning) are affected by information-processing biases (i.e. schema) found in paranoia (Rector, 2004). These biases appear to be especially sensitive to threatening stimuli, such as negative emotional expressions (Locascio and Synder 1975; Brennan and Hemsley 1984; Miller and Karoni 1996; Freeman et al. 2002; Green et al. 2003c; Phillips et al. 2000b; Green and Phillips 2004). Information-processing biases are considered important factors in the both the development and maintenance of persecutory delusions (Freeman et al. 2002). These biases can affect what the individual attends to and also how this information is interpreted and recalled (Fiske and Taylor 1991; Wyer and Carlston 1979 as discussed in Fenigstein 1997; Pinkham et al. 2003). In the following sections, we review some of the constructs that may underlie impaired social and emotion perception such as an increased sensitivity for threat and the presence of visual scanning deficits for facial stimuli. This will be followed by a review of studies examining emotion perception and person perception.

Persons with elevated levels of paranoia seem to be more sensitive to threat, based on research using the Emotional Stroop Test, which measures pre-attentive or early visual processing. These individuals have greater interference (slower read times) for paranoid content words as compared to neutral and depressed words (Bentall and Kaney 1989; Kinderman 1994; Fear *et al.* 1996; Combs *et al.* 2003; Combs and Penn 2004). Also, paranoia has been shown to be associated with an increased recall for threatening words/stories and a higher tendency to form illusory correlations to threatening words, which reflects the involvement of deeper encoding or controlled processes (Brennan and Hemsley 1984; Kaney *et al.* 1992; Bentall *et al.* 1995; Fenigstein 1997). Finally, persons with elevated paranoia levels exhibit improved implicit learning for negative subtle co-variations among facial features and negative personality traits such as unfairness (Combs *et al.* 2003).

There is also evidence that persons with delusions show abnormalities in visual scanning for faces and emotional expressions. On face and emotion perception tasks, persons with deluded schizophrenia tend to focus on non-essential areas of the face or even peripheral stimuli (Gordon *et al.* 1992; Phillips and David 1997; Streit *et al.* 1997). There is also a reduction in the amount of time they view relevant facial features such as the eyes, nose, and mouth (Gordon *et al.* 1992; Swartz *et al.* 1999; Green *et al.* 2005). There also appear to be differences in the visual scanning for negative and positive emotions (Loughland *et al.* 2002). When viewing threatening expressions, normal persons show more extensive and longer fixations to facial features and these expressions are identified more rapidly, which is considered evolutionarily adaptive in the detection of threat (Green *et al.* 2003c). Similarly, both deluded and delusion-prone persons also show this extensive scanning for threat. However, there is a reduction in attention to facial features and these emotions tend to be recognized more slowly, and it is speculated that these scanning deficits may be a reason for the poorer accuracy scores found in research (Green *et al.* 2001, 2003a,b).

In terms of emotion perception, there is consistent evidence that persons with schizophrenia perform worse on emotion identification and discrimination tasks than both psychiatric (depressed and bipolar) and non-psychiatric controls (see reviews by Mandal *et al.* 1998; Edwards *et al.* 2002; Penn *et al.* 2006, 2000). These deficits appear to be relatively stable over time based on several longitudinal studies using follow-up periods between three months and one year (Addington and Addington 1998; Kee *et al.* 2003). The performance of persons with paranoia on emotion perception tasks is interesting in that contradictory predictions are possible. On one hand, the presence of an information-processing bias for social and threatening stimuli suggests that persons with persecutory delusions should show enhanced emotion perception abilities (Kline *et al.* 1992; Penn *et al.* 1997; Green and Phillips 2004; Combs *et al.* 2006a). In contrast, it is possible that there are deficits (i.e. visual scanning, etc.) in this ability since many persons with persecutory delusions also have schizophrenia. Research in this area is still developing, although several previous studies found that persons with paranoid schizophrenia are better at emotion perception than persons with non-paranoid schizophrenia (Kline *et al.* 1992; Lewis and Garver 1995), with this strength being particularly evident for naturalistic rather than posed emotions (Davis and Gibson 2000; Peer *et al.* 2004).

In terms of accuracy, there is generally no difference for positive emotions between persons with paranoid schizophrenia and normal controls (Kline *et al.* 1992; Davis and Gibson, 2000), which is a pattern consistent with the general schizophrenia literature (Dougherty *et al.* 1974; Edwards *et al.* 2002). For negative emotions, the findings largely depend on the type of comparison group used in the study. Persons with paranoid schizophrenia typically perform better than persons with non-paranoid schizophrenia (disorganized, negative/deficit type), but worse (not better) than normal controls in the recognition of negative emotions such as fear, anger, sadness, shame, and disgust (LaRusso 1978; Kline *et al.* 1992; Lewis and Garver 1995; Davis and Gibson 2000; Green *et al.* 2001). The fact that persons with non-paranoid schizophrenia show the poorest scores suggests that cognitive abilities play a major role in emotion recognition (Combs and Gouvier 2004). Thus, it should be emphasized that any improvement in recognizing negative emotions is relative to other types of schizophrenia only.

To further illustrate the relationship between paranoia and emotion perception, we present findings from a recently published study on emotion perception across the paranoia continuum (Combs *et al.* 2006a). In this study, we used four groups of participants that differed on level of paranoia. The sample was comprised of thirty clinical participants who had documented persecutory delusions based on the BPRS and three groups of sub-clinical participants ($n = 88$ college students) who showed low, medium, and high levels of sub-clinical paranoia based on the PS. We administered two measures of emotion perception: the Face Emotion Identification Test (FEIT) and the Bell–Lysaker Emotion Recognition Test (BLERT). As evident in Table 9.2, as paranoia increased in severity, emotion perception scores (composite mean score) decreased. Clinical participants with persecutory delusions had the poorest emotion perception abilities and the low paranoia group had the best. Consistent with the research findings, there was a significant difference between the groups for negative emotions, but not for positive emotions. The recognition of positive emotions was relatively unimpaired with the differences mainly arising from the negative emotions such as anger, fear, disgust, and sadness, which may be more difficult to distinguish (Phillips *et al.* 2000a;

Table 9.2 Affect perception scores by group membership

Variable (range)	Sub-clinical groups			
	Clinical	High	Moderate	Low
Mean affect score (0–20)	12.3 (3.3)	14.6 (1.6)	15.7 (1.6)	16.2 (1.4)
Mean positive score (0–5)	3.6 (1.0)	4.3 (0.58)	4.3 (0.58)	4.5 (0.41)
Mean negative score (0–11)	7.0 (1.4)	7.5 (1.1)	8.2 (1.0)	8.5 (1.1)

Note. Higher scores indicate better emotion recognition abilities.
Table reproduced with permission from Combs et al. (2006a), ©2006 British Psychological Society.

Horley *et al.* 2001; Edwards *et al.* 2002; Green *et al.*, 2003a; Kohler *et al.* 2003; Peer *et al.* 2004).

A more complex construct is social perception which consists of how persons perceive and attend to social scenes and other persons in their environment. There is not as much literature on social perception to draw upon, but there are four studies of note (Freeman *et al.* 2000, 2005b; Phillips *et al.* 2000a; Combs and Penn 2004). Similar to research on attributional style, person perception research tends to use ambiguous interactions or neutral-behaving examiners, which are believed to elicit the cognitive biases associated with paranoia. Combs and Penn (2004) examined a group of high (*n* = 29) and low (*n* = 31) participants based on scores from the PS. To assess immediate perceptions, each participant was allowed to sit as close or as far away from the examiner as possible. Persons with high paranoia scores sat significantly (almost 1 foot) father from the examiner. Also, these persons took almost twice as long to read the consent form and both of these behaviours reflect the suspiciousness of others found in paranoia. In fact, similar behaviours were found in a recent replication of this study with inpatients with persecutory delusions (Gay and Combs 2005). At the end of the study, the participants were asked to rate the examiner (who left the room), and who was trained to remain neutral during the study, on five 'in-vivo' perception items. To enhance the validity of the perceptions, the participants returned the rating form to a secure box and were assured that only the lead experimenter would review the results. As predicted, persons with high paranoia viewed the examiner as less trustworthy and more likely to be analysing their performance and influencing their performance during the study even though the examiner remained neutral. Ratings of hostility and friendliness were in the expected direction, but were not statistically significant.

Consistent with the results from Combs and Penn (2004), Freeman *et al.* (2005b) examined paranoia among 30 non-clinical participants across five virtual reality interactions with neutral-behaving computer-generated characters. Using a modified measure of persecutory ideation developed for the study, it was found that paranoid ideation was generated during these interactions. In fact, 23 out of the 30 participants reported some degree of persecutory ideation. The reporting of paranoia in virtual reality settings was also related to other external indicators, such as interview ratings, visual ana-logue ratings and self-report measures of paranoia, which provide validity to the reported symptoms. Using a regression analysis, predictors of paranoia ratings in the virtual reality setting were sub-clinical paranoia, hallucinatory experiences, timidity, anxiety, and sense of being in the simulated environment (viewed scene as more realistic).

Finally, two studies have examined visual appraisal of social scenes using eye tracking methodology. Freeman et al. (2000) found that persons with persecu-tory delusions showed a restricted scanning for happy scenes and a more extensive scanning of directly threatening and ambiguous scenes. Phillips et al. (2000a) examined the visual scanning patterns of 19 persons with persecutory delusions, eight persons without persecutory delusions and 18 normal con-trols while viewing ambiguous, threatening, and neutral social scenes. The social scenes were black-and-white images from magazines, which were rated as ambiguous, threatening, and neutral by normal controls prior to the study. Using an eye-tracking technology, each participant viewed each scene twice. The first time was a free-viewing condition and during the second time the person was instructed to look for threat. Initially, all groups showed equivalent scanning patterns to the various scenes. On the second viewing, the study found that when viewing the ambiguous scene, persons with persecutory delusions showed less scanning of overtly threatening areas, but greater scan-ning of non-threatening areas. Thus, this may reflect the sensitivity to threat and more specifically the tendency to look for threat in inappropriate places. Also this viewing of non-threatening areas instead of the threatening ones may suggest problems with context appreciation or ambiguity (which would be consistent with research on attributions). The lack of reappraisal may reflect a jumping-to-conclusions bias (seeking less information before making a decision; Huq et al. 1988; Garety et al. 1991) or impaired cognitive flexibility (Freeman et al., 2004; Garety et al., 2005) associated with delusions and paranoia (see Green and Phillips 2004 for a discussion).

Methodologically, emotion perception studies rely mainly on static, posed images and may not be ecologically valid given the brevity of expressions. In fact, persons with paranoia may over-analyse these types of expressions (Davis and Gibson, 2000). Sadly, there are no measures of emotion perception that present emotions embedded in natural social interactions, but one recent study used moving emotional expressions and found better recognition for moving versus static expressions (Tomlinson *et al.* 2006). Also, positive expressions may be easier to identify, thus hindering direct comparisons with negative emotions. The same issue is relevant for person perception studies which often use researchers playing a simulated role, which may not reflect natural interactions. Using more natural, ecologically valid stimuli would help to determine whether the findings are related to the test and measures (measurement artefact) or reflect a deficit across situations and contexts.

Drawing together the studies on emotion and social perception, it appears that paranoia affects both pre-attentive and controlled processing. When threat is identified, persons with paranoia tend to process this information more slowly and deliberately. Research on eye tracking suggests that they may actually avoid looking at threatening areas and instead examine areas of ambiguity (Green and Phillips 2004). These visual scanning deficits in paranoids when viewing threatening emotions may reflect a reduced neural response compared with normals (Phillips *et al.* 2000b). The reduced reappraisal and visual fixation to facial features may reflect the jumping-to-conclusions bias when attempting to recognize the emotional states of others. Furthermore, problems attending to the subtle facial cues important in recognizing emotions may exacerbate this deficit. It is possible that sufficient information would be obtained if subjects were instructed on how to scan emotions or social scenes (see Combs *et al.* 2006c for an example of this methodology).

Remediating social cognition: social cognition and interaction training (SCIT)

Given the number of impairments in social cognition and the consequent impact of paranoia on social functioning, attention is now turned to developing interventions that address the deficits in ToM, attributional style, and social/emotion perception (Couture *et al.* 2006). In Figure 9.1, we present a social cognitive model of paranoia, which attempts to integrate the various domains discussed in this review and their relationships.

The primary treatment of paranoia is cognitive-behavioural therapy, which is used to reduce paranoia, delusional ideation, and emotional distress through challenging evidence for those beliefs and behavioural testing (Rector 2004). In contrast, there are a number of interventions that attempt to remediate social cognition. These social cognitive interventions can be classified as either 'targeted' or 'broad-based' (see Combs *et al.* in press a; Couture *et al.* 2006 for a review; Penn and Combs 2000). Targeted interventions focus on a specific social cognitive domain (e.g. ToM or emotion perception; Kayser *et al.* 2006;

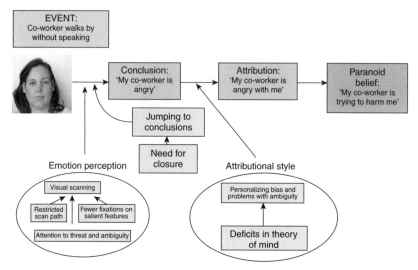

Fig. 9.1 Social cognitive model of paranoia. Adapted from Couture *et al.* (2006), with permission from Oxford University Press.

Russell *et al.* 2006), whereas broad-based interventions combine a variety of psychosocial approaches, including cognitive remediation and social skills training (Spaulding *et al.* 1999; van der Gaag *et al.* 2002; Hogarty *et al.* 2004). Although both approaches improve social cognition, several key issues remain unaddressed. First, can we expect the narrow focus of targeted interventions to yield improvements across social cognitive domains or to generalize to social functioning? Second, if targeted interventions are too narrow, are broad-based interventions too burdensome? That is, is it necessary to stack social cognitive training atop intensive cognitive remediation and social skills training, or might social cognitive training alone be sufficient to improve social functioning? Third, these interventions have not been empirically examined or developed to address the social cognitive biases found in paranoia.

We therefore developed a comprehensive, 'stand-alone' manual-based intervention called Social Cognition and Interaction Training (SCIT; D.L. Roberts *et al.* unpublished manual) that targets the three core social cognitive deficits in schizophrenia: emotion perception, ToM, and attributional style. SCIT is comprised of three phases: (1) emotion training, (2) figuring-out situations, and (3) integration, which are delivered by one or two therapists over 20–24 weekly sessions, with each session lasting 50 min. SCIT involves the use of didactic instruction, videotape and computerized learning tools, and role-play methods to improve social cognition. We will briefly describe the goals and techniques associated with each phase of treatment. Pilot testing of SCIT in a small sample of inpatients showed improvements in ToM and attributional hostility but not emotion perception (Penn *et al.* 2005).

The primary goals of phase 1 (emotion training) are to provide information about emotions and their relationship to thoughts and situations, define the basic emotions, improve emotion perception with computerized facial expression training tools, and teach clients to distinguish between justified and unjustified suspiciousness.

The primary goals of phase 2 (figuring-out situations) are to teach clients about the potential pitfalls of jumping to conclusions, to improve cognitive flexibility in social situations, and to help clients distinguish between personal and situational attributions, and between social 'facts' and social 'guesses'. Techniques include a variety of guessing games (20 question game) and fact-finding exercises (doing detecting work), and generating attributions for events in the client's lives with an emphasis on possible situational factors that should be considered.

The primary goals of phase 3 (integration) are to assess the certainty of facts and guesses surrounding events in clients' personal lives, recognize that it is sometimes necessary to obtain more information about social situations, and to teach effective social skills for checking out guesses. The purpose of the final phase is to put into practice what clients have learned in SCIT. One can view the phases of SCIT as moving from 'cold' social cognition in phase 1 (i.e. social cognition for non-personal events) to 'hot' social cognition in phase 3 (i.e. application of social cognitive skills to personally relevant situations) (Brenner *et al.* 1992). We have done this intentionally, so as to allow clients to learn social cognitive skills without become over-aroused or defensive.

To illustrate the effect of SCIT on paranoia and social cognition, we have provided some data from a recently completed outcome study on SCIT using forensic inpatients (Combs *et al.* 2007a). We present data for 13 persons with persecutory delusions as defined by scores on the Positive and Negative Syndrome Scale (PANSS) suspiciousness item of 5 (see Humphreys and Barrowclough, 2006). All of the participants were diagnosed with schizophrenia using the SCID.

Outcome measures included measures of social and emotion perception, ToM, and attributional style for ambiguous situations. We also examined scores from the engagement sub-scale for the Social Functioning Scale to reflect functioning on the treatment ward. As evident in Table 9.3, SCIT was associated with a significant reduction in level of paranoia (as measured by the PANSS), but also significant improvements across the social cognition and functioning measures. Thus, SCIT can be considered an emerging treatment

Table 9.3 Social Cognition and Interaction Training (SCIT) for inpatients with persecutory delusions (n = 13)

Variable	SCIT	
	Pre-test	**Post-test**
PANSS Suspiciousness Item	5.3 (0.48)	4.0 (1.1)*
Face Emotion Identification Test	11.3 (3.0)	15.5 (1.7)*
Social Perception Scale	12.1 (2.9)	24.5 (5.7)*
Hinting Task	13.9 (2.2)	19.0 (0.12)*
AIHQ Hostility Bias for Ambiguous Situations	1.9 (0.38)	1.2 (0.06)*
Social Functioning Scale: social engagement subscale	10.3 (1.7)	13.5 (1.0)*

Values are mean (SD).

Persecutory delusions defined by Positive and Negative Syndrome Scale (PANSS) suspiciousness scores of ≥5.

*$P < 0.01$ (dependent t-tests).

AIHQ, Ambiguous Intentions Hostility Questionnaire.

for social cognitive deficits (Penn *et al.* 2007) and several randomized trials are being planned.

Conclusions and summary

We would like to emphasize several important points about social cognition in paranoia. First, the study of social cognition illuminates the manner in which these persons attend, process, and interpret their place in the social world, which is important in its own right. As discussed, there are three main types of social cognitive deficits (ToM, attributional style, and social/emotion perception) and a number of potential underlying causes (jumping to conclusions, need for closure, visual scanning deficits for faces). In addition, some of the biases are found in clinical samples, but not in sub-clinical ones (attributional style), while others are found across the continuum (ToM in high-risk samples and social/emotion perception in sub-clinical samples). It is possible that some of these deficits emerge at clinical levels of paranoia, but this remains to be consistently demonstrated. Thus, the pattern of social cognitive impairment may become more pervasive as symptoms become more severe, which is akin to the way an ordinary belief becomes delusional. Longitudinal studies of sub-clinical and clinical samples would help answer this question. Second, once an understanding of these processes is obtained, work can continue on remediating these deficits with the ultimate goal of improving social functioning and community outcome. It would be wise for treatment outcome studies to include measures of social cognition in addition to symptom measures.

Paranoia has both clinical and research implications and can be approached from a number of perspectives, We feel that a continued emphasis on social cognition is a key component in understanding this debilitating condition.

References

Addington, J. and Addington, D. (1998) Facial emotion recognition and information processing in schizophrenia and bipolar disorder. *Schizophrenia Research*, 32, 171–181.

Adolphs, R. (2001) The neurobiology of social cognition. *Current Opinion in Neurobiology*, 11, 231–239.

Adolphs, R. (2003) Cognitive neuroscience of human social behaviour. *Nature Reviews: Neuroscience*, 4, 65–178.

Anderson, S.W., Bechara, A., Damasio, H., Tranel, D. and Damasio, A.R. (1999) Impairment of social and moral behavior related to early damage in human prefrontal cortex. *Nature Neuroscience*, 2, 1032–1037.

Appelo, M.T., Woonings, F.M.J., van Nieuwenhuizen, C.J., Emmelkamp, P.M.G., Slooff, C.J. and Louwerens, J.W. (1992) Specific skills and social competence in schizophrenia. *Acta Psychiatrica Scandinavica*, 85, 419–422.

Bentall, R. and Kaney, S. (1989) Content specific information processing and persecutory delusions: an investigation using the emotional stroop test. *British Journal of Medical Psychology*, 62, 355–364.

Bentall, R.P. and Kaney, S. (2005) Attributional lability in depression and paranoia. *British Journal of Clinical Psychology*, 44, 475–488.

Bentall, R.P. and Kinderman, P. (1997) Causal attributions in paranoia and depression: internal, personal, and situational attributions for negative events. *Journal of Abnormal Psychology*, 106, 341–345.

Bentall, R.P. and Swarbrick, R. (2003) The best laid schemas of paranoid patients: autonomy, sociotropy, and need for closure. *Psychology and Psychotherapy: Theory, Research and Practice*, 76, 163–171.

Bentall, R., Jackson, H.F. and Pilgrim, D. (1988) Abandoning the concept of schizophrenia: some implications of validity arguments for psychological research into psychotic phenomena. *British Journal of Clinical Psychology*, 27, 156–169.

Bentall, R., Kinderman, P. and Kaney, S. (1994) The self, attributional processes and abnormal beliefs: towards a model of persecutory delusions. *Behavior Research and Therapy*, 32, 331–341.

Bentall, R., Kaney, S. and Bowen-Jones, K. (1995) Persecutory delusions and recall of threat related, depression related, and neutral words. *Cognitive Therapy and Research*, 19, 445–457.

Bentall, R.P., Corcoran, R., Howard, R., Blackwood, N. and Kinderman, P. (2001) Persecutory delusions: a review and theoretical interpretation. *Clinical Psychology Review*, 21, 1143–1192.

Blackwood, N.J., Howard, R.J. Bentall, R.P. and Murray, R.M. (2001) Cognitive neuropsychiatric models of persecutory delusions. *American Journal of Psychiatry*, 158, 527–539.

Blair, R.J.R. and Cipolotti, L. (2000) Impaired social response reversal: a case of 'acquired sociopathy.' *Brain*, 123, 1122–1141.

Blakemore, S.J. and Frith, C.D. (2004) How does the brain deal with the social world? *Neuroreport: For Rapid Communication of Neuroscience Research*, 15, 119–128.

Bozikas, V.P., Kosmidis, M.H., Anezoulaki, D., Giannakou, M. and Karavatos, A. (2004) Relationship of affect recognition with psychopathology and cognitive performance in schizophrenia. *Journal of the International Neuropsychological Society*, 10, 549–558.

Brennan, J.H. and Hemsley, D.R. (1984) Illusory correlations in paranoid and non-paranoid schizophrenia. *British Journal of Clinical Psychology*, 23, 225–226.

Brenner, H.D., Hodel, B., Roder, V. and Corrigan, P.W. (1992) Treatment of cognitive dysfunctions and behavioral deficits in schizophrenia. *Schizophrenia Bulletin*, 18, 21–26.

Brothers, L. (1990) The social brain: a project for integrating primate behavior and neurophysiology in a new domain. *Concepts in Neuroscience*, 1, 27–61.

Brüne, M. (2003) Theory of mind and the role of IQ in chronic disorganized schizophrenia. *Schizophrenia Research*, 60, 57–64.

Brüne, M. (2005a) Emotion recognition, 'theory of mind,' and social behavior in schizophrenia. *Psychiatry Research*, 133, 135–147.

Brüne, M. (2005b) "Theory of mind" in schizophrenia: a review of the literature. *Schizophrenia Bulletin*, 31, 21–42.

Bryson, G., Bell, M.D. and Lysaker, P.H. (1997) Affect recognition in schizophrenia: a function of global impairment or a specific cognitive deficit. *Psychiatry Research*, 71, 105–113.

Candido, C.L. and Romney, D.M. (1990) Attributional style in paranoid vs. depressed patients. *British Journal of Medical Psychology*, 63, 355–363.

Chung, G.Y. and Lee, M.K. (1998) Self-concept and self-discrepancy in paranoid students. *Korean Journal of Clinical Psychology*, 17, 127–138.

Colbert, S.M. and Peters, E.R. (2002) Need for closure and jumping to conclusions in delusion-prone individuals. *Journal of Nervous and Mental Disease*, 170, 27–31.

Combs, D.R. and Gouvier, W.D. (2004) The role of attention in affect perception: an examination of Mirsky's four factor model of attention in chronic schizophrenia. *Schizophrenia Bulletin*, 30, 727–738.

Combs, D.R. and Penn, D.L. (2004) The role of sub-clinical paranoia on social perception and behavior. *Schizophrenia Research*, 69, 93–104.

Combs, D.R., Penn, D.L. and Mathews, R. (2003) Implicit learning in sub-clinical paranoia: does content matter? *Personality and Individual Differences*, 34, 143–157.

Combs, D.R., Michael, C.O. and Penn, D.L. (2006a) Paranoia and emotion perception across the continuum. *British Journal of Clinical Psychology*, 45, 19–31.

Combs, D.R., Penn, D.L., Cassisi, J. *et al.* (2006b) Perceived racism as a predictor of paranoia among African Americans. *Journal of Black Psychology*, 32, 87–104.

Combs, D.R., Tosheva, A., Wanner, J. and Basso, M.R. (2006c) Remediation of emotion perception deficits in schizophrenia: the use of attentional prompts. *Schizophrenia Research*, 87 (1–3), 340–341.

Combs, D.R., Adams, S.D., Penn, D.L. Roberts, D.L, Tiegreen, J.A. and Stem, P. (2007a) Social cognition and interaction training for schizophrenia spectrum disorders: preliminary findings. *Schizophrenia Research*, 91, 112–116.

Combs, D.R., Penn, D.L., Chadwick, P.D.J., Trower, P., Michael, C. and Basso, M.R. (2007b) Subtypes of paranoia in a non-clinical sample. *Cognitive Neuropsychiatry*, 12, 537–553.

Combs, D.R. Penn, D.L., Wicher, M. and Waldheter, E. (2007c) The ambiguous intentions hostility questionnaire (AIHQ): a new measure for evaluating hostile social cognitive biases in paranoia. *Cognitive Neuropsychiatry*, 12, 128–143.

Corcoran, R. (2001) Theory of mind and schizophrenia. In Corrigan, P.W. and Penn, D.L. (eds), *Social Cognition and Schizophrenia*, pp. 149–174. Washington, DC: American Psychological Association.

Costello, C.G. (1994) Two dimensional views of psychopathology. *Behavior Research and Therapy*, 32, 391–402.

Couture, S.M., Penn, D.L. and Roberts, D.L. (2006) The functional significance of social cognition in schizophrenia: a review. *Schizophrenia Bulletin*, 32 (Suppl. 1), S44–63.

Craig, J.S., Hatton, C., Craig, F.B. and Bentall, R.P. (2004) Persecutory beliefs, attributions, and theory of mind: comparison of patients with paranoid delusions, Asperger's syndrome, and healthy controls. *Schizophrenia Research*, 69, 29–33.

Crick, N.R. and Dodge, K.A. (1994) A review and reformulation of social information-processing mechanisms in children's social adjustment. *Psychological Bulletin*, 115, 74–101.

Davis, P.J. and Gibson, M.G. (2000) Recognition of posed and genuine facial expressions of emotion in paranoid and nonparanoid schizophrenia. *Journal of Abnormal Psychology*, 109, 445–450.

Dougherty, E.E. Bartlett, E.S. and Izard, C.E. (1974) Responses of schizophrenics to expressions of fundamental emotions. *Journal of Clinical Psychology*, 30, 243–246.

Drury, V.M., Robinson, E.J. and Birchwood, M. (1998) 'Theory of mind' skills during an acute episode of psychosis and following recovery. *Psychological Medicine*, 28, 1101–1112.

Edwards, J., Jackson, H.J. and Pattison, P.E. (2002) Emotion recognition via facial expression and affective prosody in schizophrenia: a methodological review. *Clinical Psychology Review*, 22, 789–832.

Ellett, L., Lopes, B. and Chadwick, P. (2003) Paranoia in a non-clinical population of college students. *Journal of Nervous and Mental Disease*, 191, 425–430.

Fear, C., Sharp, H. and Healy, D. (1996) Cognitive processes in delusional disorders. *British Journal of Psychiatry*, 168, 61–67.

Fenigstein, A. (1997) Paranoid thought and schematic processing. *Journal of Social and Clinical Psychology*, 16, 77–94.

Fenigstein, A. and Vanable, P.A. (1992) Paranoia and self-consciousness. *Journal of Personality and Social Psychology*, 62, 129–138.

Fine, C., Lumsden, J. and Blair, R.J.R. (2001) Dissociation between "theory of mind" and executive functions in a patient with early left amygdala damage. *Brain*, 124, 287–298.

Fiske, S.T. and Taylor, S. (1991) *Social Cognition*, 2nd edn. New York: McGraw-Hill.

Freeman, D. and Garety, P.A. (2000) Comments on the content of persecutory delusions: does the definition need clarification? *British Journal of Clinical Psychology*, 39, 407–414.

Freeman, D. and Garety, P.A. (2003) Connecting neurosis and psychosis: The direct influence of emotion on delusions and hallucinations. *Behavior Research and Therapy*, 41, 923–947.

Freeman, D., Garety, P.A., Fowler, D. *et al.* (1998) The London–East Anglia randomized controlled trial of cognitive-behavior therapy for psychosis. IV: Self-esteem and persecutory delusions. *British Journal of Clinical Psychology*, 37, 415–430.

Freeman, D., Garety, P.A. and Phillips, M.L. (2000) The examination of hypervigilance for external threat in individuals with generalized anxiety disorder and individuals with persecutory delusions using visual scan paths. *Quarterly Journal of Experimental Psychology: Human Experimental Psychology*, 53A, 549–567.

Freeman, D., Garety, P., Kuipers, E., Fowler, D. and Bebbington, P.E. (2002) A cognitive model of persecutory delusions. *British Journal of Clinical Psychology*, 41, 331–347.

Freeman, D., Garety, P.A., Fowler, D., Kuipers, E., Bebbington, P.E. and Dunn, G. (2004) Why do people fail to choose more realistic explanations for their experiences? An empirical investigation. *Journal of Consulting and Clinical Psychology*, 72, 671–660.

Freeman, D., Dunn, G., Garety, P.A. *et al.* (2005a) The psychology of persecutory ideation. I: A questionnaire survey. *Journal of Nervous and Mental Disease*, 193, 302–308.

Freeman, D., Garety, P.A., Bebbington, P.E. *et al.* (2005b) The psychology of persecutory ideation II: A virtual reality experimental study. *Journal of Nervous and Mental Disease*, 193, 309–315.

Freeman, D., Garety, P.A., Bebbington, P.E. *et al.* (2005c) Psychological investigation of the structure of paranoia in a non-clinical population. *British Journal of Psychiatry*, 186, 427–35.

Frith, C.D. (1992) *The Cognitive Neuropsychology of Schizophrenia*. Hove: Lawrence Erlbaum.

Frith, C.D. and Corcoran, R. (1996) Exploring 'theory of mind' in people with schizophrenia. *Psychological Medicine*, 26, 521–30.

Garety, P.A. and Freeman, D. (1999) Cognitive approaches to delusions: a critical review of theories and evidence. *British Journal of Clinical Psychology*, 38, 113–154.

Garety, P.A., Freeman, D., Jolley, S. *et al.* (2005) Reasoning, emotions, and delusional conviction in psychosis. *Journal of Abnormal Psychology*, 114, 373–384.

Garety, P.A., Hemsley, D.R. and Wessely, S. (1991) Reasoning in deluded schizophrenic and paranoid patients: biased in performance on a probabilistic inference task. *Journal of Nervous and Mental Disease*, 179, 194–201.

Gay, N.W. and Combs, D.R. (2005) Social behaviors in persons with and without persecutory delusions. *Schizophrenia Research*, 80, 361–362.

Gilbert, D.T. Pelham, B.W. and Krull, D.S. (1988) On cognitive busyness: when person perceivers meet persons perceived. *Journal of Personality and Social Psychology*, 54, 733–40.

Gordon, E., Coyle, S., Anderson, J. *et al.* (1992) Eye movement response to a facial stimulus in schizophrenia. *Biological Psychiatry*, 31, 626–29.

Green, M.J. and Phillips, M.L. (2004) Social threat perception and the evolution of paranoia. *Neuroscience and Biobehavioral Reviews*, 28, 333–342.

Green, M.J., Williams, L.M. and Davidson, D.J. (2001) Processing of threat-related affect is delayed in delusion-prone individuals. *British Journal of Clinical Psychology*, 40, 157–165.

Green, M.J., Williams, L.M. and Davidson, D.J. (2003a) Visual scanpaths to threat-related faces in deluded schizophrenia. *Psychiatry Research*, 119, 271–285.

Green, M.J., Williams, L.M. and Davidson, D.J. (2003b) Visual scanpaths and facial affect recognition in delusion-prone individuals: increased sensitivity to threat? *Cognitive Neuropsychiatry*, 8, 19–41.

Green, M.J., Williams, L.M. and Davidson, D.J. (2003c) In the face of danger: specific viewing strategies for facial expressions of threat? *Cognition and Emotion*, 17, 779–786.

Green, M.J., Uhlhaas, P.J. and Coltheart, M. (2005) Context processing and social cognition in schizophrenia. *Current Psychiatry Reviews*, 1, 11–22.

Greig, T.C., Bryson, G.J. and Bell, M.D. (2004) Theory of mind performance in schizophrenia: diagnostic, symptom, and neuropsychological correlates. *Journal of Nervous and Mental Disease*, 192, 12–18.

Harrington, L., Langdon, R., Siegert, R.J. and McClure, J. (2005a) Schizophrenia, theory of mind, and persecutory delusions. *Cognitive Neuropsychiatry*, 10, 87–104.

Harrington, L., Siegert, R.J. and McClure, J. (2005b) Theory of mind in schizophrenia: a critical review. *Cognitive Neuropsychiatry*, 10, 249–286.

Herold, R., Tényi, T., Lénárd, K. and Trixler, M. (2002) Theory of mind deficit in people with schizophrenia during remission. *Psychological Medicine*, 32, 1125–1129.

Hooker, C. and Park, S. (2002) Emotion processing and its relationship to social functioning in schizophrenia patients. *Psychiatry Research*, 112, 41–50.

Hogarty, G.E., Flesher, S., Urlich, R. *et al.* (2004) Cognitive enhancement therapy in schizophrenia. *Archives of General Psychiatry*, 61, 866–876.

Horley, K., Gonsalvz, C., Williams, L., Lazzaro, I., Bahramali, H. and Gordon, E. (2001) Event-related potentials to threat-related faces in schizophrenia. *International Journal of Neuroscience*, 107, 113–130.

Humphreys, L. and Barrowclough, C. (2006) Attributional style, defensive functioning and persecutory delusions: symptom-specific or general coping strategy. *British Journal of Clinical Psychology*, 45, 231–246.

Huq, S.F., Garety, P.A. and Hemsley, D.R. (1988) Probablistic reasoning in deluded and non-deluded subjects. *Quarterly Journal of Experimental Psychology*, 40A, 801–812.

Janssen, I., Krabbendam, L., Jolles, J. and van Os, J. (2003) Alterations in theory of mind in patients with schizophrenia and non-psychotic relatives. *Acta Psychiatrica Scandinavica*, 108, 110–117.

Johns, L.C. (2004) Hallucinations in the general population. *Current Psychiatry Reports*, 7, 162–167.

Johns, L.C. and van Os, J. (2001) The continuity of psychotic experiences in the general population. *Clinical Psychology Review*, 21, 1125–1141.

Jones, W., Bellugi, U., Lai, Z. *et al.* (2000) Hypersociability in Williams Syndrome. *Journal of Cognitive Neuroscience*, 12, 30–46.

Kaney, S. and Bentall, R.P. (1989) Persecutory delusions and attributional style. *British Journal of Medical Psychology*, 62, 191–198.

Kaney, S., Wolfenden, M., Dewey, M.E. and Bentall, R.P. (1992) Persecutory delusions and recall of threatening propositions. *British Journal of Clinical Psychology*, 31, 85–87.

Kanwisher, N. (2000) Domain specificity in face perception. *Nature Neuroscience*, 3, 759–763.

Kayser, N., Sarfati, Y., Besche, C. and Hardy-Bayle, M.C. (2006) Elaboration of a rehabilitation method based on a pathogenetic hypothesis of 'theory of mind' impairment in schizophrenia. *Neuropsycholological Rehabilitation*, 16, 83–95.

Kee, K.S., Kern, R.S. and Green, M.F. (1998) Perception of emotion and neurocognitive functioning in schizophrenia: what's the link? *Psychiatry Research*, 81, 57–65.

Kee, K.S., Green, M.F., Mintz, J. and Brekke, J.S. (2003) Is emotion processing a predictor of functional outcome in schizophrenia? *Schizophrenia Bulletin*, 29, 487–497.

Kinderman, P. (1994) Attentional bias, persecutory delusions and the self-concept. *British Journal of Medical Psychology*, 67, 53–66.

Kinderman, P. and Bentall, R.P. (1996a) A new measure of causal locus: The Internal, Personal, and Situational Attributions Questionnaire. *Personality and Individual Differences*, 20, 261–264.

Kinderman, P. and Bentall, R.P. (1996b) Self-discrepancies and persecutory delusions: evidence for a model of paranoid ideation. *Journal of Abnormal Psychology*, 105, 106–113.

Kinderman, P. and Bentall, R.P. (1997) Causal attributions in paranoia and depression: internal, personal, and situational attributions for negative events. *Journal of Abnormal Psychology*, 106, 341–345.

Kinderman, P., Dunbar, R.I.M. and Bentall, R.P. (1998) Theory of mind deficits and causal attributions. *British Journal of Psychology*, 71, 339–349.

Kline, J.S., Smith, J.E. and Ellis, H.C. (1992) Paranoid and nonparanoid schizophrenic processing of facially displayed affect. *Journal of Psychiatric Research*, 26, 169–182.

Kohler, C., Bilker, W.B., Hagendoorn, M., Gur, R.E. and Gur, R.C. (2000) Emotion recognition deficit in schizophrenia: association with symptomatology and cognition. *Biological Psychiatry*, 48, 127–136.

Kohler, C., Turner, T.H., Bilker, W.B. *et al.* (2003) Facial emotion recognition in schizophrenia: Intensity effects and error patterns. *American Journal of Psychiatry*, 160, 1768–1774.

Kristev, H., Jackson, H. and Maude, D. (1999) An investigation of attributional style in frist-episode psychosis. *British Journal of Clinical Psychology*, 88, 181–194.

Langdon, R. and Coltheart, M. (1999) Mentalising, schizotypy, and schizophrenia. *Cognition*, 71, 43–71.

LaRusso, L. (1978) Sensitivity of paranoid patients to nonverbal cues. *Journal of Abnormal Behavior*, 3, 463–471.

Lee, H.J. (1999) An exploratory study on the cause of paranoia: the self-concept and reasoning bias. *Korean Journal of Clinical Psychology*, 18, 1–15.

Lee, H.J. and Won, H.T. (1998) The self-concepts, the other-concepts, and attributional styles in paranoia and depression. *Korean Journal of Clinical Psychology*, 17, 105–125.

Lee, K.H., Farrow, T.F.D., Spence, S.A. and Woodruff, P.W.R. (2004) Social cognition, brain networks, and schizophrenia. *Psychological Medicine*, 34, 391–400.

Lee, D.A., Randall, F., Beattie, G. and Bentall, R.P. (2004) Delusional discourse: an investigation comparing the spontaneous causal attributions of paranoia and non-paranoid individuals. *Psychology and Psychotherapy: Theory, Research, and Practice*, 77, 525–540.

Lewis, S.F. and Garver, D.L. (1995) Treatment and diagnostic subtype in facial affect recognition in schizophrenia. *Journal of Psychiatry Research*, 29, 5–11.

Locascio, J.J. and Synder, C.R. (1975) Selective attention to threatening stimuli and field independence as factors in the etiology of paranoid behavior. *Journal of Abnormal Psychology*, 84, 637–643.

Loughland, C.M., Williams, L.M. and Gordon, E. (2002) Visual scan paths to positive and negative facial emotions in an outpatient schizophrenia sample. *Schizophrenia Research*, 55, 159–170.

Lyon, H.M., Kaney, S. and Bentall, R.P. (1994) The defensive function of persecutory delusions: Evidence from attributional tasks. *British Journal of Psychiatry*, 164, 637–646.

Mandal, M.K., Pandey, R. and Prasad, A.B. (1998) Facial expressions of emotions and schizophrenia: a review. *Schizophrenia Bulletin*, 24, 399–412.

Marjoram, D., Miller, P., McIntosh, A.M. *et al.* (2006) A neuropsychological investigation into 'Theory of Mind' and enhanced risk of schizophrenia. *Psychiatry Research*, 144, 29–37.

Martin, J.A. and Penn, D.L. (2001) Social cognition and sub-clinical paranoid ideation. *British Journal of Clinical Psychology*, 40, 261–265.

Martin, J. and Penn, D.L. (2002) Attributional style among outpatients with schizophrenia with and without persecutory delusions. *Schizophrenia Bulletin*, 28, 131–141.

Mazza, M., DeRisio, A., Surian, L., Roncone, R. and Casacchia, M. (2001) Selective impairments of theory of mind in people with schizophrenia. *Schizophrenia Research*, 47, 299–308.

McKay, R., Langdon, R. and Coltheart, M. (2005) Paranoia, persecutory delusions and attributional biases. *Psychiatry Research*, 136, 233–245.

McKay, R., Langdon, R. and Coltheart, M. (2006) The persecutory ideation questionnaire. *Journal of Nervous and Mental Disease*, 194, 628–631.

McKay, R., Langdon, R. and Coltheart, M. (2007) The defensive function of persecutory delusions: an investigation using the Implicit Association Test. *Cognitive Neuropsychiatry*, 12, 1–24.

Miller, E. and Karoni, X. (1996) The cognitive psychology of delusions: a review. *Applied Cognitive Psychology*, 10, 487–502.

Moritz, S. and Woodward, T.S. (2005) Jumping to conclusions in delusional and non-delusional schizophrenic patients. *British Journal of Clinical Psychology*, 44, 193–207.

Mueser, K.T., Doonan, R., Penn, D.L., Blanchard, J.J., Bellack, A.S. and Nishith, P. (1996) Emotion recognition and social competence in chronic schizophrenia. *Journal of Abnormal Psychology*, 105, 271–275.

Newhill, C.H. (1990) The role of culture in the development of paranoid symptomatology. *American Journal of Orthopsychiatry*, 60, 176–188.

Peer, J.E., Rothmann, T.L. Penrod, R.D., Penn, D.L. and Spaulding, W.D. (2004) Social cognitive biases and neurocognitive deficits in paranoid symptoms: evidence for an interaction effect and changes during treatment. *Schizophrenia Research*, 71, 463–471.

Penn, D.L. and Combs, D. (2000) Modification of affect perception deficits in schizophrenia. *Schizophrenia Research*, 46, 217–229.

Penn, D.L., van der Does, A.J.W., Spaulding, W., Garbin, C., Linszen, D. and Dingemans, P. (1993) Information processing and social-cognitive problem solving in schizophrenia: Assessment of inter-relationships and changes over time. *Journal of Nervous and Mental Disease*, 181, 13–20.

Penn, D.L., Spaulding, W., Reed, D. and Sullivan, M. (1996) The relationship of social cognition to ward behavior in chronic schizophrenia. *Schizophrenia Research*, 20, 327–335.

Penn, D.L., Corrigan, P.W., Bentall, R., Racenstein, J.M. and Newman, L. (1997) Social cognition in schizophrenia. *Psychological Bulletin*, 121, 114–132.

Penn, D.L., Combs, D.R., Ritchie, M. *et al.* (2000) Emotion recognition in schizophrenia: further investigation of generalized versus specific deficit models. *Journal of Abnormal Psychology*, 109, 512–516.

Penn, D.L., Ritchie, M., Francis, J., Combs, D. and Martin, J. (2002) Social perception in schizophrenia: The role of context. *Psychiatry Research*, 109, 149–159.

Penn, D.L., Roberts, D., Munt, E.D., Silverstein, E., Jones, N. and Sheitman, B. (2005) A pilot study of social cognition and interaction training (SCIT) for schizophrenia. *Schizophrenia Research*, 80, 357–359.

Penn, D.L., Addington, J. and Pinkham, A. (2006) Social cognitive impairments. In: Lieberman, J.A., Stroup, T.S. and Perkins, D.O. (eds), *American Psychiatric Association Textbook of Schizophrenia*, pp. 261–274. Arlington, VA: American Psychiatric Publishing Press.

Penn, D.L., Roberts, D., Combs, D.R. and Sterne, A. (2007) *Psychiatric Services*. The development of the social cognition and interaction training (SCIT) program for schizophrenia spectrum disorders. *Psychiatric Services*, 58, 449–451.

Peters, E. and Garety, P.A. (2006) Cognitive functioning in delusions: a longitudinal analysis. *Behaviour Research and Therapy*, 44, 481–514.

Peters, E., Day, S. and Garety, P. (1997) From preconscious to conscious processing: where does the abnormality lie in delusions. *Schizophrenia Research*, 24, 120.

Peters, E.R., Joseph, S.A. and Garety, P.A. (1999) Measurement of delusional ideation in the normal population: introducing the PDI (Peters *et al.*, Delusions Inventory). *Schizophrenia Bulletin*, 25, 553–76.

Peterson, C., Semmel, A., Von Baeyer, C., Abramson, L., Metalsky, G.I. and Seligman, M.E.P. (1982) The Attributional Style Questionnaire. *Cognitive Therapy and Research*, 3, 287–300.

Phillips, M.L. and David, A.S. (1997) Visual scan paths are abnormal in deluded schizophrenics. *Neuropsychologia*, 35, 99–105.

Phillips, M.L., Senior, C. and Davis, A.S. (2000a) Perception of threat in schizophrenics with persecutory delusions: An investigation using visual scan paths. *Psychological Medicine*, 30, 157–167.

Phillips, M.L., Williams, L. and Senior, C. *et al.* (2000b) A differential neural response to threatening and non-threatening negative facial expressions in paranoia and non-paranoia schizophrenics. *Psychiatry Research: Neuroimaging section*, 92, 11–31.

Phillips, M.L., Drevets, W.C., Rauch, S.L. and Lane, R. (2003) Neurobiology of emotion perception I: The neural basis of emotion perception. *Biological Psychiatry*, 54, 504–514.

Pickup, G.J. (2006) Theory of mind and its relation to schizotypy. *Cognitive Neuropsychiatry*, 11, 117–192.

Pickup, G.J. and Frith, C.D. (2001) Theory of mind impairments in schizophrenia: symptomatology, severity and specificity. *Psychological Medicine*, 31, 207–220.

Pilowsky, T., Yirmiya, N., Arbelle, S. and Mozes, T. (2000) Theory of mind abilities of children with schizophrenia, children with autism, and normally developing children. *Schizophrenia Research*, 42, 145–155.

Pinkham, A.E. and Penn, D.L. (2006) Neurocognitive and social cognitive predictors of social skill in schizophrenia. *Psychiatry Research*, 143 (2–3), 167–178.

Pinkham, A.E., Penn, D.L., Perkins, D.O. and Lieberman, J. (2003) Implications for the neural basis of social cognition for the study of schizophrenia. *American Journal of Psychiatry*, 160, 815–824.

Randall, F., Corcoran, R., Day, J.C. and Bentall, R.P. (2003) Attention, theory of mind, and causal attributions in people with persecutory delusions. *Cognitive Neuropsychiatry*, 8, 287–294.

Rector, N. (2004) Cognitive theory and therapy of schizophrenia. In: Leahy, R.L. (ed.), *Contemporary Cognitive Therapy: Theory, Research, and Practice*, pp. 244–268. New York: Guilford Press.

Roncone, R., Falloon, I.R.H., Mazza, M. *et al.* (2002) Is theory of mind in schizophrenia more strongly associated with clinical and social functioning than with neurocognitive deficits? *Psychopathology*, 35, 280–288.

Russell, T.A., Chu, E. and Phillips, M.L. (2006) A pilot study to investigate the effectiveness of emotion recognition remediation in schizophrenia using the micro-expression training tool. *British Journal of Clinical Psychology*, 45, 579–583.

Sachs, G., Steger-Wuchse, D., Krypsin-Exner, I., Gur, R.C. and Katschnig, H. (2004) Facial recognition deficits and cognition in schizophrenia. *Schizophrenia Research*, 68, 27–35.

Schenkel, L., Spaulding, W. and Silverstein, S.M. (2005) Poor premorbid social functioning and theory of mind deficit in schizophrenia: evidence of reduced context processing? *Journal of Psychiatric Research*, 39, 499–508.

Schneider, F., Gur, R.C., Gur, R.E. and Shtasel, D.L. (1995) Emotional processing in schizophrenia: neurobehavioral probes in relation to psychopathology. *Schizophrenia Research*, 17, 67–75.

Sergi, M.J. and Green, M.F. (2002) Social perception and early visual processing in schizophrenia. *Schizophrenia Research*, 59, 233–241.

Sergi, M.J., Rassovsky, Y., Nuechterlein, K.H. and Green, M.F. (2006) Social perception as a mediator of influence of early visual processing on functional status in schizophrenia. *American Journal of Psychiatry*, 163, 448–454.

Silver, H. and Shlomo, N. (2001) Perception of facial emotions in chronic schizophrenia does not correlate with negative symptoms but correlates with cognitive and motor dysfunction. *Schizophrenia Research*, 52, 265–273.

Spaulding, W.D., Reed, D., Sullivan, M., Richardson, C. and Weiler, M. (1999) Effects of cognitive treatment in psychiatric rehabiltation. *Schizophrenia Bulletin*, 25, 657–676.

Streit, M., Wölwer, W. and Gaebel, W. (1997) Facial-affect recognition and visual scanning behaviour in the course of schizophrenia. *Schizophrenia Research*, 24, 311–317.

Swartz, B.L., Rosse, R.B., Johri, S. and Deutsch, S.I. (1999) Visual scanning of facial expressions in schizophrenia. *Journal of Neuropsychiatry and Clinical Neuroscience*, 11, 103–106.

Taylor, J.L. and Kinderman, P. (2002) An analogue study of attributional complexity, theory of mind deficits and paranoia. *British Journal of Psychology*, 93, 137–140.

Tager-Flusberg, H., Boshart, J. and Baron-Cohen, S. (1998) Reading the windows into the soul: evidence for domain-specific sparing in Williams syndrome. *Journal of Cognitive Neuroscience*, 10, 631–639.

Tomlinson, E.K., Jones, C.A., Johnston, R.A. Meaden, A. and Wink, B. (2006) Facial emotion recognition from moving and static point-light images in schizophrenia. *Schizophrenia Research*, 85(1–3), 96–105.

Toomey, R., Wallace, C.J., Corrigan, P.W., Schuldberg, D. and Green, M.F. (1997) Social processing correlates of nonverbal social perception in schizophrenia. *Psychiatry*, 60, 292–300.

Trower, P. and Chadwick, P. (1995) Pathways to a defense of the self: a theory of two types of paranoia. *Clinical Psychology: Science and Practice*, 2, 263–278.

Turkat, I.D., Keane, S.P. and Thompson-Pope, S.K. (1995) Social processing errors among paranoid personalities. *Journal of Psychopathology and Behavioral Assessment*, 12, 263–269.

Van der Gaag, M., Kern, R.S., van den Bosch, R.J. and Liberman, R.P. (2002) A controlled trial of cogntive remediation in schizophrenia. *Schizophrenia Bulletin*, 28, 167–176.

Vauth, R., Rusch, N., Wirtz, M. and Corrigan, P.W. (2004) Does social cognition influence the relation between neurocognitive deficits and vocational functioning in schizophrenia? *Psychiatry Research*, 128, 155–165.

van Os, J., Hanssen, M., Bijl, R.V. and Ravelli, A. (2000) Strauss (1969) revisited: a psychosis continuum in the general population. *Schizophrenia Research*, 45, 11–20.

Verdoux, H. and van Os, J. (2002) Psychotic symptoms in non-clinical populations and the continuum of psychosis. *Schizophrenia Research*, 54, 59–65.

Walston, F. (2000) "Theory of mind", persecutory delusions, and the somatic marker mechanism. *Cognitive Neuropsychiatry*, 5, 161–174.

Whaley, A.L. (2001) Cultural mistrust: an important psychological construct for diagnosis and treatment of African-Americans. *Professional Psychology: Research and Practice*, 32, 555–562.

Williams, L.M., Loughland, C.M., Gordon, E. and Davidson, D. (1999) Visual scanpaths in schizophrenia. Is there a deficit in face recognition? *Schizophrenia Research*, 40, 189–199.

Won, H.T. and Lee, H.J. (1997) The self-concept and attributional style in a paranoid group. *Korean Journal of Clinical Psychology*, 16, 173–182.

Wyer, R. and Carlston, D. (1979) *Social Cognition, Inference, and Action*. Hillsdale, NJ: Erlbaum.

Wykes, T., Hamid, S. and Wagstaff, K. (2001) Theory of mind and executive functions in the non-psychotic siblings of patients with schizophrenia. (Abstract.) *Schizophrenia Research*, 49 (Suppl. 1), 148.

Zigler, E. and Glick, M. (1988) Is paranoid schizophrenia really camouflaged depression? *American Psychologist*, 43, 284–290.

Chapter 10

Persecutory delusions and theory of mind: longstanding debates and emerging issues

Rhiannon Corcoran and Suzanne Kaiser

Introduction

The rapidity with which interest grew in the topic of 'theory of mind' (ToM) in schizophrenia during the latter half of the 1990s took those of us who were involved in the earliest studies of this socio-cognitive skill by surprise. The popularity of the topic probably comes down to two factors. The first is the elegance of Frith's (1992) meta-representational model of schizophrenia into which the ToM studies fell. Using his highly convincing overarching model, he was able to conduct symptom-based studies which he could ally to diagnosis. Like no other in the field, this model managed to provide a synthesis between the controversial diagnosis on the one hand and the heterogeneity of the symptoms associated with it on the other. Furthermore, in doing so it tackled the polarity between advocates of the biological perspective and those whose understanding of psychosis came from a more psychological perspective. The second reason for the popularity of the ToM proposal was the intuitively compelling suggestion that a misunderstanding of other people's intentions lay at the heart of paranoia. While this suggestion teeters towards tautology, it was nevertheless open to scientific scrutiny by the adoption of carefully designed empirical tests, some of which were borrowed from the child development literature and others which emerged expressly for the purpose of studying mentalizing in the adult brain. The popularity of this approach to understanding the signs and symptoms of schizophrenia has carried over into genetic and evolutionary accounts of schizophrenia through proposals such as those of Brüne (2001) and Burns (2004) which argue that schizophrenia is the price that must be paid for the significant and rapid advancement in social cognition of Homonids.

We will not here present an exhaustive review of the ToM literature in this area but we would suggest that readers look at the two excellent reviews of the wider area presented by Harrington *et al.* (2005) and Brüne (2005). We begin with a definition of the term 'theory of mind' as it was originally used in association with psychosis, and go on to summarize and assess the arguments that Frith put forward about how and why this socio-cognitive skill may be linked with persecutory delusions (PD). We will follow this with a presentation of key studies which have led to the present state of knowledge within what are now relatively longstanding debates about the relationship of ToM to PD. This will emphasize both what we know and what we still do not know. Some suggestions about how to take current debates forward will be offered. We will proceed with an investigation of some of the emerging issues in the literature including a brief review of studies of the remediation of ToM, transdiagnostic issues, studies of implicit ToM and the fit of the mentalizing model to the situation.

Longstanding debates

The definition and origins of ToM in the context of persecutory delusions

According to Frith's model, problems with ToM result from a more general problem with meta-representation, the super-ordinate skill of thinking about the contents of the mind. Thus, meta-representation involves the secondary, as opposed to the primary, representation of the world. Indeed, Brüne (2005) has suggested that it may be the failure to distinguish secondary representations from primary representations that underlies the firmly held beliefs that we refer to as delusions. The ability to meta-represent enables introspection and self-awareness as well as reflection on the mental states of others. It is the ability to think about the thoughts, intentions and beliefs of others, that will be used as the working definition of ToM in this chapter because it is this precise ability that was originally argued to be relevant to persecutory delusions (PD).

The possession of a functioning ToM enables one to mentalize or 'mind-read', in other words, to infer the mental states of other people. Experience tells us that individual differences exist in the efficiency of this skill. We all know people who have a tendency to 'put their foot in it', who fail to 'take a hint', who lack tact or who tend to 'get the wrong end of the stick'. These are familiar terms which people use to reflect a relative lack of aptitude in this key socio-cognitive skill. Some studies exploring mentalizing in healthy adult samples have linked a relative impoverishment of this ability to levels of schizotypal personality wherein people endorse sub-clinical psychotic-like beliefs and experiences (Langdon and Coltheart 1999; Pickup 2006). It is significant that the particular beliefs and experiences sampled in these questionnaires resemble the positive symptoms of psychosis of which PD are probably the most common (Garety *et al.* 1988; Jorgensen and Jensen 1994; Stompe *et al.* 1999). According to Wing *et al.* (1974) PD arise when 'the subject believes that someone, or some organization, or some force or power, is trying to harm him/her in some way: to damage his/her reputation, to cause him/her bodily injury, to drive him/her mad or to bring about his/her death' (p. 170). This definition alongside the DSM-IV criteria which asserts that a delusion is 'a false personal belief based on incorrect inference about external reality …', makes the proposal that PD stem from incorrect inferences about another's intention (i.e. a ToM difficulty) very obvious.

Frith suggested that people who hold beliefs that others mean them harm do so as a result of a temporary malfunction of the meta-representational mechanism when it is engaged in inferring the intentions of other people. The specificity of this malfunction implies that for people who suffer from PD, in the absence of any other psychotic sign or symptom, the stages of meta-representation prior to mentalizing will be intact (Fig. 10.1). In other words, the abilities to introspect, engage in wilful acts and to self-monitor, will be intact in such patients. However, in practice, PD do not occur in isolation but instead tend to present alongside auditory hallucinations as well as other delusions and sometimes thought disorder (e.g. Liddle 1987). Also integral in the original formulation was the assumption that the ToM problem is associated with the acute state and that when symptoms remit this is because the temporary meta-represetational fault has been rectified. It therefore follows that

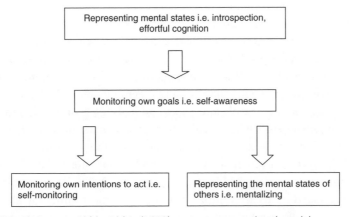

Fig. 10.1 The stages within Frith's (1992) meta-representational model.

patients who have had PD in the past but who are now in remission should have intact ToM skills. Again, because of the presence of other signs and symptoms, it is difficult to assess adequately the veracity of this claim, and the debate about state and trait continues in the literature as discussed below. The assumption that the difficulty is linked to the deluded state explained, in part, by the content of the incorrect inferences that are made in the context of PD. The misinterpretations are characteristically malign because patients are used to drawing inferences about others' intentions efficiently and accurately, and they anticipate being able to do so consistently in the future. Consequently when they begin to have difficulties, they make an external attribution to account for this and conclude that the reason for their difficulty is that the other person is trying to conceal his/her intentions. Following from that conclusion, one likely default assumption to account for the concealment of intention is that the other person's intentions towards one are not benign. This series of speculations could be scrutinized by examining the ability of patients with PD to understand the intention to deceive when the motive is more clearly benign, for example when one tries to conceal a surprise party or a present. To our knowledge no studies of this sort have been conducted.

More recently other researchers have tried to account for the content of PD by suggesting that the ToM difficulty is not a deficit but rather a bias which leads to them holding a default 'nasty ToM'. This is an idea drawn originally from Happé and Frith's (1996) work on children with conduct disorder but which recent work by J. Taylor (personal communication) has shown to relate to PD in forensic populations. The idea of a bias rather than a deficit in ToM gives the socio-cognitive problems a further aetiological perspective where it fits with the growing literature showing a link between positive symptoms and histories of abuse (e.g. Read *et al.* 2005). If mentalizing is like other skills in having a learned element, then one can deduce that a history characterized by abuse may lead to the development of a 'ToM store' which is rich in malign intentions. A further neglected issue that comes through clearly in the growing literature on the psychology of violent behaviour in the context of PD is the importance of empathic as opposed to mental state inferences in this group of patients. Abu-Akel and Khalid (2004) found intact ToM in combination with deficient empathic inferences and high levels of hostility towards others in participants who had a history of violence towards others. The extent to which the ability to infer the cognitive states of others should be regarded as distinct from the ability to infer others' emotional states has arisen quite often in the wider ToM literature (e.g. Stone 2000). Recently this issue has been clarified by functional magnetic resonance imaging showing both shared and separable components in these two types of social inference, with the amygdala in particular being more active when participants think about others' emotions (Völlm *et al.* 2006). The pattern of activity is consistent with the arguments of LeDoux (1996) who proposed that both cortical and limbic circuits exist for decision-making (i.e. 'hot' and 'cold' cognition). It would seem that those with a tendency to act in a violent manner on the basis of their PD are, possibly as a result of increased levels of hostility arising from negative emotional experiences with others now and in the past, less capable of accurately inferring the emotions of other people. It would be valuable to examine the corresponding amygdala activity associated with the emotional inferences that such patients draw during empathic inference tests focusing on strangers versus people known to them, a distinction which has come to a head very recently in the mentalizing literature and to which we return in the section on 'Theory-theory or simulation theory: the role of different contexts' (Mitchell *et al.* 2006).

Another aspect of the original model that has remained untested to date is the specificity of the ToM difficulty to others' intentions. Much of the work carried out so far has focused on false belief understanding as opposed to the understanding of intentions (e.g. Langdon *et al.* 1997; Sarfati *et al.*, 1999). Some of the early work did look specifically at intentions, for example when they were hidden behind indirect speech acts, and found difficulties in patients with paranoid symptoms (Corcoran *et al.* 1995). More recently Corcoran and Frith (2003) have suggested that it is intention to deceive which appears to be most robustly associated with the ToM difficulty in schizophrenia. However, a real test of whether belief, knowledge or intention attributions are differentially affected in the context of PD remains to be conducted.

So far we have looked at questions deriving directly from Frith's original model. While all of them are still relevant, perhaps the most challenging of these remains the specific link of ToM problems to PD. As we shall see, this link is far from clearly established.

Are ToM difficulties related to PD at all?

The literature on schizophrenia consistently shows that neuropsychological deficits are not associated with positive symptoms (e.g. Keefe *et al.* 2006). In the context of these very robust negative findings, the evidence associating ToM problems to PD looks quite convincing on the face of it. However, a proper review of the literature demonstrates that the situation is far from straightforward.

The two excellent reviews of the literature on ToM in schizophrenia by Harrington *et al.* (2005) and Brüne (2005) provide us with enough information to assess whether or not the weight of evidence supports the existence of a

ToM difficulty in relation to PD. Having assessed the methodological issues which make the assessment of this question difficult—for example, how the presence of PD are established; whether or not other symptoms were present; the chronicity of the disorder; the extent of the contribution made to any ToM difficulty by problems with other 'domain-general' cognitive skills and the nature of the ToM task itself—Harrington *et al.* concluded 'it is clear that current evidence points to thought disorder and paranoid symptoms as being most consistently associated with the well-established ToM deficit present in schizophrenia.' (p. 275). Brüne is a little less firm in his assessment of the evidence overall but is nevertheless happy to conclude that: 'It is therefore conceivable that patients with persecutory delusions are particularly compromised when they have to "mentalize on the spot" but may perform quite normally on standard ToM tests when not under time pressure.' (p. 34).

One study by Walston *et al.* (2000) indicated that no clear problems are associated with ToM when circumscribed PD exist in isolation of other signs and symptoms of psychosis. These authors examined a small number of patients with 'pure' PD in the context of delusional disorder using a range of ToM tasks including stories to second-order, hints and jokes. The good performance on ToM tasks by this group led the authors to suggest that PD should be distinguished from other paranoid-type symptoms when assessing ToM. However, these patients did have difficulties when they were asked to try to understand the mental states of their 'persecutors'. This may support the presence of a circumscribed ToM deficit existing alongside the circumscribed delusion.

Compelling evidence for the association between ToM and PD comes from recent studies taking a transdiagnostic approach to the psychology of PD (see 'Transdiagnostic issues' below) and on the basis of these findings and the conclusions of the reviews referred to above, we think it is reasonable to conclude that ToM difficulties are associated with the presence of PD specifically.

Abu-Akel (1999) has suggested that some people with schizophrenia may over-attribute the intentions of others and thus show hyper-ToM as opposed to a deficit or bias. Interestingly, the results of a recent study by Russell *et al.* (2006) support this proposal to some extent. Russell *et al.* used animations which showed geometric shapes moving in a random fashion, in an apparently goal-directed way (e.g. resembling foraging) or finally in a way that looked like they were interacting on the basis of a knowledge of mental states (e.g. resembling teasing). What these authors noticed was that with the lower-level stimuli (i.e. random and goal-directed), some patients in their paranoid group (which included PD and other symptoms) had a tendency to attribute mental states to these animations. On the other hand, when the interaction animations were considered, there was good evidence that the paranoid group tended not to attribute mental states as much as controls. Perhaps the association between ToM and paranoia is more complex than early studies imply. Russell *et al.* suggested that people with paranoid-type delusions can attribute mental states on-line but do so unreliably and rather inappropriately—which was effectively the same argument as originally proposed by Frith (1992). A slightly different interpretation of the diversity of the ToM difficulty seen in schizophrenia was offered by Abu-Akel and Bailey (2000) who suggested that there may be three types of ToM malfunction; impaired ToM, intact ToM with compromised capacity to apply the information, and hyper-ToM. This tripartite model is eminently testable and we await further work by this group.

State or trait?

The debate about whether the ToM difficulty associated with the diagnosis of schizophrenia is state- or trait-related is ongoing, as both Harrington *et al.* and Brüne point out. However, recent evidence suggests that perhaps the best way to summarize the literature with respect to PD is to propose that the ToM difficulty is present during remission of these beliefs, and is seen in relation to high schizotypy (Pickup 2006) and in unaffected relatives of people with schizophrenia (Janssen *et al.* 2003). However, the level of difficulty associated with the skill appears to increase during episodes of acute illness. Amongst the studies that would be consistent with such an interpretation would be the cross-sectional study conducted by Randall *et al.* (2003) which looked specifically at PD and the findings of Drury *et al.* (1998) which included a short follow-up period. These authors concluded that the case for the ToM difficulty being a consistent trait-like feature for those showing a propensity for PD was strong.

Resolving the longstanding debates

In order to bring the debates addressed above to firmer conclusions, longitudinal studies of first-onset or 'at-risk' cohorts are required. Such studies should include several ToM tasks assessing intentions and false beliefs, testing explicit and implicit forms of mental state inference (see section on 'Measuring implicit or 'on-line' ToM' below) and using both verbal and non-verbal paradigms to do so. Prior to this, however, groups conducting this type of research should endeavour to establish the psychometric properties of the measures they use (e.g. see Shryane *et al.* 2007). They should explore the construct validity of their measures and the test–retest and inter-rater reliability of the measures. Furthermore, the measurement of PD needs to be explicit and based upon accepted criteria for the presence of delusions with clear evidence of their persecutory nature established by appropriate standardized assessments which also assess the presence, severity and chronicity of other signs and symptoms of psychosis. Studies should continue to assess the potential impact of 'domain-general skills' on ToM as the specificity of this skill is far from well-established (e.g. Russell 1998); but the search for candidate cognitive sub-components or contributors to social cognition should be widened to include not only IQ, but also aspects of higher order cognition which could theoretically underpin mentalizing. Such skills are generally not included in standard neuropsychological batteries. Some suggestions as to what these might be are presented in 'How to mentalize when ToM malfunctions: the use of domain-general skills' below, but assessments of the general ability to simulate *per se* (i.e. the ability to run through scenarios in the head with a view to generating solutions to a problem) would be important. Finally, attempts need to be made to establish the impact of the duration and chronicity of the illness on social cognition as well as antipsychotic drug treatment, a factor which has been conspicuously absent in previous studies of ToM.

Emerging issues

Transdiagnostic issues

We would like now to move away from debates which have been in the forefront of research for some time and instead consider themes that are beginning to emerge in the more recent literature. The first of these is the issue of whether the ToM impairment associated with PD is seen across diagnoses. As the majority of published studies on ToM in psychosis have been on samples of patients with schizophrenia, this issue has been largely avoided. Early work by Doody et al. (1998) reported that ToM was intact in a group of patients with affective disorder in spite of a shared symptom profile with a group of patients with schizophrenia whose ToM was impaired. Kerr et al. (2003) went on to demonstrate poor ToM in patients with bipolar disorder. However, these studies did not specifically focus on PD. Moore et al. (2006) did look exclusively at PD in patients with very-late-onset schizophrenia-like psychosis and found evidence of impairments in the understanding of deception on a story task which tested both deception and false belief to second-order level. This study agrees with the suggestion of Corcoran and Frith (2003) that it may be the understanding of the intention to deceive that is core to PD. Other work of a transdiagnostic nature conducted by R. Corcoran et al. (2007) has demonstrated that the presence of PD is associated with ToM difficulty in the context of both schizophrenia spectrum disorders and affective disorders. Evidence is therefore beginning to accrue to support the idea that, although ToM problems are robustly associated with a diagnosis of schizophrenia (and that within that diagnosis, several signs and symptoms appear to be related to ToM problems), these same difficulties are central to PD wherever they originate.

How to mentalize when ToM malfunctions: the use of domain-general skills

According to Dennett (1987), humans take the intentional stance by default. In other words we cannot help but interpret others' behaviours as resulting from their thoughts and intentions. While it may very well be the case that people with autistic spectrum disorders and possibly people with the negative features of schizophrenia are exceptions to this rule in that they may not be driven, by default, to think about others (or themselves) in this way (Frith 1992; Baron-Cohen 1995), it would seem that people with PD do take the intentional stance. The weight of evidence (from formal empirical studies and clinical experience) indicates that people with PD do have a ToM, in the sense that they understand that others are driven by mental states, but that their inferences about these mental states are compromised. If we assume that the default adoption of the intentional stance indicates the working of an evolved mechanism (an assumption that not everyone would agree with, of course) then it follows that this mechanism fails in the presence of PD but that patients are still driven to understand the intentions of others. How do they do this? Some work proposes that people rely on domain-general skills to answer mentalizing questions when their ToM modules 'crash', and this, alongside the fact that these domain-general skills may themselves be compromised, results in the drawing of unreliable ToM inferences. Three studies have demonstrated that skills needed to draw inductive inferences are compromised in patients with schizophrenia who show ToM problems. The idea is that because the ToM 'module' is malfunctioning, people with schizophrenia have to rely on a poor or biased autobiographical memory in conjunction with impaired social conditional reasoning to draw ToM conclusions (Corcoran 2003; Corcoran and Frith 2003, 2005). It is possible that if these domain-general skills were intact, then the ToM output resulting from them would be reliable and there would be no need for a devoted ToM module at all. Some later work has looked at heuristic reasoning, a form of fast experience-based reasoning thought to be relied on for everyday problem-solving situations, in patients with PD. Corcoran *et al.* (2006) reported that patients with PD tended not to use information about themselves as a basis for inferences about the experiences of other people. This result is consistent with there being poor simulation-based mentalizing in patients with PD (see 'Theory-theory or simulation theory: the role of different contexts' below).

Amongst other work focusing on less-well-established cognitive correlates or models of ToM is that of Charlton *et al.* who propose that ToM is intact in patients with PD (in the sense of understanding that others behave according to the contents of their minds) but their ToM judgments go wrong because these judgements are arrived at using the somatic marker mechanism (Damasio 1995). This means that people work backwards from their emotional body states (e.g. fear) to guess which intentions of others would cause such body states (e.g. intention to harm). It is the bias towards particular emotional states that informs mentalizing in people with PD. Although not directly tested, this hypothesis is consistent with the general findings of Corcoran *et al.* (2006) of biased heuristic reasoning in the context of threatening situations. Charlton's (2001) somatic marker proposal could be more directly tested in patients with PD using the tasks derived by Damasio *et al.* in their studies of patients with ventromedial lesions such as the Iowa Gambling Task (Bechara *et al.* 1994).

The remediation of ToM

It has taken a relatively long time for studies aimed at improving ToM in people with schizophrenia to emerge. It is not clear what led to this relative inertia as researchers were interested in the topic from an early stage. The lack of publications may reflect a lack of success at establishing these trials or a lack of positive findings. To date there have been three published attempts to remediate ToM in people with schizophrenia spectrum disorders (Roncone *et al.* 2004; Penn *et al.* 2005; Kayser *et al.* 2006). All three of these studies reported some success, though they all suffer from methodological problems, casting doubt on the validity of their findings. The problems include failure to take account of regression to the mean (Penn *et al.* 2005), use of inappropriate psychiatric control groups (Roncone *et al.* 2004; Kayser *et al.* 2006), lack of a control group against which to compare the ToM therapy (Penn *et al.* 2005), confounding of general and directed therapies (Roncone *et al.* 2004), and weak analyses (Kayser *et al.* 2006). Of the three studies Roncone *et al.*'s is perhaps the best designed. It offers some evidence that ToM may be improved. However, the fact that Roncone *et al.* embedded a directed therapy for ToM within a more general cognitive therapy means that it is impossible to determine what aspect of their remediation programme was responsible for the positive results. These studies have used heterogeneous groups of patients with various signs and symptoms of psychosis. Frith (1992) argued, and empirical evidence indicates, that patients with negative signs have a severe and enduring ToM impairment similar in extent to that seen in people with autism (e.g. Corcoran *et al.* 1995). Attempts at remediation including such severely impaired participants may jeopardize findings which may be more fruitful if they were to focus on patients with PD.

Measuring implicit or 'on-line' ToM

Implicit ToM is more automatic, more moment-to-moment, and less effortful than explicit ToM, which requires overt reasoning and effort. Implicit ToM is the type of mentalizing employed in everyday social situations, particularly conversation, and it is possible that implicit ToM might be more driven by fast emotionally based reasoning. The significant neglect of this type of ToM reasoning in favour of the ecologically less sound use of empirical tests has, in our opinion, hindered advance in the understanding of how ToM really functions and relates to PD and psychosis more generally. The few studies that have been conducted have used diverse methods and reached differing conclusions. Quantitative work by Langdon *et al.* (1997) showed that people with schizophrenia used fewer mental state terms when describing their responses to a picture-sequencing task than healthy controls. This finding was replicated by Russell *et al.* (2006) in the context of descriptions of scenarios involving animated triangles. However, both Langdon *et al.* and Russell *et al.* examined mental state references in the context of monologue, even though mental state referents would most likely occur during dialogue. Conducting an examination of dialogue, McCabe *et al.* (2004) used a qualitative analysis of conversations between people with positive symptoms of psychosis and mental health professionals. They concluded that implicit ToM was intact since patients could maintain conversation and because they recognized that others did not share their delusional beliefs. However, an alternative explanation to account for McCabe *et al.*'s observations is presented below.

As part of the work conducted for her PhD, Kaiser (2007) attempted to improve on the published studies in the area by using a measure of implicit ToM and empathic inference based on dialogues between the experimenter and the participant probing brief stories written by the participant in response to verbal or pictorial prompts. Controlling for total speech produced, Kaiser compared ratings of mental state and emotional references about story characters, positive references to own mental state (e.g. 'I think', 'In my opinion'), and references to the conversational partner's mental states. Eighteen people with schizophrenia spectrum disorders with chronic histories and often persistent positive symptoms including PD participated in this study along with nine healthy adults with similar age, sex and IQ profiles. Kaiser found that the patients made significantly fewer mental state and emotional references and references to the conversational partner's mental state than the healthy controls. However, there was no difference between the groups for references to own mental states. According to this more rigorous study of implicit mentalizing, operationalized as references to both the story characters' mental states and the conversational partner's mental state, this type of mentalizing is impaired, as is implicit empathizing in patients with schizophrenia spectrum disorders. These results support the findings of Langdon *et al.* (1997) and Russell *et al.* (2006) but not the conclusions of McCabe *et al.* (2004).

We believe that the conclusions drawn by McCabe *et al.* on the basis of transcribed therapy session of patients with positive symptoms are incorrect. We propose that the ability of patients to converse and exchange views with their therapists, and indeed with other people more generally, in meaningful ways can be accounted for by their intact processes of alignment (Garrod and Pickering 2004). Alignment is an automatic process that begins with the first utterance of a dialogue and continues over the course of the interaction to make the interlocutors' representations at several levels become more similar. It is relevant here that, according to Garrod and Pickering, the ultimate form of alignment takes place at the level of 'situation models', global representations of a situation that take into account information about sequence, space, time, contributing individuals, and causality. Each interlocutor creates and updates his or her own situation model based on contributions to the interaction, and the extent of the similarity between interlocutors' situation models influences the success of the conversation. Garrod and Pickering also illustrate clearly how alignment can produce meaningful conversation in the presence of impoverished ToM.

S.L. Kaiser *et al.* (unpublished) examined the process of alignment in a sample of 59 patients with schizophrenia and 38 age-, sex- and IQ-matched controls. The task examined the ability to align responses to requests for level of politeness while also establishing the ability of participants to infer the knowledge state of one of the characters involved in the scenarios used. Using this quantitative task, she showed that patients were able to align for politeness to the same degree as controls while demonstrating relatively impoverished knowledge attribution (i.e. ToM). While the sample used here was a mixed group of patients with *DSM-IV*-defined schizophrenia, some (~40%) had active PD alongside other signs and symptoms. This process, which appears to enable interaction with others despite poor ToM, requires more investigation in those with delusions as well as in patients with formal thought disorder where it is possible that processes of alignment might very well fail.

Theory-theory or simulation theory: the role of different contexts

Recent imaging work by Mitchell *et al.* (2006) has led to the proposal that the ToM system contains both theory-based and simulation-based elements, depending on the target of the mentalizing process. This has implications for the debate over the relationship between ToM and PD. Mitchell *et al.*'s findings showed that different regions of the medial prefrontal cortex were activated in healthy controls depending on the subjective degree of similarity of the target to the participant. These authors argue that nearly all traditional ToM tasks used in imaging studies consist of characters who will be seen as dissimilar to the participant, triggering theory-based mentalizing (e.g. Russell *et al.* 2000; Brunet *et al.* 2003; Calarge *et al.* 2003; Völlm *et al.* 2006). This is also true of ToM studies in people with PD where, to our knowledge, patients have never been asked to infer the mental states of people known to them or judged to be similar to them. Thus, the findings relating ToM to PD refer only to theory-based mentalizing. If faults in the theory-based mentalizing system play a role in the development and maintenance of PD, it would mean that people with PD have learned mentalizing rules that are incorrect. If these incorrect rules are applied during the mentalizing process, the person will be unable accurately to discern others' intentions, leading them to conclude that the target is hiding (presumably malevolent) intentions. However, if Mitchell *et al.* are correct, this process will only occur when targets are perceived as dissimilar to the participant. Currently it is not known whether simulation-based mentalizing is impaired in psychosis, but on the basis of the evidence available it seems that PD in part results from a combined process of judgements of dissimilarity and inaccurate theory-based mentalizing. These speculations raise several questions for future research. It is unknown whether judgements of similarity (which would trigger theory-based or simulation-based mentalizing) are affected by psychosis in general or differ among people with different symptom profiles. If these judgements are affected, people with psychosis may employ theory-based versus simulation-based mentalizing differently from healthy populations. Clearly, suitable tests of similarity/familiarity judgments, simulation *per se* and simulation-based mentalizing should be developed and applied to samples with psychosis.

The future

In this chapter we have presented an overview of the findings which concern the nature of the relationship between PD and ToM. Many questions deriving from Frith's (1992) original proposal still remain to be answered by future studies with improved methodological rigour. However, the emerging issues in this area are clearly relevant to the association of ToM with PD. These extend the field of future research outward to include different aspects of ToM and related processes into various diagnoses where PD present.

References

Abu-Akel, A. (1999) Impaired theory of mind in schizophrenia. *Pragmatics and Cognition*, 7, 247–282.

Abu-Akel, A. and Bailey, A.L. (2000) Letter to the editor. *Psychological Medicine*, 30, 735–738.

Abu-Akel, A. and Khalid, A. (2004) 'Theory of mind' in violent and non-violent patients with paranoid schizophrenia. *Schizophrenia Research*, 69, 46–53.

Baron-Cohen, S. (1995) *Mindblindness. An Essay on Autism and Theory of Mind*. Cambridge, MA/London: MIT Press.

Bechara, A., Damasio, A.R., Damasio, H. and Anderson, S. (1994) Insensitivity to future consequences following damage to the human prefrontal cortex. *Cognition*, 50, 7–12.

Brüne, M. (2001) Social cognition and psychopathology in an evolutionary perspective. *Psychopathology*, 34, 85–94.

Brüne, M. (2005) 'Theory of mind' in schizophrenia: a review of the literature. *Schizophrenia Bulletin*, 31, 21–42.

Brunet, E., Sarfati, Y., Hardy-Baylé, M.-C. and Decety, J. (2003) Abnormalities of brain function during a nonverbal theory of mind task in schizophrenia. *Neuropsychologia*, 41, 1574–1582.

Burns, J.K. (2004) An evolutionary theory of schizophrenia: cortical connectivity, metarepresentation, and the social brain. *Behavioral and Brain Sciences*, 27, 831–855.

Calarge, C., Andreasen, N.C. and O'Leary, D.S. (2003) Visualizing how one brain understands another: a PET study of theory of mind. *American Journal of Psychiatry*, 160, 1954–1964.

Charlton, B.G. (2001) Theory of mind and the "somatic marker mechanism" (SMM). *Behavioral and Brain Sciences*, 24, 1141–1142.

Corcoran, R. (2003) Inductive reasoning and the understanding of intention in schizophrenia. *Cognitive Neuropsychiatry*, 8, 223–235.

Corcoran, R. and Frith, C. D. (2003) Autobiographical memory and theory of mind: evidence of a relationship in schizophrenia. *Psychological Medicine*, 33, 897–905.

Corcoran, R. and Frith C.D. (2005) Thematic reasoning and theory of mind. Accounting for social inference difficulties in schizophrenia. *Evolutionary Psychology*, 3, 1–19.

Corcoran, R., Mercer, G. and Frith, C.D. (1995) Schizophrenia, symptomatology and social inference: investigating 'theory of mind' in people with schizophrenia. *Schizophrenia Research*, 17, 5–13.

Corcoran, R., Cummins, S., Rowse, G. *et al.* (2006) Reasoning under uncertainty: heuristic judgments in patients with persecutory delusions or depression. *Psychological Medicine*, 36, 1109–1118.

Corcoran, R., Rowse, G., Moore, R. *et al.* (2007) A transdiagnostic investigation of 'theory of mind' and 'jumping to conclusions' in patients with persecutory delusions. *Psychological Medicine* doi: 10.1017/S0033291707002152.

Damasio, A.R. (1995) Towards a neurobiology of emotion and feeling: operational concepts and hypotheses. *The Neuroscientist*, 1, 19–25.

Dennett, D.C (1987) *The Intentional Stance*. Cambridge, MA: MIT Press.

Doody, G.A., Götz, M., Johnstone, E.C., Frith, C.D. and Cunningham Owens, D.G. (1998) Theory of mind and psychoses. *Psychological Medicine*, 28, 397–405.

Drury, V.M., Robinson, E.J. and Birchwood, M. (1998) 'Theory of mind' skills during an acute episode of psychosis and following recovery. *Psychological Medicine*, 28, 1101–1112.

Frith, C.D. (1992) *The Cognitive Neuropsychology of Schizophrenia*. Hove: Erlbaum.

Garety, P.A., Everitt, B.S. and Hemsley, D.R. (1988) The characteristics of delusions: a cluster analysis of deluded subjects. *European Archives of Psychiatry and Neurological Sciences*, 237, 112–114.

Garrod, S. and Pickering, M.J. (2004) Why is conversation so easy? *Trends in Cognitive Sciences*, 8, 8–11.

Happé, F.G.E. and Frith, U. (1996) theory of mind and social impairment in children with conduct disorder. *British Journal of Developmental Psychology*, 14, 385–398.

Harrington, L., Siegart, R.J. and McClure, J. (2005) Theory of mind in schizophrenia: a critical review. *Cognitive Neuropsychiatry*, 10, 249–286.

Janssen, I., Krabbendam, L., Jolles, J. and van Os, J. (2003) Alterations in theory of mind in patients with schizophrenia and non-psychotic relatives. *Acta Psychiatrica Scandinavica*, 108, 110–117.

Jorgensen, P. and Jensen, J. (1994) Delusional beliefs in first admitters. *Psychopathology*, 27, 100–112.

Kaiser, S.L. (2007) Theory of mind and cognitive processes in psychosis. Unpublished doctoral dissertation, University of Manchester, Manchester, UK.

Kayser, N., Sarfati, Y., Besche, C., and Hardy-Baylé, M.-C. (2006) Elaboration of a rehabilitation method based on a pathogenetic hypothesis of "theory of mind" impairment in schizophrenia. *Neuropsychological Rehabilitation*, 16, 83–95.

Keefe, R.S., Bilder, R.M., Harvey, P.D. *et al.* (2006) Baseline neurocognitive deficits in the CATIE schizophrenia trial. *Neuropsychopharmacology*, 31, 2033–2046.

Kerr, N., Dunbar, R.I.M., Bentall, R.P. (2003) Theory of mind deficits in bipolar affective disorder. *Journal of Affective Disorders*, 73, 253–259.

Langdon, R. and Coltheart, M. (1999) Mentalising, schizotypy, and schizophrenia. *Cognition*, 71, 43–71.

Langdon, R., Michie, P.T., Ward, P.B., McConaghy, N., Catts, S.V. and Coltheart, M. (1997) Defective self and/or other mentalising in schizophrenia: a cognitive neuropsychological approach. *Cognitive Neuropsychiatry*, 2, 167–193.

LeDoux, J. (1996) *The Emotional Brain*. Simon & Schuster, New York.

Liddle, P.F. (1987) The symptoms of chronic schizophrenia: a re-examination of the positive–negative dichotomy. *British Journal of Psychiatry*, 151, 145–151.

McCabe, R., Leudar, I. and Antaki, C. (2004) Do people with schizophrenia display theory of mind deficits in clinical interactions? *Psychological Medicine*, 34, 1–12.

Mitchell, J.P., Macrae, C.N. and Banaji, M.R. (2006) Dissociable medial prefrontal contributions to judgments of similar and dissimilar others. *Neuron*, 50, 655–663.

Moore, R., Blackwood, N., Corcoran, R. *et al.* (2006) Misunderstanding the intentions of others: an exploratory study of the cognitive etiology of persecutory delusions in very late-onset schizophrenia-like psychosis. *American Journal of Geriatric Psychiatry*, 14, 410–418.

Penn, D., Roberts, D.L., Munt, E.D., Silverstein, E., Jones, N. and Sheitman, B. (2005) A pilot study of social cognition and interaction training (SCIT) for schizophrenia. *Schizophrenia Research*, 80, 357–359.

Pickup, G. (2006) theory of mind and its relation to schizotypy. *Cognitive Neuropsychiatry*, 11, 177–192.

Randall, F., Corcoran, R., Day, J.C. and Bentall, R.P. (2003) Attention, theory of mind, and causal attributions in people with persecutory delusions: a preliminary investigation. *Cognitive Neuropsychiatry*, 8, 287–294.

Read, J., van Os, J., Morrison, A.P. and Ross, C. (2005) Childhood trauma, psychosis and schizophrenia: a literature review with theoretical and clinical implications. *Acta Psychiatrica Scandinavica*, 112, 330–350.

Roncone, R., Mazza, M., Frangou, I. *et al.* (2004) Rehabilitation of theory of mind deficit in schizophrenia: a pilot study of metacognitive strategies in group treatment. *Neuropsychological Rehabilitation*, 14, 421–435.

Russell, J. (1998) How executive disorders can bring about an inadequate theory of mind. In: Russell, J. (ed.), *Autism as an Executive Disorder*, pp. 256–299. Oxford: Oxford University Press.

Russell, T.A., Rubia, K., Bullmore, E.T. *et al.* (2000) Exploring the social brain in schizophrenia: left prefrontal underactivation during mental state attribution. *American Journal of Psychiatry*, 157, 2040–2042.

Russell, T.A., Reynaud, E., Herba, C., Morris, R. and Corcoran, R. (2006) Do you see what I see? Interpretations of intentional movement in schizophrenia. *Schizophrenia Research*, 81, 101–111.

Sarfati, Y., Hardy-Baylé, M.-C., Brunet, E. and Widlöcher, D. (1999) Investigating theory of mind in schizophrenia: influence of verbalization in disorganized and non-disorganized patients. *Schizophrenia Research*, 37, 183–190.

Shryane, N.M., Corcoran, R., Moore, R., Rowse, G., Cummins, S., Kinderman, P., Blackwood, N., Howard, R. and Bentall, R.P. (2007) Deception and false belief in paranoia: modeling theory of mind stones. *Cognitive Neuropsychiatry*, 13, 8–32.

Stompe, T., Friedman, A., Ortwein, G. *et al.* (1999) Comparisons of delusions among schizophrenics in Austria and Pakistan. *Psychopathology*, 32, 225–234.

Stone, V.E. (2000) The role of the frontal lobes and amygdala in theory of mind. In: Baron-Cohen S., Tager-Flusberg H. and Cohen, D. (eds), *Understanding Other Minds: Perspectives from Autism and Developmental Cognitive Neuroscience*, 2nd edn, pp. 253–273. Oxford: Oxford University Press.

Völlm, B., Taylor, A., Richardson, P. *et al.* (2006) Neural correlates of theory of mind and empathy: an fMRI study in a nonverbal task. *NeuroImage*, 29, 90–98.

Walston, F., Blennerhassett, R.C. and Charlton, B.G. (2000) 'Theory of mind,' persecutory delusions and the somatic marker mechanism. *Cognitive Neuropsychiatry*, 5, 161–174.

Wing, J.K., Cooper, J.E. and Sartorius, N. (1974) *Measurement and Classification of Psychiatric Symptoms: An Instruction Manual for the PSE and Catego Program.* Cambridge: Cambridge University Press.

Chapter 11

The cognitive neuropsychological understanding of persecutory delusions

Robyn Langdon, Ryan McKay, and
Max Coltheart

Introduction

In considering the contribution of cognitive neuropsychology to the understanding of persecutory delusions, we shall first consider the contribution of
the more conventional *clinical* neuropsychological approach to the study of
delusions. After all, cognitive neuropsychology developed as a hybrid of clinical
neuropsychology (the psychological study of brain-injured people) and cognitive psychology (the study of the mental information-processing procedures
that people use to perform such activities as speaking and understanding
speech, and recognizing objects). Second, we shall outline the cognitive neuropsychological approach with brief reference to its history. Third, we shall
describe how this approach has been applied to the study of delusions with
reference to our two-deficit cognitive neuropsychological model of monothematic delusions. Finally we shall evaluate the applicability of this model to the
explanation of other delusions that are not so obviously neuropsychological;
here we shall focus on persecutory delusions.

The clinical neuropsychology of delusions

Conventional clinical neuropsychological studies proceed by administering
standard batteries of tasks that are known to reliably demonstrate performance deficits in patients with identifiable lesions. The primary clinical aims
include: (a) specifying which cognitive abilities have been impaired and which
remain intact, consequent to the brain injury, so as to target remediation; and
(b) identifying the likely sites of underlying neuropathology so as to assist in
diagnosis. Standard neuropsychological batteries typically carve up cognition

into relatively coarse-grained domains—e.g. executive function (linked to frontal brain regions) and spatial abilities (linked to parietal regions).

Most conventional clinical neuropsychological studies do not, however, adopt a symptom-focused approach so as to identify the neuropsychological impairments that are associated with a particular symptom—say delusions. More often, the focus will be on a particular diagnostic category, regardless of symptomatology, or, if clinical symptoms are of interest, researchers will examine the associations between neuropsychological impairments and characteristic clusters of symptoms. Delusions might be of interest but they will be grouped together with other co-occurring symptoms so as to form a symptom cluster.

If we consider first those clinical neuropsychological studies that have adopted a symptom-focused approach so as to investigate delusions, these studies are more common when the delusions occur in the context of known neurological illness. Such delusions are termed 'organic' (or such patients are referred to as suffering 'organic psychoses') and are distinguished traditionally from 'functional' delusions (or the 'functional psychoses', including for example schizophrenia). In the latter case, there is less consensus concerning the nature and the role (if any, for some researchers) of underlying neuropathy. A common example of this type of work is the clinical neuropsychological study of delusions in dementia. Results from such studies generally indicate that delusions in dementia are associated with greater cognitive impairment and a more rapid cognitive decline (Haupt et al. 1996). There are also indications of more specific associations with executive function and semantic memory deficits (Fischer et al. 2006).

The focus of this volume, however, is persecutory delusions, and although persecutory delusional themes are seen in the organic psychoses, they are also very common in the functional psychoses. Clinical neuropsychological studies of psychotic conditions that focus, in some regard, on delusions, are most common in the field of schizophrenia research (see Heinrichs and Zakzanis 1998, and Bilder et al. 2000, for reviews). These studies do not, however, examine associations with single symptoms (including delusions); they focus instead on symptom clusters, in particular the positive and negative symptoms of schizophrenia. Delusions are grouped together, for example, with hallucinations and positive thought disorder, all of which are considered 'positive' due to the presence of something which is abnormal. Negative symptoms (e.g. apathy) are instead characterized by the absence of something that should normally be present. The general finding from clinical neuropsychological studies of schizophrenia is that, whenever associations are found between neuropsychological impairment and symptoms, it is the negative symptoms and not the positive symptoms that are involved (see e.g. Addington and Addington 1999, 2000).

Even when we turn to the few clinical neuropsychological studies of the functional psychoses that have adopted more of a symptom-focused approach to investigate delusions, there is still little to suggest a critical contribution from neuropsychological impairment. Baddeley *et al.* (1996), for example, compared memory (episodic and semantic) and executive function in five patients with schizophrenia who were currently delusional and five patients who were no longer delusional; these authors found few differences between the groups. Mortimer *et al.* (1996) adopted instead a correlational approach with two much larger samples ($n = 79$ and $n = 67$) yet still found no evidence that impairments of general intellectual ability, memory, or executive function were associated with delusions in schizophrenia.

While we are aware of no clinical neuropsychological studies that have focused even more specifically on persecutory delusions (e.g. to compare persecutory deluded patients and non-persecutory deluded patients), several studies have categorized patients according to diagnostic sub-types or differing symptom profiles so as to compare 'paranoid' and 'non-paranoid' subgroups (e.g. Hill *et al.* 2001; Savage *et al.* 2003). Generally speaking these studies report that, even when differences are found, it is the paranoid individuals who appear less neuropsychologically impaired (see Bentall and Taylor 2006, for discussion).

So what are we to take from these more conventional, clinical neuropsychological studies? One might conclude that neuropsychological abnormalities are only implicated in the generation of delusions when delusions arise in the context of organic psychoses; but we suggest that this conclusion is premature. It might be the case that there are also neuropsychological abnormalities associated with delusions in the psychotic conditions traditionally conceived of as functional psychoses. These have so far not been discovered, however, because the standard batteries of tasks used in conventional studies do not tap adequately the specific nature of the neuropsychological abnormalities that contribute to delusion formation. This leads us to consider the possible contribution of a cognitive neuropsychological approach to the study of delusions.

Cognitive neuropsychology

Cognitive neuropsychology developed as a blend of clinical neuropsychology and cognitive psychology. The primary aims were twofold: (1) to explain the symptoms of brain-injured patients in terms of what has been lost and what remains intact in a cognitive model (or theory) of the normal system for mental information processing; and (2) to evaluate such models in terms of how well they explain the patterns of spared and dysfunctional capacities observed in brain-injured populations (Coltheart 1984; Ellis and Young 1998).

Cognitive neuropsychologists attempt to develop such cognitive theories by breaking up the cognitive system into subcomponents and connections so as to model the representations, computations and transformations of information that relate to a particular domain of interest.

Up until the 1990s, this approach was applied primarily to such 'lower-level' domains as reading, memory, attention and visual object recognition, in contrast to such 'higher-level' domains as belief formation, decision-making, 'theory of mind' and pragmatics. Because disorders in these high-level domains often fall under the rubric of psychiatry, the application of cognitive neuropsychology to the study of these kinds of disorders came to be called 'cognitive neuropsychiatry' (David and Halligan 1996).

The cognitive neuropsychiatry of delusions

Hadyn Ellis and his colleagues were pioneers in the field of cognitive neuropsychiatry. These researchers were primarily interested in the misidentification delusions (e.g. Capgras delusion—the belief that someone emotionally close to you, typically a spouse, has been replaced by an impostor, and Fregoli delusion—the belief that one is being followed by familiar people in disguise). Ellis and Young (1990), for example, sought to explain these various types of misidentification delusion in terms of different patterns of breakdown in the normal cognitive system for face recognition.

Our own cognitive neuropsychological approach to the study of delusions is far more general. We advocate the adoption of a general explanatory framework in which the normal cognitive system is conceived of as sub-divided into those components which, when disrupted, explain the initial generation of an implausible thought and those components which, when disrupted, account for the uncritical acceptance of the implausible thought as a belief.

Consider Capgras delusion, for example. It has been shown that sufferers from this delusion do not exhibit the autonomic response to familiar faces that is normally found in non-deluded individuals (Ellis *et al.* 1997; Hirstein and Ramachandran, 1997; Brighetti *et al.* 2007). Note that face recognition itself is not seriously impaired in people with Capgras: if it were, they would not say 'This woman looks exactly like my wife (but it is not her)'. The cognitive abnormality here is instead a disconnection between intact face recognition and the autonomic response which recognition of a familiar face should normally trigger. It is the viewing of a face that matches the loved one's face in the absence of an expected autonomic sense of familiarity which explains the generation of the impostor content—the initial thought that the person being seen is a stranger who looks like the spouse.

But the presence of this particular deficit, even if it is necessary for the occurrence of Capgras delusion, is not sufficient. We know, for example, that there are patients with damage to bilateral ventromedial regions of frontal cortex who also show evidence of a disconnection between intact face recognition and autonomic responses, yet are not delusional (Tranel *et al.* 1995). And we know that those patients who do develop Capgras delusion are provided with ample evidence (e.g. from the spouse and other family members) that their belief is false. We have therefore argued that a second deficit must also be present in people with Capgras delusion that explains these people's *failure to reject* the implausible impostor-thought after it has come to mind.

In considering what this second deficit might be, we shall turn to other monothematic delusions with thematic content that also appears (at first sight) just as incomprehensible as the impostor content of Capgras. Patients with mirrored-self misidentification, for example, believe that the person they see when they look in the mirror is not them, but some stranger. How could such an implausible thought come to mind? In one such case (see Breen *et al.* 2001), the answer was an impaired appreciation of mirror spatial relations and a consequent inability to interact appropriately with mirrors, elsewhere termed 'mirror agnosia' (Ramachandran *et al.* 1997). For this patient, a mirror was effectively a window or a hole in the wall. Any person seen through a window or a hole in the wall is occupying a different region of space from you, and therefore can't be you: this is what we suggest prompted the initial implausible thought in our patient with mirrored-self misidentification delusion.

Take another example: people with sufficiently large right temporoparietal lesions will suffer left-sided paralysis. Some of these people will exhibit anosognosia for their hemiplegia (i.e. will deny the paralysis of the left limbs), and some of these anosognosic patients will attribute ownership of the paralysed limbs to other people. This is an example of somatoparaphrenia, the belief that some part of your body—say, your left arm—is not yours but belongs to some other person (often your neurological examiner). If your examiner places your left arm in your intact visual field and asks you to move your paralysed arm, the arm will not move. This is an arm that you cannot accept as paralysed due to your anosognosia. Therefore you must find some explanation of the fact that it did not move other than that it is paralysed. If it were not your arm but instead someone else's, that would provide such an explanation. That, we suggest, is what generates this thought about the arm in patients with somatoparaphrenia who have anosognosia for their hemiplegia.

The conclusion we draw is that the left hemisphere is typically intact in these cases of Capgras, mirrored-self misidentification and somatoparaphrenia. So, if we want to pursue the hypothesis that the second deficit of belief evaluation is the same across a variety of monothematic delusions, we are led to conclude that the second deficit has something to do with the right hemisphere: some region of the right hemisphere is critically involved in the evaluation and rejection of implausible beliefs.

Our current thinking is that this region lies in the right frontal lobe (see Coltheart 2007, and Coltheart *et al.* 2007, for detailed discussion). For example, Staff *et al.* (1999) conducted neuropsychological testing and single-photon emission tomography imaging of deluded and non-deluded patients with Alzheimer's disease. The two groups were matched on general severity of cognitive deterioration. While the conventional neuropsychological testing revealed no significant differences between groups, the imaging results revealed a consistent pattern of hypoperfusion in the right frontal (and limbic) brain regions in the deluded group compared to the non-deluded group. Consider also Papageorgiou *et al.* (2003) who conducted an event-related potential (ERP) study of nine patients experiencing misidentification delusions (a mixed group of Capgras and/or Fregoli sufferers) and 11 healthy controls. The deluded patients showed a significant reduction in the P300 amplitude at the right frontal brain region compared to the healthy controls. Papageorgiou *et al.* described the P300 ERP component as 'the physiological correlate of updating a cognitive hypothesis, or the working memory (WM) update of what is expected in the environment' (p. 366). The process of updating a cognitive hypothesis of what is occurring in the environment is clearly a major component of belief evaluation.

We have therefore proposed that two distinct neuropsychological deficits need both be present to explain monothematic delusions with thematic content that defies everyday commonsense: Deficit-1 is responsible for the theme of the delusional belief and will necessarily differ from delusion to delusion, while Deficit-2, conceptualized as a right frontal impairment of the capacity to reject the implausible thought triggered by Deficit-1, may be the same across many delusions.

Thus far we have focused on monothematic delusions with apparent nonsensical content. However, there are many delusions associated with schizophrenia—including persecutory delusions, grandiose delusions, erotomanic delusions and delusional jealousy—that seem less bizarre and so perhaps are not so well-explained by our two-deficit model. In the next section we shall evaluate the applicability of the two-deficit account to the explanation of persecutory delusions.

A two-deficit cognitive neuropsychological account of persecutory delusions?

We begin by considering neuropsychological impairments of the first type (Deficit-1) which might contribute to the generation of persecutory delusional themes. Appropriate candidates are not difficult to find, e.g. hearing loss consequent to a failing auditory nerve. Claims of a connection between paranoia and deafness have long been made (e.g. Piker 1937; Houston and Royse 1954; Cooper 1976) and, despite some inconsistent findings (e.g. Thomas 1981; Blazer *et al.* 1996; Thewissen *et al.* 2005; Stefanis *et al.* 2006), it is nevertheless plausible that the experience of surrounding voices at lower than expected volume will prompt the initial thought, 'People are whispering.' If a deficit in belief evaluation is also present, this initial thought, which should be deemed implausible in the light of evidence of hearing loss (including that provided by doctors), will be accepted as true and will persist. This false belief will itself prompt further thoughts, 'Why do they whisper? It must be because they don't want me to hear what they are saying. Why don't they want me to hear what they are saying? It must be that they are plotting against me.'

Memory impairment is another likely candidate. Consider delusions of theft, common in dementia and associated with persecutory elaborations (Hwang *et al.* 1997). Likely scenarios are not difficult to imagine: A patient opens his top drawer expecting to find his wallet, only to discover it gone. Having forgotten that he had earlier moved his wallet, the patient will naturally think, 'Someone has moved my wallet'. Now imagine what might happen if this initial thought is accepted uncritically as true and never revised in light of evidence of memory loss. This patient will question others about moving his wallet, only to be met with general denials. Similar incidents, each triggered by an initial thought that should be rejected as implausible yet is not despite the evidence of memory loss, will likely promote persecutory themes.

These rather convoluted chains of thought seem, however, quite different to the more direct links between neuropsychological impairments and the themes of Capgras, mirrored-self misidentification and somatoparaphrenia suggested above. Perhaps we can get a bit closer to a Capgras-like explanation of persecutory delusional themes if we consider the involvement of hallucinations. Hallucinations and delusions reliably co-occur in factor-analytic studies of symptom ratings in schizophrenia (see e.g. Liddle 1987) and hallucinatory experiences are also strongly associated with delusional ideation in the nonclinical population (see e.g. van Os *et al.* 2000). We shall focus on auditory verbal hallucinations. These are the most common type of hallucination in schizophrenia and are typically unpleasant experiences which lend themselves rather naturally to persecutory elaborations. Auditory verbal hallucinations are associated with disruption to left-side language areas of the brain (David 2004). The cognitive impairment here is conceived of as an impaired capacity to monitor the source of inner speech (see e.g. Johns *et al.* 2001). The initial thought of a person who first experiences unpleasant voices, however, is likely to be, 'Someone is saying nasty things to me'. It is only after this thought is accepted uncritically as true (and never revised) and further reflection follows ('Hearing such nasty things upsets me; Why should the speaker want to upset me in this way? They must be trying to hurt me'), that a persecutory delusional theme emerges.

Ideas of reference fall into a similar category (i.e. we can get closer, but not quite close enough, to a Capgras-like explanation). Ideas of reference and persecutory delusions are reported to be associated in factor-analytic and multi-dimensional scaling studies which use ratings of individual symptoms rather than global symptom ratings (see e.g. Minas *et al.* 1992; Kitamura *et al.* 1998). These co-occurrences may reflect the self-referential quality of both phenomena (see Freeman and Garety 2000, for discussion of key characteristics of persecutory ideation, e.g. that harm is being done to oneself; and Startup and Startup 2005, for discussion of the self-referential quality of referential ideas). Ideas of reference include experiences of innocuous events (e.g. the location of a crumpled brown paper bag on the pavement) appearing to have special significance uniquely for the patient. Kapur (2003) suggests that such experiences reflect aberrant states of salience that attach inappropriately to events which ought normally to be screened from attention rather than becoming the focus of attention. The underlying cause, Kapur further suggests, is dopamine hyperactivity. But why should experiences of this type prompt thoughts of *harm*, also characteristic of persecutory ideation (Freeman and Garety, 2000; McKay *et al.* 2006)? When, for example, an aberrant state of salience attaches to the image of Kylie Minogue performing on television, might not the affected viewer think, 'She's secretly sending a message to me. Why? It must be because she secretly loves me.'—in other words, an example of Clérambault syndrome?

Perhaps a complicating factor here is in assuming that referential ideas are unitary. Some referential ideas concern the inappropriate perception of meaningful contingencies between coincidental events. Empirical support for a link between referential thoughts of this type and persecutory delusions was provided by Blakemore *et al.* (2003) who found that persecutory-deluded patients perceived contingencies between shapes (e.g. one shape seen as launching another shape) when non-persecutory-deluded patients and healthy controls did not. Startup and Startup (2005) have also suggested a distinction between referential ideas of communication (e.g. thinking that others say things with double meanings) and referential ideas of observation (e.g. thinking that one is under surveillance). These authors found that only the referential ideas of observation were associated with persecutory delusions. What type of neuropsychological impairment, if any, could prompt ideas of observation? One intriguing possibility, we suggest, is disruption to the cognitive system for monitoring other people's gaze. This system is sustained by a neural network linking the superior temporal sulcus, amygdala, and orbitofrontal cortex which is reported to be disrupted in schizophrenia (e.g. Emery 2000). People with schizophrenia have also been found to consciously misjudge the averted gaze of others as directed towards themselves (Rosse *et al.* 1994). At the same time, these individuals also show some evidence of an unconscious hypersensitivity to signals of intentionality from other people's gaze-direction (Langdon *et al.* 2006).

We think these findings intriguing, if complex. But even if future work were to tease apart the multi-faceted nature of ideas of reference and identify the various types (and combinations) of neuropsychological impairment that might be involved, we suspect that an explanatory gap would remain. If, for example, neuropsychological impairment(s) were to prompt the initial thought, 'Others are *intentionally* observing *me*', why should a threat-related persecutory interpretation be favoured over say a grandiose interpretation?

What our examples illustrate is that, while neuropsychological impairments like those listed above might precipitate a train of thought leading (more or less directly) to a persecutory delusion, the tendency to threat-related persecutory elaboration exists prior to and independently of these neuropsychological events. Is a neuropsychological impairment then necessary to trigger the persecutory train of thought? Elsewhere we have allowed that a neuropsychological impairment of the first type (Deficit-1) might not be necessary when the delusional content does not have the same apparent non-sensical quality of say Capgras or somatoparaphrenia (Langdon and Coltheart 2000). In cases of 'everyday' persecutory content (e.g. the neighbours are spying on me), attentional biases to threat-related material in the environment might be sufficient to set the persecutory train of thought rolling.

But what causes the attentional bias to threat? It may have something to do with latent negative self-beliefs. Bentall and colleagues (Bentall and Kaney 1996; Kinderman and Bentall 1996, 1997) have argued that persecutory delusions are purposive constructions that serve to avoid the activation of negative self-beliefs, thus maintaining self-esteem. A prediction of their model is that persecutory delusions will be associated with a discrepancy between relatively high measures of conscious, overt self-esteem and relatively low measures of unconscious, covert self-esteem. This prediction has received empirical support (Kinderman 1994; Lyon *et al.* 1994; McKay *et al.* 2007; Moritz *et al.* 2006). Freeman and colleagues (e.g. Freeman and Garety, 1999, 2003) have highlighted the role of emotional factors, in particular social anxiety, in the explanation of threat anticipation in persecutory-deluded individuals. Their view has also received considerable support (see Freeman 2007, for a review). However, the contribution of neuropsychological factors ought not to be ignored even here. For example, neuropsychological and neuroimaging studies have implicated the amygdala and prefrontal circuits in the interpretation of social signals of threat. These neural networks are disrupted in schizophrenia and such disruptions might explain the abnormally heightened perception of social threat that is associated with persecutory delusions in this disorder (Green and Phillips 2004).

Let's now consider why the persecutory-deluded patient clings so tenaciously to his or her delusional belief when there is so much pressure to reject it. Might disruption to the normal cognitive system for belief evaluation (caused by right frontal brain dysfunction: Deficit-2) contribute to the failure to reject a persecutory thought, even when that thought has been prompted by threat-related attentional biases that are unrelated to neuropsychological deficits?

We noted earlier that delusions in Alzheimer's disease are associated with greater hypoperfusion in right frontal (and limbic) brain regions. Persecutory themes are common in these delusions (Heinik *et al.* 2001; Cook *et al.* 2003). It therefore follows that right frontal brain damage might contribute to the maintenance of persecutory delusions in cases of dementia. Persecutory themes are also common in the delusions that can arise after traumatic brain injury (TBI: Sachdev *et al.* 2001; Zhang and Sachdev 2003). Frontal brain regions are frequently damaged in TBI, although the brain damage is typically quite diffuse. Nevertheless, it is plausible that right frontal damage also contributes to the failure to reject persecutory thoughts in TBI patients.

When we turn to the functional psychoses, however, the findings are less convincing. In support of the involvement of right frontal dysfunction is the historical view that paranoid schizophrenia (identified according to traditional diagnostic subtypes) is associated with right hemisphere dysfunction while non-paranoid schizophrenia is characterized by left hemisphere deficits (e.g. Magaro and Page 1983). Current evidence also suggests right frontal abnormalities in schizophrenia (e.g. Coltheart *et al.* 2007, for details). For example, structural magnetic resonance imaging (MRI) work has indicated right but not left frontal hypergyria (Vogeley *et al.* 2001; Narr *et al.* 2004). Regional cerebral blood flow (rCBF) studies, which employ neuroimaging techniques to measure the blood supply to specific brain regions at given times, have also reported abnormal metabolism in right but not left frontal lobe in schizophrenia patients (Hook *et al.* 1995; Malaspina *et al.* 2000). But despite such findings of right frontal abnormalities in schizophrenia and despite the prominence of persecutory delusions in this disorder there is little consistent evidence of a direct link between right frontal dysfunction and persecutory delusions. Some studies, for example, report disturbances of right hemisphere function in patients with paranoid (and not non-paranoid) schizophrenia (Magaro and Chamrad 1983; Romney *et al.* 2000). At the same time, other studies report evidence of left hemispheric abnormalities in relation to paranoid ideation. Sallet *et al.* (2003), for example, investigated cortical folding in different subgroups of schizophrenia patients. They found that the paranoid subtype showed reduced cortical folding that was restricted to the left hemisphere. Kohno *et al.* (2006) evaluated the relationship between rCBF and clinical symptoms in schizophrenia. These authors found that the suspiciousness score on the Brief Psychiatric Rating Scale was positively correlated with rCBF in the left inferior temporal gyrus; no other associations reached statistical significance.

Conclusions

While our two-deficit model has proven useful for the explanation of monothematic delusions with themes that defy everyday commonsense (Langdon and Coltheart, 2000; Davies *et al.* 2001), the applicability of this model to the explanation of ordinary persecutory delusions appears somewhat limited in contrast. Threat-related attentional biases might be sufficient to trigger a persecutory train of thought in the absence of a precipitating neuropsychological event. And, although a heightened anticipation of social threat might be related to deregulation of a neural network linking amygdale and prefrontal circuits, the chicken-and-egg question remains: Which comes first, the neural disturbance or the experiences of harm from others? As for the involvement of right frontal disruption to the normal cognitive system for belief evaluation, the findings concerning persecutory delusions in the functional psychoses are equivocal. In light of such considerations, we have recently explored the need to incorporate motivational factors into a model of the normal system for belief generation and evaluation so as to explain those delusions that appear somewhat resistant to a strictly neuropsychological account (e.g. Reverse Othello[1]—see McKay *et al.* 2005). This work has led

---

[1] This was a patient reported by Butler (2000) who had sustained severe head injuries in a car accident. The accident left him a quadriplegic, unable to speak without reliance on an electronic communicator. One year after his injury, the patient developed a delusion

us to advocate a more general two-factor account of delusions in which we propose that, regardless of the delusional theme and regardless of the aetiology, one needs to answer two questions in order to explain the presence of any delusion:

1 What gave rise to the belief in the first place—what caused the patient to first entertain a thought with this particular content?

2 Having once entertained this particular thought, why does the patient cling to it rather than rejecting it?

For some patients, the answers to these two questions will be wholly neuropsychological. For other patients they will not. We suggest that both questions are best addressed on a case-by-case basis. Neither motivational nor neuropsychological factors should be ruled out automatically because of either the aetiology or the thematic content of a delusion. The fact that certain delusions are conceived of traditionally as functional (e.g. persecutory delusions) does not mean that neuropsychological impairment will not feature in the explanation of such delusions in all patients. And, likewise, the fact that a delusion is conceived of traditionally as organic does not mean that motivational factors should be ruled out as significant explanatory forces.

References

Addington, J. and Addington, D. (1999) Neurocognitive and social functioning in schizophrenia. *Schizophrenia Bulletin*, 25, 173–192.

Addington, J. and Addington, D. (2000) Neurocognitive and social functioning in schizophrenia: a 2.5 year follow-up study. *Schizophrenia Research*, 44, 47–56.

Baddeley, A.D., Thornton, A., Chua, S.E. and McKenna, P. (1996), Schziophrenic delusions and the construction of autobiographical memory. In: Rubin, D.C. (ed.), *Remembering our Past: Studies in Autobiographical Memory*. Cambridge: Cambridge University Press.

Bentall, R.P. and Kaney, S. (1996) Abnormalities of self-representation and persecutory delusions: A test of a cognitive model of paranoia. *Psychological Medicine*, 26, 1231–1237.

Bentall, R. and Taylor, J.L. (2006) Psychological processes and paranoia: implications for forensic behavioural science. *Behavioral Sciences and Law*, 24, 277–294.

Bilder, R.M., Goldman, R.S., Robinson, D. *et al.* (2000) Neuropsychology of first-episode schizophrenia: initial characterization and clinical correlates. *American Journal of Psychiatry*, 157, 549–559.

....

concerning the continuing fidelity of his partner (who had in fact severed all contact with him soon after his accident). The patient became convinced that he and his former partner had recently married, and he was eager to persuade others that he now felt sexually fulfilled.

Blakemore, S.J., Sarfati, Y., Bazin, N. and Decety, J. (2003) The detection of intentional contingencies in simple animations in patients with delusions of persecution. *Psychological Medicine*, 33, 1433–41.

Blazer, D.G., Hays, J.C. and Salive, M.E. (1996) Factors associated with paranoid symptoms in a community sample of older adults. *Gerontologist*, 36, 70–75.

Breen, N., Caine, D. and Coltheart, M. (2001) Mirrored-self misidentification: two cases of focal onset dementia. *Neurocase*, 7, 239–254.

Brighetti, G., Bonifacci, P., Borlimi, R. and Ottaviani, C. (2007) "Far from the heart far from the eye": evidence from the Capgras delusion. *Cognitive Neuropsychiatry*, 12(3), 189–197.

Butler, P. V. (2000) Reverse othello syndrome subsequent to traumatic brain injury. *Psychiatry: Interpersonal and Biological Processes*, 63, 95–92.

Coltheart, M. (1984) Editorial. *Cognitive Neuropsychology*, 1, 1–8.

Coltheart, M. (2007) Cognitive neuropsychiatry and delusional belief: the 33rd Bartlett Lecture. *Quarterly Journal of Experimental Psychology*, 60, 1041–1062.

Coltheart, M., Langdon, R. and McKay, R. (2007) Schizophrenia and monothematic delusions. *Schizophrenia Bulletin*, 33, 642–647.

Cook, S.E., Miyahara, S., Bacanu, S.A. *et al.* (2003) Psychotic symptoms in Alzheimer disease: evidence for subtypes. *American Journal of Geriatric Psychiatry*, 11, 406–413.

Cooper, A.F. (1976) Deafness and psychiatric illness. *British Journal of Psychiatry*, 129, 216–226.

David, A.S. (2004) The cognitive neuropsychiatry of auditory verbal hallucinations: an overview. *Cognitive Neuropsychiatry*, 9(1–2), 107–123.

David, A.S. and Halligan, P.W. (1996) Editorial. *Cognitive Neuropsychiatry*, 1, 1–3.

Davies, M., Coltheart, M., Langdon, R. and Breen, N. (2001) Monothematic delusions: towards a two-factor account. *Philosophy, Psychiatry and Psychology*, 9(2–3), 133–159.

Ellis, H.D. and Young, A.W. (1998) Faces in their social and biological context. In: Young, A.W. (ed.), *Face and Mind*, pp. 67–95. New York: Oxford University Press.

Ellis, H.D. and Young, A.W. (1998) Accounting for delusional misidentifications. *British Journal of Psychiatry*, 157, 239–249.

Ellis, H.D., Young, A.W., Quayle, A.H. and de Pauw, K.W. (1997) Reduced autonomic responses to faces in Capgras delusion. *Proceedings of the Royal Society of London B*, 264, 1095–1092.

Emery, N. (2000) The eyes have it: the neuroethology, function and evolution of social gaze. *Neuroscience and Biobehavioral Reviews*, 24, 591–604.

Fischer, C., Ladowsky-Brooks, R., Millikin, C., Norris, M., Hansen, K. and Rourke, S.B. (2006) Neuropsychological functioning and delusions in dementia: a pilot study. *Aging and Mental Health*, 10, 27–32.

Freeman, D. (2007) Suspicious minds: the psychology of persecutory delusions. *Clinical Psychology Review*, 27, 425–457.

Freeman, D. and Garety, P.A. (1999) Worry, worry processes and dimensions of delusions: an exploratory investigation of a role for anxiety processes in the maintenance of delusional distress. *Behavioural and Cognitive Psychotherapy*, 27, 47–62.

Freeman, D. and Garety, P.A. (2000) Comments on the content of persecutory delusions: does the definition need clarification? *British Journal of Clinical Psychology*, 39, 407–414.

Freeman, D. and Garety, P.A. (2003) Connecting neurosis and psychosis: the direct influence of emotion on delusions and hallucinations. *Behaviour Research and Therapy*, 41, 923–947.

Green, M.J. and Phillips, M.L. (2004) Social threat perception and the evolution of paranoia. *Neuroscience and Biobehavioral Reviews*, 29, 333–342.

Haupt, M., Romero, B. and Kurz, A. (1996) Delusions and hallucinations in Alzheimer's disease: Results from a two-year longitudinal study. *International Journal of Geriatric Psychiatry*, 11, 965–972.

Heinik, J., Solomesh, I., Shein, V., Mester, R., Bleich, A. and Becker, D. (2001) Correlation between clock-drawing test and paranoid and delusional ideation in dementia of the alzheimer's type. *International Journal of Geriatric Psychiatry*, 16, 735–736.

Heinrichs, R. and Zakzanis, K.K. (1999) Neurocognitive deficit in schizophrenia: a quantitative review of the evidence. *Neuropsychology*, 12, 426–445.

Hill, S., Ragland, J., Gur, R.C. and Gur, R.E. (2001) Neuropsychological differences among empirically derived clinical subtypes of schizophrenia. *Neuropsychology*, 15, 492–501.

Hirstein, W.S. and Ramachandran, V.S. (1997) Capgras syndrome: a novel probe for understanding the neural representation of the identity and familiarity of persons. *Proceedings of the Royal Society of London B*, 264, 437–444.

Hook, S., Gordon, E., Lazzaro, I. *et al.* (1995) Regional differentiation of cortical activity in schizophrenia: a complementary approach to conventional analysis of regional cerebral blood flow. *Psychiatry Research: Neuroimaging*, 61, 95–93.

Houston, F. and Royse, A.B. (1954) Relationship between deafness and psychotic illness. *Journal of Mental Science*, 100, 990–993.

Hwang, J.-P., Yang, C.-H., Tsai, S.-J. and Liu, K.-M. (1997) Delusions of theft in dementia of the alzheimer type: a preliminary report. *Alzheimer Disease and Associated Disorders*, 11, 110–112.

Johns, L.C., Rossell, S., Frith, C. *et al.* (2001) Verbal self-monitoring and auditory verbal hallucinations in patients with schizophrenia. *Psychological Medicine*, 31, 705–715.

Kapur, S. (2003) Psychosis as a state of aberrant salience: a framework linking biology, phenomenology, and pharmacology in schizophrenia. *American Journal of Psychiatry*, 160, 13–23.

Kinderman, P. (1994) Attentional bias, persecutory delusions and the self-concept. *British Journal of Medical Psychology*, 67, 53–66.

Kinderman, P. and Bentall, R.P. (1996) Self-discrepancies and persecutory delusions: evidence for a model of paranoid ideation. *Journal of Abnormal Psychology*, 105, 106–113.

Kinderman, P. and Bentall, R.P. (1997) Causal attributions in paranoia and depression: internal, personal, and situational attributions for negative events. *Journal of Abnormal Psychology*, 106, 341–345.

Kitamura, T., Okazaki, Y., Fujinawa, A., Takayanagi, I. and Kasahara, Y. (1998) Dimensions of schizophrenic positive symptoms: an exploratory factor analysis investigation. *European Archives of Psychiatry and Clinical Neuroscience*, 248, 130–135.

Kohno, T., Shiga, T., Kusumi, I. *et al.* (2006) Left temporal perfusion associated with suspiciousness score on the Brief Psychiatric Rating Scale in schizophrenia. *Psychiatry Research*, 147(2–3), 163–171.

Langdon, R. and Coltheart, M. (2000) The cognitive neuropsychology of delusions. *Mind and Language*, 15, 194–219.

Langdon, R., Corner, T., McLaren, J., Coltheart, M. and Ward, P.B. (2006) Attentional orienting triggered by gaze in schizophrenia. *Neuropsychologia*, 44, 417–429.

Liddle, P.F. (1987) The symptoms of chronic schizophrenia: a re-examination of the positive–negative dichotomy. *British Journal of Psychiatry*, 151, 145–151.

Lyon, H.M., Kaney, S. and Bentall, R.P. (1994) The defensive function of persecutory delusions: evidence from attribution tasks. *British Journal of Psychiatry*, 164, 637–646.

Magaro, P.A. and Chamrad, D.L. (1983) Hemispheric preference of paranoid and nonparanoid schizophrenics. *Biological Psychiatry*, 18, 1269–1285.

Magaro, P.A. and Page, J. (1983) Brain disconnection, schizophrenia, and paranoia. *Journal of Nervous and Mental Disease*, 171, 133–140.

Malaspina, D., Bruder, G., Furman, V., Gorman, J.M., Berman, A. and Van Heertum, R. (2000) Schizophrenia subgroups differing in dichotic listening laterality also differ in neurometabolism and symptomatology. *Journal of Neuropsychiatry and Clinical Neurosciences*, 12, 495–492.

McKay, R., Langdon, R. and Coltheart, M. (2005) "Sleights of mind": delusions, defences, and self-deception. *Cognitive Neuropsychiatry*, 10, 305–326.

McKay, R., Langdon, R. and Coltheart, M. (2006) The Persecutory Ideation Questionnaire. *Journal of Nervous and Mental Disease*, 194(9), 629–631.

McKay, R., Langdon, R. and Coltheart, M. (2007) The defensive function of persecutory delusions: an investigation using the Implicit Association Test. *Cognitive Neuropsychiatry*, 12, 1–24.

Minas, I.H., Stuart, G.W., Klimidis, S., Jackson, H.J., Singh, B.S. and Copolov, D.L. (1992) Positive and negative symptoms in the psychoses: Multidimensional scaling of saps and sans items. *Schizophrenia Research*, 9, 143–156.

Moritz, S., Werner, R. and von Collani, G. (2006) The inferiority complex in paranoia readdressed. A study with the Implicit Association Test. *Cognitive Neuropsychiatry*, 11(4), 402–415.

Mortimer, A.M., Bentham, P., McKay, A.P. *et al.* (1996) Delusions in schizophrenia: a phenomenological and psychological exploration. *Cognitive Neuropsychiatry*, 1, 299–303.

Narr, K. L., Bilder, R. M., Kim, S. *et al.* (2004) Abnormal gyral complexity in first-episode schizophrenia. *Biological Psychiatry*, 55, 959–967.

Papageorgiou, P., Ventouras, E., Lykouras, L., Uzunoglu, N. and Christodoulou, G.N. (2003) Psychophysiological evidence for altered information in delusional misidentification syndromes. *Progress in Neuro-Psychopharmacology and Biological Psychiatry*, 27, 365– 372.

Piker, P. (1937) Psychologic aspects of deafness. *Laryngoscope*, 47, 499–507.

Ramachandran, V.S., Altschuler, E.L. and Hillyer, S. (1997) Mirror agnosia. *Proceedings of the Royal Society of London B*, 264, 645–647.

Romney, D.M., Mosley, J.L. and Addington, D.E. (2000) Hemispheric processing deficits in patients with paranoid schizophrenia. *Journal of Genetic Psychology*, 161, 99–114.

Rosse, R.B., Kendrick, K., Wyatt, R.J. *et al.* (1994) Gaze discrimination in patients with schizophrenia: Preliminary report. *American Journal of Psychiatry*, 151, 919–921.

Sachdev, P., Smith, J.S. and Cathcart, S. (2001) Schizophrenia-like psychosis following traumatic brain injury: a chart-based descriptive and case-control study. *Psychological Medicine*, 31, 231–9.

Sallet, P.C., Elkis, H., Alves, T.M. *et al.* (2003) Reduced cortical folding in schizophrenia: an MRI morphometric study. *American Journal of Psychiatry*, 160, 1606–1613.

Savage, R.M., Jackson, W.T. and Sourathathone, C.M. (2003) A brief neuropsychological test battery for evaluating patients with schizophrenia. *Psychological Medicine*, 29, 613–620.

Staff, R.T., Shanks, M.F., Macintosh, L., Pestell, S.J., Gemmell, H.G. and Venneri, A. (1999) Delusions in alzheimer's disease: SPET evidence of right hemispheric dysfunction. *Cortex*, 35, 549–560.

Startup, M. and Startup, S. (2005) On two kinds of delusion of reference. *Psychiatry Research*, 137(1–2), 97–92.

Stefanis, N., Thewissen, V., Bakoula, C., van Os, J. and Myin-Germeys, I. (2006) Hearing impairment and psychosis: a replication in a cohort of young adults. *Schizophrenia Research*, 95, 266–272.

Thewissen, V., Myin-Germeys, I., Bentall, R., de Graaf, R., Vollebergh, W. and van Os, J. (2005) Hearing impairment and psychosis revisited. *Schizophrenia Research*, 76, 99–103.

Thomas, A.J. (1981) Acquired deafness and mental health. *British Journal of Medical Psychology*, 54, 219–229.

Tranel, D., Damasio, H. and Damasio, A.R. (1995) Double dissociation between overt and covert face recognition. *Journal of Cognitive Neuroscience*, 7, 425–432.

van Os, J., Hanssen, M., Bijl, R.V. and Ravelli, A. (2000) Straus (1969) revisited: a psychosis continuum in the general population? *Schizophrenia Research*, 45(1–2), 11–20.

Vogeley, K., Tepest, R., Pfeiffer, U. *et al.* (2001) Right frontal hypergyria differentiation in affected and unaffected siblings from families multiply affected with schizophrenia: a morphometric MRI study. *American Journal of Psychiatry*, 159, 494–496.

Zhang, Q. and Sachdev, P.S. (2003) Psychotic disorder and traumatic brain injury. *Current Psychiatry Reports*, 5, 197–201.

Part 4

Biological processes

Chapter 12

Dopamine and persecutory delusions

Marc Laruelle

Introduction

Schizophrenia is the prototypical condition associated with persecutory delusions. It is a severe and chronic illness (or group of illnesses) with high prevalence (~0.5–1% of the population suffers from this condition). Symptoms of schizophrenia usually emerge during adolescence or early adulthood. Psychotic symptoms include hallucinations, typically auditory, and delusions, which frequently involve persecution and/or megalomania. Psychotic symptoms and severe thought disorganization are often grouped under the term 'positive symptoms'. Deficit symptoms, also commonly referred to as 'negative symptoms', manifest themselves in many dimensions, such as affect (affect flattening), volition (apathy), speech (poverty), pleasure (anhedonia), and social life (withdrawal).

While the aetiology and fundamental pathology of schizophrenia remain unclear, a large body of evidence suggests that alterations in several neurotransmitter systems are involved in the pathophysiological processes of the illness. Among these transmitters, dopamine (DA) has received the most attention, although other systems such as the glutamatergic, gamma-aminobutyric acid (GABA)-ergic, serotonergic, cholinergic and the opioid systems have also been implicated.

The putative role of DA systems in the pathophysiology and treatment of schizophrenia has been the subject of intense research efforts over the last fifty years. The first formulation of the DA hypothesis of schizophrenia proposed that hyperactivity of DA transmission was responsible for the positive symptoms observed in the disorder (Carlsson and Lindqvist 1963; Rossum 1966). This hypothesis was based on the recognition that antipsychotic drugs were DA D_2 receptor antagonists (Carlsson and Lindqvist 1963; Seeman and Lee 1975; Creese et al. 1976) and that DA-enhancing drugs were psychotogenic (for review see Angrist and van Kammen 1984; Lieberman et al. 1987a).

D_2 receptors being mainly expressed in the striatum, several authors proposed that hyperactivity of DA systems in the limbic striatum was associated with the emergence of psychosis (Snyder 1973; Stevens 1973; Matthysse 1974). As D_2 receptor antagonists are most effective in treating positive symptoms, the classical DA hypothesis of schizophrenia provided a putative base for the positive symptoms, among which persecutory delusions are a prominent feature.

This chapter reviews the evidence suggesting that positive symptoms in general, and persecutory delusions more specifically, are associated with increased DA activity at D_2 receptors in the striatum.

Overview of DA transmission

Dopaminergic projections are divided among nigro-striatal, mesolimbic and mesocortical systems (Lindvall and Björklund 1983). The nigro-striatal system projects from the substantia nigra (SN) to the dorsal striatum and is involved in cognitive integration, habituation, sensorimotor co-ordination and initiation of movement. The mesolimbic system projects from the ventral tegmental area (VTA) to the limbic structures such as the ventral striatum, the hippocampus, and the amygdala. The mesocortical system projects from the VTA to the cortical regions. The mesolimbic and the mesocortical systems are involved in the regulation of motivation, attention and reward (Mogenson *et al.* 1980).

DA receptors were originally classified into two types: the D_1 receptors, which stimulate adenylate cyclase, and the D_2 receptors, which are neither coupled to nor inhibiting this effector (Kebabian and Calne 1979). The advent of molecular biology techniques in the late 1980s enabled the cloning of these two receptors (Bunzow *et al.* 1988; Dearry *et al.* 1990; Monsma *et al.* 1990; Zhou *et al.* 1990), as well as three newer DA receptors, termed D_3, D_4 and D_5 (Sokoloff *et al.* 1990; Sunahara *et al.* 1991; Tiberi *et al.* 1991; Van Tol *et al.* 1991). The pharmacological characterization of these receptors revealed that D_1 and D_5 share similar properties, while the pharmacological profiles of D_3 and D_4 are similar to the D_2 type. Thereby, the D_1–D_2 classification of the DA receptors has been elaborated upon to consist of a D_1-like family (D_1 and D_5 receptors) and a D_2-like family (D_2, D_3 and D_4 receptors) (for review, see Palermo-Neto 1997; Missale *et al.* 1998).

DA receptors differ in their regional localization in the human brain (for reviews see Seeman 1992; Meador-Woodruff *et al.* 1996; Joyce and MeadorWoodruff 1997). D_1 receptors show a widespread neocortical distribution, including the prefrontal cortex, and are also present in high concentration in striatum. D_5 receptors are concentrated in the hippocampus and the entorhinal cortex. D_2 receptors are concentrated in the striatum, with low concentration in the medial temporal structures (hippocampus, entorhinal cortex, amygdala) and the thalamus. The concentration of D_2 receptors in the prefrontal cortex is extremely low. D_3 receptors are present in the striatum with their concentration being particularly high in the ventral striatum. D_4 receptors are present in the prefrontal cortex and the hippocampus but are undetected in the striatum.

Unlike 'fast' transmitters such as glutamate, DA does not directly gate ion channels, but rather, the stimulation of a G-protein linked to the DA receptor induces a cascade of intracellular signalling events that modify the response of the cell to other transmitters. DA is neither 'inhibitory' nor 'excitatory'. DA action depends on the state of the neurons at the time of the stimulation and the type of receptor involved (Yang *et al.* 1999). In the striatum, DA modulates the response of the GABAergic medium spiny neurons to the glutamatergic drive. In this structure, it has been proposed that DA is 'reinforcing', i.e. augmentation of the inhibition of neurons that are unstimulated, and of the excitatory response of neurons that are excited (Wickens 2000). In this manner, DA acts to gate glutamatergic inputs by increasing their signal-to-noise ratio. In the prefrontal cortex, DA modulates pyramidal cell excitability, both directly and through GABAergic interneurons (Smiley *et al.* 1994; Mrzljak *et al.* 1996; Yang *et al.* 1999). Here again, it has been proposed that DA increases the signal-to-noise ratio of glutamatergic afferents, i.e. augmenting the response of neurons stimulated by glutamate, and silencing the neurons not stimulated by glutamate (Seamans *et al.* 2001).

DA and persecutory delusions: review of the evidence

Pharmacological evidence

Aversive pharmacological effects. The psychotogenic effect of amphetamine and other DA-enhancing drugs such as methylphenidate and L-3, 4-dihydroxyphenylalanine (L-DOPA), is a cornerstone of the classical DA hypothesis of schizophrenia. Two sets of observations are relevant to this issue. First, repeated exposure to high doses of psychostimulants in non-schizophrenic subjects might gradually induce paranoid psychosis. This well-documented observation shows that sustained increase in DA activity is psychotogenic. Second, low doses of psychostimulants that are not psychotogenic in healthy subjects might induce or worsen psychotic symptoms in patients with schizophrenia. This observation indicates that patients with schizophrenia have an increased vulnerability to the psychotogenic effects of DA-enhancing drugs.

Although mentioned in 1938 by Young and Scoville, amphetamine-induced psychosis was not clearly recognized as a possible consequence of chronic amphetamine use until 1958 upon the publication of a 42-case monograph by Connell (1958). In this paper, Connell provided the 'classical' definition of amphetamine psychosis, as 'a paranoid psychosis with ideas of references, delusions of persecution, auditory and visual hallucinations in the setting of a clear sensorium' and concluded that 'the mental picture may be indistinguishable from acute or chronic paranoid schizophrenia' (Connell 1958).

In the early 1970s, several studies experimentally induced amphetamine psychosis in non-schizophrenic amphetamine-abusers in order to better document the clinical pattern of this syndrome (Griffith *et al.* 1968; Angrist and Gershon 1970; Bell 1973). These experiments formally established that sustained psychostimulant exposure can produce paranoid psychosis in non-schizophrenic individuals. This reaction does not occur in the context of a delirium since subjects maintain a clear sensorium during the episode and are able to recollect the episode after its resolution. Since these studies were performed before the conceptualization of the symptoms of schizophrenia into positive and negative (Crow 1980), they did not formally assess negative symptoms. These papers only include anecdotal reports of emotional blunting, withdrawal or alogia, thereby suggesting that sustained and excessive stimulation of DA systems does not consistently induce what are now defined as the 'negative' symptoms of schizophrenia.

Ellinwood *et al.* provided one of the most insightful descriptions of amphetamine-induced psychosis by conceptualizing the condition as a continuum that evolves from the gradual onset of paranoid tendencies to delusional paranoia (Ellinwood 1967; Ellinwood *et al.* 1973). The first step is characterized by stimulation of interpretive mental activities (great attention to details, intense feeling of curiosity, repetitive searching and sorting behaviour). Ellinwood saw in Sherlock Holmes, a regular cocaine user, a prototypical example of the endless search for meanings ('my mind rebels at stagnation'). With increased exposure, these paranoid tendencies and interests for the minutiae develop into an intermediate stage, which is characterized by marked enhancement of perceptual acuity, sustained 'pleasurable' suspiciousness, and compulsive probing behaviour. Finally, this inquisitive behaviour is reversed and projected to others (persecution), leading to paranoia and ideas of references. The 'enhancement of sensitive acuity' develops into hallucinations, initially auditory, then visual and tactile. The sensorium remains clear until toxic delirium is reached. Thought disorders might manifest towards the end of the continuum near the toxic stage. Kapur (2003) recently reformulated and modernized the Ellinwood 'Sherlock Holmes' theory by defining schizophrenia psychosis as a state of aberrant salience.

Another important property of psychostimulants is their ability to induce reverse tolerance or 'sensitization' (Robinson and Becker 1986; Kalivas *et al.* 1993). Long-term sensitization to psychostimulants is a process whereby repeated exposure to these drugs results in an enhanced response upon subsequent exposures. The relevance of this process for the pathophysiology of schizophrenia has been reviewed recently (Lieberman *et al.* 1997; Laruelle 2000b). Subjects who abused psychostimulants and experienced stimulant-induced psychotic episodes are reported to remain vulnerable to low doses of psychostimulants (Connell 1958; Ellinwood *et al.* 1973; Sato *et al.* 1983). In these subjects, exposure to psychostimulants at doses that do not normally produce psychotic symptoms can trigger a recurrence of these symptoms. The similarity between these patients and the patients with schizophrenia in terms of vulnerability to the psychotogenic effects of psychostimulants has led to the proposal that schizophrenia might be associated with an 'endogenous' sensitization process (Lieberman *et al.* 1990; Glenthoj and Hemmingsen 1997; Laruelle 2000b).

Considerable research efforts have been devoted to the identification of neuronal substrates involved in sensitization. Several studies have shown that sensitization is associated with increased stimulant-induced DA release in the axonal terminal fields (for references, see Laruelle 2000b). A recent brain-imaging study confirmed that, in humans, sensitization to the effects of amphetamine involves increased amphetamine-induced DA release (Boileau *et al.* 2003). The imaging studies reviewed below show that patients with schizophrenia display an enhanced amphetamine-induced DA release, supporting the notion of an endogenous sensitization process of subcortical DA system in schizophrenia.

A number of studies, reviewed by Lieberman *et al.* (1987b), provided evidence that patients with schizophrenia, as a group, display increased sensitivity to the psychotogenic effects of acute psychostimulant administration. In other words, some, but not all patients with schizophrenia present emergence or worsening of psychotic symptoms after acute exposure to psychostimulants at doses that do not induced psychosis in healthy subjects. The psychotic response appears to be state dependent. First, patients who responded with a psychotic reaction to a psychostimulant challenge during an acute episode failed to show such a response when they were in remission. Second, the propensity to present a psychotic reaction to a psychostimulant challenge is predictive of relapse upon antipsychotic discontinuation. Thus, the clinical response to stimulants might 'reveal' an active phase of the illness that is not readily identifiable by the clinical symptomatology in the absence of a psychostimulant administration.

Therapeutic pharmacological effects. Since the recognition in 1952 of the antipsychotic properties of chlorpromazine (Delay *et al.* 1952), antipsychotic medications have fundamentally altered the course and the prognosis of schizophrenia. They have proven effective at reducing the severity of symptoms and preventing episodes of illness exacerbation. To date, D_2 receptor antagonism is the only pharmacological property shared by all antipsychotic drugs. The clinical dose of these drugs is related to their affinity for D_2 receptors. D_2 receptor antagonism appears both necessary and sufficient for antipsychotic action (as demonstrated by the selective D_2 receptor antagonist amisulpride). The fact that patients with schizophrenia improve following administration of D_2 receptor antagonists is one of the few incontestable pieces of evidence in schizophrenia (Weinberger 1987).

D_2 receptor blockade by antipsychotic drugs has been confirmed by a large number of imaging studies (reviewed in Talbot and Laruelle 2002). In general, these studies failed to observe a relationship between the degree of D_2 receptor occupancy and the quality of the clinical response. However, most studies reported doses achieving more than 50% occupancy. The minimum occupancy required for a therapeutic response remains somewhat uncertain. Two studies performed with low doses of relatively selective D_2 receptor antagonists (haloperidol and raclopride) suggest that a minimum of 50% occupancy is required to observe a rapid clinical response (Nordstrom *et al.* 1993; Kapur *et al.* 2000). Imaging studies have repeatedly confirmed the existence of a striatal D_2 receptor occupancy threshold (about 80%) above which extrapyramidal symptoms (EPS) are likely to occur (Farde *et al.* 1992). Thus, these data suggest the existence of a therapeutic window between 50 and 80% striatal D_2 receptor occupancy. Within this window, the relationship between occupancy and response is unclear, presumably because of the variability in endogenous DA (Frankle *et al.* 2004). Furthermore, the occupancy threshold required for therapeutic effects might differ between drugs.

The introduction of a second generation of antipsychotic (SGA) drugs since the early 1990s has not fundamentally altered the prominence of D_2 receptor antagonism in the current treatment of schizophrenia. Most SGAs also potently interact with other receptors, such as the serotonin (hydroxytryptamine) $5HT_{2A}$ receptors, but the possibility of achieving an 'atypical' profile with a pure D_2 receptor antagonist such as amisulpride indicates that serotonin pharmacological effects are not absolutely required to produce this effect.

Post-mortem evidence

The discovery of the antipsychotic effect of D_2 receptor blockade inspired decades of post-mortem research seeking to determine if schizophrenia was associated with alterations of DA transmission parameters. This large body of research has so far failed to provide definitive answers, in part, because of the confounding effect of ante-mortem antipsychotic treatment.

Tissue DA and HVA. Direct measures of the tissue content of DA and its metabolites have failed to demonstrate consistent and reproducible abnormalities (for review see Cross and 1981; Reynolds 1989; Davis *et al.* 1991). It should be noted, however, that some studies comparing samples taken from patients with schizophrenia with samples taken from controls have reported higher DA tissue levels in the subcortical regions such as the caudate (Owen *et al.* 1978), the accumbens (Mackay *et al.* 1982) and the amygdala (Reynolds 1983), and that no studies have reported lower DA content in these regions in the patients compared to the controls.

D_1 *receptors.* Striatal D_1 receptors have been reported as unaltered in schizophrenia (Pimoule *et al.* 1985; Seeman *et al.* 1987; Joyce *et al.* 1988; Reynolds and Czudek 1988), although one study reported decreased density (*Hess et al.* 1987).

D_2 *receptors.* Increased density of striatal D_2 receptors in patients with schizophrenia measured with [^{3}H]spiperone and other [^{3}H]neuroleptic drugs has been a consistent finding in a large number of post-mortem studies (Lee *et al.* 1978; Owen *et al.* 1978; Mackay *et al.* 1982; Cross *et al.* 1983; Seeman *et al.* 1984; Mita *et al.* 1986; Hess *et al.* 1987; Reynolds *et al.* 1987; Seeman *et al.* 1987; Joyce *et al.* 1988). However, chronic neuroleptic administration upregulates D_2 receptor density, (Burt *et al.* 1977), making it unclear whether these post-mortem findings are related to prior neuroleptic exposure or to the disease process *per se.*

D_3 *receptors.* Gurevich *et al.* (1997) reported a significant increase (almost two-fold) in the D_3 receptor number in post-mortem samples of ventral striatum from patients with schizophrenia that were off neuroleptics at the time of death. In contrast, the D_3 receptor binding was normal in patients on neuroleptics at the time of death, suggesting that treatment might normalize these receptors. However, these interesting findings have not yet been replicated, and D_3 receptor mRNA levels have been reported to be normal in the accumbens (Meador-Woodruff *et al.* 1997).

D_4 *receptors.* Based on ligand subtraction techniques, several studies have reported an increase in striatal D_4-like receptors in schizophrenia (Seeman *et al.* 1993; Murray *et al.* 1995; Sumiyoshi *et al.* 1995; Marzella *et al.* 1997). These findings, combined with the higher affinity of clozapine for D_4 relative to other DA receptors, prompted the hypothesis that D_4 receptors might play a critical role in the pathophysiology of the illness (Seeman et al. 1995). Yet, the elevation of D_4-like receptors in the striatum in patients with schizophrenia was neither confirmed by other studies using the same subtraction technique (Reynolds and Mason 1994; Lahti et al. 1996b), nor found in one study using the selective D_4 ligand [^{3}H]NGD 94–1 (Lahti et al. 1996a).

DA transporters (DAT). DAT terminate the action of synaptic DA by transporting DA from the synapse back to the intracellular space of the presynaptic neurons. A large number of post-mortem studies have reported unaltered DAT concentration in the striatum of patients with schizophrenia (Hirai et al. 1988; Joyce et al. 1988; Czudek and Reynolds 1989; Pearce et al. 1990; Chinaglia et al. 1992; Knable et al. 1994).

In conclusion, post-mortem measurements of the indices of DA transmission have generated a number of consistent observations: (i) the binding of the radioligand to D_2-like receptors in the striatum of patients with schizophrenia is increased, but it has been difficult to exclude the contribution of pre-mortem antipsychotic exposure to this set of findings; (ii) striatal DAT and D_1 receptor densities are unaffected in schizophrenia.

Imaging evidence

DA receptors and transporters. Striatal D_2 receptor density in schizophrenia has been extensively studied with positron emission tomography (PET) and single-photon emission computed tomography (SPECT) imaging, and these studies have been reviewed elsewhere (Laruelle 1998; Laruelle 2003). The vast majority of these studies have been negative, but meta-analysis of the results revealed a nonrandom distribution of the results consistent with a modest elevation of D_2 receptors in schizophrenia. Interestingly, studies performed with radiolabelled N-methyl spiperone ([^{11}C]NMSP, $n = 7$) showed elevated D_2 receptor binding in the striatum of patients with schizophrenia, while studies performed with radiolabelled benzamides, such as [^{11}C]raclopride and [^{123}I]iodobenzamide (IBZM), did not. To explain this discrepancy, Seeman noted that the in-vivo binding of benzamide is affected by competition with endogenous DA, whereas the binding of [^{11}C]NMSP is not (Seeman 1988; Seeman et al. 1989). It follows that, if endogenous DA is elevated in schizophrenia, D_2 receptor density measured *in vivo* with [^{11}C]raclopride and [^{123}I]IBZM would be 'underestimated' to a greater extent in patients with schizophrenia than in control subjects.

Several PET studies have reported no alteration in D_1 transporters in the striatum of patients with schizophrenia, a finding consistent with post-mortem studies (Okubo et al. 1997; Abi-Dargham et al. 2002; Karlsson et al. 2002).

Also consistent with post-mortem findings are the results of imaging studies reporting unaltered levels of DAT and of the vesicular transporters in schizophrenia (Laakso *et al.* 2000; Laruelle *et al.* 2000; Taylor *et al.* 2000; Lavalaye *et al.* 2001), although one study reported decreased DAT level in chronic patients (Laakso *et al.* 2001).

Striatal DOPA decarboxylase activity. Seven studies have reported rates of DOPA decarboxylase (an enzyme responsible for the precursor DOPA into dopamine) in patients with schizophrenia, using $[^{18}F]$DOPA (Reith *et al.* 1994; Hietala *et al.* 1995, 1999; Dao-Castellana *et al.* 1997; Meyer-Lindenberg *et al.* 2002; McGowan *et al.* 2004) or $[^{11}C]$DOPA (Lindstrom *et al.* 1999). Six out of seven studies reported an increased accumulation of DOPA in the striatum of patients with schizophrenia. Several studies reported high DOPA accumulation in psychotic paranoid patients. While the relationship between DOPA decarboxylase and the rate of DA synthesis is unclear (DOPA decarboxylase is not the rate-limiting step of DA synthesis), these observations are compatible with higher DA synthesis activity in patients experiencing psychotic symptoms.

Striatal amphetamine-induced DA release. The decrease in $[^{11}C]$raclopride and $[^{123}I]$IBZM in-vivo binding following acute amphetamine challenge has been well-validated as a measure of the change in D_2 receptor stimulation by DA due to amphetamine-induced DA release (Breier *et al.* 1997; Laruelle *et al.* 1997a; Villemagne *et al.* 1999; Laruelle 2000a; Piccini *et al.* 2003). Three out of three studies (Laruelle *et al.* 1996; Breier *et al.* 1997; Abi-Dargham *et al.* 1998) have demonstrated that amphetamine-induced decrease in $[^{11}C]$raclopride or $[^{123}I]$IBZM binding was elevated in untreated patients with schizophrenia compared to well-matched controls (Fig. 12.1). A significant relationship has been observed between the magnitude of DA release and the transient induction or worsening of positive symptoms, including paranoid ideations (Fig. 12.2).

These studies provided evidence that an exaggerated stimulation of D_2 receptors appears to be an important step for the expression of these symptoms. However, dopamine-mediated stimulation of D_2 receptors explained only about 30% of the variance in the positive symptom change, indicating that other factors play a role in the exacerbation of these symptoms following amphetamine. In addition, a psychotic response was never observed in healthy controls, even in the controls who showed large (i.e. >15%) amphetamine-induced $[^{123}I]$IBZM displacement. The unique qualitative features of the psychotic response in each patient also support the idea that dopamine stimulation leads to activation of pre-existent and specific dysfunctional neuronal circuits and re-entrant ensembles that are specific to each patient.

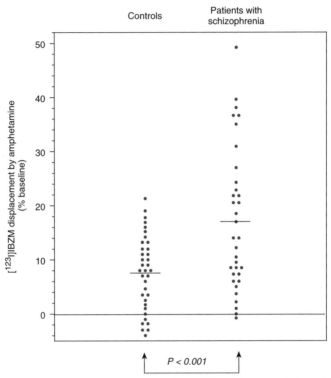

Fig. 12.1 Effect of amphetamine (0.3 mg/kg) on [123I]iodobenzamide (IBZM) binding in healthy controls and untreated patients with schizophrenia. The y-axis shows the percentage decrease in [123I]IBZM binding potential induced by amphetamine, which is a measure of the increased occupancy of D_2 receptors by DA following the challenge.

The increased amphetamine-induced DA release has been observed in both first episode/drug-naïve patients and patients previously treated by antipsychotic drugs scanned during an episode of illness exacerbation, but not in patients scanned during a remission phase (Laruelle *et al.* 1999). Thus, just like the enhanced vulnerability to the psychotogenic effects of stimulants (Lieberman *et al.* 1987b), the enhanced DA response to stimulants in schizophrenia appears to be state-dependent.

This exaggerated response of the DA system to amphetamine exposure did not appear to be a non-specific effect of stress, as elevated anxiety before the experiment was not associated with a larger amphetamine effect. Furthermore, non-psychotic subjects with unipolar depression, who reported levels of anxiety similar to the schizophrenic patients at the time of the scan, showed normal amphetamine-induced displacement of [123I]IBZM (Parsey *et al.* 2001).

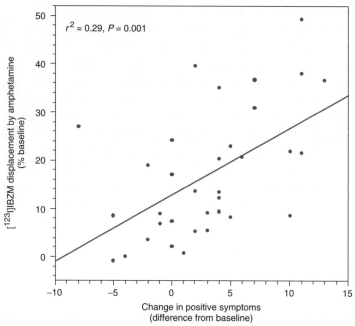

Fig. 12.2 Relationship between striatal amphetamine-induced dopamine release (y-axis) and amphetamine-induced changes in positive symptoms measured with the positive subscale of the Positive and Negative Symptom Scale (PANSS) in patients with schizophrenia. Stimulation of D_2 receptors was associated with emergence or worsening of positive symptoms and accounted for about 30% of the variance in this behavioural response.

These findings were generally interpreted as reflecting a larger DA release following amphetamine in the schizophrenic group. Another interpretation of these observations would be that schizophrenia is associated with increased affinity of D_2 receptors for DA. The development of D_2 receptor imaging with radiolabelled agonists is needed to settle this issue (Hwang *et al.* 2000; Narendran *et al.* 2004). Another limitation of this paradigm is that its measures change in synaptic DA transmission following a nonphysiological challenge (i.e. amphetamine) and do not provide any information about synaptic DA levels at baseline, i.e. in the unchallenged state.

Baseline occupancy of striatal D_2 receptors by DA. In rodents, acute depletion of synaptic DA is associated with an acute increase in the in-vivo binding of [^{11}C]raclopride or [^{123}I]IBZM to D_2 receptors (for review, see Laruelle 2000a). The increased binding is observed *in vivo* but not *in vitro*, indicating that it is not due to receptor upregulation, but to the removal of endogenous DA and the unmasking of D_2 receptors previously occupied by DA. The acute

DA depletion technique was developed in humans using α-methyl-p-tyrosine, to assess the degree of occupancy of D_2 receptors by DA (Laruelle *et al.* 1997b; Fujita *et al.* 2000; Verhoeff *et al.* 2002a,b). Using this technique, higher occupancy of D_2 receptors by DA was recently reported in patients with schizophrenia experiencing an episode of illness exacerbation compared to healthy controls (Abi-Dargham *et al.* 2000). Again assuming normal affinity of D_2 receptors for DA, the data are consistent with higher DA synaptic levels in patients with schizophrenia. A higher occupancy of D_2 receptors by DA in patients with schizophrenia was predictive of a good therapeutic response of these symptoms following six weeks of treatment with atypical antipsychotic medications. The fact that high levels of synaptic DA at baseline predicted a better or faster response to atypical antipsychotic drugs suggested that the D_2 receptor blockade induced by these drugs remains a key component in their initial mode of action.

Discussion

While the studies reviewed above are generally consistent with the DA imbalance hypothesis of schizophrenia, it is important to examine these results in light of the more recent views of schizophrenia as a neurodevelopmental illness, involving dysconnectivity of cortico-subcortical and intracortical networks. In this discussion, I will speculate about the possible relationships between the imaging results reviewed above and this contemporary view of schizophrenia. The model proposed here suggests that neurodevelopmental abnormalities of intra-cortical and cortico-limbic connectivity set the stage for the development of intermittent episodes of endogenous sensitization of the mesolimbic DA system that lead to the abnormal gating of information flow in the limbic loops underlying the psychotic experience. If sustained, this aberrant gating leads to plastic adaptation and remodelling of these circuits. As a result of these neuroplastic changes, the psychotic symptoms might become independent of sustained DA hyperactivity and resistant to D_2 receptor blockade.

Cortical regulation of subcortical DA transmission. While it cannot be definitively ruled out that the DA dysregulation revealed by these studies would result from a primary abnormality of DA neurons, it seems more likely that these abnormalities are a consequence of cortico-subcortical dysconnectivity involving regulation of DA cells' activity. Moreover, given the weight of evidence implicating prefrontal cortex (PFC) connectivity as a central deficient node in the brains of people with schizophrenia, it is tempting to speculate that a dysregulation of the firing activity of dopaminergic neurons might stem from a failure of the PFC to regulate this process. In fact, it has long been hypothesized that dysregulation of subcortical DA function in schizophrenia may be secondary to a failure of the PFC to adequately control subcortical dopaminergic function (Weinberger *et al.* 1986; Grace 1991).

In patients with schizophrenia, low *N*-acetyl-aspartate (NAA) concentration in the dorsolateral prefrontal cortex (DLPFC), a marker of DLPFC pathology, is associated with increased amphetamine-induced DA release (Bertolino *et al.* 2000). This result provides direct support to the hypothesis that disinhibition of subcortical DA activity might be secondary to prefrontal pathology in schizophrenia. Yet, the nature of the PFC pathology in schizophrenia and how it might affect subcortical DA function remains to be elucidated.

According to the model introduced by Carlsson (1999), the PFC modulates activity of mesolimbic midbrain DA neurons via both an activating pathway (the 'accelerator') and an inhibitory pathway ('the brake'), allowing fine tuning of dopaminergic activity by the PFC. The activating pathway is provided by direct and indirect glutamatergic projections onto the dopaminergic cells. Recent electron microscopy evidence suggest that direct stimulation of DA neurons by prefrontal afferents is restricted to DA neurons that project back to the cortex, while a polysynaptic mechanism, possibly involving the pedunculopontine tegmentum, mediates the prefrontal activation of mesolimbic DA neurons (see discussion and reference in Carr and Sesack 2000). The inhibitory pathway is provided by PFC glutamatergic efferents to midbrain GABAergic interneurons and striatomesencephalic GABA neurons. The model of dual modulation of the mesolimbic DA system by the PFC has been recently confirmed by studies demonstrating that extracellular DA concentration in the accumbens is decreased and increased following low- and high-frequency PFC stimulation, respectively (Jackson *et al.* 2001). Furthermore, blockade of glutamate transmission in the VTA increases DA release in the accumbens and decreases DA release in the PFC (Takahata and Moghaddam 2000). This observation demonstrates a glutamatergic-mediated tonic inhibitory regulation of mesoaccumbens neurons and a tonic excitatory regulation of mesoprefrontal DA neurons. In other words, under baseline conditions, the 'accelerator' mainly activates mesocortical systems, while the 'brake' mainly inhibits mesolimbic DA systems.

With this model, we could speculate that a reduced prefrontal activity, possibly secondary to *N*-methyl-D-aspartate (NMDA) transmission deficiency (Javitt and Zukin 1991; Olney and Farber 1995; Jentsch and Roth 1999), would result in a reduction of mesocortical DA activity (worsening prefrontal-related cognitive impairment and perhaps involved in negative symptoms), and, under conditions of stress (such as under stimulation of DA system by the amygdala), failure of the PFC to properly regulate DA activity in subcortical territories (Jackson and Moghaddam 2001). If sustained, this dysregulation of mesolimbic DA might precipitate positive symptoms.

The inhibition of dopaminergic cell firing following amphetamine is an important feedback mechanism by which the brain reduces the effect of amphetamine on DA release. The inhibition of dopaminergic cell firing induced by amphetamine is mediated both by stimulation of presynaptic D_2 autoreceptors, and by stimulation of this inhibitory pathway (Bunney and Aghajanian 1978; Carlsson *et al.* 1999). Following administration of amphetamine (i.e. under conditions in which the inhibitory pathway should be activated), NMDA receptor blockade results in a failure of activation of the inhibitory pathway, resulting in exaggerated amphetamine-induced DA release (Miller and Abercrombie 1996).

Kegeles *et al.* (2000) recently confirmed this mechanism in humans: pretreatment with the NMDA non-competitive antagonist ketamine significantly enhanced amphetamine-induced DA release. The increase in amphetamine-induced DA release induced by ketamine (more than two-fold) was comparable in magnitude to the exaggerated response seen in patients with schizophrenia. These data are consistent with the hypothesis that the alteration of DA release revealed by the amphetamine challenge in schizophrenia results from a disruption of glutamatergic neuronal systems regulating dopaminergic cell activity. Moreover, these data provide a direct link between the DA hypothesis and the NMDA receptor hypofunction hypothesis of schizophrenia (Javitt and Zukin 1991; Olney and Farber 1995; Jentsch and Roth 1999).

Alternatively, the failure of PFC control of subcortical DA release might stem from mechanisms other than NMDA hypofunction. For example, glutamatergic projections from the PFC to the VTA are under tonic inhibition by prefrontal GABA (see Karreman and Moghaddam 1996, and references therein). It follows that deficit in GABAergic function in the PFC is also expected to lead to disinhibition of the subcortical DA response to amphetamine. Alteration of GABAergic function in the PFC is one of the most consistently noted post-mortem abnormalities in schizophrenia. Gene expression for GABA synthetic enzyme glutamic acid decarboxylase$_{67}$ appears to be reduced in the PFC (Akbarian *et al.* 1995; Volk *et al.* 2000). GABAergic markers in axon terminals of chandelier neurons might be substantially reduced (Woo *et al.* 1998). One study reported decreased density of GABAergic interneurons in PFC in layer II (Benes *et al.* 1991), although this finding has not been replicated (Akbarian *et al.* 1995; Woo *et al.* 1997). Increased binding of the GABA$_A$ receptors was also observed (Hanada *et al.* 1987; Benes *et al.* 1992, 1996), which has been interpreted as a compensatory upregulation induced by GABA deficit.

Since the seminal work of Pycock *et al.* (1980), many laboratories described the reciprocal and opposite regulations between cortical and subcortical dopaminergic system: stimulation of cortical DA leads to inhibition of subcortical DA (Kolachana *et al.* 1995; Karreman and Moghaddam 1996), while destruction of cortical DA projections leads to subcortical disinhibition (Deutch 1990; Wilkinson 1997). In the cortex, DA has an inhibitory effect on pyramidal neurons that stimulate DA release at the VTA level (Karreman and Moghaddam 1996), an effect mediated in part by DA stimulation of GABAergic interneurons (Deutch 1993). Thus, deficits in PFC DA function in schizophrenia might represent another avenue leading to the disinhibition of subcortical DA revealed by these imaging studies.

Moreover, preclinical studies have documented that dysregulation of subcortical DA function might be a delayed and enduring consequence of neurodevelopmental abnormalities of limbic–cortical connectivity. Studies in rodents have shown that alteration of cortico-limbic development induced by prenatal exposure to the antimitotic agent methylazoxymethanol acetate (MAM) results in increased subcortical DA release in adulthood (Watanabe *et al.* 1998). The increase in subcortical DA transmission in MAM-treated rodents correlated strongly with the severity of cerebral cortical thinning resulting from altered development. Adult rhesus monkeys with neonatal ablation of the amygdala–hippocampal formation exhibit lower NAA concentration in the PFC and impaired PFC inhibition of subcortical DA functions (Bertolino *et al.* 1997; Saunders *et al.* 1998). Thus, several lines of evidence, both at the preclinical and clinical levels, suggest that hyperactivity of subcortical DA release in schizophrenia might be secondary to neurodevelopmental events affecting primarily connectivity within the PFC or between the PFC and the limbic system.

Schizophrenia and endogenous sensitization. While the evidence reviewed above is consistent with the model that dysregulation of subcortical DA function in schizophrenia is an enduring consequence of neurodevelopmental abnormalities involving PFC connectivity, these models *per se* do not account for the apparent episodic nature of this dysregulation. In the imaging studies reviewed above, elevated amphetamine-induced DA release was observed only in patients experiencing a first episode of illness or an episode of illness exacerbation, but not in patients studied during a period of illness remission. Confirmation of this observation by studying the same subjects during and between episodes is warranted. Nonetheless, this observation, combined with the clinical evidence of the fluctuating nature of positive symptomatology, suggests that subcortical hyperdopaminergia is episodic in the schizophrenic brain.

Neurochemical sensitization of mesolimbic DA systems has been proposed by several authors as one mechanism that might underlie the progression of a 'silent' vulnerability into overt symptomatology, resulting in further 'toxic' effects on the brain (Robinson and Becker 1986; Lieberman *et al.* 1990, 1997; Glenthoj and Hemmingsen 1997; Pierce and Kalivas 1997). Sensitization is a process whereby exposure to a given stimulus such as a drug or a stessor results in an enhanced response to subsequent exposures. This phenomenon has been well-characterized in rodents: repeated exposure to psychostimulants such as amphetamine induces an increase in the behavioural (locomotion) and biochemical (DA release) response to amphetamine, other stimulants, or stressors (for review see Kalivas *et al.* 1993; Robinson and Becker 1986; Kalivas and Stewart 1991; Sorg *et al.* 1994). Under certain conditions, sensitization is a long-lasting adaptation: animals sensitized to stimulants continue to display enhanced response after months of abstinence (Magos 1969; Robinson and Becker 1986). Sensitization is a form of learning and is essentially a non-homeostatic, positive feedback mechanism. Sensitization makes individuals more vulnerable rather than more resistant to a number of pharmacological or environmental stimulations.

Subjects who abused psychostimulants and experienced stimulant-induced psychotic episodes have been reported to remain vulnerable to low doses of psychostimulants (Connell 1958; Ellinwood *et al.* 1973; Sato *et al.* 1983). In these subjects, exposure to psychostimulants at doses that do not normally produce psychotic symptoms can trigger recurrence of these symptoms. The similarity between these patients and patients with schizophrenia in terms of vulnerability to the propsychotic effects of psychostimulants has already been noted and led to the suggestion that schizophrenia might be associated with an 'endogenous' sensitization process (Lieberman *et al.* 1990; Glenthoj and Hemmingsen 1997).

The brain-imaging data reviewed above provide support for the hypothesis that dysfunction of DA systems in schizophrenia results from a process similar to the sensitization phenomenon described following repeated psychostimu-lant exposure in rodents, since both conditions are associated with increased psychostimulant-induced DA release. In turn, this proposition suggests that neurodevelopmental abnormalities associated with schizophrenia may set the stage for the development of an endogenous sensitization process (Lieberman *et al.* 1997; Laruelle 2000b).

We have reviewed elsewhere (Laruelle 2000b) the preclinical literature sug-gesting that early brain lesions that affect the development of cortical connectivity might result in enhanced vulnerability to sensitization of mesolimbic DA systems. During late adolescence, alteration in cortical connectivity in schizophrenia might limit the capacity of the brain to modulate stress-related increased activity of mesolimbic DA neurons. This failure of normal homeostatic and buffering mechanisms results in endogenous sensitization of mesolimbic DA neurons, a response not observed in humans under normal circumstances. While increased DA activity is initially associated with environmental stressors, the sensitization process is self-perpetuating, and, beyond a given threshold, becomes independent of the environmental factors responsible for its initiation. This positive feedback loop, in which more DA leads to more DA, results ultimately in profound gating alterations in the corticostriatal-thalamo-cortical loops and to the expression of positive symptoms.

With treatment, chronic blockade of D_2 receptors and/or neuroleptic-induced depolarization blockade of dopaminergic neurons (Bunney and Grace 1978) might allow a progressive extinction of this sensitized state of the mesolimbic DA system. This proposition is suggested by the failure to detect an increase in amphetamine-induced DA release in currently untreated patients with schizophrenia during periods of illness stabilization. However, the high rate of relapse during prolonged treatment discontinuation suggests that the vulnerability to develop endogenous sensitization endures. Upon environmental, physiological, or pharmacological stress, this process might be reactivated, leading to clinical relapse.

Conclusion

The neurobiological basis of persecutory delusions remains to be elucidated, but robust evidence suggests that, in schizophrenia, hyperactivity of DA systems in the striatum is an important factor associated with their genesis, expression, and maintenance. This evidence rests both on solid pharmacological ground (repeated exposure to DA-enhancing drugs induces psychosis, blocking D_2 receptors alleviates psychosis) and on a growing body of direct-imaging evidence that has documented that, at least during an episode of illness exacerbation, schizophrenia is associated with increases in activity of DA neurons projecting to the striatum, and that this hyperactivity is associated with the severity of positive symptoms. Additional research is warranted to better understand both the causes and the consequences of this DA hyperactivity in patients with schizophrenia.

The observation that D_2 receptor blockade is not completely effective at alleviating chronic delusions suggested that increased DA activity might trigger neuroplastic adaptation 'downstream' from the mesolimbic dopaminergic synapse and that, once established, these neuroplastic changes become independent of increased DA activity. Positive symptom circuits might become 'hard wired' in prefrontal–ventrostriatal–ventropallidal–mediodorsal–thalamic–prefrontal loops described above. The established role of DA in modulating long-term potentiation and long-term depression of glutamatergic synapses (Arbuthnott *et al.* 2000; Kerr and Wickens 2001) provides a potential cellular mechanism by which sustained excess of DA activity might shape and remodel these circuits. Following these neuroplastic changes, excessive DA stimulation maintains the potential to activate these neuronal ensembles (as demonstrated by the relationship between D_2 receptor stimulation and worsening of positive symptoms), but the evidence suggests that, at least in some patients, these symptoms might become independent of continuous DA stimulation (as demonstrated by the observation that some patients exhibit severe positive symptoms in the absence of detectable abnormalities in synaptic DA). Thus, the emergence of treatment-resistant positive symptoms suggest that these symptoms have taken 'a life of their own', i.e. have become independent of DA stimulation. A better understanding of the consequences of sustained dopaminergic activity on the plasticity of prefrontal–striatal–thalamic loops is needed to further characterize the neurobiological effects of a sustained hyperdopaminergic state.

References

Abi-Dargham, A., Gil, R., Krystal, J. *et al.* (1998) Increased striatal dopamine transmission in schizophrenia: confirmation in a second cohort. *American Journal of Psychiatry*, 155, 761–767.

Abi-Dargham, A., Rodenhiser, J., Printz, D. *et al.* (2000) Increased baseline occupancy of D2 receptors by dopamine in schizophrenia. *Proceedings of the National Academy of Sciences of the USA*, 97, 8104–8109.

Abi-Dargham, A., Mawlawi, O., Lombardo, I. *et al.* (2002) Prefrontal dopamine D1 receptors and working memory in schizophrenia. *J Neuroscience*, 22, 3708–3719.

Akbarian, S., Kim, J.J., Potkin, S.G. *et al.* (1995) Gene expression for glutamic acid decarboxylase is reduced without loss of neurons in prefrontal cortex of schizophrenics. *Archives of General Psychiatry*, 52, 258–266.

Angrist, B. and van Kammen, D.P. (1984) CNS stimulants as a tool in the study of schizophrenia. *Trends Neuroscience*, 7, 388–390.

Angrist, B.M. and Gershon, S. (1970) The phenomenology of experimentally induced amphetamine psychosis—preliminary observation. *Biological Psychiatry*, 2, 95–107.

Arbuthnott, G.W., Ingham, C.A. and Wickens, J.R. (2000) Dopamine and synaptic plasticity in the neostriatum. *Journal of Anatomy*, 196, 587–596.

Bell, D.S. (1973) The experimental reproduction of amphetamine psychosis. *Archives of General Psychiatry*, 29, 35–40.

Benes, F.M., McSparren, J., Bird, E.D., Vincent, S.L. and SanGiovani, J.P. (1991) Deficits in small interneurons in schizophrenic cortex. *Archives of General Psychiatry*, 48, 996–1001.

Benes, F.M., Vincent, S.L., Alsterberg, G., Bird, E.D. and SanGiovanni, J.P. (1992) Increased GABAa receptor binding in superficial layers of cingulate cortex in schizophrenics. *Journal of Neuroscience*, 12, 924–929.

Benes, F.M., Vincent, S.L., Marie, A. and Khan, Y. (1996) Up-regulation of GABAA receptor binding on neurons of the prefrontal cortex in schizophrenic subjects. *Neuroscience*, 75, 1021–1031.

Bertolino, A., Saunders, R.C., Mattay, V.S., Bachevalier, J., Frank, J.A. and Weinberger, D.R. (1997) Altered development of prefrontal neurons in rhesus monkeys with neonatal mesial temporo-limbic lesions: a proton magnetic resonance spectroscopic imaging study. *Cerebral Cortex*, 7, 740–748.

Bertolino, A., Breier, A., Callicott, J.H. *et al.* (2000) The relationship between dorsolateral prefrontal neuronal *N*-acetylaspartate and evoked release of striatal dopamine in schizophrenia. *Neuropsychopharmacology*, 22, 125–132.

Boileau, I., Dagher, A., Leyton, M., Gunn, R., Diksic, M. and Benkelfat, C. (2003) Sensitization to psychostimulants: a PET/[11C]-Raclopride study in healthy volunteers. *ACNP Annual Meeting Abstracts.*

Breier, A., Su, T.P., Saunders, R., Carson, R.E. *et al.* (1997) Schizophrenia is associated with elevated amphetamine-induced synaptic dopamine concentrations: evidence from a novel positron emission tomography method. *Proceedings of the National Academy of Sciences of the USA*, 94, 2569–2574.

Bunney, B.S. and Aghajanian, G.K. (1978) d-Amphetamine-induced depression of central dopamine neurons: evidence for mediation by both autoreceptors and a striato-nigral feedback pathway. *Naunyn-Schmiedebergs Archiv für Pharmacologie*, 304, 255–261.

Bunney, B.S. and Grace, A.A. (1978) Acute and chronic haloperidol treatment: comparison of effects on nigral dopaminergic cell activity. *Life Sciences*, 23, 423–435.

Bunzow, J.R., Van Tol, H.H., Grandy, D.K. *et al.* (1988) Cloning and expression of a rat D2 dopamine receptor cDNA. *Nature*, 336, 783–787.

Burt, D.R., Creese, I. and Snyder, S.S. (1977) Antischizophrenic drugs: chronic treatment elevates dopamine receptors binding in brain. *Science*, 196, 326–328.

Carlsson, A. and Lindqvist, M. (1963) Effect of chlorpromazine or haloperidol on formation of 3-methoxytyramine and normetanephrine in mouse brain. *Acta Pharmacologica et Toxicologica*, 20, 140–144.

Carlsson, A., Waters, N. and Carlsson, M.L. (1999) Neurotransmitter interactions in schizophrenia—therapeutic implications. *Biological Psychiatry*, 46, 1388–1395.

Carr, D.B. and Sesack, S.R. (2000) Projections from the rat prefrontal cortex to the ventral tegmental area: target specificity in the synaptic associations with mesoaccumbens and mesocortical neurons. *Journal of Neuroscience*, 20, 3864–3873.

Chinaglia, G., Alvarez, F.J., Probst, A. and Palacios, J.M. (1992) Mesostriatal and mesolimbic dopamine uptake binding sites are reduced in Parkinson's disease and progressive supranuclear palsy: a quantitative autoradiographic study using [3H]mazindol. *Neuroscience*, 49, 317–327.

Connell, P.H. (1958) *Amphetamine Psychosis*. London: Chapman & Hill.

Creese, I., Burt, D.R. and Snyder, S.H. (1976) Dopamine receptor binding predicts clinical and pharmacological potencies of antischizophrenic drugs. *Science*, 19, 481–483.

Cross, A.J., Crow, T.J. and Owen, F. (1981) 3H-Flupenthixol binding in post-mortem brains of schizophrenics: evidence for a selective increase in dopamine D2 receptors. *Psychopharmacology*, 74, 122–124.

Cross, A.J., Crow, T.J., Ferrier, I.N. *et al.* (1983) Dopamine receptor changes in schizophrenia in relation to the disease process and movement disorder. *Journal of Neural Transmission* (Suppl. 18), 265–272.

Crow, T.J. (1980) Molecular pathology of schizophrenia: more than one disease process? *British Medical Journal*, 280, 66–68.

Czudek, C. and Reynolds, G.P. (1989) [3H] GBR 12935 binding to the dopamine uptake site in post-mortem brain tissue in schizophrenia. *Journal of Neural Transmission*, 77, 227–230.

Dao-Castellana, M.H., Paillere-Martinot, M.L., Hantraye, P. *et al.* (1997) Presynaptic dopaminergic function in the striatum of schizophrenic patients. *Schizophrenia Research*, 23, 167–174.

Davis, K.L., Kahn, R.S., Ko, G. and Davidson, M. (1991) Dopamine in schizophrenia: a review and reconceptualization. *American Journal of Psychiatry*, 148, 1474–1486.

Dearry, A., Gingrich, J.A., Falardeau, P., Fremeau, R., Jr, Bates, M.D. and Caron, M.G. (1990) Molecular cloning and expression of the gene for a human D1 dopamine receptor. *Nature*, 347, 72–76.

Delay, J., Deniker, P. and Harl, J. (1952) Therapeutic use in psychiatry of phenothiazine of central elective action (4560 RP). *Annales Medicopsychologiques*, 110, 112–117.

Deutch, A.Y. (1993) Prefrontal cortical dopamine systems and the elaboration of functional corticostriatal circuits: implications for schizophrenia and Parkinson's disease. *Journal of Neural Transmission, General Section*, 91, 197–221.

Deutch, A., Clark, W.A. and Roth, R.H. (1990) Prefrontal cortical dopamine depletion enhances the responsiveness of the mesolimbic dopamine neurons to stress. *Brain Research*, 521, 311–315.

Ellinwood, E.H., Jr (1967) Amphetamine psychosis: I. Description of the individuals and process. *Journal of Nervous and Mental Diseases*, 144, 273–283.

Ellinwood, E.H., Sudilovsky, A. and Nelson, L.M. (1973) Evolving behavior in the clinical and experimental amphetamine model psychosis. *American Journal of Psychiatry*, 130, 1088–1093.

Farde, L., Nordström, A.L., Wiesel, F.A., Pauli, S., Halldin, C. and Sedvall, G. (1992) Positron emission tomography analysis of central D1 and D2 dopamine receptor occupancy in patients treated with classical neuroleptics and clozapine. *Archives of General Psychiatry*, 49, 538–544.

Frankle, W.G., Gil, R., Hackett, E. *et al.* (2004) Occupancy of dopamine D2 receptors by the atypical antipsychotic drugs risperidone and olanzapine: theoretical implications. *Psychopharmacology (Berlin)*, 175, 473–480.

Fujita, M., Verhoeff, N.P., Varrone, A. *et al.* (2000) Imaging extrastriatal dopamine D(2) receptor occupancy by endogenous dopamine in healthy humans. *European Journal of Pharmacology*, 387, 179–188.

Glenthoj, B.Y. and Hemmingsen, R. (1997) Dopaminergic sensitization: implications for the pathogenesis of schizophrenia. *Progress in Neuropsychopharmacology and Biological Psychiatry*, 21, 23–46.

Grace, A.A. (1991) Phasic versus tonic dopamine release and the modulation of dopamine system responsivity: a hypothesis for the etiology of schizophrenia. *Neuroscience,* 41, 1–24.

Griffith, J.J., Oates, J. and Cavanaugh, J. (1968) Paranoid episodes induced by drugs. *Journal of the American Medical Association,* 205, 39.

Gurevich, E.V., Bordelon, Y., Shapiro, R.M., Arnold, S.E., Gur, R.E. and Joyce, J.N. (1997) Mesolimbic dopamine D-3 receptors and use of antipsychotics in patients with schizophrenia—a postmortem study. *Archives of General Psychiatry,* 54, 225–232.

Hanada, S., Mita, T., Nishino, N. and Tanaka, C. (1987) [3H]Muscimol binding sites increased in autopsied brains of chronic schizophrenics. *Life Sciences,* 40, 259–266.

Hess, E.J., Bracha, H.S., Kleinman, J.E. and Creese, I. (1987) Dopamine receptor subtype imbalance in schizophrenia. *Life Sciences,* 40, 1487–1497.

Hietala, J., Syvalahti, E., Vuorio, K. *et al.* (1995) Presynaptic dopamine function in striatum of neuroleptic-naive schizophrenic patients. *Lancet,* 346, 1130–1131.

Hietala, J., Syvalahti, E., Vilkman, H. *et al.* (1999) Depressive symptoms and presynaptic dopamine function in neuroleptic-naive schizophrenia. *Schizophrenia Research,* 35, 41–50.

Hirai, M., Kitamura, N., Hashimoto, T. *et al.* (1988) [3H]GBR-12935 binding sites in human striatal membranes: binding characteristics and changes in parkinsonians and schizophrenics. *Japanese Journal of Pharmacology,* 47, 237–243.

Hwang, D.R., Kegeles, L.S. and Laruelle, M. (2000) (–)-N-[(11)C]Propyl-norapomorphine: a positron-labeled dopamine agonist for PET imaging of D(2) receptors. *Nuclear Medicine and Biology,* 27, 533–539.

Jackson, M.E. and Moghaddam, B. (2001) Amygdala regulation of nucleus accumbens dopamine output is governed by the prefrontal cortex. *Journal of Neuroscience,* 21, 676–681.

Jackson, M.E., Frost, A.S. and Moghaddam, B. (2001) Stimulation of prefrontal cortex at physiologically relevant frequencies inhibits dopamine release in the nucleus accumbens. *Journal of Neurochemistry,* 78, 920–923.

Javitt, D.C. and Zukin, S.R. (1991) Recent advances in the phencyclidine model of schizophrenia. *American Journal of Psychiatry,* 148, 1301–1308.

Jentsch, J.D. and Roth, R.H. (1999) The neuropsychopharmacology of phencyclidine: from NMDA receptor hypofunction to the dopamine hypothesis of schizophrenia. *Neuropsychopharmacology,* 20, 201–225.

Joyce, J.N. and Meador-Woodruff, J.H. (1997) Linking the family of D-2 receptors to neuronal circuits in human brain: insights into schizophrenia. *Neuropsychopharmacology,* 16, 375–384.

Joyce, J.N., Lexow, N., Bird, E. and Winokur, A. (1988) Organization of dopamine D1 and D2 receptors in human striatum: receptor autoradiographic studies in Huntington's disease and schizophrenia. *Synapse,* 2, 546–557.

Kalivas, P.W. and Stewart, J. (1991) Dopamine transmission in the initiation and expression of drug- and stress-induced sensitization of motor activity. *Brain Research, Brain Research Reviews,* 16, 223–244.

Kalivas, P.W., Sorg, B.A. and Hooks, M.S. (1993) The pharmacology and neural circuitry of sensitization to psychostimulants. *Behavioural Pharmacology,* 4, 315–334.

Kapur, S. (2003) Psychosis as a state of aberrant salience: a framework linking biology, phenomenology, and pharmacology in schizophrenia. *American Journal of Psychiatry*, 160, 13–23.

Kapur, S., Zipursky, R., Jones, C., Remington, G. and Houle, S. (2000) Relationship between dopamine D(2) occupancy, clinical response, and side effects: a double-blind PET study of first-episode schizophrenia. *American Journal of Psychiatry*, 157, 514–520.

Karlsson, P., Farde, L., Halldin, C. and Sedvall, G. (2002) PET study of D(1) dopamine receptor binding in neuroleptic-naive patients with schizophrenia. *American Journal of Psychiatry*, 159, 761–767.

Karreman, M. and Moghaddam, B. (1996) The prefrontal cortex regulates the basal release of dopamine in the limbic striatum: an effect mediated by ventral tegmental area. *Journal of Neurochemistry*, 66, 589–598.

Kebabian, J.W. and Calne, D.B. (1979) Multiple receptors for dopamine. *Nature*, 277, 93–96.

Kegeles, L.S., Abi-Dargham, A., Zea-Ponce, Y. *et al.* (2000) Modulation of amphetamine-induced striatal dopamine release by ketamine in humans: implications for schizophrenia. *Biological Psychiatry*, 48, 627–640.

Kerr, J.N. and Wickens, J.R. (2001) Dopamine D-1/D-5 receptor activation is required for long-term potentiation in the rat neostriatum in vitro. *Journal of Neurophysiology*, 85, 117–124.

Knable, M.B., Hyde, T.M., Herman, M.M., Carter, J.M., Bigelow, L. and Kleinman, J.E. (1994) Quantitative autoradiography of dopamine-D1 receptors, D2 receptors, and dopamine uptake sites in postmortem striatal specimens from schizophrenic patients. *Biological Psychiatry*, 36, 827–835.

Kolachana, B.S., Saunders, R. and Weinberger, D. (1995) Augmentation of prefrontal cortical monoaminergic activity inhibits dopamine release in the caudate nucleus: an in vivo neurochemical assessment in the rhesus monkey. *Neuroscience*, 69, 859–868.

Laakso, A., Vilkman, H., Alakare, B. *et al.* (2000) Striatal dopamine transporter binding in neuroleptic-naive patients with schizophrenia studied with positron emission tomography. *American Journal of Psychiatry*, 157, 269–271.

Laakso, A., Bergman, J., Haaparanta, M. *et al.* (2001) Decreased striatal dopamine transporter binding in vivo in chronic schizophrenia. *Schizophrenia Research*, 52, 115–120.

Lahti, R.A., Roberts, R.C., Conley, R.R. and Tamminga, C.A. (1996a) Dopamine D2, D3 and D4 receptors in human postmortem brain sections: comparison between normals and schizophrenics. *Schizophrenia Research*, 18, 173.

Lahti, R.A., Roberts, R.C., Conley, R.R., Cochrane, E.V., Mutin, A. and Tamminga, C.A. (1996b) D2-type dopamine receptors in postmortem human brain sections from normal and schizophrenic subjects. *Neuroreport*, 7, 1945–1948.

Laruelle, M. (1998) Imaging dopamine transmission in schizophrenia. A review and meta-analysis. *Quarterly Journal of Nuclear Medicine*, 42, 211–221.

Laruelle, M. (2000a) Imaging synaptic neurotransmission with in vivo binding competition techniques: a critical review. *Journal of Cerebral Blood Flow and Metabolism*, 20, 423–451.

Laruelle, M. (2000b) The role of endogenous sensitization in the pathophysiology of schizophrenia: Implications from recent brain imaging studies. *Brain Research, Brain Research Reviews*, 31, 371–384.

Laruelle, M. (2003) Dopamine transmission in the schizophrenic brain. In: Weinberger, D.R. and Hirsch, S. (eds), *Schizophrenia*, 2nd edn, pp. 365–387. Oxford: Blackwell.

Laruelle, M., Abi-Dargham, A., van Dyck, C.H. *et al.* (1996) Single photon emission computerized tomography imaging of amphetamine-induced dopamine release in drug free schizophrenic subjects. *Proceedings of the National Academy of Sciences of the USA*, 93, 9235–9240.

Laruelle, M., Iyer, R.N., Al-Tikriti, M.S. *et al.* (1997a) Microdialysis and SPECT measurements of amphetamine-induced dopamine release in nonhuman primates. *Synapse*, 25, 1–14.

Laruelle, M., DSouza, C.D., Baldwin, R.M. *et al.* (1997b) Imaging D-2 receptor occupancy by endogenous dopamine in humans. *Neuropsychopharmacology*, 17, 162–174.

Laruelle, M., Abi-Dargham, A., Gil, R., Kegeles, L. and Innis, R. (1999) Increased dopamine transmission in schizophrenia: relationship to illness phases. *Biological Psychiatry*, 46, 56–72.

Laruelle, M., Abi-Dargham, A., van Dyck, C. *et al.* (2000) Dopamine and serotonin transporters in patients with schizophrenia: an imaging study with [123I]beta-CIT. *Biological Psychiatry*, 47, 371–379.

Lavalaye, J., Linszen, D.H., Booij, J. *et al.* (2001) Dopamine transporter density in young patients with schizophrenia assessed with [123]FP-CIT SPECT. *Schizophrenia Research*, 47, 59–67.

Lee, T., Seeman, P., Tourtelotte, W.W., Farley, I.J. and Hornykiewicz, O. (1978) Binding of 3H-neuroleptics and 3H-apomorphine in schizophrenic brains. *Nature*, 274, 897–900.

Lieberman, J.A., Kane, J.M. and Alvir, J. (1987a) Provocative tests with psychostimulant drugs in schizophrenia. *Psychopharmacology*, 91, 415–433.

Lieberman, J.A., Kane, J.M., Sarantakos, S. *et al.* (1987b) Prediction of relapse in schizophrenia. *Archives of General Psychiatry*, 44, 597–603.

Lieberman, J.A., Kinon, B.L. and Loebel, A.D. (1990) Dopaminergic mechanisms in idiopathic and drug-induced psychoses. *Schizophrenia Bulletin*, 16, 97–110.

Lieberman, J.A., Sheitman, B.B. and Kinon, B.J. (1997) Neurochemical sensitization in the pathophysiology of schizophrenia: deficits and dysfunction in neuronal regulation and plasticity. *Neuropsychopharmacology*, 17, 205–229.

Lindstrom, L.H., Gefvert, O., Hagberg, G. *et al.* (1999) Increased dopamine synthesis rate in medial prefrontal cortex and striatum in schizophrenia indicated by L-(beta-11C) DOPA and PET. *Biological Psychiatry*, 46, 681–688.

Lindvall, O. and Björklund, A. (1983) Dopamine- and norepinephrine-containing neuron systems: their anatomy in the rat brain. In: Emson, P. (ed.), *Chemical Neuroanatomy*, pp. 229–255. New York: Raven Press.

Mackay, A.V., Iversen, L.L., Rossor, M. *et al.* (1982) Increased brain dopamine and dopamine receptors in schizophrenia. *Archives of General Psychiatry*, 39, 991–997.

Magos, L. (1969) Persistence of the effect of amphetamine on stereotyped activity in rats. *European Journal of Pharmacology*, 6, 200–201.

Marzella, P.L., Hill, C., Keks, N., Singh, R. and Copolov, D. (1997) The binding of both [H-3]nemonapride and [H-3]raclopride is increased in schizophrenia. *Biological Psychiatry*, 42, 648–654.

Matthysse, S. (1974) Dopamine and the pharmacology of schizophrenia: the state of the evidence. *Journal of Psychiatric Research*, 11, 107–113.

McGowan, S., Lawrence, A.D., Sales, T., Quested, D. and Grasby, P. (2004) Presynaptic dopaminergic dysfunction in schizophrenia: a positron emission tomographic [18F]fluorodopa study. *Archives of General Psychiatry*, 61, 134–142.

Meador-Woodruff, J.H., Damask, S.P., Wang, J., Haroutunian, V., Davis, K. and Watson, S.J. (1996) Dopamine receptors mRNA expression in human striatum and neocortex. *Neuropsychopharmacology*, 15, 17–29.

Meador-Woodruff, J.H., Haroutunian, V., Powchik, P., Davidson, M., Davis, K.L. and Watson, S.J. (1997) Dopamine receptor transcript expression in striatum and prefrontal and occipital cortex. Focal abnormalities in orbitofrontal cortex in schizophrenia. *Archives of General Psychiatry*, 54, 1089–1095.

Meyer-Lindenberg, A., Miletich, R.S., Kohn, P.D. *et al.* (2002) Reduced prefrontal activity predicts exaggerated striatal dopaminergic function in schizophrenia. *Nature: Neuroscience*, 5, 267–271.

Miller, D.W. and Abercrombie, E.D. (1996) Effects of MK-801 on spontaneous and amphetamine-stimulated dopamine release in striatum measured with in vivo microdialysis in awake rats. *Brain Research Bulletin*, 40, 57–62.

Missale, C., Nash, S.R., Robinson, S.W., Jaber, M. and Caron, M.G. (1998) Dopamine receptors: from structure to function. *Physiology Reviews*, 78, 189–225.

Mita, T., Hanada, S., Nishino, N. *et al.* (1986) Decreased serotonin S2 and increased dopamine D2 receptors in chronic schizophrenics. *Biological Psychiatry*, 21, 1407–1414.

Mogenson, G.J., Jones, D.L. and Yim, C.Y. (1980) From motivation to action: functional interface between the limbic system and the motor system. *Progress in Neurobiology*, 14, 69–97.

Monsma, F., Jr, Mahan, L.C., McVittie, L.D., Gerfen, C.R. and Sibley, D.R. (1990) Molecular cloning and expression of a D1 dopamine receptor linked to adenylyl cyclase activation. *Proceedings of the National Academy of Science of the USA*, 87, 6723–6727.

Mrzljak, L., Bergson, C., Pappy, M., Huff, R., Levenson, R. and Goldman-Rakic, P.S. (1996) Localization of dopamine D4 receptors in GABAergic neurons of the primate brain. *Nature*, 381, 245–248.

Murray, A.M., Hyde, T.M., Knable, M.B. *et al.* (1995) Distribution of putative D4 dopamine receptors in postmortem striatum from patients with schizophrenia. *Journal of Neuroscience*, 15, 2186–2191.

Narendran, R., Hwang, D.R., Slifstein, M. *et al.* (2004) In vivo vulnerability to competition by endogenous dopamine: comparison of the D2 receptor agonist radiotracer (−)-N-[11C]propyl-norapomorphine ([11C]NPA) with the D2 receptor antagonist radiotracer [11C]-raclopride. *Synapse*, 52, 188–208.

Nordstrom, A.L., Farde, L., Wiesel, F.A. *et al.* (1993) Central D2-dopamine receptor occupancy in relation to antipsychotic drug effects: a double-blind PET study of schizophrenic patients. *Biological Psychiatry*, 33, 227–235.

Okubo, Y., Suhara, T., Suzuki, K. *et al.* (1997) Decreased prefrontal dopamine D1 receptors in schizophrenia revealed by PET. *Nature*, 385, 634–636.

Olney, J.W. and Farber, N.B. (1995) Glutamate receptor dysfunction and schizophrenia. *Archives of General Psychiatry*, 52, 998–1007.

Owen, F., Cross, A.J., Crow, T.J., Longden, A., Poulter, M. and Riley, G.J. (1978) Increased dopamine-receptor sensitivity in schizophrenia. *Lancet*, 2, 223–226.

Palermo-Neto, J. (1997) Dopaminergic systems. Dopamine receptors. *Psychiatric Clinics of North America*, 20, 705–721.

Parsey, R.V., Oquendo, M.A., Zea-Ponce, Y. *et al.* (2001) Dopamine D(2) receptor availability and amphetamine-induced dopamine release in unipolar depression. *Biological Psychiatry*, 50, 313–322.

Pearce, R.K., Seeman, P., Jellinger, K. and Tourtellotte, W.W. (1990) Dopamine uptake sites and dopamine receptors in Parkinson's disease and schizophrenia. *European Neurology*, 30 (Suppl. 1), 9–14.

Piccini, P., Pavese, N. and Brooks, D.J. (2003) Endogenous dopamine release after pharmacological challenges in Parkinson's disease. *Annals of Neurology*, 53, 647–653.

Pierce, R.C. and Kalivas, P.W. (1997) A circuitry model of the expression of behavioral sensitization to amphetamine-like psychostimulants. *Brain Research: Brain Research Reviews*, 25, 192–216.

Pimoule, C., Schoemaker, H., Reynolds, G.P. and Langer, S.Z. (1985) [3H]SCH 23390 labelled D1 dopamine receptors are unchanged in schizophrenia and Parkinson's disease. *European Journal of Pharmacology*, 114, 235–237.

Pycock, C.J., Kerwin, R.W. and Carter, C.J. (1980) Effect of lesion of cortical dopamine terminals on subcortical dopamine receptors in rats. *Nature*, 286, 74–77.

Reith, J., Benkelfat, C., Sherwin, A. *et al.* (1994) Elevated dopa decarboxylase activity in living brain of patients with psychosis. *Proceedings of the National Academy of Sciences of the USA*, 91, 11651–11654.

Reynolds, G.P. (1983) Increased concentrations and lateral asymmetry of amygdala dopamine in schizophrenia. *Nature*, 305, 527–529.

Reynolds, G.P. (1989) Beyond the dopamine hypothesis. The neurochemical pathology of schizophrenia. *British Journal of Psychiatry*, 155, 305–316.

Reynolds, G.P. and Czudek, C. (1988) Status of the dopaminergic system in post-mortem brain in schizophrenia. *Psychopharmacology Bulletin*, 24, 345–347.

Reynolds, G.P. and Mason, S.L. (1994) Are striatal dopamine D-4 receptors increased in schizophrenia? *Journal of Neurochemical*, 63, 1576–1577.

Reynolds, G.P., Czudek, C., Bzowej, N. and Seeman, P. (1987) Dopamine receptor asymmetry in schizophrenia. *Lancet*, 1, 979.

Robinson, T.E. and Becker, J.B. (1986) Enduring changes in brain and behavior produced by chronic amphetamine administration: a review and evaluation of animal models of amphetamine psychosis. *Brain Research: Brain Research Reviews*, 11, 157–198.

Rossum, V. (1966) The significance of dopamine receptor blockade for the mechanism of action of neuroleptic drugs. *Archives Internationales de Pharmacodynamie et de Therapie*, 160, 492–494.

Sato, M., Chen, C.C., Akiyama, K. and Otsuki, S. (1983) Acute exacerbation of paranoid psychotic state after long-term abstinence in patients with previous methamphetamine psychosis. *Biological Psychiatry*, 18, 429–440.

Saunders, R.C., Kolachana, B.S., Bachevalier, J. and Weinberger, D.R. (1998) Neonatal lesions of the medial temporal lobe disrupt prefrontal cortical regulation of striatal dopamine. *Nature*, 393, 169–171.

Seamans, J.K., Gorelova, N., Durstewitz, D. and Yang, C.R. (2001) Bidirectional dopamine modulation of GABAergic inhibition in prefrontal cortical pyramidal neurons. *Journal of Neuroscience*, 21, 3628–3638.

Seeman, P. (1988) Brain dopamine receptors in schizophrenia: PET problems. *Archives of General Psychiatry*, 45, 598–560.

Seeman, P. (1992) Dopamine receptor sequences. Therapeutic levels of neuroleptics occupy D2 receptors, clozapine occupies D4. *Neuropsychopharmacology*, 7, 261–284.

Seeman, P. and Lee, T. (1975) Antipsychotic drugs: direct correlation between clinical potency and presynaptic action on dopamine neurons. *Science*, 188, 1217–1219.

Seeman, P., Ulpian, C., Bergeron, C. *et al.* (1984) Bimodal distribution of dopamine receptor densities in brains of schizophrenics. *Science*, 225, 728–731.

Seeman, P., Bzowej, N.H., Guan, H.C. *et al.* (1987) Human brain D1 and D2 dopamine receptors in schizophrenia, Alzheimer's, Parkinson's, and Huntington's diseases. *Neuropsychopharmacology*, 1, 5–15.

Seeman, P., Guan, H.-C. and Niznik, H.B. (1989) Endogenous dopamine lowers the dopamine D2 receptor density as measured by [^{3}H]raclopride: implications for positron emission tomography of the human brain. *Synapse*, 3, 96–97.

Seeman, P., Guan, H.C. and Van Tol, H.H.M. (1993) Dopamine D4 receptors elevated in schizophrenia. *Nature*, 365, 411–445.

Seeman, P., Guan, H.C. and Van Tol, H.H. (1995) Schizophrenia: elevation of dopamine D4-like sites, using [3H]nemonapride and [125I]epidepride. *European Journal of Pharmacology*, 286, R3–5.

Smiley, J.F., Levey, A.I., Ciliax, B.J. and Goldman-Rakic, P.S. (1994) D1 dopamine receptor immunoreactivity in human and monkey cerebral cortex: predominant and extrasynaptic localization in dendritic spines. *Proceedings of the National Academy of Sciences of the USA*, 91, 5720–5724.

Snyder, S.H. (1973) Amphetamine psychosis: a "model" schizophrenia mediated by catecholamines. *American Journal of Psychiatry*, 130, 61–67.

Sokoloff, P., Giros, B., Martres, M.-P., Bouthenet, M.-L. and Schwartz. J.-C. (1990) Molecular cloning and characterization of a novel dopamine receptor D3 as a target for neuroleptics. *Nature*, 347, 146–151.

Sorg, B.A., Hooks, M.S. and Kalivas, P.W. (1994) Neuroanatomy and neurochemical mechanisms of time-dependent sensitization. *Toxicology and Industrial Health*, 10, 369–386.

Stevens, J. (1973) An anatomy of schizophrenia? *Archives of General Psychiatry*, 29, 177–189.

Sumiyoshi, T., Stockmeier, C.A., Overholser, J.C., Thompson, P.A. and Meltzer, H.Y. (1995) Dopamine D4 receptors and effects of guanine nucleotides on [3H]raclopride binding in postmortem caudate nucleus of subjects with schizophrenia or major depression. *Brain Research*, 681, 109–116.

Sunahara, R.K., Guan, H.-C. and O'Dowd, B.F. *et al.* (1991) Cloning of the gene for a human dopamine D5 receptor with higher affinity for dopamine than D1. *Nature*, 350, 614–619.

Takahata, R. and Moghaddam, B. (2000) Target-specific glutamatergic regulation of dopamine neurons in the ventral tegmental area. *Journal of Neurochemistry*, 75, 1775–1778.

Talbot, P.S. and Laruelle, M. (2002) The role of in vivo molecular imaging with PET and SPECT in the elucidation of psychiatric drug action and new drug development. *European Neuropsychopharmacology*, 12, 503–511.

Taylor, S.F., Koeppe, R.A., Tandon, R., Zubieta, J.K. and Frey, K.A. (2000) In vivo measurement of the vesicular monoamine transporter in schizophrenia. *Neuropsychopharmacology*, 23, 667–675.

Tiberi, M., Jarvie, K.R., Silvia, C. *et al.* (1991) Cloning, molecular characterization, and chromosomal assignment of a gene encoding a second D1 dopamine receptor subtype: differential expression pattern in rat brain compared with the D1A receptor. *Proceedings of the National Academy of Sciences of the USA*, 88, 7491–7495.

Van Tol, H.H.M., Bunzow, J.R., Guan, H.-C. *et al.* (1991) Cloning of the gene for a human dopamine D4 receptor with high affinity for the antipsychotic clozapine. *Nature*, 350, 610–614.

Verhoeff, N.P., Hussey, D., Lee, M. *et al.* (2002a) Dopamine depletion results in increased neostriatal D(2), but not D(1), receptor binding in humans. *Molecular Psychiatry*, 7, 233, 322–238.

Verhoeff, N.P., Kapur, S., Hussey, D. *et al.* (2002b) A simple method to measure baseline occupancy of neostriatal dopamine D2 receptors by dopamine in vivo in healthy subjects. *Neuropsychopharmacology*, 25, 213–223.

Villemagne, V.L., Wong, D.F., Yokoi, F. *et al.* (1999) GBR12909 attenuates amphetamine-induced striatal dopamine release as measured by [(11)C]raclopride continuous infusion PET scans. *Synapse*, 33, 268–273.

Volk, D.W., Austin, M.C., Pierri, J.N., Sampson, A.R. and Lewis, D.A. (2000) Decreased glutamic acid decarboxylase67 messenger RNA expression in a subset of prefrontal cortical gamma-aminobutyric acid neurons in subjects with schizophrenia. *Archives of General Psychiatry*, 57, 237–245.

Watanabe, M., Nonaka, R., Hagino, Y. and Kodama, Y. (1998) Effects of prenatal methylazoxymethanol treatment on striatal dopaminergic systems in rat brain. *Neuroscience Research*, 30, 135–144.

Weinberger, D.R. (1987) Implications of the normal brain development for the pathogenesis of schizophrenia. *Archives of General Psychiatry*, 44, 660–669.

Weinberger, D.R., Berman, K.F. and Zec, R.F. (1986) Physiological dysfunction of dorsolateral prefrontal cortex in schizophrenia: I. Regional cerebral blood flow evidence. *Archives of General Psychiatry*, 43, 114–124.

Wickens, J.R. (2000) Dopamine regulation of synaptic plasticity in the neostriatum: a cellular model of reinforcement. In: Miller, R. and Wickens, J.R. (eds), *Brain Dynamics and the Striatal Complex*, pp 65–76. Amsterdam: Harwood.

Wilkinson, L.S. (1997) The nature of interactions involving prefrontal and striatal dopamine systems. *Journal of Psychopharmacology*, 11, 143–150.

Woo, T.U., Miller, J.L. and Lewis, D.A. (1997) Schizophrenia and the parvalbumin-containing class of cortical local circuit neurons. *American Journal of Psychiatry*, 154, 1013–1015.

Woo, T.U., Whitehead, R.E., Melchitzky, D.S. and Lewis, D.A. (1998) A subclass of prefrontal gamma-aminobutyric acid axon terminals are selectively altered in schizophrenia. *Proceedings of the National Academy of Sciences of the USA*, 95, 5341–5346.

Yang, C.R., Seamans, J.K. and Gorelova, N. (1999) Developing a neuronal model for the pathophysiology of schizophrenia based on the nature of electrophysiological actions of dopamine in the prefrontal cortex. *Neuropsychopharmacology*, 21, 161–194.

Young, D. and Scoville, W.B. (1938) Paranoid psychosis in narcolepsy and the possible dangers of benzedrine treatment. *Medical Clinics of North America*, 22, 637.

Zhou, Q.Y., Grandy, D.K., Thambi, L. *et al.* (1990) Cloning and expression of human and rat D1 dopamine receptors. *Nature*, 347, 76–80.

Chapter 13

The role of cannabis in inducing paranoia and psychosis

Cécile Henquet, Marta Di Forti,
Robin M. Murray, and Jim van Os

Introduction

In this chapter the acute and long-term effects of cannabis on psychotic symptoms, in particular on paranoia, will be discussed. Cannabis is the world's most popular illicit drug. An estimated 4% of the world's adult population consumes it each year, more than all the other illicit drugs combined. The rates of use, and dosage, based on the levels of active compound present in street drugs, have increased over the last quarter of the twentieth century in the UK and Europe. As a result, 40% of 15-year-olds in the UK have tried the drug. In addition, the age of first use has been decreasing across Europe. For example, a large study carried out in The Netherlands showed that between 1992 and 1996, the number of children starting cannabis use by age 13 years or younger had doubled (Monshouwer *et al.* 2005). Finally, there is some evidence that the proportion of the active psychotogenic ingredient, Δ-9-tetrahydrocannabinol (THC), has been rising in street preparations of cannabis. As a consequence, for the very first time the United Nations (2006) devoted much of its annual report on drug abuse to cannabis. There is much interest in whether heavy use of cannabis can impair cognition (Solowij *et al.* 2007) but here we shall concentrate on the effects of its acute and chronic use on psychotic symptoms.

Experimental studies of acute effects of cannabis on psychosis

It has been known for a century and a half that use of cannabis can induce acute paranoia and other psychotic symptoms. Thus, in 1845 Moreau published the results of his studies in which, after taking THC himself (most probably up to several hundred milligrams) and giving it to some of his students and patients, he concluded that THC could precipitate 'acute psychotic reactions, generally lasting but a few hours, but occasionally as long as a week' (Moreau, 1973 translation). The reaction seemed dose-related and its main features included paranoid ideation, illusions, hallucinations, delusions, depersonalization, confusion, restlessness and excitement. As a result of this and subsequent reports, it became widely accepted that cannabis intoxication can cause brief psychotic episodes or short-term relapses of pre-existing psychotic symptoms (Negrete et al. 1986; Thornicroft 1990; Mathers and Ghodse 1992).

However, the scientific study of the effects of cannabis began only half a century ago. Ames (1958) exposed medical staff members to controlled doses of cannabis. In the majority of cases, delusions and visual hallucinations emerged. Paranoid ideation was most apparent during cannabis intoxication, whereby subjects reported fear of being hypnotized and had ideas that the experimenters were asking questions with hidden implications. Fear of being monitored by a hidden tape recorder and beliefs of secretly receiving electro-convulsive therapy were also noted. Other early experimental studies (Isbell et al. 1967) and clinical case reports (Talbott and Teague 1969; Chopra and Smith 1974; Voruganti et al. 2001) investigated the effects of THC. They showed that THC can both induce transient psychotic symptoms in healthy subjects and acutely exacerbate symptoms in individuals with established psychosis. Furthermore, these experimental studies consistently showed that the effects of THC on psychosis are dose-related. Isbell et al. (1967) exposed healthy individuals to various doses of cannabis and described a dose-related intensity of visual and auditory hallucinations, depersonalization and derealization.

In contrast, however, other experimental studies found no effects of cannabis on psychotic symptoms, while significant effects on cognition and driving performance were observed (Ramaekers et al. 2006). These diverging observations may be due to the fact that individuals differ in their sensitivity to THC, a finding that has been described in epidemiological studies (van Os et al. 2002; Henquet et al. 2005a). Recently, Favrat et al. (2005) observed differential sensitivity to the acute effects of THC on psychosis outcome in a study originally designed to investigate the effects of cannabis on cognition and driving. The majority of the cases did not experience any psychotic symptoms after 15.8 or 45.7 mg synthetic THC (dronabinol). However, two of the participants had to be withdrawn from the study because of adverse events. Both subjects demonstrated severe anxiety, derealization and depersonalization following the low dose of 15.8 mg dronabinol. One subject experienced frank paranoia, as evidenced by the belief that the experimenters were concealing some problems during the experiment. Other studies illustrated similar variation in the psychotogenic effects of THC and showed that both environmental factors, such as expectations and stressful situations, and personality characteristics (e.g. introversion) may moderate the effects of THC on paranoid symptoms (Jones 1971; Gregg *et al.* 1976). However, most of the aforementioned studies were not sensitive enough to investigate the specific effects of cannabis on individual psychotic symptoms or to identify the moderating factors thereof.

Melges (1976) conducted a placebo-controlled study and exposed healthy controls to three conditions, including 20 mg THC via pulmonary uptake, placebo and a dose of alcohol which was calculated to be as intoxicating as the THC doses. In line with the above reports, this study clearly showed that symptoms of persecutory ideation were more likely to emerge in the THC than in the placebo or alcohol condition. Leweke and Schneider (1999) used a semi-placebo controlled design, and found persecutory delusions and delusions of thought insertion after exposure to dronabinol (20 mg). They also showed negative effects of THC on binocular depth inversion (BDI), a complex neuropsychological phenomenon that has been found to be related to schizophrenia. BDI is the illusion that occurs when a three-dimensional object is presented pseudoscopically, thereby giving rise to an inverted percept of the object. Healthy controls, under normal conditions, will continue to perceive the object as convex. This mechanism is hypothesized to result from top-down processes by which implausible contents of perception are adjusted so that they become consistent with the current context. It has been shown that individuals with established psychosis show impairments in this 'correcting mechanism' (Schneider *et al.* 2002). Koethe *et al.* (2006) further investigated the effects of dronabinol (120 µg per kg body weight) on binocular depth inversion in healthy controls using a similar design as described by Leweke and Schneider (1999) and compared these to non-exposed patients with schizophrenia and individuals in prodromal states of schizophrenia. In healthy controls, THC acutely impaired the correcting mechanism underlying BDI; after exposure to dronabinol, the BDI values of the healthy controls were similar to those of the patients and the individuals in prodromal states. In addition to the cognitive effect, exposure to dronabinol caused thought disturbance, hostility and suspiciousness.

D'Souza *et al.* (2005) investigated the acute effects of 2.5 and 5 mg intravenous THC on cognition in a double-blind placebo-controlled study. They found that patients with schizophrenia showed greater impairment of memory and attention after THC administration compared to healthy controls. This indicates that individuals with an increased vulnerability for psychosis (i.e. being a patient) show abnormal sensitivity to the cognitive effects of THC. This finding is relevant as cognitive impairments are a fundamental feature of psychotic illness and mild cognitive impairments are present in individuals with genetic vulnerability for psychosis (Krabbendam *et al.* 2001). D'Souza *et al.* (2005) also found that THC intravenously significantly increased both positive psychotic and negative symptoms as assessed by the Positive and Negative Syndrome Scale (PANSS) in patients and controls (Fig. 13.1).

Effects of chronic use of cannabis

Understandably, there have not been experimental studies of the effects of chronic cannabis use. For this we must rely on epidemiological and clinical studies.

Cohort studies

Most cohort studies have examined the relationship been cannabis use and schizophrenia or psychotic symptoms as a whole rather than paranoia specifically. Thus, Andreasson *et al.* (1987) described an association between cannabis use and diagnosis of schizophrenia. This landmark cohort-study of 45 000 Swedish male conscripts (representing 97% of men aged 18–20 years in the population at that time) followed up for 15 years, found that heavy use of marijuana at age 18 years increased the risk of schizophrenia later in life by a

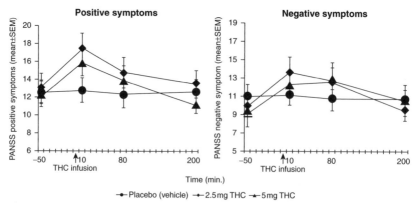

Fig. 13.1 Subjects assessed by the Positive and Negative Syndrome Scale (PANSS) show a significant exacerbation of positive and negative symptoms in the 2.5 mg (squares) and 5 mg (triangles) Δ-9-tetrahydrocannabinol (THC) condition compared to the placebo condition (circles). Modified with permission from D'Souza *et al.* (2005).

factor of six. There was a dose–response relationship in the association between cannabis use at age 18 years and schizophrenia diagnosis in the ensuing 15 years. Zammit *et al.* (2002) extended the follow-up of the same Swedish Army Cohort to 25 years. Heavy cannabis users were 6.7 times more likely than non-users to be diagnosed with schizophrenia later in life. The same risk was described in a sub-sample of conscripts who only smoked cannabis as opposed to using other drugs as well. Zammit challenged the self-medicating hypothesis that explains the association between cannabis and schizophrenia as a consequence of an attempt to treat prodromal symptoms of psychosis. He repeated the analyses in those individuals who developed schizophrenia only five years after conscription. He found no difference between the results obtained and those from the entire cohort. Therefore, he concluded that his study supported a causal role for cannabis in the onset of schizophrenia.

Van Os *et al.* (2002) conducted analyses of the Netherlands Mental Health Survey and Incidence Study (NEMESIS), examining the effect of cannabis use on psychotic symptoms among the general population. In this study, 4045 psychosis-free individuals and 59 subjects with self-reported symptoms of psychosis were assessed at baseline, and then at one-year and three-year follow-up. Even after statistical adjustment for factors including ethnic group, marital status, educational level, urbanicity and discrimination, the individuals using cannabis at baseline were three times more likely to report psychotic symptoms at follow-up. The results confirm that cannabis is an independent risk factor for the onset of psychosis in previously healthy individuals and that cannabis use is associated with poor outcome in individuals with established psychosis vulnerability.

In one of the most detailed studies, a general population birth cohort of 1034 children born in Dunedin, New Zealand, in 1972–1973, was assessed 10 times from age 3 years. At age 11 years, they were interviewed by a child psychiatrist, and at ages 15 and 18 years they were asked about drug consumption. At age 26 years, 96% were interviewed using a standardized psychiatric interview schedule (*Diagnostic and Statistical Manual of Mental Disorders*: *DSM-IV*). Of these, 3.7% met criteria for schizophreniform psychosis (Arseneault *et al.* 2002). Study participants who used cannabis at ages 15 and 18 years reported higher rates of psychotic symptoms at age 26 years compared to non-users. Thus, 10% of those who smoked cannabis at age 15 years were diagnosed with schizophreniform disorder at age 26 years compared with 3% of the non-using control group. This study also elegantly indicates 'specificity of outcome': cannabis use by age 15 years did not predict depressive outcomes at age 26 years and 'specificity of exposure': the use of other illicit drugs in adolescence did not predict schizophreniform outcomes over and above the effect of cannabis use (Arseneault et al. 2002). This study also controlled for the presence of minor psychotic symptoms at age 11 years. When these were taken into consideration, the association with schizophreniform disorder was no longer significant but that between cannabis use at age 15 years and schizophrenic symptoms at 26 years remained so.

Several studies have focused on the direction of the relationship between cannabis use and psychotic symptoms. In the Christchurch Health & Development Study, a birth cohort of 1055 children was studied annually throughout childhood, and then data on cannabis use and psychotic symptoms (10 items from the SCL-90) were collected at ages 18, 21, and 25 years (Fergusson 2003; Fergusson et al. 2005). This study used statistical modelling in an attempt to distinguish between the causal and self-medication hypotheses, and reported that the data were more compatible with a causal rather than a self-medication explanation (Fergusson et al. 2005). Thus, cannabis use had a positive and significant effect on psychotic symptoms ($P < 0.001$) implying that increasing cannabis use was associated with increasing symptom levels. The effect of psychotic symptoms on cannabis use was negative; if anything the development of psychotic symptoms appeared to have inhibited rather than encouraged cannabis use.

In a prospective cohort study of 2437 young German people (aged 14–24 years), Henquet et al. (2005a) analysed data on cannabis use and psychotic symptoms at four-year follow-up. The results showed that cannabis use at baseline increased the cumulative incidence of psychotic symptoms at follow-up, even after adjusting for age, sex, socio-economic status, urbanicity, childhood trauma, predisposition for psychosis at baseline, and use of other drugs, tobacco and alcohol (Henquet et al. 2005a). In this study, Henquet et al. reported, as in the Christchurch study, that baseline psychosis liability (attenuated psychotic symptoms) did not predict later cannabis use.

Ferdinand et al. (2005), in a 14-year follow-up study of 4–16-year-olds ($n = 1580$) drawn randomly from the Dutch population, also assessed the direction of effect between cannabis use and psychotic symptoms. The results confirmed that cannabis use predicted future psychotic symptoms in individuals who did not have such symptoms before they began using cannabis. Thus the study agreed with the consensus in this regard. However, in contrast to the studies of Fergusson and of Henquet, Ferdinand and colleagues found that the reverse was also true; the presence of psychotic symptoms in those who had never used cannabis predicted future cannabis use (Ferdinand et al. 2005).

Some criticism can be made of the above studies in the context of the present discussion. Their lack of homogeneity of measures of outcome makes it difficult to draw a firm conclusion on paranoia from the findings reported. However, they all consistently show that cannabis users have an elevated risk for psychosis later in life. Another limitation derives from the fact that measures of cannabis use were based on self-report and not supplemented by urine tests or hair analyses. The Dunedin study is so far the only study to clearly establish temporal priority between cannabis use and adult psychosis. Some have claimed that these studies may be confounded by the effect of using other drugs such as amphetamines, phenylcycline and LSD (lysergic acid diethylamide) which are thought to be psychotogenic (Murray *et al.* 2003); use of other drugs among young adults is almost always preceded by cannabis consumption (Fergusson *et al.* 2000). Nevertheless the evidence for the association between cannabis use and later schizophrenia in the Dunedin, NEMESIS and Swedish studies held even when adjusting for the use of other drugs (Arseneault *et al.* 2002; Van Os *et al.* 2002; Zammit *et al.* 2002). Henquet *et al.* (2005b), who conducted a meta-analysis of the above studies, came to the conclusion that cannabis consumption is associated with approximately a doubling in risk of later schizophrenia.

Clinical samples

Arendt *et al.* (2005) investigated whether individuals who receive a diagnosis of cannabis psychosis go on to subsequently develop persistent psychotic illness. Data on 535 patients treated for cannabis-induced psychotic symptoms between 1994 and 1999 were extracted from the Danish Psychiatric Central Register, and the patients were followed for at least three years. Almost half of the patients who received a diagnosis of cannabis-induced psychosis developed a schizophrenia-spectrum disorder one year or more later, and at a significantly younger age than a comparison group of patients with similar symptoms with no history of cannabis use (Arendt *et al.* 2005).

In patients with established psychosis, Grech *et al.* (2005) showed that continued use of cannabis is associated with poor outcome and with more frequent and earlier relapses, more frequent hospitalization and poorer psychosocial functioning (Grech *et al.* 2005). Also, in first-episode psychosis, Pencer *et al.* (2005) showed that cannabis use correlates with increased severity and chronicity of symptoms, and risk of relapse (Pencer *et al.* 2005).

A further contribution to the understanding of the association between cannabis use and schizophrenia comes from the Edinburgh High-Risk study, which showed that both individuals at high genetic risk of schizophrenia (with two affected relatives) as well as individuals with no family history of schizophrenia were at increased risk of developing psychotic symptoms after cannabis use (Miller *et al.* 2001).

In an imaginative study, J. Thirtalli *et al.* (unpublished) interviewed 477 intravenous drug users in St Louis, MO, USA on their views concerning the effects of the various psychotropic agents that they had tried. The percentage of dependent persons reporting psychotic symptoms in relation to use of specific drugs was 85% for hallucinogens, 80% for cocaine, 64% for cannabis, 56% for amphetamine, 54% for opioids, 41% for alcohol and 32% for sedatives. There was a tendency for certain drugs to be associated with particular psychotic symptoms. Not surprisingly, hallucinogens and PCP (Phencyclidine) were rated as most likely to cause hallucinations whereas cannabis was rated as more likely to be associated with delusions than hallucinations. Unfortunately, the investigators did not enquire especially concerning paranoia.

How does cannabis cause persecutory delusions?

The most influential model of psychosis posits that this arises from excess striatal dopamine (DA). Laruelle *et al.* (1996) demonstrated that acutely psychotic patients release excessive striatal dopamine in response to an amphetamine challenge; furthermore, the degree of dopamine release correlates positively with the severity of positive symptoms and with subsequent response to dopamine blockers. The likely mechanism has been described by Kapur (2005) who has integrated evidence concerning the normal biological role of dopamine with data on motivational salience to produce an attractive theory. 'Motivational salience' is the process whereby reward-associated stimuli 'grab the attention' of the individual and lead to goal-directed behaviour. This process is driven by striatal release of dopamine; thus, increased release of dopamine, as occurs in acute psychosis (Abi-Dargham *et al.* 2000), results in increased attention and excessive significance ('salience') being attributed to everyday stimuli. In this way, an unexpected sound, the comments of a television newsreader or eye contact with a stranger are transformed from trivial everyday occurrences into highly salient events of great personal meaning to the psychotic individual. Secondary to these altered perceptions, persecutory delusions can be understood as an attempt to explain these experiences and resolve the resultant perplexity, confusion and dysphoria (Bentall *et al.* 1994; Krabbendam *et al.* 2004).

Recent studies have shown that cannabis markedly increases dopaminergic neuronal firing, including burst-firing, and that Cannabinoid 1 (CB1) receptor agonists such as THC increase the release of dopamine at terminal fields in the striatum and prefrontal cortex (Lupica and Riegel 2005). It is tempting therefore to suggest that cannabis exerts its effects by increasing striatal release of dopamine. However, there have been no investigations directly testing this in humans, although there is one imaging study in which it was found that when a subject broke the protocol by smoking cannabis, there was evidence suggesting increased dopamine at dopamine D_2 receptors (Voruganti *et al.* 2001)

An obvious question is why only a minority of those who take cannabis, even in large quantities, experience psychotic symptoms. Verdoux *et al.* (2003) studied the acute effects of cannabis in an everyday setting. She divided her sample of college students into those who were psychosis-prone on the bases of their responses to a questionnaire. Individuals without this proneness generally respond to cannabis by feeling more relaxed and at ease with the world, and experience minor perceptual changes. However, those who scored as psychosis-prone reported more marked perceptual changes and a feeling of increased suspicion and hostility after taking cannabis.

Recently, it was found that a functional polymorphism in the catechol-O-methyltransferase (COMT Val[158]Met) gene may moderate the psychosis-inducing effect of THC. This suggests an interaction between cannabis use and vulnerability to psychosis. Caspi *et al.* (2005) reasoned that part of the vulnerability might lie in inheritance. They therefore studied the interaction in the Dunedin Birth Cohort between cannabis use and variation at the COMT gene. Due to a functional polymorphism, involving a Met to Val substitution at codon 158, this gene has two common allelic variants (Met and Val) which cause variation in the efficiency with which dopamine is broken down in the prefrontal cortex. Findings from positron emission tomography and post-mortem studies indicate that the Val allele is associated with markedly increased dopamine synthesis in midbrain neurons projecting to the ventral striatum (Meyer-Lindenberg and Weinberger 2006). Caspi *et al.* found that while use of cannabis in adolescence had no effect on the risk of psychosis in those homozygous for the Met allele, adolescent smokers with the Val/Val genotype were much more likely to develop schizophreniform psychosis than those with the same genotype who did not take cannabis (Fig. 13.2). Perhaps Val/Val individuals have a greater pool of releasable dopamine which makes them more susceptible to the psychotogenic effects of exogenous cannabis.

Henquet *et al.* (2006) further investigated possible genetic moderators of the acute effects of THC on psychosis and cognition outcome in a double-blind placebo-controlled study. Patients with a psychotic disorder, relatives of patients with a psychotic disorder and healthy controls were exposed to 300 µg THC/kg body weight or placebo followed by cognitive assessment and assessment of current psychotic experiences. Overall vulnerability for psychosis (psychometric psychosis liability) was assessed with the CAPE (Community Assessement of Psychic Experiences), a questionnaire developed to measure subclinical psychotic experiences. In line with work by Caspi *et al.* (2005),

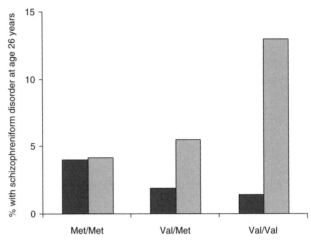

Fig. 13.2 Cannabis use during adolescence significantly increased the risk of developing a schizophreniform disorder at age 26 years, but only in those individuals who carried one or two COMT Va1158Met Val alleles. Black bars: individuals who never used cannabis; grey bars: those who used cannabis during adolescence. Modified with permission from Caspi *et al.* (2005).

moderating effects of a functional polymorphism in the COMT Va1158Met gene on the effects of THC were also investigated. This study showed that carriers of the Val/Val genotype were more sensitive to the effects of THC on positive psychotic symptoms, but this was conditional on prior evidence of psychometric psychosis liability. Carriers of the Val allele were also more sensitive to THC-induced memory and attention impairments compared to carriers of the Met allele.

Conclusion

In conclusion, there is convincing evidence from experimental studies that cannabis can acutely induce paranoid symptoms, and epidemiological studies indicate an increase risk for later psychosis in cannabis users. These effects seem dose-related and conditional upon prior genetic vulnerability for psychosis. However, the extent to which the drug preferentially elicits paranoid as opposed to more general psychotic symptoms is largely unknown, as are the neurochemical mechanisms. More experimental studies and investigations of gene–environment interaction are essential to further explore the role of cannabis in the development of psychosis and to understand the biological mechanisms involved (Caspi and Moffitt 2006).

References

Abi-Dargham, A., Rodenhiser, J., Printz, D., Zea-Ponce, Y., Gil, R., Kegeles, L.S. *et al.* (2000) Increased baseline occupancy of D2 receptors by dopamine in schizophrenia. *Proceedings of the National Academy of Science of the USA,* 97(14), 8104–8109.

Ames, F. (1958) A clinical and metabolic study of acute intoxication with *Cannabis sativa* and its role in the model psychoses. *Journal of Mental Science,* 104, 972–999.

Andreasson, S., Allebeck, P., Engstrom, A., Rydberg, U. (1987) Cannabis and schizophrenia. A longitudinal study of Swedish conscripts. *Lancet* 2(8574), 1483–1486.

Arendt, M., Rosenberg, R., Foldager, L., Perto, G. and Munk-Jorgenson, P. (2005) Cannabis-induced psychosis and subsequent schizophrenia-spectrum disorders: follow-up study of 535 incident cases. *British Journal of Psychiatry,* 187, 510–515.

Arsenault, L., Cannon, M., Poulton, R., Murray, R., Caspi, A., Moffitt, T.E. (2002) Cannabis use in adolescence and risk for adult psychosis: longitudinal prospective study. *British Medical Journal,* 325(7374), 1212–1213.

Bentall, R.P., Kinderman, P. and Kaney, S. (1994) The self, attributional processes and abnormal beliefs: towards a model of persecutory delusions. *Behaviour Research and Therapy,* 32, 331–341.

Caspi, A. and Moffitt, T.E. (2006) Gene–environment interactions in psychiatry: joining forces with neuroscience. *Nature Reviews Neuroscience,* 7, 583–590.

Caspi, A., Moffitt, T.E., Cannon, M. *et al.* (2005) Moderation of the effect of adolescent-onset cannabis use on adult psychosis by a functional polymorphism in the catechol-*O*-methyltransferase gene: longitudinal evidence of a gene X environment interaction. *Biological Psychiatry,* 57, 1117–1127.

Chopra, G.S. and Smith, J.W. (1974) Psychotic reactions following cannabis use in East Indians. *Archives of General Psychiatry,* 30, 24–27.

D'Souza, D.C., Abi-Saab, W.M., Madonick, S. *et al.* (2005) Delta-9-tetrahydrocannabinol effects in schizophrenia: implications for cognition, psychosis, and addiction. *Biological Psychiatry,* 57, 594–608.

Favrat, B., Menetrey, A., Augsburger, M. *et al.* (2005) Two cases of "cannabis acute psychosis" following the administration of oral cannabis. *BMC Psychiatry,* 5, 17.

Ferdinand, R.F., Sondeijker, F., van der Ende, J., Selten, J.P., Huizink, A. and Verhulst, F.C. (2005) Cannabis-psychosis pathway independent of other types of psychopathology. *Schizophrenia Research,* 79(2–3): 289–295.

Fergusson, D.M. and Horwood, L.J. (2000) Does cannabis use encourage other forms of illicit drug use? *Addiction,* 95(4), 505–520.

Fergusson, D.M., Horwood, L.J. and Ridder, E.M. (2005) Tests of causal linkages between cannabis use and psychotic symptoms. *Addiction,* 100, 354–366.

Fergusson, D.M., Horwood, L.J., Swain-Campbell, N.R. (2003) Cannabis dependence and psychotic symptoms in young people. *Psychological Medicine,* 33(1), 15–21.

Grech, A.J., Van Os, J., Jones, P.B., Lewis, S.W. and Murray, R.M. (2005) Cannabis use and outcome of recent onset psychosis. *European Psychiatry,* 20, 349–353.

Gregg, J.M., Small, E.W., Moore, R., Raft, D. and Toomey, T.C. (1976) Emotional response to intravenous delta9tetrahydrocannabinol during oral surgery. *Journal of Oral Surgery,* 34, 301–313.

Henquet, C., Krabbendam, L., Spauwen, J. et al. (2005a) Prospective cohort study of cannabis use, predisposition for psychosis, and psychotic symptoms in young people. British Medical Journal, 330(7481), 11–15.

Henquet, C., Murray, R., Linszen, D., van Os, J. (2005b) The environment and schizophrenia: the role of cannabis use. Schizophrenia Bulletin, 31(3), 608–612.

Henquet, C., Rosa, A., Krabbendam, L. et al. (2006) An experimental study of catechol-O-methyltransferase val(158)met moderation of delta-9-tetrahydrocannabinol-induced effects on psychosis and cognition. Neuropsychopharmacology, 31, 2748–2757.

Isbell, H., Gorodetzsky, C.W., Jasinski, D., Claussen, U., von Spulak, F. and Korte, F. (1967) Effects of delta-9-trans-tetrahydrocannabinol in man. Psychopharmacologia, 11, 184–188.

Jones, R.T. (1971) Marihuana-induced "high": influence of expectation, setting and previous drug experience. Pharmacological Reviews, 23, 359–369.

Kapur, S., Mizrahi, R., Li, M. (2005) From dopamine to salience to psychosis—linking biology, pharamacology and phenomenology of psychosis. Schizophrenia Research, 79(1), 59–68.

Koethe, D., Gerth, C.W., Neatby, M.A. et al. (2006) Disturbances of visual information processing in early states of psychosis and experimental delta-9-tetrahydrocannabinol altered states of consciousness. Schizophrenia Research, 88(1–3): 142–150.

Krabbendam, L., Marcelis, M., Delespaul, P., Jolles, J. and van Os, J. (2001) Single or multiple familial cognitive risk factors in schizophrenia? American Journal of Medical Genetics, 105, 183–188.

Krabbendam, L., Myin-Germeys, I., Hanssen, M. et al. (2004) Hallucinatory experiences and onset of psychotic disorder: evidence that the risk is mediated by delusion formation. Acta Psychiatrica Scandinavica, 110, 264–272.

Laruelle, M., Abi-Dargham, A., van Dyck, C.H., Gil, R., D'Souza, C.D., Erdos, J. et al. (1996) Single photon emission computerized tomography imaging of amphetamine-induced dopamine release in drug-free schizophrenic subjects. Proceedings of the National Academy of Science of the USA, 93(17), 9235–9240.

Leweke, F.M. and Schneider, U. (1999) Effects of synthetic delta9-tetrahydrocannabinol on binocular depth inversion of natural and artificial objects in man. Psychopharmacology (Berlin), 142, 230–235.

Lupica, C.R. and Riegel, A.C. (2005) Endocannabinoid release from midbrain dopamine neurons: a potential substrate for cannabinoid receptor antagonist treatment of addiction. Neuropharmacology, 48, 1105–1116.

Mathers, D.C., Ghodse, A.H. (1992) Cannabis and psychotic illiness. British Journal of Psychiaty 161, 648–653.

Melges, F.T. (1976) Tracking difficulties and paranoid ideation during hashish and alcohol intoxication. American Journal of Psychiatry, 133, 1024–1028.

Meyer-Lindenberg, A. and Weinberger, D.R. (2006) Intermediate phenotypes and genetic mechanisms of psychiatric disorders. Nature Reviews Neuroscience, 7, 818–827.

Miller, P., Lawrie, S.M., Hodges, A., Clafferty, R., Cosway, R., Johnstone, E.C. (2001) Genetic liability, illicit drug use, life stress, and psychotic symptoms: preliminary findings from the Edinburgh study of people at high risk for schizophrenia. Social Psychiatry and Psychiatric Epidemiology, 36(7), 338–342.

Monshouwer, K., Smit, F., de Graaf, R., van Os, J. and Vollebergh, W. (2005) First cannabis use: does onset shift to younger ages? Findings from 1988 to 2003 from the Dutch National School Survey on Substance Use. *Addiction*, 100, 963–970.

Moreau, J.J. (1845; trans. 1973) *Hashish and Mental Illness*. New York: Raven Press.

Murray, R.M., Grech, A., Phillips, P., Johnson, S. (2003) What is the relationship between substance abuse and schizophrenia? In R. Murray, P. Jones, E. Susser, J. van Os and M. Cannon (eds), *The Epidemiology of Schizophrenia*, pp. 317–342. Cambridge: Cambridge University Press.

Negrete, J.C., Knapp, W.P., Douglas, D.E., Smith, W.B. (1986) Cannabis affects the severity of schizophrenic symtoms: results of a clinical survey. *Psychological Medicine*, 16(3), 515–520.

Pencer, A., Addington, J. and Addington, D. (2005) Outcome of a first episode of psychosis in adolescence: a 2-year follow-up. *Psychiatry Research*, 133, 35–43.

Ramaekers, J.G., Kauert, G., van Ruitenbeek, P., Theunissen, E.L., Schneider, E. and Moeller, M.R. (2006) High-potency marijuana impairs executive function and inhibitory motor control. *Neuropsychopharmacology*, 31, 2296–2303,

Schneider, U., Borsutzky, M., Seifert, J. *et al.* (2002) Reduced binocular depth inversion in schizophrenic patients. *Schizophrenia Research*, 53(1–2), 101–108.

Solowij, N., Michie, P.T. (2007) Cannabis and cognitive dysfunction: parallels with endophenotypes of schizophrenia? *Journal of Psychiatry and Neuroscience*, 32(1), 30–52.

Talbott, J.A. and Teague, J.W. (1969) Marihuana psychosis. Acute toxic psychosis associated with the use of cannabis derivatives. *Journal of the American Medical Association*, 210, 299–302.

Thorricroft, G. (1990) Cannabis and psychosis. Is there epidemiological evidence for an assocation? *British Journal of Psychiatry*, 157, 25–33.

United Nations (2006) *Drug Abuse*. www.unodc.org/unodc/en/world_drug_report.html

van Os, J., Bak, M., Hanssen, M., Bijl, R.V., de Graaf, R. and Verdoux, H. (2002) Cannabis use and psychosis: a longitudinal population-based study. *American Journal of Epidemiology*, 156, 319–327.

Verdoux, H., Gindre, C., Sorbara, F., Tournier, M., Swendsen, J.D. (2003) Effects of cannabis and psychosis vulnerability in daily life: an experience sampling test study. *Psychological Medcine*, 33, 23–32.

Voruganti, L.N., Slomka, P., Zabel, P., Mattar, A. and Awad, A.G. (2001) Cannabis induced dopamine release: an in-vivo SPECT study. *Psychiatry Research*, 107, 173–177.

Zammit, S., Allebeck, P., Andreasson, S., Lundberg, I., Lewis, G. (2002) Self reported cannabis use as a risk factor for schizophrenia in Swedish conscripts of 1969: historical cohort study. *British Medical Journal*, 325(7374), 1199.

14

Imaging and delusions

Matthew R. Broome and Philip K. McGuire

Introduction

Over the last 15 years neuroimaging has been deployed to study psychopathology scientifically and to elucidate the anatomical correlates of the symptoms and signs of psychiatry. This approach has been applied particularly in the characterization of the pathophysiology of auditory hallucinations (McGuire et al. 1995; Shergill et al. 2003). By contrast, delusion has been relatively understudied, yet is, if anything, an even more fundamental element of psychosis. In this chapter we outline the scope and limits of functional imaging, particularly functional magnetic resonance imaging (fMRI), as a method to study psychopathology and we survey findings from imaging studies relevant to persecutory delusions. Our discussion is based around studies that address steps in the cognitive model, and finally, we offer suggestions as to how neuroimaging may be employed to further research into the formation, maintenance, and treatment of abnormal beliefs.

Imaging and psychopathology

Functional MRI is a powerful technique for studying the function of the brain in mental illness. It relies on the biophysics of haemoglobin: in blood, as the ratio of oxyhaemoglobin to deoxyhaemoglobin changes, so does the paramagnetic signal. An increase in blood flow to an area of the brain will lead to an increase in this ratio, and hence a change in signal, detectable by MRI. Thus, fMRI measures blood oxygenation and flow, with this in turn serving as an indicator of, and proxy for, neural activity (Gjedde, 2001; Matthews, 2001). The important question is how, if at all, blood flow and neural activity relate to psychopathology. In the research paradigm entitled 'cognitive neuropsychiatry' (CNP), there is an explicit link between abnormal mental state and deficits in normal cognitive mechanisms (David et al. 2000; Halligan et al. 2001). Further, this approach explicitly links such mechanisms to their neural substrates in the brain. Thus, there is a stepwise progression from the clinical phenomenon to a cognitive neuropsychological model, in terms of deficits or alterations of normal functions, and in turn the anatomical areas, and pathology therein, that instantiate such mechanisms. Given such an approach, one can see the potential of functional neuroimaging in providing a means of bridging the gap from clinical psychopathology to cognitive neuropsychology and neuroanatomy.

In addition to studying anatomical and neurocognitive changes with respect to both vulnerability to, and progression of, a disorder the CNP approach allows the symptoms of mental illness to be examined. There are two broad types of approach. First, the investigator can use neuroimaging to measure brain activity while the symptom is being experienced by the patient ('capturing'). For example, the participant may indicate the presence of the symptom of interest by button-pressing when it begins and ends whilst being scanned, with images being retrospectively classified according to the patient's signal. However, the range of psychopathology amenable is relatively small. One needs a well-demarcated experience, which the participant can reliably access and report on, and further, the participant needs to have a certain degree of insight in being able to pick out 'that symptom' from other mental events. Thus, this approach is feasible for discrete events like auditory hallucinations but not for other symptoms, such as delusions. An alternative approach is to study cognitive processes putatively linked to the production of that symptom or sign of interest (Fu *et al.* 1999; Honey 2002; McGuire and Matsumoto 2004; Fusar-Poli and Broome 2006). This approach is clearly more flexible and has been applied widely to many areas of psychiatric morbidity. However, many assumptions are involved (Honey 2002; Fusar-Poli and Broome 2006; Kanaan and McGuire in press), for example that psychopathology is an expression of a quantitative difference from normal cognitive processes, and further, that mental function and psychopathology are modular in terms of function and anatomical localization. If the latter is indeed the case then a realist approach to the symptoms of mental illness such that they should smoothly reduce to abnormalities in discrete neural circuits is, at least in theory, sensible (Broome 2006). However, this prospect may in turn be hampered by concern as to whether it is coherent to define neural states in terms of psychological properties, which are properties of people rather than brains (Bennett and Hacker 2003).

Putting such concerns to one side, delusions pose a special case. Unlike some other symptoms of psychosis, delusions are not discrete either temporally or in terms of their demarcation from other mental states (it would seem inconceivable to instruct a participant to button-press when deluded and when non-deluded, for example). Delusions can be thought of as propositional attitudes whose content is false but as any clinician can attest, there is a lot more to a delusion than merely being wrong. Most contemporary accounts of delusion view them as a non-discrete mental state, a symptom when a certain number of differing dimensional attitudes to a belief, and characteristics of that belief—such as implausibility, conviction, being unfounded, distressing, preoccupying, and not being shared by others—are adopted or met (Freeman 2007). Delusions lead to the participant's whole experience of themselves and the world to be altered. The meaningful structures of existence are altered and that which was once banal, and beneath conscious attention, becomes salient and self-referential (Hemsley 1993; Gray *et al.* 1995; Kapur 2003, Kapur *et al.* 2005b; Broome *et al.* 2005b). Essentially, the normative, socially conditioned, rules for linking reasons, causes and explanations are disrupted, and we are left with the hallmark of delusion: namely, that the reasons the deluded give for holding their beliefs either do not look like reasons or are not very good reasons when presented to another (L. Bortolotti and M.R. Broome unpublished). Further, the degree of certainty engendered is such that, as with beliefs we all hold, the giving of and asking of reasons for holding that belief do not make sense (Campbell 2001). As such, delusions are incorrigible. For these reasons the 'capturing' functional imaging approach is closed to the investigator, but further, it may begin to be appreciated how imaging and cognitive psychology may have difficulties in understanding and explaining delusions as the product of problems of reasoning.

Imaging and the cognitive model

Given that we cannot 'capture' delusions whilst scanning participants we can at least try to examine the neurocognitive basis of the various biases and deficits putatively linked to the formation of delusions (Garety and Freeman, 1999; Bentall *et al.* 2001; Garety *et al.* 2001; Freeman *et al.* 2002; Freeman and Garety 2003; Freeman 2007). Most accounts are indebted to the Maherian model (Maher 1988) or bottom-up approach whereby the delusion is a (rational) explanation of an anomalous experience. Thus, the current cognitive models of delusion formation focus on the generation of anomalous experiences and how the sufferer then views such experiences and searches for meaning, with biases and deficits in the reasoning mechanisms also invoked. We now review the imaging literature on these various stages.

Imaging and anomalous experiences

Garety *et al.* (2001) propose that the most common route to psychosis is via a 'basic cognitive dysfunction' or disturbance of automatic processing. Possible mechanisms include difficulties in (i) integrating information into its temporal and spatial context (Hemsley 1993, 1994a,b, 2005; Gray *et al.* 1995) or (ii) in the self-monitoring of intentions and actions that lead to the individual's own actions being experienced as alien (Frith 1992). These disturbances are assumed to lead to anomalous conscious experiences, such as heightened perception, actions experienced as unintended, thoughts appearing to be broadcast, thoughts experienced as voices, and events that are unconnected appearing to be causally linked.

Both cognitive and neurobiological models propose that a critical factor in the development of psychosis is the faulty appraisal or interpretation of anomalous experiences or events (Garety and Freeman 1999; Garety et al. 2001, and in press; Freeman et al. 2002; Kapur 2003, Kapur et al. 2005b; Broome et al. 2005a). In particular, appraising experiences as being externally generated and/or caused by a personal agency, and as being personally meaningful may lead to an increase in their severity, associated distress, and the need for care (Bak et al. 2001; Escher et al. 2002; Krabbendam et al. 2004). This is consistent with evidence that anomalous experiences can occur in healthy people (Johns and van Os 2001), and that the frequency and form of these experiences is similar in people who do not seek clinical care as in those who do, these groups being more distinguished by the way they appraise and react to their symptoms (Brett 2004).

Several groups have attempted to explain how anomalous perceptual experiences are transformed into psychotic symptoms. Maher (1988) pointed out that the experiences are often puzzling and associated with intense emotion, and may seem extremely personally relevant to the individual; not surprisingly, they trigger a search for explanation as to their cause. Kapur (2003) makes a similar point that the experience of being bombarded by apparently salient stimuli causes great anxiety and arousal in the acutely psychotic individual, and this in turn might lead to a continued disruption of contextual integration and consequent vulnerability to intrusions into awareness. One way to resolve this anxiety and arousal is to develop a delusional explanation of the experiences. There are two approaches in the literature where anomalous experiences have been studied using imaging: the first is functional neurochemical imaging of the dopaminergic system and the second is fMRI using paradigms explicitly designed to create unusual and anomalous experiences.

Dopamine, PET, and salience

A powerful way of approaching the genesis of anomalous experiences is through positron emission tomography (PET) and imaging of the dopaminergic system. This technique involves using positron-emitting isotopes which are incorporated into particular molecules to allow imaging of cerebral blood flow, metabolism, or neurotransmitter and receptor systems (Patterson II and

Kotrla 2004). There has been a recent resurgence of interest in dopamine and how it links to cognitive models of psychosis (Kapur 2003; Broome *et al.* 2005b; Kapur *et al.* 2005) and PET has been used as a tool to investigate these relationships.

Hemsley (1993) described how in the acutely psychotic individual 'Meaningful connections are created between temporary coincident external impressions ... or perceptions with thoughts that happen to be present, or events and recollections happening to occur in consciousness at the same time.' He and his colleagues (Gray *et al.* 1991) pointed out that, normally, input from the hippocampus controls the mesolimbic dopamine system, and they speculated that damage to it causes a loss of this control, with the resultant heightened dopamine transmission facilitating the formation of 'meaningful connections' between coincident events. Laruelle *et al.* (1996), who demonstrated increased striatal dopamine release following amphetamine challenge in acute schizophrenic patients, revealed the long-suspected link between dopamine dysregulation and psychosis. Furthermore, the degree of dopamine release correlated positively with extent of acute positive symptoms and with subsequent response to dopamine blockers (Laruelle and Abi-Dargham, 1999; Laruelle *et al.* 1999; Abi-Dargham *et al.* 2000).

Kapur elaborated on the link between dopamine and the positive symptoms of psychosis (Kapur 2003, 2004; Kapur *et al.* 2005a,b), and drew on theories of the role of mesolimbic dopamine in the healthy brain derived from studies using experimental animals. It has been argued that in the normal individual, mesolimbic dopamine acts to provide significance or salience, transforming an affectively neutral mental representation of a stimulus into an attractive or aversive one (Berridge and Robinson 1998). Thus, mesolimbic dopamine activity may determine whether an intrusion into awareness from either external perceptual or internal mental sources receives a positive or negative 'hedonic vector', and thus 'grabs the attention' of the individual. If psychosis were associated with increased, often stimulus-independent, release of dopamine, salience would be granted to what would otherwise be relatively innocuous events and stimuli. In this way, it is argued, dopamine provides 'the wind of psychotic fire' (Laruelle and Abi-Dargham 1999).

For Kapur *et al.* (2005b) the prodromal phase of psychosis is characterized by context-independent or context-inappropriate firing of dopamine neurons and dopamine release. Clinically, there may be anomalous experiences of altered novelty and salience without any clear explanation for them. This may progress until a delusion is formed which seeks to explain such an experience, and the formation of a stable delusion marks the transition from the prodromal phase to onset of psychotic illness. 'With this delusional atmosphere we always find an 'objective something' there, even though quite vague, a something which lays the seed of objective validity and meaning. This general delusional atmosphere with all is vagueness of content must be unbearable. Patients obviously suffer terribly under it and to reach some definite idea at last is like being relieved from some enormous burden. ... Experiences such as these give rise to convictions of persecution, of having committed crime, of being accused or, by contrast, of some golden age, transfiguration, sanctification, etc.' (Jaspers 1959/1997). In people at clinically high risk of developing psychosis, there is evidence of both a 'jumping to conclusions' (JTC) bias (Broome et al. 2007) and of elevated presynaptic dopamine synthesis (Howes et al. 2006), although as yet, it is unclear how the two variables are related to one another, or how they relate to clinical course and the progression to frank psychosis.

Based around this formulation, anti-psychotics do not engage directly with the positive symptoms of psychosis *per se*, but rather attenuate the generation of salience, whether pathologically determined or the result of normal motivational processes (Kapur et al. 2005b). Delusions, following Maher, are thus a top-down response of the individual to the anomalous experience of inappropriate novelty, salience, and experience of chaotic demands for goal-directed behaviour. The delay of antipsychotic action is an artefact of the two steps—anomalous experience and delusional explanation—being treated as a unit (Agid et al. 2003, 2006; Kapur et al. 2005b). Antipsychotics will aid the former immediately, but a psychological resolution of the latter may take longer (Garety et al. 2007; van der Gaag 2006).

In the light of our discussion of the role of dopamine, it may be that Garety's 'basic cognitive dysfunction' corresponds to heightened mesolimbic dopamine transmission (Gray et al. 1995; Kapur 2003). As Gray et al. (1991, 1995) point out, damage to the hippocampus will therefore result in a 'weakening of the influence of stored memories of regularities of previous input on current perception', and this in turn will lead to ambiguous and unstructured sensory input (Hemsley 1993, p. 635). Further, both dopamine-generated salience and the JTC bias (see below) may be working in tandem at every stage of the model of psychosis: initial misattribution of salience, detected by the JTC bias, and the clinical phenomenology of novelty, inappropriate deployment of attention, and anomalous experiences, examined by PET. At the second stage, that of formation of delusions, this state JTC vulnerability may be exaggerated (Van Dael et al. 2006), as may the dopamine transmission (McGowan et al. 2004; Howes 2006).

Thus, theories implicating impaired contextual integration and abnormal appraisal on the one hand and dopamine dysregulation on the other may be attempts at explaining the same processes at the levels of information-processing and neurochemistry respectively. It is the ability of dopamine to attribute salience that makes this neurotransmitter of interest to psychiatrists and psychologists, and it is salience, a term that can only be understood as a psychological property, that links in with current cognitive models of psychosis in terms of both pathophysiology and treatment.

We are currently studying how JTC relates both to PET measures of dopamine and to correlates of working memory and executive functions, obtained using fMRI, in an at-risk group (Broome *et al.* 2005, 2007; Howes 2006; M.R. Broome *et al.* unpublished).

Self-monitoring as fMRI paradigm

In a verbal self-monitoring paradigm a distorted voice is used as an anomalous experience (Allen *et al.* 2004; Johns *et al.* 2006). Participants are asked to speak and judge whether the distorted voice they hear is their own, another, or whether they are unsure. Participants with an acute psychosis tend to judge distorted feedback of their own voice as 'other' to a greater extent than controls, and this may reflect problems in verbal self-monitoring and/or the appraisal of ambiguous sensory material (Johns *et al.* 2006). This paradigm has been studied with functional imaging in healthy participants (Fu *et al.* 2006), and in both remitted and symptomatic patients with schizophrenia (C.H.Y. Fu *et al.* in press). The latter study suggests that the actively psychotic patients show greater superior temporal activation when making external misattributions than correct self-attributions. The converse pattern in seen in both remitted patients and healthy controls: greater activation with correct self-attributions than incorrect external misattributions. These findings are consistent with self-monitoring hypotheses, as the temporal activation is associated with a mismatch between expected and perceived auditory feedback which may reflect an impairment in self-monitoring. Thus, this method allows some anatomical characterization of the purported mechanism underlying the 'basic cognitive dysfunction' that may generate certain types of anomalous experiences (in this case unusual auditory experiences) which a delusion is an attempt to explain.

Imaging and cognitive biases

Cognitive biases limit the search for explanations of anomalous experiences, hence settling on a fantastical conclusion, as well as constraining and skewing the content of such explanations. The JTC bias is an example of the former: the participant will attest to being certain at lower levels of information than healthy controls and this bias has been demonstrated not only in those with active persecutory delusional ideation (Huq *et al.* 1988; Garety 1991; Garety *et al.* 1991), but also in volunteers with high levels of delusional ideation (Linney *et al.* 1998), relatives (Van Dael *et al.* 2006), and those with the 'at-risk mental state' (ARMS) for transition to psychosis (Broome *et al.* 2007). Further, the degree of bias is linked with the intensity of delusional ideation (Garety and Freeman, 1999; Linney *et al.* 1998; Peters *et al.* 1999; Garety *et al.* 2005; Van Dael *et al.* 2006; Broome *et al.* 2007). Other important biases relevant to delusion formation include the externalizing attributional bias (Kinderman *et al.* 1992; Bentall *et al.* 1994, 2001, 2005; Kinderman and Bentall 1997, 2000; Moore *et al.* 2006) and deficits in understanding social situations and the intentions of others ('theory of mind') (Frith 1992; Corcoran *et al.* 1995, 1997; Frith and Corcoran, 1996; Langdon and Coltheart, 1999; Langdon *et al.* 2002, 2006; Corcoran and Frith 2003; McKay *et al.* 2005). The former tend to lead to the blaming of others for negative events, whereas the latter may lead to errors in reading the intentions of other people.

Jumping to conclusions

The JTC style of thinking has, as yet, not been studied using functional imaging in a clinical group. However, probabilistic reasoning and decision-making in conditions of uncertainty have been investigated in healthy controls in the scanner (Blackwood *et al.* 2004b). The active condition was analogous to the 'beads' task outside of the scanner (Huq *et al.* 1988) with either an abstract ('balls in a jar') or a more ecological version (negative or positive comments from a personality survey). The reference or baseline condition was one of counting. The decision-making under conditions of uncertainty task was mediated by the neocerebellum, premotor cortex, inferior parietal lobule, and medial occipital cortex (Blackwood *et al.* 2004a). The authors suggest that internal models used in inductive predictive reasoning are created by the cerebellum and that it is a converse method from that which is utilized to predict the effects of our physical movements: from an uncertain ambiguous state of affairs, causes are investigated and various explanations modelled.

Theory of mind and social cognition

The idea behind 'theory of mind' (ToM) deficits resulting in persecutory delusions is that the individual finds it harder to read others' intentions towards him or herself. In this void, a malign intent is posited and thus the individual feels persecuted. However, considerable empirical work suggests that ToM deficits are neither related to nor specific for persecutory delusions (Garety and Freeman 1999; Freeman 2007). Indeed, thought disorder was most strongly associated with, and predicted performance on, ToM performance (Grieg *et al.* 2004). There is a further conceptual problem: if the start is ignorance of others' mental states, why is the persecution circumscribed rather than generalized, and why is it a malign intent that is posited rather than other attitudes? (Freeman in press). Others, however, suggest that, despite the conflicting data, there is likely to be a link between ToM performance and the presence of delusions (Brune 2005; see also Chapter 10, this volume).

Although deficits in ToM *per se* may not be relevant in the genesis of persecutory delusions, social cognition and emotional recognition more generally may be a factor (Aleman *et al.* 2006). The imaging literature on emotional recognition in schizophrenia does seem to indicate an abnormality, specifically with respect to negative emotions (Kohler and Martin 2006; Russell *et al.* 2007). Further, a recent fMRI study of patients with schizophrenia, with and without persecutory delusions, and healthy controls viewing changing fearful faces revealed differences in neural activation between the three groups. The non-paranoid clinical group demonstrated increased hippocampal activation, but with abnormal bilateral amygdala activation only in the group with active persecutory delusions (Russell *et al.* in press). The authors suggest that the former changes may reflect a trait abnormality in schizophrenia, whereas the latter activations may reflect a state abnormality related to the presence of paranoid symptoms.

Attentional and attributional biases

Blackwood and colleagues have used fMRI to examine attentional and attributional biases in both healthy volunteers (Blackwood *et al.* 2000) and participants with active persecutory delusions and a diagnosis of schizophrenia (Blackwood *et al.* 2004b). An individual may tend to focus selectively on self-referential or threatening information, and thus offer explanations that are viewed as delusional by others, and further may have an exaggeration of the normal 'self-serving bias' whereby we tend to accept praise and credit for good things, but deny and externalize responsibility for negative events and failure (Blackwood *et al.* 2000). In their study, attention to threatening stimuli relevant to the individual activated a network involving the left inferior frontal gyrus, the right caudate, and right anterior cingulate. The self-serving bias (present in us all, but enhanced in those with persecutory delusions) was associated with increased activity in the left precentral gyrus. The authors interpreted this finding as the activation reflecting an inhibition of a 'pre-potent' response underpinning the self-serving bias. Thus, their hypothesis would be that in a deluded sample there would be a relative hypoactivation of this area and a resultant enhanced bias. In their study on patients with delusions, again using statements that were ambiguous, neutral, or threatening, and self- or other-relevant (Blackwood *et al.* 2004), the clinical group demonstrated an absence of rostral anterior cingulate activation and increased

posterior cingulate activation and it was interpreted that the delusional participants tended to view ambiguous self-referential material as more emotionally
salient than healthy controls.

Imaging and role of affect in delusions

The links between persecutory delusions and affect are rather commonsensical:
if one believes that one is under threat of harm it is appropriate to feel anxious,
and if chronic and unremitting, this may lead to 'learned helplessness' and
depression. However, what is perhaps of greater interest is how such affects
may impact on the pathogenesis of delusions and, further, their maintenance
once established.

Retrospective studies show that depression and anxiety are among the first
noticeable psychological disturbances in individuals who later become psychotic; indeed most patients with a first-episode of schizophrenia will have
had a depressed mood and at least one frank episode of depression, in the year
prior to hospitalisation (an der Heiden and Hafner 2000). From studies of
those with the 'at-risk mental state' (ARMS), it is clear that prior to the onset
of frank psychosis there are prominent mood symptoms, many of which reach
DSM-IV diagnostic criteria (Broome *et al.* 2005a,b; Yung *et al.* 1996, 1998,
2003). Such affective symptomatology may play a role in the genesis of positive
symptoms such as hallucinations and delusions. Freeman and Garety (2003)
suggest that anxiety also facilitates the development of aberrant cognitive
schema and beliefs, and influences the generation of anomalous experiences
and then the maintenance of delusions once formed (Freeman and Garety
2003). Fowler *et al.* (2006) demonstrated, in a non-clinical population, how
paranoid ideation was associated with negative beliefs: both about the individuals themselves, but also negative beliefs about others and anxiety. Paranoia
may well build upon such negative beliefs about the self ('bad me') or others
('poor me'). Anxiety is predictive of the occurrence of paranoid thoughts and
of the persistence of persecutory delusions (Freeman *et al.* 2005; Freeman
2007). Further, there are analogies to the behaviour one sees in 'neurotic' illnesses such as obsessive-compulsive disorder (OCD), or phobias: patients
with persecutory ideation may carry out safety behaviours to allay their anxiety
regarding threat (Freeman *et al.* 2001).

As yet there are no imaging data focusing specifically on the role of affect
in delusions, but there are some tangential data that may be of relevance.
For example, imaging has been used to study self appraisal and reflection
and thus core schema and attribution biases. It seems that the medial prefrontal cortex is activated by material deemed to be self-descriptive, with the

ventral anterior cingulate activations correlating with the attribution of valence (positive or negative) (Moran *et al.* 2006). One could hypothesise that a person with schema that may be relevant to the formation of persecutory delusions may have greater activation of the medial prefrontal cortex with statements to do with harm and threat, reflecting them to be personally relevant. Interestingly, the neural correlates of how one view's oneself are different to how one believes another views oneself and different areas of the medial pre-frontal cortex are activated. First-person appraisal is associated with posterior cingulate activation whereas reflection on how others' view us is asscoiated with areas linked more to memory and emotion, such as the insula, orbitofrontal, and temporal cortex (Ochsner *et al.* 2004).

Compulsive behaviour, designed to allay, yet reinforce ultimately, the anxiety provoked by obsessional thoughts may have some parallels with the 'safety behaviour' observed in delusions, and posited as a maintaining factor of the belief (Freeman *et al.* 2001). There is a wide imaging literature on OCD (Friedlander and Desrocher 2006), but imaging has recently begun to study specific components of the disorder such as particular types of compulsive behaviour. It has been demonstrated that there are distinct neural correlates of various types of behaviour (washing, checking, hoarding) (Mataix-Cols *et al.* 2004), but participative anxiety, in both patient and control groups, was asso-ciated with similar activation in bilateral ventral prefrontal, limbic, dorsal prefrontal, and visual areas (Mataix-Cols *et al.* 2003). Checking-relevant anxiety predominantly activated the dorsal prefrontal regions.

Imaging and the transition to psychosis

A further approach to studying the formation of persecutory delusions using imaging is by focusing on the onset of frank psychosis. The latter is defined by the presence of delusions and/or hallucinations; given the frequency of perse-cutory delusions in the initial episode of psychotic illness, the transition to the first episode can be a useful proxy for studying longitudinally the develop-ment of delusions of persecution. This approach has recently been possible due to the development of research strategies involving the follow-up of groups at high risk of later developing psychosis (Yung *et al.* 1996; Klosterkotter *et al.* 2001; Cornblatt 2002; Johnstone *et al.* 2002; McGlashan *et al.* 2003; Morrison *et al.* 2004; Broome *et al.* 2005a). These samples may be at high risk because they comprise the non-psychotic co-twins or relatives of patients with psychosis (Johnson *et al.* 2003; van Erp *et al.* 2004; Whyte *et al.* 2006), or because they have 'prodromal' symptoms. The latter group are said to have an 'at-risk mental state' (ARMS), with clinical features such as attenuated psychotic symptoms, brief limited intermittent psychotic symptoms (BLIPS) or a recent decline in functioning, characteristics that significantly increase the risk for imminent onset of psychosis (Yung and McGorry 1996).

The relatives of patients affected with psychosis, the co-twins of patients and participants with an ARMS appear to share similar neurocognitive abnormalities (Fusar-Poli et al. 2007) that are qualitatively similar but less severe than those observed in the first episode of illness. These have mainly been described in the prefrontal and anterior cingulated cortex, the basal ganglia, hippocampus and cerebellum. In the genetic high-risk studies, participants who latter developed psychosis demonstrated increased activation of the parietal lobe, decreased activation of the anterior cingulate, and smaller increases in activation with increasing task difficulty in the right lingual gyrus and bilateral temporal regions, whilst undertaking a sentence completion task (Whalley et al. 2006).

Structural imaging studies of the clinical at-risk group (Phillips et al. 2002), using a region-of-interest analysis, reported that hippocampal volume in participants with an ARMS was smaller than that in controls but not in patients with first-episode psychosis. In addition, within the at-risk group, the subset who developed a psychotic disorder when followed up subsequent to scanning had a larger left hippocampal volume than the subgroup that did not. More recently, in a voxel-based analysis of MRI data (which examined the entire brain) from the same centre, Pantelis et al. (2003) found that within a group of participants with the ARMS, those who later became psychotic had smaller inferior frontal, cingulate, superior temporal and hippocampal volumes than those who did not. However, in a cross-sectional study, using a region-of-interest approach, Velakoulis et al. (2006) reported that ARMS patients had normal baseline hippocampal and amygdala grey matter volumes whether or not they subsequently developed psychosis. These results suggest that some structural brain changes occur closer to the transition to psychosis than suggested by the traditional neurodevelopmental hypothesis of schizophrenia (Murray and Lewis 1987; Weinberger 1987; Murray et al. 1998; Cardno et al. 1999; Weinberger and McClure 2002; Broome et al. 2005b). A recent study from Basel (S.J. Borgwardt et al. 2007), again using voxel-based morphometry, demonstrated that in comparison to controls, at-risk participants who go on to develop psychosis had smaller grey matter volume in left parietal/posterior temporal region. It does seem that brain abnormalities are already present before the transition to psychosis, whereas others become apparent during the transition to the episode of psychosis. These early abnormalities may reflect developmental or later maturational processes in adolescence and early adulthood and are markers of an increased trait vulnerability to psychosis. Additional volumetric brain abnormalities within the ARMS group are then associated with the state changes and the development of psychosis.

Directions for the future

Delusions are remarkably heterogeneous phenomena and it has been notoriously difficult to offer an all-inclusive definition or to operationalize criteria to enable their reliable detection. This is not so much due to conceptual woolliness or confusion, but rather because the term 'delusion' does not pick out or index a discrete psychological state or natural kind. Over the years there have been numerous ways to subclassify delusions: primary or autochthonous ('delusions') or secondary ('delusion-like ideas') (Jaspers 1959/1997), based upon whether the interviewer's empathic skills (*Verstehen*) can be used to understand the narrative genesis of the belief or not; Schneiderian; by theme or content; by congruity with mood; or by degree of fixity and conviction. This volume has focused on a subtype of delusion defined by theme, namely persecutory delusions. Despite an explicit definition being offered (Freeman and Garety 2000), persecutory delusions are still a complex phenomenon psychologically. Nevertheless clinicians can usually agree whether delusions are present or not, and despite being difficult to define themselves, they serve as important criteria in the diagnosis of mental illness in the psychiatric classifications. This may be because delusions show themselves when a belief tends to have characteristics that lie at the extreme end of several related, but not necessarily dependent, dimensions. These dimensions include such things as plausibility, foundation of the belief, conviction, level of distress incurred, preoccupation evoked, and degree of being shared by others (Freeman 2007). The problem in defining delusions becomes clear: how are the dimensions weighted? Are they normally distributed? Do they correlate with one another? Can patients who score 'low' on one dimension be deluded if they score 'high' on the other dimensions? What are the cut-offs for each dimension for 'delusionality' and are they altered by the scores on other dimensions? Which elements are necessary for a diagnosis of delusion? Some of the answers to these questions, particularly those of cut-off, threshold, and interaction will lie outside of natural science: what does society view as being deluded? This cannot be determined by biological or psychological research in itself, as the dimensions integral to delusions are themselves defined using normative criteria, some of which may be more socially constructed (for example, plausibility) whereas others link into more basic and profound issues in rationality and judgement (foundedness). Further, certain beliefs have special rules of justification (such as religious belief). However, cognitive neuropsychology will have a crucial role in understanding the various processes, including perceptual and affective, as well as information-processing, that may underpin shifts up and down the dimensions linked to 'delusionality'. Given this framework, one can appreciate the role functional imaging may have. However, delusion on this analysis is not amenable to a smooth reduction from symptom to circuits, as hoped for by a realist biological psychiatry, but is rather deconstructed into several discrete phenomena. Imaging will have a crucial role in determining the neural correlates of the processes that may impact upon shifts in these dimensions, and, with PET, may also allow progress into the biological physiology of such dimensions (for example, dopaminergic salience in relation to preoccupation, foundedness, and distress). A further methodological advance is linking longitudinal research with imaging: fMRI when used in high-risk studies (such as the clinical and genetic studies outlined above) is a powerful method of linking biological variables (neural activations) with cognitive variables (such as reasoning biases) and the evolution of psychopathology, such as delusions, and the transition to psychosis.

Conclusions

Imaging is unlikely to find a brain location specifically linked to the presence of delusions. However, it is a crucial tool in examining the neurocognitive, neurochemical and anatomical variables that may well be related to factors in the formation and maintenance of delusions. How such variables, dimensions, and biases interact is a question imaging by itself is unable to answer. Our own approach in studying the formation of delusions and the transition to psychosis has been to relate variables from different methodologies longitudinally when examining how, for example, working memory, dopamine, and the JTC reasoning bias may themselves change over time with clinical course but also how they inter-relate and effect the pathogenesis of psychosis and the formation of delusions.

Acknowledgements

We are very grateful to Paul Allen, Stefan Borgwardt, Lisa Bortolotti, Daniel Freeman, Cindy Fu, Paolo Fusar-Poli, Louise Johns, Nick Medford, Tamara Russell and James Woolley for advice and recommendations during the writing of this chapter.

References

Abi-Dargham, A., Rodenhiser, J., Printz, D. *et al.* (2000) Increased baseline occupancy of D2 receptors by dopamine in schizophrenia. *Proceedings of the National Academy of Sciences of the USA*, 97, 8104–8109.

Agid, O., Kapur, S., Arenovich, T. *et al.* (2003) Delayed-onset hypothesis of antipsychotic action: a hypothesis tested and rejected. *Archives of General Psychiatry*, 60, 1228–1235.

Agid, O., Seeman, P. and Kapur, S. (2006) The "delayed onset" of antipsychotic action—an idea whose time has come and gone. *Journal of Psychiatry and Neuroscience*, 31, 93–100.

Aleman, A., Medford, N. and David, A.S. (2006) Dissecting the cognitive and neural basis of emotional abnormalities. In: Aleman, A., Medford, N. and David, A.S. (eds), *The Cognitive Neuropsychiatry of Emotion and Emotional Disorders*, pp. 193–197. Hove: Psychology Press.

Allen, P.P., Johns, L.C., Fu, C.H.Y. *et al.* (2004) Misattribution of external speech in patients with hallucinations and delusions. *Schizophrenia Research*, 69, 277–287.

an der Heiden, W. and Hafner, H. (2000) The epidemiology of onset and course of schizophrenia. *European Archives of Psychiatry and Clinical Neuroscience*, 250, 292–303.

Bak, M., van der Spil, F., Gunther, N. *et al.* (2001) MACS-II: does coping enhance subjective control over psychotic symptoms? *Acta Psychiatrica Scandinavica*, 103, 460–464.

Bennett, M.R. and Hacker, P.M.S. (2003) *Philosophical Foundations of Neuroscience*. Oxford: Blackwell.

Bentall, R.P., Kinderman, P. and Kaney, S. (1994) The self, attributional processes and abnormal beliefs: towards a model of persecutory delusions. *Behaviour Research and Therapy*, 32, 331–341.

Bentall, R.P., Corcoran, R., Howard, R. *et al.* (2001) Persecutory delusions: a review and theoretical integration. *Clinical Psychology Review*, 21, 1143–1192.

Bentall, R.P., Kinderman, P. and Manson, K. (2005) Self-discrepancies in bipolar disorder: comparison of manic, depressed, remitted and normal participants. *British Journal of Clinical Psychology*, 44, 457–473.

Berridge, K.C. and Robinson, T.E. (1998) What is the role of dopamine in reward: hedonic impact, reward learning, or incentive salience? *Brain Research Brain Research Reviews*, 28, 309–369.

Blackwood, N.J., Howard, R.J., ffytche, D.H. *et al.* (2000) Imaging attentional and attributional bias: an fMRI approach to the paranoid delusion. *Psychological Medicine*, 30, 873–883.

Blackwood, N., Ffytche, D. Simmons, A. *et al.* (2004a) The cerebellum and decision making under uncertainty. *Cognitive Brain Research*, 20, 46–53.

Blackwood, N.J., Bentall, R.P., Ffytche, D.H. *et al.* (2004b) Persecutory delusions and the determination of self-relevance: an fMRI investigation.[see comment]. *Psychological Medicine*, 34, 591–596.

Borgwardt, S.J., McGuire, P.K., Aston, J., Berger, G.E., Dazzan, P., Gschwandtner, U., Pfluger, M., D'Souza, M.D., Radue, E.W., Riecher-Rossler, A. (2007) Structural brain abnormalities in individuals with an At Risk Mental State who later develop psychosis. *British Journal of Psychiatry*, 191, s69–s75.

Brett, C. (2004) *Anomalous Experiences and Cognitive Processes in the Development of Psychosis*. London: University of London.

Broome, M.R. (2006) Taxonomy and Ontology in Psychiatry. *Philosophy, Psychiatry, and Psychology*, 13(4), 303–319.

Broome, M.R., Woolley, J.B., Johns, L.C. *et al.* (2005a) Outreach and support in South London (OASIS): implementation of a clinical service for prodromal psychosis and the at risk mental state. *European Psychiatry*, 20, 372–378.

Broome, M.R., Woolley, J.B., Tabraham, P. *et al.* (2005b) What causes the onset of psychosis? *Schizophrenia Research*, 79, 23–34.

Broome, M.R., Johns, L.C., Valli, I. *et al.* (2007) Delusion formation and reasoning biases in those at clinical high risk for psychosis. *British Journal of Psychiatry,* 191, s38–s42.

Brune, M. (2005) "Theory of mind" in schizophrenia: a review of the literature. *Schizophrenia Bulletin*, 31, 21–42.

Campbell, J. (2001) Rationality, analysis, and the meaning of delusion. *Philosophy, Psychiatry, and Psychology*, 8, 89–100.

Cardno, A.G., Marshall, E.J., Coid, B. *et al.* (1999) Heritability estimates for psychotic disorders: the Maudsley twin psychosis series. *Archives of General Psychiatry*, 56, 162–168.

Corcoran, R. and Frith, C.D. (2003) Autobiographical memory and theory of mind: evidence of a relationship in schizophrenia. *Psychological Medicine*, 33, 897–905.

Corcoran, R., Mercer, G. and Frith, C.D. (1995) Schizophrenia, symptomatology and social inference: investigating "theory of mind" in people with schizophrenia. *Schizophrenia Research*, 17, 5–13.

Corcoran, R., Cahill, C. and Frith, C.D. (1997) The appreciation of visual jokes in people with schizophrenia: a study of 'mentalizing' ability. *Schizophrenia Research*, 24, 319–327.

Cornblatt, B., Lencz, T. and Obuchowski, M. (2002) The schizophrenia prodrome: treatment and high-risk perspectives. *Schizophrenia Research*, 54, 177–186.

David, A.S., Halligan, P.W., David, A.S. *et al.* (2000) Cognitive neuropsychiatry: potential for progress. *Journal of Neuropsychiatry and Clinical Neurosciences*, 12, 506–510.

Escher, S., Romme, M., Buiks, A. *et al.* (2002) Independent course of childhood auditory hallucinations: a sequential 3-year follow-up study. *British Journal of Psychiatry*, 181, s10–s18.

Fowler, D., Freeman, D., Smith, B. *et al.* (2006) The Brief Core Schema Scales (BCSS): psychometric properties and associations with paranoia and grandiosity in non-clinical and psychosis samples. *Psychological Medicine*, 36, 749–759.

Freeman, D. (2007) Suspicious minds: the psychology of persecutory delusions. *Clinical Psychology Review*, 27, 425–457.

Freeman, D. and Garety, P.A. (2000) Comments on the content of persecutory delusions: Does the definition need clarifying? *British Journal of Clinical Psychology*, 39, 407–414.

Freeman, D. and Garety, P.A. (2003) Connecting neurosis and psychosis: the direct influence of emotion on delusions and hallucinations. *Behaviour Research and Therapy*, 41, 923–947.

Freeman, D., Garety, P. and Kuipers, E. (2001) Persecutory delusions: Developing the understanding of belief maintenance and emotional distress. *Psychological Medicine*, 31, 1293–1306.

Freeman, D., Garety, P.A. Kuipers, E. *et al.* (2002) A cognitive model of persecutory delusions. *British Journal of Clinical Psychology*, 41, 331–347.

Freeman, D., Garety, P.A., Bebbington, P. *et al.* (2005) The psychology of persecutory ideation. II: A virtual reality experimental study. *Journal of Nervous and Mental Disease*, 193, 309–315.

Friedlander, L. and Desrocher, M. (2006) Neuroimaging studies of obsessive-compulsive disorder in adults and children. *Clinical Psychology Review*, 26, 32–49.

Frith, C. (1992) *The Cognitive Neuropsychology of Schizophrenia*. Hove: LEA.

Frith, C.D. and Corcoran, R. (1996) Exploring 'theory of mind' in people with schizophrenia. *Psychological Medicine*, 26, 521–530.

Fu, C.H., McGuire, P.K., Fu, C.H. *et al.* (1999) Functional neuroimaging in psychiatry. *Philosophical Transactions of the Royal Society of London B*354, 1359–1370.

Fu, C.H.Y., Vythelingum, G.N., Brammer, M.J. *et al.* (2006) An fMRI study of verbal self-monitoring: neural correlates of auditory verbal feedback. *Cerebral Cortex*, 16, 969–977.

Fu, C.H.Y., Brammer, M.J., Yaguez, L., Allen, P., Matsumoto, K., van Haren, N., Johns, L., Weinstein, S., Borgwardt, S., Broome, M., *et al.* (in press) Increased superior temporal activation associated with external misattribution of self-generated speech in schizophrenia. *Schizophrenia Research.*

Fusar-Poli, P. and Broome, M.R. (2006) Conceptual issues in psychiatric neuroimaging. *Current Opinion in Psychiatry*, 16, 608–612.

Fusar-Poli, P., Perez, J. Broome, M.R. *et al.* (2007) Neurofunctional correlates of liability to psychosis: a systematic review of the literature and meta-analysis. *Neuroscience and Biobehavioural Reviews*, 31(4), 405–484.

Garety, P. (1991) Reasoning and delusions. *British Journal of Psychiatry*, 159, 14–18.

Garety, P.A. and Freeman, D. (1999) Cognitive approaches to delusions: a critical review of theories and evidence. *British Journal of Clinical Psychology*, 38, 113–154.

Garety, P., Hemsley, D. and Wessely, S. (1991) Reasoning in deluded schizophrenic and paranoid patients: Biases in performance on a probabilistic inference task. *Journal of Nervous and Mental Disease*, 179, 194–201.

Garety, P., Kuipers, E., Fowler, D. *et al.* (2001) A cognitive model of the positive symptoms of psychosis. *Psychological Medicine*, 31, 189–195.

Garety, P.A., Freeman, D., Jolley, S. *et al.* (2005) Reasoning, Emotions, and Delusional Conviction in Psychosis. *Journal of Abnormal Psychology*, 114, 373–384.

Garety, P.A., Bebbington, P., Fowler, D. *et al.* (2007) Implications for neurobiological research of cognitive models of psychosis. *Psychological Medicine*, 37, 1377–1391.

Gjedde, A. (2001) Brain energy metabolism and the physiological basis of the haemodynamic response. In: Jezzard, P. Matthews, P.M. and Smith, S.M. (eds), *Functional MRI: An Introduction to Methods*, pp. 37–65. Oxford: Oxford University Press.

Gray, J., Feldon, J., Rawlins, J. *et al.* (1991) The neuropsychology of schizophrenia. *Behavioral and Brain Sciences*, 14, 1–84.

Gray, J.A., Joseph, M.H., Hemsley, D.R. *et al.* (1995) The role of mesolimbic dopaminergic and retohippocampal afferents to the nucleus accumbens in latent inhibition: Implications for schizophrenia. *Behavioural Brain Research*, 71, 19–31.

Grieg, T.C., Bryson, G.J. and Bell, M.D. (2004) Theory of mind performance in schizophrenia. *Journal of Nervous and Mental Disease*, 192, 12–18.

Halligan, P.W., David, A.S., Halligan, P.W. *et al.* (2001) Cognitive neuropsychiatry: towards a scientific psychopathology. *Nature Reviews Neuroscience*, 2, 209–215.

Hemsley, D.R. (1993) A simple (or simplistic?) cognitive model for schizophrenia. *Behaviour Research and Therapy*, 31, 633–645.

Hemsley, D.R. (1994a) A cognitive model for schizophrenia and its possible neural basis. *Acta Psychiatrica Scandinavica Supplementum*, 90(384), 80–86.

Hemsley, D.R. (ed.) (1994b) Perceptual and cognitive abnormalities as the bases for schizophrenic symptoms. In David, A.S. and Cutting, J.C. (eds), *The Neuropsychology of Schizophrenia*, pp. 97–116. East Sussex: Psychology Press.

Hemsley, D.R. (2005) The development of a cognitive model of schizophrenia: placing it in context. *Neuroscience and Biobehavioral Reviews*, 29, 977–988.

Honey, G.D., Fletcher, P.C. and Bullmore, E.T. (2002) Functional brain mapping of psychopathology. *J Neurol Neurosurg Psychiatry*, 72, 432–439.

Howes, O.M.A.J. Asselin, M-C. Murray, R.M. McGuire, P. Grasby, P.M. (2006) The pre-synaptic dopaminergic system before and after the onset of psychosis: initial results from an ongoing [18F]FLUORO-DOPA PET study. *Schizophrenia Research*, 81, 14.

Huq, S., Garety, P. and Hemsley, D. (1988) Probabilistic judgements in deluded and non-deluded subjects. *Quarterly Journal of Experimental Psychology A: Human Experimental Psychology*, 40, 801–812.

Jaspers, K. (1959/1997) *General Psychopathology* (trans. Hoenig, J. and Hamilton, M.W.). Baltimore: Johns Hopkins University Press.

Johns, L.C. and van Os, J. (2001) The continuity of psychotic experiences in the general population. *Clinical Psychology Review*, 21, 1125–1141.

Johns, L.C., Gregg, L. Allen, P. *et al.* (2006) Impaired verbal self-monitoring in psychosis: effects of state, trait and diagnosis. *Psychological Medicine*, 36, 465–474.

Johnson, J.K., Tuulio-Henriksson, A. Pirkola, T. *et al.* (2003) Do schizotypal symptoms mediate the relationship between genetic risk for schizophrenia and impaired neuropsychological performance in co-twins of schizophrenic patients? *Biological Psychiatry*, 54, 1200–1204.

Johnstone, E.C., Cosway, R. and Lawrie, S.M. (2002) Distinguishing characteristics of subjects with good and poor early outcome in the Edinburgh High-Risk Study. *British Journal of Psychiatry* Suppl 43, s26–29.

Kanaan, R.A. and McGuire, P.K. (in press) Methodological and conceptual challenges for psychiatric neuroimaging. *Philosophy, Psychiatry, and Psychology*.

Kapur, S. (2003) Psychosis as a state of aberrant salience: a framework linking biology, phenomenology, and pharmacology in schizophrenia. *American Journal of Psychiatry*, 160, 13–23.

Kapur, S. (2004) How antipsychotics become anti-"psychotic"—from dopamine to salience to psychosis. *Trends in Pharmacological Sciences*, 25, 402–406.

Kapur, S., Arenovich, T. Agid, O. *et al.* (2005a) Evidence for onset of antipsychotic effects within the first 24 hours of treatment. *American Journal of Psychiatry*, 162, 939–946.

Kapur, S. Mizrahi, R. and Li, M. (2005b) From dopamine to salience to psychosis–linking biology, pharmacology and phenomenology of psychosis. *Schizophrenia Research*, 79, 59–68.

Kinderman, P. and Bentall, R.P. (1997) Causal attributions in paranoia and depression: internal, personal, and situational attributions for negative events. *Journal of Abnormal Psychology*, 106, 341–345.

Kinderman, P. and Bentall, R.P. (2000) Self-discrepancies and causal attributions: studies of hypothesized relationships. *British Journal of Clinical Psychology*, 39, 255–273.

Kinderman, P., Kaney, S. Morley, S. *et al.* (1992) Paranoia and the defensive attributional style: deluded and depressed patients' attributions about their own attributions. *British Journal of Medical Psychology*, 65, 371–383.

Klosterkotter, J., Hellmich, M., Steinmeyer, E.M. *et al.* (2001) Diagnosing schizophrenia in the initial prodromal phase. *Archives of General Psychiatry*, 58, 158–164.

Kohler, C.G. and Martin, E.A. (2006) Emotional processing in schizophrenia. In: Aleman, A., Medford, N. and David, A.S. (eds), *The Cognitive Neuropsychiatry of Emotion and Emotional Disorders*, pp. 250–271. Hove: Psychology Press.

Krabbendam, L., Myin-Germeys, I. Hanssen, M. *et al.* (2004) Hallucinatory experiences and onset of psychotic disorder: evidence that the risk is mediated by delusion formation. *Acta Psychiatrica Scandinavica*, 110, 264–272.

Langdon, R. and Coltheart, M. (1999) Mentalising, schizotypy, and schizophrenia. *Cognition*, 71, 43–71.

Langdon, R., Coltheart, M., Ward, P.B. *et al.* (2002) Disturbed communication in schizophrenia: the role of poor pragmatics and poor mind-reading. *Psychological Medicine*, 32, 1273–1284.

Langdon, R., Coltheart, M. and Ward, P.B. (2006) Empathetic perspective-taking is impaired in schizophrenia: evidence from a study of emotion attribution and theory of mind. *Cognitive Neuropsychiatry*, 11, 133–155.

Laruelle, M. and Abi-Dargham, A. (1999) Dopamine as the wind of the psychotic fire: new evidence from brain imaging studies. *Journal of Psychopharmacology*, 13, 358–371.

Laruelle, M., Abi-Dargham, A., van Dyck, C.H. *et al.* (1996) Single photon emission computerized tomography imaging of amphetamine-induced dopamine release in drug-free schizophrenic subjects. *Proceedings of the National Academy of Sciences of the USA*, 93, 9235–9240.

Laruelle, M., Abi-Dargham, A., Gil, R. *et al.* (1999) Increased dopamine transmission in schizophrenia: relationship to illness phases. *Biological Psychiatry*, 46, 56–72.

Linney, Y.M., Peters, E.R. and Ayton, P. (1998) Reasoning biases in delusion-prone individuals. *British Journal of Clinical Psychology*, 37, 285–302.

Maher, B. (1988) Anomalous experience and delusional thinking: the logic of explanations. In: Oltmanns, T.F. (ed.), *Delusional Beliefs*, pp. 15–33. Oxford: Wiley.

Mataix-Cols, D., Cullen, S., Lange, K. *et al.* (2003) Neural correlates of anxiety associated with obsessive–compulsive symptom dimensions in normal volunteers. *Biological Psychiatry*, 53, 482–493.

Mataix-Cols, D., Wooderson, S., Lawrence, N. *et al.* (2004) Distinct neural correlates of washing, checking, and hoarding symptom dimensions in obsessive–compulsive disorder. *Archives of General Psychiatry*, 61, 564–576.

Matthews, P.M. (2001) An introduction to functional magnetic resonance imaging of the brain. In Jezzard, P., Matthews, P.M. and Smith, S.M. (eds), *Functional MRI: An Introduction to Methods*, pp. 3–34. Oxford: Oxford University Press.

McGlashan, T.H., Zipursky, R.B., Perkins, D. *et al.* (2003) The PRIME North America randomized double-blind clinical trial of olanzapine versus placebo in patients at risk of being prodromally symptomatic for psychosis. I. Study rationale and design. *Schizophrenia Research*, 61, 7–18.

McGowan, S., Lawrence, A.D., Sales, T. *et al.* (2004) Presynaptic dopaminergic dysfunction in schizophrenia: a positron emission tomographic [18F]fluorodopa study. *Archives of General Psychiatry*, 61, 134–142.

McGuire, P. and Matsumoto, K. (2004) Functional neuroimaging in mental disorders. *World Psychiatry*, 3, 6–11.

McGuire, P.K., Silbersweig, D.A., Wright, I. *et al.* (1995) Abnormal monitoring of inner speech: a physiological basis for auditory hallucinations.[see comment]. *Lancet*, 346, 596–600.

McKay, R., Langdon, R. and Coltheart, M. (2005) Paranoia, persecutory delusions and attributional biases. *Psychiatry Research*, 136, 233–245.

Moore, R., Blackwood, N., Corcoran, R. *et al.* (2006) Misunderstanding the intentions of others: an exploratory study of the cognitive etiology of persecutory delusions in very late-onset schizophrenia-like psychosis. *American Journal of Geriatric Psychiatry*, 14, 410–418.

Moran, J.M., Macrae, C.N., Heatherton, T.F. *et al.* (2006) Neuroanatomical evidence for distinct cognitive and affective components of self. *Journal of Cognitive Neuroscience*, 18, 1586–1594.

Morrison, A.P., French, P., Walford, L. *et al.* (2004) Cognitive therapy for the prevention of psychosis in people at ultra-high risk: randomised controlled trial. *British Journal of Psychiatry*, 185, 291–297.

Murray, R.M. and Lewis, S.W. (1987) Is schizophrenia a neurodevelopmental disorder? *British Medical Journal (Clinical Research Edition)*, 295, 681–682.

Murray, R.M., Lewis, S.W., Owen, M.J. *et al.* (1998) The neurodevelopmental origins of Dementia Praecox. In: Bebbington, P. and McGuffin, P. (eds), *Schizophrenia: The Major Issues*, pp. 90–107. London: Heinemann.

Ochsner, K.N., Knierim, K., Ludlow, D.H. *et al.* (2004) Reflecting upon feelings: an fMRI study of neural systems supporting the attribution of emotion to self and other. *Journal of Cognitive Neuroscience*, 16, 1746–1772.

Pantelis, C., Velakoulis, D., McGorry, P.D. *et al.* (2003) Neuroanatomical abnormalities before and after onset of psychosis: a cross-sectional and longitudinal MRI comparison. *Lancet*, 361, 281–288.

Patterson II, J.C. and Kotrla, K.J. (2004) Functional Neuroimaging in Psychiatry. In: Yudofsky, S. C. and Hales, R.E. (eds), *Essentials of Neuropsychiatry and Clinical Neurosciences*, pp. 109–138. Washington, DC: American Psychiatric Publishing, Inc.

Peters, E.R., Joseph, S.A. and Garety, P.A. (1999) Measurement of delusional ideation in the normal population: Introducing the PDI (Peters *et al.* Delusions Inventory). *Schizophrenia Bulletin*, 25, 553–576.

Phillips, L.J., Velakoulis, D., Pantelis, C. *et al.* (2002) Non-reduction in hippocampal volume is associated with higher risk of psychosis. *Schizophrenia Research*, 58, 145–158.

Russell, T.A., Reynaud, E., Kucharska-Pietura, K. *et al.* (2007) Neural responses to dynamic expressions of fear in schizophrenia. *Neuropsychologia*, 45(1), 107–123.

Shergill, S.S., Brammer, M.J., Fukuda, R. *et al.* (2003) Engagement of brain areas implicated in processing inner speech in people with auditory hallucinations. *British Journal of Psychiatry*, 182, 525–531.

Van Dael, F., Versmissen, D., Janssen, I. *et al.* (2006) Data gathering: biased in psychosis? *Schizophrenia Bulletin*, 32, 341–351.

van der Gaag, M. (2006) A neuropsychiatric model of biological and psychological processes in the remission of delusions and auditory hallucinations. *Schizophrenia Bulletin*, 32, S113-S122.

van Erp, T.G., Saleh, P.A., Huttunen, M. *et al.* (2004) Hippocampal volumes in schizophrenic twins. *Archives of General Psychiatry*, 61, 346–353.

Velakoulis, D., Wood, S.J., Wong, M.T. *et al.* (2006) Hippocampal and amygdala volumes according to psychosis stage and diagnosis: a magnetic resonance imaging study of chronic schizophrenia, first-episode psychosis, and ultra-high-risk individuals. *Archives of General Psychiatry*, 63, 139–149.

Weinberger, D.R. (1987) Implications of normal brain development for the pathogenesis of schizophrenia. *Archives of General Psychiatry*, 44, 660–669.

Weinberger, D.R. and McClure, R.K. (2002) Neurotoxicity, neuroplasticity, and magnetic resonance imaging morphometry: what is happening in the schizophrenic brain? *Archives of General Psychiatry*, 59, 553–558.

Whalley, H.C., Simonotto, E., Moorhead, W. *et al.* (2006) Functional imaging as a predictor of schizophrenia. *Biological Psychiatry*, 60, 454–462.

Whyte, M.C., Brett, C., Harrison, L.K. *et al.* (2006) Neuropsychological performance over time in people at high risk of developing schizophrenia and controls. *Biological Psychiatry*, 59, 730–739.

Yung, A.R. and McGorry, P.D. (1996) The prodromal phase of first-episode psychosis: past and current conceptualizations. *Schizophrenia Bulletin*, 22, 353–370.

Yung, A.R., McGorry, P.D., McFarlane, C.A. *et al.* (1996) Monitoring and care of young people at incipient risk of psychosis. *Schizophrenia Bulletin*, 22, 283–303.

Yung, A.R., Phillips, L.J., McGorry, P.D. *et al.* (1998) Prediction of psychosis—a step towards indicated prevention of schizophrenia. *British Journal of Psychiatry*, 172, 14–20.

Yung, A.R., Phillips, L.J., Yuen, H.P. *et al.* (2003) Psychosis prediction: 12-month follow up of a high-risk ("prodromal") group. *Schizophrenia Research*, 60, 21–32.

Part 5

Treatment: overviews

Chapter 15

Pharmacological management of persecutory delusions

Paul Bebbington, Stephen Pilling, and
Craig Whittington

Introduction

Persecutory delusions are non-specific psychiatric phenomena. As they are
acknowledged to be a common feature of a range of psychiatric disorders, principally schizophrenia spectrum disorders (World Health Organization 1973) but
also severe affective disorders (Black and Nasrallah 1989), they are not of themselves
diagnostic. Strongly paranoid ideation is also associated with several personality
disorders: paranoid personality disorder, obviously, but also schizotypal and borderline personality disorder. However, new evidence suggests that paranoid
ideation is, in fact, widespread, occurring regularly in 15–20% of respondents in
general population surveys (Eaton *et al.* 1991; Olfson *et al.* 2002; Johns
et al. 2004; Freeman *et al.* 2005a). Indeed, it can be induced in many non-clinical
individuals by seemingly neutral virtual reality environments (Freeman *et al.*
2003, 2005b). Because of this, persecutory delusions call in question the nature of
the genetic origins of schizophrenia, while at the same time suggesting possible
mechanisms linking genotype and phenotype.

However, this increasing appreciation of the way paranoia is distributed has
certainly not yet been reflected in research studies. This is particularly true in
relation to pharmacological treatments, where there are two key problems. The
first is that the pharmacological treatment of persecutory delusions has never
been studied in separation from the inclusive category of positive symptoms. The
second is that the treatment of psychotic symptoms has never been investigated
in conditions other than frank psychosis. Any general statements about the treatment of persecutory delusions must therefore come from pharmacotherapeutic
extrapolation, bolstered by inferences from neurobiological studies. However,
few neurobiological investigations have focused on persecutory delusions,
and positive symptoms have rarely been studied in people who do not meet the
definitional requirements for psychosis.

The consequence is that, in this chapter, we are required to focus on the treatment of persecutory delusions within the broader context of the pharmacological treatment of psychotic disorders and in particular the treatment of schizophrenic disorders. It is therefore inevitable that our conclusions about the pharmacological treatment of persecutory delusions must draw on inferences from the treatment of disorders in which the presenting symptoms are both extensive and variable, albeit often including persecutory delusions.

Differentiating symptoms in schizophrenia

Although there has been a long tradition of differentiating delusions from one another phenomenologically, these 'item-level' distinctions were almost never used to inform research. At best, delusions have been treated as a unitary category, but in most cases they have been regarded merely as members of the class of positive symptoms. Only recently has this changed (e.g. Kimhy *et al.* 2005).

While there have been many studies differentiating symptom groups in psychosis, these have generally been based on statistical techniques of data reduction such as factor analysis or principal component analysis. The analyses start from a theoretical position (or at least hunch) defining the domain of interest. This is important, because the domain chosen constrains the degree of differentiation: wide domains usually make for coarse-grained clusters because of the tendency of these statistical techniques to generate relatively restricted numbers of factors. This does not matter if they are the right clusters, but they may not be. The early studies aimed to establish empirical groupings for genetic and prognostic research, and to an extent for pharmacotherapeutic investigations. They trawled the totality of psychotic symptoms for significant groupings, and established the now traditional distinctions between positive, negative and cognitive symptoms. These divisions had face validity: they certainly looked distinct from each other, and it was thereby argued that they might have different biological causes and a differential impact on outcome. Investigators of pharmacological treatments have adopted the positive, negative and cognitive divisions of symptoms, mainly with the intention of demonstrating the potential advantages of new pharmacological products as they emerge. In fact, the negative symptom cluster has demonstrated its utility and it has been consistently associated with structural and functional abnormalities in the brain (Min *et al.* 1999; Potkin *et al.* 2002; Ho *et al.* 2003; Szeszko *et al.* 2003). However, the findings in relation to positive symptoms have been much less conclusive (Min *et al.* 1999; Potkin *et al.* 2002; Arango *et al.* 2003). This may indicate that positive symptoms are a rather heterogeneous group, and that they need further refinement if they are to serve successfully as the basis of theory-driven investigation (Toomey *et al.* 1997).

So far, four studies have analysed symptom structures based on item-level symptoms. In the context of the present chapter, it is of particular interest that all of them generated factor structures that separate off persecutory delusions from most other aspects of positive symptomatology. In three cases, the persecutory delusions are bundled with delusions of reference (Kitamura *et al.* 1995; Toomey *et al.* 1997; Peralta and Cuesta 1999), whereas Kimhy *et al.* (2005) found, in a drug-naïve sample of people with schizophrenia, a separate factor relating to persecutory delusions, while delusions of reference clustered with grandiose, religious, and guilty delusions (which they termed delusions of self-significance).

Peralta and Cuesta (2001) put forward a hierarchical system of symptom classification as an aid to finding the most appropriate level for studying symptoms in relation to neurobiological mechanisms. Individual symptoms (e.g. thought insertion) lie at the foot of the hierarchy, followed by broader categories of symptoms (for instance, all forms of anomalous experience). These in turn participate in constructs at a still higher level (in this case, positive symptoms). This hierarchical conceptualization helps to clarify thinking. However, while there may be a tendency to regard the more differentiated levels as having more validity, this is not necessarily true. The appropriate level depends on the theory-driven purposes of the investigator, and at a given level, some elements may not be useful, partly because they have been defined for pragmatic rather than theoretical reasons. Thus, some item-level categorizations of delusions based on content (e.g. delusions of changing appearance or jealousy) may not be helpful in finding links with postulated psychological or neurobiological processes.

Nevertheless, attempts to link symptoms to neurobiology have so far primarily employed the global symptom level (i.e. the totality of positive symptoms). Thus, persecutory delusions have rarely been studied in their own right, usually being bundled together with the other positive symptoms. Until recently there has been no theoretical interest in studying delusion formation *per se*.

Biological theories and the pharmacotherapy of psychosis

Although it is broadly accepted that most major psychiatric disorders have strong biological and genetic components, the precise mechanism by which these elements operate and their role in the development and maintenance of the disorders are not well understood (Garety *et al.* 2007). In schizophrenia, the dopamine hypothesis has remained the most influential and resilient theory of schizophrenia, despite the growing interest in glutamate dysregulation (Kapur and Mamo 2003; Stone *et al.* 2007). Put crudely, the brain of someone with schizophrenia behaves as if there is too much dopamine activity in some areas, too little in others. The first element in the argument for the involvement of dopamine came from a consideration of the action of antipsychotic drugs. It was discovered that dopamine D_2 receptor blockade was common to all known antipsychotic drugs, and that their clinical potency correlated with their affinity for this receptor (Seeman *et al.* 1975; Burt *et al.* 1976).

However, despite the D_2 receptor antagonism of most antipsychotic drugs, dopamine receptors do not seem abnormal in people with schizophrenia, at least before exposure to antipsychotic medication. Single-photon emission computed tomography (SPECT) and positron emission tomography (PET) carried out with drug-naïve patients generally found no difference in dopamine D_2 receptor density compared with controls (Farde *et al.* 1990; Martinot *et al.* 1991; Pilowsky *et al.* 1994). Whatever differences exist are small, and probably of little aetiological weight (Zakzanis and Hansen 1998).

Laruelle *et al.* (1996) used SPECT to demonstrate, for the first time, significantly perturbed dopamine neurotransmission in living patients with schizophrenia. They used amphetamine challenge to cause release of stored dopamine in presynaptic neurons. People with schizophrenia showed significantly greater amphetamine-induced dopamine release than healthy controls, albeit with considerable overlap between the two groups. Moreover, positive symptoms increase after amphetamine administration, and this correlates with the amount of dopamine release (Abi-Dargham *et al.* 1998). This is usually interpreted as evidence of increased dopamine synthesis, which in turn is taken as the reason for increased uptake of DOPA (a dopamine precursor) in the striatum of patients with schizophrenia (McGowan *et al.* 2004; see also Chapter 11).

Kapur (2003) has put forward an explanatory model for the positive symptoms of schizophrenia derived from the *incentive salience theory* of addiction (Robinson and Berridge 1993). He proposed that dopamine release in the ventral striatum would signal that a given stimulus or event was 'salient'. Ordinarily, the activation of this system requires the presence of significant appetitive or threat stimuli, enabling animals to learn to seek out or avoid similar experiences in the future. Other neural systems deliver the appropriate affective valency of salience, whether pleasurable or fearful. Kapur (2003) hypothesized that enhanced dopamine release by striatal dopaminergic neurons might underlie hallucinations and delusions in schizophrenia by attaching abnormal salience (and thus personal significance) to normal internal and external events. For the person with schizophrenia, every stimulus becomes loaded with significance and meaning.

In contrast to over-activity in the striatum, there is good evidence that there is actually dopamine hypofunction in the prefrontal cortex (Abi-Dargham and Moore 2003). This is regarded as being instrumental in the generation of negative symptoms in schizophrenia. However, it may also contribute to striatal dopaminergic over-activity, as there seems to be a reciprocal influence operating between cortical and subcortical dopamine systems (Abi-Dargham and Moore 2003). Current research suggests that dopamine and glutamate disturbances may give rise to different aspects of psychopathology: drugs aimed at alleviating glutamate abnormalities primarily improve negative symptoms (although this may have little therapeutic value: Buchanan *et al.* 2007), and have no significant effect on positive symptoms (Tuominen *et al.* 2005; Javitt 2006). In contrast, amphetamine-induced dopamine release acerbates positive symptoms, but leaves negative ones untouched (Abi-Dargham *et al.* 1998).

Biological research in psychiatry has involved distinctions between positive and negative symptoms, but has generally not relied on further refinements of symptoms to drive research. Thus, Kapur's (2003) theory is pitched essentially at the global level of positive symptoms. Aetiological and mediational studies of subgroups of positive symptoms have largely been the province of psychologists and psychopathologists (Garety *et al.* 2007). However, if specific delusional characteristics can be distinguished, it is possible that particular patterns of cerebral function may be associated with them. Thus, Sabri *et al.* (1997) found that grandiosity was strongly associated with hyper-perfusion in the anterior caudate, medial prefrontal cortex and frontal regions. Persecutory delusions, on the other hand, were associated with reduced perfusion in these areas. In this context, Blackwood *et al.* (2004) reported significantly lower anterior cingulate and medial prefrontal cortex activation during a task determining self-relevance among individuals with paranoid delusions compared with controls.

Imaging studies have also provided some evidence in identifying the biological substrate underlying delusional ideas (Blackwood *et al.* 2001), including a PET study of people with chronic schizophrenia (Liddle *et al.* 1992) which showed positive correlations between the reality distortion dimension and regional rCBF in left frontal, ventral striatal, and temporal areas. A further PET study in schizophrenia demonstrated a significant positive correlation between the reality distortion dimension and left-sided temporal activity (Kaplan *et al.* 1993). Although the direction of effect thus remains unclear at this stage (in part owing to differing patient characteristics in the different studies), this research highlights the potential importance of the medial temporal and ventral striatal limbic areas in delusion formation.

Research revealing discriminative dysfunction in neurobiological systems has, interestingly, also been productive at the item-level of symptoms in non-schizophrenic disorders. Thus Pearlson *et al.* (1995) found that increased density of dopamine D_2 receptors in the caudate only occurred in those bipolar patients who had psychotic symptoms. Moreover, D_2 receptor density correlated with scores on psychotic items of the Present State Examination. Dopamine also seems to be associated with paranoid ideation in depressive disorder (Cubells *et al.* 2002; Wood *et al.* 2002). Dopamine theories have been implicated in schizotypal and borderline personality disorder (Abi-Dargham *et al.* 2004; Friedel 2004; Joyce *et al.* 2006), but there have been no studies in paranoid personality disorder that we have been able to find.

With regard to the genetic basis of persecutory delusions, Schulze *et al.* (2005) report on a genetic linkage study in which an association was identified between the D-amino acid oxidase activator gene and persecutory delusions in bipolar disorder. Detera-Wadleigh and McMahon (2006) in a meta-analysis report further evidence for the involvement of similar genes in the development both of schizophrenic and of bipolar disorders, and Schurhoff et al. (2003) report findings suggesting a familial proneness to develop delusional symptoms in both disorders.

There is thus some tentative evidence suggesting a common biological propensity to delusions extending beyond the central category of schizophreniform disorder. This may be the strongest justification for using psychopharmacological agents in the treatment of persecutory delusions wherever they appear. This can be seen in the clinical reviews of the pharmacological treatment of those personality disorders in which paranoia is a common feature (Tyrer and Bateman 2004), and antipsychotic medication is recommended, albeit from a very weak evidence base.

Others in this book (Chapters 14–17 and 19) have described the psychological interventions which may be of value in the treatment of persecutory delusions. These psychological treatments are often delivered in conjunction with pharmacological interventions, an approach we support.

The effectiveness of pharmacological treatments for persecutory delusions

Although a sizeable number of people will recover from an acute psychotic episode, the majority will relapse without treatment (and a significant number will relapse even with treatment). Thus in a study of people with first-episode schizophrenia, 82% relapsed within five years of initial response, although this risk could be reduced by maintenance therapy with antipsychotic medication (Robinson et al. 1999). In an exploratory meta-analysis of relapse prevention and risk of treatment failure in people with schizophrenia, Leucht et al. (2003) examined 11 trials of second-generation 'atypical' antipsychotics (SGAs). When the results were pooled across trials of different drugs, the risk of relapse in the SGA and placebo groups was 16% and 33%, respectively, while the risk of treatment failure was 43% versus 72%. High relapse rates may be partly explained by the relatively large numbers of people that discontinue treatment; with 74% discontinuing medication over a period of 18 months in a recent study (Lieberman et al. 2005). With regard to response to treatment (most often defined as a 20–30% reduction in scores on a symptom rating scale), the rate of people with chronic schizophrenia responding to a trial of antipsychotic medication was quite variable (between 20 and 74%, depending on the medication tested, compared to 26% of those given placebo) (Bagnall et al. 2003).

There is also a paucity of evidence regarding the differential response of individual psychotic symptoms to different pharmacological approaches; a problem that arises from several causes. These include: the focus of many pharmacological treatment trials on obtaining a license for the treatment of schizophrenic and related disorders; the lack of reporting of the outcome of pharmacological treatments on the individual symptoms in psychotic disorders; and the lack of a proper theoretical understanding of the nature of persecutory delusions such as would guide both pharmacological and psychological treatment strategies.

Nevertheless, pharmacological treatments play a central role in the treatment of psychotic symptoms, and, by extension, of persecutory delusions. However, treatment is shaped by the intensity, duration and degree of personal or social impairment associated with the delusional ideas. Previous response to treatment is also an important indicator, but beyond these broad principles, there is little specifically to guide or direct the treatment of persecutory delusions by pharmacological means. This is largely because individual clinical trials of antipsychotic medication have been carried out for licensing purposes, thereby focusing on broad diagnostic groups: schizophrenia, schizoaffective disorder, treatment-resistant schizophrenia, bipolar disorder and psychotic depression. In addition, the choice of outcomes is not driven by particular symptom clusters or profiles but by broader aspects of mental state. They rely on a limited range of measures, usually the Positive and Negative Syndrome Scale or, in earlier trials, the Brief Psychiatric Rating Scale. Sub-analyses, where they are made, have concentrated on positive and negative symptoms, and, more recently, cognition, mood and quality of life.

Existing clinical guidelines produced by leading international bodies in the field, for example, the National Institute for Clinical Excellence (NICE) clinical guidelines on schizophrenia (Kendall *et al.* 2003) or bipolar disorder (National Collaborating Centre for Mental Health 2006), the American Psychiatric Association (2004) guideline on schizophrenia, and the Royal Australian and New Zealand College of Psychiatrists Clinical Practice Guidelines Team (2004) provide no significant direct reference to the pharmacological treatment of persecutory delusions.

In order to address this problem, we decided to look for dedicated systematic reviews in the area. We began with a search for recent systematic reviews on the pharmacological treatment of schizophrenia, updating the search strategy used in the NICE clinical guideline on schizophrenia in the process (Kendall *et al.* 2003). An initial search of CINAHL, EMBASE, MEDLINE, PSYCINFO (January 2002 to February 2007) produced 3574 hits after removal of duplicates. An additional search of the Cochrane central register of controlled trials (January 2002 to February 2007) produced 763 hits. Scanning titles and abstracts identified 163 systematic reviews, of which 41% were Cochrane reviews. Of the non-Cochrane reviews, 33% used meta-analysis to synthesize the results of individual studies. However, further examination of these titles and abstracts (and an electronic key word search of the Cochrane reviews) failed to identify any significant reviews specifically related to the pharmacological treatment of persecutory delusions.

This meant that, by default, we were obliged to draw heavily on the pharmacological data relating to the symptoms of schizophrenia as a whole.

As a basis for establishing principles of prescribing antipsychotic medication for conditions characterized by paranoid delusions, three factors need to be taken into consideration. These are:

- the effectiveness of antipsychotic medication (including the comparative effectiveness of first- and second-generation antipsychotic drugs);
- the differential effectiveness of antipsychotic medication for particular sets of symptoms or problems;
- the possible side-effects associated with the use of antipsychotic medication.

The following review is built around these three questions.

The effectiveness of antipsychotic medication

A major concern of recent meta-analyses of antipsychotic medication has been whether the SGAs such as olanzapine and risperidone confer significant clinical advantage over and above that associated with the use of first-generation antipsychotics (FGAs). From the late 1990s, a significant number of reviews have addressed this question. The conclusions reached by Geddes *et al.* (2000) are typical of such reviews. They state that the SGAs appear on average to confirm no advantage in terms of efficacy and overall tolerability over FGAs when used at standard doses. There may, however, be a reduced risk of extrapyramidal side-effects. The review of Geddes *et al.* (2000), in common with other reviews, did not find any evidence of differential effects of the SGAs and so treated them as a class. However, more recent evidence (Lieberman *et al.* 2005) would suggest that, when both the efficacy and side-effects of the SGAs are taken into account, differences may emerge in terms of the overall benefit. Indeed, these differences may be greater than between some FGAs and SGAs. Similar differences between the SGAs may exist in relation to the treatment of persecutory delusions.

Unfortunately, the more recent systematic reviews of the use of antipsychotic medication in schizophrenic disorders do little to clarify the picture, particularly in relation to differences between SGAs. The major review for the Health Technology Assessment programme (Bagnall *et al.* 2003) included 171 randomized controlled trials (RCTs) and 52 observational studies. The authors concluded that the evidence for the superior effectiveness of the SGAs compared with FGAs was generally of poor quality, with high attrition from study protocols. In terms of alleviating overall symptoms of psychosis, SGAs were generally held to have an advantage over FGAs. However, the authors noted some differences; for example, the evidence suggested that quetiapine and sertindole were no more effective than FGAs.

Other reviews, for example that by Davis *et al.* (2003), which included 124 RCTs, concluded that some SGAs (i.e. amisulpride, clozapine, olanzapine and risperidone) were more efficacious than FGAs, while others (aripiprazole, quetiapine, remoxipride, sertindole, ziprasidone and zotepine) were not. They concluded that SGAs are not a homogeneous group, and that some of them alleviate a wider range of symptoms (i.e. positive symptoms, negative symptoms, cognition, impulse control/excitement and mood) than FGAs. In an attempt to provide answers more useful for clinical practice, a recent meta-analysis focused on the number of people leaving trials early for any reason or due to adverse events (Martin *et al.* 2006). Twenty-eight RCTs (7754 patients) met the authors' inclusion criteria. The results suggested that, in both short- and long-term trials, SGAs had advantages over FGAs (haloperidol and chlorpromazine), although this was more evident in flexible-dose studies than in medium-to-high fixed-dose studies. Whether SGAs are uniformly superior in terms of their risk-benefit profile was debated at the American Psychiatric Association's 2005 annual meeting in Atlanta (Moran 2005), with the only real consensus being that treatment must be individualized for each patient because SGAs are not a homogeneous group of drugs.

Most systematic reviews have failed to address the issue of cost-effectiveness (but see Bagnall *et al.* 2003), and, as noted above, the primary studies reviewed were generally set up for licensing purposes. Moreover, the majority of the reviews have concentrated on the differential efficacy of FGAs and SGAs, with less emphasis on the comparative effectiveness of the SGAs themselves. In addition, trial methodologies may have favoured SGAs over FGAs (although this has been disputed, see Davis *et al.* 2007). The FGA comparator was often prescribed at relatively high doses, but also without prophylactic anticholinergic medication. This raises the risk of parkinsonian akinesia, a side-effect that may be difficult to differentiate from the negative symptoms of psychosis (Rosenheck 2005). Thus, there is a possibility that differences in negative symptoms are an artefact of this treatment side-effect. Moreover, the statistical technique used by many trials for imputing missing data (known as last observation carried forward) probably favours SGAs over FGAs in terms of symptoms (Rosenheck 2005). This is because participants leaving the trial early (most probably due to side-effects) would have less time to respond, yet their scores would be carried forward as if they were end-point scores. Many trials also excluded people from participating who had previously failed to respond to the experimental drug, but did not apply this criterion to the comparator (Volavka *et al.* 2002). Finally, the majority of the primary studies, if not the systematic reviews, have been industry-sponsored, and the reported conclusions must therefore be treated with some caution (see Als-Nielsen *et al.* 2003; Heres *et al.* 2006). With this in mind, a cautious reading of the reviews would suggest that for some patients there may be a clinical advantage to using a particular SGA, but there is no specific evidence relating to persecutory delusions.

Recent pragmatic trials

In the light of these difficulties and the provenance of much of these recent studies, two large-scale pragmatic trials (practical clinical trials) were initiated to look at the effectiveness of FGAs and SGAs. Importantly, neither trial was commercially funded. These were the Clinical Antipsychotic Trials of Intervention Effectiveness (CATIE) (Stroup *et al.* 2003; Lieberman *et al.* 2005), funded by the US National Institute of Mental Health (NIMH), and the Cost Utility of the Latest Antipsychotic Drugs in Schizophrenia (CUtLASS 1 and 2) (Jones *et al.* 2006; Lewis *et al.* 2006; Davies *et al.* 2007), funded by the British NHS Research and Development Health Technology Assessment Programme. In phase 1 of the CATIE trial 1493 people with chronic schizophrenia were randomized to an SGA: olanzapine (7.5–30 mg/day), quetiapine (200–800 mg/day), risperidone (1.5–6.0 mg/day), or ziprasidone (40–160 mg/day); or an FGA: perphenazine (8–32 mg/day), for up to 18 months. Perphenazine was chosen as a comparator FGA because its propensity to cause extrapyramidal side-effects was lower than that of other FGAs. The primary measure of clinical effectiveness was discontinuation of medication. The results suggest that perphenazine performed as well on this measure as most of the SGAs. The exception was olanzapine, but the latter was also associated with greater increases in weight and abnormalities in indices of glucose and lipid metabolism. Furthermore, there was no evidence that any antipsychotic was superior in terms of social functioning, as measured by the Quality of Life Scale (Swartz *et al.* 2007). Cost-effectiveness was measured in relation to QALY (quality-adjusted life year) ratings, a combined measure of symptoms and side-effects. The FGA perphenazine was less costly and no less effective than the SGAs (Rosenheck *et al.* 2006).

In phase 2 of the CATIE trial (McEvoy *et al.* 2006), 99 people who discontinued SGA treatment in phase 1 were randomized between clozapine and other SGAs (olanzapine, quetiapine, risperidone, or ziprasidone). The results show that switching to clozapine was more effective than switching to another SGA (McEvoy *et al.* 2006), although it should be noted that clozapine carries a potentially significant side-effect burden (Joint Formulary Committee 2007).

The CUtLASS 1 trial involved 227 people with schizophrenia whose medication was being changed because of intolerance or inadequate clinical response. They were randomized to an SGA (amisulpride, olanzapine, quetiapine, or risperidone) or an FGA (most commonly sulpiride). The results showed that there were no advantages in using SGAs in preference to FGAs in terms of quality of life, symptoms, or associated costs of care. CUtLASS 2 involved 136 people with schizophrenia, whose medication was being changed because of treatment resistance. They were randomized between clozapine and other SGAs. While clozapine had the advantage of other SGAs in symptom improvement, this was not so in quality of life, and the drug may not be cost-effective. The outcomes of both these trials were succinctly summarized by Lieberman (2006) in a recent editorial: '... any reasoned and objective view of the evidence in light of CUtLASS 1 and CATIE must lead to the conclusion that, with the possible exception of clozapine, the SGAs are not the great breakthrough in therapeutics they were once thought to be; rather, they represent an incremental advance at best.' More recently, the discussion about the interpretation of CUtLASS and CATIE has continued in letters to the editor of the *Archives of General Psychiatry* (e.g. Jones *et al.* 2007; Tandon *et al.* 2007) and the *American Journal of Psychiatry* (Leucht *et al.* 2007; Stroup *et al.* 2007).

Given Lieberman's rather stark conclusion, the impact of side-effects becomes more significant in determining the choice of antipsychotic medication. This is important not only because of the potential impact on the individual's physical health, but because a significant number of patients in pragmatic trials stop or change medication precisely because of side-effects (Lieberman *et al.* 2005).

Intermittent treatment regimes

While the general consensus has been that relapse rates in psychosis are minimized by continuous treatment with antipsychotic medication, the long-term risks and subjective discomfort associated with adverse effects of medication led to the promotion of targeted or intermittent treatment regimes (Carpenter *et al.* 1987; Hirsch and Barnes 1994). Under these regimes, patients would be taken off medication when they had recovered fully from an episode of psychosis. They would then be closely monitored, and antipsychotic medication would be reintroduced if they showed signs of relapse. The chosen signs of relapse might be those associated with re-emergence of psychotic symptoms, or of prodromal symptoms of an affective type. This strategy has been evaluated in several large-scale controlled studies (Gaebel 1995; Kane 1999). It is generally found that relapse rates with intermittent treatment are around twice those with continuous psychotic treatment. Over half the samples in these trials did poorly on intermitted treatment, which also let to an increased drop-out rate. Targeted treatment was associated with increased risk of relapse and rehospitalization in the NIMH study (Schooler *et al.* 1997). However, Herz *et al.* (1991) found no difference in admission rates or symptom recurrence for those patients who remained in their study, whether they were on continuous or intermittent treatment.

There is some evidence from the large trial by Pietzcker *et al.* (1994) that, if treatment has been discontinued, it is more effective to intervene when affective symptoms suggestive of a prodrome emerge, rather than waiting for the re-emergence of psychotic symptoms. However, it is problematic to use affective prodromes as an indicator of impending psychotic relapse, as many psychotic episodes occur without affective prodromes, and many affective prodromes are not followed by full psychotic relapse (Malla and Norman 1994).

Intermittent treatment does not appear overall to improve social functioning, nor does it improve the sense of well-being (Jolley *et al.* 1989). Interestingly, intermittent therapy had no effect in improving extrapyramidal side-effects or tardive dyskinesia, despite an overall decrease in neuroleptic exposure (Hirsch and Barnes 2004).

There is some evidence that a low-dose medication regime, combined with a low-dose augmentation when prodromal or early symptoms of relapse appear, is as effective as full-dose maintenance therapy (Marder *et al.* 1987; Hogarty *et al.* 1988). Moreover, the study by Marder *et al.* (1994) suggests that patients and clinicians become more effective over time in identifying the indicators of individual relapse.

Part of the problem with these studies is that, although patients treated with continuous medication do better than those on some kind of intermittent regime, there is still a substantial proportion of people on the intermittent regimes who remain relapse-free. However, there seems to be no way of identifying these patients a priori.

We have no evidence about the effect of intermittent treatment on persecutory delusions occurring outside a psychiatric diagnosis of psychosis. However, there has always been a presumption that in such cases treatment with low doses on an ad-hoc basis is appropriate, and this may be so. However, evidence to support this strategy is lacking.

The side-effects of antipsychotic medication
Neurological side-effects

The primary neurological side-effects associated with the use of antipsychotic medication include extrapyramidal side-effects, such as parkinsonian symptoms, acute dystonic reactions, akathisia, and with long-term treatment, tardive dyskinesia or dystonia. There is reasonable evidence from systematic reviews that some if not all SGAs have a reduced risk of acute extrapyramidal side-effects such as akathisia and dystonia, while over the longer-term, there is a possible reduction in the risk of tardive dyskinesia (Correll *et al.* 2004). This conclusion is supported by the CATIE trial, where perphenazine had a higher risk of discontinuation due to extrapyramidal effects than any of the SGAs (Lieberman *et al.* 2005). However, some have suggested that if FGAs are used in low doses (e.g. Leucht *et al.* 2003), or if low side-effect potency FGAs are used (e.g. Schillevoort *et al.* 2001, 2005), the advantages identified in other reviews (e.g. Geddes *et al.* 2000) may not be sustained (with the possible exception of clozapine). Nevertheless, given the distressing nature of extrapyramidal side-effects and their negative impact on medication adherence and on quality of life, the possible reduced risk of these side-effects at standard doses for SGAs versus FGAs may suggest an advantage for SGAs.

Effects on weight gain and other metabolic effects of antipsychotic medications

Recent years have seen increasing concern about the potential endocrine and metabolic effects of antipsychotic medication. Much of this has focused on the SGAs, although a number of metabolic effects of the FGAs have been known for some time, for example, hyperprolactinaemia and gynaecomastia (Joint Formulary Committee 2007). Much of the concern about SGAs has been directed at the related issues of weight gain, disturbances in glucose metabolism and the *metabolic syndrome.*

Weight gain

Although systematic reviews have produced a rather conflicting picture, some clarity emerges from the CATIE trial, in which significant weight gain was associated with some of the SGAs, in particular clozapine and olanzapine (Lieberman *et al.* 2005; McEvoy *et al.* 2006).

Glucose level and diabetes

A number of reviews conclude that SGAs are associated with a high incidence of problems with glucose metabolism (e.g. Jin *et al.* 2004), and evidence for a link with diabetes mellitus comes from large-scale observational studies (Sernyak *et al.* 2002; Lambert *et al.* 2005, 2006). This was confirmed by the CATIE study, in which olanzapine was associated with greater abnormalities in glucose and lipid metabolism (Lieberman *et al.* 2005). Recent guidance suggests that clinicians should consider the metabolic risks when starting SGAs, and perform both baseline screening and regular monitoring (American Diabetes Association, American Psychiatric Association, American Association of Clinical Endocrinologists, and the North American Association for the Study of Obesity 2004). However, it is uncertain whether this regime is necessary for all antipsychotic medication, or whether certain drugs, for example olanzapine, may require closer and more careful monitoring.

Metabolic syndrome

There has been a growing interest in the metabolic syndrome, which comprises glucose and lipid metabolic abnormalities, obesity and hypertension (Grundy *et al.* 2004). It may have a prevalence of up to 30% in people with chronic schizophrenia, representing a two-fold increase in prevalence over non-psychotic cohorts of equivalent age (De Hert *et al.* 2006; Van Gaal 2006). Given the problems composing this cluster, it is not surprising that the metabolic syndrome increases risk for cardiovascular disease and is associated with higher morbidity and mortality (Grundy *et al.* 2004; De Hert *et al.* 2006; Van Gaal 2006). While all antipsychotics have the potential to contribute to the development of the metabolic syndrome, SGAs, most notably olanzapine, may confer the greatest risk

(Lieberman *et al.* 2005). Further analyses of the CATIE dataset could shed more light on this important topic (Meyer *et al.* 2005).

Cardiovascular side-effects

Because of the metabolic syndrome, poor lifestyle and coronary heart disease, people with schizophrenia (and more generally, severe mental illness) have a two-fold increase in mortality due to cardiovascular disease over the general population (Meyer and Koro 2004; Auquier *et al.* 2006; Van Gaal 2006; Osborn *et al.* 2007). Several reviews have suggested an association of SGAs (especially those that are dibenzodiazepine-derived) with dyslipidaemia and cardiovascular disease (Casey 2004; Meyer and Koro 2004; Haupt 2006).

Use of antipsychotic medication in non-schizophrenic conditions

This has been subject to much less research, which in any case is not generally germane to persecutory delusions *per se*. Antipsychotic drugs have long been used in the treatment of acute episodes of bipolar disorder (Tohen *et al.* 2001). However, the recent interest in SGAs in bipolar disorder has focused on the rectification of mood rather than of psychotic symptoms, with the conclusion that normalization is best achieved by combining SGAs and traditional mood stabilizers (such as lithium) (Cousins and Young 2007; Scherk *et al.* 2007) or possibly by SGAs alone (Ferrier *et al.* 2006). As the inferred mechanism involves action on the dopamine system, it might be thought that part of the benefit might nevertheless operate through effects on specific psychotic symptoms.

Finally, a useful Cochrane review (Wijkstra *et al.* 2005) has summarized the evidence for the pharmacological treatment of depressive psychosis. The authors conclude that treatment with antipsychotic medication alone is not advised. Treatment with an antidepressant either with an antipsychotic at the same time or added in later is likely to be most appropriate.

Pharmacological studies and the mechanisms of delusion generation

The results of studies of pharmacological interventions on outcome are obviously central to the provision of the clearest possible guidance for individual treatment. However, they also have potentially interesting implications for the mechanisms lying behind the generation of persecutory delusions. Thus repeated symptomatic assessments following the initiation of drug treatment might indicate temporal differences in improvement of individual symptoms. These might in turn suggest causal links: for instance, if anomalous experiences improved more quickly than delusional ideas it might suggest that the latter were being driven by the experiences, but that the beliefs took longer to dissipate, having a momentum of their own. This might lie behind the frequent clinical observation that, as the mental state begins to improve in response to medication, delusions become fixed on past rather than current experiences. Unfortunately no drug trial has published data of this type, even though it is probably generally available.

The studies of antipsychotic medication in bipolar disorder and in unipolar psychotic depression do offer some insight. Thus it is clear that significant benefit in the treatment of bipolar disorder by antipsychotic medication comes from mood stabilization, rather than from the antipsychotic effect. Moreover, in psychotic unipolar depression, it seems that the crucial effect of medication is through the rectification of mood, not the direct elimination of delusional symptoms (Wijkstra et al. 2005). The latter seem to improve as the mood improves. This tallies with other work suggesting the significance of mood disturbance in psychotic processes (Garety et al. 2005; Smith et al. 2006). However, there seems to be a discrepancy between bipolar disorder and unipolar depression, in that antipsychotic medication probably both stabilizes mood and controls psychotic symptoms in the former, while in the latter it is insufficient on its own to rectify the mood imbalance. The implications of this are unclear, although one might speculate about the relative salience of dopaminergic and serotonergic pathways in bipolar and unipolar depression.

Clinical implications

Developing guidance for the pharmacotherapy of persecutory delusions from a literature that exists mainly at a tangent to the key questions must lead to recommendations that are necessarily tentative. The inferences from the considerable literature on the treatment of disorders from the schizophrenic spectrum can be taken as reasonably secure. Where the delusions clearly form part of the mental state of such a disorder, the treatment is that of the condition as a whole. This will usually involve the prescription of antipsychotic medication within the *British National Formulary* dose range, preferably in monotherapy. The choice of drug would usually depend on the side-effect profile and other characteristics of the drug, and the prior experience of treatment and preference of the person being treated. However, in cases where an FGA has been used successfully in the past without much in the way of side-effects and this continues to represent the preference of the client, there are no grounds for a change. This position does not deviate substantially from the NICE guideline on schizophrenia (Kendall et al. 2003). The antipsychotic medication should generally be used on a long-term basis, rather than intermittently.

In bipolar disorder the general argument for the use of antipsychotic medication, for example in order to assist mood stabilization, is strengthened by the presence of persecutory delusions. These seem likely to be ameliorated whether the route involves mood stabilization or direct action on the delusional propensity.

As the strongest evidence for antipsychotic medication in bipolar disorder has been established using SGAs, it is best to use a drug from this group. Because a key aim is likely to be mood stabilization, treatment should ideally be long term.

Where persecutory delusions form part of a psychotic unipolar depressive disorder, the literature so far suggests that there is little to choose between antidepressant monotherapy and combined treatment with an antidepressant and an antipsychotic, preferably an SGA. There is an argument for using antipsychotics only on a short- to medium-term basis in depressive psychosis, although the decision should be made in the light of the course of illness in individual clients.

Judgements about treatment are more difficult where persecutory ideation occurs in the context of some kind of personality disorder, or where the ideation can be seen as the extreme end of a normal continuum of paranoia, perhaps characterized by anxious threat (Freeman *et al.* 2005a). In such circumstances, the clinician has to share with the client the uncertainty of the guidance provided by the literature, and present the option of pharmacological treatment as very much a jointly decided experiment, with constant review and no a-priori decisions about the ultimate length of treatment. Treatment may only need to be short-term, and should start with low doses, which may or may not need to be increased. The negotiation should proceed in the context of consideration of other treatment, alternative or simultaneous, particularly using psychological techniques. The implications of this review suggest that antipsychotics should be used with caution for such individuals.

The choice of an SGA (or indeed an FGA) needs to acknowledge they are not a homogeneous group, although differences in effectiveness are modest at best. It is therefore likely that the side-effects experienced by each individual and their preference relating to these will be important factors influencing choice. Before prescribing antipsychotics, clinicians must therefore take considerable time to discuss the potential side-effects associated with each drug, institute an appropriate system for monitoring them, and seek to ameliorate the effects. It is likely that the individual differences in response to antipsychotic medication will be key determinants of what happens. These are difficult to identify from clinical trials, and remain a challenge for the clinician and patient to address together.

Conclusion

Antipsychotic medication has an important part to play in the overall treatment of persecutory delusions, but evidence directly related to the effect of these drugs on persecutory delusions is absent. Individual responses, both in terms of benefits and harms, should therefore be central to decisions about appropriate treatment.

References

Abi-Dargham, A. and Moore, H. (2003) Prefrontal DA transmission at D1 receptors and the pathology of schizophrenia. *Neuroscientist*, 9, 404–416.

Abi-Dargham, A., Gil, R., Krystal, J. *et al.* (1998) Increased striatal dopamine transmission in schizophrenia: confirmation in a second cohort. *American Journal of Psychiatry* 155, 761–767.

Abi-Dargham, A., Kegeles, L.S., Zea-Ponce, Y. *et al.* (2004) Striatal amphetamine-induced dopamine release in patients with schizotypal personality disorder studied with single photon emission computed tomography and [123I]iodobenzamide. *Biological Psychiatry*, 55, 1001–1006.

Als-Nielsen, B., Chen, W., Gluud, C., Kjaergard, L.L. (2003) Association of funding and conclusions in randomized drug trials: a reflection of treatment effect or adverse events? *Journal of the American Medical Association*, 290, 921–928.

American Diabetes Association; American Psychiatric Association; American Association of Clinical Endocrinologists; North American Association for the Study of Obesity (2004) Consensus development conference on antipsychotic drugs and obesity and diabetes. *Diabetes Care*, 27, 596–601.

American Psychiatric Association (2004) *Practice Guideline for the Treatment of Patients with Schizophrenia*, 2nd edn. Washington: APA.

Arango, C., Breier, A., McMahon, R., Carpenter, W.T. and Buchanan, R.W. (2003) The relationship of clozapine and haloperidol treatment response to prefrontal, hippocampal, and caudate brain volumes. *American Journal of Psychiatry*, 160, 1421–1427.

Auquier, P., Lançon, C., Rouillon, F., Lader, M. and Holmes, C. (2006) Mortality in schizophrenia. *Pharmacoepidemiology Drug Safety*, 15, 873–879.

Bagnall, A-M., Jones, L., Ginnelly, L. *et al.* (2003) A systematic review of atypical antipsychotic drugs in schizophrenia. *Health Technology Assessment*, 7 (13).

Black, D.W. and Nasrallah, A. (1989) Hallucinations and delusions in 1715 patients with unipolar and bipolar affective disorders. *Psychopathology*, 22, 28–34.

Blackwood, N.J., Howard, R.J., Bentall, R.P. and Murray, R.M. (2001) Cognitive Neuropsychiatric Models of Persecutory Delusions. *American Journal of Psychiatry*, 158, 527–539.

Blackwood, N.J., Bentall, R.P., Ffytche, D.H., Simmons, A., Murray, R.M. and Howard, R.J. (2004) Persecutory delusions and the determination of self-relevance: An fMRI investigation. *Psychological Medicine*, 34, 591–596.

Buchanan, R.W., Javitt, D.C., Marder, S.R. *et al.* (2007) The Cognitive and Negative Symptoms in Schizophrenia Trial (CONSIST): the efficacy of glutamatergic agents for negative symptoms and cognitive impairments. *American Journal of Psychiatry*, 164, 1593–1602.

Burt, D.R., Creese, I. and Snyder, S.H. (1976) Properties of [3H]haloperidol and [3H]dopamine binding associated with dopamine receptors in calf brain membranes. *Molecular Pharmacology*, 12, 800–812.

Carpenter, W.T.J., Heinrichs, D.W. and Hanlon, T.E. (1987) A comparative trial of pharmacologic strategies in schizophrenia. *American Journal of Psychiatry*, 144, 1466–1470.

Casey, D.E. (2004) Dyslipidemia and atypical antipsychotic drugs. *Journal of Clinical Psychiatry*, 65 (Suppl 18), 27–35.

Correll, C.U., Leucht, S. and Kane, J.M. (2004) Lower risk for tardive dyskinesia associated with second-generation antipsychotics: a systematic review of 1-year studies. *American Journal of Psychiatry*, 161, 414–25.

Cousins, D.A. and Young, A.H. (2007) The armamentarium of treatments for bipolar disorder: a review of the literature. *Internal Journal of Neuropsychopharmacology*, 10, 411–431.

Cubells, J.F., Price, L.H., Meyers, B.S. *et al.* (2002) Genotype-controlled analysis of plasma dopamine beta-hydroxylase activity in psychotic unipolar major depression. *Biological Psychiatry*, 51, 358–364.

Detera-Wadleigh, S.D. and McMahon, F.J. (2006) G72/G30 in schizophrenia and bipolar disorder: review and meta-analysis. *Biological Psychiatry*, 60, 106–114.

Davies, L.M., Lewis, S., Jones, P.B. *et al.*; CUtLASS team (2007) Cost-effectiveness of first- v. second-generation antipsychotic drugs: results from a randomised controlled trial in schizophrenia responding poorly to previous therapy. *British Journal of Psychiatry*, 191, 14–22.

Davis, J.M., Chen, N. and Glick, I.D. (2003) A meta-analysis of the efficacy of second-generation antipsychotics. *Archives of General Psychiatry*, 60, 553–564.

Davis, J. M., Chen, N. and Glick, I. D. (2007) Issues that may determine the outcome of antipsychotic trials: industry sponsorship and extrapyramidal side effect. *Neuropsychopharmacology*, DOI 10.1192/bjp.bp.106.028654.

De Hert, M.A., van Winkel, R., Van Eyck, D. *et al.* (2006) Prevalence of the metabolic syndrome in patients with schizophrenia treated with antipsychotic medication. *Schizophrenia Research*, 83, 87–93.

Eaton, W.W., Romanoski, A., Anthony, J.C. and Nestadt, G. (1991) Screening for psychosis in the general population with a self-report interview. *Journal of Nervous and Mental Disease*, 179, 689–693.

Farde, L., Wiesel, F.A., Stone-Elander, S. *et al.* (1990) D2 dopamine receptors in neuroleptic-naive schizophrenic patients. A positron emission tomography study with [11C]raclopride. *Archives of General Psychiatry*, 47 213–219.

Ferrier, N., Pilling, S., Bazire, S. *et al.* (2006) *Bipolar Disorder: The Management of Bipolar Disorder in Adults, Children and Adolescents, in Primary and Secondary Care*. London: British Psychological Society and Gaskell Press.

Freeman, D., Slater, M., Bebbington, P.E. *et al.* (2003) Can virtual reality be used to investigate persecutory ideation? *The Journal of Nervous and Mental Disease*, 191, 509–514.

Freeman, D., Garety, P.A., Bebbington, P.E. *et al.* (2005a) Psychological investigation of the structure of paranoia in a non-clinical population. *British Journal of Psychiatry*, 186, 427–435.

Freeman, D., Garety, P.A., Bebbington, P. *et al.* (2005b) The psychology of persecutory ideation II: A virtual reality experimental study. *Journal of Nervous and Mental Disease*, 193, 309–315.

Friedel, R.O. (2004) Dopamine dysfunction in borderline personality disorder: a hypothesis. *Neuropsychopharmacology*, 29, 1029–1039.

Gaebel, W. (1995) Is intermittent, early intervention medication an alternative for neuroleptic maintenance treatment? *International Clinical Psychopharmacology*, 9 (Suppl. 5), 11–16.

Garety, P.A., Freeman, D., Jolley, S. *et al.* (2005) Reasoning, emotions and delusional conviction in psychosis. *Journal of Abnormal Psychology*, 114, 373–384.

Garety, P.A., Bebbington, P., Fowler, D., Freeman, D. and Kuipers, E. (2007) Implications for neurobiological research of cognitive models of psychosis: a theoretical paper. *Psychological Medicine*, 37, 1377–1391.

Geddes, J., Freemantle, N., Harrison, P. and Bebbington, P. (2000) Atypical antipsychotics in the treatment of schizophrenia: systematic overview and meta-regression analysis. *British Medical Journal*, 321, 1371–1376.

Grundy, S.M., Brewer, H.B. Jr, Cleeman, J.I., Smith, S.C. Jr, Lenfant, C.; American Heart Association; National Heart, Lung, and Blood Institute (2004) Definition of metabolic syndrome: Report of the National Heart, Lung, and Blood Institute/American Heart Association conference on scientific issues related to definition. *Circulation* 109, 433–438.

Haupt, D.W. (2006) Differential metabolic effects of antipsychotic treatments. *European Neuropsychopharmacoogy*, 16 (Suppl. 3), S149–S155.

Heres, S., Davis, J., Maino, K., Jetzinger, E., Kissling, W. and Leucht, S. (2006) Why olanzapine beats risperidone, risperidone beats quetiapine, and quetiapine beats olanzapine: an exploratory analysis of head-to-head comparison studies of second-generation antipsychotics. *American Journal of Psychiatry*, 163, 185–194.

Herz, M.I., Glazer, W.M., Mostert, M.A. *et al.* (1991) Intermittent versus maintenance medicaiton in schizophrenia. Two year results. *Archives of General Psychiary*, 48, 333–339.

Hirsch, S.R. and Barnes, T.R.E. (1994) Clinical use of high-dose neuroleptics. *British Journal of Psychiatry*, 164, 94–96.

Hogarty, G.E., McEvoy, J.P., Munetz, M. *et al.* (1988) Dose of fluphenazine, familial expressed emotion, and outcome in schizophrenia. Results of a two-year controlled study. *Archives of General Psychiatry*, 45, 979–905.

Ho, B.C., Andreasen, N.C., Nopoulos, P., Arndt, S., Magnotta, V. and Flaum, M. (2003) Progressive structural brain abnormalities and their relationship to clinical outcome: A longitudinal magnetic resonance imaging study early in schizophrenia. *Archives of General Psychiatry*, 60, 585–594.

Javitt, D. C. (2006) Is the glycine site half saturated or half unsaturated? Effects of glutamatergic drugs in schizophrenia patients. *Current Opinions in Psychiatry*, 19, 151–157.

Jin, H., Meyer, J.M. and Jeste, D.V. (2004) Atypical antipsychotics and glucose dysregulation: a systematic review. *Schizophrenia Research*, 71 195–212.

Johns, L.C., Cannon, M., Singleton, N. *et al.* (2004) The prevalence and correlates of self-reported psychotic symptoms in the British population. *British Journal of Psychiatry*, 185, 298–305.

Jolley, A.G., Hirsch, S.R., McRink, A. and Manchanda, R. (1989) Trial of brief intermittent neuroleptic prophylaxis for selected schizophrenic outpatients: clinical outcome at one year. *British Journal of Psychiatry* 298, 985–990.

Joint Formulary Committee (2007) *British National Formulary*, 53rd edn. London: British Medical Association and Royal Pharmaceutical Society of Great Britain.

Jones, P.B., Barnes, T.R., Davies, L. *et al.* (2006) Randomized controlled trial of the effect on Quality of Life of second- vs first-generation antipsychotic drugs in schizophrenia: Cost Utility of the Latest Antipsychotic Drugs in Schizophrenia Study (CUtLASS 1) *Archives of General Psychiatry*, 63 1079–1087.

Jones, P.B., Barnes, T.R., Elton, P. *et al.* (2007) First- vs second-generation antipsychotic drugs in schizophrenia—reply. *Archives of General Psychiatry*, 64, 979–980.

Joyce, P.R., McHugh, P.C., McKenzie, J.M. *et al.* (2006) A dopamine transporter polymorphism is a risk factor for borderline personality disorder in depressed patients. *Psychological Medicine*, 36, 807–813.

Kane, J.M. (1999) Pharmacologic treatment of schizophrenia. *Biological Psychiatry*, 46, 1396–1408.

Kaplan, R.D., Szechtman, H., Franco, S. *et al.* (1993) Three clinical syndromes of schizophrenia in untreated subjects: relation to brain glucose activity measured by positron emission tomography (PET). *Schizophrenia Research*, 11, 47–54.

Kapur, S. (2003) Psychosis as a state of aberrant salience: a framework linking biology, phenomenology, and pharmacology in schizophrenia. *American Journal of Psychiatry*, 160, 13–23.

Kapur, S. and Mamo, D. (2003) Half a century of antipsychotics and still a central role for dopamine D2 receptors. *Progress in Neuropsychopharmacology and Biological Psychiatry*, 27, 1081–1090.

Kendall, T.J.G., Pilling, S., Barnes, T.R.E. *et al.* (2003) *Schizophrenia: Full National Clinical Guideline on Core Interventions in Primary and Secondary Care.* London: Gaskell Press.

Kimhy, D., Goetz, R., Yale, S., Corcoran, C. and Malaspina, D. (2005) Delusions in individuals with schizophrenia: factor structure, clinical correlates, and putative neurobiology. *Psychopathology*, 38: 338–344.

Kitamura, T., Okazaki, Y., Fujinawa, A., Takayanagi, I. and Kasahara, Y. (1995) Dimensions of schizophrenic positive symptoms: an exploratory factor analysis investigation. *European Archives of Psychiatry and Clinical Neuroscience*, 248, 130–135.

Lambert, B.L., Chou, C.H., Chang, K.Y., Tafesse, E. and Carson, W. (2005) Antipsychotic exposure and type 2 diabetes among patients with schizophrenia: a matched case–control study of California Medicaid claims. *Pharmacoepidemiology and Drug Safety* 14, 417–25.

Lambert, B.L., Cunningham, F.E., Miller, D.R., Dalack, G.W. and Hur, K. (2006) Diabetes risk associated with use of olanzapine, quetiapine, and risperidone in veterans' health administration patients with schizophrenia. *American Journal of Epidemiology*, 164, 672–81.

Laruelle, M., Abi-Dargham, A., van Dyck, C. H. *et al.* (1996) Single photon emission computerized tomography imaging of amphetamine-induced dopamine release in drug-free schizophrenic subjects. *Proceedings of the National Academy of Sciences USA*, 93, 9235–9240.

Leucht, S., Wahlbeck, K., Hamann, J. and Kissling, W. (2003) New generation antipsychotics versus low-potency conventional antipsychotics: a systematic review and meta-analysis. *Lancet*, 361(9369), 1581–1589.

Leucht, S., Heres, S., Hamann, J. and Kissling, W. (2007) Pretrial medication bias in randomized antipsychotic drug trials. *American Journal of Psychiatry*, 164, 1266.

Lewis, S.W., Davies, L., Jones, P.B. *et al.* (2006) Randomised controlled trials of conventional antipsychotic versus new atypical drugs, and new atypical drugs versus clozapine, in people with schizophrenia responding poorly to, or intolerant of, current drug treatment. *Health Technology Assessment*, 10, 1–165.

Liddle, P.F., Friston, K.J., Frith, C.D. *et al.* (1992) Patterns of cerebral blood flow in schizophrenia. *British Journal of Psychiatry*, 160, 179–186.

Lieberman, J.A., Stroup, T.S., McEvoy, J.P. *et al.* (2005) Clinical Antipsychotic Trials of Intervention Effectiveness (CATIE) Investigators. Effectiveness of antipsychotic drugs in patients with chronic schizophrenia. *New England Journal of Medicine*, 353, 1209–1223.

Lieberman, J.A. (2006) Comparative effectiveness of antipsychotic drugs. A commentary on: Cost Utility of the Latest Antipsychotic Drugs in Schizophrenia Study (CUtLASS 1) and Clinical Antipsychotic Trials of Intervention Effectiveness (CATIE). *Archives of General Psychiatry*, 63, 1069–1072.

Malla, A.K. and Norman, R.M.G. (1994) Prodromal symptoms in schizophrenia. *British Journal of Psychiatry*, 164, 487–493.

Marder, S.R., Van Putten, T., Mintz, J., Lebell, M., McKenzie, J. and May, P.R. (1987) Low and conventional dose maintenance therapy with flupenazine decanoate: two-year outcome. *Archives of General Psychiatry*, 44, 518–521.

Marder, S.R., Wirshing, W.C., Van Putten, T. *et al.* (1994) Fluphenazine vs placebo supplementation for prodromal signs of relapse in schizophrenia. *Archives of General Psychiary*, 51, 280–287.

Martin, J.L., Perez, V., Sacristan, M., Rodriguez-Artalejo, F., Martinez, C. and Alvarez, E. (2006) Meta-analysis of drop-out rates in randomised clinical trials, comparing typical and atypical antipsychotics in the treatment of schizophrenia. *European Psychiatry*, 21, 11–20.

Martinot, J.L., Paillere-Martinot, M.L., Loc'h, C. *et al.* (1991) The estimated density of D2 striatal receptors in schizophrenia. A study with positron emission tomography and 76Br-bromolisuride. *British Journal of Psychiatry*, 158, 346–530.

McEvoy, J.P., Lieberman, J.A., Stroup, T.S. *et al.*; CATIE Investigators. (2006) Effectiveness of clozapine versus olanzapine, quetiapine, and risperidone in patients with chronic schizophrenia who did not respond to prior atypical antipsychotic treatment. *American Journal of Psychiatry*, 163, 600–610.

McGowan, S., Lawrence, A.D., Sales, T., Quested, D. and Grasby, P. (2004) Presynaptic dopaminergic dysfunction in schizophrenia: a positron emission tomographic [18F]fluorodopa study. *Archives of General Psychiatry*, 61, 134–142.

Meyer, J.M. and Koro, C.E. (2004) The effects of antipsychotic therapy on serum lipids: a comprehensive review. *Schizophrenia Research*, 70, 1–17.

Meyer, J.M., Nasrallah, H.A., McEvoy, J.P. *et al.* (2005) The Clinical Antipsychotic Trials of Intervention Effectiveness (CATIE) Schizophrenia Trial: clinical comparison of subgroups with and without the metabolic syndrome. *Schizophrenia Research*, 80, 9–18.

Min, S.K., An, S.K., Jon, D.I. and Lee, J.D. (1999) Positive and negative symptoms and regional cerebral perfusion in antipsychotic-naive schizophrenic patients: a high-resolution SPECT study. *Psychiatry Research*, 90, 159–168.

Moran, M. (2005) Experts square off across the antipsychotic generation gap. *Psychiatric News*, 40, 1.

National Collaborating Centre for Mental Health (2006) *Bipolar Disorder: The Management of Bipolar Disorder in Adults, Children and Adolescents, in Primary and Secondary Care.* London: British Psychological Society and Gaskell Press.

Olfson, M., Lewis-Fernández, R., Feder, A., Gameroff, M.J., Pilowsky, D. and Fuentes, M. (2002) Psychotic symptoms in an urban general medicine practice. *American Journal of Psychiatry*, 159, 1412–1419.

Osborn, D.P., Levy, G., Nazareth, I., Petersen, I., Islam, A. and King, M.B. (2007) Relative risk of cardiovascular and cancer mortality in people with severe mental illness from the United Kingdom's General Practice Research Database. *Archives of General Psychiatry*, 64, 242–249. Erratum in: *Archives of General Psychiatry*, 64, 736.

Pearlson, G.D., Wong, D.F., Tune, L.E. *et al.* (1995) In vivo D2 dopamine receptor density in psychotic and nonpsychotic patients with bipolar disorder. *Archives of General Psychiatry*, 52, 471–477.

Peralta, V. and Cuesta, M.J. (1999) Dimensional structure of psychotic symptoms: an item-level analysis of SAPS and SANS symptoms in psychotic disorders. *Schizophrenia Research*, 38, 13–26.

Peralta, V. and Cuesta, M.J. (2001) How many and which are the psychopathological dimensions in schizophrenia? Issues influencing their ascertainment. *Schizophrenia Research*, 49, 269–285.

Pietzcker, A., Gaebel, W., Kopcke, W. *et al.* (1994) Intermittent versus maintenance neuroleptic long-term treatment in schizophrenia—2-year results of a German multicentre study. *Journal of Psychiatry Research*, 27, 321–339.

Pilowsky, L.S., Costa, D.C., Ell, P.J., Verhoeff, N.P., Murray, R.M. and Kerwin, R.W. (1994) D2 dopamine receptor binding in the basal ganglia of antipsychotic-free schizophrenic patients. An 123I-IBZM single photon emission computerised tomography study. *British Journal of Psychiatry*, 164, 16–26.

Potkin, S.G., Alva, G., Fleming, K. *et al.* (2002) A PET study of the pathophysiology of negative symptoms in schizophrenia. *American Journal of Psychiatry*, 159, 227–237.

Robinson, D., Woerner, M.G., Alvir, J.M.J. *et al.* (1999) Predictors of relapse following response from a first episode of schizophrenia or schizoaffective disorder. *Archives of General Psychiatry*, 56, 241–247.

Robinson, T.E. and Berridge, K.C. (1993) The neural basis of drug craving: an incentive-sensitization theory of addiction. *Brain Research and Brain Research Reviews*, 18, 247–291.

Rosenheck, R.A. (2005) Open forum: effectiveness versus efficacy of second-generation antipsychotics: haloperidol without anticholinergics as a comparator. *Psychiatric Services*, 56, 85–92.

Rosenheck, R.A, Leslie, D.L., Sindelar, J. *et al.*; CATIE Study Investigators (2006) Cost-effectiveness of second-generation antipsychotics and perphenazine in a randomized trial of treatment for chronic schizophrenia. *American Journal of Psychiatry*, 163, 2080–2089.

Royal Australian and New Zealand College of Psychiatrists Clinical Practice Guidelines Team for the Treatment of Schizophrenia and Related Disorders (2004) Royal Australian and New Zealand College of Psychiatrists clinical practice guidelines for the treatment of schizophrenia and related disorders. *Australian and New Zealand Journal of Psychiatry*, 39, 1–30.

Sabri, O., Erkwoh, R., Schreckenberger, M., Owega, A., Sass, H. and Buell, U. (1997) Correlation of positive symptoms exclusively to hyperperfusion or hypoperfusion of cerebral cortex in never-treated schizophrenics. *Lancet*, 349, 1735–1739.

Scherk, H., Pajonk, F.G. and Leucht, S. (2007) Second-generation antipsychotic agents in the treatment of acute mania: a systematic review and meta-analysis of randomized controlled trials. *Archives of General Psychiatry*, 64, 442–455.

Schillevoort, I., de Boer, A., Herings, R.M., Roos, R.A., Jansen, P.A., Leufkens, H.G. (2001) Antipsychotic-induced extrapyramidal syndromes. Risperidone compared with low- and high-potency conventional antipsychotic drugs. *European Journal of Clinical Pharmacology*, 57, 327–31.

Schillevoort, I., Herings, R.M., Hugenholtz, G.W. *et al.* (2005) Antipsychotic-induced extrapyramidal syndromes in psychiatric practice: a case–control study. *Pharmacy and World Science*, 27, 285–289.

Schooler, N.R., Keith, S.J., Severe, J.B. *et al.* (1997) Relapse and rehospitalization during maintenance treatment of schizophrenia: the effects of dose reduction and family treatment (see comments). *Archives of General Psychiaytry*, 54, 453–463.

Schurhoff, F., Szoke, A., Meary, A., Bellivier, F., Rouillon, F., Pauls, D. and Leboyer, M. (2003) Familial aggregation of delusional proneness in schizophrenia and bipolar pedigrees. *American Journal of Psychiary*, 180, 1313–1319.

Schulze, T.G., Ohlraun, S., Czerski, P.M. *et al.* (2005) Genotype-phenotype studies in bipolar disorder showing association between the DAOA/G30 locus and persecutory delusions: a first step toward a molecular genetic classification of psychiatric phenotypes. *American Journal of Psychiatry*, 162, 2101–2108.

Seeman, P., Chau-Wong, M., Tedesco, J. and Wong, K. (1975) Brain receptors for antipsychotic drugs and dopamine: direct binding assays. *Proceedings of the National Academy of Science of the USA*, 72, 4376–4380.

Sernyak, M.J., Leslie, D.L., Alarcon, R.D., Losonczy, M.F. and Rosenheck, R. (2002) Association of diabetes mellitus with use of atypical neuroleptics in the treatment of schizophrenia. *American Journal of Psychiatry*, 159, 561–566.

Smith, B., Fowler, D.G., Freeman, D. *et al.* (2006) Emotion and psychosis: links between depression, self-esteem, negative schematic beliefs and delusions and hallucinations. *Schizophrenia Research*, 86, 181–188.

Stone, J.M., Morrison, P.D. and Pilowski, L.S. (2007) Glutamate and dopamine dysregulation in schizophrenia—a synthesis and selective review. *Journal of Psychopharmacology*, 21, 440–452.

Stroup, T.S., McEvoy, J.P., Swartz, M.S. *et al.* (2003) The National Institute of Mental Health Clinical Antipsychotic Trials of Intervention Effectiveness (CATIE) project: schizophrenia trial design and protocol development. *Schizophrenia Bulletin*, 29, 15–31.

Stroup, T.S., Rosenheck, R.A. Essock, S.E. and Lieberman, J.A. (2007) Drs. Stroup, Rosenheck, Essock, and Lieberman reply. *American Journal of Psychiatry*, 164, 1266–1267.

Swartz, M.S., Perkins, D.O., Stroup, T.S. *et al.*; CATIE Investigators (2007) Effects of antipsychotic medications on psychosocial functioning in patients with chronic schizophrenia: findings from the NIMH CATIE study. *American Journal of Psychiatry*, 164, 428–436.

Szeszko, P.R., Gunning-Dixon, F., Ashtari, M., Snyder, P.J., Lieberman, J.A. and Bilder, R.M. (2003) Reversed cerebellar asymmetry in men with first episode schizophrenia. *Biological Psychiatry*, 53, 450–459.

Tandon, R. Carpenter, W.T. and Davis, J.M. (2007) First- and second-generation antipsychotics: learning from CUtLASS and CATIE. *Archives of General Psychiatry*, 64, 979–980.

Tohen, M., Zhang, F., Taylor, C.C. *et al.* (2001) A meta-analysis of the use of typical antipsychotic agents in bipolar disorder. *Journal of Affective Disorders*, 65, 85–93.

Toomey, R., Kremen, W.S., Simpson, J.C. *et al.* (1997) Revisiting the factor structure for positive and negative symptoms: evidence from a large heterogeneous group of psychiatric patients. *American Journal of Psychiatry*, 154, 371–377.

Tuominen, H.J., Tiihonen, J. and Wahlbeck, K. (2005) Glutamatergic drugs for schizophrenia: a systematic review and meta-analysis. *Schizophrenia Research*, 72, 225–234.

Tyrer, P. and Bateman, A.W. (2004) Drug treatment for personality disorders. *Advances in Psychiatric Treatment*, 10, 389–398.

Van Gaal L.F. (2006) Long-term health considerations in schizophrenia: metabolic effects and the role of abdominal adiposity. *European Neuropsychopharmacology*, 16 (Suppl. 3), S142–814.

Volavka, J., Czobor, P., Sheitman, B. *et al.* (2002) Clozapine, olanzapine, risperidone, and haloperidol in the treatment of patients with chronic schizophrenia and schizoaffective disorder. *American Journal of Psychiatry*, 159, 255–62. Erratum in: *American Journal of Psychiatry*, 59, 2132.

Wijkstra, J., Lijmer, J., Balk, F., Geddes, J. and Nolen, W.A. (2005) Pharmacological treatment for psychotic depression. *Cochrane Database of Systematic Reviews*, Issue 4. Art. No. CD004044. DOI: 10.1002/14651858.CD004044.pub2.

Wood, J.G., Joyce, P.R., Miller, A.L., Mulder, R.T. and Kennedy, M.A. (2002) A polymorphism in the dopamine beta-hydroxylase gene is associated with "paranoid ideation" in patients with major depression. *Biological Psychiatry*, 51, 365–369.

World Health Organization (1973) *The International Pilot Study of Schizophrenia*, Vol. 1. Geneva: World Health Organization.

Zakzanis, K.K. and Hansen, K.T. (1998) Dopamine D_2 densities and the schizophrenic brain. *Schizophrenia Research*, 32, 201–206.

Chapter 16

Research evidence of the effectiveness of cognitive behavioural therapy for persecutory delusions: more work is needed

Philippa Garety, Richard P. Bentall, and Daniel Freeman

Introduction

Elsewhere in this book, we read that the very first report of cognitive behavioural therapy (CBT) by its founder, Aaron Beck, concerned successful work with a persecutory delusion (Beck 1952; see Chapter 20 of this volume). In this section, the other chapters describe the process and main elements of therapy with persecutory delusions, and illustrative case examples are provided, together with a first-person account of the experience of therapy. These accounts indicate that CBT is an increasingly popular and acceptable approach for working with persecutory delusions: but what is the research evidence for its effectiveness? In this chapter, we offer a descriptive summary of the relevant research in CBT, note that the evidence for effectiveness is mixed and modest, and highlight key questions for future development.

The development of CBT for psychosis

Beck's 1952 case report did not immediately stimulate the development of CBT for psychosis. Instead, Beck turned his gaze on depression and the serendipitous discovery of antipsychotic effects of chlorpromazine in the same year (1952) initiated an era dominated by pharmacological treatments for psychosis. However, in time, the limitations of the antipsychotic medications, in terms of their effectiveness, acceptability and side-effects, came to be recognized and the search for other treatment approaches, to supplement medication, gained ground (Curson *et al.* 1988; Garety *et al.* 2000). By the late 1980s/early 1990s, a new generation of largely British psychologists and psychiatrists started to experiment with CBT approaches for delusions and hallucinations, influenced by the evidence supporting CBT for anxiety and depression, the emerging cognitive theories of delusions and hallucinations (e.g. Hemsley and Garety 1986; Bentall 1990) and a number of behavioural and coping-focused case studies targeting psychotic symptoms, published in the preceding decade. Encouraging case reports and small controlled trials of CBT were first published (e.g. Fowler and Morley 1989; Chadwick and Lowe 1990; Kingdon and Turkington 1991; Tarrier et al. 1993; Garety et al. 1994). These were soon to be followed by the development of treatment manuals as the basis for more substantial randomized controlled trials (RCTs) of CBT (Kingdon and Turkington 1994; Chadwick et al. 1996; Fowler et al. 1995).

The evidence from randomized controlled trials

The study populations: do they include people with persecutory delusions?

A major difficulty in reviewing the literature on the effectiveness of CBT for persecutory delusions is that no RCT has yet been published. In this respect, the lack of formal evidence for the evaluation of the psychological treatment of persecutory delusions mirrors the situation in pharmacology (see Chapter 15). The first generation of CBT case studies was focused on people with persistent and generally distressing delusions and hallucinations, since these were the medication-unresponsive symptoms for which new treatment approaches were seen to be needed. The first wave of RCTs therefore also largely selected people meeting the same criterion of positive symptom persistence, all in the context of a diagnosis in the schizophrenia spectrum (Tarrier et al. 1993, 1998; Kuipers et al. 1997; Pinto et al. 1999; Sensky et al. 2000). None of these studies was focused on people with persecutory delusions; although, of course, as persecutory delusions are the second most common positive symptom, after ideas of reference (Freeman 2007), CBT in these studies will frequently have been targeted on persecutory delusions. (Typically persecutory delusions occur in about 50% of those with schizophrenia and in a higher proportion, above 80%, of those with delusions.) Only one trial, that by Kuipers et al. (1997), has reported outcomes for persecutory delusions (combined with ideas of reference). Since 2000, there have been further RCTs for people with persistent positive symptoms and a diagnosis of schizophrenia (Durham et al. 2003; Cather et al. 2005; Valmaggia et al. 2005).

Very soon, however, CBT broadened its scope beyond people with persistent positive symptoms and RCTs were reported with populations selected by a wide variety of new criteria, only some of which used a diagnostic criterion of schizophrenia. These include: acute psychosis (Drury *et al.* 1996; Bach and Hayes 2002; Startup *et al.* 2004; Bechdolf *et al.* 2004; Gaudiano and Herbert 2006; Garety *et al.* in press); early psychosis (Haddock *et al.* 1999a; Lewis *et al.* 2002; Jolley *et al.* 2003; Jackson *et al.* 2005); people with co-morbid substance misuse (Barrowclough *et al.* 2001); people with negative and positive symptoms (Rector *et al.* 2003); community patients (Turkington *et al.* 2002) and older community patients (Granholm *et al.* 2005); people stable in the community and at risk of relapse (Gumley *et al.* 2003); people with hallucinations (Wykes *et al.* 1999; Jenner *et al.* 2004; Trower *et al.* 2004) and people considered at high risk of developing psychosis (Morrison *et al.* 2004). Many, but not all, of these populations will include a substantial, but generally unknown, proportion of people with persecutory delusions. It should also be noted that therapies in most of these studies were delivered individually, while a small number used a group format. This review therefore can only offer an overview of outcomes for psychosis and, where measured, positive symptoms; and, with one exception (Kuipers *et al.* 1997), we need to extrapolate from these studies to make any inferences about outcomes for persecutory delusions. Since studies targeting hallucinations or at-risk mental states explicitly do not directly target persecutory delusions, we will not consider them further in this review.

Study design: choice of control group

The RCTs differ not only in respect of the study populations, and individual or group format, but also in terms of design, a key difference being the choice of control condition. The majority of studies compare CBT added to Routine care or 'Treatment as usual (TAU, typically drug treatment and case management)' with TAU alone. Another group of studies compares CBT plus TAU with another psychological intervention (e.g. supportive counselling) plus TAU. Rarely, there are three conditions, with CBT (plus TAU), an active intervention (plus TAU) and a TAU-only condition. Clearly these designs have different strengths and limitations. The CBT comparison with TAU allows investigation of the effects of CBT when added to standard care; however, it does not permit inferences about the specific benefits of CBT rather than any psychological approach. However, the comparison of CBT with an active psychological intervention, in the absence of a TAU-only condition, does not enable us to infer whether CBT is beneficial, only whether it is more or less beneficial than an alternative psychological approach. In this review, we therefore separately examine comparisons of CBT with TAU and with another active treatment. We do not report analyses which combine outcomes from two different psychological interventions (e.g. CBT and supportive therapy) and compare both with TAU.

CBT approach

Most studies have used a generic CBT for psychosis approach, based on the early manuals or variants of these. All of these emphasize the importance of engagement, collaboration, considering the personal meaning and appraisals of psychotic experiences, normalizing and gently exploring alternative explanations, and work with affective symptoms and relapse prevention. It has been suggested that in the studies with generic CBT for psychosis, some CBT therapists and trial research groups have practised a more behavioural style of CBT, in contrast with a more purely cognitive approach (Tarrier and Wykes 2004); however, whether any such differences affect outcome has not been prospectively investigated. There are also some studies which explicitly describe some differences in emphasis of CBT, as delivered. For example, a number of CBT approaches report a particular focus on social functioning (e.g. 'functional CBT': Cather *et al.* 2005; and 'cognitive behavioural social skills training': Granholm *et al.* 2005).

There is also a new variant of CBT for psychosis, with distinctive theory and therapy elements, sometimes called 'third wave', Acceptance and Commitment Therapy (ACT) [the first wave being behavioural therapies and the second cognitive therapies (Hayes 2004)]. ACT differs from traditional CBT in emphasizing acceptance and mindfulness, aiming for a new relationship to negative thoughts and emotions, in contrast to 'formal disputation of dysfunctional thought content' (Gaudiano *et al.* 2006). Two studies of acute psychosis have used ACT (Bach and Hayes 2002; Gaudiano and Herbert 2006). These will therefore be considered separately.

Outcomes

One important issue for the evaluation of RCT evidence concerns the selection of trial outcomes. There are of course a wide variety of potentially important outcomes from therapy for psychosis, and different trials have had different intended benefits. Initially, trials concentrated particularly on reducing positive symptoms and measured this using standardized scales, such as the Brief Psychiatric Rating Scale (BPRS; Overall and Gorham 1967) and the Positive and Negative Symptom Scales (PANSS; Kay *et al.* 1989). This approach has been criticized by some authors, notably Birchwood and Trower (2006), who argue that the goals of CBT should not be assumed to be the same as the goals of drug treatment, that is symptom reduction. They propose, instead, that CBT should be focused on emotional dysfunction and reactions to psychotic experiences. Indeed, from early on, many CBT studies have also targeted the distress associated with symptoms, and measured this using multi-dimensional scales (e.g. PSYRATS, Haddock *et al.* 1999b) as well measures of affective symptoms and social functioning. More recent trials with other specific targets of treatment have measured these other outcomes, such as relapse, appraisals of hallucinations and transition to psychosis. In this overview, we consider the most commonly measured outcomes: positive and negative symptoms, depression, social functioning and relapse.

Methodological requirements

There has been considerable variability in the methodological conduct of trials and a growing awareness that these methodological differences might have had an impact on intervention effects, through contributing to sources of hidden bias (Tarrier and Wykes 2004). Methods to reduce bias include independent randomization in allocation to treatment, blind assessment, and improving rates of follow-up. Recent years have therefore witnessed a greater sophistication in the methodology of trials, influenced both by this awareness and by the requirements set by consensus good practice statements, such as the CONSORT group statement (Altman *et al*. 2001). We note in particular whether blind assessment has been undertaken, since this has been found to be a particular source of bias (Tarrier and Wykes 2004). It is worth adding that, in general, the methodology of many CBT trials has been superior to that of many pharmacological investigations, for example those comparing first- and second-generation anti-psychotics, which have been compromised by short follow-up periods and high drop-out rates (Geddes *et al*. 2000).

Summary of outcomes from RCTs for CBT for psychosis

In Tables 16.1, 16.2 and 16.3a and 16.3b we present a summary of the effects of individually delivered CBT for psychosis, at the end of the treatment phase and at follow-up, grouped by treatment population, separately for comparisons with TAU and with an active treatment. Group treatments are shown together in Tables 16.4a and 16.4b.

The most consistent evidence for reductions in positive symptoms occurs in trials of individual CBT with people with persistent positive symptoms, where the CBT intervention is compared to a TAU control. One trial in this subgroup (Kuipers *et al*. 1997) specifically reports a positive effect on persecutory delusions and ideas of reference (BPRS suspiciousness item). This is the largest sub-group of studies and we can conclude that individual CBT is effective for reducing persistent positive symptoms and is, by extrapolation, very likely to have benefits for the treatment of persistent persecutory delusions. To add a note of caution, we note that these studies are generally small, with fewer than 100 participants, and include a number of the earlier, less methodologically robust trials.

Table 16.1 Evaluations of individual cognitive-behavioural therapy (CBT) for the positive symptoms of psychosis that compare CBT plus treatment as usual (TAU) and a TAU control

Study	Patients	n	Groups	Blind assessment	Assessment points	Treatment length	End of CBT treatment effects				Relapse over trial
							Positive symptoms	Negative symptoms	Depression	Social functioning	
Persistent symptoms											
Tarrier et al. (1993)	Persistent positive symptoms	39	1. Coping strategy enhancement 2. Problem solving 3. Waiting list control	No	Pre-waiting period, pre-treatment, post-treatment (6 weeks), 6-month follow-up	6 weeks	Yes	No	No	No	No
Garety et al. (1994)	Persistent distressing positive symptoms	20	1. CBT 2. Waiting list control	No	Monthly for 6 months	6 months	Yes		Yes	No	
Kuipers et al. (1997)	Persistent distressing positive symptoms	60	1. CBT 2. TAU control	No	0, 3, 6, 9, 18 months	9 months	Yes*		No	No	
Tarrier et al. (1998)	Persistent positive symptoms	87	1. CBT 2. Supportive counselling 3. TAU control	Yes	Baseline, 3 months, 12 months	10 weeks	Yes				No

		N	Conditions	Assessment		Length				
Durham et al. (2003)	Persistent distressing positive symptoms	66	1. CBT 2. Supportive therapy 3. TAU control	0, post-treatment, 3-month follow-up	Yes	9 months	Yes			
Rector et al. (2003)	Persistent positive and negative symptoms	42	1. CBT 2. TAU control	0, 6 (post-treatment), 12 months	Yes	6 months	No	No	No	
Outpatients										
Turkington et al. (2002)	Outpatients with a diagnosis of schizophrenia	422	1. Brief CBT 2. TAU control	Baseline, post therapy, 12 months	No	6 sessions over an average of 20 weeks	No	No	Yes	Yes
Gumley et al. (2003)	Patients with schizophrenia, vulnerable to relapse and no current severe positive symptoms	144	1. CBT 2. TAU control	0, 12, 26, 52 weeks	No	5 sessions in first 12 weeks plus additional sessions at signs of relapse	Yes	Yes	Yes	Yes

Table 16.1 (Continued) Evaluations of individual cognitive-behavioural therapy (CBT) for the positive symptoms of psychosis that compare CBT plus treatment as usual (TAU) and a TAU control

Study	Patients	n	Groups	Blind assessment	Assessment points	Treatment length	End of CBT treatment effects				Relapse over trial
							Positive symptoms	Negative symptoms	Depression	Social functioning	
Acute psychosis											
Lewis et al. (2002)	Acute psychosis (first or second episode)	315	1. CBT 2. Supportive counselling 3. TAU control	Yes	0, 2, 3, 4, 5 weeks. 6-10-week and 18-month follow-ups	5 weeks	Yes				No
Jolley et al. (2003)	Schizophrenia diagnosed in the last 5 years and symptoms present within last 3 months	21	1. CBT 2. TAU control	Yes	0, 2, 4, 6, months	6 months	No		No		No
Startup et al. (2004)	Acute psychosis	90	1. CBT 2. TAU control	No	0, 6, 12, 24 months	Up to 25 sessions over year	Yes	Yes		Yes	No
Garety et al. (in press)	Acute psychosis	301	1. CBT 2. Family intervention 3. TAU control	Yes	0, 3, 6, 12, 24 months	9 months	No	No	No	No	No

ACT/acute psychosis

Study	Population	N	Groups	Assessment					
Bach and Hayes (2002)	Acute psychosis	80	1. ACT 2. TAU control	Baseline, 4-month follow-up	No	4 sessions	No	No	No
Gaudiano and Herbert (2006)	Acute psychosis	40	1. ACT 2. TAU control	Baseline, discharge, 4-month follow-up	No	Length of inpatient stay	Yes	No	Yes

Substance misuse

Barrowclough et al. (2001)	Schizophrenia and substance abuse	36	1. Motivational interviewing, CBT and family intervention 2. TAU control	0, 9, 12 months	Yes	9 months	Yes	No	No

Early psychosis

Jackson et al. (2005)	Early psychosis	91	1. COPE 2. TAU control	0, 6, 12 months	Yes	12 months	No	No	No

*Improvement in persecutory ideation.

ACT, Acceptance and Commitment Therapy; COPE, cognitively oriented psychotherapy for early psychosis.

Table 16.2 Trials comparing cognitive-behavioural therapy (CBT) with another active psychological intervention

Study	Patients	n	Groups	Assessment points	Blind assessment	Treatment length	End of CBT treatment effects				Relapse over trial
							Positive symptoms	Negative symptoms	Depression	Social functioning	
Persistent positive/psychotic symptoms											
Pinto et al. (1999)	Persistent psychotic symptoms	41	1. CBT and social skills training 2. Supportive therapy	0, 6 (post-treatment) months	No	6 months	Yes	No			No
Sensky et al. (2000)	Persistent distressing psychotic symptoms	90	1. CBT 2. Befriending	0, 9 (post-treatment), 18 months	Yes	9 months	No	No	No		
Cather et al. (2005)	Persistent psychotic symptoms	30	1. Functional CBT 2. Psycho-education	0, 4 (post-treatment)	Yes	4 months	No	No	No	No	
Valmaggia et al. (2005)	Persistent positive symptoms in long-term patients	62	1. CBT 2. Supportive counselling plus psycho-education	0, 4 (post-treatment) 6 months	Yes	4 months?	No Yes (hallucinations, some aspects)	No	No	No	

Acute psychosis

Drury et al. (1996)	Acute psychosis	40	1. Individual and group CBT 2. Activity control group	Weekly for 6 months. Follow-up at 9 months.	No	8 h per week during inpatient admission	Yes	No	No
Haddock et al (1999)	Acute psychosis (and onset <5 years)	21	1. CBT 2. Supportive counselling and psycho-education	0, 5 weeks (post treatment) 5–6 months, 2 years	Yes	5 weeks	No		

Table 16.3a Outcomes at follow-up for comparisons of individual cognitive-behavioural therapy (CBT) plus treatment as usual (TAU) and TAU control

Study	Duration of treatment	Duration of follow-up	Positive symptoms	Negative symptoms	Depression	Social functioning	Relapse or readmission
Kuipers et al. (1997, 1998)	9 months	18 months	Yes				No
Tarrier et al. (1998, 1999, 2000)	10 weeks	12 months / 24 months	Yes / Yes	No / Yes			No
Durham et al. (2003)	9 months	3 months	Yes				
Rector et al. (2003)	6 months	6 months	No	Yes	No		
Turkington et al. (2002, 2006b)	6 sessions over an average of 20 weeks	12 months	No	Yes	No	No	Yes
Lewis et al. (2002); Tarrier et al. (2004)	5 weeks	18 months	No data on CBT vs TAU	No data on CBT vs TAU			No
Startup et al. (2004, 2005)	Up to 25 sessions over year	24 months	No	Yes		Yes	No
Garety et al. (in press)	9 months	24 months	No	No	Yes	No	No
Bach and Hayes (2002)	4 sessions	4 months	No				Yes
Gaudiano and Herbert (2006)	Length of inpatient stay.	4 months	No				No
Barrowclough et al. (2001); Haddock et al. (2003)	9 months	18 months	No	Yes		Yes	No
Jackson et al. (2005)	12 months	4 years					No

Table 16.3b Outcomes at follow-up for comparisons of individual cognitive-behavioural therapy (CBT) and an active psychological intervention

Study	Duration of treatment	Duration of follow-up	Positive symptoms	Negative symptoms	Depression	Social functioning	Relapse or readmission
Persistent positive/psychotic symptoms							
Sensky et al. (2000); Turkington et al. (2008)	9 months	18 months 5 years	Yes No	Yes Yes	Yes No		No
Valmaggia et al. (2005)	4 months?	10 months	No	No			No
Drury et al. (1996, 2000)	8 h per week during inpatient admission	5 years	No				No

Table 16.4a Evaluation of group cognitive-behavioural therapy (CBT) trials

Study	Patients	n	Groups	Assessment points	Blind assessment	Treatment length	End of CBT treatment effects				Relapse over trial
							Positive symptoms	Negative symptoms	Depression	Social functioning	
Group CBT trials (TAU comparison)											
Barrowclough et al. (2006)	Persistent positive symptoms of schizophrenia	113	1. Group CBT 2. Control	Baseline, 6 (post-treatment), 12 months	Yes	6 months	No	No	No Yes (hopelessness/ self-esteem)	No	No
Granholm et al. (2005)	Older patients (aged 42–74 years) with schizophrenia in the community	76	1. CBT and social skills training 2. Control	0, 3, 6 (post-treatment) months	Yes	6 months	No	No	No	Yes	
Group CBT trials (CBT and active psychological intervention comparison)											
Bechdolf et al. (2004)	Inpatients with schizophrenia	88	1. Group CBT 2. Group psycho-education	Baseline, 2 (post-treatment) 6 months	No	8 weeks	No (6 months)	No (6 months)			No Yes (rehospitalized at 6 months)

TAU, treatment as usual.

Table 16.4b Outcomes at follow-up for group cognitive-behavioural therapy (CBT) trials

Study	Length of treatment	Length of follow-up	Positive symptoms	Negative symptoms	Depression	Social functioning	Relapse over trial
Group CBT trials (CBT and TAU comparison)							
Granholm *et al.* (2005)	6 months	12 months	No	No	No	Yes	
Group CBT trials (active psychological intervention comparison)							
Bechdolf *et al.* (2004, 2005)	8 weeks	24 months	No	No			No

TAU, treatment as usual.

The results are less consistent for all the other sub-groups of studies. It is noteworthy that, when CBT for persistent positive symptoms is compared to an active psychological intervention (supportive counselling, befriending or psycho-education), although the number of studies is small, CBT does not show significantly greater effects than other treatment, at the end of treatment, on positive symptoms (see Table 16.2). However, most of these studies suggest that both groups show improvements and that there are trends to greater effects for CBT. In one study (Sensky *et al.* 2000), effects on 'schizophrenia change scores' were significantly greater for CBT than the befriending control at follow-up (see Table 16.3b). Some trials report enduring effects, up to two or even five years. However, in general, effects are less often significant at follow-up.

There is also, at present, some more limited and mixed evidence for benefits of CBT for positive symptoms in acute psychosis (Table 16.1). It is perhaps noteworthy that only one trial using blind assessment shows post-treatment improvements in positive symptoms in acute psychosis. Furthermore, this set of studies includes two of the larger and more methodologically robust studies (Lewis *et al.* 2002; Garety *et al.* in press). It is acknowledged in these latter studies that patients generally show a positive response to medication in the acute phase and thus demonstrating an additional effect of CBT in the context of this improving course is challenging.

The ACT studies (Bach and Hayes 2002; Gaudiano and Herbert 2006) are intriguing, in that both report some positive results in the context of very brief interventions in acute psychosis, lasting only three or four sessions. This is apparently very different from the effects of the other CBT studies. However, some points might elucidate these differences, before firm conclusions are drawn. Both trials had a very short total duration, including follow-up (four months), which is arguably too early for assessing relapse as a primary outcome, as reported by Bach and Hayes (2002). (Both studies nevertheless reported unusually high and non-significantly different rates of relapse within this short period, of 20% and 28% in the treatment and 40% and 45% in the control arm.) The trials were also less methodologically robust in that neither used blind assessment. The Gaudiano and Herbert (2006) study had an unusually high proportion of participants with major mood disorder (42%) rather than schizophrenia spectrum psychosis, and only eight of these (total $n = 40$) reported self-rated delusions, although all reported hallucinations. We therefore consider it premature to draw any conclusions from these studies about the effectiveness of ACT with persecutory delusions.

There is only a small number of group CBT treatment studies: Granholm *et al.* (2005), Barrowclough *et al.* (2006), and that of Bechdolf *et al.* (2004) employing an active intervention control (see Table 16.4a). Two of these studies have so far published an analysis of outcomes at follow-up (Bechdolf *et al.* 2005;

Granholm *et al.* 2005) (see Table 16.4b). There are therefore limited conclusions we can draw; however, the evidence so far does not support significant benefits for positive symptoms for CBT in a group format.

Meta-analyses and reviews

Recent reviews and meta-analyses are consistent with the evidence presented in the tables (Gould *et al.* 2001; Pilling *et al.* 2002; Tarrier and Wykes 2004; Zimmerman *et al.* 2005; Pfammater *et al.* 2006; Turkington *et al.* 2006a). They all conclude that there is good evidence that CBT is effective for the reduction in positive symptoms. Effect sizes are generally modest and are most consistent for persistent positive symptoms (for example, an effect size of 0.47 is cited by Pfammater *et al.* 2006 based on analysis of data from 12 trials for persistent positive symptoms). Zimmerman *et al.* (2005), in an analysis of 17 studies, report a mean effect size of 0.35 for positive symptoms. In contrast to the general conclusion of the reviews, Zimmerman *et al.* (2005), also conclude that effect sizes are larger for treatment in the acute episode compared to treatment in the 'chronic' condition, although this conclusion is only based on three studies in the acute episodes.

Gaudiano (2006) assessed the clinical significance of symptomatic improvement in response to CBT and also contrasted effects between comparison conditions. He concludes that reliable and clinically significant improvements in psychotic symptoms are demonstrated in RCTs of CBT. As seen in Table 16.2, he also notes that the clear advantage of CBT consistently demonstrated when the comparison condition is TAU is less unequivocal when CBT is compared to a credible alternative intervention. Gaudiano argues that supportive interventions appear also to be efficacious.

In summary, then, meta-analyses support our conclusion that individually delivered CBT is effective for persistent positive symptoms. We can extrapolate from these findings with reasonable confidence to conclude that CBT is effective for persistent persecutory delusions. The size of the effect is generally small–medium. However, although CBT appears to be somewhat more effective than other psychological treatments, the trials do not unequivocally demonstrate that CBT is the most effective approach and supportive approaches are likely also to be of benefit. CBT may also have beneficial effects for persecutory delusions in acute episodes and in other subgroups, but the data so far are not consistent with these populations.

Conclusions

In this descriptive review of CBT for psychosis, we have focused on symptom outcomes, particularly on positive symptoms. We conclude that CBT for psychosis, delivered individually, has small-to-moderate effects in improving positive symptoms, particularly when symptoms are persistent. The trials of CBT in acute psychosis are generally more recent, with larger and well-conducted studies, but demonstrate less positive evidence. Treatment for persecutory delusions in groups has, as yet, little evidential basis. Although we find CBT for psychosis to be effective for persistent positive symptoms, and by extension, for persecutory delusions, little is known about the mechanisms of change. We have used the term 'generic CBT for psychosis' since most trials reviewed here have used a broad-based approach to treatment, targeting a wide range of symptoms and potential mechanisms. In this context, it is not clear that CBT is more effective than alternative less structured therapies, such as supportive counselling.

We do consider that CBT is not a 'quasi-neuroleptic' with a sole purpose of reducing symptoms (Birchwood and Trower 2006). It has an equally important role to play in working with emotional distress and the reactions of person with psychosis to their experiences of psychosis and of the self. We have not reviewed such outcomes in detail, but note that a number of trials suggest some benefits in depression, emotional distress and social functioning; we support the view that these specific targets of treatment are important and should also be evaluated.

This research literature is new and is developing rapidly. It is less than 15 years since the first trials of CBT for psychosis were published. We are witnessing and recording here the early stages of innovation and development of a new treatment approach. It would have been considered, only two decades ago, to be a radical departure from the assumptions of the time about what works with psychosis. Further experimentation and development of CBT are clearly warranted, to build on the successes demonstrated and to improve on the outcomes. In this volume, many chapters report empirical evidence of psychological processes causally implicated in persecutory delusions. It is now possible to develop new CBT approaches, which use theoretically informed strategies, to attempt to change the hypothesized causal mechanisms and thereby produce beneficial outcomes. It is particularly timely to develop and test new forms of CBT for persecutory delusions.

References

Altman, D.G., Schulz, K.F., Moher, D. *et al.*; CONSORT GROUP (Consolidated Standards of Reporting Trials) (2001) The revised CONSORT statement for reporting randomized trials: explanation and elaboration. *Annals of Internal Medicine*, 134, 663–694.

Bach, P. and Hayes, S.C. (2002) The use of acceptance and commitment therapy to prevent the rehospitalisation of psychotic patients: a randomised controlled trial. *Journal of Consulting and Clinical Psychology*, 70, 1129–1139.

Barrowclough, C., Haddock, G., Tarrier, N. *et al.* (2001) Randomized controlled trial of motivational interviewing, cognitive behaviour therapy, and family intervention for patients with comorbid schizophrenia and substance use disorders. *American Journal of Psychiatry*, 158, 1706–1713.

Barrowclough, C., Haddock, G., Lobban, F. *et al.* (2006) Group cognitive-behavioural therapy for schizophrenia. Randomised controlled trial. *British Journal of Psychiatry*, 189, 527–532.

Bechdolf, A., Knost, B., Kunterman, C. *et al.* (2004) A randomized comparison of group congitive behavioural therapy and group psycho-education in patients with schizophrenia. *Acta Psychiatrica Scandinavica*, 110, 21–28.

Bechdolf, A., Kohn, D., Knost, B., Pukrop, R. and Klosterkotter, J. (2005) A randomized comparison of group cognitive-behavioural therapy and group psycho-education in acute patients with schizophrenia: outcome at 24 months. *Acta Psychiatrica Scandinavica*, 112, 173–179.

Beck, A.T. (1952) Successful outpatient psychotherapy of a chronic schizophrenic with a delusion based on borrowed guilt. *Psychiatry*, 15, 305–312.

Bentall, R.P. (1990) The illusion of reality: a review and integration of psychological research on hallucinations. *Psychology Bulletin*, 107, 82–95.

Birchwood, M. and Trower, P. (2006) The future of cognitive behavioural therapy for psychosis: not a quasi-neuroleptic. *British Journal of Psychiatry*, 188, 107–108.

Cather, C., Penn, D., Otto, M.W., Yovel, I., Mueser, K.T. and Goff, D.C. (2005) A pilot study of functional cognitive-behavioural therapy (fCBT) for schizophrenia. *Schizophrenia Research*, 74, 201–209.

Chadwick, P.D. and Lowe, C.F. (1990) Measurement and modification of delusional beliefs. *Journal of Consulting Clinical Psychology*, 58, 225–232.

Chadwick, P.D.J., Birchwood, M. and Trower, P. (1996) *Cognitive Therapy for Delusions, Voices and Paranoia*. New York: Wiley.

Curson, D.A., Patel, M., Liddle, P.F. and Barnes, T.R. (1988) Psychiatric morbidity of a long stay hospital population with chronic schizophrenia and implications for future community care. *British Medical Journal*. 297, 819–822.

Drury, V., Birchwood, M., Cochrane, R. and MacMillan, F. (1996) Cognitive therapy and recovery from acute psychosis: a controlled trial—I. Impact on psychotic symptoms. *British Journal of Psychiatry*, 169, 593–601.

Drury, V., Birchwood, M. and Cochrane, R. (2000) Cognitive therapy and recovery from acute psychosis: a controlled trial—five-year follow-up. *British Journal of Psychiatry*, 177, 8–14.

Durham, R.C., Guthrie, M., Morton, V. *et al.* (2003) Tayside–Fife clinical trial of cognitive behavioural therapy for medication-resistant psychotic symptoms. *British Journal of Psychiatry*, 182, 303–311.

Fowler, D. and Morley, S. (1989) The cognitive behavioural treatment of hallucinations and delusions: a preliminary study. *Behavioural Psychotherapy*, 17, 267–282.

Fowler, D., Garety, P. and Kuipers, E. (1995) *Cognitive Behaviour Therapy for Psychosis: Theory and Practice*. Wiley, New York.

Freeman, D. (2007) Suspicious minds: the psychology of persecutory delusions. *Clinical Psychology Reviews*, 27, 425–457.

Garety, P., Kuipers, E., Fowler, D., Chamberlain. and Dunn, G. (1994) Cognitive behavioural therapy for drug-resistant psychosis. *British Journal of Medical Psychology*, 67, 259–271.

Garety, P.A., Fowler, D. and Kuipers, E. (2000) Cognitive-behavioural therapy for medication-resistant symptoms. *Schizophrenia Bulletin*, 26, 73–86.

Garety, P.A., Fowler, D.G., Freeman, D., Bebbington, P., Dunn, G. and Kuipers, E. (in press) A randomised controlled trial of cognitive behavioural therapy and family intervention for the prevention of relapse and reduction of symptoms in psychosis. *British Journal of Psychiatry*.

Gaudiano, B.A. (2006) Is symptomatic improvement in clinical trials of cognitive-behavioral therapy for psychosis clinically significant? *Journal of Psychiatric Practice*, 12, 11–23.

Gaudiano, B.A. and Herbert, J.D. (2006) Acute treatment of inpatients with psychotic symptoms using acceptance and commitment therapy: pilot results. *Behaviour Research and Therapy*, 44, 415–437.

Geddes, J., Freemantle, N., Harrison, P. and Bebbington, P. (2000) Atypical anti-psychotics in the treatment of schizophrenia: systematic overview and meta-regression analysis. *British Medical Journal*, 321, 1371–1376.

Gould, R.A., Mueser, K.T., Bolton, E., Mays, V. and Goff, D. (2001) Cognitive therapy for psychosis in schizophrenia: an effect size analysis. *Schizophrenia Research*, 48, 335–342.

Granholm, E., McQuaid, J.R., McClure, F.S. *et al.* (2005) A randomized controlled trial of cognitive behavioural social skills training for middle-aged and older outpatients with chronic schizophrenia. *American Journal of Psychiatry*, 162, 520–529.

Gumley, A., O'Grady, M., McNay, L., Reilly, J., Power, K. and Norrie, J. (2003) Early intervention for relapse in schizophrenia: results of a 12-month randomized controlled trial of cognitive behavioural therapy. *Psychological Medicine*, 33, 419–431.

Haddock, G., Tarrier, N., Morrison, A.P., Hopkins, R., Drake, R. and Lewis, S. (1999a) A pilot study evaluating the effectiveness of individual inpatient cognitive behavioural therapy in early psychosis. *Social Psychiatry and Psychiatric Epidemiology*, 34, 254–258.

Haddock, G., McCarron, J., Tarrier, N. and Faragher, E.B. (1999b) Scales to measure dimensions of hallucinations and delusions: the psychotic symptom rating scales (PSYRATS) *Psychological Medicine*, 29, 879–889.

Haddock, G., Barrowclough, C., Tarrier, N. *et al.* (2003) Cognitive behavioural therapy and motivational intervention for schizophrenia and substance misuse. *British Journal of Psychiatry*, 183, 418–426.

Hayes, S.C. (2004) Acceptance and commitment therapy, relational frame theory, and the third wave of behaviour therapy. *Behavior Therapy*, 35, 639–665.

Hemsley, D.R. and Garety, P.A. (1986) Formation and maintenance of delusions: a Bayesian analysis. *British Journal of Psychiatry*, 149, 51–56.

Jackson, H., McGorry, P., Edwards, J. *et al.* (2005) A controlled trial of cognitively oriented psychotherapy for early psychosis (COPE) with four year follow up re-admission data. *Psychological Medicine*, 35, 1295–1306.

Jenner, J.A., Nienhuis, F.J., Wiersma, D. and van de Willige, G. (2004) Hallucination focused integrative treatment: a randomized controlled trial. *Schizophrenia Bulletin*, 30, 133–145.

Jolley, S. Garety, P.A., Craig, T., Dunn, G. White, J and Aitken, M. (2003) CBT for early psychosis: a pilot study. *British Journal of Behavioural and Cognitive Psychotherapy*, 31, 474–478.

Kay, S.R., Opler, L.A. and Lindenmayer, J.P. (1989) The positive and negative syndrome scale (PANSS): Rationale and standardization. *British Journal of Psychiatry*, 155, 59–65.

Kingdon, D. and Turkington, D. (1994) *Cognitive Behavioral Therapy of Schizophrenia.* New York: Guilford Press.

Kingdon, D.G. and Turkington, D. (1991) The use of cognitive behaviour therapy with a normalizing rationale in schizophrenia. *Journal of Nervous and Mental Disease,* 179, 207–211

Kuipers, E., Garety, P.A., Fowler, D. *et al.* (1997) The London–East Anglia randomised controlled trial of cognitive-behaviour therapy for psychosis. I: Effects of the treatment phase. *British Journal of Psychiatry,* 171, 319–327.

Kuipers, E., Fowler, D., Garety, P. *et al.* (1998) London–East Anglia randomised controlled trial of cognitive-behavioural therapy for psychosis. III: Follow-up and economic evaluation at 18 months. *British Journal of Psychiatry,* 173, 61–68.

Lewis, S., Tarrier, N., Haddock, G. *et al.* (2002) Randomised controlled trial of cognitive behavioural therapy in early schizophrenia: acute phase outcomes. *British Journal of Psychiatry,* 181, S91–97.

Morrison, A.P., French, P., Walford, L. *et al.* (2004) Cognitive therapy for the prevention of psychosis in people at ultra-high risk: randomized controlled trial. *British Journal of Psychiatry,* 185, 291–297.

Overall, J. and Gorham, D. (1967) Brief Psychiatric Rating Scale. *Psychological Reports,* 10, 799–812.

Pfammater, M., Junghan, U.M. and Brenner, H.D. (2006) Efficacy of psychological therapy in schizophrenia: conclusions from meta-analyses. *Schizophrenia Bulletin,* 32, S64–80.

Pilling, S., Bebbington, P., Kuipers, E. *et al.* (2002) Psychological treatments in schizophrenia: I. Meta-analysis of family intervention and cognitive behaviour therapy. *Psychological Medicine,* 32, 763–782.

Pinto, A., La Pia, S., Mannella, R., Domenico, G. and DeSimone, L. (1999) Cognitive behavioural therapy and clozapine for clients with treatment-refractory schizophrenia. *Psychiatric Services,* 50, 901–904.

Rector, N.A., Seeman, M.V. and Segal, Z.V. (2003) Cognitive therapy for schizophrenia: a preliminary randomized controlled trial. *Schizophrenia Research,* 63, 1–11.

Sensky, T., Turkington, D., Kingdon, D. *et al.* (2000) A randomized controlled trial of cognitive behavioural therapy for persistent symptoms in schizophrenia resistant to medication. *Archives of General Psychiatry,* 57, 165–172.

Startup, M., Jackson, M.C. and Bendix, S. (2004) North Wales randomized controlled trial of cognitive behaviour therapy for acute schizophrenia spectrum disorders: outcomes at 6 and 12 months. *Psychological Medicine,* 34, 413–422.

Startup, M., Jackson, M.C., Evans, K.E. and Bendix, S. (2005) North Wales randomized controlled trial of cognitive behaviour therapy for acute schizophrenia spectrum disorders: two-year follow-up and economic evaluation. *Psychological Medicine,* 35, 1307–1316.

Tarrier, N. and Wykes, T. (2004) Is there evidence that cognitive behaviour therapy is an effective treatment for schizophrenia? A cautious or cautionary tale? *Behaviour Research and Therapy,* 42, 1377–1401.

Tarrier, N., Beckett, R., Harwood, S., Baker, A., Yusupoff, L. and Ugarteburu, I. (1993) A trial of two cognitive behavioural methods of treating drug-resistant residual psychotic symptoms in schizophrenic patients: I. Outcome. *British Journal of Psychiatry,* 162, 524–532.

Tarrier, N., Yusupoff, L., Kinney, C. *et al.* (1998) Randomized controlled trial of intensive cognitive behaviour therapy for patients with chronic schizophrenia. *British Medical Journal*, 317, 303–307.

Tarrier, N., Wittkowski, A., Kinney, C., McCarthy, E., Morris, J. and Humphreys, L. (1999) Durability of the effects of cognitive behavioural therapy in the treatment of chronic schizophrenia: 12 month follow-up. *British Journal of Psychiatry*, 174, 500–504.

Tarrier, N., Kinney, C., McCarthy, E., Humphreys, L. and Wittkowski, A. (2000) Two year follow-up of cognitive behavioural therapy and supportive counselling in the treatment of persistent symptoms in chronic schizophrenia. *Journal of Consulting and Clinical Psychology*, 68, 917–922.

Tarrier, N., Lewis, S., Haddock, G. *et al.* (2004) Cognitive-behavioural therapy in first-episode and early schizophrenia—18-month follow-up of a randomised controlled trial. *British Journal of Psychiatry*, 184, 231–239.

Trower, P., Birchwood, M., Meaden, A., Byrne, S., Nelson, A. and Ross, K. (2004) Cognitive therapy for command hallucinations: randomized controlled trial. *British Journal of Psychiatry*, 184, 312–320.

Turkington, D., Kingdon, D. and Turner, T. (2002) Effectiveness of a brief cognitive behavioural therapy intervention in the treatment of schizophrenia. *British Journal of Psychiatry*, 180, 523–527.

Turkington, D., Kingdon, D. and Weiden, P.J. (2006a) Cognitive behaviour therapy for schizophrenia. *American Journal of Psychiatry*, 163, 365–373.

Turkington, D., Kingdon, D., Rathod, S., Hammond, K., Pelton, J. and Mehta, R. (2006b) Outcomes of an effectiveness trial of cognitive-behavioural intervention by mental health nurses in schizophrenia. *British Journal of Psychiatry*, 189, 36–40.

Turkington, D., Sensky, T., Scott, J. *et al.* (2008) A randomized controlled trial of cognitive behaviour therapy for persistent symptoms in schizophrenia: a five year follow-up. *Schizophrenia Research*, 98, 1–17.

Valmaggia, L.R., van der Gaag, M., Tarrier, N., Pignenborg, M. and Slooff, C.F. (2005) Cognitive behavioural therapy for refractory psychotic symptoms of schizophrenia resistant to atypical antipsychotic medication. Randomised controlled trial. *British Journal of Psychiatry*, 186, 324–330.

Wykes, T., Parr, A.M. and Landau, S. (1999) Group treatment of auditory hallucinations. Exploratory study of effectiveness. *British Journal of Psychiatry*, 175, 180–185.

Zimmerman, G., Favrod, J., Trieu, V.H. and Pomini, V. (2005) The effect of cognitive behavioural treatment on the positive symptoms of schizophrenia spectrum disorders: a meta-analysis. *Schizophrenia Research*, 77, 1–9.

Chapter 17

Family intervention in psychosis: working with persecutory delusions

Juliana Onwumere, Ben Smith, and Elizabeth Kuipers

The most likely thing to trigger (my paranoia) is a comment or question that could have more than one meaning, or at least that's how it seems at the time. It can be a comment that feels critical and that I dwell on afterwards. These comments are usually from people I know well, especially family.

Karl Murphy (2004)

Introduction

This chapter highlights issues in providing family interventions (FIs) to families where one individual has persecutory beliefs, particularly in relation to another family member. It describes the main components of evidence-based FIs in psychosis, and particularly emphasises some of the features of FI that we have found to be relevant for patients with paranoid presentations.

Individuals with psychosis tend to have smaller social networks; these are more likely to comprise family members and dependant relationships (informal carers) (Macdonald *et al.* 2000; Evert *et al.* 2003; Elisha *et al.* 2006). A large majority live with and/or maintain close contact with informal carers (e.g. Thornicroft *et al.* 2004). Informal carers, who are likely to be the mothers or partners of patients, play an important role in promoting recovery and maintaining the well-being of individuals with psychosis (e.g. Czuchta and McCay 2001; Oyebode 2003; Jeppesen *et al.* 2005).

Caregiving, however, can have a negative impact on a carer's physical and emotional well-being (Kuipers and Bebbington 2005). High rates of emotional disturbance (e.g. anxiety and depression symptoms) are commonly found in carers (e.g. Harvey *et al.* 2001; Singleton *et al.* 2002; Ukpong 2006). Further, carers experience high levels of burnout (e.g. emotional exhaustion), at similar levels to those reported in psychiatric nurses (Angermeyer *et al.* 2006). Individuals with psychosis are vulnerable to the type of care they receive (Oyebode 2003). Highly distressed and burned-out carers may be unable to provide care and engage in adaptive forms of coping (Perlick *et al.* 2001; Quinn *et al.* 2003; Moller-Leimkuhler 2005). In turn, this is likely to have negative implications for client outcomes (Vitaliano *et al.* 2003).

Higher levels of relapse are found among individuals with psychosis living with or in close contact with carers with high levels of expressed emotion (EE); these are carers who report above-threshold levels of critical and/or hostile attitudes towards the individual with psychosis and/or engage in high levels of emotionally over-involved behaviours (Bebbington and Kuipers 1994; Butzlaff and Hooley 1998; King and Dixon 1999). Higher levels of carer burden and distress are associated with high EE (Shimodera *et al.* 2000; Raune *et al.* 2004). Further, highly critical and/or hostile carers are more inclined to attribute the clients' symptoms and illness-related behaviour (e.g. social withdrawal, hostility) to internal causes (i.e. to the individual and their personality rather than to the illness). They are also more likely to perceive the individual with psychosis as being able to control their illness (Hooley and Campbell 2002; Barrowclough and Hooley 2003).

Caregiving and symptoms of psychosis

Psychosis symptoms are associated with carer burden; carers report higher levels of burden for individuals with psychosis who are more symptomatic (Wolthaus *et al.* 2002; Lowyck *et al.* 2004; Roick *et al.* 2006). Debate continues over which particular symptom groups prove most burdensome. Negative symptoms have traditionally been found to be related to burden (Dyck *et al.* 1999; Ukpong 2006); however, positive symptoms (e.g. delusions) have also been associated with higher burden levels (e.g. Magliano *et al.* 1998; Wolthaus *et al.* 2002). Positive symptoms have also been associated with higher rates of critical comments from carers (e.g. Shimodera *et al.* 1998).

Delusions, particularly those defined as persecutory, form a core feature of schizophrenia symptomatology (Jaspers 1963). Their impact on individuals' behaviour and their social cognition has been well-documented (e.g. Freeman *et al.* 2002, 2006; Freeman and Garety 2006). To date, most authors have focused on the theoretical frameworks (e.g. perceptual anomalies or reasoning biases) purported to underpin the development and/or maintenance of persecutory delusions within clinical (e.g. Garety and Freeman 1999; Bentall *et al.* 2001; Garety *et al.* 2005) and non-clinical populations (Freeman *et al.* 2003, 2005a,b). However, despite the large numbers of patients in regular contact with informal carers, the specific impact of persecutory delusions within a family setting, and in the context of a caregiving relationship, has not been subjected to the same level of critical review (Taylor 2006). So far, investigations have been predominately limited to descriptive accounts (e.g. Ulzen and Carpenter 1997) or to studies reporting on the variability in levels of carer burden in response to the degree and/or severity of client symptoms (e.g. Lauber *et al.* 2003). However, we do know that, first, as part of their persecutory delusions, many individuals with psychosis live with an ongoing belief that their persecutor is going to kill them or will force them to kill others either imminently (i.e. within seven days), or within a few weeks (e.g. Startup *et al.* 2003; Green *et al.* 2006). Second, many individuals with psychosis can specifically identify their persecutor(s), of which many are personally known to them (e.g. friends and family) (e.g. Green *et al.* 2006; Stompe *et al.* 1999). Third, high levels of distress are known to accompany persecutory beliefs, with some early indications that distress levels may be higher when the identity of the persecutor is personally known (e.g. Freeman *et al.* 2001; Green *et al.* 2006).

Although individuals with psychosis do not necessarily universally present a risk of violence to others (Taylor and Gunn 1999; Walsh *et al.* 2001), when compared to the general population, there are sub-groups who have a higher risk of committing a violent act (Arseneault *et al.* 2000; Brennan *et al.* 2000). Where such acts are committed, members of the clients' immediate social network (e.g. friends and family members) are more likely to be the victims of serious violence compared to all other groups (e.g. strangers) (Johnston and Taylor 2003; Joyal *et al.* 2004; Nielssen *et al.* 2007). This is particularly the case for mothers living with individuals with psychosis (Estroff *et al.* 1998; Nordstrom and Kullgren 2003a,b). Persecutory delusions are one of the symptom groups most strongly associated with the execution of violent acts (e.g. Arsenault *et al.* 2000; Nordstrom *et al.* 2006).

Family intervention in psychosis

Family interventions in psychosis have a strong evidence base (see Pilling *et al.* 2002; Pharoah *et al.* 2006); they are known to reduce significantly rates of patient relapse and readmission (e.g. Dixon *et al.* 2000; Bustillo *et al.* 2001; Pilling *et al.* 2002). They also have a positive impact on carer burden (e.g. Cuijpers 1999; Pilling *et al.* 2002); social functioning in patients (e.g. Barrowclough and Tarrier 1990; Leff *et al.* 1990), and medication non-adherence (e.g. Mari and Striener 1994; Pilling *et al.* 2002). Their effectiveness within routine clinical services has also been demonstrated (e.g. Barrowclough *et al.* 1999; Kelly and Newstead 2004; Magliano *et al.* 2006).

Due to their proven efficacy, evidence-based FI in psychosis is currently included within UK and US clinical treatment recommendations for individuals with schizophrenia (Lehman and Steinwachs 1998; National Institute for Clinical Excellence (NICE) 2003; American Psychiatric Association 2004; Lehman *et al.* 2004). The formats of FIs can vary, and different treatment manuals are available (e.g. Falloon *et al.* 1984; Barrowclough and Tarrier 1992; Kuipers *et al.* 2002).

Evidence-based FIs have been designed to minimize the negative impact of clients' symptoms on the carer and reduce the risk of client relapse. These objectives are met, initially, by attempts to increase a carer's understanding and tolerance of psychosis symptoms and their sequelae. Particular attention is often given to facilitating a carer's cognitive reappraisal of symptoms; to help carers understand that the client's symptoms form part of a recognizable illness process.

Within the Kuipers *et al.* (2002) treatment manual, central importance is given to the task of defusing the large range of difficult emotions that psychosis can often engender in families (e.g. feelings of anger and fear). Similarly, improving communication between carer and the individual with psychosis (especially about the subjective experience of symptoms), negotiated problem solving, and improving adaptive styles of coping, all form integral parts of FIs.

Consistent with other evidence-based manuals (e.g. Falloon *et al.* 1984; Barrowclough and Tarrier 1992), Kuipers *et al.* (2002) draws upon a stress-vulnerability framework for understanding the development of psychosis in clients and their individual risk of future relapse. Intervention sessions are therefore aimed at current problems that are affecting the client and their carer and which increase the client's vulnerability to relapse. The intervention is based upon a positive view of individuals with psychosis and their carers; the strengths of the family unit are explicitly recognized and family members are mobilized as supportive therapeutic allies.

The Kuipers *et al.* (2002) manual recommends the use of two trained family workers rather than a single practitioner to deliver the intervention. The intervention sessions are often held fortnightly and are normally conducted within the family home with the individual with psychosis and carer(s) both present. As part of the overall structure of the sessions, the therapists always try to ensure that only one family member speaks at a time and that each family member is given equal talking time.

Although the content of FI will vary in line with the specific needs of the family, psycho-education, managing difficult emotions (e.g. anger, frustration) and enhancing communication skills all tend to form very prominent features of interventions with families where the identified client experiences persecutory delusions. In the next half of the chapter, we present FIs that are drawn from two cases in order to illustrate these particular features. The case of Peter and Laura was selected to illustrate the use of psycho-education techniques whilst the case of Heather and June illustrates the use of enhancing communication. Both cases involve the management of difficult emotions.

Case example 1: Peter and Laura

In our clinical experience, it is often helpful to start FI with some psycho-education sessions and this is what happens in the case of Peter and Laura. The widespread availability of the Internet and the popularity of mental health campaign groups such as Rethink (formerly known as the National Schizophrenia Fellowship) has meant that many carers now have some knowledge about psychosis. However, most say they would like an opportunity to learn more.

In FI, psycho-education sessions are individualized (i.e. based upon the clients' personal experiences and symptoms) and are used as a tool to disentangle some of the folklore that surrounds psychosis (e.g. the client is being lazy versus the client is affected by considerable negative symptoms and depression). Carers are helped to understand that the clients' symptoms are distressing and genuine rather than deliberate attempts to upset and/or harass them. The therapists encourage carers to objectify the client's symptoms and understand their behaviour in a more benign manner. The psycho-education component of FI can serve as an excellent opportunity for carers to learn more about the clients' subjective experience of their illness (e.g. content of their beliefs or hallucinations), with the aim of working towards more adaptive management responses.

Psycho-education sessions are designed to be interactive rather than didactic; all family members are encouraged to provide their own perspective and reflect, in a respectful manner, on the information they receive from the therapists and from each other. An information booklet, specifically designed for use with individuals with psychosis *and* carers, is used. These booklets are comprehensive and cover a broad range of issues relating to psychosis, including diagnosis, symptoms, causal theories, treatments and recovery, relapse prevention, and stress management for carers.

Peter, a 27-year-old man, had a four-year history of paranoid schizophrenia. He believed that he was being targeted by unknown 'others', who were controlled by 'Satan'. Satan frequently informed Peter, primarily via auditory hallucinations, that he was going to inflict unimaginable harm on him on earth and in the 'spirit' world. Peter expected to be attacked at any moment. He believed that Satan was targeting him because of previous 'minor' misdemeanors that he had committed during his adolescence.

Peter had recently moved from his family home, which he had shared with his mother and elder brother, into supported housing nearby. He tended to visit his mother on an almost daily basis and sleep over at weekends. Peter preferred to spend his time at the family home where he felt 'safer' from attack. Laura (Peter's mother) was a very busy woman, who also provided significant caregiving input to an elderly infirm relative who lived nearby.

At the start of our intervention, Laura was rated as low EE on the Camberwell Family Interview (Vaughn and Leff 1976). However, on measures of perceived carer criticism, the results suggested that Peter perceived his mother as being highly critical towards him.

At the start of our contact with the family, Peter had recently experienced an exacerbation in his beliefs following an extended period in which he had decided to cut down (or stop) his medication. The sessions were attended by Peter and his mother. Laura was keen to understand more about her son's difficulties but informed the two therapists that she already knew a considerable amount about psychosis because it had been 'in the family in the past'. She was also keen to report that Peter was not currently experiencing any of the main symptom disturbances that had led to his most recent relapse. It was also one of Peter's aims for the intervention to talk about some of his experiences and 'educate' his mother *and* the therapists about his struggles.

Initially, however, Peter was reluctant to offer any details about his experiences beyond reporting that everything was 'okay' or that he had had problems 'in the past but not now'. This is a common presentation within family meetings and can be alleviated by improving engagement. Thus, the therapists spent time trying to normalize Peter's hesitance and emphasizing that they wanted to work towards finding a way that he could be better supported both now and in the future. As the sessions progressed, he began to report, in mini-disclosures, that he continued to experience ongoing distressing thoughts about being persecuted by unknown others. Moreover, he believed that his mother was Satan; a fact that was previously unknown to his mother, the therapists and his clinical team. Peter said that there were times when he was not always totally convinced that his mother was Satan or that she was willingly orchestrating the campaign to persecute him. The therapists and Laura learnt that Peter liked to spend a lot of time in the family home, in the company of his mother, as part of an attempt to monitor her and her behaviour towards him. Peter disclosed that he found it helpful to talk about his experiences as part of the sessions, although he was unable to specify in what way.

Initial sessions which focused on psycho-education also involved work around the emotional and risk issues that followed Peter's disclosure. For example, Laura understandably expressed feelings of shock and apprehension because she thought that she knew 'almost everything' about Peter's illness and was surprised that he had kept these extremely disturbing thoughts to himself. The extent of his beliefs and their persistence also worried her: 'I really thought that he was getting better'. This prompted further discussions about Peter's irritability towards his mother during previous relapses. Laura openly wondered whether this related to his belief about her being Satan. Peter confirmed that it was. Laura went on to recall events from one of Peter's earlier episodes whereby she had woken up in the middle of the night to find Peter standing at the foot of her bed holding a knife. She reported that at the time, she knew Peter 'wasn't himself', thus she was unable to feel any anger towards him.

With some facilitation from the therapists, Laura was able to share with Peter her belief that his irritability was understandable given the context of his beliefs. She also expressed considerable sadness and concern that hitherto, he had not shared his experiences with her despite their close relationship and her willingness to listen. The therapists explicitly praised Peter for his candidness and courage in sharing his beliefs, and in the way that he had coped with his experiences for a long time whilst maintaining a close relationship with his mother.

Based on the accounts of Peter's previous episodes, the therapists were able to ascertain, and subsequently reflect with Peter and Laura, that the strength of his beliefs tended to fluctuate, particularly in relation to his low mood. The sessions led to work on issues around relapse prevention. This focused on Laura's response to signs of low mood and/or increased irritability in Peter. During previous episodes, Laura had tended to have minimal contact with the clinical team and refrained from involving them until she felt she had no other choice. Peter and Laura were encouraged to consider (i.e. problem solve) alternative response strategies that could be implemented around times of increased distress and possible relapse: a more productive crisis response. Both parties liked the straightforward strategy whereby Laura, following her observations of Peter's altered mood, would ask his community psychiatric nurse to contact him.

Based on Peter's need to monitor his mother, the therapists worked with the family and subsequently with the clinical team on issues related to Peter's daily structure. Both Laura and Peter were encouraged to see the potential benefits of Peter having something enjoyable to do, at least 'once' during the day, and preferably something that was able to take Peter away from the family home. Peter and Laura agreed to work with the team occupational therapist and social recovery worker to reconsider the issue of daytime activities.

The psycho-education sessions also led to an updated risk assessment for Peter.

Post intervention, Laura's low EE rating remained unchanged; there was also a small reduction in the levels of criticism that Peter perceived from his mother and in his anxiety symptoms.

Case example 2: Heather and June

Communication, both in terms of content and quality, is often negatively affected by clients' symptoms, as illustrated by the case of Heather and June. For example, in clients with negative symptoms, communication may be limited. In contrast, clients with paranoid beliefs, particularly those which relate to a close relative, might frequently question the relative about their behaviour. In turn, this can precipitate interpersonal conflict and distress. Although it is understandable, clinical experience suggests that entering into arguments and/or debates with clients about the content of their beliefs is often unhelpful to carers and clients alike, due to clients with strong beliefs having limited alternatives available (Freeman *et al.* 2004).

Consequently, facilitating optimal levels of communication between the individual with psychosis and their carers is an important and ongoing activity during FI sessions. Primarily, it aims to minimize the degree of negative exchanges through encouraging carers and clients to speak directly to each other (it is much easier to deliver negative comments when talking about a person instead of directly to a person). It encourages family members to specify the actual problem rather than being vague or generalizing an issue (e.g. compare: 'he is so lazy' with 'it upsets me that John cannot make me a cup of tea once or twice a week'). Improving communication also involves helping individuals with psychosis and carers report on the personal impact of negative comments; something that is often overlooked in the middle of an emotionally charged and difficult relationship.

Heather, aged 26 years, had an 18-month history of schizophrenia and lived at home with her mother and younger sister (aged 15 years). Heather believed that her biological father and his partner were involved in a covert plot to physically harm and publicly humiliate her. She was made aware of these machinations through the loud and continuous voices that she heard. Heather was considerably distressed by the overall experience and tended to oscillate between attempts at confronting her father in a verbally aggressive manner (i.e. via phone, in writing, or on some occasions in person) or by repeatedly questioning her mother about why the plotting was occurring and what she knew of it. On three previous occasions, Heather had taken an overdose of analgesics when she reported feeling acutely distressed and hopeless about her ability to defend herself against the plot.

June (Heather's mother) worked as a part-time healthcare worker in a nursing home. She had been divorced from Heather's father for approximately ten years. Her relationship with her daughter was becoming increasingly characterized by frequent arguments and hostility. June found it very difficult to cope with Heather's behaviour, particularly her frequent accusations about her biological father and the regular outbursts towards him. She also found it difficult to understand why Heather was unable to accept her explanation (or those from anyone else in the family) that 'there was no plot against her'. June said that she had told her daughter a 'thousand times' that no plot existed and Heather's 'refusal' to accept her explanation frequently led to their arguments. At the start of the intervention June was worried because she felt that she was unable to cope with any further stresses at home. She reported moderate levels of burden, whilst Heather reported mild levels of anxiety symptoms.

Initially, as part of the focus on psycho-education, Heather was able to share with her mother her ongoing sense of foreboding and how vulnerable she felt to being harmed. With some encouragement from the therapists, Heather explained to her mother that her style of responding to her questions left her feeling more distressed. June (mother) was asked to listen and comment. June became visibly upset whilst acknowledging the distress that her daughter was experiencing. She reported that she was finding the 'entire' experience really difficult to cope with on her own and that there was no one available to support her. She revealed that she was having problems at work and was constantly worried about the impact of Heather's difficulties on her youngest daughter. June said that she found it hard to be confronted with the same question from Heather, particularly from the moment she arrived home from work or was about to prepare the evening meal. June reported that her greatest fears related to Heather getting herself into trouble with her father, or harming herself when the distress became overwhelming.

Heather appeared to be somewhat shocked by her mother's response. She said that she was unaware that her mother was struggling and spontaneously offered words of sympathy and support. The therapists chose to focus on the warmth between Heather and June and tried to use what seemed to be examples of genuine concern for each other as the rationale to address the issue of their frequent arguments (i.e. facilitating communication). This was a way of both defusing the upset and of dealing with the concern that had led to it, but in a positive way (i.e. through positively reframing their behaviour).

Heather and June were encouraged to think about alternative strategies for coping with Heather's questions and their timing. It was collaboratively agreed that June would allow her daughter to ask the question uninterrupted and would reply, in a clear, gentle and reassuring tone, that she was not aware of any plot to harm her and was not involved in any plot. Their coping strategy represented a 'new way of doing things' and due to the expectation that they would experience a few difficulties, June and Heather were given 'homework' to practice the new strategy and report back on how it felt. Within sessions, and through therapists' modelling, the therapists worked with June on trying to develop a more gentle (or empathic) tone in her responses to Heather's questions rather than her usual style, which tended to be more critical and harsh in tone.

The therapists also encouraged the family to problem solve the issue about the timing of Heather's questions, which appeared to be at their peak when June arrived home from work and was pressed for time when trying to prepare the evening meal. Both Heather and June agreed that when Heather was engaged in a neutral activity (e.g. household chores, brisk walk) she appeared to be less preoccupied with the voices and the ongoing issue of the plot. Thus, in an attempt to introduce some additional focal points in their interactions, it was agreed that Heather would help her mother prepare the family meals and on two occasions during the week she would take responsibility for preparing the family meal before her mother arrived back from work. The therapists also worked with the clinical team on the issue of trying to find a subsidized fitness club that Heather could access on a regular basis, which could form part of her daily schedule of activities.

Given the stress that she was under, the therapists were keen to encourage June to address her own needs for emotional and social support through attendance at a local carers' support group (which was also open to her youngest daughter to attend). June was happy for the therapists to make a referral to the carer link worker within the clinical team. This can often be interpreted as the therapists giving 'permission' to carers to address their own needs, a task that is frequently overlooked by many carers.

Post intervention, June's reported levels of burden had decreased. Although Heather continued to remain symptomatic, her anxiety symptoms had reduced to minimal levels. Heather and June both reported an improvement in their relationship; June stated that they had begun to 'talk' more, and their conversations were not limited to Heather's distressing beliefs.

Conclusion

Persecutory beliefs are distressing for individuals with psychosis and for those in their social network. Evidence-based FIs can play a central role in helping to reduce interpersonal difficulties that often arise directly from the delusional beliefs and indirectly from their negative sequelae. Their positive contributions to patient and carer functioning in psychosis are widely acknowledged.

Suggested further reading and key resources

Jones, S. and Hayward, P. (2004) *Coping with Schizophrenia: A Guide for Patients, Families and Caregivers*. London: Oneworld Publications.

Kuipers, E. and Bebbington, P. (2005) *Living with Mental Illness: A Book for Relatives and Friends*, 3rd edn. London: Souvenir Press.

Kuipers, E., Leff, J. and Lam, D. (2002) *Family Work for Schizophrenia. A Practical Guide*, 2nd edn. London: Gaskell Press.

Psycho-education leaflet (requests to first author).

www.rethink.org

www.mentalhealthcare.org.uk

www.carersonline.org.uk

www.understandingpsychosis.com

References

American Psychiatric Association (2004) Practice guideline for the treatment of patients with schizophrenia. *American Journal of Psychiatry*, 161 (Suppl. 2), 1–56.

Angermeyer, M.C., Bull, N., Bernert, S., Dietrich, S. and Kopf, A. (2006) Burnout of caregivers: a comparison between partners of psychiatric patients and nurses. *Archives of Psychiatric Nursing*, 20, 158–165.

Arseneault, L., Moffitt, T.E., Caspi, A., Taylor, P.J. and Silva, P.A. (2000) Mental disorders and violence in a total birth cohort: results from the Dunedin study. *Archives of General Psychiatry*, 57, 979–986.

Barrowclough, C. and Hooley, J.M. (2003) Attributions and expressed emotion: a review. *Clinical Psychology Review*, 23, 849–880.

Barrowclough, C. and Tarrier, N. (1990) Social functioning in schizophrenic patients: 1. The effects of expressed emotion and family intervention. *Social Psychiatry and Psychiatric Epidemiology*, 25, 125–129.

Barrowclough, C. and Tarrier, N. (1992) *Families of Schizophrenic Patients: Cognitive Behavioural Intervention*. Cheltenham: Stanley Thornes.

Barrowclough, C., Tarrier, N., Lewis, S. *et al.* (1999) Randomised controlled effectiveness trial of a needs-based psychosocial intervention service for carers of people with schizophrenia. *British Journal of Psychiatry*, 174, 505–511.

Bebbington, P. and Kuipers, L. (1994) The clinical utility of expressed emotion in schizophrenia. *Acta Psychiatrica Scandinavica*, 89, 46–53.

Bentall, R.P., Corcoran, R., Howard, R., Blackwood, N. and Kinderman, P. (2001) Persecutory delusions: A review and theoretical integration. *Clinical Psychology Review*, 21, 1143–1192.

Brennan, P.A., Mednick, S.A. and Hodgins, S. (2000) Major mental disorders and criminal violence in a Danish birth cohort. *Archives of General Psychiatry*, 57, 494–500.

Bustillo, J.R., Lauriello, J., Horan, W.P. and Keith, S.J. (2001) The psychological treatment of schizophrenia: an update. *American Journal of Psychiatry*, 158, 163–175.

Butzlaff, R.L. and Hooley, J.M. (1998) Expressed emotion and psychiatric relapse: a meta-analysis. *Archives of General Psychiatry*, 55, 547–552.

Cuijpers, P. (1999) The effects of family intervention on relatives' burden: a meta analysis. *Journal of Mental Health*, 8, 275–285.

Czuchta, D.M. and McCay, E. (2001) Help-seeking for parents of individuals experiencing a first episode of schizophrenia. *Archives of Psychiatric Nursing*, 15, 159–170.

Dixon, L., Adams, C. and Luckstead, A. (2000) Update on family psychoeducation for schizophrenia. *Schizophrenia Bulletin*, 26, 5–20.

Dyck, D.G. and Short, R. and. V.P.P. (1999) Predictors of burden and infectious illness in schizophrenia caregivers. *Psychosomatic Medicine*, 61, 411–419.

Elisha, D., Castle, D. and Hocking, B. (2006) Reducing social isolation in people with mental illness: the role of the psychiatrist. *Australasian Psychiatry*, 14, 281–284.

Estroff, S.E., Swanson, J.W., Lachicotte, W.S., Swartz, M. and Bolduc, M. (1998) Risk reconsidered: targets of violence in the social networks of people with serious psychiatric disorders. *Social Psychiatry and Psychiatric Epidemiology*, 33, S95–S101.

Evert, H., Harvey, C., Trauer, T. and Herrman, H. (2003) The relationship between social networks and occupational and self-care functioning in people with psychosis. *Social Psychiatry and Psychiatric Epidemiology*, 38, 180–188.

Falloon, I.R.H., Boyd, J.L. and McGill, C.W. (1984) *Family Care of Schizophrenia*. New York: Guilford Press.

Freeman, D. and Garety, P.A. (2006) Helping patients with paranoid and suspicious thoughts: a cognitive-behavioural approach. *Advances in Psychiatric Treatment*, 12, 404–415.

Freeman, D., Garety, P.A. and Kuipers, E. (2001) Persecutory delusions: developing the understanding of belief maintenance and emotional distress. *Psychological Medicine*, 31, 1293–1306.

Freeman, D., Garety, P.A., Kuipers, E., Fowler, D. and Bebbington, P.E. (2002) A cognitive model of persecutory delusions. *British Journal of Clinical Psychology*, 41, 331–347.

Freeman, D., Slater, M., Bebbington, P. E. *et al.* (2003) Can virtual reality be used to investigate persecutory ideation? *Journal of Nervous and Mental Disease*, 191, 509–514.

Freeman, D., Garety, P.A., Fowler, D., Kuipers, E., Bebbington, P.E. and Dunn, G. (2004) Why do people with delusions fail to choose more realistic explanations for their experiences? An empirical investigation. *Journal of Consulting and Clinical Psychology*, 72, 671–680.

Freeman, D., Garety, P.A., Bebbington, P.E., Smith, B., Rollinson, R. and Fowler, D. (2005a) Psychological investigation of the structure of paranoia in a non-clinical population. *British Journal of Psychiatry*, 186, 427–435.

Freeman, D., Dunn, G., Garety, P.A. *et al.* (2005b) The psychology of persecutory ideation. I.—A questionnaire survey. *Journal of Nervous and Mental Disease*, 193, 302–308.

Freeman, D., Freeman, J. and Garety, P. (2006) *Overcoming Paranoid and Suspicious Thoughts: A Self Help Guide Using Cognitive Behavioural Techniques*. London: Robinson Constable.

Garety, P. A. and Freeman, D. (1999) Cognitive approaches to delusions: a critical review of theories and evidence. *British Journal of Clinical Psychology*, 38, 113–154.

Garety, P.A., Freeman, D., Jolley, S. *et al.* (2005) Reasoning, emotions, and delusional conviction in psychosis. *Journal of Abnormal Psychology*, 114, 373–384.

Green, C., Garety, P.A., Freeman, D. *et al.* (2006) Content and affect in persecutory delusions. *British Journal of Clinical Psychology*, 45, 561–577.

Harvey, K., Burns, T., Fahy, T., Manley, C. and Tattan, T. (2001) Relatives of patients with severe psychotic illness: factors that influence appraisal of caregiving and psychological distress. *Social Psychiatry and Psychiatric Epidemiology*, 36, 456–461.

Hooley, J.M. and Campbell, C. (2002) Control and controllability: beliefs and behaviour in high and low expressed emotion relatives. *Psychological Medicine*, 32, 1091–1099.

Jaspers, K. (1963) *General Psychopathology*. Manchester University Press.

Jeppesen, P., Petersen, L., Thorup, A. *et al.* (2005) Integrated treatment of first-episode psychosis: effect of treatment on family burden—OPUS trial. *British Journal of Psychiatry*, 187, S85–S90.

Johnston, I. and Taylor, P.J. (2003) Mental disorder and serious violence; the victims. *Journal of Clinical Psychiatry*, 64, 819–824.

Joyal, C.C., Putkonen, A., Paavola, P. and Tiihonen, J. (2004) Characteristics and circumstances of homicidal acts committed by offenders with schizophrenia. *Psychological Medicine*, 34, 433–442.

Kelly, M and Newstead, L. (2004) Family intervention in routine practice: it is possible. *Journal of Psychiatric and Mental Health Nursing*, 11, 64–72.

King, S. and Dixon, M. (1999) Expressed emotion and relapse in young schizophrenia outpatients. *Schizophrenia Bulletin*, 25, 377–386.

Kuipers, E. and Bebbington, P. (2005) Research on burden and coping strategies in families of people with mental disorders: problems and perspectives. In: Sartorius, N., Leff, J., Lopez-Ibor, J.J., Maj, M., Okasha, A. (eds), *Families and Mental Disorders: From Burden to Empowerment*, pp. 217–234. Chichester: Wiley.

Kuipers, E., Lam, D. and Leff, J. (2002) *Family Work for Schizophrenia: A Practical Guide*. London: Gaskell Press.

Lauber, C., Eichenberger, A., Luginbuhl, P., Keller, C. and Rossler, W. (2003) Determinants of burden in caregivers of patients with exacerbating schizophrenia. *European Psychiatry*, 18, 285–289.

Leff, J., Berkowitz, R., Shavit, N., Strachan, A., Glass, I. and Vaughn, C. (1990) A trial of family therapy versus a relatives' group for schizophrenia. Two-year follow-up. *British Journal of Psychiatry*, 157, 571–577.

Lehman, A.F. and Steinwachs, D.M. (1998) Patterns of usual care for Schizophrenia: Initial results from the Schizophrenia Patient Outcomes Research Team (PORT) client survey. *Schizophrenia Bulletin*, 24, 11–20.

Lehman, A.F., Kreyenbuhl, J., Buchanan, R.W. *et al.* (2004) The Schizophrenia Patient Outcomes Research Team (PORT): updated treatment recommendations 2003. Schizophrenia Bulletin, 30, 193–217.

Lowyck, B., De Hert, M., Peeters, E., Wampers, A., Gilis, P. and Peuskens, J. (2004) A study of the family burden of 150 family members of schizophrenic patients. *European Psychiatry*, 19, 395–401.

Macdonald, E.M., Hayes, R.L. and Baglioni, A.J. (2000) The quantity and quality of the social networks of young people with early psychosis compared with closely matched controls. *Schizophrenia Research*, 46, 25–30.

Magliano, L., Fadden, G., Madianos, M. *et al.* (1998) Burden on the families of patients with schizophrenia: results of the BIOMED I study. *Social Psychiatry and Psychiatric Epidemiology*, 33, 405–412.

Magliano, L., Fiorillo, A., Malangone, C., De Rosa, C. and Maj, M. (2006) Implementing psychoeducational interventions in Italy for patients with schizophrenia and their families. *Psychiatric Services*, 57, 266–269.

Mari, J.J. and Striener, D.L. (1994) An overview of family interventions and relapse on schizophrenia: meta analysis of research findings. *Psychological Medicine*, 24, 565–578.

Moller-Leimkuhler, A.M. (2005) Burden of relatives and predictors of burden. Baseline results from the Munich 5-year-follow-up study on relatives of first hospitalized patients with schizophrenia or depression. *European Archives of Psychiatry and Clinical Neuroscience*, 255, 223–231.

National Institute of Clinical Excellence (NICE) (2003) *Schizophrenia; Full National Clinical Guidelines on Core Interventions in Primary and Secondary Care*. London: Gaskell Press.

Nielssen, O.B., Westmore, B.D., Large, M.M.B. and Hayes, R.A. (2007) Homicide during psychotic illness in New South Wales between 1993 and 2002. *Medical Journal of Australia*, 186, 301–304.

Nordstrom, A. and Kullgren, G. (2003a) Victim relations and victim gender in violent crimes committed by offenders with schizophrenia. *Social Psychiatry and Psychiatric Epidemiology*, 38, 326–330.

Nordstrom, A. and Kullgren, G. (2003b) Do violent offenders with schizophrenia who attack family members differ from those with other victims? *International Journal of Forensic Mental Health*, 2, 195–200.

Nordstrom, A., Dahlgren, L. and Kullgren, G. (2006) Victim relations and factors triggering homicides committed by offenders with schizophrenia. *Journal of Forensic Psychiatry and Psychology*, 17, 192–203.

Oyebode, J. (2003) Assessment of carers' psychological needs. *Advances in Psychiatric Treatment*, 9, 45–53.

Perlick, D.A., Rosenheck, R.R., Clarkin, J.F., Raue, P. and Sirey, J. (2001) Impact of family burden and patient symptom status on clinical outcome in bipolar affective disorder. *Journal of Nervous and Mental Disease*, 189, 31–37.

Pharoah, F.M., Mari, J., Rathbone, J. and Wong, W. (2006) Family intervention for schizophrenia (Cochrane Review). Cochrane Database of Systematic Review, Issue 4.

Pilling, S., Bebbington, P., Kuipers, E. *et al.* (2002) Psychological treatments in schizophrenia: I. Meta-analysis of family intervention and cognitive behaviour therapy. *Psychological Medicine*, 32, 763–782.

Quinn, J., Barrowclough, C. and Tarrier, N. (2003) The Family Questionnaire (FQ): a scale for measuring symptom appraisal in relatives of schizophrenic patients. *Acta Psychiatrica Scandinavica*, 108, 290–296.

Raune, D., Kuipers, E. and Bebbington, P.E. (2004) Expressed emotion at first-episode psychosis: investigating a carer appraisal model. *British Journal of Psychiatry*, 184, 321–326.

Roick, C., Heider, D., Toumi, M. and Angermeyer, M.C. (2006) The impact of caregivers' characteristics, patients' conditions and regional differences on family burden in schizophrenia: a longitudinal analysis. *Acta Psychiatrica Scandinavica*, 114, 363–374.

Singleton, N., Maung, N., Cowie, A., Sparks, J., Bumpstead, R. and Meltzer, H. (2002) *Mental Health of Carers*. London: Office for National Statistics.

Shimodera, S., Inoue, S., Tanaka, S. and Mino, Y. (1998) Critical comments made to schizophrenic patients by their families in Japan. *Comprehensive Psychiatry*, 39, 85–90.

Shimodera, S., Mino, Y., Inoue, S., Izumoto, Y., Fujita, H. and Ujihara, H. (2000) Expressed emotion and family distress in relatives of patients with schizophrenia in Japan. *Comprehensive Psychiatry*, 41, 392–397.

Startup, M., Owen, D.M., Parsonage, R.K. and Jackson, M.C. (2003) Anomalous experiences and the contents of persecutory delusions during acute psychotic episodes. *Psychology and Psychotherapy—Theory Research and Practice*, 76, 315–322.

Stompe, T., Friedman, A., Ortwein, G. *et al.* (1999) Comparison of delusions among schizophrenics in Austria and in Pakistan. *Psychopathology: International Journal of Descriptive and Experimental Psychopathology, Phenomenology and Psychiatric Diagnosis*, 32, 225–234.

Taylor, P.J. (2006) Delusional disorder: is there a risk of violence in social interactions about the core symptom? *Behavioural Sciences and the Law*, 24, 313–331.

Taylor, P.J. and Gunn, J. (1999) Homicides by people with mental illness: myth and reality. *British Journal of Psychiatry*, 174, 9–14.

Thornicroft, G., Tansella, M., Becker, T. *et al.* (2004) The personal impact of schizophrenia in Europe. *Schizophrenia Research*, 69(2–3), 125–132.

Ukpong, D.I. (2006) Demographic factors and clinical correlates of burden and distress in relatives of services users experiencing schizophrenia: a study from south-western Nigeria. *International Journal of Mental Health Nursing*, 15, 54–59.

Ulzen, T.P.M. and Carpenter, R. (1997) The delusional parent: family and multisystemic issues. *Canadian Journal of Psychiatry—Revue Canadienne de Psychiatrie*, 42, 617–622.

Vaughn, C. and Leff, J. (1976) Measurement of expressed emotion in families of psychiatric-patients. *British Journal of Social and Clinical Psychology*, 15, 157–165.

Vitaliano, P.P., Zhang, J.P. and Scanlan, J.M. (2003) Is caregiving hazardous to one's physical health? A meta-analysis. *Psychological Bulletin*, 129, 946–972.

Walsh, E., Buchanan, A. and Fahy, T. (2001) Violence and schizophrenia: examining the evidence. *British Journal of Psychiatry*, 180, 490–495.

Wolthaus, J.E.D., Dingemans, P.M.A.J., Schene, A.H. *et al.* (2002) Caregiver burden in recent-onset schizophrenia and spectrum disorders: the influence of symptoms and personality traits. *Journal of Nervous and Mental Disease*, 190, 241–247.

Part 6

Therapy examples

Chapter 18

Coping with paranoia: a first-person account developed during cognitive behavioural therapy for psychosis

Karl Murphy and Ben Smith

There is a stigma about paranoia that stops us talking about it openly. I believe it should be talked about so we can share ways of coping with it.

Karl Murphy (2003)

Introduction

During 2003 we worked together in cognitive behavioural therapy (CBT) for psychosis. Karl had recently experienced an increase in his paranoid thinking and Ben was working as a research clinical psychologist. It was in response to Karl's statement (above) that we decided that the CBT sessions should have a specific focus. That focus was to work towards developing a short article about coping with paranoia. At that stage neither of us quite knew what the article would contain nor who would read it. However, we hoped that it would be of benefit to both of us, to some of Karl's friends and to Ben's colleagues. This chapter aims to explain how the article was developed in CBT and to provide a forum through which the article itself can reach a wider audience.

Contexts

At the start of CBT the referral information regarding Karl, available to Ben, was as follows: he has paranoid and suspicious beliefs; he believes that others are watching him or spying on him (65% belief conviction); he has no hallucinatory experiences; he is prescribed low-dose antipsychotic medication; and he has recently had a brief hospital admission.

CBT sessions started in March 2003 with a comprehensive engagement and assessment phase. This aimed to establish a working collaborative therapeutic relationship, allowing for the collection of information that would inform cognitive behavioural formulation (Fowler *et al*. 1995). Despite this initial attempt at engagement, Karl had mixed feelings about the CBT sessions and did not attend five of the first six sessions offered. It was not clear to Karl how CBT could help him. He felt that he had developed his own coping strategies and that although they weren't perfect, they were good enough.

It was August by the time we had reached our second session. Karl made his statement (above) and we decided to investigate just how much information there was available in the public domain about the experience of paranoia. Although Karl felt that he was coping well (most of the time) with his paranoia he knew that others often struggled with it more than he and that a stigma was still attached to paranoia. He also recognized that he had never read anything about paranoia himself and had developed his own coping strategies without guidance or help.

Our investigations revealed only a very small number of articles written as first-hand accounts of psychosis. However, the academic literature yielded some interesting findings. The research of Freeman *et al*. (2005) suggested that paranoia seems to reach across the population, rather than be the domain of only a few mental health patients. We resolved to write a short article based on Karl's experiences about coping with paranoia. The aim was that others may benefit from reading about what Karl had learnt and that Karl may gain an even better insight into his own paranoia. In total we met for 15 sessions of CBT, working towards the article as our main focus. The article is below.

Coping with paranoia

Summary

'There is a stigma about paranoia that stops us talking about it openly. I believe it should be talked about so we can share ways of coping with it. In my experience paranoia is made up of different factors. In this article I will try to summarize the important factors in paranoia as I see it. I am speaking from personal experience and Ben, who has helped me with this, is a clinical psychologist. I would like to give a summary of my personal experiences of paranoia. I hope this might help others understand their own paranoia and realise that paranoia is not such an uncommon thing and that it can be dealt with.

My background

'If there is a history of paranoia in your family you may have had to witness other people's paranoia. I saw my Dad go through intense paranoia and suffer a lot with it. I always thought I wanted to deal with it differently to the way he did. Things haven't gone well for my Dad and I have always looked for a different way to deal with my paranoia.

'I believe I have inherited a tendency to get things wrong sometimes. I have a tendency to think in a certain way and to put 2 and 2 together and get 5. Over the years I have realised that I have this tendency. Most of the time this is in the background and I have no problems. Sometimes, though, with certain people or at certain times it gets activated and I get paranoid. What follows is the nitty-gritty of how it works and how I have learnt to deal with it. Sometimes I deal with it better than others and I am still learning.

Personal weaknesses

'I think most of us have some personal weaknesses. Mine come from things that have gone wrong in my life and have been stored up in my memory. This is a drawback because some personal weaknesses crop up as triggers for my paranoia. The bits of my personality that are a drawback are my guilty conscience and my tendency to bottle things up.

Triggers

'It has taken me a long time to figure out the triggers for my paranoia. I think triggers can be really hard to spot. The most likely thing to trigger me off is a comment or a question that could have more than one meaning, or at least that is how it seems at the time. It can be a comment that feels critical and that I dwell on afterwards. These comments are usually from people I know well, especially family. The comments can trigger off my guilty conscience especially if I feel people are having a go at me. It is like the triggers can push me into a different state of mind.

'It helps me to know what my triggers for paranoia are. At least then, if I suddenly feel paranoid I can spot what triggered me off. If you don't know what has triggered you off it is even harder to deal with the paranoid state of mind.

'Triggers that are a bit unclear are the worst. In my experience, not knowing what someone really means is hard to tolerate. Not knowing is the worst bit. The problem is that I then have a burning desire to find out the truth. Even if the conclusion I come to is paranoid at least I know where I stand. For years I went through this and kept getting paranoid.

What I mean by 'paranoia'

'It is like a bubble of thinking. I feel alone and threatened when I am in it. It is like a build-up of information and thoughts that haven't been stored away yet.

They start racing around my head. I keep thinking "people are against me—they are watching me" and "people can't be trusted—they will let me down". It is like I am in a different zone from everyone else around me, and that feels lonely.

'When I am in this bubble I get desperate to work things out. It is in this state when I am most likely to put two and two together and get five. This state can last up to a few minutes but always leaves me thinking about things and dwelling on my paranoid worries. I worry that "they are all against me" and "I can't trust anyone". I usually get scared that I have offended people and that they will hold this against me. I go over and over things and feel more scared and alone. I used to cope with this by isolating myself and avoiding people. As a result I got very depressed and usually even more paranoid.

'For me, paranoia isn't just fear. It is a mental state that can make you do things that you wouldn't normally do. It is like a chain of events that leads to an idea—a theory—especially if it is reinforced by evidence. Then you feel you are right and that is reassuring. Then the fear comes.

How I deal with paranoia

'The trick is to try to reverse it. The first thing I do is take myself away from the triggers, either by going home or changing my scenery. This often releases me from the paranoid state. Once I have calmed down I try to go over what happened in my mind. I ask myself some important questions:

1 What triggered me off?
2 Am I getting this right?
3 Have I got this all in perspective?
4 Am I getting this out of proportion?

I come up with the answers by carefully going through what happened. I try to do this slowly and calmly. I always do this on my own but I can see how it might help to talk it through with someone you trust. If I cannot come up with an answer I try to come up with alternative possible answers. I tell myself: "Stay in neutral. There is always an alternative answer."

'Sometimes I come to the conclusion that it isn't me getting paranoid. If I come up with an answer that someone *was* making a dig at me then I have two choices. Either shut it off or ask them why they said what they said. I am getting better at knowing my condition and whether it is me being paranoid or just real-life hassles. In some ways it is good that I get paranoid sometimes as it gives me practice at dealing with it. Practice makes perfect.

Conclusion

'I think everyone has to find his or her own way of dealing with paranoia. There is now evidence that lots of people in the UK have paranoid thoughts on a regular basis. It is not as uncommon as we might think.'

Dissemination

We hope that mental health professionals who read the article will share it with people who experience paranoia and who may find it of interest or benefit.

Acknowledgement

This work was supported by a programme grant from the Wellcome Trust (No. 062452).

References

Fowler, D., Garety, P.A. and Kuipers, E.K. (1995) *Cognitive Behaviour Therapy for Psychosis: Theory and Practice.* Chichester: Wiley.

Freeman, D., Garety, P.A., Bebbington, P.E. et al. (2005) Psychological investigation of the structure of paranoia in a non-clinical population. *British Journal of Psychiatry*, 186, 427–435.

Chapter 19

Cognitive therapy for suspiciousness and paranoia in individuals at high risk of developing psychosis

Sophie K. Parker, Samantha E. Bowe, and Anthony P. Morrison

Introduction

Paranoia is one of the most distressing symptoms of psychosis, and can have a profound effect upon social, interpersonal and occupational functioning, often leading to hospitalization. Paranoia *per se* is a normal experience that all of us can relate to at times. Experiencing thoughts that friends, acquaintances, or strangers might be hostile is a common experience (Freeman *et al.* 2005). Furthermore, being wary of other peoples' intentions is adaptive under certain circumstances. Consequently, it is accepted that paranoia/suspiciousness lies on a continuum with normal experience. Suspicious thoughts become a clinical problem when they are excessive, exaggerated or unfounded, and distressing.

The prodromal phase of psychosis is associated with cognitive, emotional and behavioural changes. During this phase it is common to experience psychotic symptoms that are below the threshold for frank psychosis (e.g. low-level voice hearing, etc.). Such sub-threshold symptoms put an individual 'at risk' of developing psychosis. For a typical at-risk individual, suspiciousness starts to move outside the range of 'normal experience' and becomes more distressing, has a bigger impact on behaviour (e.g. avoiding going out/spending more time ruminating about the problem), and a belief system develops to explain what is happening.

This chapter aims to outline the use of cognitive therapy for paranoia/suspiciousness with individuals who are considered to be at ultra-high risk of developing psychosis. We begin by defining who is considered to be at high risk of developing psychosis, and provide a brief summary of interventions for this client group. Cognitive therapy intervention strategies are then described and illustrated with a case example.

Who is at ultra-high risk of developing psychosis?

As part of the international drive to develop early intervention services for psychosis, the early detection and prevention of psychosis has become a topic of growing interest. The influential work of Yung *et al.* (1998) led to the development of operational criteria that identify at-risk mental states (ARMS). Using these criteria, they found that 40% of individuals identified as ultra-high risk made transition to psychosis over a nine-month period (Yung *et al.* 1998).

The criteria identify four groups who are at ultra-high risk using a combination of state and trait risk factors. With regards to the state factors, these involve individuals experiencing: (i) attenuated or sub-threshold psychotic symptoms; and (ii) brief limited intermittent psychotic symptoms (BLIPS) which remit without treatment within a week. The trait factors are: (i) experiencing a recent deterioration in functioning and having a family history (first degree relative) of psychosis; and (ii) a diagnosis of schizotypal personality disorder also coupled with the experience of a recent deterioration in functioning. For the purposes of this chapter, our focus will be on the group with attenuated symptoms as they make up approximately 80% of at-risk clients seen by early detection services.

What are attenuated psychotic symptoms?

Attenuated psychotic symptoms refer to psychotic-like experiences that are below the clinical threshold for frank psychotic symptoms. They differ from frank psychotic symptoms in their intensity, frequency and/or duration (Yung *et al.* 2005). For example, a persecutory idea that is held with less than delusional conviction is attenuated as it has less intensity than a persecutory delusion, being held with less conviction and having less impact on behaviour and emotion. If an individual fleetingly holds a persecutory belief with delusional conviction (100% conviction) but only for one hour, this does not meet the standard criteria (e.g. in the *DSM-IV*, American Psychiatric Association 1994) for a frank psychotic symptom on the basis of duration. Similarly, if an individual had paranoid ideas only twice within a month, these would be considered attenuated psychotic symptoms as the frequency is below the threshold for frank psychosis (duration of at least one month).

Interventions for individuals at ultra-high risk

Advances in the identification of individuals at risk have raised the possibility of preventing transition to psychosis. To date, the efficacy of a number of interventions has been evaluated in three randomized controlled trials: a combination of psychological and pharmacotherapy (McGorry *et al.* 2002); cognitive therapy alone (Morrison *et al.* 2004); and pharmacotherapy alone (McGlashan *et al.* 2006).

McGorry *et al.* (2002) found that, in comparison with supportive therapy and case management (needs-based intervention; NBI), a combination of psychological therapy and specific pharmacotherapy (specific preventive intervention; SPI) reduced the risk of transition to psychosis (10% transition rate compared with 36% in the NBI group). However, results were not maintained at six-month follow-up. Thus it was concluded that it might be possible to delay transition to psychosis rather than prevent it. Morrison *et al.* (2004) carried out a randomized controlled trial (RCT) ($n = 58$), the EDIE (Early Detection, Intervention and Evaluation) study, comparing cognitive therapy with monitoring alone (no treatment). Cognitive therapy significantly reduced transition to psychosis at the end of treatment (6% transition rate compared with 22% in the treatment-as-usual group) and this result was maintained at 12-month follow-up. Consequently, it was concluded that it may be possible to prevent transition to psychosis (currently a large multi-site RCT based on EDIE is ongoing to test this proposition further). This significant difference remained at three-year follow-up when cognitive therapy factors were included in the analysis. However, McGlashan *et al.* (2006), on a trial comparing olanzapine to placebo ($n = 60$), did not find a significant difference in the numbers of transitions to psychosis at 12 months (16.1% transition rate in the olanzapine group compared with 37.9% in the placebo group), suggesting that antipsychotic medication does not delay or prevent transition to psychosis in at-risk individuals. McGlashan *et al.* (2006) reported a trend towards significance and acknowledged deficient power as a potential cause for the lack of statistical significance. In addition to the lack of supporting evidence, there are also ethical issues to consider (e.g. side-effects, stigma) in relation to using antipsychotic medication with this clinical group (Bentall and Morrison 2002).

Cognitive model of psychosis

A cognitive model that accounts for the formation and maintenance of psychotic experiences, including paranoia, has been proposed (Morrison 2001) and is shown in Fig. 19.1. The EDIE trial has provided preliminary evidence that cognitive therapy based upon this model can prevent or delay psychosis in those at high risk (Morrison *et al.* 2004). The model implies that it is the interpretation of intrusions (e.g. mood states, external perceptions or intrusive thoughts) that is important. Essentially, a person is seen to be psychotic if they endorse a culturally unacceptable interpretation of intrusions (e.g. to assume that hearing one's first

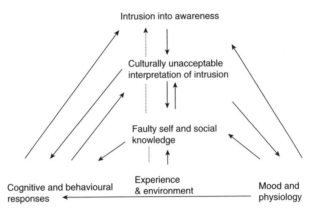

Fig. 19.1 Morrison's (2001) cognitive model of the formation and maintenance of psychotic experiences, including paranoia.

name on television is evidence that everyone is talking about you). Morrison (2001) also states that similar processes are involved in the development of psychotic and non-psychotic disorders. Consequently, the model encompasses key aspects of Wells and Matthews' (1994) S-REF (self-regulatory executive function) model of emotional dysfunction.

Morrison (2001) proposes that culturally unacceptable interpretations of intrusions are maintained by safety behaviours (e.g. watching people from window), procedural beliefs (beliefs about information-processing strategies; e.g. paranoia keeps me safe), faulty self- and social knowledge (meta-cognitiive beliefs such as that thinking about something means it will happen), mood and physiology. The model implies that unhelpful cognitive responses (e.g. selective attention/thought control strategies), behavioural responses (e.g. avoidance/safety behaviours) and emotion (e.g. anxiety) maintain distress and psychotic symptoms.

The purpose of this model is to facilitate the collaborative development of idiosyncratic case formulations, from which intervention strategies can be derived. This process is described using the case example below. Table 19.1 lists some of the intervention strategies that can be utilized.

Case example: 'at-risk' client with attenuated paranoia

Background and assessment information

Martin was a 22-year-old man who had dropped out of college and was working in a call centre. He lived with a close friend in a flat and had regular contact with his family who lived in a neighbouring city. He was becoming increasingly suspicious of people around him. He found this distressing and

Table 19.1 Intervention strategies

Cognitive	Behavioural
Verbal reattribution methods (e.g. on content and/or interpretation of cognitions)	Behavioural experiments
	Safety behaviour manipulation
Provision of normalizing information	Behavioural surveys
Pie charts	Action plans
Advantages and disadvantages of cognitions/beliefs/strategies	
Working with imagery	

confusing and was becoming increasingly preoccupied with his suspicious ideas. This was also starting to impact upon relationships with friends and work colleagues. He was also feeling more anxious, self-conscious and low in mood. Recently, Martin had started to think that his friends were talking about him and plotting behind his back. He had become more hypervigilant: watching out for 'suspicious behaviour' and questioning the meaning of things people said in conversations. He indicated that his conviction that others were talking and plotting against him was 70%. This belief rating fluctuated considerably; when he was directly in a situation in which he felt threatened it would rise to 100% and outside it could drop to 40%. He was very confused by what he was thinking and was unsure whether his beliefs were realistic or whether it was 'all in his mind'. This alternative explanation was also threatening to him as it would mean he was 'going mad' and 'losing it'. In the weeks leading up to the referral he had started to confront others. He had walked out of work and received a written warning. His friends had unsuccessfully tried to reassure him that they were not against him in any way.

Problem list and goals of therapy

In his initial cognitive therapy sessions, Martin identified the following difficulties for his 'problem list': (i) not trusting others/not knowing when to believe others; (ii) thinking others were out to get him; and (iii) feeling awkward and self-conscious when out. His main therapy goals were: (i) to reduce how suspicious he felt about others (particularly his friends); (ii) to be able to work out accurately whether or not people were really out to get him; (iii) to feel more comfortable (less self-conscious and anxious) when out; and (iv) to stop leaving difficult situations.

Formulation

In the early sessions the therapist looked at specific situations in which Martin felt paranoid and attempted to develop a case conceptualization which would help him to understand his difficulties and guide the selection of intervention strategies. These conceptualizations can range from very basic event–thought–feeling–behaviour chains through to fairly complex historical formulations that incorporate relevant early experiences, schemas and assumptions, critical incidents and current environmental factors. It is useful to adopt a parsimonious approach, utilizing the simplest formulation where possible, but always baring in mind the client's early experiences and the beliefs that have been formed as a consequence. These early experiences can often be incorporated in the explicit, shared-case conceptualization when working with at-risk cases. In addition, it can be useful to provide a historical or developmental perspective in order to facilitate the normalization of the client's psychotic experiences (for instance, when a client's history of abuse makes sense of current paranoid ideation).

All formulations should, ideally, be based upon an empirically supported cognitive model of the difficulties in question. The model of psychosis outlined above is easily translated into idiosyncratic case conceptualizations that can be used to explain the development and maintenance of psychosis in individual cases, and this was done for Martin (see Fig. 19.2).

A number of life experiences shaped how Martin viewed himself, the world and those around him. These experiences included being bullied at school, not knowing the identity of his father and, more recently, being thrown out of a shared house after his co-tenants plotted against him. These experiences gave rise to a number of beliefs that Martin held, such as 'I am weird/different,' 'Others cannot be trusted,' and 'Paranoia keeps me safe.' Therefore, when Martin is in situations like the one depicted in the formulation where he feels anxious and self-conscious, his appraisals reflect these underlying beliefs, for example, 'My friend has taken me here deliberately to make me feel uncomfortable (anxious), he will tell everyone how weird I look.' When these thoughts run through his mind Martin feels anxious, self-conscious, depressed and angry.

Martin engages in a number of behaviours which help him to cope with this difficult situation, for instance, keeping himself safe by using behaviours which he feels will reduce the likelihood of others noticing him as weird/different, such as putting his hands in his pockets to stop others from noticing them shaking. Other things that Martin does in these situations are to remain hypervigilant, for example, paying attention to his body as well as to others around him.

Interventions

Once a case conceptualization has been collaboratively developed and problems and goals negotiated, then intervention strategies can be discussed and chosen on the basis of what is likely to achieve quick success or what will have the

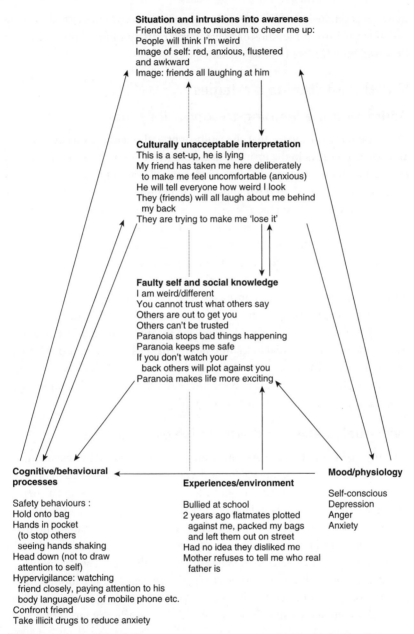

Situation and intrusions into awareness
Friend takes me to museum to cheer me up:
People will think I'm weird
Image of self: red, anxious, flustered
and awkward
Image: friends all laughing at him

Culturally unacceptable interpretation
This is a set-up, he is lying
My friend has taken me here deliberately
  to make me feel uncomfortable (anxious)
He will tell everyone how weird I look
They (friends) will all laugh about me behind
  my back
They are trying to make me 'lose it'

Faulty self and social knowledge
I am weird/different
You cannot trust what others say
Others are out to get you
Others can't be trusted
Paranoia stops bad things happening
Paranoia keeps me safe
If you don't watch your
  back others will plot against you
Paranoia makes life more exciting

**Cognitive/behavioural
processes**

Safety behaviours :
Hold onto bag
Hands in pocket
 (to stop others
 seeing hands shaking
Head down (not to draw
 attention to self)
Hypervigilance: watching
 friend closely, paying attention to his
 body language/use of mobile phone etc.
Confront friend
Take illicit drugs to reduce anxiety

Experiences/environment

Bullied at school
2 years ago flatmates plotted
 against me, packed my bags
 and left them out on street
Had no idea they disliked me
Mother refuses to tell me who real
 father is

Mood/physiology

Self-conscious
Depression
Anger
Anxiety

Fig. 19.2 Case formulation of attenuated paranoia in a client at high risk of developing psychosis.

most effect on quality of life. Most change strategies can be described as being verbal reattribution methods or behavioural reattribution methods; each of these will be considered in more detail.

Verbal reattribution strategies

Addressing the jumping-to-conclusions bias

Cognitive models propose that the faulty appraisal of anomalous experiences and events is crucial in the formation and maintenance of delusions (Freeman *et al.* 2002) and making probabilistic judgements is an important part of this appraisal (Garety *et al.* 1991). It appears that a jumping-to-conclusions style is evident in individuals at risk of psychosis as well as in those with frank persecutory delusions (Broome *et al.* 2007). Thus, this bias may play a role in the formation of persecutory delusions/paranoia and is an important target within cognitive therapy for those at risk of psychosis.

In Martin's case, it was useful to share this information with him, and through guided discovery he considered a number of possible advantages and disadvantages to thinking in this way. This process allowed Martin to consider if it may be useful to find a way of addressing the information available to him prior to fixing on the initial thought/concern that he has. It was also helpful to remind Martin of his second goal (being able to work out accurately whether or not people were really out to harm him) and to consider how jumping to conclusions may hinder him in achieving this.

Evidential analysis and alternative explanations

Clients usually benefit from learning how to generate alternative explanations before considering the evidence for and against these possibilities in order to evaluate the accuracy of their thoughts (Beck 1976). For example, in an attempt to help Martin work out whether people were intending him harm, a range of possible explanations were generated for the situation Martin had found troubling (friends taking him to a museum to cheer him up). It is helpful to develop an exhaustive list of explanations, taking time to do this well. The creative use of Socratic dialogue will aid this process. Using the list, belief ratings for each of the possible explanations can be obtained with values ranging from 0 to 100%, which allow enough room to be sensitive to change. Anchor points for the scale are set out by the therapist (for example, 0 = do not believe this at all, and 100 = believe it to be completely true, with no doubt at all) and the scale is written down to aid the process. In Martin's case, the alternative explanations and associated belief ratings can be seen in Table 19.2. Once this list has been agreed it is

Table 19.2 Alternative explanations

- Situation: friends take me to museum to cheer me up
- Current explanation (belief rating): my friend has taken me here deliberately to make me feel uncomfortable (70%)
- Current mood associated with this belief: anxiety

Other explanations	Belief rating	Associated mood
It was a genuine act of kindness	20%	Happy
He was going anyway, so he took me along	35%	OK
He didn't want to go alone and asked me as company	25%	Alright
He was scared of going and so wanted me there to feel safe	5%	OK for me

then possible to take each explanation in turn and consider the evidence for and against it (see Table 19.3 for an example).

Meta-cognitive beliefs

Meta-cognition refers to thoughts or beliefs that people have about their own thoughts and mental processes; for example, believing that your thoughts are uncontrollable or that all of your thoughts should be 'pure'. Meta-cognition is defined as any knowledge or cognitive process that is involved in the appraisal, monitoring or control of cognition (Flavell 1979). Morrison (2001) proposes that meta-cognitive processes maintain persecutory delusions/paranoia. One study found that meta-cognition is involved in the development of, and distress associated with, paranoia in a non-clinical population (Morrison *et al.* 2005). A study investigating meta-cognition in 58 at-risk individuals found that, in comparison with a non-clinical group (matched on age and occupational status), at-risk individuals had higher measures of negative meta-cognitive beliefs (Morrison *et al.* 2006). The negative meta-cognitive beliefs included: negative beliefs about uncontrollability; general negative beliefs about thoughts (superstitiousness, punishment and responsibility); and cognitive self-consciousness. Interestingly, higher levels of negative meta-cognitive beliefs were associated with higher attenuated psychotic symptom scores (e.g. paranoia).

The finding that at-risk individuals score higher on measures of meta-cognitive beliefs is consistent with Morrison's (2001) cognitive model of psychosis, and with the S-REF model (Wells and Matthews, 1994). According to

Table 19.3 An example of an 'evidence for and against' sheet

Belief to be examined	My friend took me to the museum as a genuine act of kindness
Associated mood	Happy
Belief rating	20%
Evidence for:	Evidence against:
He knew that I like doing that sort of thing He is always asking how I am See him make time for others He seemed happy to offer help Does voluntary work, maybe he's a kind person When I said I was going he looked concerned and came home with me	I'm not sure I can trust him Not done that before for me
Belief rating (re-rating)	60%
Alternative thought	Maybe asking me to go was a genuine act of kindness to cheer me up but I am not trusting of others so I didn't see it for what it was
Associated mood	Happy

these models, positive beliefs about paranoia should be associated with the frequency of psychotic-like experiences, whereas negative beliefs should be associated with the resulting distress. Consequently, it is the evolution of such beliefs that may underlie transition to psychosis.

Martin held positive beliefs about paranoia (e.g. 'paranoia will keep me safe'), as well as negative beliefs (e.g. 'my paranoia interferes with my life'). In order to explore the impact of such beliefs, it was first necessary to consider the advantages and disadvantages of holding them (see Table 19.4). This afforded Martin the opportunity to consider some of the disadvantages of adopting paranoia as a strategy while acknowledging that it holds some advantages for him. Discussion of some of the drawbacks of this strategy in addition to reminding Martin of his first goal of therapy (to reduce how suspicious he felt about others, particularly with friends) provided an opening for Martin to review his belief that paranoia keeps him safe. The use of Socratic dialogue allowed Martin to consider how this belief developed and to review how it fitted into his daily life. We can see from Martin's formulation that there have been times in his life (e.g. when bullied) when being paranoid could have been a useful strategy to employ to keep him safe. While acknowledging this, it was possible for Martin to explore the impact of this belief in his current environment.

Table 19.4 Advantages and disadvantages of paranoia

Advantages	Disadvantages
Keeps me safe	Makes me feel anxious
Makes me feel as though I'm being pro-active	I worry all the time about what other people are up to and thinking
Makes life more exciting	Sometimes when I worry too much I can't make sense of what is real and what is not
	Stops me from keeping from friends
	Stops me from being able to enjoy the things I used to do
	Stops me from going to places
	Makes me preoccupied with everything around me

A useful analogy to use at this stage is that of an alarm with several sensitivity levels each of which will result in a different threshold for triggering the alarm. There may be times when we would want an alarm to be highly sensitive; for example, when there have been a number of intruders in the area. However, keeping the alarm at this level when this threat has reduced may mean that the alarm is repeatedly set off accidentally (e.g. by spiders or pets), keeping the householder on high alert unnecessarily. When offered this analogy, Martin was given the opportunity to consider how his own sensitivity to threat related to his current situation. In this way Martin reviewed his position in relation to things that he had experienced in his past but which were not present to the same degree in his current environment. This then led to Martin designing a behavioural experiment in which he examined the safety behaviours which arose from his belief that paranoia kept him safe (see below for a detailed description).

Trauma

Previous traumatic events have been identified as contributing to the development of persecutory delusions/paranoia (Morrison 2001; Freeman *et al.* 2002). Several comprehensive reviews of the relationship between trauma and psychosis have been published that support this view (Morrison *et al.* 2003; Read *et al.* 2005). To date there is no published literature specifically examining the role of trauma in people at high risk of psychosis.

It has been suggested that experiencing traumatic events such as bullying, and childhood physical abuse, are likely to lead to the development of negative beliefs about others (e.g. 'others are harmful') and the self (e.g. 'I am vulnerable'), which in turn may contribute to the development and maintenance of persecutory delusions/paranoia (Morrison *et al.* 2003).

It is evident in the formulation that in Martin's case, there is an example of perceived trauma, although this is not an event that would meet criterion A for post-traumatic stress disorder; it is interpersonal in nature (i.e. housemates plotting behind his back and then returning home to find all of his belongings thrown out of the house). This is likely to have resulted in him using paranoia as a strategy to manage the interpersonal threat that others pose, which in turn influenced his information processing (e.g. seeking confirmatory information to justify his suspicious thoughts). Furthermore, the content of his paranoia relates directly to the humiliating event he experienced in the past (friends deliberately making him anxious to laugh at him behind his back).

In the case of Martin, a number of core beliefs were identified using the downward arrow technique. This is a common technique used to access core beliefs in relation to negative thoughts by employing questions such as 'What would be the worst thing about that?' By using questions like this, it is possible to identify the underlying concerns and beliefs about negative thoughts; for example, one of Martin's core beliefs was 'Others can't be trusted.' By using the formulation it was possible for Martin to discover what experiences may have contributed to the development of this belief and to make sense of the strategies he uses in relation to it. Core beliefs can be evaluated in a number of ways, for example by examining evidence for and against them, by generating alternative explanations, by role-play and by the use of flashcards (Beck 1995). Flashcards are used as a way of linking current affect with an individual's schematic beliefs, and help them to challenge these beliefs in a way that is systematic. For example, by using Judy Beck's Core Belief Worksheet (Beck 1995) evidence can be gathered in support of alternative beliefs, comparing these with original beliefs and documenting the extent to which each is believed. Similar to the work that Martin had done previously, we worked together to consider the advantages and disadvantages of holding such beliefs. We then evaluated the accuracy of these beliefs in relation to his current situation. These strategies can also be very useful for helping to re-evaluate negative beliefs about the self, such as Martin's belief that 'I am weird.' This is important since there is evidence that paranoia in at-risk participants can be associated with high levels of discrepancy between clients' beliefs about themselves and their ideals (Morrison *et al.* 2006), as would be expected on the basis of theories that suggest a defensive function for persecutory ideas (Bentall *et al.* 2001).

Paranoia and social anxiety

Does social anxiety play a role in the development of paranoia/persecutory delusions? Social anxiety commonly presents co-morbidly with persecutory delusions in psychosis and with at-risk individuals experiencing attenuated paranoia. Furthermore, there is obvious overlap between the two conditions.

In social anxiety, threat beliefs are related to an excessive fear of social performance and scrutiny of others, whereas persecutory delusions involve threat beliefs concerning fears about a persecutor intentionally causing harm to the individual. However, both disorders involve attentional biases to threat-related information, involve heightened self-focused attention and view of the self as a target, and the use of safety behaviours (e.g. avoidance). By contrast, the explanation for threat across the disorders is somewhat different. In the case of persecutory delusions an external, but personal, attribution is made for negative events (Kinderman and Bentall 1997) whereas in social anxiety an internal and personal attribution is made for negative events.

Is it possible that, due to an external attribution style, individuals with psychosis misinterpret social anxiety as evidence of a threat from others? Once such threat-beliefs about others develop, cognitive and behavioural processes may then play a role in contributing to the development of attenuated paranoia and then to the formation of persecutory delusions. Although this idea is speculative, Martin's case example illustrates this notion to some degree. In addition to attenuated psychotic symptoms (e.g. paranoia), this client also met *DSM-IV* criteria (American Psychiatric Association 1994) for social anxiety. Even when his paranoid ideas were less frequent and distressing, he continued to experience social anxiety. Because of this, he is likely to have felt anxious as soon as he entered the museum with his friend. It is possible that, because of his previous traumatic experiences with friends, and because he had positive beliefs about paranoia as a strategy for managing interpersonal threat, he then misinterpreted his anxiety and self-consciousness as evidence of an external threat (i.e. 'My friend is deliberately trying to make me look anxious to tell everyone and laugh at me'). Providing education about social anxiety and the criteria for social phobia helped to normalize these experiences for Martin. Exploring Martin's formulation with him in order to re-examine his social anxiety in a manner of 'Is it a feeling or is it true?' helped Martin to question the validity of his distressing cognitions relating to social anxiety and to provide a rationale for generating alternative explanations. Tackling the image he had of himself using behavioural experiments, in a similar manner to those recommended for clients with social phobia (Clark and Wells 1995), also helped Martin to reduce his social anxiety.

Behavioural reattribution strategies

Safety behaviours and behavioural experiments

To date there have been no at-risk studies carried out exploring safety behaviours specifically, despite the evidence that safety behaviours are associated with paranoia in people with psychosis (Freeman *et al.* 2001). Certainly, safety behaviours are evident in the at-risk population and they have been identified in the literature as important targets for cognitive therapy for individuals at ultra-high risk of psychosis (French and Morrison 2004). Evaluation of paranoid thoughts using behavioural experiments can be one of the most effective ways of achieving belief change (Chadwick and Lowe 1990), although verbal reattribution strategies are likely to be required to allow the client to feel sufficiently safe to do so.

As can be seen in the case formulation, safety behaviours were employed by Martin, who used typical safety behaviours associated with social anxiety (e.g. holding his bag tightly), which makes sense in terms of the emotions he was experiencing (anxiety/self-consciousness) and the perceived threat (friends deliberately making him anxious to laugh at him) and associated cognitions (image of self as red and flustered). He used less avoidance safety behaviours, but used illicit drugs to reduce his social anxiety, which in turn put him at greater risk of psychosis and maintained his paranoia. Interestingly, he used aggressive safety behaviours (e.g. confronting friends), which fits with his emotional response (e.g. anger) and the perception that the threat is underserved (see 'poor me' paranoia: Trower and Chadwick 1995).

During a session exploring Martin's belief that paranoia keeps him safe (see above), Martin identified a number of strategies which result from this belief. At this stage, a number of metaphors can be used to provide a rationale for engaging in an experiment to examine the use of safety behaviours (Wells 1997), for example, discussion of the use of garlic and crucifixes to ward off vampires, of dancing to prevent volcanic eruptions, or using compulsive rituals to prevent train derailment by elephants. These metaphors can foster an understanding of how the safety behaviours help to keep the person feeling safe in the short term but may be maintaining a belief in their usefulness in the long-term. Once this rationale has been explored, Martin was open to testing the usefulness of the identified strategies by designing a behavioural experiment. The use of Socratic dialogue facilitated this process so that Martin could create an experiment which would allow him to test out his predictions while remaining in control of what would be happening to him.

Once an experiment has been designed and adequately thought through, it is vital to set out the belief that will be tested in addition to rating the belief level (see above). The client is then encouraged to make a prediction of what they think will happen as a result of the experiment and also to think through any potential obstacles to completing the task. This latter phase is essential as it is often possible to problem solve around these obstacles to maximize the likelihood of the experiment taking place. An outline of the experiment designed by Martin, in which he modified his safety behaviours (in this case, gripping his bag tightly, with his other hand in pocket and keeping his head down) and observed the effects on others' reactions and himself (using video feedback) is provided in Table 19.5 (using a behavioural experiment form; Greenberger and Padesky, 1995). As a result of this experiment, Martin discovered that some of the things he does to cope with his situation are not necessarily useful and he started to consider alternative ways in which he might practice being in such situations.

Other problems

As discussed previously, anxiety plays an important role in the development and maintenance of persecutory delusions (Freeman *et al.* 2002). In at-risk individuals, anxiety is a typical emotional reaction in response to threat-related thoughts and beliefs. When experiencing attenuated paranoia, an individual often feels confused as to what is really happening, alternating between two possible explanations: believing the paranoid ideas (external attribution), or believing that the individual is going mad (internal attribution). Both of these induce anxiety as they are threatening. The client's conviction in these beliefs varies, impacting upon the intensity of the anxiety experienced. The level of anxiety will influence information processing (e.g. jumping to conclusions) and the extent to which safety behaviours are utilized. Normalizing information and the formulation can help to provide an alternative explanation that is less threatening than either of these options.

Table 19.5 Outline of behavioural experiment

- Thought to be tested: When I feel anxious other people will notice my hands shaking and will think I'm weird and laugh at me

- Belief in thought: (0–100%); before experiment: 100%; after experiment: 40%

Experiment to test thought	Likely problems	Strategies to deal with problems	Expected outcome	Actual outcome	Alternative thought
Do usual, e.g. hold on tightly to my bag (5 min), exaggerate this behaviour (5 min), drop this behaviour (5 min)	I will feel too scared to do what's asked of me	Tell my self that this is worth a go, that nothing else is working, it's only for 15 min	People will think I'm weird	I looked more anxious when I did my usual things	Maybe some things I do don't help me

Co-morbidity with other psychological disorders is common in at-risk individuals. Typical co-morbid disorders include panic, generalized anxiety disorder, depression, anger, low self-esteem, social anxiety and substance misuse (French and Morrison 2004). Although this chapter focuses on paranoia and suspiciousness, it is important to work with whatever is on the person's problem list.

Outcome

The example of Martin comprises a number of cases which have been amalgamated in order to protect anonymity. Therefore, it is not possible to describe the specific outcome in this case; however, it is possible to discuss possible outcomes in such cases, which may provide an indication that therapy has been successful.

When clients have been identified with an at-risk mental state, the primary tool used to assess outcome should be a valid ARMS measure such as the Comprehensive Assessments for At Risk Mental States (CAARMS; Yung *et al.* 2005). Achieving a reduction in the clients at risk-status so that they no longer meet criteria for an at-risk mental state is one useful outcome. However, other goals may be just as important, if not more so, such as reducing the distress associated with unusual experiences and beliefs, helping to evaluate problematic appraisals and improving social and occupational functioning.

Addressing clients' idiosyncratic problem lists and meeting their goals of therapy are essential outcomes to aim for. For example, in the case of Martin, important outcomes would be for him to feel less suspicious about other people, feel confident that he is making accurate assessments of other people's intentions by utilizing all of the evidence available to him and to both feel comfortable while he is out in social situations and to feel able to stay in those situations even if he feels anxious. It is also important to consider other outcomes such as an increase in meaningful activity, as might have been an indicated need in the assessment and formulation with a client. These outcomes may be monitored in relation to specific and measurable goals that are set collaboratively or using standardized measures (such as self-report measures of mood, anxiety, quality of life, etc.).

Conclusion

Paranoia and suspiciousness are common experiences for people at risk of developing psychosis, although they are usually held with less conviction and associated distress than in the case of clients with an established psychotic disorder. The application of cognitive behavioural strategies derived from a case formulation based on a cognitive model appears to be an acceptable and effective approach to preventing transition to psychoses and reducing problems associated with paranoia for this population.

References

American Psychiatric Association (1994) *Diagnostic and Statistical Manual for Mental Disorders*, 4th edn. Washington, DC: American Psychiatric Association.

Beck, A.T. (1976) *Cognitive Therapy and the Emotional Disorders*. New York: International Universities Press.

Beck, J.S. (1995) *Cognitive Therapy: Basics and Beyond*. New York: Guilford Press.

Bentall, R.P. and Morrison, A.P. (2002) More harm than good: the case against using antipsychotic drugs to prevent severe mental illness. *Journal of Mental Health*, 11, 351–365.

Bentall, R.P., Corcoran, R., Howard, R., Blackwood, R. and Kinderman, P. (2001) Persecutory delusions: a review and theoretical integration. *Clinical Psychology Review*, 22, 1–50.

Broome, M.R., Johns, L.C., Valli, I., Woolley, J.B., Tabraham, P., Brett, C., Valmaggia, L., Peters, E., Garety, P.A. and McGuire, P. (2007) Delusion formation and reasoning biases in those at clinical high risk for psychosis. *British Journal of Psychiatry*, 191, s38–s42.

Chadwick, P. and Lowe, C.F. (1990) The measurement and modification of delusional beliefs. *Journal of Consulting and Clinical Psychology*, 58, 225–232.

Clark, D.M. and Wells, A. (1995) A cognitive model of social phobia. In: Heimberg, R.G. and Liebowitz, M.R. (eds), *Social Phobia: Diagnosis, Assessment, and Treatment*, pp. 69–93. New York: Guilford Press.

Flavell, J.H. (1979) Metacognition and metacognitive monitoring: a new area of cognitive-developmental inquiry. *American Psychologist*, 34, 906–911.

Freeman, D., Garety, P.A. and Kuipers, E. (2001) Persecutory delusions: developing the understanding of belief maintenance and emotional distress. *Psychological Medicine*, 31, 1293–1306.

Freeman, D., Garety, P.A., Kuipers, E., Fowler, D. and Bebbington, P.E. (2002) A cognitive model of persecutory delusions. *British Journal of Clinical Psychology*, 41, 331–347.

Freeman, D., Garety, P.A., Bebbington, P.E. *et al.* (2005) Psychological investigation of the structure of paranoia in a non-clinical population. *British Journal of Psychiatry*, 186, 427–435.

French, P. and Morrison, A.P. (2004) *Early Detection and Cognitive Therapy for People at High Risk of Developing Psychosis: A Treatment Approach*. London: Wiley.

Garety, P. A., Hemsley, D.R. and Wessely, S. (1991) Reasoning in deluded schizophrenic and paranoid patients. *Journal of Nervous and Mental Disease*, 179, 194–201.

Greenberger, D. and Padesky, C.A. (1995) *Mind Over Mood: A Cognitive Therapy Treatment Manual for Clients*. New York: Guilford Press.

Kinderman, P. and Bentall, R.P. (1997) Causal attributions in paranoia and depression: internal, personal, and situational attributions for negative events. *Journal of Abnormal Psychology*, 106, 341–345.

McGlashan, T.H., Zipursky, R.B., Perkins, D. *et al.* (2006) Randomized, double-blind trial of olanzapine versus placebo in patients prodromally symptomatic for psychosis. *American Journal of Psychiatry*, 163, 790–799.

McGorry, P.D., Yung, A.R., Phillips, L.J. *et al.* (2002) Randomized controlled trial of interventions designed to reduce the risk of progression to first-episode psychosis in a clinical sample with subthreshold symptoms. *Archives of General Psychiatry*, 59, 921–928.

Morrison, A.P. (2001) The interpretation of intrusions in psychosis: an integrative cognitive approach to hallucinations and delusions. *Behavioural and Cognitive Psychotherapy*, 29, 257–276.

Morrison, A.P., Frame, L. and Larkin, W. (2003) Relationships between trauma and psychosis: a review and integration. *British Journal of Clinical Psychology*, 42, 331–353.

Morrison, A.P., French, P., Walford, L. *et al.* (2004) Cognitive therapy for the prevention of psychosis in people at ultra-high risk: randomised controlled trial. *British Journal of Psychiatry*, 185, 291–297.

Morrison, A.P., Gumley, A.I., Schwannauer, M. *et al.* (2005) The beliefs about paranoia scale: preliminary validation of a metacognitive approach to conceptualising paranoia. *Behavioural and Cognitive Psychotherapy*, 33, 153–164.

Morrison, A.P., French, P., Lewis, S.W. *et al.* (2006) Psychological factors in people at ultra-high risk of psychosis: comparisons with non-patients and associations with symptoms. *Psychological Medicine*, 36, 1395–1404.

Read, J., van Os, J., Morrison, A.P. and Ross, C.A. (2005) Childhood trauma, psychosis and schizophrenia: a literature review and clinical implications. *Acta Psychiatrica Scandinavica*, 112, 330–350.

Trower, P. and Chadwick, P. (1995) Pathways to defense of the self: a theory of two types of paranoia. *Clinical Psychology: Science and Practice*, 2, 263–278.

Wells, A. (1997) *Cognitive Therapy for Anxiety Disorders*. London: Wiley.

Wells, A. and Matthews, G. (1994) *Attention and Emotion*. Hove: Lawrence Erlbaum Associates.

Yung, A., Phillips, L.J., McGorry, P.D. *et al.* (1998) A step towards indicated prevention of schizophrenia. *British Journal of Psychiatry*, 172 (Suppl. 33), 14–20.

Yung, A.R., Yuen, H.P., McGorry, P.D. *et al.* (2005) Mapping the onset of psychosis: the Comprehensive Assessment of At-Risk Mental States. *Australian and New Zealand Journal of Psychiatry*, 39(11–12), 964–971.

Chapter 20

Cognitive behavioural therapy for persecutory delusions: three case examples

David Kingdon, Katie Ashcroft, and
Douglas Turkington

Introduction

The development of an integrated cognitive behavioural therapy (CBT) for
persecutory delusions has evolved over the past few decades since Beck
(Beck 1952; Kingdon and Turkington 2005) first described his process of therapy of a man with a delusional system involving surveillance and persecution
by the FBI. The basic principles of his therapeutic approach then apply equally
now. He engaged with the patient by taking his beliefs seriously and trying to
understand them in a collaborative manner. They together examined evidence
that either supported or refuted his delusional beliefs. They investigated further and tried to understand the belief system better by specifically focusing
on individuals who were thought to be FBI agents involved in surveillance.
It is clear from Beck's description that they established a good working
alliance in which trust and reality testing could proceed and the delusional
system which had been so intrusive gradually receded. This chapter will discuss engagement, assessment, formulation and specific techniques for working
with delusions including use of guided discovery and Socratic questioning.
Techniques will also be described for establishing homework exercises, working at the schema level and for relapse prevention. It will also explore ways of
working with individuals who present difficulties in engaging and have beliefs
which seem particularly resistant to change (grandiose delusions and
delusional systems).

Paranoia can present differently in the varied sub-groups within the broad
psychosis and schizophrenia spectrum of disorders (Kingdon and Turkington
2005). Possible groupings include those where initial onset is associated with
(a) severe traumatic experiences, (b) use of hallucinogenic drugs, (c) significant

stress-sensitivity and where (d) anxiety symptoms are converted into system-atized delusions, thereby relieving the anxiety, by the sense of understanding 'what's been going on' albeit delusionally. These sub-groups have a lengthy history: Kraepelin differentiated between dementia praecox and late-onset paranoid ('delusional') states, and hysteria (similar to borderline personality disorder) as well as manic depressive psychosis (Kraepelin 1919). Drug-related psychosis emerged at a later date.

Trauma in schizophrenia (often presenting with co-morbid borderline personality disorder) is very commonly and understandably associated with paranoia as fear of the perpetrator of the trauma often remains, even after that person is no longer apparently in a position to cause harm (e.g. has died or is imprisoned). Bad experiences from hallucinogenic drugs precipitating psychotic experiences frequently involve paranoia which may be due to the chemical effect of the drug itself or associated experiences, e.g. with drug deal-ers or police or simply the fear of association with them. Stress sensitivity may be associated with bullying and social anxiety on a continuum with overval-ued ideas and delusions of persecution. Later-onset delusional systems, where personality and relationships have been previously well-formed, can arise where stress—particularly where it is perceived as unfair—is misunderstood, for example, indigestion can be misconstrued as poisoning, paraesthesiae from hyperventilation as electrocution. Grandiose beliefs, e.g. of being responsible for inventing the CD player, when not accepted by others, can be supplemented by persecutory delusions, e.g. they stole it from me and are doing everything they can to prevent me getting recognition.

Engagement

Developing a strong therapeutic relationship is the foundation of any thera-peutic work, without which little progress can be made. A key component of this is the development and maintenance of trust. Where trust is lost, rebuild-ing can be very difficult and sometimes the damage left can mean that, at least for that therapist, meaningful work can prove impossible. This is particularly the case with persecutory delusions simply because their essence is mistrust. It is too easy to confirm that mistrust by being caught out deceiving the indi-vidual, even if it is only through patronizing. For example, a question such as 'Will this medication help me?' will often receive the response 'Yes ... definitely' or 'Does it have side-effects?' with minimization 'Not many.' The person is much more likely to engage with a more considered response—'It does help a lot of people, but not by any means everyone' or 'Well, there are quite a lot listed but these are the commoner ones ...'—and may indeed be deliberately checking out the veracity of the mental health worker, fully aware of the answers already. It may seem trite to emphasize honesty but being pedantic about answers can pay dividends.

In general terms, the 'non-specific factors' described as fundamental to good therapy are especially important with paranoia. Specific cognitive behavioural techniques can have added benefit over and above that of the relationship alone but a good relationship is the indispensable foundation on which therapy is built. Expertise in developing empathy, genuineness and warmth, is sometimes assumed, rather than recognized as requiring training, experience and practice, observing in a reflective way and reacting to any negative, or lack of positive, responses within the relationship. Warmth may be particularly engaging—conveyed in smiling with the person, gentleness in voice and manner, use of humour where it can seem likely to be reciprocated and self-disclosure especially on request of a type relevant to the nature of the relationship at that time. Conveying empathy may be better done non-verbally—by asking the relevant question or a well-placed 'mmm …'—overt statements to confirm understanding can seem forced or be rejected. Being able to convey competence can also enhance the relationship by providing a secure base and engendering hopefulness that changes for the better are possible. Our experience of using 'befriending' as a control intervention in clinical trials reinforced to us just how valuable simple conversation respecting the other's point of view was in building trust and forming a foundation for reducing persecutory delusions.

Assessment

Focusing on the key symptoms and concerns of the individual is very important but unless the full personal context within which these issues have arisen, including social and physical factors, is assessed, it can be very difficult to progress. For example, when assessing a client with concerns about going out in a certain area, the information that the client has a history of being sexually assaulted by someone who lives in that area is of considerable importance. A full systematic chronological personal history gives a holistic view which can supply a wealth of relevant material and allow the person themselves to understand all the issues within which their particular concern resides—and be sure that the therapist appreciates them as well. Understanding the development of their concerns, tracing the path they took which led them to the particular belief that they had, allows understanding of how that came about and can inform all involved. So often, taking this broad perspective in a way which is non-threatening, logical and not challenging helps engagement and brings a little flexibility to previously rigid positions. At the start of therapy it is important to do a rating of the impact of the major presenting symptom, for example using the Psychotic Symptoms Rating Scales (PSYRATS; Haddock *et al.* 1999). This allows the patient systematically to explain all aspects of their experience of the persecution; how much they act upon it or hide away from it; what the major emotional component is and just how much flexibility there is in relation to this belief. Ratings of anxiety (e.g. Beck Anxiety Inventory) and depression (e.g. Beck Depression Inventory) may also be relevant. A global rating scale covering social and psychological aspects, such as Global Assessment of Functioning (GAF) or Health of the Nation Outcome Scale (HoNOS) can also be informative. Use of the individual items which score highly can be used to track progress session by session with completion of the full scales at around session 6 and end of therapy to assess and document progress.

Formulation

This process of gathering personal information helps therapist and client make sense of the client's difficulties in the context of present and past experience. Formulation allows this to happen by concisely drawing together key facts, concerns, thoughts, feelings, behaviours and experiences and then providing a format to see how links have developed with both positive and negative consequences. Formulation can be used to focus on specific links between activating events, beliefs and consequences (ABC) based on Rational Emotive Therapy models as described by Chadwick and colleagues in psychosis (Chadwick 2006); for an example of such a formulation see the case of Margaret later in this chapter.

Developmental formulations, e.g. Beck (2005), can show a person with a persecutory delusion how they developed low self-esteem which is very common among patients with persecutory delusions and may act as a vulnerability factor predisposing to their development. We have taken things a step further with development of the area described as 'early childhood experiences' to include predisposing, precipitating, perpetuating and protective factors which can be especially relevant in psychosis. Choice of formulation needs to be adapted to client and therapist and may be used sequentially. It can be useful for the therapist to draw information together into a broader comprehensive formulation after initial assessment to plan a therapeutic strategy but the amount of information may be overwhelming at that stage, at least to the client. In such cases an ABC formulation can be of use as it allows the therapist to identify key areas to begin working with. When the therapy needs a new focus or is getting 'stuck', returning to the broader picture can provide new productive areas or simply different aspects of the same issue to work on. It can also be a useful check near the end of therapy that the major issues have indeed been tackled. Formulations can also be presented in the form of letters (see Chadwick 2006).

Work with persecutory delusions

Assessment, engagement and formulation constitute important components of work with paranoia but work which focuses more directly on the content of the beliefs themselves also has an important place. Discussion with the individual about their beliefs and its implications and consequences is not only a very important part of assessment, engagement and formulation but also a method for instilling a modicum of doubt where appropriate. As the process of guided discovery leads the therapist through the pre-existing circumstances and subsequent genesis of the belief, the process of questioning inevitably draws out evidence for and against the proposition being made by the client. This in turn leads to some examination by the client and questioning of it – albeit this may not be voiced and indeed would usually be denied if challenged (which is why such challenging can be disengaging if used too early, if at all). A good shared understanding of the beliefs and their development should emerge, clarifying the reasons why such a belief is held by the client and eventually where and why the therapist may differ in their conviction about it. Such a process is helpful in engagement and assessment: the evidence supporting the paranoid beliefs in clients who have been traumatized will have been clarified and there may be appropriate safety measures that can be taken, e.g. in relation to personal protection. Where drugs have been an issue, specific measures to avoid at-risk situations or limit damaging drug use may be reasonable. Stress-sensitivity can lead to avoidance which in turn reinforces low confidence and paranoia and may benefit from graded re-exposure and pre-emptive management of other symptoms, e.g. delusions of reference. It is often useful with patients to normalize paranoid thinking by using self-disclosure around paranoid thoughts and explaining circumstances in which paranoia has a protective function, e.g. there are certain areas of every city where it would be very wise to have a regular look over your shoulder to see who is approaching you.

Systematized delusions need specific approaches which build on the initial reasoning processes. This reasoning often allows sufficient engagement to occur for the individual to attend regularly and work with the beliefs they have. At some stage however, agreement-to-differ may be needed to avoid prolonged repetitive and frustrating discussion. The content of the beliefs is reviewed and agreed; the evidence for them is set out by the client and the evidence which is not supportive developed, if possible, collaboratively—with use of homework assignments by client and therapist. At this stage, clients may begin to discuss other issues in their lives spontaneously—loneliness, lack of achievement, etc.—and the client may allow work with these to occur. These often appear to be clearly related to the beliefs being expressed, e.g. poor self-esteem being linked to grandiosity. If this is not happening spontaneously, techniques to work with underlying beliefs may open up these areas. However, caution is needed in relation to exposing distress which can lead to retrenchment of beliefs or symptomatic worsening with increased risk including suicidality. Again where distress is exposed, collaboration with the client on the pace of intervention and nature of the discussion is vital. Key underlying beliefs can sometimes be detected by asking clients hypothetically about what would be the positive and negative consequences for them if others did accept their interpretations of situations or specifically beliefs about themselves, especially grandiose beliefs. For example, if others agreed that they were holders of eminent positions, e.g. king or pop star, why would that matter to them? Answers are not always those anticipated but often refer to being respected or accepted by others, no longer isolated. It may then be possible to work further with these beliefs, e.g. if being respected is a problem, what can we do about that? Who do you feel doesn't respect you? And so forth.

Summary

Work with paranoia particularly involves the development and maintenance of a therapeutic relationship. When this is the prime focus of the intervention, it is possible to engage even with patients with a very high level of conviction in their delusional beliefs. Debate and discussion can then allow them to cope better with their situation and behaviour to change in the direction of improved relationships generally. The following three case studies illustrate working with paranoia in circumstances where traumatic experiences have particular but differing relevance.

Case studies

Schema-focused CBT for a persecutory and grandiose delusional system linked to underlying trauma

Presenting complaint

Anger towards his previous employers.

Assessment

David is a 25-year-old man who was referred for CBT following failed trials of antipsychotic medication. He had been prescribed flupenthixol 60 mg depot weekly for 6 months in the community. He was then admitted as an inpatient due to the fact that he was acting on his delusions in a manner considered to be potentially dangerous to others. As an inpatient he did not settle on olanzepine even with the dose eventually being increased to 30 mg daily. He was encouraged to accept a trial of clozapine but utterly refused as he viewed the issue about blood testing in a delusional manner.

During the assessment session he exhibited very marked euphoria in relation to his grandiose beliefs and also expressed anger about his previous employers whom he believed had stolen one of his ideas for a new type of milk carton. He was rated using the Maudsley Assessment of Delusions Schedule (Taylor *et al.*, 1994). This revealed the intensity and systematization of his delusional beliefs as well as showing little in the way of cognitive flexibility and complete lack of insight. It seemed that discharge from hospital in the near future was going to be impossible due to his propensity to act on his beliefs. David believed that he was in training for the Olympics and would often break off from the session to do press-ups and sit-ups. At all times he was dressed in sports wear.

Therapy
Early sessions

These early sessions involved engaging and attempting to assess the ongoing risk. He would endlessly talk about his anger at his previous employers and about his milk carton which he believed the company had now patented. Very little progress was made until we attempted inductively to work our way through an examination of the antecedents of his psychosis. He informed the therapist that two months prior to the breakdown he had been the subject of bullying in the workplace. This was done by one particular worker who was calling him 'a queer' because 'I liked to be well turned out, clean and tidy at work.' The verbal abuse turned into physical abuse with provocation and with David being bumped and nudged at the factory. The 'joke' spread and David was increasingly the butt of all the work-floor jibes. At about the same time he was under pressure from the Child Support Agency (a government agency established to ensure child support is paid) as his ex-girlfriend was demanding £100 per week for the support of their child. This was money that David could not afford as he was already receiving red letters about falling behind on his mortgage. He then mentioned that he had gone to the Millennium Bridge on the eve of the millennium and then visited the house where he used to stay at the time that he was sexually abused by an older boy. This had never been disclosed before but it appears from the notes that there was no evidence that anyone had specifically asked this question. He disclosed this in a matter of fact way with little in the way of emotional distress. The rape by a teenager occurred when he was only 4 years old. The effect of this assault was to leave him wondering why it had happened and specifically whether there was something odd or different about him that made the perpetrator choose him in particular. Following this he did reasonably well at school, though he was 'picked on' to a degree. He worked in the factory making cartons until the bullying took place at work. He then became increasingly anxious and developed grandiose ideas that Dairylea had accepted his new carton design for a major contract. He started to believe that he was about to appear on *Gladiators* (a TV programme) and then that he had been tipped to win three Olympic gold medals. Just prior to admission he had knocked the staircase down in his house to give him a climbing wall for training. He came to believe that his colleague at work was actually his Olympic trainer and also that he was about to marry his childhood sweetheart. This led eventually to admission under the Mental Health Act after a violent situation at work when he interrupted a board Meeting demanding that they sign the milk carton patent back to him. He also demanded the return of the money which he believed was being kept back from him and overturned the Chief Executive's desk and tore up the minutes of the meeting.

Formulation

We attempted to produce a formulation connecting these various strands of information. He had been abused and had come to believe that he was 'different', he was then bullied at work and had other stresses, leading to increasing anxiety with the emergence of paranoid and grandiose delusions which seemed to be linked to the anxiety resolving. He had obviously always tried hard to be accepted and approved by others but this had eventually broken down with all the jokes about him at work. A key schema-forming event was of sexual assault aged 4 years. He therefore developed a core maladaptive schema of being different from others and a compensatory schema vulnerability linked to a need for approval. The critical incident which triggered the emergence of the delusional system was bullying at work. This led to such high levels of increasing anxiety that an approval-maintaining schema emerged.

Middle sessions

David refused to do any homework of any kind and all the CBT had to be done in the sessions. Attempts at reality testing by viewing the Olympic athlete lists to introduce doubt were unsuccessful. His name was always just about to appear. Attempts to reduce the intensity of his anger with his employers using rational responses were similarly unhelpful. An inference chain was done which led to disapproval by colleagues as a matter of great shame and despair, if it did turn out to be the case that his carton hadn't been taken on as a contract. Further, there was a very painful core personal belief that he was a 'misfit'.

relating to the flat. Margaret cited a number of evictions in support of her conspiracy belief. However, the reasons for these were rent arrears, damage to property or her frequent shouting. At the time of referral she was no longer confronting her perceived persecutors as she had no desire for further contact with the criminal justice system.

Second, Margaret was of the opinion that people were trying to make her lose her sense of smell (50%). This belief appeared to be triggered by experiencing her nose itching. However, this belief did not have as great an impact on her life. She would experience the thought, avoid it by reading and as the itching passed so did the preoccupation with the belief.

Finally, Margaret believed that people would be critical of her, dismissing her as they wanted to distress her and they disliked her. If this were to happen she would feel hurt, and believe that she was a failure and disliked. This appeared to be the longest-standing belief; she gave examples of experiencing distress associated with this in her late twenties. When in social situations she would either try to agree with people to the point of being obsequious or go on the defensive and be verbally aggressive. She reported that either response led to the same reaction in others, that of them disengaging both immediately and/or in the long term. Consequently, over the decades, she had developed a strategy of being critical of others before they had a chance to be critical of her, which led to her being very socially isolated. Margaret had two goals for therapy: not to be so lonely and to feel that she was acceptable to others.

During the assessment sessions it became clear that the belief that caused the most intense distress was the one regarding the accommodation providers; it was also established that Margaret believed 100% in the conspiracy against her. When asked by the therapist 'How would it be if we were to explore the possibility that there may be other explanations for things moving in the flat?' She replied 'If you were to say that you would be saying that I was mad and not worth talking too.'

From this response the therapist was left in no doubt that direct exploration of this belief was likely to prompt disengagement. Also, exploration of this belief did not fit with Margaret's goals for therapy. Her greatest concern was that of loneliness. It was agreed that the belief that contributed to this was the third of those listed above. Additionally, what little sense of self-esteem Margaret experienced was solely reliant on 'being right' and this also contributed to her interpersonal style.

Formulation

A formulation letter was constructed and given to Margaret in a session at the end of the assessment period. The letter was structured as described by

Chadwick (2006). The therapist acknowledged the effort Margaret put into attending sessions, acknowledging that Margaret found it challenging to focus on her difficulties and that, as she was always waiting to be let down by people, it must be effortful to confide and trust in the therapeutic relationship. The themes of failure, fear of criticism and low self-esteem were outlined followed by the treatment options.

It was also important for Margaret and the therapist to formulate some of their interactions using the ABC framework. The formulation in Table 20.1 illustrates how the previously mentioned themes unfolded; labelling prevented these becoming challenges to progress in therapy.

Therapy

As the ABC demonstrates, the importance of being right also led to behaviour that was incompatible with a two-way conversation and social success. Margaret and the therapist explored in depth how 'getting in first' played out in the therapy sessions. The therapist noted a pattern of Margaret starting to lecture her when she felt uneasy. They clarified the experience for Margaret using the ABC framework. Over a number of sessions they were able to establish that Margaret engaged in such behaviour when feeling anxious as manifested by tension in her neck. She was then able to notice anxiety in other parts of her body, and finally to relax by slower breathing. In a relatively short space of time Margaret was able to notice her anxiety, reduce it and resist the urge to lecture the therapist.

Having learned how to drop the 'getting in first' behaviour in sessions, the challenge was for Margaret to apply it on a day-to-day basis. This homework

Table 20.1 Case example of formulating specific links between 'activating events, beliefs and consequences' (ABC) (Chadwick 2006)

A	B	C
In therapy session, start to feel uneasy	I need to prove I am right; if I don't the therapist will only contradict me	Anxiety 8/10 Tension in neck Start to lecture the therapist
	↓	
	That will mean I am wrong	
	↓	
	She will criticize me	
	↓	
	I am a failure	

took careful setting up. After assessment Margaret had requested therapy sessions once every three weeks as she found them very challenging. The therapist was cognizant of how effortful therapy and behaving differently was and agreed with the proposed frequency of meetings.

Margaret decided to make the most of a hairdressing appointment and a behavioural experiment was designed. She predicted that the hairdresser would be critical within five minutes of starting to cut her hair (95% belief). This was noted down along with Margaret's fear of feeling hurt and her behavioural fallback position of being rude in return. Her alternative behaviour was planned and rehearsed in session: noticing the anxiety, doing the breathing, resisting the urge to be critical, engaging in safe topics of conversation. She agreed to make a note on returning home as to how it went. At the following session considerable time was spent on homework review—what had happened and what had been learnt from the experience of having a very pleasant chat with the hairdresser. Margaret's percentage rating of the belief that 'people will be critical or contradict me' went down a little but it took many repetitions of the same experiment, with Margaret cautiously selecting the next individual, for the percentage rating to reduce further. However, as therapy progressed she reported needing less preparation time 'to "psych" myself up to be civil' and the number of people she could talk too reached double digits.

The second strand of therapeutic work focused on her view of herself as being a failure and, through this, unacceptable to others. Simple checking of the evidence for 'I am a failure' proved productive. While there were many things Margaret hadn't achieved in her life it became apparent that she hadn't aspired to some of them, e.g. marriage or children. Furthermore, slowly, she was able to list achievements such as political work, staying out of hospital, achieving good A-levels, and more recent stability regarding housing. Margaret then saw the task as 'learning to tolerate the positives in my life.' This was effortful and acknowledging the positives prompted anxiety, so a flash card was constructed to support daily reading of 'my achievements.' The flash card, which Margaret carried with her, was as follows: 'I try to avoid positive things about myself. When I was growing up I absorbed the way others thought about me, a failure and not good enough. That is how people behaved towards me. Now I know this wouldn't happen but I still behave in a way that I think it would. Now it is OK for me to think positively about myself.'

At session 14 of therapy, Margaret was able to notice her anxiety without prompting from the therapist and link it to the discussion. She stated: 'I've started to feel tense because we are getting close to the fact that I have a lot of ideas that I feel put down by everyone when I am not put down. I can acknowledge that

I am OK.' Shortly after this session therapy work was reviewed and Margaret felt that she had achieved her goals.

Outcome

Margaret allowed people to be friendly towards her and was friendly in response, and building upon this she had started to form friendships. She received Christmas cards and felt excited and pleased about this change in her life. She had gone from only having contact with mental health professionals to three or more social contacts a week with her peers. She described being proud of her achievements and proud of the mistakes she hadn't made. These changes were noted in the relapse prevention planning along with very specific plans for behaviour so that Margaret could be clear in terms of what she needed to continue doing. Consideration was given to what might prompt setbacks in the future and how to deal with such events.

With reference to the conspiracy belief, Margaret was significantly less preoccupied. It was still a concern for her, she felt safer in her flat (maintaining her tenancy for 18 months—a huge achievement) but Margaret had not unpacked properly and at times of stress believed her flat *might* be broken into. At these times she talked of her plan to phone the police if she noticed that something had been moved. To the care team's knowledge she did not make contact with the police. Three years after discharge Margaret continues to do well. She is still in the same flat, has a number of friends and now goes on day trips. She has not done any more unpacking.

Summary

The case of Margaret provides an example of work with someone who had fixed persecutory beliefs. It demonstrates that significant work can be undertaken on less firmly held beliefs, particularly those associated with the client's goals, even though some aspects of core persecutory beliefs persist. Such work can lead to significant changes, in Margaret's case to improvement in social functioning.

Cognitive therapy for paranoia arising from childhood trauma

Presenting complaint

Auditory and visual hallucinations of Satan, with overwhelming feelings of despair.

Assessment

Jan is 41 years old, married but not currently working. She lives with her husband. She grew up locally. Her father heavily abused alcohol and she developed a great fear of him. He sexually abused her during her late childhood and early teens leaving her feeling unloved and ashamed. Her relationship with her mother also was distant and not a happy one. She was the middle child of five with two older brothers and younger sisters. She had lost contact with family over the past twenty years. School was uneventful. After school she then did reasonably well at her exams and started working full time as secretary for many years at a local firm until aged 36 years.

Her husband works locally as shop manager. She doesn't feel she can talk to him but he has been very loyal to her expressing his own strong concerns about medication and hospitalization used by her mental health team. She has a good relationship with her two sons and a daughter who are working away or at college locally.

She had a brief hospital admission in her late teens but had then stayed out of treatment until the age of 36 years when she had been attacked on the way home from work. Although she managed to run away and was not harmed, this led to her becoming increasingly distressed and angry leading to hospitalization on three occasions over four years. She was readily tearful and had suicidal ideas. She had intrusive thoughts about killing her husband which distressed her. She was hearing voices telling her she was worthless and to take an overdose which she felt compelled to obey. She was also experiencing visual hallucinations—seeing the people 'turning into the Satan'. She had seriously self-harmed in the recent past, on one occasion cutting which led to tendon damage ('the accident'). She did not use alcohol or illicit drugs. When frightened and convinced that she was being followed and in danger, she would carry a hammer to protect her self. When an attempt was made to remove the hammer on one admission to hospital, this had led to a threatening situation to which the police had been called.

She had been referred for psychodynamic psychotherapy and was offered a number of sessions which she attended initially but then discontinued when admitted to hospital. She was then referred for cognitive therapy, but after a few sessions the issue of the hammer being bought to therapy emerged. She felt unable to leave it outside the session, so the sessions were discontinued. She continued to see a psychiatrist who was trained in cognitive therapy. Forensic opinion sought at the time was that risk was present but the only occasion when risk to others had occurred was when attempts to disarm her occurred. Risk to herself was significant and needed to be monitored. Hospitalization including compulsory admission was used when ideation, i.e. suicidal thoughts, increased to intent to act on voices and passivity (i.e. the conviction that she was controlled by the voices and had to do what they commanded).

Formulation

Such a complex case involves many factors which are summarized in the 'Making sense' formulation. Margaret's expressed current concern is central and directly elicited and noted. Predisposing, precipitating, perpetuating and protective factors are listed. Thoughts, feelings, behaviour and social factors are also described. The underlying belief that she is worthless reverberated throughout contact with her. There are many potential links from worthlessness to the thoughts, feelings, and behaviours that she was experiencing and to its origin in her early life experiences. Establishing and understanding these links provides focus for therapy. Paying sufficient attention to the immediate concerns presented is sometimes difficult but important, and work is needed with all the inter-related factors, e.g. influence of isolation and distant relationships along with risk concerns (Fig. 20.1).

Therapy

Maintaining engagement was the major focus of each session through discussion of family issues, daily activities, medication needs and wishes with relevant self-disclosure. This involved cautious teasing out of key concerns

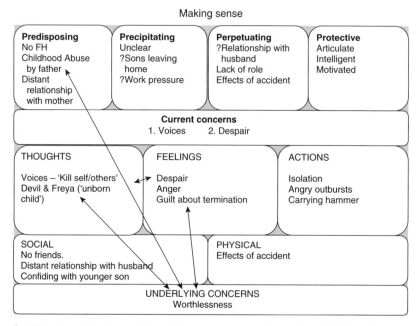

Fig. 20.1 Cognitive therapy formulation for paranoia arising from childhood trauma

relevant to the previous period between interviews. Discussion of daily activities and those of family members, her mood, sleep and the current level of her symptoms and relationships within the family occurred whilst being able to tactfully develop as positive and hopeful an atmosphere as was credible in the circumstances. Sufficient focus on negative aspects was necessary for Jan to feel she was being listened to and as far as possible understood without the interview being solely focused on her despair. Refocusing on positive developments occurring often over quite a lengthy period of time, e.g. her sons' development, was attempted. Assessment information was gathered and a formulation drawn up but shared piecemeal as was relevant to discussion. The paranoid beliefs related directly to childhood fears, and shame and guilt to the abusive experiences. Making these connections could be achieved by asking about when these beliefs had originally arisen and relating these in general terms to the context:

Therapist: So when did you first feel this frightened?

Client: As long as I remember.

Therapist: So back when you were a kid.

Client: Yes.

Therapist: That was pretty understandable then with all that was going on ... but do you know why you feel the same now?

Client: No but I know what I feel.

Such discussions were important in exploring beliefs about self and risk to self and with time have begun to reduce conviction. Specific events in childhood were discussed only very briefly—occasional contacts with duty professionals when assessments of these events were attempted had an aversive effect. However, it was possible to express the therapist's view that she could not be held responsible for the events that occurred and that far from being evil herself, evil had been done to her, thus her suspicion of others was very understandable. Beliefs about self which related to these events could therefore be gently discussed, e.g. 'I'm threatened and unsafe,' 'I'm evil,' and 'I'm ashamed of myself.' Work within the clinical team enabled engagement with a female mental health social worker whose aim was to provide support and develop community links. Regular discussions and exchange of copy letters to the family doctor led to interchange of risk and mood information. Maintaining relationships using relatively brief weekly-to-fortnightly sessions over a period of two to three years has allowed a dialogue to be continued, hospitalization to be avoided and risk to self and others not materialized.

Summary

Jan presented with a range of symptoms: voices, visions, depression and paranoia with major issues of risk to herself and others. The formulation developed as she described a severely disrupted and distressing childhood in which she had been severely traumatized. Her paranoid symptoms were a very natural reaction to those experiences. Medication had very limited effect and hospitalization when used in desperation had very short-term protective benefits but soon became counter-productive. The key therapeutic aim was to establish and sustain a relationship which engaged her with the service and to offer ways of understanding and countering her distressing experiences. CBT was used to build collaboration, normalize her response to very abnormal experiences and counter her feelings of utter unworthiness. It has been possible to maintain the relationship over a period of a few years with some reduction in the distress experienced.

References

Beck, A.T. (1952) Successful outpatient psychotherapy of a chronic schizophrenic with a delusion based on borrowed guilt. *Psychiatry: Journal for the Study of Interpersonal Processes*, 15, 305–312.

Beck, J.S. (2005) *Cognitive Therapy for Challenging Problems*. Guilford, New York.

Callcott, P. and Turkington, D. (2006) CBT for traumatic psychosis. In: Larkin,W. and Morrison, A.P. (eds), *Trauma and Psychosis*, pp. 222–238. Hove: Routledge.

Chadwick, P.D. (2006) *Person Based Cognitive Therapy for Distressing Psychosis*. Chichester: Wiley.

Haddock, G., McCarron, J., Tarrier, N. and Faragher, E.B. (1999) Scales to measure dimensions of hallucinations and delusions: the psychotic symptom rating scales (PSYRATS). *Psychological Medicine*, 29, 879–889.

Kingdon, D. and Turkington, D. (2002) *A Case Study Guide to Cognitive Therapy for Psychosis*. Chichester: Wiley.

Kingdon, D.G. and Turkington, D. (2005) *Cognitive Therapy of Schizophrenia*. Guilford: New York.

Kraepelin, E. (1919) *Dementia Praecox and Paraphrenia*. Bristol: Thoemmes Press.

Taylor, P.J., Garety, P., Buchanan, A. *et al.* (1994) Delusions and violence. In: Monahan, J.E. and Steadman, H.J.E. (eds), *Violence and Mental Disorder: Developments in Risk Assessment*, pp. 161–182. Chicago: University of Chicago Press.

Chapter 21

Person-based cognitive therapy for paranoia: the challenges of 'poor me'

Paul Chadwick and Peter Trower

Introduction

In this chapter we consider how to use person-based cognitive therapy (PBCT) to help people with what Trower and Chadwick (1995) called 'poor me' paranoia. We focus on 'poor me' because several issues combine to make cognitive therapy for individuals with 'poor me' paranoia particularly challenging. We first describe the 'poor me'–'bad me' distinction and give a research update. We then describe five key developments that take PBCT for distressing psychosis (Chadwick 2006) beyond standard cognitive therapy for psychosis. These are: greater emphasis on a person-based relationship; a new approach to case formulation; integrating mindfulness; more work with self; and a clearer focus on meta-cognition. We explore in each area a number of key challenges facing a therapist working with people with 'poor me' paranoia. These challenges are illustrated with case material.

Two types of paranoia: 'poor me' and 'bad me'

James, aged 26 years, was referred for cognitive behavioural therapy (CBT) for persecutory beliefs and was seen by a clinical psychologist specializing in CBT for psychosis. He reports being assaulted around the body and head: 'I hear voices and they constantly threaten and attack. It's been going on for two-and-a-half years. I hear them and see images, pictures in my head. The assaults are chopping away my identity and my identity gets more faded. It feels like they are trying to capture my head, my personality, my thoughts and opinions, trying to take me over. I tell them to clear off but they get worse. I try to switch off. My main fear is that I would be fully trapped and my identity sucked out of me completely. It feels like they are moving my arms and head and sending signals out to people.'

James knows who 'they' are: 'Some bloke who lives down the bottom of the road and his daughter. They're psychic. They're trying to take over control of me and do me in. They also attack my back, groin and legs. It feels like they're cutting the vein, like the inside of my head collapses, is sore and tight.'

The persecutor's voice repeatedly identifies itself as the most dominant, valuable person on the planet and says James was rude to him. James did take his daughter for a walk, just as a friend, and afterwards had an altercation with the man, who thought James was being rude. When he got home James noticed his urine was luminous, which showed 'something was wrong.' James says of the persecution. 'I don't deserve this; it's unfair, not right. Why don't they pick on someone bad?' He sees them as 'getting fun and entertainment out of seeing him suffer' and views them as 'bad, malicious.'

James's experience is illustrative of classical persecution paranoia—what we call 'poor me' paranoia (Trower and Chadwick 1995) defined in terms of a central perception of *undeserved* persecution. We identified a second type of paranoia, 'bad me', which we argued shares many features with the classical 'poor me' profile, yet also is different in some aspects of phenomenology. A central difference is that in 'bad me' paranoia, others' malevolence and mistreatment are perceived as deserved—a punishment for an inherent badness. Often there are linked traumatic experiences that established this sense of badness, such as trauma, abuse, bullying and loss. Conscious self-esteem is low, in contrast to the classical 'poor me' persecution, where conscious self-esteem is typically normal.

Our separation of two types of paranoia challenged the contemporary presentation of a uniform paranoid process. In a seminal paper, Zigler and Glick (1988) anticipate the possibility of two types of paranoia, proposing in a developmental approach to psychopathology that some forms of paranoid schizophrenia might be camouflaged depression. Certain paranoias, they argue, will be genotypically schizophrenia; others may well be genotypically depression.

First and foremost, the 'poor me'–'bad me' distinction concerns understanding a person's current experience—the phenomenology of paranoia. This includes current emotional, cognitive (automatic thoughts, underlying assumptions and core beliefs) and behavioural experience. Empirical evidence for the two types has accumulated slowly over the past decade. Five research studies have found evidence for the 'poor me'–'bad me' distinction (Freeman *et al.* 2001; Startup *et al.* 2003; Chadwick *et al.* 2005; Fornells-Ambrojo and Garety 2005; Melo *et al.* 2006). Freeman *et al.* (2001) and Chadwick *et al.* (2005) further supported Trower and Chadwick's (1995) predictions about differences in depression and self-evaluation or self-esteem. Chadwick *et al.*'s (2005) study of 53 people with psychosis showed that the crucial differences in self-esteem and self-evaluation between those with 'poor me' and 'bad me' paranoia were not simply artefacts of differences in depression. Two further studies offer indirect evidence for the two types in people with psychosis (Peters and Garety 2006) and in college students highly disposed to paranoia (Combs et al. 2007). In addition to phenomenology, Trower and Chadwick (1995) offer distinct cognitive developmental formulations for the origins of the two types. These theoretically derived models remain to be tested, and their usefulness is an issue separate from that of the phenomenological distinction itself.

In our writing we have tended to describe 'poor me' and 'bad me' paranoia through different clients. This is largely for ease of expression. In fact they are different psychological processes. Whilst it is often the case that individuals present as strongly one or the other, our intention has never been to force a dichotomy. Also, although many clients remain characteristically 'poor me' or 'bad me', we have never asserted that this must be so. It is possible for some people either not to fit neatly into either profile, or to move between the two psychological processes. Indeed, Melo et al. (2006) found that approximately a third of their sample shifted in perception of deservedness of persecution over time.

The distinction has implications for psychological therapy. Chadwick et al. (1996) spelled out some of the key differences in therapeutic approach to 'poor me' and 'bad me' paranoia. Over the past decade our own clinical experience, and that of supervisees and colleagues, suggests that psychological therapy for 'poor me' paranoia is particularly challenging. This reflects difficulty establishing a collaborative relationship and focus for therapy, problems with formulation, and also what can be considerable difficulty in exploring the persecutory beliefs in a way that is acceptable to clients. No therapeutic work with people with distressing psychosis is ever simple, but with 'bad me' paranoia the building blocks for the relationship and process of therapy are often more easily located: a common focus on easing distress and promoting self-acceptance, perhaps a clear formulation linking current beliefs and formative traumatic experience, and so on. In this chapter we focus on the particular challenges of working with 'poor me' paranoia.

Person-based cognitive therapy for 'poor me' paranoia: formulation

In PBCT the approach to formulation (see Chadwick 2006; Chapter 3, this volume) is to identify four distinct sources of distress and potential well-being (see Fig. 21.1). There is no requirement or endeavour to establish one, linear developmental diagram, as is done in traditional CBT. Indeed, Chadwick (2006) has argued that 'poor me' paranoia often lacks the clear developmental links with formative life experience such as trauma, loss and abuse, which are so characteristic of 'bad me' paranoia. That is to say, therapists and clients can seek to understand the onset and maintenance of paranoia without having to make links to early experience that can feel forced and spurious. The four domains are conceptualized in terms of Vygotsky's Zone of Proximal Development (ZoPD: Vygotsky 1979). Vygotsky defined the ZoPD as follows: 'It is the distance between the actual developmental level as determined by independent problem solving and the level of potential development as determined through problem solving under adult guidance or in collaboration with more capable peers' (p. 86). In PBCT the ZoPD concept is used almost as a metaphor. In no way is it intended to imply that therapists are experts or more capable peers, but rather to express how within PBCT change occurs because of and through a social and collaborative process of exploration of a client's potential to let go of sources of distress and disturbance and move

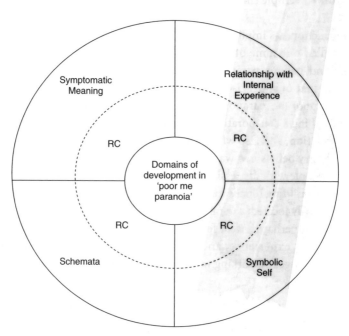

Fig. 21.1 Four domains of radically collaborative (RC) exploration of proximal development. Reproduced with permission from P.D.J. Chadwick, *Person-based Cognitive Therapy for Distressing Psychosis.* ©2006 John Wiley & Sons Ltd.

towards well-being and acceptance in each of the four domains of proximal development. In each domain, a client's current strengths, positive qualities and potentialities are as important as current sources of distress.

The four sources of distress illusrated in Figure 21.1 are: Symptomatic Meaning; Relationship to Internal Experience; Schemata; Symbolic Self. Symptomatic meaning concerns paranoia, voices and linked beliefs, images etc. In the present context this is where 'bad me' and James's 'poor me' beliefs lie. Relationship to inner experience concerns how a person reacts in the moment of awareness of an unpleasant psychotic sensation, such as a voice, image, tactile sensation or paranoid intrusion. Where symptomatic meaning concerns how a person makes sense of psychotic sensations, this domain is *relational*—does the person react with experiential avoidance, struggle, rumination, or judgement? This is where mindfulness is integrated within PBCT (Chadwick 2006: Chapters 1 and 5, this volume). For James, this means understanding how he relates in the moment of experiencing voices, images and tactile sensations. Schemata concern work with negative schemata, principally of self but also others, and the development of positive self-schemata. Whilst James has not described negative self-schemata, there is a striking absence of positive schematic experience—a powerful potential source of proximal development and well-being. Symbolic Self concerns working towards an overarching meta-cognitive insight into the nature of self—that it is an emotionally complex, contradictory and changing process. It is this insight which forms the basis for self-acceptance, encapsulated for example by Rogers (1961) and in Ellis's concept of unconditional self-acceptance (Ellis 1994). James appears to have lost a sense of Symbolic Self altogether, attributing this to the persecutors sucking out his identity. The ZoPD allows therapists to work flexibly across all four domains while retaining a coherent framework for the process of therapy.

Challenges building and maintaining relationships

James's therapist describes James as big, solid, motionless, his face almost expressionless. What little body language there is says: 'Don't try, I don't trust you. You're going to try to interrogate me; I'm not going to let you. Keep out.' He sits very erect, head held high, looking down at the therapist, frowning, just a hint of narrowing his eyes. He gives mainly monosyllabic answers, never asks questions, rarely volunteering information. He talks a little more freely about 'safe' interests, like martial arts or popular myths that take the focus off psychological aspects to do with himself. He looks tough (though the therapist does not feel threatened); smiles are rare and controlled quickly. There is no sign of anxiety; he is very composed, still. Initially he admits to having no emotions, only 'confusion' and low motivation. When pressed he admits to finding the hallucinations 'annoying.' It takes several sessions for him to disclose the emotional intensity of the 'battle' with 'them' and how he has the attacks 'pretty much all the time.' Only well into therapy, when reporting how during mindfulness he feels 'refreshed and calm,' does he state how 'most of the time he is stressed.'

People with 'poor me' paranoia experience others as being fundamentally malevolent without justification. They are victims of an unjust world. This might be expressed in the Schemata domain of the ZoPD in terms of an underlying rule or assumption, 'If other people get the chance, they will harm me without cause.' Where mistrust is assumption-based, moments of mistrust of therapists are common, even to be expected. As well as schematic mistrust of therapists, clients might also incorporate therapists into their symptomatic beliefs, believing them to be involved in the persecution. This usually poses a stronger threat to relationship building. Chadwick (2006, pp. 74–77) offers some guidance to therapists on this issue—it is helpful for therapists to anticipate with clients times of mistrust, collaboratively to explore how to be aware of and manage it, and accept and seek to understand it when it does happen.

It is important to 'meet the person, not the problem' (Chadwick 2006, p. 23). Talking about martial arts, for example, is already an invitation to form a warm, collaborative relationship that embraces all that the person is and not only psychosis. James' interests are potential sources of positive schematic experience (Schemata domain) and valued goals which may later help James accept psychosis as merely one aspect of a complex and emotionally varied self (Symbolic Self).

Relationship building depends upon therapists remaining steadfastly Rogerian throughout therapy. Experience over many years both giving and receiving supervision in CBT reveals how easily therapists can cease to be person-centred with people with psychosis. For example, therapists might be person-centred (or at least passive) for one or two sessions, and then 'change gear' or 'switch modes' and begin to push model, goals and techniques. Therapists' pushing or striving behaviour blocks relationship building, and this problem is magnified greatly when working with 'poor me' paranoia. When therapist 'pushing' behaviour is analysed in supervision, it is commonly found to be driven by therapists' own anxiety, despondency, frustration, hopelessness, and sense of failure.

Addressing this issue, Burns and Auerbach (1996) clarify that therapists' emotional arousal in therapy often reflects their own cognitions, and not psychoanalytic empathy—a process whereby therapists feel what their clients are feeling, or even repressing. Consistent with this, Chadwick (2006) argues that therapist anxiety and striving behaviour stems from their own underlying anticollaborative assumptions about how therapy *should* progress—for example, that clients must engage in therapy, must not drop out, and must change. Therapists are thrown into feeling responsible for clients' behaviour and the process of therapy. If unchecked, therapists' anticollaborative assumptions not only support anxiety, frustration, despondency, etc., but also linked pushing and controlling therapist behaviours that are not Rogerian and can establish self-defeating interpersonal patterns within therapy (e.g. making clients more likely to drop out).

In PBCT therapists aspire to embody radical collaboration—that is, a therapist stance that is free from assumptions about how therapy *must* progress. The process of therapy is to explore what proximal development is possible in the four domains, accepting whatever emerges. Radical collaboration does not diminish a therapist's effectiveness or commitment to supporting a client to change—it is about letting go of needing this to happen. How then are therapists to remain Rogerian and radically collaborative? First, it is important for therapists to become more aware of their emotional arousal and any underlying anticollaborative beliefs as they occur during therapy. As one supervisee said, 'whenever I feel anxious with a client, I ask myself "what is my goal at the moment," and I find it is trying to *make* the client change.'

Second, we encourage therapists to articulate their own positive assumptions about person-based therapy that support radical collaboration: for example, 'My responsibility is to be committed, open, collaborative and to accept my client's decisions and the unfolding process of therapy.' A third way to support radical collaboration is in supervision to ask therapists 'what are your goals working with this client?' Supervisees usually reply by naming something they want to change in the client. With prompting, therapists articulate goals, such as 'to be more aware of my emotional arousal and anticollaborative assumptions,' or 'to become more aware of the limits of my acceptance.' Rogerian acceptance is a process, not a milestone.

PBCT emphasizes working with the therapeutic relationship. This is not about interpretation, or working with transference from formative relationships—it is about openness and a commitment both to understanding and collaboration in the here-and-now. The one thing James brought reliably to therapy was himself, even usually arriving early. Why? When the therapist explored this, after being prompted James said that he 'was willing to give therapy a go because he thought meditation might help.' This was movement, offering opportunity for gentle Socratic exploration. The therapist might explore: How does James think meditation might help? How does he find the sessions? What does he find most helpful and least helpful? When does he feel most emotionally comfortable within sessions, when least? Openness and understanding is two-way, with therapists exploring ways to be themselves more fully with clients. When James's therapist felt frustrated or lost at the start of sessions, working with the relationship meant finding a way to share that feeling: 'James, I find sometimes at the start of our sessions that I don't know how you are feeling or what you want us to work on. I can feel a little lost, cut off from you, even frustrated at these times. It would really help me to understand how you feel at the start of the sessions'. It is far better to start this way, than once again drawing a blank by asking for agenda items, reflections from last week or progress on any homework.

Challenges exploring 'poor me' beliefs

The 'activating events, beliefs and consequences' (ABC) framework (Chadwick *et al.* 1996) remains the basic formulation within the Symptomatic meaning domain of the ZoPD. When working in this domain, at no point is a person being told what to think, or how to think. The aim is not to try to change minds (Padesky 1993) but rather to explore what development is possible. Development is proximal, so exploration needs to begin from the client's current position. When James describes his experience of persecution, in his own mind he is not describing a belief at all. He is telling someone what is happening to him. It is crucial to recognize and respect *the way in which the belief is real for the client*. This is the essence of Rogerian acceptance and underpins relationship building. It would not be sensible for the therapist to come straight back with an invitation to consider that this is a belief that may or may not be true. Therapists often do this because they feel that in suspending their own disbelief they are meeting a person halfway. However, halfway requires a client to move from a starting position of 'this persecution is a fact of my experience,' to viewing it as a belief which may or may not be true; this is unlikely to fall within the zone of proximal development. It should also be remembered that clients with paranoia are usually waiting for therapists to communicate disbelief, a threat to relationship building.

Yet therapists must not feel gagged. It is as much a mistake to avoid discussing the perceived persecution as it is to challenge it head on. It is better to stay with the client, remain Socratic and explore first evidence *for* the belief, and second to explore the client's own doubt. With James, this means exploring: Does James currently have any doubt whatsoever; has he ever had any doubt in the past, however fleeting; and what would have to happen today for him to doubt his belief? At present James had no doubt whatsoever that the persecution was occurring. He reported how people—family, doctors—were always telling him that it is not real, but all part of an illness, schizophrenia.

James says 'They don't know, its not happening to them.' He could not think of any eventuality that would make him doubt his belief, other than 'if the attacks stopped.' In the past there had been times of doubt. This is movement. When a time of doubt was drawn out using an ABC framework (Table 21.1), James stated of his persecutors: 'They would be rich if they could read my mind and had all these powers, and they are not.' In this moment, belief conviction was 35% and his overall subjective rating of distress was far lower. These two experiences—current 100% certainty with high distress, and past doubt with only 35% certainty with low distress—are written down as in Table 21.1 and used to share the cognitive ABC model Socratically through James's own experience. This explores James' capacity to decentre from his experiences, and gain meta-cognitive insight into how meaning (B) shapes distress (C).

And so on: all standard CBT methods for working with persecutory beliefs (behavioural experiments, etc.) are used, but always in a radically collaborative and accepting way to explore proximal development. With James, belief conviction remained unchanged through exploration and testing of his central persecutory belief. Therapists can easily become frustrated or despondent if belief conviction remains fixed. Rogerian acceptance applies to all aspects of a person, including fixed beliefs. A distinct advantage of the ZoPD is that it

Table 21.1 Sharing the cognitive mediational model through 'activating events, beliefs and consequences' (ABC) analysis of accessible cognition during moments of certainty and doubt

A Situation, mood, sensations	B Meaning, imagery	C Emotions, body state, behavioural urge and action
	Time of 100 % certainty I know it's real, it's happening to me I don't deserve these attacks, they should be stopped	*Distress rating (9/10)* Very stressed and angry Body tense, agitated Urge: go and 'get them'
Alone, stressed Unpleasant tactile sensations, voices and images	They enjoy seeing me suffer They're bad, malicious	Action: resisting, battling with voices
	Time of doubt (35% conviction) They can't have all these powers. If they had them, they'd have money, be rich and famous. No one's even heard of them	*Distress rating (4/10)* Confused, with slight irritation and stress Body more relaxed Not battling

illustrates how the symptomatic meaning domain is but one source of distress and potential well-being, thereby giving therapists clarity and flexibility. It was important for James's therapist was to explore in a radically collaborative way what change was possible in belief conviction, to accept that none was possible, while *concurrently* working to explore proximal development in other domains (see Figure 21.1). Moreover, development in another domain (e.g. Mindfulness) might through generalization influence symptomatic beliefs.

Relationship to internal experience

A strength of the ZoPD formulation is that therapists can work flexibly with diverse sources of distress, and push where it moves. Working with 'poor me' persecutory beliefs can be very challenging. There are times when a client can feel that any discussion, however gentle and Socratic, is confrontational and an expression of disbelief. At such times, therapists can be especially glad of the opportunity through mindfulness to explore relationship to internal experience. This also addresses distress directly linked to psychotic sensations, but does so without getting into meaning and hence potential confrontation.

Mindfulness as used within PBCT has two main aspects. On the one hand there is the experiential practice of clear, open and gentle awareness of whatever is present, marked by acceptance and an absence of reaction (avoidance, struggle, rumination, etc.). Within PBCT mindfulness practice has been adapted for distressing psychosis (see Chadwick 2006; Chapter 5, this volume). Practice lasts 10 min, beginning with a brief body scan, then a focus on sensations of breathing for 2 or 3 min, and then opening awareness to whatever is present, such that attention moves naturally among breathing, body sensations, voices, images, thoughts, etc. On the other hand, there is an explicit focus on supporting meta-cognitive insight (Teasdale *et al.*, 2002), especially about sources of distress and well-being. This aim shapes preparation for, guidance during, and subsequent reflection on mindfulness practice. It is often during reflection that important meta-cognitive insights are made, rather than during the experiential practice itself. These two sides of mindfulness—awareness and insight—are equally important, and share a dialectical relationship.

It is important to repeatedly assert that mindfulness will not get rid of voices, images, thoughts, or feelings. Notwithstanding this, after several sessions of practice James expressed disappointment in mindfulness: 'It was not getting rid of the attacks.' Motivation to practice mindfulness comes from a careful consideration of current coping reactions and their advantages and disadvantages (Chadwick 2006; Chapter 5, this volume). James is by no means alone when he states: 'I challenge them, what they are doing is wrong, but they don't listen or care, they carry on attacking: nothing I do works.' Recognition of the limits of his current coping motivates James to practice mindfulness.

To make this specific, how is mindfulness relevant to James's experience? First, like the ABC framework, it distinguishes between sensations and reactions to them. Sensations are the voices, images and tactile sensations that James experiences in his head, legs, and groin. Through mindfulness practice, James is invited to see if he can experience all these sensations with decentred awareness, without reacting to them, watching them come and go, stripped of his reactions, accepting what is present in each moment. Typically James first tries experiential avoidance and, if this fails, reacts with struggle, fight and paranoid rumination. In meditation practice, as he is able to decentre; even for only a few moments, he can explore how it feels to not react in his habitual ways. When he catches himself in the midst of reacting with rumination and struggle, he is encouraged to notice how this feels emotionally and in his body, and how it feels to let go of struggling and ruminating, and allow his awareness to move back to sensations of breathing. This supports meta-cognitive insight into how he might alleviate his distress through mindfulness (Abba *et al.* 2008).

James, like many clients, finds it very difficult to give up fighting and getting entangled with his 'attacks' because his habitual reactions are maintained by meta-cognitive beliefs. A main belief for him is, 'Unless I fight, I will be overwhelmed and my very identity will be taken from me.' Mindfulness practice is in part a behavioural experiment to test this belief—in moments of decentred awareness of voices, images, and tactile sensations, does it feel overwhelming, and does his identity feel diminished? Like very many clients James found it difficult to take the 'risk' and could let go of reacting 'only for a few moments at a time.' This is realistic progress; James's therapist elicited from James how during these few moments he felt peaceful and more in touch with himself, not less so, thus experientially challenging the meta-cognitive belief.

The self and 'poor me' paranoia: schemata and symbolic self

Experiential methods, such as two chair enactments (Greenberg *et al.* 1993) form the basis of exploration in the Schemata and Symbolic Self domains of the ZoPD (Chadwick 2006; Chapters 6 and 7, this volume). In PBCT, self is conceptualized as a process. Within PBCT, work in these domains is aimed at (i) decentring from negative schematic experience and seeing clearly its nature and impact, (ii) developing positive self-schemata, with development of linked behaviour and goals, (iii) accepting negative and positive schematic experience,

(iv) gaining meta-cognitive insight into the self as an emotionally complex, contradictory and changing process (Chadwick 2006; Chapters 6 and 7, this volume).

With 'bad me' paranoia, negative self-schematic experiences are conscious. They, like psychotic sensations (voices, images …) are accepted as a phenomenological reality, one part of a person's self. It is the metacognitive belief that the negative schematic experience is the person's entire self that is questioned experientially. Chadwick *et al.* (1996) suggested that with 'poor me' one option for therapists is to ask clients to imagine for a moment that their beliefs are false. ABC assessment and thought chaining is then used to explore what feelings and cognitions might result. Sometimes this reveals negative self-schemata, and sometimes not. Our position is not that in all cases there are negative self-schemata underlying 'poor me' beliefs. Indeed we have argued that people with 'poor me' paranoia may develop persecutory beliefs through a lack of sense of self (see Trower and Chadwick 1995) rather than through defending a negative one. Rather we described a method for exploring whether, for a particular person, negative schemata might exist and be brought into awareness through ABC analysis and thought chaining. If no such beliefs emerge, we would not assume that they exist and are too well-defended by paranoia. There is a danger that cognitive theories become immunized against refutation (Popper 1977).

A key facet of ongoing work with James is to establish positive schematic experience. As with many clients with paranoia, his social, occupational, and sexual life is greatly diminished. This involves supporting James to pursue valued goals in spite of psychosis and other obstacles (Kushlick *et al.* 1997, pp. 147–148; Hayes *et al.* 1999)—a vital aspect of working with clients with psychosis. The therapeutic relationship and work in all domains of proximal development are for James opportunities to experience and gain insight into the richness, variety, emotional complexity and changeability of his self, which supports self-acceptance, perhaps the end point of PBCT.

At the time of writing, James has had 15 sessions of PBCT spaced over ~15 months. Relationship building and exploration of proximal development have been challenging. James reports little change in the frequency of, and his preoccupation with, the 'attacks'. Nor has there been any change in his level of conviction that the attackers are real, intend to do him harm and are actually harming him. However, he feels he has 'adapted' to the attacks, he is less distressed by them, and he feels that they are less important and interfere less with his life. He is now more active; he attends a gym, is learning kick boxing and attends a centre for meditation monthly. James particularly values the meditation, because it enables him to experience the attacks without reacting so much and being able to remain relatively calm. Therapy continues, with meditation always a part of the sessions.

References

Abba, N.A., Chadwick, P.D.J. and Stevenson, C. (2008) Responding mindfully to distressing psychosis: a grounded theory analysis. *Psychotherapy Research*, 18, 77–87.

Burns, D. and Auerbach, A. (1996) Therapeutic empathy in cognitive-behavioral therapy: does it really make a difference? In: Salkovskis, P. (ed.), *Frontiers of Cognitive Therapy*, pp. 135–165. New York: Guilford Press.

Chadwick, P.D.J. (2006) *Person-based Cognitive Therapy for Distressing Psychosis*. Chichester: Wiley.

Chadwick, P.D.J., Birchwood, M.J. and Trower, P. (1996) *Cognitive Therapy for Delusions, Voices and Paranoia*. Chichester: Wiley.

Chadwick, P.D.J., Trower, P., Juusti-Butler, T. and Maguire, N. (2005) Phenomenological evidence for two types of paranoia. *Psychopathology*, 38, 327–333.

Combs, D.R., Penn, D.L., Chadwick, P.D.J., Trower, P., Michael, C. and Basso, M.R. (2007) Subtypes of paranoia in a non-clinical sample. *Cognitive Neuropsychiatry*, 12, 537–553.

Ellis, A. (1994) *Reason and Emotion in Psychotherapy*, revised edn. New York: Lyle Stuart.

Fornells-Ambrojo, M. and Garety, P. (2005) Bad me paranoia in early psychosis: a relatively rare phenomenon. *British Journal of Clinical Psychology*, 44, 521–528.

Freeman, D., Garety, P.A. and Kuipers, E. (2001) Persecutory delusions: developing the understanding of belief maintenance and emotional distress. *Psychological Medicine*, 31, 1293–1306.

Greenberg, L., Rice, L. and Elliott, R. (1993) *Facilitating Emotional Change: The Moment-by-moment Process*. New York: Guilford.

Hayes, S.C., Strosahl, K.D. and Wilson, K.G. (1999) *Acceptance and Commitment Therapy: An Experiential Approach to Behaviour Change*. New York: Guilford Press.

Kushlick, A., Trower, P. and Dagnan, D. (1997) Applying cognitive-behavioural approaches to the carers of people with learning disabilities who display challenging behaviour. In: Kroese, B.S., Dagnan, D. and Loumidis, K. (eds), *Cognitive-Behaviour Therapy for People with Learning Disabilities*, pp. 141–161. London and New York: Routledge.

Melo, S.S., Taylor, J.L. and Bentall, R. (2006) 'Poor me' versus 'bad me' paranoia and the instability of persecutory ideation. *Psychology and Psychotherapy: Theory, Research and Practice*, 79, 271–288.

Peters, E. and Garety, P.A. (2006) Cognitive functioning in delusions: a longitudinal analysis. *Behaviour Research and Therapy*, 44, 481–514.

Popper, K.R. (1977) On hypotheses. In: Johnson-Laird, P.N. and Wason, P.C. (eds), *Thinking: Readings in Cognitive Science*. Cambridge: Cambridge University Press.

Rogers, C. (1961) *On Becoming a Person*. London: Constable.

Startup, M., Owen, D.M., Parsonage, R.K. and Jackson, M.C. (2003) Anomalous experiences and the contents of persecutory delusions during acute psychotic episodes. *Psychology and Psychotherapy: Theory, Research and Practice*, 76 (Pt 3), 315–322.

Teasdale, J.D., Moore, R.G., Hayhurst, H., Pope, M., Williams, S. and Segal, Z.V. (2002) Metacognitive awareness and prevention of relapse in depression: empirical evidence. *Journal of Consulting and Clinical Psychology*, 70, 275–287.

Trower, P. and Chadwick, P.D.J. (1995) Pathways to defence of the self: a theory of two types of paranoia. *Clinical Psychology: Science and Practice*, 2, 263–278.

Vygotsky, L.S. (1979) *Mind in Society*. Cambridge, MA: MIT Press.

Zigler, E. and Glick, M. (1988) Is paranoid schizophrenia really camouflaged depression? *American Psychologist*, 43, 284–290.

Index

Please note that page numbers relating to Figures or Tables will be in *italic* print. Any references to 'PD' stand for 'persecutory delusions', while references to 'ToM' stand for 'Theory of Mind'.